Zephyr RTOS Embedded C Programming

Using Embedded RTOS POSIX API

Andrew Eliasz

Apress®

Zephyr RTOS Embedded C Programming: Using Embedded RTOS POSIX API

Andrew Eliasz
First Technology Transfer
Croydon, Surrey, UK

ISBN-13 (pbk): 979-8-8688-0106-8 ISBN-13 (electronic): 979-8-8688-0107-5
https://doi.org/10.1007/979-8-8688-0107-5

Copyright © 2024 by Andrew Eliasz

This work is subject to copyright. All rights are reserved by the Publisher, whether the whole or part of the material is concerned, specifically the rights of translation, reprinting, reuse of illustrations, recitation, broadcasting, reproduction on microfilms or in any other physical way, and transmission or information storage and retrieval, electronic adaptation, computer software, or by similar or dissimilar methodology now known or hereafter developed.

Trademarked names, logos, and images may appear in this book. Rather than use a trademark symbol with every occurrence of a trademarked name, logo, or image we use the names, logos, and images only in an editorial fashion and to the benefit of the trademark owner, with no intention of infringement of the trademark.

The use in this publication of trade names, trademarks, service marks, and similar terms, even if they are not identified as such, is not to be taken as an expression of opinion as to whether or not they are subject to proprietary rights.

While the advice and information in this book are believed to be true and accurate at the date of publication, neither the authors nor the editors nor the publisher can accept any legal responsibility for any errors or omissions that may be made. The publisher makes no warranty, express or implied, with respect to the material contained herein.

> Managing Director, Apress Media LLC: Welmoed Spahr
> Acquisitions Editor: Susan McDermott
> Development Editor: Laura Berendson
> Project Manager: Jessica Vakili

Cover designed by eStudioCalamar

Cover image by Pixabay

Distributed to the book trade worldwide by Springer Science+Business Media New York, 1 New York Plaza, New York, NY 10004. Phone 1-800-SPRINGER, fax (201) 348-4505, e-mail orders-ny@springer-sbm.com, or visit www.springeronline.com. Apress Media, LLC is a California LLC and the sole member (owner) is Springer Science + Business Media Finance Inc (SSBM Finance Inc). SSBM Finance Inc is a **Delaware** corporation.

For information on translations, please e-mail booktranslations@springernature.com; for reprint, paperback, or audio rights, please e-mail bookpermissions@springernature.com.

Apress titles may be purchased in bulk for academic, corporate, or promotional use. eBook versions and licenses are also available for most titles. For more information, reference our Print and eBook Bulk Sales web page at http://www.apress.com/bulk-sales.

Any source code or other supplementary material referenced by the author in this book is available to readers on the Github repository: https://github.com/Apress/Zephyr-RTOS-Embedded-C-Programming. For more detailed information, please visit https://www.apress.com/gp/services/source-code.

If disposing of this product, please recycle the paper

TABLE OF CONTENTS

Counting Semaphore 35
Mutual Exclusions Semaphore (Mutex) 36
Priority Inversion Avoidance 37
Using Semaphores and Mutexes in Interrupt Service Routines 38
Semaphore Usage Patterns and Scenarios 38
Wait and Signal Synchronization 38
Credit Tracking Synchronization 39
Synchronizing Access to a Shared Resource Using a Binary Semaphore 40
Message Queueing and Message Queues 41
Interlocked, One-Way Data Communication 43
Interlocked, Two-Way Data Communication 44
Pipes 45
Event Objects (Event Registers) 47
Condition Variables 48
Interrupts and Exceptions 49
Timing and Timers 52
Memory Management 53
Synchronization Patterns and Strategies 56
Communication Patterns 58
Patterns Involving the Use of Critical Sections 59
Common Activity Synchronization Design Patterns 59
Common Resource Synchronization Design Patterns 61
Some More Advanced Thread Interaction Patterns 62
Handling Multiple Data Items and Multiple Inputs 65
Sending Urgent/High Priority Data Between Tasks 66
Device Drivers 66
References 67

Table of Contents

About the Author xvii

About the Technical Reviewer xix

Chapter 1: An Introduction 1
    What This Book Is "All About" 1
    What Is an RTOS and When and Why "Do You Need One"? 2
    What Is an RTOS? 4
    Using Open Source RTOS in Systems Requiring Functional Safety 5
    Reconciling Certification with Open Source 10
    Zephyr As a Modular RTOS 11
    Zephyr As a Fully Featured RTOS 12
    Arguments for Choosing Zephyr OS 14
    What Makes Zephyr RTOS Special 15
    Zephyr and Security 15
    References 17

Chapter 2: A Review of RTOS Fundamentals 19
    Embedded System Software Development Strategies/Options 23
    Multitasking and Interprocess Communication and Synchronization
    Concepts and Patterns 29
        Tasks 29
    Intertask Communication 33
    Semaphore 34
    Binary Semaphore 34

iii

TABLE OF CONTENTS

Emulator Use Cases 119
Advantages of Simulators and Emulators 119
Disadvantages of Simulators and Emulators 120
Summarizing Renode 121
References 122

Chapter 4: Zephyr RTOS Multithreading 123

Kconfig 124
Devicetrees and Devicetree Configuration 126
Kconfig and Devicetree Usage Heuristics 127
Multithreading in Zephyr 127
Zephyr Kernel Mode and User Mode Threads 133
An Overview of Generic Zephyr Features Pertaining to Privilege Modes, Stack Protection and Separation, User Mode Threads, and Memory Domains ... 134
Privilege Modes 134
Safety Model and Threats That Zephyr RTOS Applications Need to Protect Against 135
ARM Cortex M Memory Protection Unit (MPU): An Overview 137
User syscalls 138
Zephyr RTOS Thread Priorities 139
Thread Custom Data 141
Dropping Privileges 141
Thread Termination 142
System Threads 142
Basic Multithreading Scenarios 144
Simple Multithreading Example 145
FIFOs in Zephyr 147
Synchronizing Threads Using Semaphores and Sleeping 151

TABLE OF CONTENTS

Chapter 3: Zephyr RTOS Application Development Environments and Zephyr Application Building Principles 69

Setting Up a Zephyr SDK CLI (Command-Line Interface) Development Environment on Microsoft Windows 71

Choices of Boards and Development Kits for Getting Started 74

Setting Up an nRF Connect SDK Development Environment Using a Microsoft VS Code–Based IDE 81

Working in VS Code 85

Global Actions 91

Application-Specific Actions 92

Build-Specific Actions 92

Details View 93

Devicetree View 94

Actions View 95

Exercise: Building and Running a Zephyr Sample Application Using VS Code 95

Introduction to the Zephyr RTOS Device Driver Model and the Zephyr RTOS Device Driver APIs and Data Structures 97

GPIO Inputs 106

UART Communications Between a Target Board and a PC 108

Zephyr Logging Module 111

Plan of Action for Exploring Multithreading and Thread Synchronization 114

Using Simulation and Simulators for Testing and Developing Zephyr RTOS Applications 114

Zephyr Applications Using Renode 115

Renode and Firmware Testing 116

Building Machines in Renode 116

Emulators vs. Simulators 117

Simulator Use Cases 118

v

TABLE OF CONTENTS

Signalling Using a Condition Variable 157

The Dining Philosophers Problem 162

Producers and Consumers and Multithreading.. 170

The Zephyr RTOS Producer-Consumer Example 171

Using Zephyr RTOS System Calls: Essential Concepts and Overview 176

Producer-Consumer Example Sample Driver Part 179

Shared Memory Partition, System Heap, Memory Pool, and Kernel Queues Part 185

Application A Part.. 186

APP B Part... 194

Shared Memory, Protected Memory Partitions, and Memory Domains 200

Memory Partitions.. 200

Zephyr Shared Memory Example 205

References 215

Chapter 5: Message Queues, Pipes, Mailboxes, and Workqueues 217

Zephyr Message Queue 218

Message Queue – Technical Details and the Message Queue API 219

Overview of the Message Queue API Functions 221

Message Queue Example 222

Exercise Scenario Description 223

Zephyr Mailbox.. 236

Mailbox Message Format.. 237

Mailbox Message Life Cycle.. 238

Mailbox Sending and Receiving Thread Compatibility 238

Mailbox Message Sending – Synchronous and Asynchronous 239

The Mailbox API – Data Types and Functions.. 239

Message Descriptors 240

vii

TABLE OF CONTENTS

Sending and Receiving Zephyr Mailbox Messages 242
Sending a Message 243
Receiving a Mailbox Message 246
Introductory Zephyr Mailbox Example 251
Zephyr RTOS Workqueues 256
Delayable Work 258
Simple Workqueue Example 1 259
Simple Workqueue Example 2 261
Simple Workqueue Example 3 263
Summary 267

Chapter 6: Using Filesystems in Zephyr Applications 269

Quad-SPI (QSPI) 270
SDC and MMC Cards 276
SD Card Support via SPI 277
Zephyr RTOS Disk Access API 278
Zephyr File System API 279
Working with Directories 283
File Systems – A High-Level Overview 284
Overview of the FAT File System and FatFs 285
Overview of the LittleFS File System 288
Walkthrough of a LittleFS Example Program 288
Summary 302
References 302

Chapter 7: Developing Zephyr BLE Applications 305

BLE: A Short History 306
Uses of BLE 307
BLE Architecture 307

TABLE OF CONTENTS

BLE Physical Layer 308
BLE Link Layer 309
BLE Unicast Connection Scenario 310
BLE Broadcast Connect Scenario..311
BLE Link Layer Addressing..312
BLE Packet Types 312
Connections and Connection Events..313
HCI (Host Controller Interface) Layer...314
Logical Link Control and Adaptation Protocol (L2CAP) Layer 314
BLE Actors – Peripherals, Broadcasters, Centrals, and Observers...................315
BLE Peripheral...315
BLE Central 315
HCI – Generic Access Profile (GAP) 316
Attribute Protocol (ATT) 317
Data Attributes 317
GATT Attribute and Data Hierarchy...319
Characteristics 319
Profiles 320
Attribute Operations 322
Requests – Flow Control, Reading Attributes, and Writing to Attributes 323
Bluetooth 5...324
BLE Security..325
Building and Testing Peripheral and Central BLE Applications........................327
The nRF52840 Dongle and Its Uses 327
nRF Connect Bluetooth Low Energy Applications 328
Setting Up an nRF52840 Dongle for Use with the nRF Connect for
Desktop nRF BLE Application 329

ix

TABLE OF CONTENTS

Using the Dongle in BLE Central Mode..331
BLE Network Connection Map..333
Using the Dongle in BLE Peripheral Mode..336
Using the Power Mode Emulation to Set Up an Emulated Battery Service.......339
BLE Application Development APIs Provided by Zephyr and the nRF
Connect SDK 343
The Source BLE Structure in the Zephyr Source Code......................................347
Building, Programming, and Configuring Host Roles 347
Basic Peripheral Example 347
Bluetooth: Central/Heart Rate Monitor 356
Overview of the Connected Function 365
Is It Possible to Run Both a Peripheral and a Central on the Same Board? 371
What Next?..372
Summary...372
References 372

Chapter 8: Zephyr RTOS and Ethernet, Wi-Fi, and TCP/IP 375

Zephyr and Network Management...379
The Nucleo-F767ZI Board 382
Building and Troubleshooting the Zephyr Network Programming
Examples Using the STM32 Nucleo-F767ZI Board...385
The BSD Sockets API..386
A Zephyr Echo Server Example Overview 387
Zephyr OS Services Module 388
Strategies for Studying and Reverse Engineering (Where Necessary)
Zephyr Application Code 393
Zephyr Network Management API...397
How to Request a Defined Procedure 397

x

TABLE OF CONTENTS

Listening for Network Events 398

How to Define a Network Management Procedure 399

Signalling a Network Event 400

Network Management Interface Functions 401

Zephyr Shell Module 404

Shell Commands 404

Command Creation Macros 405

Creating Static Commands 405

Dictionary Commands 406

The Shell and the Echo Server Example 408

Configuring a TCP Server Application to Use a Separate Thread for
Each Connection 424

Data Structures Associated with TCP/IP Server-Side Connections 424

Thread Structures Pool for Handling Threads Involved in TCP/IP Server
Connections 426

Echo Server on the STM32 Nucleo-F767ZI Board 431

Summary 434

References 435

Chapter 9: Understanding and Working with the Devicetree in General and SPI and I2C in Particular 437

Firmware Development Aspects of Application Development 438

Overview of SPI and I2C 442

SPI Explained 443

Advantages and Disadvantages of SPI 446

I2C Explained 446

Devicetree Configuration 448

Device Tree Source (DTS) Representation of Devicetrees 449

xi

TABLE OF CONTENTS

Unit Addresses and the Devicetree 453

Devicetree Processing 457

Devicetree Bindings 460

The Syntax of Binding Files 462

Binding and Bus Controller Nodes 469

Phandles, Phandle-Array Type Properties, and Specifier Cell Names 471

Including .yaml Binding Files 473

Accessing the Devicetree in C and C++ Application Code 475

Working with Devices in Applications 476

Working with reg and interrupts Properties 480

Working with Devices 481

Overview of How the DEVICE_DT_GET Macro Works 492

I2C Case Study Example 497

Summary 505

References 505

Chapter 10: Building Zephyr RTOS Applications Using Renode 507

Simulator Use Cases 509

Emulator Use Cases 509

Advantages of Simulators and Emulators 510

Disadvantages of Simulators and Emulators 511

Renode 511

Renode Installation 513

Renode Scripts 520

What Is Needed to Emulate a Zephyr Application Using Renode? 521

Boards and Processors Supported by Zephyr That Are Also Supported
by Renode 522

TABLE OF CONTENTS

Building an nRF52840 DK Application and Running It in Renode 526

Summary and Where Next? 530

References 530

Chapter 11: Understanding and Using the Zephyr ZBus in Application Development 531

Zephyr ZBus 531

ZBus Architecture 532

The ZBus and Code Reusability 535

Limitations of the ZBus 535

ZBus Message Delivery Guarantees and Message Delivery Rates 535

ZBus Message Delivery Sequence Guarantees 536

ZBus Programming in Practice 537

Hard Channels and Message Validation 543

Overview of ZBus Features and Their Uses 544

Publishing and Reading to and from a Channel 544

Claiming and Finishing a Channel 545

Ensuring a Message Will Not Be Changed During a Notification 546

Iterating over Channels and Observers 547

Overview of the Virtual Distributed Event Dispatcher (VDED) 550

Walkthrough of a VDED Execution Scenario 551

Walking Through Some Selected Zephyr ZBus Examples 556

Zephyr ZBus Hello World 557

Zephyr Bus Workqueue Example 565

xiii

TABLE OF CONTENTS

Chapter 12: Zephyr RTOS Wi-Fi Applications 573
Approaches to Tackling the Various Wi-Fi MAC Problems.................................574
Security Issues...575
WPA3 SAE Key Exchange Protocol 577
How Wi-Fi Uses the Radio Spectrum Allocated to It...577
Wi-Fi Frames and the 802.11 Packet Structure – An Overview 579
Access Points...580
Discovering an Access Point 581
Authentication and Association..581
Zephyr RTOS and Wi-Fi Application Development..585
nRF7002 DK Board – An Overview 586
Wi-Fi Scanning Example Walkthrough Using the nRF7002 DK 587
Zephyr Network Management – An Overview...588
Requesting a Defined Network Management Procedure 589
Listening to Network Events 589
Defining Network Management Procedures 590
Signalling Network Events 591
Building the Wi-Fi Scan Example from the nRF Connect SDK Repository.........591
Structured Overview of the Code of the Scan Example from the nRF Connect SDK Repository 592
Exploring the nRF Connect SDK Wi-Fi Shell Example 607
Basic TCP/IP Application Programming Using the nRF7002 DK........................614
Structured Exploration of the nRF Connect SDK Wi-Fi sta Example 615
Wi-Fi BSD Sockets Programming..631
nRF7002 DK – Basic TCP and UDP Example 631
Project source code directory structure...633
The Led Toggling Task 636

xiv

About the Author

Andrew Eliasz is the Founder and Head at Croydon Tutorial College as well as the Director of First Technology Transfer Ltd. First Technology Transfer runs advanced training courses and consults on advanced projects in IT, real-time, and embedded systems. Most courses are tailored to customers' needs. Croydon Tutorial College evolved from Carshalton Tutorial College, which was established to provide classes, distance-level teaching, workshops, and personal tuition in computer science, maths, and science subjects at GCSE, A Level, BTEC, undergraduate, and master's levels. It has now changed its name and location to Croydon Tutorial College at Weatherill House, Croydon. In addition to teaching and tutoring, they also provide mentoring and help for students having difficulties with assignments and projects (e.g., by suggesting how to add to a project to obtain a better grade as well as reviewing project content and writing styles).

UDP Server Task on Target Board 637
Python UDP Client to Test Out UDP Server on Target Board 641
TCP Server Task on Target Board 642
UDP Echo Client Task on Target Board 646
TCP Echo Client Task on Target Board 648
Testing Out the BSD Sockets Example 651
References 651

Index 653

About the Technical Reviewer

Jacob Beningo is an embedded software consultant with over 15 years of experience in microcontroller-based real-time embedded systems. After spending over ten years designing embedded systems for automotive, defense, and space industries, Jacob founded Beningo Embedded Group in 2009. He has worked with clients in more than a dozen countries to dramatically transform their businesses by improving product quality, cost, and time to market. Jacob has published more than 500 articles on embedded software development techniques and is a sought-after speaker and technical trainer who holds three degrees that include a Master of Engineering from the University of Michigan. He is an avid writer, trainer, consultant, and entrepreneur who transforms the complex into simple and understandable concepts that accelerate technological innovation. Jacob has demonstrated his leadership in the embedded systems industry by consulting and training at companies such as General Motors, Intel, Infineon, and Renesas along with successfully completing over 50 projects. He holds bachelor's degrees in Electronics Engineering, Physics, and Mathematics from Central Michigan University and a master's degree in Space Systems Engineering from the University of Michigan.

In his spare time, Jacob enjoys spending time with his family, reading, writing, and playing hockey and golf. In clear skies, he can often be found outside with his telescope, sipping a fine scotch while imaging the sky.

CHAPTER 1

An Introduction

What This Book Is "All About"

This book is a foundational guidebook introducing programming embedded and IoT/IIoT (Internet of Things/Industrial Internet of Things) applications in C using the Zephyr RTOS framework. It is for engineers and programmers planning to embark on a project involving the use of Zephyr RTOS, or evaluating the potential advantages of using Zephyr RTOS in an upcoming project.

You, the reader, probably have a digital electronics and embedded systems programming background building specialized embedded systems applications in C and assembler. Maybe the requirements of upcoming applications are such that a classical bare metal programming approach may not be the best way to go. Maybe you have inherited some poorly documented complex multitasking code and the developers or consultants involved in developing this code have left the project and your company is considering migrating the code to use a real-time multitasking operating system.

The aims of this book are to show you what Zephyr is capable of and to introduce you to the basic RTOS programming skills required before embarking on a real-world real-time RTOS-based project. The book can also be thought of as a guide to the rich and complex framework that makes up Zephyr RTOS and to the examples that are part of the Zephyr code repository.

CHAPTER 1   AN INTRODUCTION

Alternatively, you may have embedded Linux programming experience and have to develop applications on processors that, though powerful, are too small to run a full Linux system. Here, again, one of the things that makes Zephyr special is that it has embraced and adapted many of the concepts and technologies that make Linux so special, things such as support for the POSIX API and the use of Linux technologies such as Kconfig and devicetree.

What Is an RTOS and When and Why "Do You Need One"?

Modern microcontrollers come in a wide variety of sizes and complexity ranging from 8-bit microcontrollers with less than 10 kilobytes (10K) Flash and less than 2 kilobytes (2K) RAM through to multiprocessor 64-bit microcontrollers interfacing with gigabytes of memory. There are SoC (System on Chip) processor architectures at the lower end of the embedded computing spectrum and SoM (System on a Module) boards at the upper end.

For tiny systems performing a single specialized task, or a small number of fixed tasks, such as a motor controller in a toothbrush or power drill controlling a motor, the code can be implemented as a bare metal application. The complexity of modern connected applications means that they are not best suited to being implemented as bare metal applications. Modern microcontroller vendors often provide IDEs that provide a graphical interface for configuring peripherals and "pulling in" driver code into the project, thus allowing developers to focus on the application they are trying to build. Examples include Microchip's Harmony tool and STMicroelectronics STM32CubeIDE. Embedded systems applications can also be developed using an IDE such as Microsoft's VS Code with suitable plug-ins.

CHAPTER 1   AN INTRODUCTION

An operating system can be thought of as software that provides services that can be used for developing applications where multiple pieces of work (tasks) have to be worked on concurrently. At the center of an operating system is the scheduler, whose job is to decide which task is to run next. In a cooperative multitasking operating system, a task runs till it decides to suspend what it is doing and transfer control to the scheduler, which will determine which task to run next. In a preemptive multitasking operating system, a task can be preempted by the operating system at any point. Preemption may occur because a higher priority task is ready to run, or because the running task needs to access a resource that is currently not available because it is being used by another task. The concept of Real Time refers to how long it takes the system to respond to some event, such as a button press, or arrival of data at a communications peripheral, or completion of an ADC (Analog to Digital) conversion. A distinction is often made between hard and soft real-time systems. In a hard real-time system, it is an error if the time taken for a response exceeds some specified duration. In a soft real-time system, the response time is interpreted in a statistical sense in which most of the time the required time-to-completion limits are met, but, occasionally, they are not.

Classical bare metal multitasking, typically, involves a combination of a "superloop" that handles non-time-critical work, with time-critical work being done in interrupt handlers. The classical Arduino IDE also follows this pattern.

In the modern world of networked devices (both wired and wireless networking) running relatively complex network protocol stacks and doing so in a secure manner, the standard bare metal approach runs into difficulties. A networked device may have several interfaces, for example, wired or wireless Ethernet, USB, and serial communications such as CAN bus, RS232, or RS485. The code involved is quite complex, and having to handle the low-level details together with the other tasks being performed by the device, such as, for example, taking sensor readings on a periodic basis, adds further complexity. A networked device may have to interact

CHAPTER 1   AN INTRODUCTION

with a number of other devices, and the communication traffic patterns may be unpredictable. Worse still traffic may be bursty, and the system will need to protect itself against overloading by heavy bursts of traffic.

Packet-oriented communications protocols such as TCP/IP are multilayered, and a packet will contain multiple headers corresponding to the various layers and the functionality they provide. It is not uncommon for protocols to support multiplexing. For example, the TCP/IP stack handles both UDP and TCP traffic as well as ICMP traffic, and in the case of UDP and TCP, there may be traffic associated with different processes running on the device each identified by a particular identifier (port number).

From the design and implementation point of view, a multitasking approach allows the various tasks to be worked on separately and then combined together, courtesy of the scheduling and intertask communication and synchronization mechanisms such as semaphores and message queues provided by the RTOS.

The key motivation underlying the use of an RTOS to build embedded applications is that it provides a framework and its associated abstractions, APIs that support developing code that can handle the time, priorities, and preemptibility of the tasks that constitute that application so that task deadlines can be met and the system exhibits deterministic behavior. From a developer's point of view, an RTOS can be thought of as providing services, not only scheduling, synchronization, and intertask communication services but also, if required, file systems services, communications services, and security services.

What Is an RTOS?

The OS in RTOS stands for Operating System. An operating system can be thought of as a collection of modules (libraries) that provide task scheduling and control services, where a task is code that carries out a particular piece of the overall application's work. A modern advanced operating system will also provide device drivers for widely used devices and peripherals, communications protocol stacks and application layer modules on which actual applications can be layered, security and memory protection or memory management services, and much more besides. The RT in RTOS stands for Real Time.

Real Time here refers to predictable and reproducible behavior. This behavior may be predictable in a statistical sense, for example, where the response times to some event will follow a statistical distribution with a certain mean and variance. This is "soft" real time. For certain applications, there may be a requirement that the response time is always less than some specified value. Such applications are referred to as "hard" real-time applications. It is also possible to have systems that involve both "hard" and "soft" real-time aspects.

Using Open Source RTOS in Systems Requiring Functional Safety

In the case of applications where a high degree of functional safety is involved, the question also arises as to whether open source software can be used for systems for which "functional safety" is a mandatory requirement.

The use of RTOS code in safety-critical systems generally involves the use of code that has been rigorously tested and validated so that it conforms to one or more of the published safety standards. In the case of FreeRTOS, for example, there is an open source version of FreeRTOS and a validated version called SAFERTOS pre-certified to IEC 61508 for safety-critical applications. Currently, there is no pre-certified version of Zephyr RTOS. The Zephyr project is aiming to, eventually, be able to provide a version that has been certified for use in safety-critical applications. This is reflected in the Zephyr development and code review process.

CHAPTER 1   AN INTRODUCTION

Issues arising in the use of open source software in systems requiring functional safety include considerations such as those listed here:

- Open source software usually requires major transformation before it can be used.

- Mostly such transformation happens behind closed doors (if the license allows that).

- There may be a complete disconnect between original source and "certified" code.

- Transformation of open source code to be functionally safe is "expensive."

- Following standards very early in a project life cycle is a key factor.

- There are many standards dealing with safety-critical systems and software, and some members of this family are shown in the schematic partial family tree (Figure 1-1).

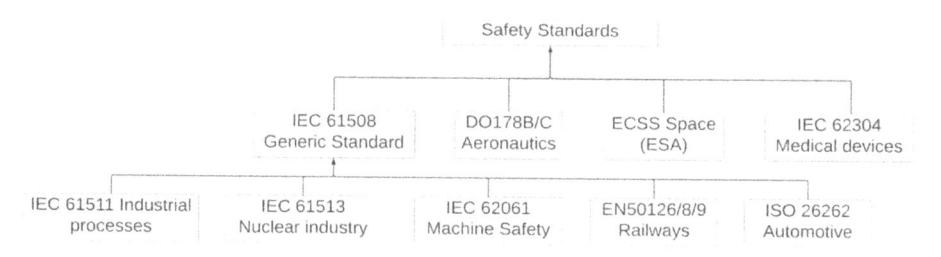

```
                        Safety Standards
                               |
        ┌──────────────┬───────┴───────┬──────────────┐
     IEC 61508      DO178B/C       ECSS Space      IEC 62304
  Generic Standard  Aeronautics       (ESA)       Medical devices
        |
┌───────┼───────┬──────────────┬──────────────┐
IEC 61511    IEC 61513     IEC 62061     EN50126/8/9    ISO 26262
Industrial   Nuclear       Machine        Railways      Automotive
processes    industry      Safety
```

Figure 1-1. *Safety Standards, a partial family tree*

An example of going from an open source project to a system certified for use in safety-critical systems is FreeRTOS. SAFERTOS started with the functional model of the FreeRTOS kernel, but the kernel code was, then, redesigned, analyzed, and tested from a HAZOP perspective, and implemented according to an IEC 61508-3 SIL 3 development life cycle.

CHAPTER 1   AN INTRODUCTION

An ambition of the Zephyr RTOS initiative is to, eventually, provide an open source RTOS that can be used in safety-critical systems. Zephyr RTOS already provides many of the features expected of a safety-critical RTOS, but the real crux of the matter is the formal validation and testing of the system and its development process. The next few sections consider some of these issues.

Characteristics of an open source OS that would make it suitable for functional safety-oriented applications include the following:

- Open source implementation
- Small trusted code base (in terms of LoC)
- Safety-oriented architecture
- Built-in security model
- POSIX-compliant C library
- Support for deterministic thread scheduling
- Support for multi-core thread scheduling
- Proof that ISO-compliant development was done
- Accountability for the implementation
- Industry adoption
- Certification-friendly interfaces

The mission statement for Zephyr [1] is "to deliver the best-in-class RTOS for connected resource-constrained devices, built to be secure and safe." The Zephyr RTOS website contains presentations describing the various steps and approaches being followed that follow standard procedures for developing and testing safety-critical systems software. These include following the Verification and Validation aspects as formalized in the V-Model of software development. A useful discussion held during Open Source Summit Europe 2022 concerning these issues is worth viewing [2].

CHAPTER 1   AN INTRODUCTION

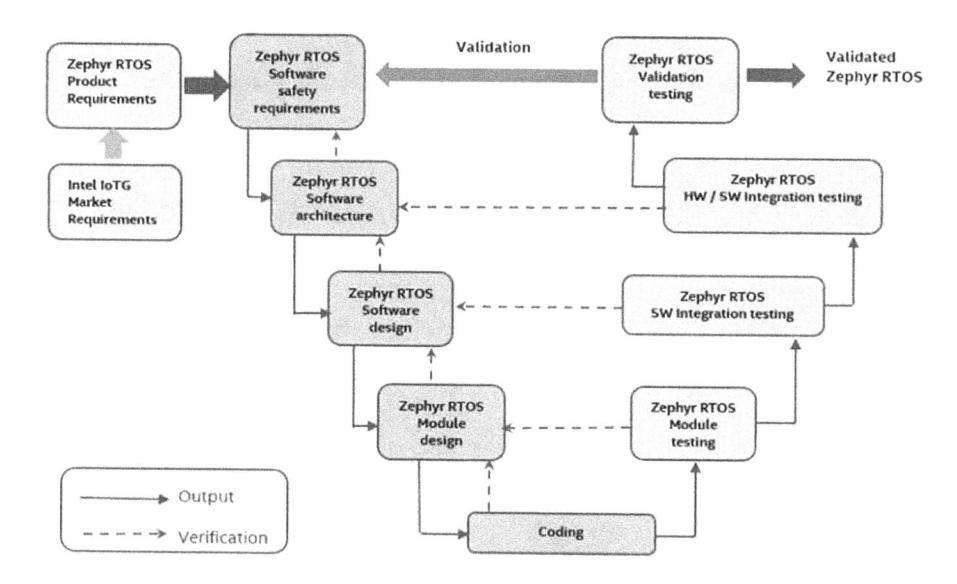

Figure 1-2. *Zephyr RTOS functional safety work products mapping to IEC 61508-3 V model [1]*

From the point of view of developing a safety-critical system quality RTOS, following the V-Model open source projects runs into issues such as the formal specification of features, producing comprehensive document, being able to produce traceability from requirements to source code, and being able to provide full information about the number of committers and information about them.

From the point of view of certification authorities, there is the problem that they are not familiar with open source development and there are no tried and tested methods for the certification of open source software.

Currently the standards being followed by Zephyr in regard to coding for Safety, Security, Portability, and Reliability in Embedded Systems are MISRA C:2012 (with Amendment 1, following MISRA C Compliance:2016 guidance) and the use of SEI CERT C and JPL (Jet Propulsion Laboratory

CHAPTER 1   AN INTRODUCTION

California Institute of Technology) as reference. As regards functional safety, the aim is to follow IEC 61508: 2010 (SIL 3 initially, eventually aiming to get to SIL 4). IEC 61508 is widely used by companies developing robotics systems and autonomous vehicles.

Writing embedded C code that conforms to MISRA guidelines is, these days, a widely accepted practice. Issues with MISRA and open source code that arise include the following:

- Some rules are very controversial; how to deal with those?
- Deciding which guidelines to deviate from and why
- MISRA C is proprietary; how can it be made more widely available?
- Finding the "open source" tools that check code and integrating these with CI

An example of a MISRA rule that is widely followed in embedded systems development is the following Rule 15.5 – A function should have a single point of exit at the end:

- Most readable structure
- Less likelihood of erroneously omitting function exit code
- Required by many safety standards
- IEC 61508
- ISO 26262

CHAPTER 1   AN INTRODUCTION

Reconciling Certification with Open Source

Reconciling an open source project with many potential contributors with a project that can produce safety-critical system certified software is tricky and represents "work in progress."

Various approaches are being explored and tried out. These include the following:

- Snapshotting a Source Tree (branch), validating it then controlling updates, which is a viable approach to software qualification.

- Defining the supported feature set as an up-front decision, bearing in mind that the more features that are supported, the greater the amount of documentation that will need to be provided and the amount of software testing that will need to be carried out. In this context, it will be important to automate as much of the information tracking as possible and to auto-generate documents from test and issue tracking systems.

- Obtaining proof-of-concept approval from a certification authority as early as possible.

An ideal project process that can combine the best aspects of open source development and critical system certification will be one based on a split development model having a flexible open instance path and an auditable instance path [3]. Aligning the auditable path with the open instance path will be dictated by the need to add new features and the costs of the certification process.

CHAPTER 1　AN INTRODUCTION

Zephyr As a Modular RTOS

The idea behind a modular RTOS is to develop it as a set of components that can be combined to be able to construct an application that incorporates only the functionality required for the application. This is not a new approach. The early versions of Microsoft's Windows NT operating system were modular with the possibility of being able to build operating system variants best suited to the task at hand.

Zephyr therefore tries to provide a solution to RTOS application development centered around a modular open source architecture appropriate for implementing a wide variety of use cases and design architectures running on connected, resource-constrained embedded controllers. Zephyr has an Apache 2.0 license, hosted at the Linux Foundation, and has extensive support for Bluetooth and for TCP/IP.

The modular aspects of the Zephyr OS can be conceptualized as a layered model shown in Figure 1-3 [3].

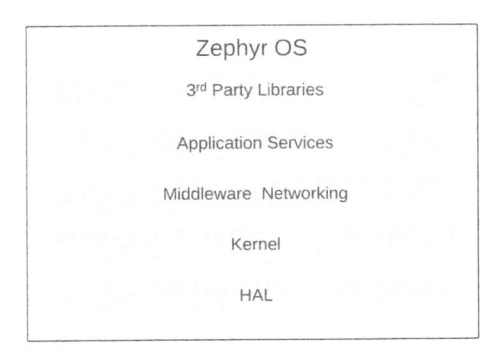

```
┌─────────────────────────────────┐
│          Zephyr OS              │
│                                 │
│        3rd Party Libraries      │
│                                 │
│        Application Services     │
│                                 │
│       Middleware  Networking    │
│                                 │
│             Kernel              │
│                                 │
│              HAL                │
└─────────────────────────────────┘
```

Figure 1-3. *Zephyr layered modular architecture*

CHAPTER 1   AN INTRODUCTION

Zephyr As a Fully Featured RTOS

An important aspect of Zephyr to be aware of is that Zephyr is not an ingredient – it provides a complete solution. Features supported by Zephyr include the following:

Safety features:

- Thread isolation
- Stack protection (HW/SW)
- Quality management (QM)
- Build time configuration
- No dynamic memory allocation
- Funtional SAfety (FuSA) (2019)

Security features:

- User-space support
- Crypto support
- Software updates

Configurable and modular kernel:

- Can configure the Zephyr kernel to run in 8K RAM
- Makes for scalable application code
- Only need to include what is required for the application

Cross-platform capabilities:

- Zephyr supports multiple architectures (ARM Cortex M, RISC-V, ARC, MIPS, Extensa).
- Native porting.
- Applications can be developed on Linux, Windows, and macOS platforms.

CHAPTER 1   AN INTRODUCTION

Open source:

- Licensed under the Apache II license
- Managed by the Linux Foundation
- Transparent development process
- Can be forked on GitHub

Connected:

- Full Bluetooth 5.0 support
- Bluetooth controller
- BLE mesh
- Thread support
- Full featured native networking stack
- Device Firmware Upgrade (DFU) (IP + BLE)

The richness of the Zephyr framework is well illustrated in Figure 1-4 [4].

CHAPTER 1 AN INTRODUCTION

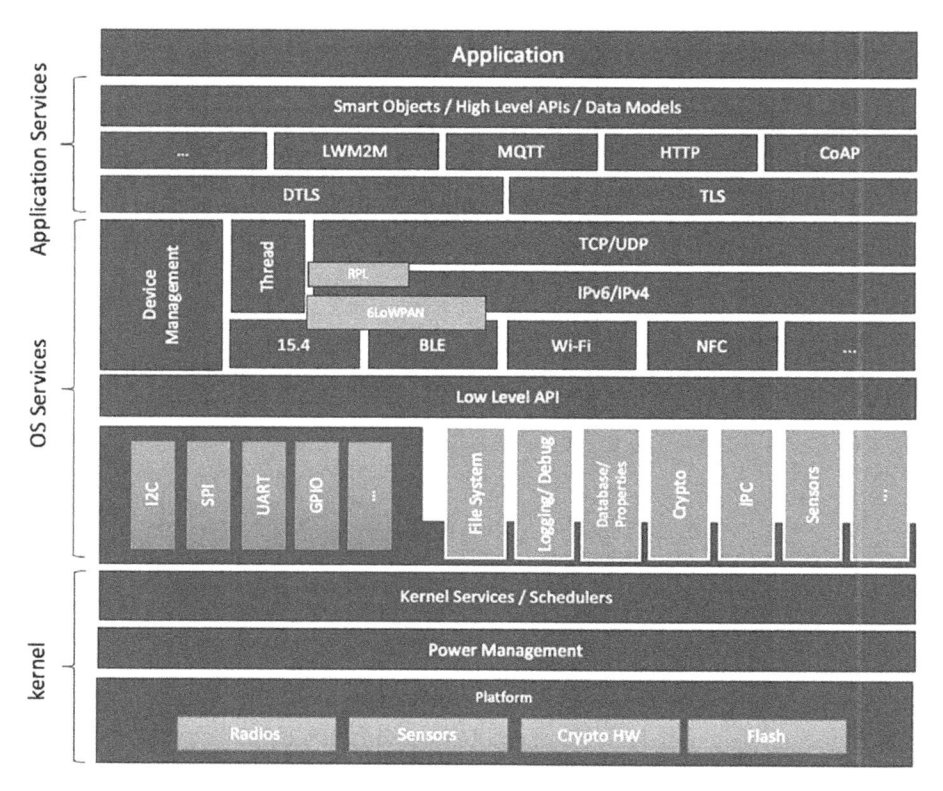

Figure 1-4. Zephyr framework components underlying Zephyr-based applications

Arguments for Choosing Zephyr OS

A major argument in favor of Zephyr is its modularity, the range of use cases it addresses, and the broad set of platforms it supports. Zephyr OS covers issues such as address fragmentation, infrastructure modularity, and support for standards such as the POSIX API. The underlying goal is to allow developers to focus on end user facing interfaces instead of having to reimplement low-level interfaces.

Zephyr provides long-term support, which is product focused. The emphasis is on hardening the functionality of existing features, as opposed to introducing new ones. The Zephyr auditable code base is established from a subset of Zephyr OS features.

What Makes Zephyr RTOS Special

Zephyr is not controlled by any one company, unlike many other RTOSes. The Zephyr project is managed by the Linux Foundation, a nonprofit organization whose mission is to create sustainable ecosystems around open source projects, thereby accelerating technology development and commercial application of that technology. Because of its independence in the sense of not being tied to a controlling commercial organization, and because of being developed and adopted in the open source GitHub repository, Zephyr has attracted more contributions when compared with FreeRTOS, backed by Amazon, and Azure RTOS (ThreadX), supported by Microsoft.

Zephyr and Security

The Zephyr project maintains a security overview that sets out security compliance requirements for developers and the security process steps to be followed.

These are outlined in Figure 1-5 [4].

CHAPTER 1　AN INTRODUCTION

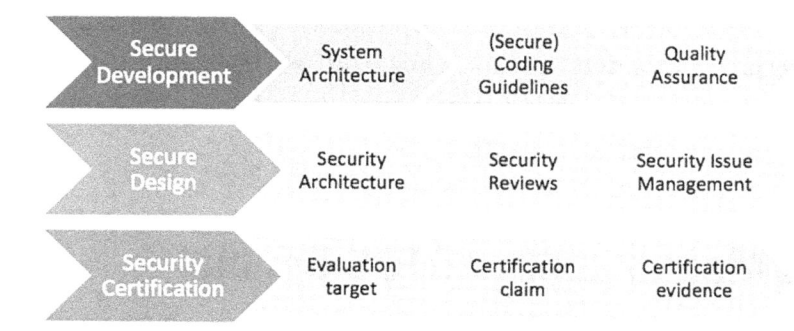

Secure Development	System Architecture	(Secure) Coding Guidelines	Quality Assurance
Secure Design	Security Architecture	Security Reviews	Security Issue Management
Security Certification	Evaluation target	Certification claim	Certification evidence

Figure 1-5. Zephyr security perspective

Interesting commercial projects based on Zephyr include the following:

- GRUSH gaming toothbrush...: `https://youtu.be/LVGKZUxuVIc`

- HereO GPS watch for children...: `https://youtu.be/N1QyZ-L3fpc`

- ProGlove wearable scanner...: `https://youtu.be/QP2xw52QAzM`

- Minut smart home alarm...: `https://youtu.be/vhsDCwOEPi8`

- Whoop personal fitness tracker...: `https://youtu.be/JJqgGEBmBes`

References

1. www.zephyrproject.org/wp-content/uploads/sites/38/2022/02/Zephyr-Overview-2022Q1-Public.pdf

2. Zephyr in Safety Critical Applications www.zephyrproject.org/zephyr-in-safety-critical-applications/

3. Developing Open-Source Software RTOS with Functional Safety in Mind? https://elinux.org/images/7/70/Elce_2018_Anas_nashif.pdf

4. https://docs.zephyrproject.org/latest/security/security-overview.html

CHAPTER 2

A Review of RTOS Fundamentals

Traditional embedded systems were stand-alone systems that were not extensively networked to other systems. Communication, when present, typically, was over a simple communications serial link such as RS232, or HART. HART [1] is an industrial protocol that can communicate over legacy 4–20 mA analog instrumentation current loops, but these days there is also a wireless version of HART and there are HART modems that can be used to run HART over RS232. Later specialized serial communications such as SPI and I2C were developed for communicating with small specialized devices such as, for example:

- Digital sensors such as temperature sensors, pressure sensors, and accelerometers
- Port expanders
- Digital-to-analog converters

The microcontrollers used in early embedded systems were, typically, 8-bit or 16-bit microcontrollers such as those from AVR (now owned by Microchip and widely used in early Arduino devices), Silabs 8051 processor architecture controllers, and Microchip PIC16 and PIC18 devices. These devices were SoC (System on Chip) devices that contained not only the processor core but also memory as well as peripherals such as timers, general-purpose IO (GPIO), I2C, SPI, ADC (analog-to-digital conversion), and PWM (pulse-width modulation). These devices had relatively simple instruction sets, and applications were code either entirely in assembler or a C compiler developed to compile code for these processor architectures. Programs were stored in on chip flash memory, and the program code ran from flash memory. Memory for nonstatic data and variables, also on chip, was RAM (SRAM).

Over time the requirements and expected capabilities of applications and the devices they run have become more and more demanding. If we consider consumer devices, then, for example:

- Some washing machines can report the time remaining to complete a wash cycle via a smartphone app

- A smoke detector, instead of being able to just blink an LED and beep, may have the ability to communicate with other smoke detectors

    - Collectively the network of smoke detectors may be able to locate the source of the fire, send messages to the emergency services, and even issue voice messages to evacuate a given area.

Users of "smart devices" that can connect to the Internet but choose not to do so may miss out on bug fixes if they are not connected. Whirlpool, not that long ago, had an issue where some of their dryers were catching on fire due to a software bug. When they tried to push new firmware to these devices, they discovered that only a small percentage were actually connected to the Internet, thus hampering the possibility of updating these devices in the field. Users, however, have concerns over privacy issues concerning such technologies. For instance, could data be collected about their use of these devices without their knowledge, or could these devices be "hacked into"?

CHAPTER 2   A REVIEW OF RTOS FUNDAMENTALS

Applications that previously used only buttons and LEDs and possibly an LCD display for user interaction can, these days, communicate over channels such as BLE, Zigbee, and LTE.

Adding such features, which superficially might appear quite straightforward, actually places considerable demands both on the underlying hardware as well as on software developers. One of the great challenges faced by modern product and application developers lies in being able to cope with and manage increased code size and complexity and the need to provide feature-rich applications and deliver them with tight time constraints.

Traditionally embedded systems code is developed in a linear fashion.

In such systems, real-time requirements are taken care of with the help of on-chip and off-chip (board-level) components. As new requirements and features are added, the ability to fine-tune the system behavior becomes more and more limited, till a point is reached where a complete redesign becomes necessary, or the implementation of fixes by, for example, adding an extra microcontroller to the board. Fine-tuning, tweaking, and adapting the application code pose serious problems as far as code maintainability and code reusability are concerned.

A typical standard embedded systems approach uses a "big loop design" supplemented with interrupts for dealing with "time-critical event handling." The basic pattern for this kind of programming is outlined in the left-hand-side flowchart of Figure 2-1.

CHAPTER 2   A REVIEW OF RTOS FUNDAMENTALS

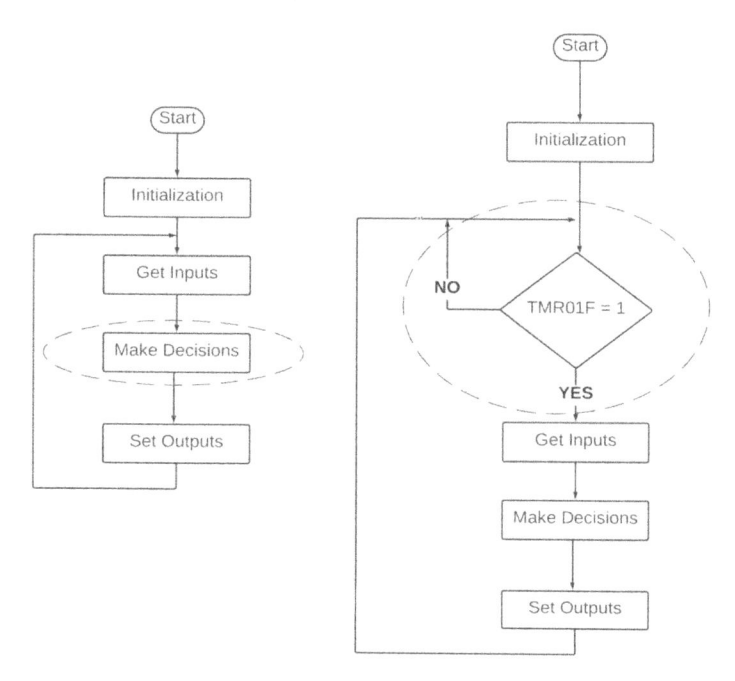

Figure 2-1. Big loop approach to embedded real time

A timer interrupt–driven "gate" (as illustrated in the schematic on the right of Figure 2-1) can be used at the start of the big loop so as to provide more predictable behavior.

It is possible to embed a basic task-oriented approach into this pattern by using "skip timers" to provide a basic "scheduling mechanism" and using state machine techniques to handle the complexities of data and event processing and task/work scheduling. The result is a coding pattern somewhat like what is shown in Figure 2-2.

CHAPTER 2 A REVIEW OF RTOS FUNDAMENTALS

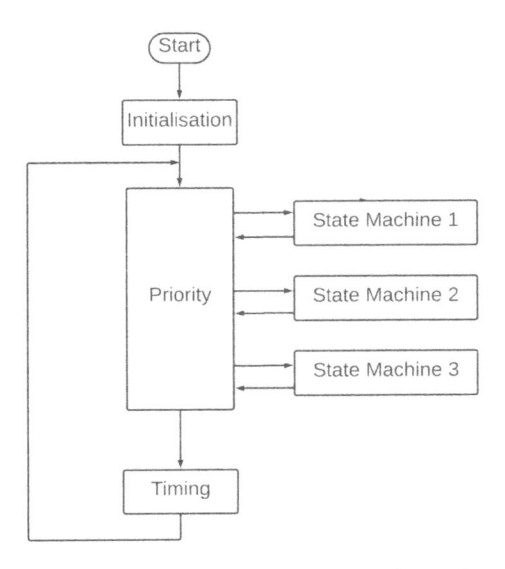

Figure 2-2. *Incorporating priority-based multitasking into a big loop approach*

As the number of tasks that need to be handled and the complexity of these tasks increase, however, the limitations of this approach become more and more apparent. As task interactions and the exchange of data between tasks become more intricate, so even more "difficulties" have to be dealt with.

Embedded System Software Development Strategies/Options

At its simplest, the possible choices are between the following:

- A bare metal implementation that does not use an (RT)OS
- An implementation based on an "in-project" "home-brewed" (RT)OS
- An open source (RT)OS
- A commercial (RT)OS

23

CHAPTER 2   A REVIEW OF RTOS FUNDAMENTALS

An application with characteristics such as the following will probably not require an (RT)OS:

1. The application is relatively simple and involves a small number of tasks that do not require any complex scheduling. The on-chip and on-board peripherals can handle any necessary real-time or scheduling requirements. As a simple example, timers can be used to blink LEDs, and edge-triggered interrupts can be used to react to button presses.

2. The application involves the monitoring of only a few external signals, and the number of actions needed to produce the required/expected behavior is small. In such a system, the use of a sophisticated scheduler would be excessive, and it would probably make the code more difficult to follow. Furthermore, incorporating a scheduler would increase the total code size. In such an application, the gains from separating the application out into clearly demarcated tasks would be small. Code reusability might probably be realized at the driver level.

3. The realization/implementation of a more complex scenario might involve the use of global variables for data exchange and the use of state machines and interrupts. Task flexibility would favor code reusability. However, at the application level, the requirements and needs of the particular tasks involved would need to be considered carefully as the requirements of one task could impose constraints on the resources available for another

task. There are many applications of intermediate complexity, and establishing stable and clear-cut requirements as to where such an approach will work and represents a sensible approach is something that developer teams should try and establish.

At the next "level of complexity," an application may involve tasks making use of more complex hardware components and protocols such as USB, TCP/IP and embedded Ethernet, CAN bus, Wi-Fi, and BLE interfaces, not singly but in combination where multiple communication interfaces and protocols need to be used concurrently. An example might be a node in an automotive system that has a wired Ethernet interface and a CAN bus interface that is interacting with several CAN bus nodes. The IoT (Internet of Things) and IIoT (Industrial Internet of Things) universes provide many case studies where suitably sophisticated (RT)OSes with rich software libraries supporting a variety of network protocols, secure communications profiles, and sophisticated signal processing are essential if code for new applications is to be developed rapidly using modern agile software development techniques. For such applications, an operating system such as Linux may be too big, too complex, and too "resource hungry." This is where operating systems such as AWS FreeRTOS, Azure RTOS ThreadX, and Zephyr RTOS come into play. Of these, Zephyr RTOS is a "true" open source project. AWS FreeRTOS is, essentially, FreeRTOS rebadged by AWS after they purchased FreeRTOS, and Azure RTOS ThreadX is ThreadX rebadged after Microsoft purchased Express Logic, the original developer of ThreadX. Although the source code for FreeRTOS and ThreadX is available to be studied for free, the commercial exploitation of both FreeRTOS and ThreadX is "not entirely without any constraints."

CHAPTER 2   A REVIEW OF RTOS FUNDAMENTALS

The reasons for selecting Zephyr RTOS for many projects in preference to either AWS FreeRTOS or Azure RTOS ThreadX have already been discussed previously.

Considerations for choosing to use an (RT)OS for developing embedded system applications and the kind of applications that would benefit from this have been discussed previously.

The remainder of this chapter will focus on general patterns of multitasking (multithreading) and how these patterns can be implemented using Zephyr RTOS. Wherever possible, the "official" Zephyr RTOS sample code will be used to illustrate these patterns, adapted and elaborated on where necessary.

The Zephyr RTOS code framework supports a wide range of microprocessors and development boards. If you are working for a company planning to develop a product that will be based on Zephyr RTOS, then the chances are that a particular processor has already been chosen, and maybe even a development kit/board to try initial ideas out on.

Many developers are building products using Nordic Semiconductor processors such as the nRF52840, or the nRF5340 or the nRF9160. These processors have on-chip wireless peripherals such as BLE (Bluetooth Low Energy) or LTE (Long-Term Evolution). The wireless technologies on the chip depend on the particular processor chosen. Wireless technologies such as BLE and LTE are widely used in many IoT (Internet of Things) applications. Although this course will not go into applications involving wireless networking in depth, if you will be working on such applications, then it is a good idea to start gaining familiarity with a development system that supports the wireless technology your application will be using.

All of the Nordic processors mentioned are ARM Cortex M devices. The nRF52840 processor is an ARM Cortex M4 device, whereas the nRF5340 and nRF9160 processors are ARM Cortex M33-based devices. ARM Cortex M33 (and ARM Cortex M23) processors are of great interest because they can include support for cryptographic hardware extensions that can

CHAPTER 2 A REVIEW OF RTOS FUNDAMENTALS

be used to implement secure applications based on ARM's TrustZone technology. The nRF5340 device is the most interesting device as it is a dual core device having two ARM Cortex M33 cores, one of which incorporates the cryptographic hardware extensions needed to implement secure TrustZone-based applications and the other used for applications not involving extensive mathematical processing.

Most of the basic Zephyr RTOS code examples will be based on the Nordic Semiconductor nRF52840 DK (Development Kit) (a Cortex M4-based board). This kit is widely used because many commercial BLE sensor devices use this processor.

Nordic Semiconductor has moved its SDK (Software Development Kit) from a bare metal development kit to a kit based around the Zephyr framework. This development kit is called the nRF Connect SDK. To facilitate developing applications using its processor, Nordic Semiconductor provides a desktop application running on Windows, and now also on Linux and Mac OS X machines, called nRF Connect for Desktop that greatly simplifies the setup and installation of Zephyr RTOS development tools and also the installation of the Microsoft VS IDE and the various plug-ins needed to build, load, and debug applications on its various devices. The IDE covered in this book will be the Microsoft VS IDE with the nRF Connect SDK plug-in and other tools installed such as the GNU cross compiler and the GNU debugger.

The advantage of using an IDE such as the Microsoft VS IDE is that it enables things such as being able to edit multiple files from within the IDE, to search and replace across multiple files, color highlighting, autocompletion, and indication of possible syntax errors in the code.

Many other ARM Cortex M0, M4, and M7 processors and associated development kits are available from companies such as STMicroelectronics, Microchip, Silabs, and NXP. Many of these boards are supported by the Zephyr OS framework.

27

CHAPTER 2   A REVIEW OF RTOS FUNDAMENTALS

Zephyr RTOS has also been ported to ESP32 devices and RISC-V devices, and the examples covered in this course can be run, without too much modification, on a variety of ESP32 and RISCV32 boards as well.

Instead of using an IDE such as a Microsoft VS Code–based IDE, it is perfectly possible to develop and test applications using command-line interface (CLI) tools and text-based editors for editing code and configuration files. This is possible because the Zephyr RTOS software development system includes a very effective CLI-based tool called west, which can be used to drive the build and code flashing processes. The Zephyr application building approach makes extensive use of CMake. CMake, though very powerful, is associated with quite a steep learning curve, and west hides the details working with CMake. The VS Code IDE has a terminal window in which west commands can be run. The use of west both within the VS Code IDE and at the command line will be explained in the context of describing how to build the examples, and further details describing west can be found in the corresponding appendix in this book.

Although the various RTOSes mentioned have differing APIs (Application Programming Interfaces), the underlying RTOS components and their APIs are functionally and conceptually very similar. Understanding the various behaviors, patterns, and uses of these objects will provide a deeper understanding of how to build multitasking embedded RTOS applications. It will also be useful when evaluating and comparing different RTOSes and when porting an application from one RTOS to another.

Zephyr, like other operating systems, makes use of OS abstraction layers (OSALs). An OSAL provides wrapper function APIs that encapsulate many of the common system functions provided by the underlying operating system. OSALs supported by Zephyr are POSIX and CMSIS v2. Full details of the features supported and how they differ in detail from the corresponding POSIX and CMSIS v2 APIs can be found in the Zephyr documentation [2].

CHAPTER 2   A REVIEW OF RTOS FUNDAMENTALS

Multitasking and Interprocess Communication and Synchronization Concepts and Patterns

Tasks

Formally a task (thread) is an independent thread of execution that has to compete with other threads for processor execution time. Concurrency in a single processor system is really an illusion that is illustrated in Figure 2-3.

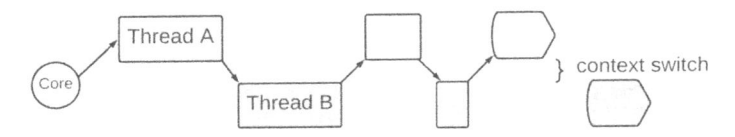

Figure 2-3. *Context switching and the illusion of concurrency*

The illusion of concurrency is realized because context switching between one thread and another is fast. However, it is not free because of the context-switching overhead of storing and restoring execution state when switching between one thread and another.

The actual multitasking context-switching schedule depends on the type of scheduling algorithm (strategy) used. Zephyr RTOS can be configured to use various scheduling strategies such as the following:

- Thread priority–based preemptive multitasking where a running lower priority thread can be preempted by a higher priority thread when the conditions needed for that thread to run have been met

- Cooperative multitasking where threads decide when to pause so that other threads have a chance to run

CHAPTER 2   A REVIEW OF RTOS FUNDAMENTALS

- Round-robin scheduling where threads are given a slice of time in which to run in sequence
- And other variations

When a thread is created, it is given a distinct set of parameters and, also, supporting data structures such as

- Name
- Unique ID
- Priority (if associated with a preemptive scheduler)
- A task control block for holding state information
- A stack
- A task routine

Typically, when a real-time kernel starts, it will create some system tasks as well as user tasks that are associated with appropriate priorities and privileges. The finer details will vary from RTOS to RTOS.

The kinds of system tasks provided by the kernel can include tasks for handling kernel startup, an idle task that uses up CPU cycles when there is no work to do, a logging task that logs system message to some logging system, an exception-handling task that runs when exceptions are detected, and, when debugging code, a debug agent task. In systems that must minimize energy consumption, the idle task may also be responsible for putting the system into a low power mode/sleep mode.

Tasks in a multitasking system may be in one of a number of defined states. A basic enumeration of states envisages a task as being either in a ready-to-run state, a waiting or blocked state in which the task is waiting for a resource to become available, or an event to occur, or a task sleep interval to expire, or in an actually running state. An RTOS may also be able to suspend or terminate a task.

CHAPTER 2   A REVIEW OF RTOS FUNDAMENTALS

The behavior of a task in a preemptive multitasking system can be described in terms of a Finite State Machine such as the one shown in Figure 2-4, which is the FSM given in the Zephyr documentation.

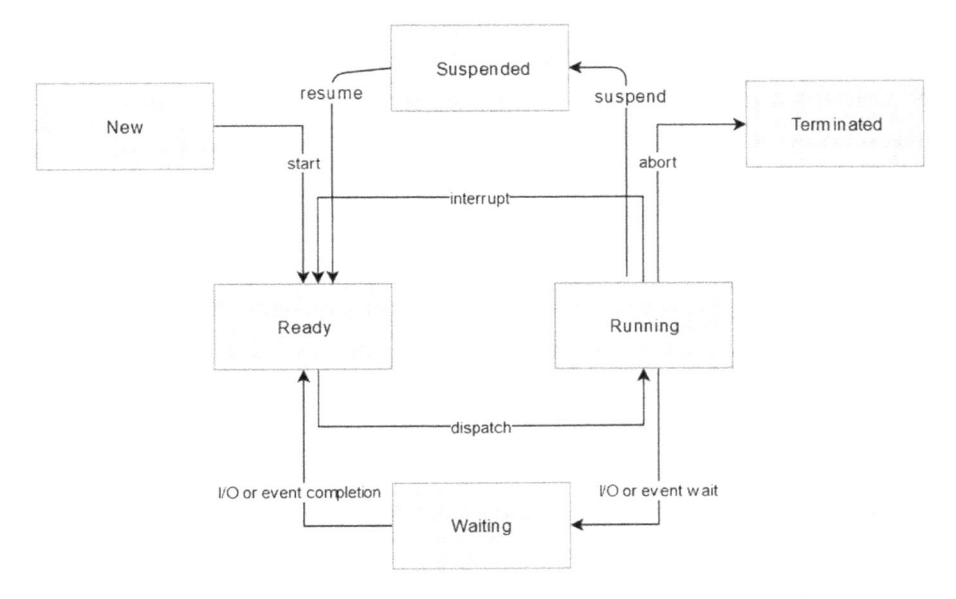

Figure 2-4. Finite State Machine (FSM) model of multitasking in Zephyr

A task may block for a number of reasons such as waiting for a synchronization object such as a mutex of a semaphore to be released, waiting for a message to arrive in a message queue, or waiting for a time delay imposed on the task to expire.

When a task becomes unblocked, it will start running if it is the highest priority task that is eligible to run or placed into the appropriate position in the queue of ready-to-run tasks otherwise. In Zephyr, actually, **Running** is a schedule state that only applies to **Ready** threads. At the risk of stating the obvious, only one thread can actually be running at any one time. The kernel is responsible for the creation and management of thread tasks and provides methods for doing things such as creating and deleting tasks, controlling the scheduling of tasks, and getting information about tasks.

31

CHAPTER 2   A REVIEW OF RTOS FUNDAMENTALS

    Managing tasks and their associated resources is a critical aspect of implementing real-time applications. For instance, when a task is terminated (deleted), it is important that any resources it was using are released or freed correctly. For systems with limited resources running on processors not having a memory management unit, dynamically creating and deleting multiple tasks can cause problems such as difficulties of guaranteeing deterministic behavior, and the continuous creation and deletion of tasks increase the risk of memory fragmentation. Task creation may make sense where the target system is running a server supporting multiple clients. The need for testability and determinism in constrained embedded systems favors designs in which the number of tasks and the work they do as well as their priorities is fixed as part of the application design process.

    Many RTOS kernels, including Zephyr, provide an API that can control task scheduling. Such APIs contain methods for doing things such as suspending, resuming, delaying, and restarting tasks, as well as methods for getting and setting the priority of a task.

    RTOS APIs also, typically, provide methods for obtaining task details such as the IDs of the installed tasks, task control block information, and resources owned by a task.

    The tasks in an application may be either "run-to-completion" tasks or "infinite loop" tasks.

    A common scenario involving a "run-to-completion" task is that it is a high priority task that initializes and starts up a set of tasks associated with the application and then ends itself. Most tasks in an application are "infinite loop tasks."

    There is some debate about the merits of describing application code using pseudocode as part of the design and documentation process and using this pseudocode as a source of documentation. An alternative approach favors a "clean code" approach in which the only comments permitted in the code pertain to engineering decisions, and implicit documentation is contained in the use of descriptive names for functions and variables.

CHAPTER 2 A REVIEW OF RTOS FUNDAMENTALS

The pseudocode for a run-to-completion task might follow a pattern like the following:

```
ARunToCompletionTask()
{
    InitialiseApplication;
    Create a number of infinite loop tasks;
    Create required kernel objects/resources
    Delete/Suspend this task
}
```

An infinite loop task might follow a pattern such as the following:

```
InfiniteLoopTask()
{
    Initialisation steps
    Loop Forever
    {
        body of loop code which, typically
        includes one or more blocking calls
    }
}
```

Intertask Communication

Mastering RTOS programming requires an understanding of the various intertask communication methods supported by the RTOS such as mutexes, semaphores, queues, message queues, and workqueues.

Every RTOS provides semaphores and mutexes, which are the most fundamental synchronization and communication mechanisms.

33

CHAPTER 2   A REVIEW OF RTOS FUNDAMENTALS

Semaphore

Formally, a semaphore can be described as a kernel object that one or more threads of execution (tasks) can acquire or release for the purposes of synchronization or mutual exclusion. The use of binary semaphores for mutual exclusion is better avoided, and mutexes are used instead. This is because in modern RTOS such as Zephyr, mutexes implement a priority inheritance mechanism that prevents a priority inversion situation in which a low priority process, in effect, blocks a higher priority process because it holds a resource needed by the higher priority process. Another important feature provided by modern mutexes is that they function recursively, thus preventing certain deadlock situations from arising, as will be discussed later.

When a semaphore object is created, the kernel assigns a data structure – a semaphore control block (SCB) – to it as well as a unique ID, a count value, and a task-waiting list. A semaphore can be thought of as a key which a task must acquire in order to access some resource or other. If the task can acquire the semaphore, then it can access the resource. If the task cannot acquire the semaphore, then it must wait till some other task releases it. From a programming perspective, there are two main kinds of binary semaphores that can only have a value of 0 or 1 and counting semaphores that can count over a greater range of numbers. A binary semaphore can be thought of as a specialized counting semaphore.

Binary Semaphore

A binary semaphore can have only two possible values: 0 and 1. When a binary semaphore is not held by any task, it has the value 1, and when a task acquires a semaphore, its value is set to 0. No other task can acquire the semaphore while its value is 0. In use, a binary semaphore is a global resource – shared by all tasks that need it, and it is possible for a task

CHAPTER 2   A REVIEW OF RTOS FUNDAMENTALS

other than the task that initially acquired the semaphore to release the semaphore. It is the choreography of semaphore usage among tasks that makes semaphores effective.

Figure 2-5 depicts the behavior of a binary semaphore as an FSM (Finite State Machine).

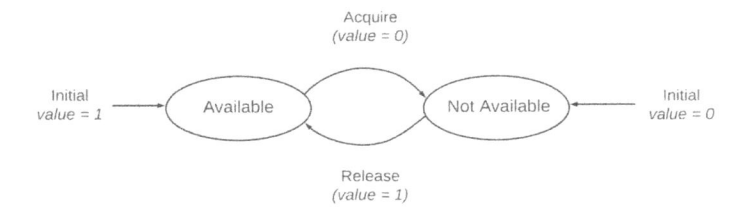

```
                        Acquire
                       (value = 0)
                       ─────────→
   Initial                                            Initial
   value = 1  ──→  ( Available )    ( Not Available ) ←──  value = 0
                       ←─────────
                        Release
                       (value = 1)
```

Figure 2-5. *State machine for a binary semaphore*

Counting Semaphore

A counting semaphore can be acquired or released multiple times. It does this via a counter. If the count value is 0, the counting semaphore is in the unavailable state. If the count is greater than 1, then the semaphore is available. When a counting semaphore is created, its initial count can be specified. In some operating systems, the maximum count value can also be specified – that is, the counting semaphore is a bounded semaphore (the count is bounded). In other operating systems, the count may be unbounded. Acquiring a counting semaphore reduces the counter value by 1, and releasing the counting semaphore increases the counter value by 1.

The behavior of a counting semaphore is described by the FSM shown in Figure 2-6.

CHAPTER 2   A REVIEW OF RTOS FUNDAMENTALS

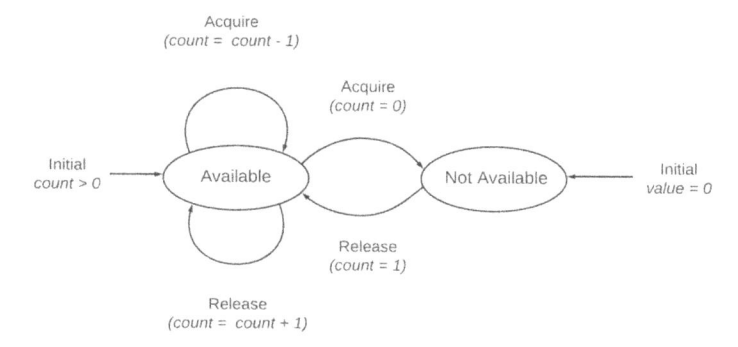

Figure 2-6. *State machine for a counting semaphore*

Mutual Exclusions Semaphore (Mutex)

A mutex such as the Zephyr RTOS mutex is sometimes described as a special kind of binary semaphore that has the properties of ownership, recursive locking, task deletion safety, and priority inversion avoidance protocol behavior. It is probably better to think of semaphore and mutexes as serving separate purposes. The mutex is an object to be used for mutual exclusion, and the semaphore is an object to be used for task synchronization.

The mutex can be in one of two states: locked (0) or unlocked (1). When created, it is in the unlocked state – and can be acquired by a task. Once a mutex is acquired, its state becomes the locked state, and that mutex can only be released by the task that acquired ownership of that mutex when it obtained the mutex. Once released, its state becomes the unlocked state.

Recursive locking means that a task that owns a mutex can acquire it multiple times in the locked state. A recursive mutex permits nesting of attempts to lock the mutex in the sense that a function that acquires the mutex can call another function that can acquire the mutex again, and can release the mutex just before it returns. In practice, the use of this recursive feature is best avoided even though it is supported.

The property of task deletion safety means that a task cannot be deleted while it owns the mutex.

CHAPTER 2 A REVIEW OF RTOS FUNDAMENTALS

Priority Inversion Avoidance

Typically, priority inversion occurs when a higher priority task is blocked because it is waiting for a lower priority task to release a needed mutex, and where the lower priority task has itself been preempted by an intermediate level priority task. In effect, the priority of the high priority task has been inverted to that of the low priority task. Where the RTOS implements a priority inversion avoidance scheme, such as Zephyr, the thread that has locked a mutex is eligible for priority inheritance. Here, the kernel will temporarily elevate the thread's priority when a higher priority thread tries to acquire that mutex. The intention is that the owning thread will now be able to complete its work and release the mutex sooner by executing at the same priority as the waiting thread. When the owning thread releases the lock (or if the high priority waiting thread times out), the kernel restores the base priority of that thread from the value saved in the mutex data structure.

An FSM description of the behavior of the mutex is shown in Figure 2-7.

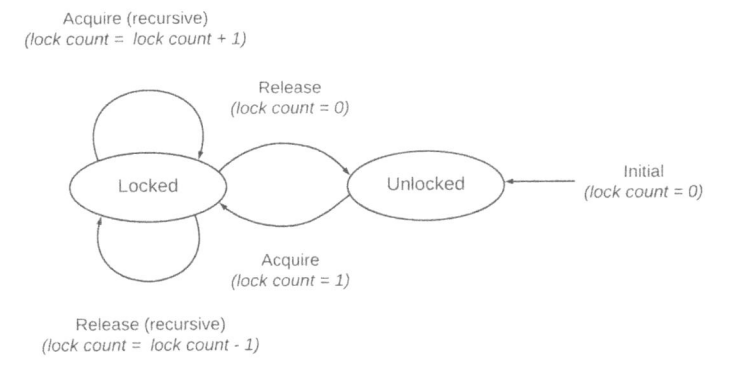

Figure 2-7. State machine for a recursive mutex

Using Semaphores and Mutexes in Interrupt Service Routines

An interrupt service routine must be responsive; hence, the code involved must be of short duration. This means that invoking an operation that might block is not permissible in an interrupt service routine. Hence, releasing a binary semaphore or a counting semaphore is allowed, but attempting to acquire a binary semaphore or a counting semaphore is not allowed. In general, mutexes should not be used in interrupt service routines.

Semaphore Usage Patterns and Scenarios

In this section, a number of well-known semaphore usage patterns will be described. These usage patterns are used for the purposes of waiting, signalling, and tracking and for controlling access to shared resources. Some of the patterns depend on the use of semaphores combined with tasks running at appropriate priority levels. Some of the patterns can become quite complex, and only the simpler, generally used, patterns will be considered here.

Wait and Signal Synchronization

Here, two tasks communicate for the purpose of synchronization without any data/information being exchanged. The Wait and Signal Synchronization pattern involves a binary semaphore and having different priority levels for the two tasks involved. In this pattern, the binary semaphore is initially unavailable (its value is 0). The higher priority task runs first, and at some point, it makes a request for the semaphore. At this point, the task will block because the semaphore is not available. The lower priority task (the signalling task) now has a chance to run. At some point, the signalling task releases the semaphore. The higher priority task is now eligible to run, and it will preempt the lower priority task. The cycle is repeated. The higher priority task sets the semaphore to zero. Then at some later point in time, it tries to acquire the semaphore and will block (because a binary semaphore is not recursive) and so the signalling cycle can go around again once more.

Credit Tracking Synchronization

In this pattern, the signalling task executes at a higher rate than the signalled task (the wait task), and the signalling task runs at a higher priority than the signalled task.

    The signalling task signals by incrementing the counting semaphore. When the signalled task is able to run, it tries to acquire the counting semaphore and will either block (if the semaphore counter is at zero) or succeed and decrement the semaphore count (atomically) by one otherwise. The scenario underlying this pattern is that the signalling task may signal in bursts, and if this pattern is used, the signalled task has a chance to "catch up" in between bursts. For example, an interrupt service routine (ISR) may execute at high priority when an interrupt is triggered, perform essential interrupt handling, and then offload the remaining processing required to handle the interrupt by signalling on a counting semaphore. The lower priority task (which is acting as a second-level (deferred) handler) can then unblock and carry out the remainder of the interrupt handling work.

    The pseudocode illustrating this synchronization pattern is really simple:

```
tWaitTask()
{
    ...
```

```
        Acquire counting semaphore
        ...
}
tSignalTask()
{
    ...
    Acquire counting semaphore
    ...
}
```

Synchronizing Access to a Shared Resource Using a Binary Semaphore

The objective underlying this pattern is to ensure that only one task/concurrent thread of execution at a time can access a shared resource. It involves the use of a binary semaphore that is initially in the available state. In order to gain access to the shared resource, a task must first acquire the semaphore. Once this is done, then, any other task attempting to acquire this semaphore will now block. When the task that has the semaphore has finished with the shared resource, it releases the semaphore. Now, a task that was blocked in its attempt to acquire the semaphore is unblocked and can make use of the shared resource in turn.

The pseudocode for this pattern is quite simple:

```
tAccessingTask ()
{
      ...
      Acquire binary semaphore
      Make use of the shared resource ( e.g. read or
      write to it )
```

```
    Release the binary semaphore
    ..;
}
```

A potential risk with this approach is that a task that has not acquired the binary semaphore may release it. And this is why a safer approach is to use a mutex instead of a binary semaphore, as only a task that has ownership of the mutex can release it.

A variant of this pattern for controlling access to multiple, equivalent, shared resources involves replacing a binary semaphore with a counting semaphore. In this case, great care must be taken to ensure that a task only releases a semaphore it has actually acquired.

Message Queueing and Message Queues

The purpose of a message queue is to provide a mechanism that can be used by tasks as well as ISRs to communicate and to synchronize while at the same time conveying data. The mechanism involves the use of a buffer-like object – a pipeline that, temporarily, holds messages from a sender(s) till the target receiver is able to read them. A beneficial effect of this approach is that it decouples the sending and receiving tasks. When a message queue is created, then, typically, an associated Queue Control Block (QCB), a message queue name, a unique ID, and a memory buffer(s) are assigned to it. The amount of memory allocated will depend on factors such as queue length and maximum message length.

Blocking is built into the message queue in the sense that a sending task blocks when the message queue is full, and a reading task blocks when the message queue is empty.

The schematic illustrated in Figure 2-8 shows the typical parameters and data structure associated with a message queue.

CHAPTER 2   A REVIEW OF RTOS FUNDAMENTALS

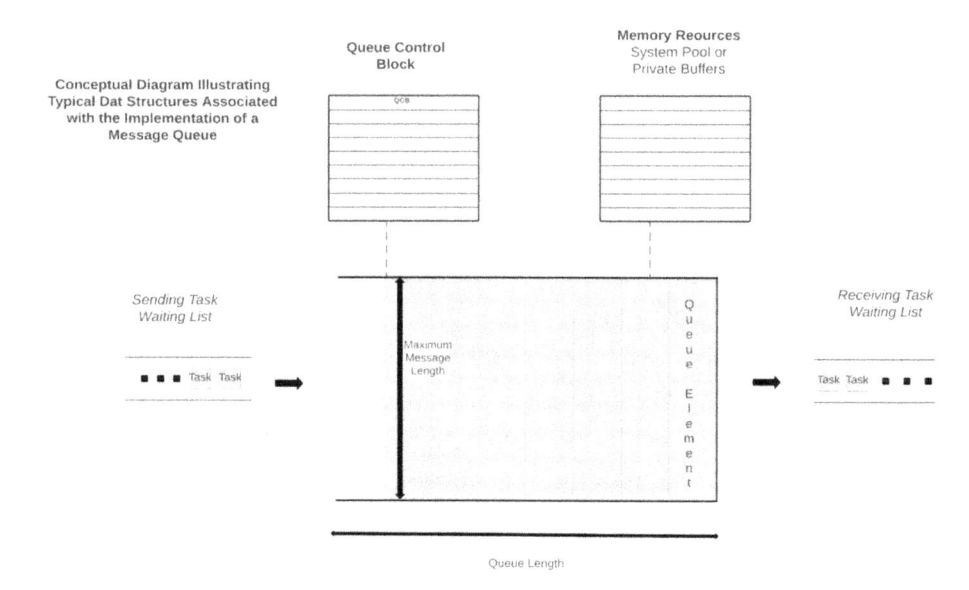

Figure 2-8. *Structure and components of a message queue*

The behavior of a message queue is outlined in the FSM diagram shown in Figure 2-9.

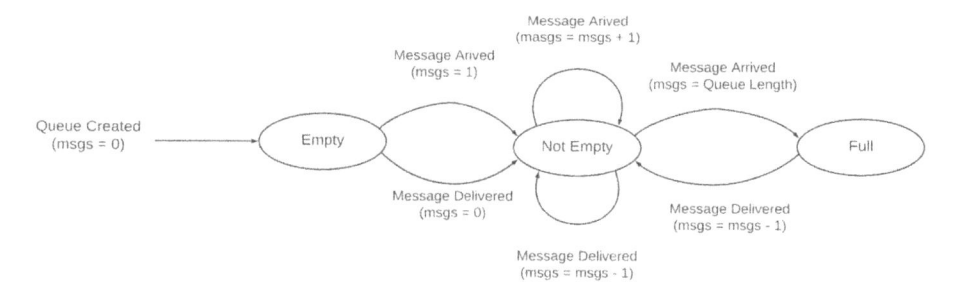

Figure 2-9. *State machine for a message queue*

The detailed mechanisms by which data is transferred whether by reference or by value (copying) are implementation dependent. The Zephyr RTOS message queue implementation uses a circular (ring) buffer of messages of a given size (which is specified at creation time) and copies data into the buffer. The Zephyr API also provides a mechanism for flushing data out of the buffer when it is full, thereby making it possible to discard older (stale) data and release space for storing new data (messages).

In practice, message queues can, by implementing the appropriate application code, be used in various ways (protocols) such as non-interlocked one-way communication, interlocked one-way communication, and interlocked two-way communication. It is also possible, with suitable extensions, to provide message queue functionality with message broadcast capabilities. In the case of Zephyr RTOS, it is the Zephyr mailbox that provides enhanced mail queue capabilities.

Interrupt service routines (ISRs) typically use the non-interlocked, one-way data communication pattern in which the receiving task runs and waits on a message queue. In this scenario, the ISR, when triggered, places one or more messages on the message queue. This needs to be done in a nonblocking way and consideration being given when implementing code to the possibility that when the message queue is full, then messages may be lost or overwritten.

Interlocked, One-Way Data Communication

In this pattern, the sending task sends a message and waits to see if the message has been received. If the message is, for some reason, not received correctly, then it can be retransmitted. The main use of this pattern is to implement a closed loop form of synchronization in which the sending and receiving tasks operate in lockstep with one another. There are various ways of implementing such a pattern. One possible way is to use a sending task, a message queue (with a length of 1), a receiving task, and a binary semaphore. In this implementation, the initial value of the binary semaphore is 0. The sending task sends a message to the message queue and blocks on the binary semaphore. The receiving task receives the message and increments the binary semaphore, which will unblock the sending task, which can then send the next message. In this implementation, the semaphore is acting as a simple acknowledgment to the sender that it is OK to send the next message.

The following pseudocode illustrates a one-way data communication implementation pattern:

```
tSendingTask()
{
      ...
      Send message to message queue
      Acquire binary semaphore
      ...
}

tReceivingTask()
{
      ...
      Receive message from message queue
      Release binary semaphore
      ...
}
```

Interlocked, Two-Way Data Communication

Interlocked, two-way data communication involves two tasks and two message queues. The details of the synchronization process depend on the kind of data that needs to be exchanged. For example, two message queues are required for a two-way exchange of data, whereas a semaphore can be used in the case where only a simple acknowledgment is required.

CHAPTER 2   A REVIEW OF RTOS FUNDAMENTALS

A pseudocode snippet illustrating two-way data communication follows here:

```
tClientTask()
{
    ...
    Send message to server's requests message queue
    Acquire binary semaphore
    ...
}

tServerTask()
{
    ...
    Receive message from server's responses message queue
    Release binary semaphore
    ...
}
```

Pipes

Pipes are kernel objects provided by operating systems such as Unix/Linux and Windows and, also, Zephyr RTOS. A pipe implements a mechanism for unidirectional stream-oriented data exchange. A pipe is associated with two descriptors: one for the reading end and one for the writing end. Data is held (buffered) in the pipe as an unstructured byte stream and read from the pipe in FIFO (first in, first out) order. Synchronizing of the reader and writer process involves the reader process blocking when the pipe is empty and the writer process blocking when the pipe is full. In contrast to a message queue, the data in a pipe is not structured, and there is no mechanism for prioritizing data in a pipe.

Schematically the architecture of a pipe is like that shown in Figure 2-10.

45

CHAPTER 2   A REVIEW OF RTOS FUNDAMENTALS

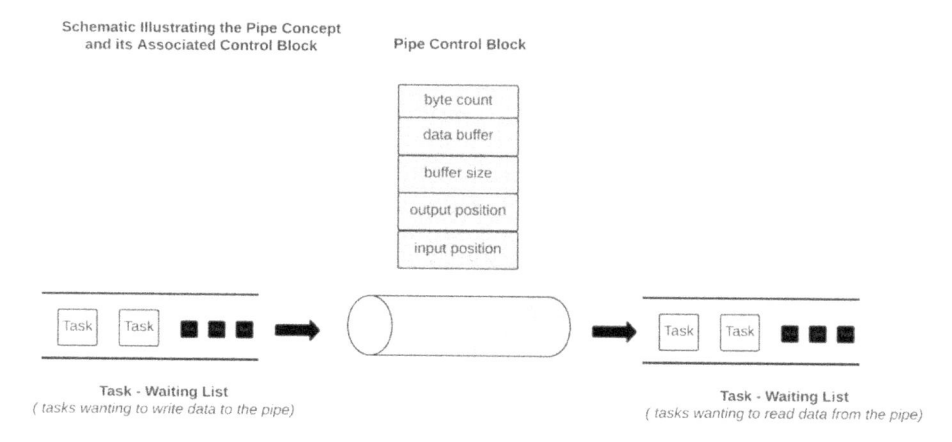

Figure 2-10. *Schematic of a pipe and its associated control block*

The creation of a pipe and its associated queues and control blocks requires allocation of memory. Pipes can be created and destroyed dynamically. The pipe control block, instantiated when the pipe instance is created, contains pipe-specific information such as the size of the pipe buffer, the amount of data (byte count) in the pipe, input and output position indicators, as well as a list of tasks waiting to write to the pipe (blocked because the buffer is full) and a list of tasks waiting to read from the pipe (blocked when the buffer is empty).

Figure 2-11 outlines the behavior of a pipe mechanism.

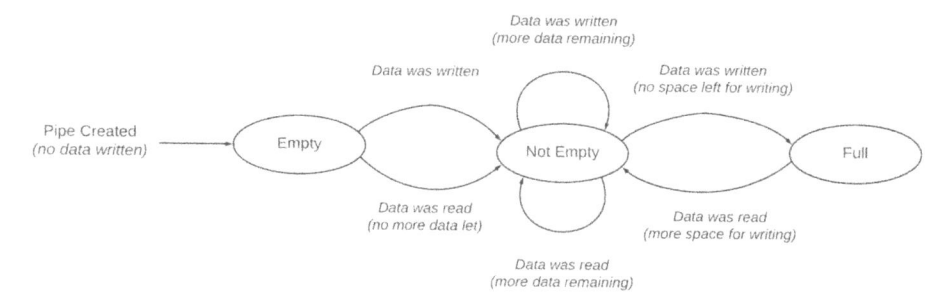

Figure 2-11. *State machine for a pipe*

46

Most implementations of pipes, including the Zephyr RTOS implementation, provide a mechanism for explicitly flushing the pipe buffer.

Event Objects (Event Registers)

An event object is associated with a task. The implementation details are hardware and kernel specific. It is, essentially, a collection of binary event flags, typically 32 bits, where every bit is associated with some specific event. These bits can be set or cleared and are used by a task to check for the occurrence/non-occurrence of a particular event. An ISR can, for example, set a bit in an event object to inform a task that a particular event has occurred. A task can perform conditional checks specified by a combination (using ANDs and ORs) of the event register bit flags. Event checking strategies can be not to wait (block), to wait indefinitely, or to wait with a timeout.

In Zephyr RTOS, there is no fixed limit on the number of event objects that can be defined. Each event object is referenced by its memory address, and one or more threads may wait on an event object until some specified set of events has been delivered to the event object. When new events are delivered to an event object, all the threads whose wait conditions are met, simultaneously, become ready to run. In Zephyr RTOS, events may be **delivered** by a thread or an ISR that may either overwrite the existing set of events or add to it in a bitwise fashion.

When working with event objects, it is worth noting that no data is associated with an event when an event is delivered (sent) through an event object (register) and that identifying protocols need to be agreed upon between senders and receivers, that is, a particular task sends a particular event by setting a particular flag (bit) in the event object. The events in an event object are not queued, and an event object cannot count the number of occurrences of an event while it is pending.

CHAPTER 2   A REVIEW OF RTOS FUNDAMENTALS

Condition Variables

A condition variable is a kernel object that is associated with some shared resource. It is used by one to wait until some other task sets the shared resource to some specified condition. The condition is deduced by evaluating some kind of logical expression (predicate). When a task examines a condition variable, it must have exclusive access to that variable, and hence, a mutex is used in conjunction with a condition variable. The task must first acquire the mutex before evaluating the predicate. If the predicate evaluates to false, the task blocks till the desired condition is attained. The implementation is such that the operation of releasing the mutex and block-waiting for the condition is an atomic (indivisible) operation.

The following pseudocode snippet illustrates the common way of using condition variables:

```
//Task 1:
Lock Mutex
Examine shared resource
While ( shared resource is busy )
WAIT ( condition variable )
Mark shared resource as Busy
Unlock Mutex
```

```
//Task 2:
Lock Mutex
Mark shared resource as Free
SIGNAL ( condition variable )
Unlock Mutex
```

Because a signal on a condition variable is lost when there is nothing waiting on it, a task should check for the presence of the desired condition before waiting on it and should check for the presence of the desired condition after a wakeup.

Interrupts and Exceptions

The subject of interrupts and exceptions and how interrupts and exceptions are handled is complex, and here, only the key basic concepts and issues will be covered.

An exception is an event that disrupts the normal execution of the processor and forces the processor into the execution of some specified special instructions in a privileged state.

Exceptions may be either synchronous exceptions, generated as a result of the execution of some processor instructions (e.g., memory alignment exception, divide-by-zero exception), or asynchronous exceptions (normally called interrupts) that are raised by external events not directly related to the execution of processor instructions that are generally associated with hardware signals (e.g., processor reset, receipt of a packet by some network interface device).

Exceptions provide a powerful communication mechanism between the hardware and an application currently running on the processor and are used in contexts such as the handling of internal errors and special conditions, dealing with hardware concurrency, and the handling of service requests.

Special conditions are generated by the execution of special instructions such as when a task running at a user privilege level attempts to issue an instruction that can only be run at a privileged supervisor (kernel) level. These kinds of exceptions can be used to force the processor into a privileged level where it has access to the privileged instruction set.

In Zephyr RTOS, it is possible to configure an application build into user code and privileged code and so prevent user code from calling various kernel functions and services directly. This is how Zephyr user applications can be implemented that need to issue some kind of system call to access privileged services indirectly.

CHAPTER 2 A REVIEW OF RTOS FUNDAMENTALS

Exceptions can be split into two types, namely, asynchronous and synchronous. A synchronous exception arises at a chosen point in the execution of a task thread, whereas an asynchronous exception can occur at any time or place in the execution of a task thread. Asynchronous exceptions (interrupts) can be subdivided into maskable interrupts that can be blocked or enabled by software and nonmaskable interrupts that cannot be blocked by software and will always be acknowledged by the processor. A hardware reset exception, for example, is always nonmaskable. Synchronous exceptions can be subdivided into precise exceptions, where the processor's program counter points exactly to the instruction that gave rise to the exception, and imprecise exceptions, where this is not the case. Imprecise exceptions may arise in processor architectures that make extensive use of pipelining, or pre-fetch algorithms.

When an exception or external interrupt occurs (is raised), the processor will save the current state information of the processor and load address (entry point) of the function that is to handle that exception or interrupt and then transfer control to that function for it to execute. After the handler has completed its work, the processor state information that was saved is restored, and a return from the interrupt takes place. Returning from an interrupt can also be a point at which the scheduler can run and decide whether the task that was interrupted can continue to run, or whether that task should be paused and a higher priority task be scheduled to run in its place.

Best practice when implementing interrupt handling is that the interrupt handler does only the minimum amount of work needed to deal with the interrupt and then delegates the remaining work to some lower order priority task.

This approach is commonly considered a best practice approach when it comes to implementing real-world interrupt handlers.

CHAPTER 2   A REVIEW OF RTOS FUNDAMENTALS

The installation and configuration of interrupts and exception handlers are an important aspect of building Zephyr RTOS applications. It involves understanding more advanced topics such as working with Kconfig and the devicetree components of Zephyr, which will be introduced in a later chapter.

When designing an application involving interrupts, it is important to take the timing requirements of the applications and the devices used into account. This is an important part of the analysis and design part of the application development process. As part of the design process, input characteristics such as burstiness and periodicity need to be taken into account as well as speed of response and data throughput.

A developer of an ISR needs to consider the effects of disabling interrupts and using polling instead, assigning interrupt priorities, and considering the effects of disabling interrupts under certain circumstances. A critical design consideration when using polling is to take the possibility of interrupt misses into account, for example, when implementing a driver for a device using an edge-triggering mechanism to assert an interrupt.

Timing analysis in the context of developing ISRs takes into consideration the time interval between interrupts, as well as interrupt latency, which is the time between the interrupt being raised and the time when the ISR routine begins to execute. The interrupt response time is the sum of the interrupt latency and the interrupt process time.

Figure 2-12 [3] illustrates latency in terms of clock cycles as would occur in a typical microcontroller such as an ARM Cortex M microcontroller.

51

CHAPTER 2 A REVIEW OF RTOS FUNDAMENTALS

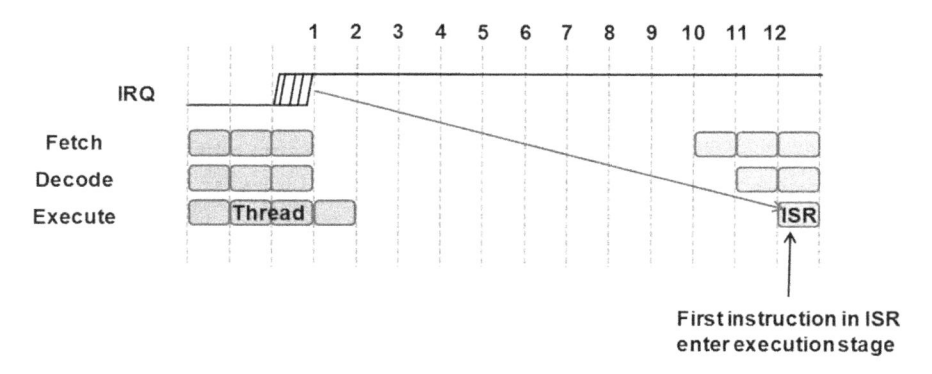

Figure 2-12. Interrupt latency of an ISR

Timing and Timers

Timers are essential in embedded systems in general and operating systems in particular.

Time-sensitive activities in an embedded system may be driven by hard timers that use physical timer circuitry that directly interrupts the processor when the timer expires, and soft timers in which timing events are generated by software. The number of hard timers is limited, but the number of soft timers that can be created is much greater. Soft timers are used where high timing precision (of the order of microseconds) is not required and where a timing resolution to within a couple of milliseconds is adequate.

Zephyr, like most operating systems, has a System Clock that tracks the time that has elapsed since system power-up. The initial value can be retrieved from a real-time clock if there is one in the application hardware. The System Clock is driven by a programmable interval timer. The timer initialization is performed as part of the startup process.

An RTOS timer API should include methods for creating and initializing a timer, a function pointer to a function to execute when the timer expires, methods for starting and stopping a timer, as well as methods for retrieving timer-related information. In Zephyr RTOS, these timers provide higher precision and/or control than can be provided by the simpler k_sleep() and k_usleep() sleep calls, which are used to suspend a thread for a specified amount of time in seconds or microseconds, respectively.

The Zephyr kernel implements efficient code to manage and index into collections of kernel timer objects. Should you wish to dig deeper into the kernel source code, then start becoming familiar with the data structure APIs used by Zephyr and the implementation of their underlying algorithms. The data structure APIs include balanced Red/Black tree, doubly linked list, flagged single-linked list, single-linked list, and ring buffers.

Memory Management

In embedded systems with limited memory resources, dynamic memory allocation and management should be avoided unless really necessary. In this section, the essential aspects of dynamic memory management in embedded system applications will be introduced. In a later section, an example of working with the Zephyr RTOS memory management APIs will be explored.

An embedded system such as Zephyr RTOS will provide some memory management services – usually via system/library calls such as malloc() and free(). A common problem with applications that make frequent, varying memory size calls to `malloc()` and `free()` is that this may lead to memory fragmentation. In its most basic form, dynamic memory allocation takes place from a contiguous block of memory called the heap. A memory management facility maintains information about the heap in a reserved (control block) area of memory, which includes things such as the start address and total size of the memory block, and will implement an allocation table, which tracks the areas of memory that are in use and those that are free, including the size of each free area of memory.

Memory is normally allocated in multiples of some fixed block size, for example, 32 bytes. When a request for memory is made, the smallest number of contiguous blocks that can satisfy that request is allocated. One possible technique for handling memory fragmentation is to use some form of memory compaction to combine small free blocks into one larger block of contiguous memory. The disadvantages of such an approach include things such as the need for block copying of data and the inability of an application to access data while it is being block copied. Memory management also needs to take architecture-specific memory alignment requirements into account (e.g., multi-byte data items such as long integers may need to be aligned on an address that is a multiple of 4). Zephyr provides a variety of memory management approaches such as shared multi-heaps, memory slab allocation, fixed block size allocation, and demand paging.

In general, in embedded system applications, it is best to avoid having a thread allocate memory dynamically. Common good practice is to allocate dynamic memory at the start of the application so that this memory will, in effect, appear to be static memory.

When allocating memory dynamically, it is important to consider whether a thread trying to allocate memory from the heap should either block indefinitely till memory becomes available, block for some specified timeout period, or return without blocking when memory is not available. Best practice here is to keep dynamic memory allocation in the middle of a running program to a minimum, performing all the dynamic memory allocation early on in the application and then working as if that dynamically allocated memory is static from then on.

A common pattern for allowing a thread to acquire extra memory when really necessary is to use a memory allocation strategy that allocates memory in fixed-size blocks only and organizes blocks of available

CHAPTER 2 A REVIEW OF RTOS FUNDAMENTALS

memory as a linked list. In the context of multithreading, the allocation of a block of memory must be atomic. One way of realizing such a design in a fixed memory block size implementation is to implement a blocking memory allocation function via the use of a mutex lock and a counting semaphore as shown in Figure 2-13.

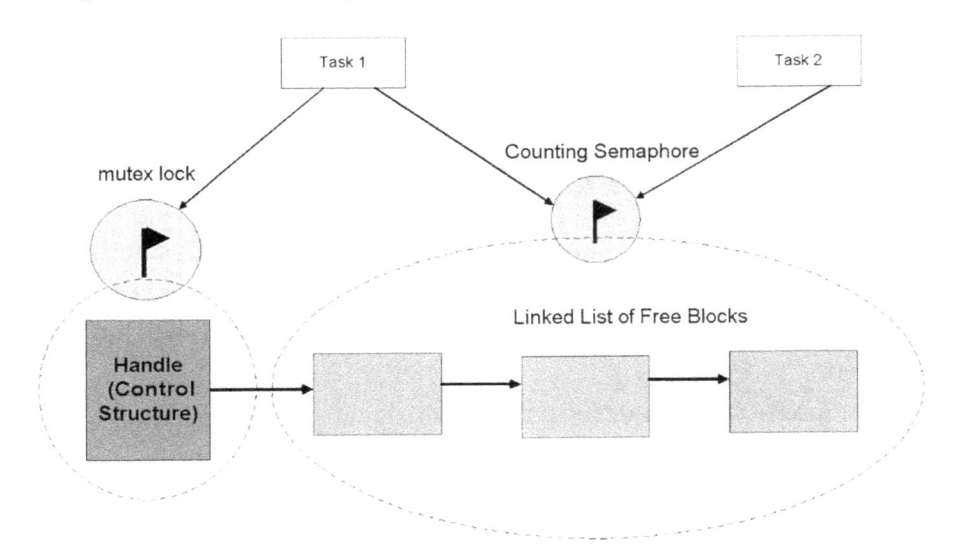

Figure 2-13. How to ensure atomic allocation of a memory block

This is a relatively basic approach, but it is necessary to be aware of the various possible approaches when, for example, looking into the Zephyr source code in order to gain a better understanding of how it implements memory management.

It is possible to implement simplified/specialized memory management using a block of memory "carved out at compile time." The following pseudocode snippet shows a possible approach:

```
/* Memory Allocation */
Acquire ( counting_semaphore )
Lock ( mutex )
```

55

```
Retrieve memory block from pool
Unlock ( mutex )
/* Memory Deallocation */
Lock ( mutex )
Release memory block back into the pool
Unlock ( mutex )
Release ( counting_semaphore )
```

Synchronization Patterns and Strategies

The patterns described next are well-known and well-studied patterns. Here, the emphasis will be on understanding the patterns. Later converting these patterns into realizations using the various Zephyr APIs will be described.

The kinds of synchronization that arise in real-world applications are resource synchronization, activity synchronization, barrier synchronization, and rendezvous synchronization. Resource synchronization is concerned with safe access to some shared resource(s) and makes use of synchronization primitives such as mutexes and semaphores in the implementation of mutual exclusion algorithms. Activity synchronization is concerned with situations in multithreaded/multitasking applications where a collection of cooperating tasks needs to, collectively, reach a certain state before they can proceed. A task in the collection will block till all the tasks have reached the required state. In barrier synchronization, a task posts its arrival at a barrier. This task then waits for other participating tasks to reach that barrier. When all the tasks have reached the barrier, then, each task will receive a notification that it can proceed beyond the barrier.

Rendezvous synchronization is quite subtle. It involves the use of synchronization and a communication point (called an entry). In this pattern, one task defines an entry and makes it public, and then, another

CHAPTER 2 A REVIEW OF RTOS FUNDAMENTALS

task calls the entry (as an ordinary function call). The issuer of the entry call is blocked if the call cannot be accepted. The task that defines the entry, normally, accepts the call, executes it, and returns the results to the caller. It is possible to have a rendezvous involving bidirectional movement of data. A rendezvous that does not involve data passing between two tasks (a simple rendezvous) can be implemented by using two binary semaphores.

Figure 2-14 illustrates the case of a simple rendezvous.

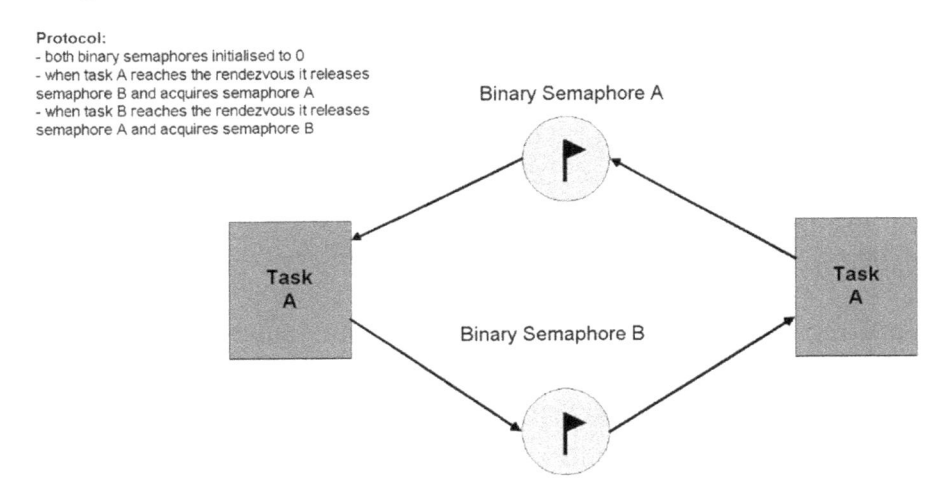

Protocol:
- both binary semaphores initialised to 0
- when task A reaches the rendezvous it releases semaphore B and acquires semaphore A
- when task B reaches the rendezvous it releases semaphore A and acquires semaphore B

Figure 2-14. Basic rendezvous

The following pseudocode snippet shows how a barrier synchronization pattern might be realized:

```
typedef struct {
      mutex_type barrier_lock;
      condition_var_type barrier_condition;
      int barrier_count;
      int number_of_threads;
} barrier_type;

barrier_call( barrier_type * barr ) {
```

57

```
        lock_mutex(&(barr->barrier_lock));
        barr->barrier_count++;
        If(barr->barrier_count < barr->number_of_threads)
        condition_wait(&(barr->barrier_condition),
        &(barr->barrier_lock));
        else {
                barr->barrier_count = 0;
                condition_broadcast(&(barr->barrier_
                condition));
        }
        unlock_mutex(&(barr->barrier_lock));
}
```

Communication Patterns

Identifying communication patterns in applications and exploiting such patterns can lead to faster code implementation as well as help make the code more maintainable and easier to understand and test.

One way of classifying communication patterns is the distinction between signal centric and data centric or a combination of the two. In signal-centric communication, all the necessary information is conveyed in the event signal itself. By contrast, in data-centric communication, information is carried in the data transferred.

Another way of classifying communication patterns is to consider how tightly coupled the communication is. When the communication is loosely coupled, the data producer does not require a response from the data consumer, for example, in the case of an ISR posting messages on a message queue.

On the other hand, in tightly coupled communication, a bidirectional transfer of data is involved. Typically, the data producer waits synchronously for a response to its data transfer before continuing execution, or a response is returned asynchronously while the producer continues processing, for example, a scenario where task A writes messages to a message queue read by task B and task B writes messages to a (different) message queue read by task A.

Patterns Involving the Use of Critical Sections

In a typical scenario, the application code may contain two critical sections of code that can access the same shared resource e.g. one that reads the shared resource and another that modifies the shared resource. The critical section code that reads the shared resource running in one task must not run when the critical section that modifies the shared resource is running in another task and vice versa. Hence, critical sections need to be guarded by a suitable mutual exclusion mechanism that will ensure that each task has exclusive use to the shared resource when it needs it (e.g., when writing to a shared area of memory). Where critical time deadlines have to be met, the size and complexity of critical section code will be important. Ideally a mutual exclusion mechanism should guarantee that only one task can enter its critical section at any given time. In practice, it is also important to ensure that multiple competing tasks are granted fair access to the shared resource and also to ensure that a task executing in its critical section does not prevent another task from executing in a noncompeting critical section.

Common Activity Synchronization Design Patterns

If you have reached this point in the course, you should be able to write some, simple, pseudocode that realizes the following patterns. Later on, when we have covered various Zephyr RTOS APIs, you should be able to convert this pseudocode into real working code and add extra details to the working code to generate more interesting behavior.

The code design strategy being exploited here is one that "postpones the detail" – in other words, it involves sketching out the solution at a high level and then filling in the details later once you are satisfied with the high-level outline. You may wish to try the following exercises.

Exercise 1. Synchronizing two tasks using a single binary semaphore. The code involves two tasks, A and B, and a semaphore. The initial value of the semaphore is 0. Task B uses the acquire operation on the shared semaphore, and task A uses the release operation on the shared semaphore.

Exercise 2. Synchronizing an ISR with a task using a single binary semaphore. Here, the initial value of the semaphore is 0. The task uses the acquire operation on the shared semaphore, and the ISR uses the release operation on the shared semaphore.

Exercises 3 and 4 are variants of 1 and 2 but use event registers instead of using a binary semaphore.

Exercise 5. Synchronizing an ISR with a task using a counting semaphore. This exercise is similar to exercise 2 except it makes use of a counting semaphore that can be used to combine the accumulation of event occurrences with event signalling. Here, the task can run as long as the counting semaphore is nonzero.

Exercise 6. This task involves implementing a simple rendezvous with data passing. It involves two tasks (task A and task B) and two message queues (message queue A and message queue B). Each message queue can hold at most one message (such structures are also called mailboxes in some operating systems). Both message queues are initially empty. When task A reaches the rendezvous, it puts a message into message queue B and waits for a message to arrive on message queue A. When task B reaches the rendezvous, it puts data into message queue A and waits for data to arrive on message queue B.

The lessons to be learned from these exercises are that there is often more than one way to tackle a problem and the best solution may not always be obvious.

Common Resource Synchronization Design Patterns

As with task synchronization, an understanding of resource synchronization design patterns is an important skill in an RTOS embedded system developer's repertoire. In real-world applications, the basic patterns serve as a conceptual starting point that can, then, be further elaborated, extended, and modified.

Exercise 1. Accessing shared memory via mutexes. This exercise involves two tasks, task A and task B, which share a common mutex and a common memory area. Each task must first acquire the mutex before it can access the shared memory, and each task must release the mutex when it has finished accessing the shared memory. Task A writes some data to the shared memory, and task B reads the data that has been written.

Exercise 2. In this scenario, control of access to shared memory is realized by the use of interrupt locks. The pattern here involves an interrupt service routine (ISR), a task, and an interrupt lock. The interrupt lock (supported by some processor architectures) is used to disable an interrupt and block all other interrupts at or below that level. The task must acquire the interrupt lock before accessing the shared memory and release it afterward. Interrupt locking is used here to prevent the ISR disrupting access to the shared memory.

The ISR, itself, does not need to be aware of the interrupt lock.

Exercise 3. In this exercise, the scenario to be implemented is one that uses preemption locking to control access to shared memory. The pattern involves two tasks, a preemption lock, and shared memory. Preemption locking involves disabling the kernel scheduler so that it will not preempt the task that has taken out the preemption lock. Each task is responsible for disabling preemption before it accesses shared memory and for re-enabling preemption when it has finished accessing the shared memory. As opposed to the situation with binary semaphores and mutexes, no waiting is involved.

Exercise 4. This exercise is concerned with the scenario of sharing multiple resource instances via counting semaphores and mutexes. Here, there are N tasks sharing M resources, one counting semaphore and one mutex. The counting semaphore is initialized to the maximum number of available resources, and a task must acquire the counting semaphore before attempting to access a resource. The mutex is used to provide a task with exclusive access to the shared resource control structure (which, for example, tracks information about which resources are currently in use and which are available), and a task must acquire this mutex before either allocating a resource instance or freeing a resource instance.

Some More Advanced Thread Interaction Patterns

Designs involving multiple tasks, multiple inputs and outputs, and multiple shared resources can be challenging. They give rise to scenarios/requirements such as controlling the flow of data being transferred, coping with the asynchronous arrival of data from multiple sources, handling multiple data and event inputs, and sending urgent data between tasks.

Data transfer with flow control is a scenario where a consumer task controls the flow of data from the producer task. A typical case involves a producer task, a consumer task, a counting semaphore, and a data buffer. For the producer to be able to write to the buffer, it must acquire

CHAPTER 2 A REVIEW OF RTOS FUNDAMENTALS

the counting semaphore. The producer will block when the value of the counting semaphore is 0, and the consumer is able to release the counting semaphore (increase its count value). Initially the counting semaphore is set to some permissible token value (less than the maximum allowable token value). The consumer is able to control the flow rate by increasing the value of the counting semaphore appropriately in relation to its ability to consume data.

An example of a pattern of handling the asynchronous reception of data from multiple data communication channels is one involving multiple ISRs, a semaphore, an interrupt lock, and a daemon task. An implementation scenario is one where each ISR inserts its data into a corresponding message queue and performs a release operation on the semaphore. The daemon task blocks and waits on the semaphore (acquire operation). When data is available, it takes out an interrupt lock (this lock is needed to protect against the various multiple interrupt sources), processes available data, and then releases the interrupt lock.

The following pseudocode snippet illustrates a starting (nonperformance optimized) approach:

```
while( acquire(Binary_semaphore))
      disable(interrupts)
      for each message_queue
            get msg_queue_length
            for (msg_queue_length)
                  retrieve message
                  enable (interrupts)
                  process message
                  disable (interrupts )
            end for
```

CHAPTER 2 A REVIEW OF RTOS FUNDAMENTALS

```
      end for
      enable (interrupts)
end while
```

The next example demonstrates an approach that makes use of an event register, a shared variable, an interrupt lock, and a semaphore. The interrupt lock is used to guard the shared variable (ISRs can generate events through the shared variable), and the semaphore blocks the task waiting on the desired event.

The pseudocode showing this scenario is shown here:

```
Event_receive(wanted_events) {
      task_cb.wanted_events = wanted_events
      while(TRUE)
            acquire(task_cb.event_semaphore)
            disable(interrupts)
            events = wanted_events XOR task_cb.received_events
            task_cb.wanted_events = task_cb.wanted_events AND
            ( NOT events )
            enable (interrupts)
            if( events is not empty )
                  return (events)
            end if
      end while
}

Event_send(events) {
      disable(interrupts)
      task_cb.received_events = task_cb.received_events
      OR events
      enable interrupts
      release (task_cb.event_semaphore)
}
```

CHAPTER 2   A REVIEW OF RTOS FUNDAMENTALS

Handling Multiple Data Items and Multiple Inputs

Use cases involving handling multiple data items and multiple inputs in a timely manner can be very challenging. One way of handling such a situation is a pattern in which there is a daemon task that has multiple data input sources (tasks generating input data) and multiple event input sources (ISRs generating input data), and an event register is used with a given input being assigned to a given bit in the event register, a counting semaphore is used for event accumulation (one for each event input source), and a message queue is used for each data input source. In this scenario, a data producer puts a message in its message queue and sets the corresponding bit in the event register. The ISR increments its counting semaphore and sets its corresponding bit in the event register.

A pseudocode snippet corresponding to a scenario involving one daemon, one timer ISR, and one data producer illustrates the key features of implementing this kind of pattern.

```
while( have_events = wait for events from event_register )
     if ( have_events & DATA_EVENT )
          while( fetch message from message_queue )
               process message
          end while
     end if
     if ( have_events & TIMER_EVENT )
          counter = 0
          disable ( interrupts )
          while ( acquire ( counting_semaphore ) )
               counter = counter + 1
          end while
          enable ( interrupts )
          if ( counter > MAX_COUNT )
```

```
                    do_recovery
        else
                    handle_tick_event
        end if
    end if
end while
```

Sending Urgent/High Priority Data Between Tasks

A streaming data channel does not support data prioritization. One way to make it possible to send high priority out of stream data is to use an urgent message queue for this purpose, with the regular data going into a normal message queue. When a data producer task or ISR has regular data, it places that data into its normal data message queue. However, when a data producer task or ISR has urgent data that need to be handled, it places that data into an urgent message queue and signals the consumer task.

The consumer task's urgent data signal handler retrieves urgent data from the urgent data message queue and deals with it. This pattern can be further enhanced by adding flow control mechanisms to control the flow of urgent data.

Device Drivers

Zephyr RTOS has implementations of device drivers for most of the devices and peripherals encountered in embedded systems such as GPIO, I2C, SPI, CAN bus, and ADC. Zephyr RTOS also provides stacks for TCP/IP, Wi-Fi, and BLE (Bluetooth Low Energy). Some specialist devices such as the nRF5x devices from Nordic Semiconductor also support proprietary BLE stacks, in addition to the open source BLE stack included with

Zephyr. Zephyr applications that need to use particular devices need to be configured so that the correct libraries are linked in when the application is built and that the correct device configuration parameters are provided as part of the application build. In Zephyr, this involves the use of the Kconfig and devicetree frameworks, and these topics will be covered in a later section.

References

1. Wikipedia entry describing the HART protocol
   https://en.wikipedia.org/wiki/Highway_Addressable_Remote_Transducer_Protocol

2. Zephyr documentation discussing portability and HAL (Hardware Abstraction Layer) aspects of Zephyr
   https://docs.zephyrproject.org/latest/services/portability/index.html

3. https://community.arm.com/arm-community-blogs/b/architectures-and-processors-blog/posts/beginner-guide-on-interrupt-latency-and-interrupt-latency-of-the-arm-cortex-m-processors

CHAPTER 3

Zephyr RTOS Application Development Environments and Zephyr Application Building Principles

Zephyr applications can be developed using either a command-line interface–based approach based on the use of tools like west and CMake from the command line or using an integrated development environment such as Microsoft VS Code with suitable extensions for Zephyr application development "plugged in." At the target platform level, the choice is between downloading and running code to an actual target board and using a simulator such as Renode or QEMU. This chapter will cover the setup of development environments, and the following chapter will cover developing applications using the simulated target environments Renode and QEMU.

CHAPTER 3   ZEPHYR RTOS APPLICATION DEVELOPMENT ENVIRONMENTS AND ZEPHYR APPLICATION BUILDING PRINCIPLES

This chapter will cover the setting up of Zephyr RTOS application development environments. Zephyr has been incorporated into the Nordic Semiconductor application development platform nRF Connect SDK [5]. The nRF Connect SDK includes the Zephyr framework as well as extra libraries and examples developed by Nordic Semiconductor for their families of processors. The nRF Connect SDK can be used to develop applications targeting other processors than nRF processors.

Zephyr has an SDK called the Zephyr SDK [6] that has toolchains for the processor architectures supported by Zephyr and also includes host tools, such as a custom QEMU and OpenOCD.

Zephyr RTOS application development can make use of IDEs for which there are suitable plug-ins. These include Eclipse and Microsoft VS Code. There are Zephyr SDK and nRF Connect SDK plug-ins for VS Code, and VS Code is widely used by Zephyr application developers.

It is also perfectly possible to follow "old-school" practices using text editors such as vim and emacs to develop code and then using west to build and flash applications. Here, setting up both VS Code and classical command-line development environments will be explored. In a later chapter, the setup of simulator/emulator-based development using QEMU and Renode will be introduced. For any given setup, a number of standard sample applications are typically built first in order to check the installation and setup. Exploring these basic examples will provide an introduction into the philosophy and mindset of the Zephyr RTOS application building process.

The intricate details of tools such as CMake and Ninja, which are used in the Zephyr application build process, will be "glossed over" at this stage, and only the "necessary details" will be covered. CMake can be thought of as a kind of DSL (Domain-Specific Language) tool. It is implemented in C++ and embeds a lot of knowledge about C and C++ compilers, and its main purpose is to generate make files or Ninja files that can then be used to drive the build process using the make and ninja commands, respectively. Craig Scott's *Professional CMake: A Practical Guide*, now in

CHAPTER 3   ZEPHYR RTOS APPLICATION DEVELOPMENT ENVIRONMENTS AND ZEPHYR APPLICATION BUILDING PRINCIPLES

its 15th edition, is a good starting point for those of you who want to study CMake in greater depth [1]. The analogy between Ninja and Make is that "ninja is to assembly" as "make is to a high-level programming language." Ninja was developed as a faster build tool than Make when building large complex projects. The intention was to have developers make use of tools such as CMake to generate ninja build scripts as opposed to writing such scripts manually. To dig deeper into Ninja, it is necessary to consult the official ninja documentation [2].

For large complex projects, the corresponding CMake files can become quite complex, because they are often built by including CMake parts from various parts of the project. This is the case with Zephyr projects. The CMake file in the application directory is usually quite small. The actual CMake file that drives the build is constructed by "pulling in" CMake files from other parts of the Zephyr source code tree. CMake has command-line options for producing verbose output (lots and lots of output in the case of Zephyr application builds), which can be invoked via the command-line options --trace, --trace-expand, and --trace-source=some_cmake_source. When trying to make sense of CMake usage in building Zephyr applications, a good approach is to learn how to "read and understand" CMake files and then to explore the various Zephyr CMake files piece by piece.

Setting Up a Zephyr SDK CLI (Command-Line Interface) Development Environment on Microsoft Windows

The basic setup steps for installing Zephyr on an up-to-date version of Windows 10 or Windows 11 are described in the Zephyr project getting started guide. The Zephyr project's dependencies include CMake (version 3.20 or newer), Python (version 3.8 or newer), and the Devicetree compiler

CHAPTER 3   ZEPHYR RTOS APPLICATION DEVELOPMENT ENVIRONMENTS AND
            ZEPHYR APPLICATION BUILDING PRINCIPLES

(version 1.4.6 or newer). Installation of these dependencies is greatly simplified by using the Chocolatey package management tool for Windows (https://docs.zephyrproject.org/latest/develop/getting_started/index.html).

The Chocolatey website provides easy-to-follow instructions (https://chocolatey.org/install) for installing Chocolatey. The Chocolatey executable, choco, can then be used to install the required packages by running the following commands, with administrator privileges, in a `cmd.exe` terminal window:

```
choco install cmake --installargs 'ADD_CMAKE_TO_PATH=System'
choco install ninja gperf python git dtc-msys2 wget unzip
```

The Zephyr SDK and associated tools can then be installed in a cmd.exe window, running as a regular user. If installing on a workstation running multiple versions of Python and, also, being used to develop other projects, then it is a good idea to use a custom Python virtual environment for working with the various Python packages required for building Zephyr applications. This can be done in either cmd.exe or PowerShell.

Installation within a Python virtual environment requires creation and activation of the Python virtual environment. The virtual environment can be created by changing into a target directory and creating the virtual environment (venv) as follows:

```
cd %HOMEPATH%
python -m venv zephyrproject\.venv
```

The commands to activate the virtual environment are `zephyrproject\.venv\Scripts\activate.bat` in cmd.exe and `zephyrproject\.venv\Scripts\Activate.ps1` in powershell.

Once the `venv` is activated, the shell prompt will be prefixed with (`.venv`). The virtual environment can be deactivated at any time by running the deactivate command.

CHAPTER 3   ZEPHYR RTOS APPLICATION DEVELOPMENT ENVIRONMENTS AND ZEPHYR APPLICATION BUILDING PRINCIPLES

The virtual environment needs to be reactivated after deactivation, or when starting a new shell window in which to work.

Having set up a working Python environment, the next step is to install the `west` tool. west is a Python package and is installed, using pip, with the following command:

```
pip install west
```

Once installed, west can be used to obtain the zephyr source code, as follows:

```
west init zephyrproject
cd zephyrproject
west update
```

The next step is to export a Zephyr CMake package to the CMake user package registry. This is needed so that CMake can download the boilerplate code needed to build a Zephyr application.

```
west zephyr-export
```

CMake is a powerful and complex tool with a steep learning curve. Fortunately, when getting started with Zephyr application programming and using west and the various samples that come with the Zephyr source code, it is possible to go a long way with only a basic knowledge of CMake.

Zephyr, itself, has a number of Python package dependencies that are listed in the text file `scripts\requirements.txt`. The necessary packages can be installed by running the following command:

```
pip install -r %HOMEPATH%\zephyrproject\zephyr\scripts\requirements.txt
```

The final step in the installation process is to install the Zephyr Software Development Kit (SDK) itself. The SDK contains toolchains for each architecture supported by Zephyr. Each toolchain includes a compiler, assembler, linker, and other programs that are required in order

CHAPTER 3   ZEPHYR RTOS APPLICATION DEVELOPMENT ENVIRONMENTS AND
            ZEPHYR APPLICATION BUILDING PRINCIPLES

to build a Zephyr application. The SDK also provides host tools, such as custom QEMU (Quick Emulator) and OpenOCD (Open On-Chip Debugger) builds and software flashing tools that can be used to emulate, flash, and debug Zephyr applications.

To test the installation, build a basic example, for example, the led blinking sample example for a particular target board. The build command template is

```
cd %HOMEPATH%\zephyrproject\zephyr
west build -p always -b <your-board-name> samples\basic\blinky
```

where the board name is the name of a particular target board.

The command west boards can be used to obtain a list of all boards that Zephyr supports. In the build command, the -p option is used to always force a pristine (brand-new) build. The -p auto option will make west use heuristics to decide whether a pristine build is required or not.

After a successful build, the executable file can be flashed to the board using the following command:

```
west flash
```

For certain boards, for flashing to work, it may be necessary to install some extra host tools.

Choices of Boards and Development Kits for Getting Started

The choice of board to start with will probably depend on longer-term interests and goals. If you are interested in developing BLE (Bluetooth Low Energy) applications, then boards based on Nordic Semiconductor nRF52 or nRF53 processors such as the nRF52840 DK board or the nRF5340 DK board are worth considering. These are relatively inexpensive and well-supported boards. Other nRF52840 boards that are less expensive are boards such as the Adafruit nRF52840 ItsyBitsy board and the SparkFun Pro nRF52840 Mini Bluetooth development board. The BBC Microbit v2 is worth considering, especially if you are interested in using it for teaching younger students. Not only does it have good support for block programming using MakeCode and for Python programming using MicroPython, it can also be used to teach C programming and RTOS programming.

Low-cost ARM Cortex M processor–based boards that are not, primarily, oriented toward BLE are the various STM32 Nucleo boards. These boards have Arduino-compatible headers and are well supported. STM also makes various Arduino header format expansion boards that provide all kinds of extra capabilities, such as motor driver control boards for DC motors and stepper control motors, and also a board with MEMS Micro-Electro-Mechanical System) and environmental sensors. STM Nucleo boards are affordable low-cost boards that are good for learning and prototyping purposes. There are Nucleo boards for various STM32 processors. For example, the Nucleo-F401RE is shown in Figure 3-1.

CHAPTER 3   ZEPHYR RTOS APPLICATION DEVELOPMENT ENVIRONMENTS AND
            ZEPHYR APPLICATION BUILDING PRINCIPLES

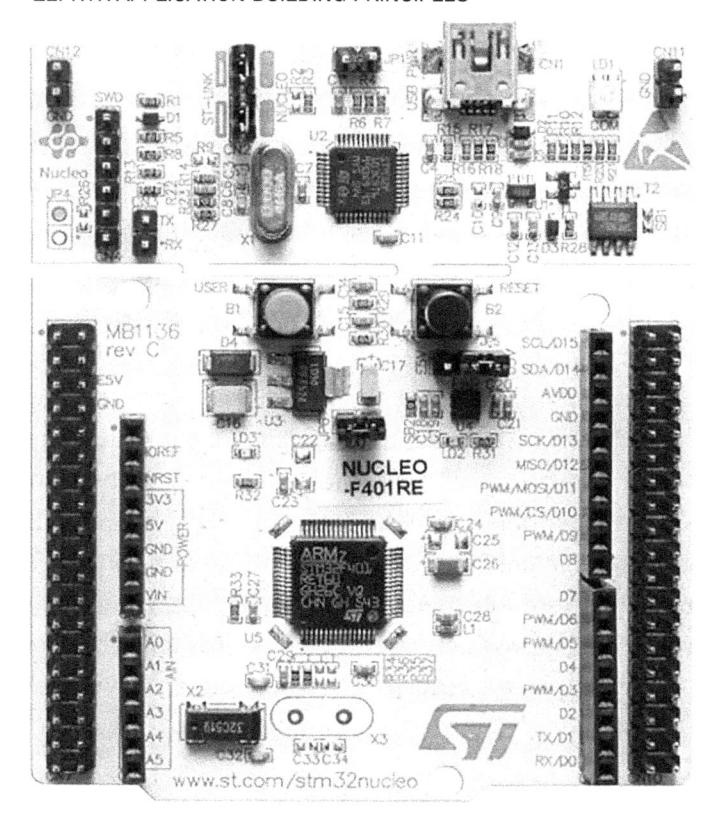

Figure 3-1. Nucleo-F401RE

For prototyping IoT (Internet of Things) applications involving various wireless networking protocols, STM produces boards such as the B-L475E-IOT01A Discovery kit for IoT node, which includes Bluetooth V4.1, 802.11 b/g/n compliant Wi-Fi, and dynamic NFC tag modules, an image of which is shown in Figure 3-2.

CHAPTER 3   ZEPHYR RTOS APPLICATION DEVELOPMENT ENVIRONMENTS AND ZEPHYR APPLICATION BUILDING PRINCIPLES

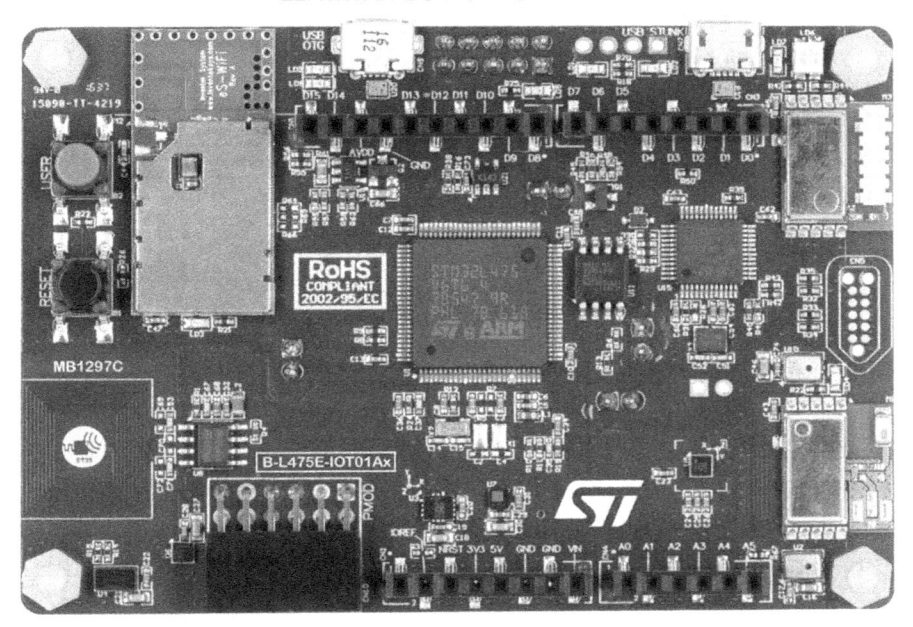

Figure 3-2. STM B-L475E-IOT01A Discovery kit

When it comes to low-cost development and prototyping boards, the feather board format is something worth knowing about. Feather boards supported by Zephyr RTOS include the Adafruit Feather M0 Basic Proto, Adafruit Feather M0 LoRa, Adafruit Feather nRF52840 Express, and Adafruit Feather STM32F405 Express boards. Figure 3-3 shows an STM32F405 board.

CHAPTER 3   ZEPHYR RTOS APPLICATION DEVELOPMENT ENVIRONMENTS AND ZEPHYR APPLICATION BUILDING PRINCIPLES

Figure 3-3. *Adafruit Feather STM32F405 Express board*

A useful prototyping technology that can be used with boards that conform to the feather board format is the feather click shield, which makes it possible to connect various Mikroe "click boards" to a "feather" board. Figures 3-4 and 3-5 show a bare feather click shield and a populated feather click shield. Mikroe has developed a wide range of "click boards," and connectors for these boards can be found in a variety of embedded systems development kits.

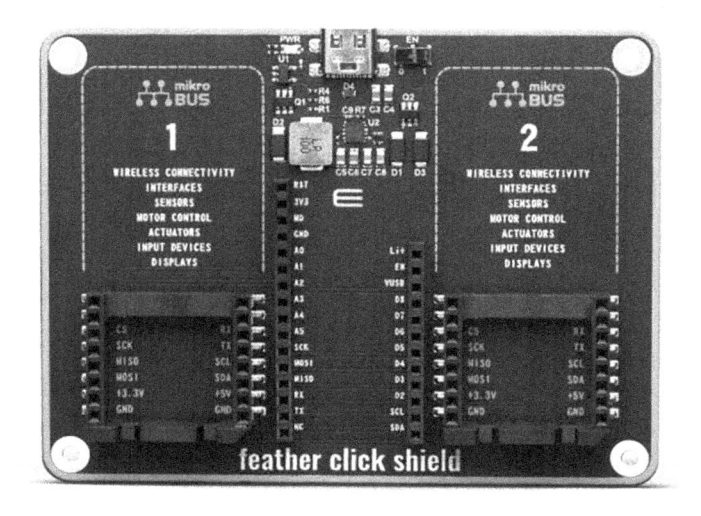

Figure 3-4. *Mikroe feather click shield*

CHAPTER 3 ZEPHYR RTOS APPLICATION DEVELOPMENT ENVIRONMENTS AND ZEPHYR APPLICATION BUILDING PRINCIPLES

Figure 3-5. *Populated feather click shield*

Espressif ESP32 processors are widely used in embedded Wi-Fi and BLE applications, partly because of their relatively low cost. ESP32 is well supported in Zephyr, and for learning purposes, boards such as the SparkFun ESP32 Thing board and the SparkFun ESP32 IoT board are useful boards to get started with.

Finally, no coverage of embedded processors supported by the Zephyr SDK would be complete without including RISC-V processor–based systems. The importance of RISC-V is that in contrast to the case for designing ARM processor core–based systems, the RISC-V core design and instruction set is fully open source. RISC-V also comes under the auspices of the Linux Foundation. There are both 32-bit and 64-bit RISC-V processor architectures. 32-bit RISC-V boards that can be used

CHAPTER 3 ZEPHYR RTOS APPLICATION DEVELOPMENT ENVIRONMENTS AND
ZEPHYR APPLICATION BUILDING PRINCIPLES

with Zephyr RTOS include SiFive's HiFive1 Rev B development kit and SparkFun's RED-V SIFIVE RISC-V REDBOARD, shown in Figure 3-6. Espressif has also developed ESP32 C3 processors, which have RISC-V core processors. Additionally, Nordic Semiconductor has started rolling out a multiprocessor family of chips that include ARM Cortex M33 and RISC-V processor cores, nRF54H20.

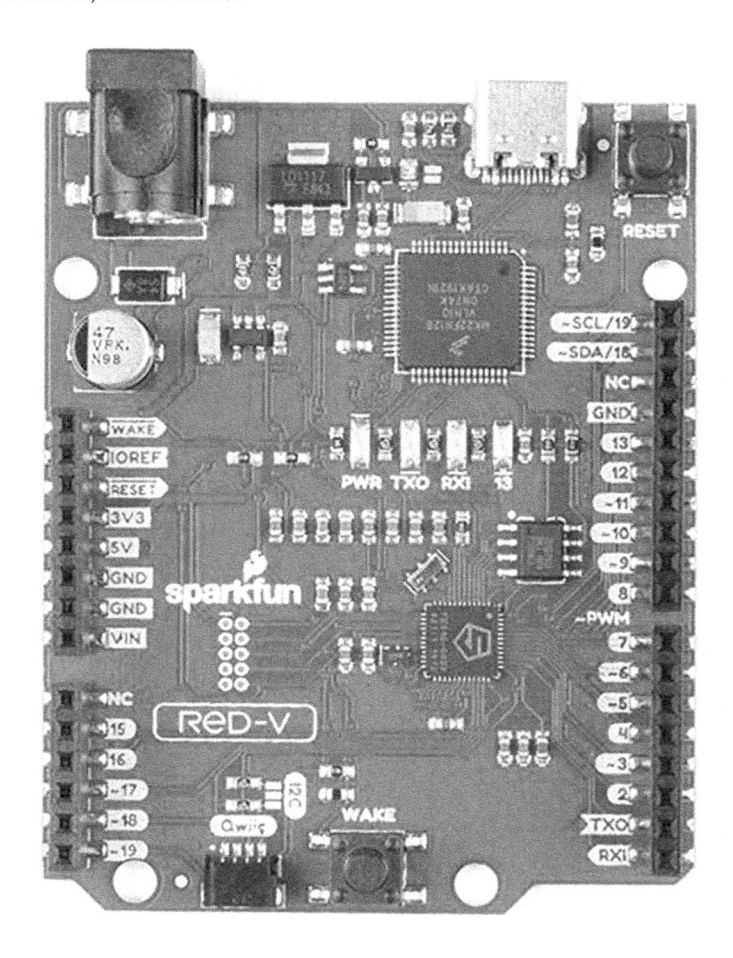

Figure 3-6. SparkFun's RED-V SIFIVE RISC-V REDBOARD

CHAPTER 3 ZEPHYR RTOS APPLICATION DEVELOPMENT ENVIRONMENTS AND
ZEPHYR APPLICATION BUILDING PRINCIPLES

Setting Up an nRF Connect SDK Development Environment Using a Microsoft VS Code–Based IDE

The Nordic Semiconductor's nRF Connect SDK is based on the Zephyr RTOS SDK. Essentially it adds a number of extra libraries and samples specifically oriented at Nordic Semiconductor processors. This SDK incorporates the Zephyr RTOS SDK and so can also be used to develop Zephyr RTOS applications targeting other boards supported by the Zephyr RTOS SDK. Nordic Semiconductor has also developed a desktop application, nRF Connect for Desktop, that greatly simplifies the installation and setup of an IDE for developing Zephyr RTOS applications. Initially developed for Microsoft Windows, there are, now, variants for Linux and Mac OS X.

nRF Connect for Desktop can be downloaded from the nordicsemi website (see Figure 3-7): `www.nordicsemi.com/Products/Development-tools/nRF-Connect-for-desktop/Download#infotabs`.

Figure 3-7. nRF Connect for Desktop download

CHAPTER 3   ZEPHYR RTOS APPLICATION DEVELOPMENT ENVIRONMENTS AND
            ZEPHYR APPLICATION BUILDING PRINCIPLES

The nRF Connect for Desktop framework is a cross-platform tool framework that facilitates developing applications on nRF devices by providing apps for monitoring, measuring, optimizing, and programming applications. It is oriented toward working with Nordic development kits and dongles.

The apps that can be installed using the nRF Connect for Desktop include the Bluetooth Low Energy app for Bluetooth Low Energy connectivity testing, a Direct Test Mode app for performing tests with Bluetooth Low Energy devices, and a Getting Started Assistant app for setting up the nRF Connect SDK and toolchain on a Linux computer. For Mac and Windows development platforms, there is the Toolchain Manager app.

Additional apps include an LTE Link Monitor app, which is a modem client application that monitors the LTE modem/link status and activity using AT commands, and a Power Profiler app, which is used with the Nordic Power Profiler Kit to analyze and export current consumption measurements.

Finally, there are a Programmer app for programming Nordic SoCs, an RSSI Viewer app for scanning the 2.4 GHz spectrum, and a Toolchain Manager app for managing the nRF Connect SDK and toolchain versions on Windows and Mac development workstations.

The Toolchain Manager takes care of installing required dependencies, namely, the Zephyr SDK, CMake, dtc (Device Tree Compiler), Girt, gperf, ninja, Python, and west.

The Toolchain Manager will install all Python dependencies into a local environment in the Toolchain Manager app. These include anytree, canopen, cbor2, click, cryptography, ecdsa, imagesize, intelhex, packaging, progress, pyelftools, pylint, PyYAML, west, and windows-curses (only when installing on Windows). Don't worry, it is not necessary to understand and be able to use these tools. The nRF Connect SDK and the Zephyr SDK make extensive use of Python scripts for managing and building Zephyr RTOS applications.

CHAPTER 3 ZEPHYR RTOS APPLICATION DEVELOPMENT ENVIRONMENTS AND
ZEPHYR APPLICATION BUILDING PRINCIPLES

After nRF Connect for Desktop has been installed, it can be used to install the Toolchain Manager by scrolling to the Toolchain Manager app entry and clicking on the Install button (see Figure 3-8).

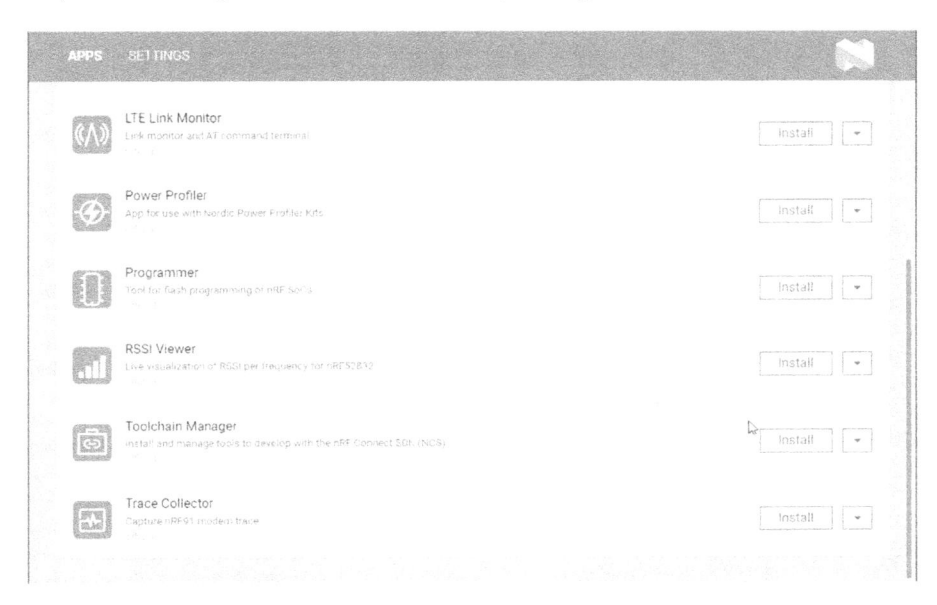

Figure 3-8. *nRF Connect for Desktop Toolchain Manager*

The Nordic recommendation is to use the Toolchain Manager to download, install, and uninstall the nRF Connect SDK for Windows, Ubuntu (20.04), and macOS machines.

The installer will check to see if the nRF Connect for Desktop dependencies (Segger J-link, Nordic drivers, and the Microsoft Visual C++ Redistributable) are already installed on the computer. If not found, they will be installed. For the installation to succeed, it is necessary to accept the installation of all the dependencies.

The next step is to use the Toolchain Manager to install the nRF Connect SDK. This is a simple procedure. First, open the Toolchain Manager by clicking on the Toolchain Manager app icon in nRF Connect

CHAPTER 3　ZEPHYR RTOS APPLICATION DEVELOPMENT ENVIRONMENTS AND
　　　　　　ZEPHYR APPLICATION BUILDING PRINCIPLES

for Desktop. Then in the Toolchain Manager, select the version of the SDK to install. Usually this will be the latest version unless you are working on a project that requires an older version (see Figure 3-9).

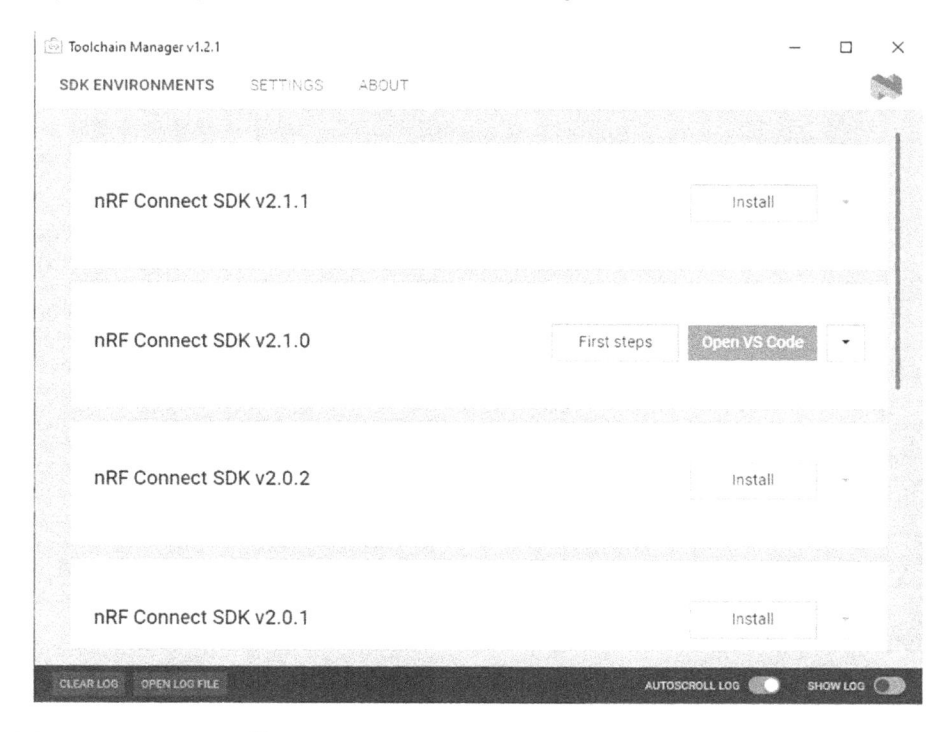

Figure 3-9. Installing nRF Connect SDK using the Toolchain Manager

In the list of available SDKs, details concerning an already-installed SDK can be seen if this is not a fresh install. To install the SDK, click SETTINGS in the navigation bar, and in the resulting dialog, specify where the nRF Connect SDK is to be installed and then in SDK, the nRF Connect SDK version to install. Once the selected nRF Connect SDK version has been installed, the Install button will change to an Open VS Code button.

CHAPTER 3   ZEPHYR RTOS APPLICATION DEVELOPMENT ENVIRONMENTS AND
            ZEPHYR APPLICATION BUILDING PRINCIPLES

Having installed the nRF Connect SDK following the previous approach, there are now two possible ways in which applications can be developed, either working in Visual Studio Code (VS Code) using the nRF Connect for VS Code extension or developing using the command line.

To develop using the VS Code IDE, click on the Open VS Code button. If this is a first installation, then a notification dialog listing missing extensions that have to be installed will appear. The list will include extensions from the nRF Connect for Visual Studio Code extension pack. Once these are installed, clicking on the Open VS Code button will start up VS Code. The nRF Connect for VS Coe extension together with VS Code results in a complete IDE in which applications for nRF91, nRF53, and nRF52 Series Nordic devices can be developed. It includes an interface to the compiler and linker, an RTOS-aware debugger, as well as an interface to the nRF Connect SDK, and a serial terminal.

Working in VS Code

Installing the nRF Connect SDK using the nRF Connect for Desktop toolchain manager also installs the nRF Connect for VS Code extension, which makes it possible to develop Zephyr projects running on nRF devices in VS Code. The next few pages, based on the nRF Connect SDK documentation [3] and a Linux Foundation blog post [4], provide an introductory overview of working with the nRF Connect SDK in VS Code. The nRF Connect SDK documentation should be consulted for more detailed information.

To create an nRF Connect SDK project in VS Code, the first step is to click on the nRF Connect icon in the Activity Bar (see Figure 3-10).

85

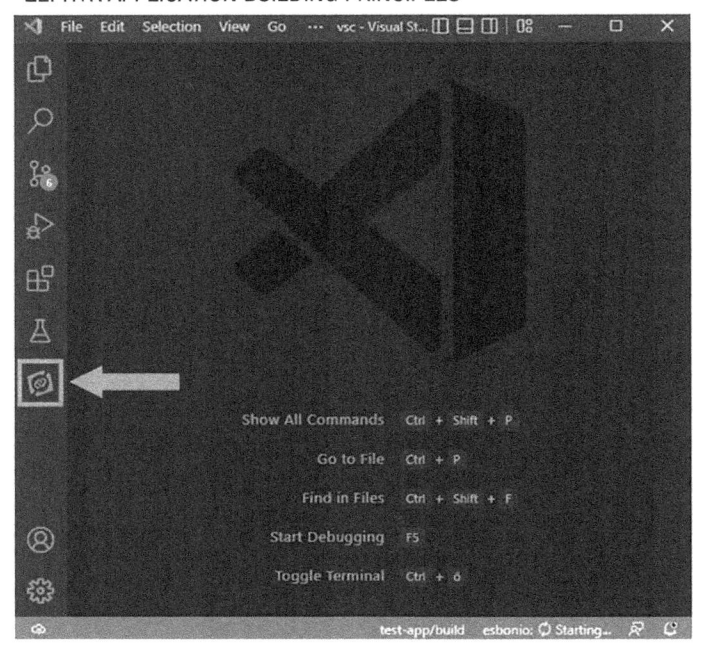

CHAPTER 3   ZEPHYR RTOS APPLICATION DEVELOPMENT ENVIRONMENTS AND
           ZEPHYR APPLICATION BUILDING PRINCIPLES

Figure 3-10. nRF Connect icon in the Activity Bar

The nRF Connect SD Extension UI VS Code user interface contains many components, which can seem a bit overwhelming at first. However, once their essential organization is grasped, much of the "apparent complexity" goes away. The four main parts of the GUI are the Extension Views, the Editor, the Panel, and the Status Bar. The majority of the tools used during development are to be found in the nRF Connect Sidebar Views in the Sidebar (see Figure 3-11).

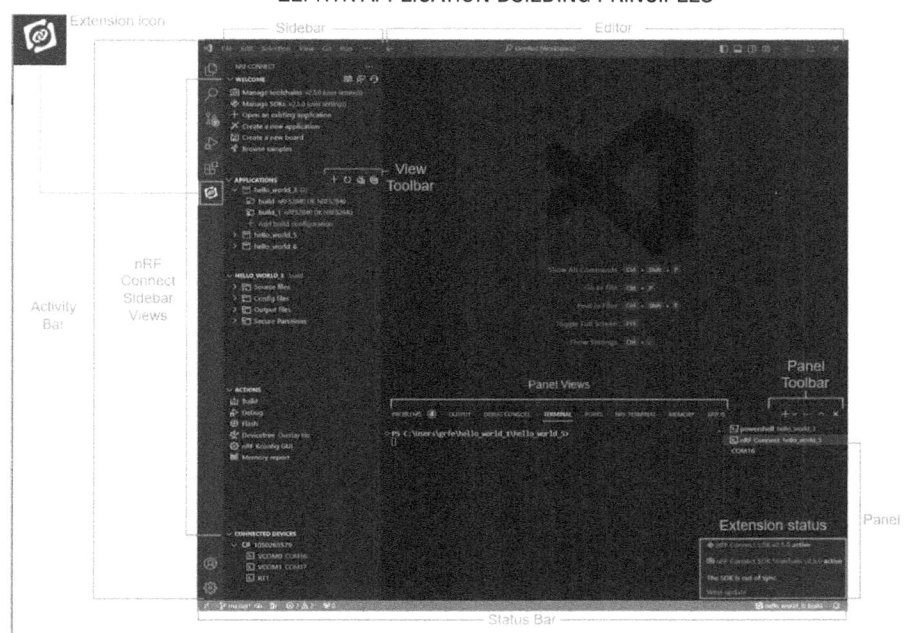

CHAPTER 3   ZEPHYR RTOS APPLICATION DEVELOPMENT ENVIRONMENTS AND
            ZEPHYR APPLICATION BUILDING PRINCIPLES

Figure 3-11. nRF Connect for VS Code Overview

Figures 3-12 and 3-13 show enlarged views of the left and right hand sides.

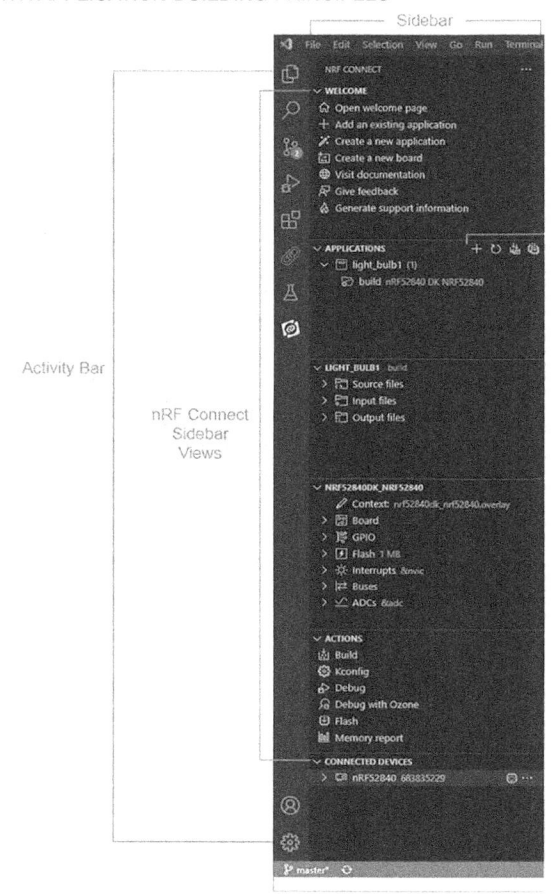

CHAPTER 3   ZEPHYR RTOS APPLICATION DEVELOPMENT ENVIRONMENTS AND
            ZEPHYR APPLICATION BUILDING PRINCIPLES

Figure 3-12. Activity Bar and nRF Connect Sidebar Views

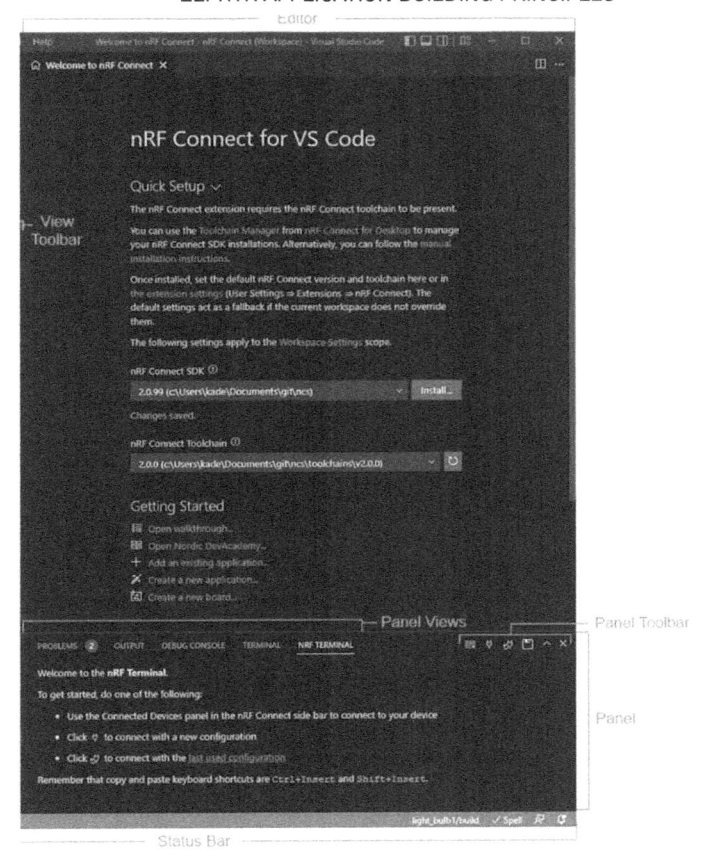

CHAPTER 3   ZEPHYR RTOS APPLICATION DEVELOPMENT ENVIRONMENTS AND
ZEPHYR APPLICATION BUILDING PRINCIPLES

Figure 3-13. *Editor Window, Panel Views, and Status Bar*

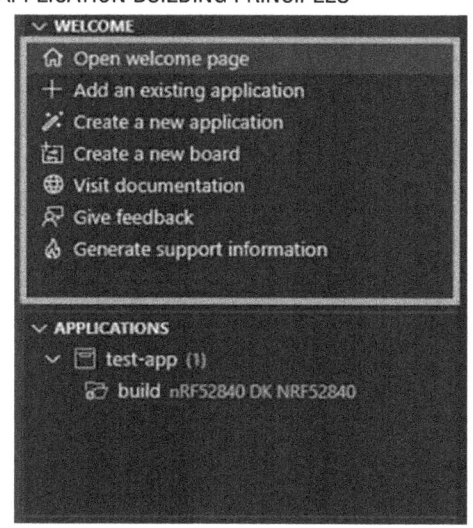

CHAPTER 3   ZEPHYR RTOS APPLICATION DEVELOPMENT ENVIRONMENTS AND
            ZEPHYR APPLICATION BUILDING PRINCIPLES

Figure 3-14. Welcome View

The Welcome View, shown in Figure 3-14, provides some helper options for creating a new application and contains several options to help you get started with creating your application. When starting for the first time, there is an Open welcome page that will appear every time VS Code is started, unless that option is deselected. If the option is deselected, the Welcome View can still be displayed by clicking the Open welcome page option in the Welcome View.

The Welcome page contains Quick Setup, Getting Started, sections, as well as a section for accessing additional documentation and support.

The Quick Setup section can be used for configuring the nRF Connect SDK and nRF Connect Toolchain versions for the application. The Welcome View has options for adding and creating applications. The option for adding an existing application can be used to build samples that come with the nRF Connect SDK and also the Zephyr SDK samples. The create a new application option is used for setting up, configuring, and creating new applications. There is also a create new board option for setting the parameters for a custom board for use as part of a build configuration.

CHAPTER 3   ZEPHYR RTOS APPLICATION DEVELOPMENT ENVIRONMENTS AND
            ZEPHYR APPLICATION BUILDING PRINCIPLES

The Applications View (Figure 3-15) is located below the Welcome View and lists all the applications in the current workspace. The icons associated with the currently selected application will be in blue instead of white.

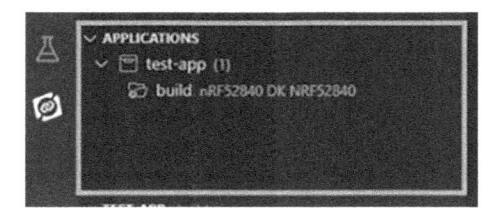

Figure 3-15. Applications View

Global Actions

Hovering over the Applications View will reveal a View Toolbar containing a number of View Actions, shown in Figure 3-16.

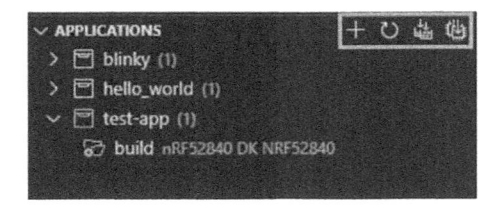

Figure 3-16. View Toolbar

There are four icons in the View Toolbar: an Add Folder as Application action icon for adding a folder containing preexisting application files to the project, a Refresh Applications application icon that prompts the extension to scan the applications folder for new build configurations if it cannot automatically detect a newly created build folder, a Build All Configurations action icon for building all configurations for all applications, and, finally, a Flash All Linked Devices action icon for flashing builds to all the associated, connected devices.

CHAPTER 3   ZEPHYR RTOS APPLICATION DEVELOPMENT ENVIRONMENTS AND
            ZEPHYR APPLICATION BUILDING PRINCIPLES

Application-Specific Actions

When hovering over an application-specific action, icons are displayed as shown in Figure 3-17.

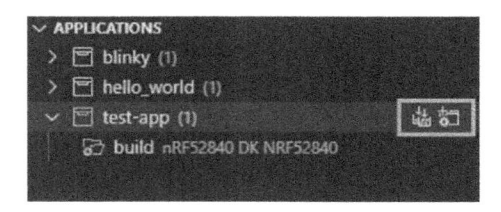

Figure 3-17. Application-specific icons appearing when hovering

There is an Add Build Configuration action that is used to set up build configurations for the application and a Build All Configurations for Application action icon that builds all the configurations for that specific application.

Build-Specific Actions

Within each application, there are build folder actions that apply to a single folder (see Figure 3-18).

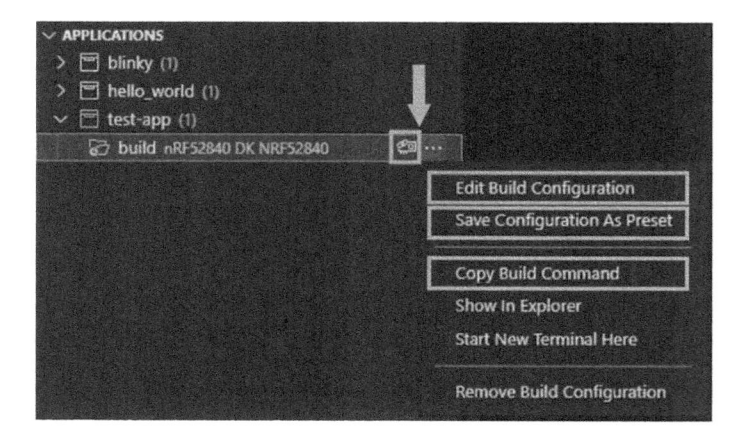

Figure 3-18. Build-specific actions

CHAPTER 3 ZEPHYR RTOS APPLICATION DEVELOPMENT ENVIRONMENTS AND ZEPHYR APPLICATION BUILDING PRINCIPLES

The Link Build Configuration And Device action is for linking a build configuration to a specific device, the Edit Configuration is for editing a preexisting build configuration for the selected application, and the Save Configuration as Preset action saves the current build configuration as a preset (which is a shortcut to the nRF Connect: Save Configuration as Preset command in the Command Palette) and saves the current build configuration to the CMakePresets.json file. The Copy Build Command can be used to save a copy of the build command for the selected build into the device's clipboard.

Details View

The Details View provides detailed access to the application project contents. It comes after the Applications View and relates to the currently selected application. Its three main sections (views) relate to the source files, input files, and output files. The source files section lists the source files used by the application, the input files section lists the CMake and devicetree configuration files, and the output files section lists the output files generated by the build process (see Figure 3-19). Hovering the mouse over any of the listed groups or folders and clicking on the magnifying glass icon will open the VS Code Search View set up (prefilled) to search only the files in the selected section.

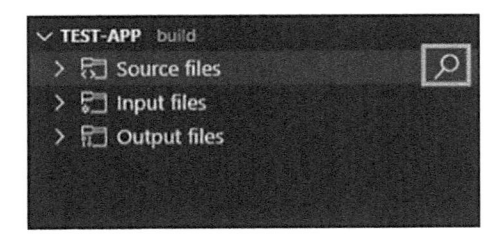

Figure 3-19. Details View

CHAPTER 3   ZEPHYR RTOS APPLICATION DEVELOPMENT ENVIRONMENTS AND
            ZEPHYR APPLICATION BUILDING PRINCIPLES

Devicetree View

The Devicetree View located under the Details View is very useful when having to examine devicetree configuration details for the application. It makes use of the nRF DeviceTree extension. A devicetree context contains the basic build target configuration and various overlay files providing use case-specific configuration details. Hovering the mouse over the View Toolbar will reveal the Show Complied Devicetree Output button, which can be used to open a Devicetree View (Figure 3-20).

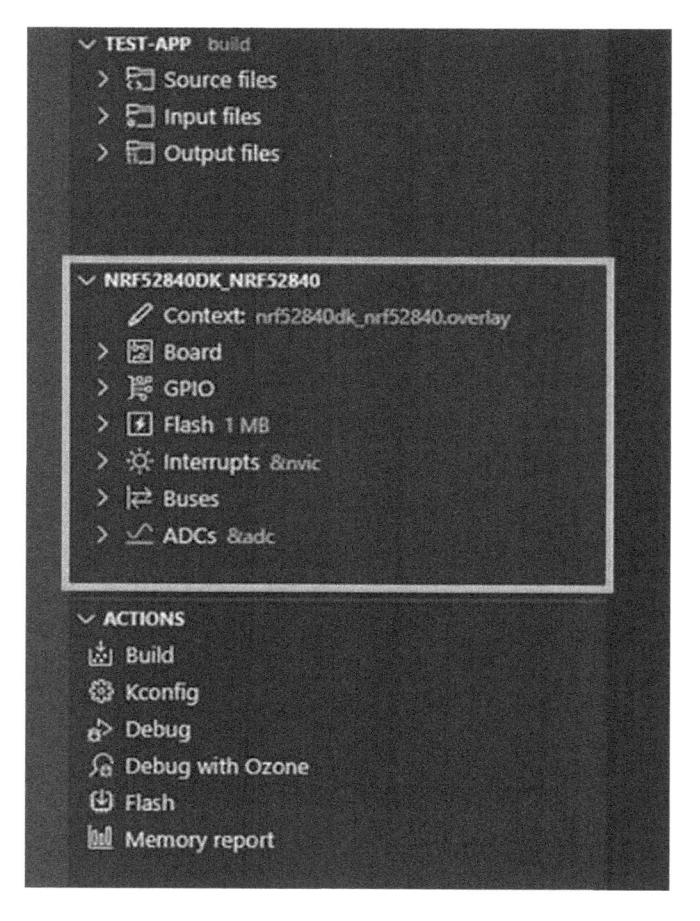

Figure 3-20. Devicetree View

Actions View

The Actions View, to be found under the Devicetree View, provides access to common actions associated with building, configuring, debugging, flashing, and seeing the memory report.

When working with the Zephyr SDK as opposed to the nRF Connect SDK, similar functionality can be obtained using the PlatformIO IDE for VS Code: https://docs.platformio.org/en/stable/integration/ide/vscode.html#ide-vscode.

Exercise: Building and Running a Zephyr Sample Application Using VS Code

The aim of this exercise is to build and run the blinky sample on a board such as the nRF52840 DK board. The sequence of steps to follow is given here.

Start by clicking on the `Create a new application` option, and enter the requisite information in the fields in the New Application View that is displayed.

The application details are that it should be a Freestanding application (linked to and using an installed version of the nRF Connect SDK) and that the nRF Connect Toolchain version corresponds to the version of the SDK installed. The directory for storing the application folder needs to be specified as well as a template on which the application is to be based. In this case, the template is to be based on the blinky sample, whose path, relative to the directory in which the nRF Connect SDK is installed will be

```
zephyr\samples\basic\blinky
```

CHAPTER 3 ZEPHYR RTOS APPLICATION DEVELOPMENT ENVIRONMENTS AND
           ZEPHYR APPLICATION BUILDING PRINCIPLES

In nRF Connect for VS Code, when creating a new application using "Create new application". Specify the application name, for example, my_blinky_1 (this will create an application folder with that name). Finally, clicking on the Create Application button will add the application code, without building it.

The next step is to add a build configuration for the application by hovering the mouse cursor over the application name, clicking on the build configuration icon, and, in the Add Build Configuration View, adding the required configuration details. These will include the target board for which the application is to be built, the project configuration file (the sample project has one already, prj.conf), Kconfig fragments (if any) for the application, extra CMake arguments (if any), and the application build directory and build directives such as whether the application is to be built automatically after the application configuration files have been generated and also whether the application is to include debugging options.

The Board ID strings corresponding to the various Nordic development kit boards are summarized in Table 3-1.

Table 3-1. *Board IDs for Nordic development kit boards*

Device	Board ID
nRF5340 DK	nrf5340dk_nrf5340_cpuapp_ns
nRF52840 DK	nrf52840dk_nrf52840
nRF52833 DK	nrf52833dk_nrf52833
nRF52 DK	nrf52dk_nrf52832
nRF9160 DK	nrf9160dk_nrf9160_ns

The build process, which will take a little while to complete, is started by clicking on the Build Configuration button.

CHAPTER 3   ZEPHYR RTOS APPLICATION DEVELOPMENT ENVIRONMENTS AND
            ZEPHYR APPLICATION BUILDING PRINCIPLES

The progress of the build can be viewed in a VS Code terminal window by clicking on the View ➤ Terminal menu option. When the build completes successfully, a mini-report showing the memory usage of the application will be displayed.

During the build process, behind the scenes as it were, services provided by west such as repository management and the driving of the application build process will be doing most of the work. These services are invoked internally by nRF Connect for VS Code.

To flash the application to the target board, the board, of course, must be connected to the workstation using a USB cable plugged into the correct USB port, used for programming, on the board, and connected to a USB port on the development workstation. If correctly plugged in, the board will be discoverable and will be visible in the boards listed in the Connected devices view. Clicking the Flash option in the Actions View will flash the application to the board. The details of the flashing process will be displayed in the Terminal Panel, if it is open. If all goes well, an LED on the board will be seen to be blinking.

Introduction to the Zephyr RTOS Device Driver Model and the Zephyr RTOS Device Driver APIs and Data Structures

The kinds of Zephyr applications commonly built to gain familiarity with building multitasking Zephyr RTOS applications typically involve things such as flashing one or more LEDs, detecting button presses, and sending messages to a PC terminal over a serial (UART) port. Because Zephyr runs on hardware platforms that do not have an MMU (Memory Management Unit) and hence do not support virtual memory, the Zephyr device driver model is not the same as the device driver models found in Linux,

Windows, or macOS systems. Hence, part of the process of learning Zephyr RTOS programming is to learn about the Zephyr RTOS device driver model and its associated APIs. The Zephyr device driver modelling framework has borrowed the devicetree language from Linux for specifying processor and board configurations. However, the way devicetree files are used in Zephyr RTOS is quite different from the way they are used in Linux.

As already mentioned, application configuration involves both Kconfig and devicetree aspects. As a rule of thumb, the devicetree is used to describe the hardware and its boot-time configuration such as the peripherals on a board, the boot-time clock frequencies, interrupt lines, etc. Kconfig is used to configure which software support to build into the final image, for example, whether to add networking support, which drivers are needed by the application, and such.

The devicetree syntax takes a certain amount of effort and practice to master. For many projects, the devicetree details do not have to be given in full as the final devicetree can be built up from processor and target board devicetree files combined with project-specific overlays. The devicetree textual description is parsed and compiled as part of the build process. The, textual, devicetree syntax is illustrated in Figure 3-21.

```
/dts-v1/;
/ {
    a-node {
        subnode_label: a-sub-node {
            foo = <3>;
        };
    };
};
```

Figure 3-21. Devicetree .dts file example

CHAPTER 3 ZEPHYR RTOS APPLICATION DEVELOPMENT ENVIRONMENTS AND
ZEPHYR APPLICATION BUILDING PRINCIPLES

The `/dts-v1/;` line means the file's contents are in version 1 of the DTS syntax. The preceding tree has three nodes: a root node "/", a node named `a-node`, which is a child of the root node, and a node named `a-sub-node`, which is a child of a-node.

Nodes can have zero or more labels. A label can be thought of as a unique shorthand that can be used to refer to the labelled node elsewhere in the devicetree. In the preceding code snippet, a-sub-node has a label subnode_label. Devicetree nodes have paths that identify their locations in the tree. A devicetree path is a string separated by slashes (/). The root node's path is a single slash "/". In general, a node path is formed by concatenating the node's ancestors' names with the name of the node itself. For example, the full path to a-sub-node is /a-node/a-sub-node.

Devicetree nodes can also have properties, which are, quite simply, name/value pairs. A property value can be any sequence of bytes. A property can be given as an array of cells, where a cell is simply a 32-bit unsigned integer. In the preceding code snippet, the node a-sub-node has a property named foo, whose value is a cell with value 3. The size and type of foo's value are implied by the enclosing angle brackets (< and >) in the DTS. Most often, devicetree nodes correspond to some piece of hardware, and the node hierarchy reflects the physical arrangement/layout of the hardware.

The devicetree also provides aliases that can be used to reference other nodes in the devicetree. It is possible to have collections of aliases. In the following devicetree snippet, the /aliases node contains properties that are aliases, in this case just a single alias. The name of the property is the name of that alias, and the value of the property is a reference to a node in the devicetree. The & is analogous to C's address of operator.

```
/ {
    aliases {
            subnode_alias = &subnode_label;
    };
};
```

99

CHAPTER 3   ZEPHYR RTOS APPLICATION DEVELOPMENT ENVIRONMENTS AND
            ZEPHYR APPLICATION BUILDING PRINCIPLES

The preceding code snippet assigns the node a-sub-node, referenced by its label subnode_label to the alias subnode_alias.

The Zephyr devicetree build process generates a C header that contains the required devicetree data abstracted behind a C macro API framework. Information about a particular devicetree node can be obtained via the corresponding C macro, which is referred to as a node identifier for that device. The two common macros used in practice are `DT_NODELABEL()`, which is used to access a node via its label, and `DT_ALIAS()`, which is used to access a node via an alias. An alias can be thought of as an abbreviation of a full node label and can be used as an easier-to-remember label as opposed to having to provide a full path. Using the preceding snippet, the node identifier of the `a-sub-node` could be obtained via `DT_NODELABEL(subnode-label)`.

The `DT_PROP()` macro can be used to retrieve the value assigned to a certain devicetree property. For example, to get the value assigned to the foo property, the macro `DT_PROP(DT_NODELABEL(subnode-label), foo)` could be used.

A specific devicetree node is referenced by the full path to that node in the devicetree, for example, `/external-bus/ethernet@0,0`. Where a user wishes to obtain an answer to a question such as "which device is eth0?" having to provide a full path may involve time spent searching through the devicetree. An aliases node can be thought of as providing a shorter user and application-friendly alias for the full device path, for example:

```
aliases {
    ethernet0 = &eth0;
    serial0 = &serial0;
};
```

CHAPTER 3   ZEPHYR RTOS APPLICATION DEVELOPMENT ENVIRONMENTS AND
ZEPHYR APPLICATION BUILDING PRINCIPLES

Writing a Zephyr application may involve getting a driver-level struct device corresponding to a particular devicetree node. The following example, based on the Zephyr documentation, illustrates how this can be done in application code. It is based on the following example devicetree fragment pertaining to a serial device serial@40002000:

```
/ {
    soc {
            serial0: serial@40002000 {
                    status = "okay";
                    current-speed = <115200>;
                    /* ... */
            };
    };
    aliases {
        my-serial = &serial0;
    };

    chosen {
        zephyr,console = &serial0;
    };
};
```

The /chosen node is a special node that contains properties that have values describing system-wide settings, and the DT_CHOSEN() macro can be used to get the node identifier for a chosen node.

Devicetree nodes can be referenced using the ampersand (&) character and the label.

To overwrite a property, the node has to be referenced using the ampersand character and the label. Devicetree entries occurring later in the devicetree overwrite earlier entries (the sequence order is important).

CHAPTER 3 ZEPHYR RTOS APPLICATION DEVELOPMENT ENVIRONMENTS AND
           ZEPHYR APPLICATION BUILDING PRINCIPLES

To obtain a device-level struct, it is necessary to provide the correct node identifier. The Zephyr framework provides a number of convenience macros for this purpose, which include the following:

- A macro that uses a node label, for example, #define MY_SERIAL DT_NODELABEL(serial0)

- A macro that uses an alias, for example, #define MY_SERIAL DT_ALIAS(my_serial)

- A macro that uses a path, for example, #define MY_SERIAL DT_PATH(soc, serial_40002000)

The Zephyr framework provides various macros that can be given a node identifier and which expand to code that returns a pointer to the corresponding struct device, for example:

```
const struct device *const uart_dev = DEVICE_DT_GET(MY_SERIAL);
if (!device_is_ready(uart_dev)) {
    /* Not ready, do not use */
    return -ENODEV;
}
Other variants of DEVICE_DT_GET() are DEVICE_DT_GET_OR_NULL()
DEVICE_DT_GET_ONE() or DEVICE_DT_GET_ANY()
```

In the interests of portability, Zephyr tries to work with generic device driver models as much as possible. In the nRF Connect SDK, as in the Zephyr SDK, the driver implementation is decoupled from its API to make it possible to switch out one low-level driver implementation and replace it with another without having to modify the application code that uses the same generic API in both cases.

CHAPTER 3 ZEPHYR RTOS APPLICATION DEVELOPMENT ENVIRONMENTS AND
ZEPHYR APPLICATION BUILDING PRINCIPLES

The generic API approach used by Zephyr borrows many ideas from Linux such as the character device driver model whose principles are used, in adapted form, in Zephyr.

Figure 3-22 shows the basic nRF Connect SDK/Zephyr SDK device driver architecture.

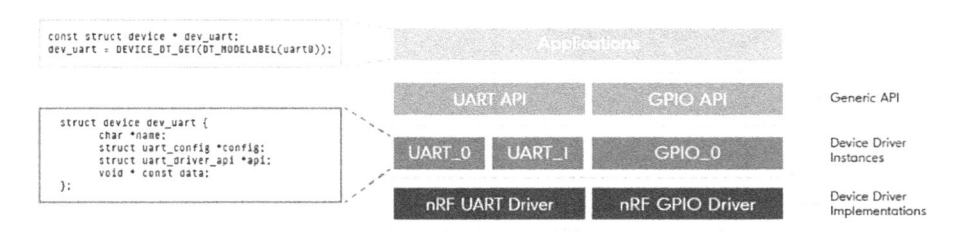

Figure 3-22. Zephyr device driver architecture

In Zephyr, there are several device driver types. They all have a similar structure for accessing the properties and methods of a device type instance. The structure consists of a set of pointers: a pointer to the device name string, a pointer to a structure containing configuration details, and a pointer to a structure containing a table of function pointers defining the behavior of the device and a pointer to data. The actual driver code functionality is provided by the functions to which the API function pointers point.

In an application, a device is accessed via a pointer (handle) to a `const struct device` instance. This pointer is initialized using the macro `DEVICE_DT_GET(<node_id>)`, which takes a devicetree node identifier as an argument. `DEVICE_DT_GET()` will fail at build time if the device is not allocated by the driver, because, for example, there is no entry for such a device in the devicetree (i.e., it does not exist in the devicetree) or the device status of that device in the devicetree is the disabled status. The failure will be detected at linker time with a linker error of the kind undefined reference to `__device_dts_ord<N>`.

CHAPTER 3   ZEPHYR RTOS APPLICATION DEVELOPMENT ENVIRONMENTS AND
             ZEPHYR APPLICATION BUILDING PRINCIPLES

The following code snippet shows a standard pattern for obtaining a handle to a device and testing for its validity by calling the Zephyr driver API function. In this example, the device in question is uart0.

```
const struct device *dev;
dev = DEVICE_DT_GET(DT_NODELABEL(uart0));
if (!device_is_ready(dev)) {
    return;
}
```

Zephyr provides utility macros for specific devices such as, for example, in the case of a GPIO pin to which an LED might be attached, the macro GPIO_DT_SPEC_GET can be used to define a device instance data structure that contains a pointer to a const struct device as one of its members.

```
static const struct gpio_dt_spec led = GPIO_DT_SPEC_GET(LED0_NODE, gpios);
```

Its use is illustrated in the following blinky sample code snippet:

```
#include <zephyr.h>
#include <drivers/gpio.h>
#define SLEEP_TIME_MS   1000
#define LED0_NODE DT_ALIAS(led0)
static const struct gpio_dt_spec led = GPIO_DT_SPEC_GET(LED0_NODE, gpios);
void main(void) {
    int ret;
    if (!device_is_ready(led.port)) {
            Return;
    }
    ret = gpio_pin_configure_dt(&led, GPIO_OUTPUT_ACTIVE);
```

CHAPTER 3   ZEPHYR RTOS APPLICATION DEVELOPMENT ENVIRONMENTS AND ZEPHYR APPLICATION BUILDING PRINCIPLES

```
if (ret < 0) {
            Return;
}
while (1) {
            ret = gpio_pin_toggle_dt(&led);
            if (ret < 0) {
                        Return;
      }
            k_msleep(SLEEP_TIME_MS);
   }
}
```

The actual driver functions such as gpio_pin_configure() and gpio_pin_toggle_dt() are passed a pointer to the device instance (obtained using the address of operator '&').

The blinky application uses the (automatically created) thread associated with the function main() and achieves led blinking by calling k_msleep() to pause this thread for the specified sleep time.

The advantage of working with an API-specific structure is that it uses a single variable to gather (encapsulate) all the information needed for working with the device. The alternative would be to extract this information from the devicetree one detail at a time.

The devicetree for a given board can be found in the directory for that board in the zephyr/boards/arm/*<board>* where the board for the nRF52840 DK is nrf52840dk_nrf52840. The devicetree file for this board is nrf52840dk_nrf52840.dts, and it contains the following section pertaining to on-board LEDs:

```
leds {
      compatible = "gpio-leds";
      led0: led_0 {
                  gpios = <&gpio0 13 GPIO_ACTIVE_LOW>;
```

```
                label = "Green LED 0";
        };
        led1: led_1 {
                gpios = <&gpio0 14 GPIO_ACTIVE_LOW>;
                label = "Green LED 1";
        };
        led2: led_2 {
                gpios = <&gpio0 15 GPIO_ACTIVE_LOW>;
                label = "Green LED 2";
        };
        led3: led_3 {
                gpios = <&gpio0 16 GPIO_ACTIVE_LOW>;
                label = "Green LED 3";
        };
};
```

Using this devicetree, the macro expansion in the statement

`static const struct gpio_dt_spec led = GPIO_DT_SPEC_GET(LED0_NODE, gpios);`

will initialize the variable led0 to a struct of type gpio_dt_spec with the device pointer pointing to the GPIO controller, &gpio0, the pin number set to 13, and the flag `led.dt_flags` set to GPIO_ACTIVE_LOW.

GPIO Inputs

Reading input pins can be accomplished in two main ways, namely, polling the pin level by repeatedly calling gpio_pin_get_dt() to keep track of the status of a pin so as to be able to detect a state change, or configuring the pin to generate edge-level change interrupts. Polling a pin continuously, though conceptually simple and simple to implement, will

CHAPTER 3   ZEPHYR RTOS APPLICATION DEVELOPMENT ENVIRONMENTS AND
ZEPHYR APPLICATION BUILDING PRINCIPLES

result in an increased power consumption. With edge-triggered interrupts, the CPU is automatically informed when there is a change in the pin status. This approach frees up the CPU from having to continually poll the status of the pin and has the extra potential advantage that the CPU can, if required, be put into sleep mode in between button presses and only woken up when there is a change in button state. Edge-triggered interrupts can only be configured on a GPIO pin configured as an output pin.

The `zephyr\samples\basic\button` example demonstrates both polling and interrupt-driven approaches for working with pins, as well as mirroring the state of a button with the state of a corresponding LED. This example illustrates the use of a thread and an interrupt in an application.

Setting up an interrupt on a GPIO pin involves configuring an interrupt on that pin and associating a callback function interrupt service routine with that interrupt.

Configuring an interrupt on the selected pin uses the `gpio_pin_interrupt_configure_dt()` function, passing in the pin specifications given in the devicetree and the interrupt configuration flags as arguments. The interrupt configuration flags configure the triggering conditions, which can be to trigger an interrupt on a rising edge, falling edge, or both – in other words, whether to trigger on a change to logical level 1, logical level 0, or both. As an example, `gpio_pin_interrupt_configure_dt(&button,GPIO_INT_EDGE_TO_ACTIVE);` will configure an interrupt being triggered on `dev.pin` when a change to logical level 1 occurs.

Setting up an interrupt handler callback requires defining (writing the code for) the interrupt service routing and then associating the callback function with the interrupt itself. The signature (function prototype) of the callback function is

```
void pin_isr(const struct device *dev, struct gpio_callback *cb, gpio_port_pins_t pins);
```

A handler that toggles the state of an LED associated with the button being pressed could be implemented along the following lines:

```
void pin_isr(const struct device *dev, struct gpio_callback *cb, uint32_t pins) {
        gpio_pin_toggle_dt(&led);
}
```

The argument, `cb`, points to a static (global) variable of type `struct gpio_callback,` which stores the address of the callback function and the bitmask corresponding to the pin being used. Initialization involves the function `gpio_init_callback()`, which takes a pointer to the pin callback data structure, a function pointer to the isr callback function, and a bitmask associated with the target pin as follows:

```
gpio_add_callback(button.port, &pin_cb_data);
```

The macro `BIT(n)` produces an unsigned integer with bit position n set. Finally, the callback function is added by calling `gpio_add_callback()` as follows:

```
gpio_add_callback(button.port, &pin_cb_data);
```

UART Communications Between a Target Board and a PC

Most modern PCs do not have DB9 connector RS232 ports. Typically a device wishing to communicate with a PC over RS232 does so over a virtual COM port realized by a chip/device that provides an RS232 to USB interface and exposes a virtual COM port on the PC.

CHAPTER 3   ZEPHYR RTOS APPLICATION DEVELOPMENT ENVIRONMENTS AND
ZEPHYR APPLICATION BUILDING PRINCIPLES

Many embedded processor development boards contain some kind of interface MCU that is involved not only in assisting with serial communications between the target board MCU but also with programming, logging, and debugging. This MCU will have a USB interface for connecting to the PC workstation and a serial interface connecting it to the core processor itself. The UART connections on the nRF52840 System on Chip (SoC) that connect to the interface MCU are summarized in Table 3-2.

The block diagram shown in Figure 3-23 for the nRF52840 DK board shows just such an approach.

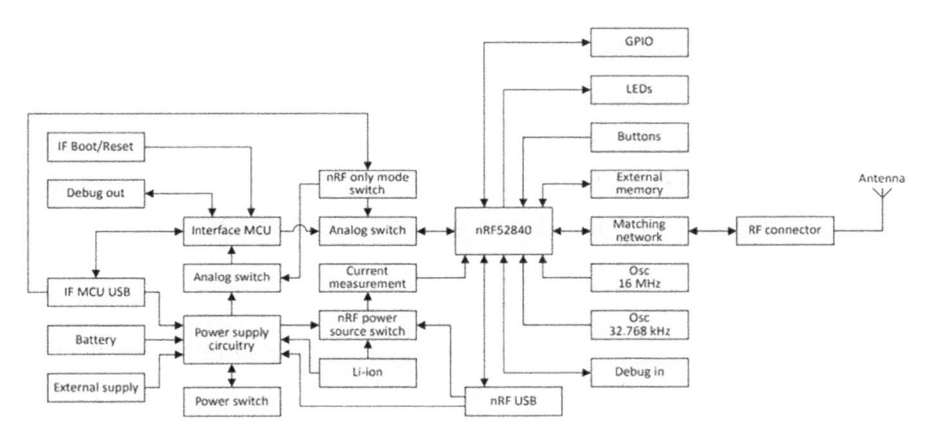

Figure 3-23. *nRF52840 DK board schematic block diagram*

Table 3-2 shows which processor GPIO pins correspond to which UART functionalities.

Table 3-2. *GPIO-UART pins*

GPIO nRF52840	nRF52840 UART
P0.05	RTS
P0.06	TXD
P0.07	CTS
P0.08	RXD

In principle, a UART only requires two signal lines to successfully communicate: a TXD (transmit data) and RXD (receive data) line as well as a common ground line (used as a reference point). When communicating with another UART device, the TXD line will be attached to a corresponding RXD line, and vice versa. No clock line is used with the UART protocol. Rather, users instead specify a particular baud rate for the two devices to operate at. The UART standard specifies two extra lines, namely, RTS (ready to send) and CTS (clear to send). The RTS and CTS lines, if connected, are responsible for flow control. If flow control is disabled, then these two pins are not used.

The USB connection between the interface MCU and the PC can forward data sent from the nRF52840 processor to the PC. From the PC's point of view, this USB connection is behaving as a serial connection, with a virtual COM port. The virtual COM port is configurable, with a flexible baud rate setting up to 1 Mbps. It also supports Dynamic Hardware Flow Control (HWFC) handling if so configured.

From the perspective of experimenting with various multithreading coding patterns, the virtual COM port–based UART is valuable because it is the port used when the Zephyr kernel `printk()` function is used to send text strings to a PC console terminal. To a certain extent, the Zephyr RTOS `printk()` mimics the corresponding `printk()` used in Linux kernel programming. `printk()` is a `printf()`-like function that supports a subset of the `printf()` format string specifiers. From the application real-time performance point of view, it is worth remembering that the output of `printk()` is not deferred but is immediately sent to the console without any mutual exclusion or buffering and that `printk()` will not return until all the bytes of the message have been sent. Bearing this in mind, the use of `printk()` in time-critical applications is best avoided.

Zephyr Logging Module

Another way of sending messages to a PC console (terminal window) is to make use of the Logger module. The Logger module's logging API provides a common interface to process messages issued by the developer code. Messages are passed through a frontend and are then processed by active backends. An advantage of working with the Logger module is that it supports deferred logging, which allows the more time-consuming aspects of message logging to be run when it is more convenient to do so, instead of processing and sending the log message immediately.

Additional features of the logging module include runtime filtering of messages, timestamping of messages, and a data dumping API. Zephyr RTOS logging borrows ideas from Linux kernel logging and syslog. Filtering is based on log message severity levels. The severity levels are summarized in Table 3-3.

Table 3-3. Log message severity levels

1 (most severe)	Error	Severe error conditions	LOG_LEVEL_ERR
2	Warning	Conditions that should be taken care of	LOG_LEVEL_WRN
3	Info	Informational messages that require no action	LOG_LEVEL_INF
4 (least severe)	Debug	Debugging messages	LOG_LEVEL_DBG

CHAPTER 3 ZEPHYR RTOS APPLICATION DEVELOPMENT ENVIRONMENTS AND
          ZEPHYR APPLICATION BUILDING PRINCIPLES

Zephyr provides several "convenience" macros for sending log messages at different severity levels, LOG_INF, LOG_DBG, LOG_WRN, and LOG_ERR, used as shown in the following example:

```
LOG_INF("Count value %d",2);
LOG_DBG("Debug I2C sensor value %d", 33);
LOG_WRN("Temp sensor reading HIGH");
LOG_ERR("Out of range setting given");
```

The Zephyr Logger module is similar to logging libraries provided with other embedded systems development environments such as, for example, the ESP32 logging library [4].

Zephyr also provides a set of LOG_HEXDUMP_X macros for dumping data as a sequence of hexadecimal byte values, where X can be DBG, INF, WRN, or ERR.

A LOG_HEXDUMP_X macro takes, as its three parameters, a pointer to the data to be dumpled, the size of that data in bytes, and a description string to describe the data, for example:

```
uint8_t data[] = { 0x00, 0x01, 0x02, 0x03, 0x04, 0x05, 0x06,
                   0x07, 'H', 'e', 'l', 'l','o' };
LOG_HEXDUMP_INF(data, sizeof(data), "hexy hello");
```

The data displayed in the terminal window will be

00 01 02 03 04 05 06 07 48 65 6c 6c 6f

The Logger module can be configured either globally or on a per-module basis. Global logging settings apply to all modules. Module-specific logging configuration can be used to specify a module logging level (LOG_LEVEL_[level]) or to disable logging from that module by using the setting LOG_LEVEL_NONE. It is also possible to override logging levels globally. However, a global override can only be used to increase the logging level.

For a module to use the logger, it must specify a unique name and register itself with the logger. Where a module is made up of multiple source files, registration is performed in one file, but each module file has to declare the module name. The logging system API can be called by general application code. The "fine control" logging capabilities of the Zephyr Logger provide a useful set of logging tuning, management, and control mechanisms. It is up to the developer to devise effective policies for the debugging, monitoring, and troubleshooting task being tackled and to move from a global logging approach to a more "fine-grained" logging approach. Log messages automatically include a timestamp and report on what part of the application they come from. The importance of each message can be specified. This makes it possible to select, at compile time, which logging messages will be included in the binary. A program can contain various debug-level messages, and messages can be included or left out of the build based on setting a build time priority level. This can be done by setting the value of CONFIG_LOG_MAX_LEVEL in the Kconfig file. This is the maximal level that is compiled in, and lower-level messages will not be compiled into the code. At runtime, it is also possible to turn off the logging of certain messages by increasing the severity threshold.

The Zephyr logging architecture design is quite sophisticated. There are three main components, namely, a frontend, which is the application logging interface; the core component, which filters messages and routes them to a given backend, which may be a network interface to send log messages to a log server in the cloud. By adding a means to send commands to the running device remotely, there is also the possibility of dynamically controlling the level of logging based on the behavior of the system under various testing scenarios.

CHAPTER 3   ZEPHYR RTOS APPLICATION DEVELOPMENT ENVIRONMENTS AND
            ZEPHYR APPLICATION BUILDING PRINCIPLES

Note   The nRF Connect for VS Code extension pack has a built-in terminal emulator called nRF Terminal, which can be used instead of an external terminal emulator, such as PuTTY in Windows. It is activated by clicking on the Connect to serial port button in the Connected Devices View.

Logging is an important debugging tool, and later on, there will be examples that explore various logging configurations and scenarios.

Plan of Action for Exploring Multithreading and Thread Synchronization

In the next section, starting from simple examples involving flashing leds, detecting button presses, and sending messages to the console, more complex scenarios involving various multithreading and thread synchronization patterns will be explored. Later sections will cover working with I2C and SPI interfaces, ADC analog data capture, and PWM output.

More advanced sections toward the end of the book will introduce Zephyr examples demonstrating the potential uses of BLE, Ethernet, and TCP/IP and lay the foundations for developing more complex IoT and IIoT applications.

Using Simulation and Simulators for Testing and Developing Zephyr RTOS Applications

Two widely used simulation/emulation frameworks for testing embedded systems are QEMU and Renode. In this section, Renode will be introduced and the potential uses of Renode in CI/CD (continuous integration/continuous deployment) approaches to the development and testing of more complex embedded systems.

CHAPTER 3   ZEPHYR RTOS APPLICATION DEVELOPMENT ENVIRONMENTS AND ZEPHYR APPLICATION BUILDING PRINCIPLES

Zephyr Applications Using Renode

Renode was developed by Antmicro, a Swedish-Polish research company, as a development tool for developing wired and wireless multinode embedded networks. Its purpose is to enable the development and testing of IoT systems, with a special emphasis on the security aspects of such systems. It provides emulators for a wide range of processor architectures and a means of adding virtual physical devices to the emulated processor cores, so that unmodified compiled software can be run on virtual boards constructed using the tools and interfaces provided by Renode. Supported processor architectures include ARMv7 and ARMv8 Cortex-A and Cortex-M, x86, and RISC-V.

Renode is implemented in C# and C, and systems can be built by connecting devices (including memory) to a system bus connected to a processor core running the corresponding processor instruction set. The devices themselves can be implemented in C# and connected to the system bus.

The Renode simulator/emulator can run "networks of devices." Renode has a command-line interface (CLI), called the Monitor, via which it is possible to control the emulation using Renode's built-in functions, which provide access to emulation objects such as peripherals, machines, and external connectors.

Renode provides a number of basic peripheral devices including UART, Timer, GPIO controller, I2C controller, SPI controller, and I2C sensor and SPI sensor examples.

Peripherals implemented in Python can also be used for the purposes of implementing devices with very simple logic.

Python code can be executed directly in the Renode Monitor using the python command. Peripherals implemented in Python can also be used for the purposes of implementing devices with very simple logic.

Renode also provides a set of hooks that make it possible to run code such as Python scripts when certain conditions arise. These hooks provide specific functionalities and include UART hooks, CPU hooks, system bus hooks, watchpoint hooks, packet interception hooks, and user state hooks.

Renode supports debugging applications running on emulated machines using the GDB debugger. It works in Renode by making use of the GDB remote protocol. Common GDB functions such as breakpoints, watchpoints, stepping, and memory access are supported.

Renode and Firmware Testing

CI/CD makes extensive use of unit testing and version control. Automated firmware testing using real hardware is difficult because it relies on stable firmware code on top of which to build the testing code as well as hardware such as code flashing tools and power supplies, and in addition providing code that will orchestrate the tests and collect the test data. The renode-test command can be used to run test scripts. The Robot framework provides many testing scripts that can either be used as is or extended (modified). Where necessary, custom testing scripts can be implemented. By combining Renode with GitHub actions, it is possible to ensure that pull requests and commits to the project repository pass the necessary tests. Although quite a steep learning process is involved, this approach is very powerful for developing complex IoT systems and for developing and testing code before the target hardware is available.

Building Machines in Renode

At a conceptual level, a machine can be thought of as a system bus to which a processor core and various (memory-mapped) peripherals can be attached. Renode provides a language for building machines and extending existing Renode provided machines.

CHAPTER 3 ZEPHYR RTOS APPLICATION DEVELOPMENT ENVIRONMENTS AND
ZEPHYR APPLICATION BUILDING PRINCIPLES

The output display in Figure 3-24 shows, schematically, a basic RISC-V machine that emulates a MiV system.

```
(machine-0) machine LoadPlatformDescription @platforms/cpus/miv.repl
(machine-0) peripherals
Available peripherals:
sysbus (SystemBus)
|
├── clint (CoreLevelInterruptor)
|       <0x44000000, 0x4400FFFF>
|
├── cpu (RiscV)
|       Slot: 0
|
├── ddr (MappedMemory)
|       <0x80000000, 0x83FFFFFF>
|
├── flash (MappedMemory)
|       <0x60000000, 0x6003FFFF>
|
├── gpioInputs (MiV_CoreGPIO)
|       <0x70002000, 0x700020A3>
|
├── gpioOutputs (MiV_CoreGPIO)
|       <0x70005000, 0x700050A3>
|
├── plic (PlatformLevelInterruptController)
|       <0x40000000, 0x43FFFFFF>
|
├── timer0 (MiV_CoreTimer)
|       <0x70003000, 0x7000301B>
|
├── timer1 (MiV_CoreTimer)
|       <0x70004000, 0x7000401B>
|
└── uart (MiV_CoreUART)
        <0x70001000, 0x70001017>
```

Figure 3-24. *A basic RISC-V machine that emulates a MiV system*

Emulators vs. Simulators

Emulators are not the same thing as simulators. A good way of distinguishing between the two is to imagine a car simulator or flight simulator. If the car or flight simulator could actually carry the user from place to place, it would be an emulator.

Real-world complex application development may involve part simulation and part emulation, for instance, emulating a microcontroller core, but simulating peripherals and sensors or communications links (see Table 3-4).

117

CHAPTER 3 ZEPHYR RTOS APPLICATION DEVELOPMENT ENVIRONMENTS AND
        ZEPHYR APPLICATION BUILDING PRINCIPLES

Table 3-4. Emulators vs. simulators

Purpose	Emulator	Simulator
Coding	Substitutes an actual device	Reveals application behavior
Environment being imitated	Both assembler and compiled high-level language code	High-level language using the simulator API
Performance	Both software and hardware aspects	End behavior of the software (what the user will experience). However, the timing in the simulator will be emulated time
	Can be slow	Typically runs compiled code, hence faster
Use cases	Testing at the level of detailed internal behavior	Testing the external (visible/experienced) behavior

Simulator Use Cases

- Developing software when the target devices have not been decided on or are not available, or are expensive

- When evaluating how an application interacts with users or some external environment

- Checking effects of using different kinds of peripheral, for example:

    - Using UI (User Interface) devices with different screen sizes and different screen resolutions

Emulator Use Cases

- Checking how application software interacts with the hardware or a combination of the hardware and an OS (Operating System).

  - Note: It may not be possible to emulate all hardware units.

- In continuous integration testing approaches, for example, when using an Agile development methodology where there is a requirement to carry out testing during the early stages of the project life cycle.

- Emulator-based automation testing makes it possible to test in parallel with the development process life cycle.

- More powerful/insightful debugging involving measuring things such as

  - CPU load
  - Memory consumption
  - Network loads

Advantages of Simulators and Emulators

- Saving money when testing network application performance as it is not necessary to actually build and administer a physical network

CHAPTER 3 ZEPHYR RTOS APPLICATION DEVELOPMENT ENVIRONMENTS AND ZEPHYR APPLICATION BUILDING PRINCIPLES

- Ability to use scalability and take advantage of the pay-as-you-go benefits of cloud computing to scale up as and when required, and also take advantage of the relative ease of cloud deployment
- The convenience of using virtual emulator and simulator devices for test automation purposes

Disadvantages of Simulators and Emulators

- Because simulators and emulators are virtual copies and not the actual devices, the test results may not be completely accurate and possibly may be quite inaccurate.
  - Hence, it is necessary to be aware of the possibility of false-positive and false-negative results.
- Not all features can be tested with emulators and simulators. Examples include features such as
  - Battery performance
  - CPU performance
  - Memory consumption
  - Video and audio quality
  - Connectivity issues involving, for example, Wi-Fi and BLE networks
  - Color display details
- Staying up to date with the underlying physical devices and their peripherals and drivers

CHAPTER 3 ZEPHYR RTOS APPLICATION DEVELOPMENT ENVIRONMENTS AND ZEPHYR APPLICATION BUILDING PRINCIPLES

Summarizing Renode

- Renode is designed to be a "whole-system emulator" that can be used in continuous integration and continuous development (CI/CD) scenarios on multiple devices.

- Renode is capable of simulating systems having multiple cores and systems having multiple heterogeneous CPUs.

- Renode has built-in support for a variety of widely used network protocols.

- Renode has built-in emulation for commonly used processor architectures such as ARM, RISC-V, PowerPC, and x86.

- Renode provides a good environment for exploring Zephyr RTOS programming in a hardware-agnostic environment.

- Renode can use the same firmware as that used in production and run it against emulated cores, peripherals, and even sensors and actuators.

- The extensive networking support and multisystem emulation capabilities provided in Renode make it a good candidate for testing systems made up of multiple communicating devices.

- Using Renode makes it possible to start development firmware code before the hardware is ready and also to test the firmware on multiple different target architectures.

CHAPTER 3   ZEPHYR RTOS APPLICATION DEVELOPMENT ENVIRONMENTS AND ZEPHYR APPLICATION BUILDING PRINCIPLES

- Using Renode can lead to faster iteration cycles by avoiding the flash loading delays inherent when loading compiled code to actual targets.
- Because Renode is built using the Mono/C# framework, it can run on multiple workstation operating systems without modification.
- Renode is focused on embedded devices, unlike QEMU, which is more focused on emulating systems designed for use with higher-level OSes (e.g., Linux computers).

The details of getting started with Renode and running Zephyr RTOS examples in Renode will be covered in a later chapter.

References

1. https://crascit.com/professional-cmake/
2. https://ninja-build.org/manual.html
3. https://nrfconnect.github.io/vscode-nrf-connect/guides/overview.html
4. ESP32 Logging library reference https://docs.espressif.com/projects/esp-idf/en/latest/esp32/api-reference/system/log.html
5. https://developer.nordicsemi.com/nRF_Connect_SDK/doc/latest/nrf/introduction.html
6. https://docs.zephyrproject.org/latest/develop/toolchains/zephyr_sdk.html

CHAPTER 4

Zephyr RTOS Multithreading

Building Zephyr application requires a basic understanding of the Zephyr build system. This involves being able to make sense of the Kconfig and devicetree files used in the sample projects and then using these as a starting point for your own projects. Mostly, the project-specific files are relatively simple and build on the Kconfig files and devicetree files in the various parts of the Zephyr source code tree. Using the west tool hides much of the underlying complexity.

The Zephyr project provides more than just an operating system kernel. It utilizes tools for developing, releasing, and maintaining a firmware application. Tools that include CMake, a toolchain with compilers, flash and debug tools together with a Zephyr repository that has the sources for the kernel itself, protocol stacks, device drivers, filesystems, and other components.

West is a multipurpose tool. It enables the management of multiple repositories. Zephyr application development makes use of libraries and features from folders that are cloned from different repositories or projects, and it is the west tool that keeps control of which commits to use from the different projects, which, considerably, simplifies the task of adding and removing modules. The concept underlying the use of west is that of a west workspace, which contains one manifest repository and multiple projects. The manifest repository, itself, controls which commits to use from the different projects on which the application will be based. The Zephyr west tool can, importantly, also pull in code from other third-party projects such as cryptographic libraries, hardware abstraction layers (HALs), protocol stacks, and the MCUboot bootloader.

west is implemented in Python 3 and has plug-in capabilities that allow extension commands and their associated features such as build tools, code flashing tools, and debugging tools to be added in.

A west command consists of the top-level west command, which can take a number of common options, followed by a sub-command to run and then options and arguments for that sub-command:

west [common-opts] <command> [opts] <args>

A west workspace is a directory on a development system consisting of a .west subdirectory and a west manifest repository. The Zephyr source code is cloned onto a development system by creating a west workspace using the west init command.

A west manifest is a YAML file, usually named west.yml, which describes the projects, or the Git repositories that make up the west workspace. When working on more advanced Zephyr applications and having to maintain and track multiple versions, knowledge of Git is essential. Git, YAML, and the structure of manifest files are covered in greater depth in more advanced follow-on courses.

Kconfig

The Zephyr project adopted the Kconfig approach used in the Linux build framework, largely because of the need to tackle the same issues as those involved in Linux kernel building, namely, having to handle a large complex code base with many components.

CHAPTER 4   ZEPHYR RTOS MULTITHREADING

Typical Zephyr application projects will use only a subset of all the available components, and building a kernel with just the components required by the application will result in a smaller executable file. Kconfig is used to configure the Zephyr kernel and subsystems at build time in order to adapt the resulting kernel for specific application and platform needs.

A Zephyr application is built by linking the kernel object code formed by compiling the kernel for the specified configuration with the object code generated by compiling the code that constitutes the application (see Figure 4-1).

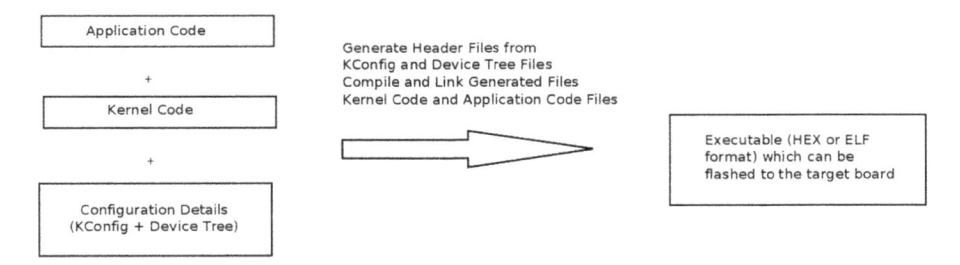

Figure 4-1. *Generating an executable*

This is different from Linux, where the kernel is built separately from the applications that run on a Linux platform. Applications, in Linux, run in a virtual memory space distinct from the Linux kernel memory space. They are loaded dynamically and access kernel (operating) system resources via system calls.

Kconfig files contain details of the required configuration options (often referred to as symbols). Kconfig files also specify dependencies between symbols that help determine which configurations are valid. Symbols can be grouped into hierarchy, which gives rise to a hierarchical menu and submenu structure. This makes it possible to develop graphical configuration tools that are simpler to use than an approach based on editing a large text file. When the project Kconfig file is processed, a header file `autoconf.h` is produced. This contains macros that can be tested at build time and used to "compile out" code for unused features. This strategy can greatly reduce the size of the final executable.

The initial configuration for an application is constructed by merging the configuration settings from three sources, namely, a BOARD-specific configuration file stored in `boards/<architecture>/<BOARD>/<BOARD>_defconfig`, CMake cache entries prefixed with `CONFIG_`, and application configuration settings provided in a project configuration file `prj.conf` by default. The `prj.conf` files for typical projects are relatively small in size and relatively easy to understand.

Devicetrees and Devicetree Configuration

The motivation underlying devicetrees is to minimize the number of separate projects involving devices and boards that are mostly similar but which differ in their details. In the earlier days of Linux before the devicetree framework was devised, there were many separate projects corresponding to various ARM processor–based boards, which led to a proliferation of projects, each of which had to be maintained separately. The number of processors and boards supported by Zephyr made the devicetree approach a "natural fit." When working with devicetrees, there are two types of devicetree input files: devicetree source files, which contain the devicetree itself, and devicetree bindings, which describe the contents, including data types, of a "correct" devicetree for a particular application.

The build system uses devicetree sources and bindings to generate a C header whose contents can be utilized in an actual application via the Zephyr `devicetree.h` API. Devicetree overlays can be used to modify larger devicetree files by overriding specific settings in the larger file. Later in this course, we will introduce the devicetree syntax and how to create suitable overlays for working with adding an I2C or SPI sensor to an application project.

CHAPTER 4   ZEPHYR RTOS MULTITHREADING

Kconfig and Devicetree Usage Heuristics

Project-specific configuration details may involve providing both Kconfig files and devicetree files that can be merged in with other Kconfig and devicetree files. There is, potentially, some degree of overlap between information provided via a project Kconfig file and a project devicetree file.

As a rule of thumb, a devicetree should be used to describe hardware and its boot-time configuration, for example, the peripherals on a board, boot-time clock frequencies, interrupt lines, and such, and Kconfig should be used to configure software support to build into the final image, such as whether to add networking support, which drivers are needed by the application, and so on. In the examples in this course, the contents of the Kconfig and devicetree files will be described without having to go into the full details of Kconfig and devicetree syntax.

Multithreading in Zephyr

A key service provided by Zephyr is multithreading. Small 32-bit SoC devices such as ARM Cortex M processor or RISC-V32 devices do not have an MMU (Memory Management Unit), and virtualization is not used in applications built using such devices. Quite a few processors used will incorporate an MPU (Memory Protection Unit), which can be used to isolate threads from one another, and Zephyr is designed to accommodate devices having an MPU. An MPU can be used to prevent threads accessing certain areas of memory that may contain privileged data and code. This can be important where, for security reasons, it is necessary to isolate certain pieces of code from others. MPUs such as those found in ARM Cortex M33 processors make trusted execution environments possible.

There is much discussion when talking about operating systems about tasks and threads and the distinction between a task and a thread. In Linux, running processes are referred to as tasks, and it is tasks which are scheduled by the Linux kernel. A Linux task runs in its own virtual memory space. Threads in Linux share the same virtual memory space but, from the scheduling point of view, are scheduled as tasks.

In Microsoft Windows, on the other hand, when a task is created, a thread (the primary thread) is also created, and this thread may then spawn other threads. Here, the task can be thought of as the holder of resources and the threads are the units of work that are scheduled. In FreeRTOS, the terms "thread" and "task" are used interchangeably. "Each task executes within its own context with no coincidental dependency on other tasks within the system or the RTOS scheduler itself. Only one task within the application can be executing at any point in time, and the real-time RTOS scheduler is responsible for deciding which task this should be."

Where FreeRTOS talks about tasks, Zephyr RTOS talks about threads. Zephyr threads are the unit of scheduling in Zephyr. In Zephyr, a thread is a kernel object that is used for application processing. Any number of threads can be defined by an application (subject to the availability of sufficient RAM), and each thread will have a unique thread id that is assigned when the thread is spawned and which can be used to reference that thread. From the application point of view, a Zephyr thread can be thought of as a "semi-independent" piece of an application that performs some specific function (carries out some specific duty) [2].

A thread will have a number of properties such as a stack area, a thread control block, an entry point function, and a thread scheduling priority. The stack area is the region of memory used for the thread's stack. The size of the stack area can be configured to conform to the actual processing needs of the thread, and Zephyr provides macros to create and make use of stack memory regions. A thread control block is used for private kernel bookkeeping of the thread's metadata and is realized as an instance of type k_thread. An entry point function, the function that is invoked when the thread is started, can take up to three argument values that can be passed to this function. The scheduling priority of a thread is used in connection with thread scheduling and the allocation of CPU time to the thread.

CHAPTER 4   ZEPHYR RTOS MULTITHREADING

A thread will also have a set of thread options that influence thread handling under certain specific circumstances. These include a start delay that specifies a waiting time delay before the thread is started and an execution mode. The execution mode can either be supervisor or user mode. By default, threads run in supervisor mode, which allows access to privileged CPU instructions, the entire memory address space, and peripherals.

User mode threads have a reduced set of privileges, depending on the CONFIG_USERSPACE option, and will have to make appropriate system calls to access services running at a higher supervisor privilege level.

The details of Zephyr user mode are described in some detail in the Zephyr documentation [1]. Zephyr support for user mode is important when developing networked applications. This is especially important in IoT and IIoT contexts, where security is an important part of the implementation and design process. The following scenarios illustrate recommended practice for having applications run user mode threads:

- To protect against unintentional programming errors where a thread with system-level privileges could corrupt the system and cause it to fail

- To sandbox complex data parsers such as interpreters, network protocols, and filesystems so that kernel or other threads will not be compromised by malicious code or data

- To make possible designs made up of multiple logical "applications," each with its own group of threads and private data structures, and isolation so that the system can continue to function if one thread crashes or is compromised in some way

The various thread states of a Zephyr thread, and the transitions between these states, are outlined in the following state chart diagram (see Figure 4-2).

CHAPTER 4   ZEPHYR RTOS MULTITHREADING

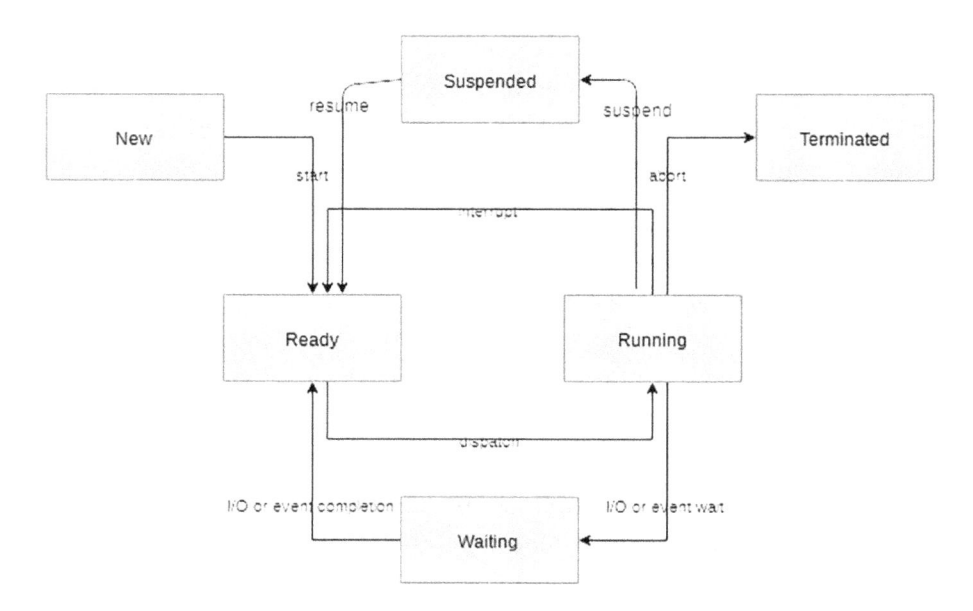

Figure 4-2. Zephyr RTOS thread states

The context of threads in the Zephyr framework is illustrated in Figure 4-3.

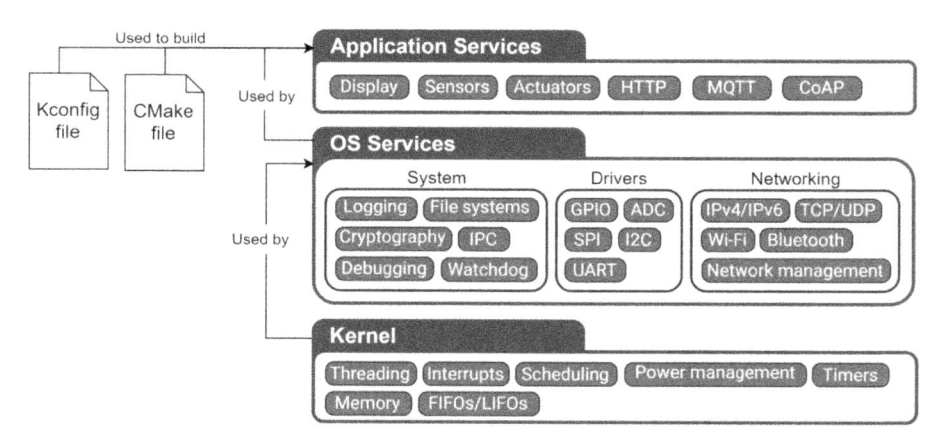

Figure 4-3. Context in which Zephyr threads run

CHAPTER 4   ZEPHYR RTOS MULTITHREADING

Essentially, the life cycle of a thread involves the following thread life cycle events: Thread Creation, Thread Termination, Thread Aborting, and Thread Suspension.

A thread must be created and initialized before it can be used. Each thread has its own stack buffer for which memory has to be allocated before the thread is created. The memory allocated may also have a part that is reserved for memory management structures. For example, if guard-based stack overflow detection is enabled, a small write-protected memory management region will be present, immediately preceding the stack buffer whose purpose is to catch overflows. If userspace is enabled, a separate fixed-size privilege elevation stack must be reserved to serve as a private kernel stack for handling system calls. Also, if userspace is enabled, the thread's stack buffer must be appropriately sized and aligned in such a way that a memory protection region may be programmed to exactly fit. The alignment constraints may be processor architecture dependent. For example, some MPUs require their regions to be of some power of two in size and aligned to the MPU size. The consequence is that portable code cannot simply pass an arbitrary character buffer to the thread create function, k_thread_create(). Zephyr provides macros to instantiate (define) stacks, K_KERNEL_STACK_DEFINE for a kernel privilege-level stack and K_THREAD_STACK_DEFINE for a userspace thread stack. When a thread is created, the kernel initializes the thread control block and one end of the stack memory. The remainder of the thread's stack is typically left uninitialized. K_THREAD_STACK_SIZEOF() gives the size for a stack object defined using K_THREAD_STACK, and K_KERNEL_STACK_SIZEOF() gives the size of a stack object defined using K_KERNEL_STACK.

The start time delay can be specified. Pass the parameter K_NO_WAIT if the thread is to start execution immediately, or K_FOREVER if the thread is start suspended and has to be started explicitly. A delayed start can be cancelled before the thread begins executing by issuing a cancellation request; however, a thread whose delayed start was successfully cancelled must be explicitly re-spawned before it can be used.

The following code snippet shows how a thread can be created at runtime. In this snippet, the thread that is created starts immediately:

```
#define MY_STACK_SIZE 500
 #define MY_PRIORITY 5
 extern void my_entry_point(void *, void *, void *);
 K_THREAD_STACK_DEFINE(my_stack_area, MY_STACK_SIZE);
 struct k_thread my_thread_data;
 k_tid_t my_tid = k_thread_create(&my_thread_data,
 my_stack_area,
 K_THREAD_STACK_SIZEOF(my_stack_area), my_entry_point,
 NULL, NULL, NULL, MY_PRIORITY, 0, K_NO_WAIT);
```

A thread can be declared at compile time by invoking the K_THREAD_DEFINE macro.

This macro defines the stack area, control block, and thread id variables automatically.

The following code snippet has the same effect as the code snippet shown previously:

```
#define MY_STACK_SIZE 500
 #define MY_PRIORITY 5
 extern void my_entry_point(void *, void *, void *);
 K_THREAD_DEFINE(my_tid, MY_STACK_SIZE,
                 my_entry_point, NULL, NULL, NULL,
                 MY_PRIORITY, 0, 0);
```

If CONFIG_USERSPACE is not enabled, the K_THREAD_STACK macros and the K_KERNEL_STACK macros will have exactly the same effects, because in this case there will be no distinction, privilege level wise between the threads. In the context where userspace is not enabled, each thread will have access to all the resources.

CHAPTER 4 ZEPHYR RTOS MULTITHREADING

Zephyr Kernel Mode and User Mode Threads

The topic of privilege levels and processor modes is a complex one, full understanding of which involves probing deeply into the instruction set, register sets, and architecture of a particular processor. In practice, application developers can work at a higher level of abstraction and think in terms of the privileges and permissions of the various threads, both kernel system threads and application threads of the running application, and the various API methods by which a privileged thread can "demote itself" and the API mechanisms that a less privileged thread can use to request some kind of service from a more privileged thread (see Figure 4-4).

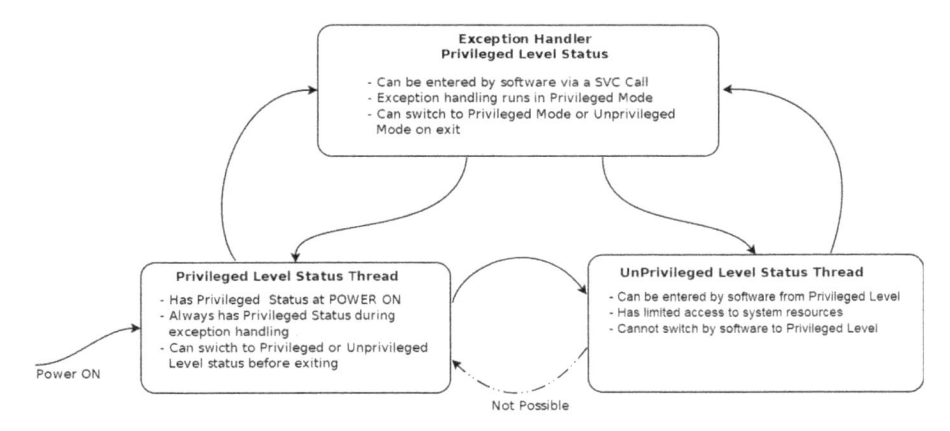

Figure 4-4. Transitions between privileged and unprivileged levels and exception handling

In Linux, there is a clear separation between kernel space and user space. In Zephyr, the distinction is not so clear cut. For example, it is possible to have all the threads, both kernel and user application threads, running at the same privilege level as the kernel threads. On the other hand, if `CONFIG_USERSPACE` is enabled, then it is possible to have threads running at the kernel privilege level or the userspace privilege level. A userspace thread is limited as to which resources it can access directly.

CHAPTER 4 ZEPHYR RTOS MULTITHREADING

An Overview of Generic Zephyr Features Pertaining to Privilege Modes, Stack Protection and Separation, User Mode Threads, and Memory Domains

Privilege Modes

By default, Zephyr runs in a single privilege mode called kernel mode, which is the privilege level of the OS kernel itself. For hardware platforms not configured to support unprivileged mode, application threads will run at the same privilege level as the kernel. The danger, here, is that a "rogue thread" might corrupt other application threads or even the kernel itself.

If the architecture supports additional modes with reduced privileges, and Zephyr is configured so as to be able to run threads at a reduced privilege level, then threads can be isolated from the kernel and isolated from other threads.

Zephyr can support hardware stack protection on systems that have stack protection capabilities. When stack protection is enabled, stack buffer overflows are detected when the system is running in supervisor mode, which will catch issues when the kernel stack buffer has overflowed. Overflows for individual stack frames will, however, not be detected. However, Zephyr can support compiler option features that enable stack canaries for individual frames. In addition to stack overflow protection, Zephyr can be configured to implement per-thread stacks that are separate from the kernel stack. When this is combined with memory protection in systems having a Memory Protection Unit (MPU), the result makes possible an MPU-backed userspace. In such a configuration, unprivileged user threads can only access their required memory regions and no other regions.

What follows next is a basic description on the use of an MPU with an RTOS. It is based on Jean Labrosse's account of the subject published in embedded computing [3] and a LinuxCon paper on Retrofitting Zephyr Memory Protection [4].

ARM Cortex M0+ and M4 processors can have up to one MPU.

The Cortex-M23 and Cortex-M33 can have up to two MPUs if the TrustZone security extension is implemented, one for Secure software and one for Non-secure software. Working with the TrustZone is an advanced topic that will not be covered in this book.

Effective use of memory protection will be important in the design and implementation of applications with demanding security requirements, and once the basic concepts are understood, the details can be studied further, starting with the examples provided in the Zephyr RTOS source tree, and then later on by studying the source code, and then progressing to studying Zephyr support for working with the TrustZone.

Safety Model and Threats That Zephyr RTOS Applications Need to Protect Against

The assumptions are that

- User threads are untrusted and need to be isolated from the kernel and each other

- The kernel thread and the kernel code are trusted and have access to all resources

- A flawed or malicious user thread must not be able to

    - Leak or modify private data of another thread unless specifically granted permission to do so

    - Interfere with or control another thread by using thread communication APIs (pipes, semaphores, etc.) provided by Zephyr RTOS

Kernel resources/kernel objects are one of the following class of data:

- Core kernel object, such as a semaphore, thread, pipe, etc.
- A thread stack, which is an array of z_thread_stack_ elements and is declared with K_THREAD_STACK_ DEFINE()
- A device driver instance (const struct device) that is one of a given set of subsystems

From the user mode perspective, Zephyr provides mechanisms to control access to kernel objects and device drivers both on a per-object and a per-thread basis, as well as system calls to access services running at a privileged level. When making system calls, the parameters passed are first validated. Zephyr also has APIs for managing user mode access to memory in systems with MMUs, so that threads cannot access the private data of other threads unless they have the necessary permissions.

By default, user threads only have privileges to read/write their own stack memory and application memory and read only/execute access to program text and ROM. User threads need to have the corresponding device drivers. Permissions can be acquired either by inheritance from a parent thread or by being granted by a thread with the permissions to do so.

A kernel object can track which user threads can access it.

A kernel thread can access all objects; however, permissions still need to be tracked to handle situations such as where the thread drops to use mode or creates user threads that have object permission inheritance enabled.

For the purposes of accessing kernel objects, Zephyr uses a hash table of kernel objects. This hash map is generated by processing an initially built .elf file to generate the final .elf executable file. This is one example of a situation where creating a Zephyr application involves running

Python scripts to generate files. Other examples include Python scripts for processing Kconfig files and devicetree files. A deep dive into the workings of Zephyr, a complex subject, requires a good understanding of what these various Python scripts do. For most practical application development purposes, this "deep knowledge" is not required.

For suitable architectures, Zephyr can provide a memory domain API, which can be used to grant access to additional blocks of memory to a user thread. The intricacies of working with MPU partitions is an advanced topic, which requires an understanding of linker scripts and how they are generated, and will not be covered in this book. However, as security is an important aspect of developing connected devices, it is something that needs to be taken seriously in design, coding, and testing.

ARM Cortex M Memory Protection Unit (MPU): An Overview

A Memory Protection Unit provides a subset of the functionality that can be provided by a Memory Management Unit (MMU) Difference between MMU and MPU. Both an MMU and an MPU are hardware components involved in memory management and protection.

The main difference between an MMU and an MPU is that an MMU provides virtual memory support while an MPU only provides physical memory protection. An MMU is used in the implementation of virtual memory systems that work by splitting up physical memory into small (say 4 Kbytes) sized pages and then mapping these pages into the virtual address space of a task running on an operating system such as Linux. Virtual memory makes it possible for an operating system to create an illusion that a process has a large address space at its disposal and also prevents a process from corrupting the "virtual" memory of another process. An MPU is much more limited in that it only provides a way to specify which areas of memory can be accessed by a given process/thread, and the number of memory regions that can be defined is relatively small. The size and complexity of an MMU make it unsuited for use in relatively small memory-constrained embedded systems. For such resource-constrained systems, an MPU can provide mechanisms for enhancing application security.

An MPU can only be configured by code running at a privileged level. Regions are defined by specifying their starting addresses and sizes. A fault is generated when a memory access that violates permissions is attempted. The key settings (flags) are as follows:

- AP (Access Privilege) – To specify whether privileged level is required for access
- XN (Execute Never) – To specify the instructions cannot be fetched and executed
- TEX (Type Extension) – Specifies the type of memory

When thread context switching occurs, the operating system (which is running at privileged level) reprograms the MPU as necessary.

User syscalls

Zephyr provides a set of system call APIs that can be used by user mode threads to call kernel services, pass arguments as part of the call, and obtain return values from the service. This is analogous to using system calls in Linux user applications to access kernel services such as file systems, input devices, and networking devices. The details, however, are not exactly the same. An example showing the use of such system calls will be explored in a later section. Although not entirely straightforward, it is possible to design and implement new custom Zephyr system calls.

Zephyr RTOS Thread Priorities

Although thread priorities are conceptually similar in preemptive multitasking operating systems, the API and implementation details do vary, and when developing Zephyr applications, it is important to be familiar with the way thread priorities are defined and handled.

Thread priority is an integer value and can be either negative or non-negative. Numerically lower priorities take precedence over numerically higher values; for example, the scheduler will treat thread A having a priority of 4 as having a higher priority than thread B having a priority of 7. Similarly, thread C of priority -2 will have a higher priority than both thread A and thread B.

Additionally, the Zephyr scheduler distinguishes between two classes of threads, based on thread priority. A cooperative thread has a negative priority value, and once it becomes the current thread, a cooperative thread remains the current thread until it performs some action that makes it unready. A preemptible thread has a non-negative priority value.

Once it becomes the current thread, a preemptible thread may be supplanted at any time if a cooperative thread, or a preemptible thread of higher or equal priority, becomes ready to run.

The initial priority value of a thread can, later, be altered up or down after the thread has been started. This means that it is possible for a preemptible thread to become a cooperative thread, and vice versa, by changing that thread's priority. Whether to make use of cooperative multithreading in an application or not is a design decision.

The Zephyr documentation suggests using cooperative threads for device drivers and other performance-critical work and also using cooperative threads to implement mutual exclusion without the need for a kernel object, such as a mutex. Preemptive threads can be used to give priority to time-sensitive processing over less time-sensitive processing [5].

The Zephyr kernel supports a virtually unlimited number of thread priority levels. Limits can be placed on priority levels via the configuration

CHAPTER 4 ZEPHYR RTOS MULTITHREADING

options CONFIG_NUM_COOP_PRIORITIES and CONFIG_NUM_PREEMPT_PRIORITIES, which specify the number of priority levels for each class of thread. With these limits in place, the usable priority ranges will be (-CONFIG_NUM_COOP_PRIORITIES) to -1 for cooperative threads and 0 to (CONFIG_NUM_PREEMPT_PRIORITIES - 1) for preemptive threads as outlined in Figure 4-5.

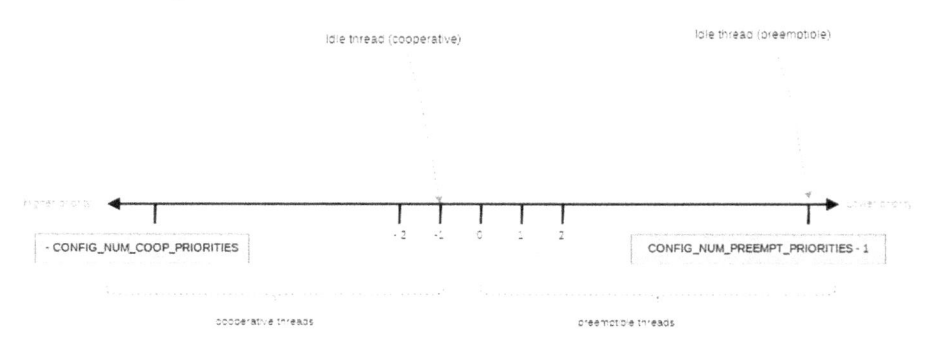

Figure 4-5. Priority ranges for cooperative and preemptive Zephyr threads

Zephyr threads may have various options associated with them, some of which may be processor architecture specific. Thread options are, essentially, bit fields corresponding to special thread handling requirements and are specified when the thread is spawned.

A thread that does not require any thread option has an option value of zero, and a thread can have multiple options by bitwise OR'ing the required option bits. A particularly significant option is K_ESSENTIAL, which tags a thread as an essential thread. Zephyr will treat the termination or aborting of an essential thread as a fatal system error.

The K_FP_REGS option is used to indicate that the thread uses the CPU's floating-point registers. If this option is set, the kernel will take additional steps to save and restore the contents of the floating-point registers when scheduling the thread, as opposed to the default behavior where the kernel does not attempt to save and restore the contents of floating-point registers when scheduling the thread. The K_USER option used when CONFIG_USERSPACE is enabled will result in a thread with reduced privileges, a user mode thread being created. Also, if CONFIG_USERSPACE is enabled, the K_INHERIT_PERMS option has the effect that a child thread will inherit all the kernel object permissions that the parent thread had, except for the parent thread object.

Thread Custom Data

Thread custom data is a 32-bit custom data area, accessible only by the thread itself, which can be used by the application for any purpose it chooses. The default custom data value for a thread is zero. By default, thread custom data support is disabled. It is enabled with the configuration option CONFIG_THREAD_CUSTOM_DATA. The Zephyr API provides the k_thread_custom_data_set() and k_thread_custom_data_get() functions to write and read a thread custom data, respectively. A thread can only access its own custom data. Typically, thread custom data is used to allow a routine to access thread-specific information, by using the custom data as a pointer to a data structure owned by the thread.

It should be noted that custom data support is not available to ISRs because they operate within a single shared kernel interrupt handling context.

Dropping Privileges

If CONFIG_USERSPACE is enabled, a thread running in supervisor mode can perform a one-way transition to user mode by using the k_thread_user_mode_enter() API function. This one-way operation will reset and zero the thread's stack memory and will mark that thread as non-essential.

Thread Termination

A thread can terminate itself by returning from its entry point function. If CONFIG_USERSPACE is enabled, aborting a thread will, additionally, mark that thread and its stack objects as uninitialized so that they may be reused.

The following code-snippet pattern illustrates a typical scenario involving thread termination:

```
void my_entry_point(int unused1, int unused2, int unused3) {
    while (true) {
        ...
        if (<some condition>) {
            return; /* thread terminates from mid-entry point
                       function */
        }
        ...
    }
    /* thread terminates at end of entry point function */
}
```

System Threads

The Zephyr RTOS startup process differs from the startup process of an RTOS such as FreeRTOS.

A FreeRTOS application starts executing in the same way as a non-RTOS bare metal application. Multitasking is started in FreeRTOS by calling the function vTaskStartScheduler(), which is commonly called in main().

Zephyr, on the other hand, spawns two threads when starting: a main thread and an idle thread. The main thread performs kernel initialization and then calls the application's main() function (if one is defined).

CHAPTER 4 ZEPHYR RTOS MULTITHREADING

By default, the main thread uses the highest configured preemptible thread priority (i.e., 0). If the kernel is not configured to support preemptible threads, the main thread uses the lowest configured cooperative thread priority (i.e., -1).

In Zephyr RTOS, the main thread is an essential thread while it is performing kernel initialization or executing the application's main() function. A fatal system error will be raised if the main thread aborts. If main() is not defined, or if it executes and then performs a normal return, the main thread terminates normally and no error is raised.

The idle thread executes when there is no other work for the system to do. If possible, the idle thread should activate the board's power management support to save power. Otherwise, the idle thread simply performs a "do nothing" loop. The idle thread remains in existence as long as the system is running and never terminates. The idle thread always uses the lowest configured thread priority. If this makes it a cooperative thread, then the idle thread repeatedly yields the CPU to allow the other application threads to run when they need to. The idle thread is also an essential thread, and a fatal system error is raised if it aborts. An application-supplied main() function begins executing once kernel initialization is complete. The kernel does not pass any arguments to the function. In other words, there are no argc and argv parameters for it.

The following code snippet illustrates a fairly typical implementation pattern for main().

```
void main(void) {
    /* initialize a semaphore */
    ...
    /* register an ISR that gives the semaphore */
    ...
    /* monitor the semaphore forever */
    while (1) {
        /* wait for the semaphore to be given by the ISR */
```

143

CHAPTER 4 ZEPHYR RTOS MULTITHREADING

```
        ...
        /* do whatever processing is now needed */
        ...
    }
}
```

Basic Multithreading Scenarios

A nontrivial aspect of design and analysis of more complex embedded system applications is working out how to "divide up" the work to be done across multiple threads, how to synchronize and interleave thread execution, and how to exchange information between threads. A related problem is how to trace and analyze application thread execution as part of application tuning and troubleshooting.

Figure 4-6 shows a possible design for an insulin infusion pump application, which is a good example of a more advanced IoT medical application.

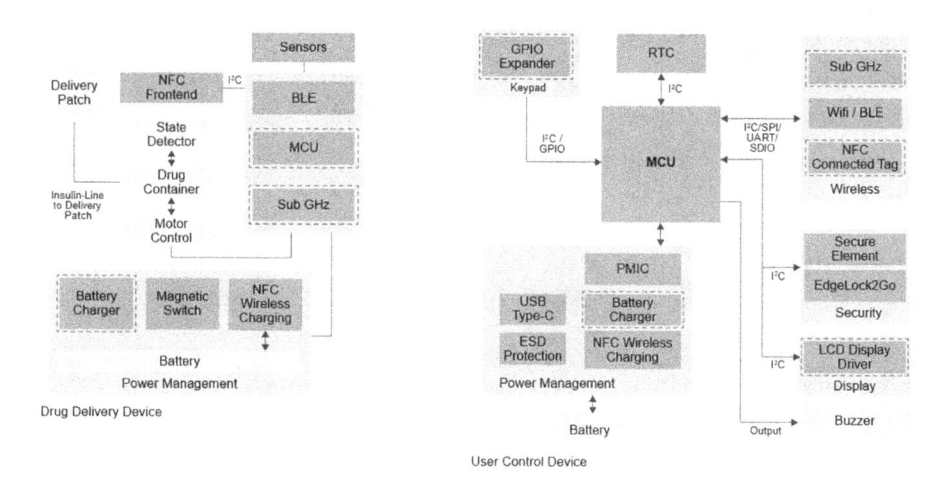

Figure 4-6. An example application for which a multithreaded design is appropriate

144

This application is made up of two components: one for insulin delivery and the other a user control device. The software has a "lot to do," and part of the design process will involve devising a suitable multithreading and interrupt handling and synchronizing scheme.

In the next section, basic multithreading and synchronization will be covered. In a later section, examples involving message queues, mailboxes, and workqueues will be explored. At that point, you should be in a good position to start exploring and thinking about more complex real-world application designs.

Simple Multithreading Example

The example studied here is the `zephyr/samples/basic/threads` sample.

This example involves three threads: one thread blinks an LED at a relatively low frequency, a second thread blinks a different LED at a higher frequency, and a third thread sends messages to a console using `printk()`. In greater detail, when either of the LED blinking threads toggles its LED, it also writes information to a FIFO queue. The data written consists of a thread/LED identifier followed by the number of times that LED has been toggled. The third thread extracts the data written to the fifo and sends it to the device console.

Before looking into the code, it is worthwhile examining the `CMakeLists.txt` and `prj.conf` files. The contents of the `prj.conf` file are as follows:

```
CONFIG_PRINTK=y
CONFIG_HEAP_MEM_POOL_SIZE=256
CONFIG_ASSERT=y
CONFIG_GPIO=y
```

CHAPTER 4   ZEPHYR RTOS MULTITHREADING

This file specifies that the application should include the libraries for using `printk()` and for working with the `gpio` peripherals. The size of the heap memory pool is specified as 256 bytes, and the use of the `__ASSERT()` macro in the kernel code is enabled.

The contents of the `CMakeLists.txt` file are as follows:

```
# SPDX-License-Identifier: Apache-2.0
cmake_minimum_required(VERSION 3.13.1)
find_package(Zephyr REQUIRED HINTS $ENV{ZEPHYR_BASE})
project(threads)
target_sources(app PRIVATE src/main.c)
```

There is only one application source file in this project, namely, `main.c`.

`main.c` starts with required #includes, some #defines for the stacksize value, thread priority value, led aliases, and a definition of a data structure defining the data items to be sent to the `fifo` being used.

```
#include <zephyr.h>
#include <device.h>
#include <drivers/gpio.h>
#include <sys/printk.h>
#include <sys/__assert.h>
#include <string.h>
/* size of stack area used by each thread */
#define STACKSIZE 1024
/* scheduling priority used by each thread */
#define PRIORITY 7
#define LED0_NODE DT_ALIAS(led0)
#define LED1_NODE DT_ALIAS(led1)
struct printk_data_t {
    void *fifo_reserved; /* 1st word reserved for use
    by fifo */
```

```
    uint32_t led;
    uint32_t cnt;
};
```

FIFOs in Zephyr

A Zephyr FIFO is a kernel object that implements a (FIFO) queue that can be used by threads and ISRs to add and remove data items of any size. The main (typical) use of a FIFO is to asynchronously transfer data items of arbitrary size in a "first in, first out" manner. The FIFO queue is implemented as a linked list that, on initialization, is empty. Because the first word of a data item is a pointer to the next item in the queue, FIFO data items must be aligned on a word boundary. The FIFO read operation k_fifo_get() is a blocking operation whose blocking behavior is defined by the second argument passed to k_fifo_get(). The possible blocking behaviors are to return at once, block for some specified amount of time, and block forever. The Zephyr FIFO API consists of the functions/MACROs K_FIFO_DEFINE, k_fifo_init(), k_fifo_alloc_put(), k_fifo_put(), k_fifo_put_list(), k_fifo_put_slist(), and k_fifo_get(), and these are described in the Zephyr documentation.

The Zephyr threads example (zephyr/samples/basic/threads/) defines the application threads at compile time by including the following macro calls inside main.c:

```
K_THREAD_DEFINE(blink0_id, STACKSIZE, blink0, NULL, NULL, NULL,
PRIORITY, 0, 0);
K_THREAD_DEFINE(blink1_id, STACKSIZE, blink1, NULL, NULL, NULL,
PRIORITY, 0, 0);
K_THREAD_DEFINE(uart_out_id, STACKSIZE, uart_out, NULL, NULL,
NULL, PRIORITY, 0, 0);
```

CHAPTER 4   ZEPHYR RTOS MULTITHREADING

The threads all have the same priority, and main.c does not contain a main() function.

The led blinking functions blink0 and blink1 make use of a led blinking helper function blink() defined as follows:

```
void blink(const struct led *led, uint32_t sleep_ms,
uint32_t id) {
    const struct device *gpio_dev;
    int cnt = 0;
    int ret;
    gpio_dev = device_get_binding(led->gpio_dev_name);
    if (gpio_dev == NULL) {
        printk("Error: didn't find %s device\n",
            led->gpio_dev_name);
        return;
    }
    ret = gpio_pin_configure(gpio_dev, led->gpio_pin, led->gpio_flags);
    if (ret != 0) {
        printk("Error %d: failed to configure pin %d '%s'\n",
            ret, led->gpio_pin, led->gpio_pin_name);
        return;
    }
    while (1) {
        gpio_pin_set(gpio_dev, led->gpio_pin, cnt % 2);
        struct printk_data_t tx_data = { .led = id, .cnt = cnt };
        size_t size = sizeof(struct printk_data_t);
        char *mem_ptr = k_malloc(size);
        __ASSERT_NO_MSG(mem_ptr != 0);
        memcpy(mem_ptr, &tx_data, size);
```

```
            k_fifo_put(&printk_fifo, mem_ptr);
            k_msleep(sleep_ms);
            cnt++;
      }
}
```

The thread entry functions blink0 and blink1 initialize a local variable containing information about the led they will be flashing and then call the blink() helper function. Each thread will then be using the same helper function code independently of the other thread, because each thread has its own stack.

The code snippet for the LED-associated data structure and for blink0 is shown in the following. blink1 is very similar to that for blink0.

```
struct led {
      const char *gpio_dev_name;
      const char *gpio_pin_name;
      unsigned int gpio_pin;
      unsigned int gpio_flags;
};
void blink0(void) {
      const struct led led0 = { #if DT_NODE_HAS_STATUS(LED0_
      NODE, okay)
            .gpio_dev_name = DT_GPIO_LABEL(LED0_NODE, gpios),
            .gpio_pin_name = DT_LABEL(LED0_NODE),
            .gpio_pin = DT_GPIO_PIN(LED0_NODE, gpios),
            .gpio_flags = GPIO_OUTPUT | DT_GPIO_FLAGS(LED0_
            NODE, gpios),
      };
      blink(&led0, 100, 0);
}
```

The example uses a fifo for sending data to the fifo object. The `uart_out` thread blocks till data to send is available in the application's global fifo. The FIFO instance is created as a global variable using the following macro invocation:

```
K_FIFO_DEFINE(printk_fifo);
```

The uart thread entry function is implemented as follows:

```
void uart_out(void) {
    while (1) {
        struct printk_data_t *rx_data =
            k_fifo_get(&printk_fifo, K_FOREVER);
        printk("Toggled led%d; counter=%d\n",
            rx_data->led, rx_data->cnt);
        k_free(rx_data);
    }
}
```

The important things to note are that the call `k_fifo_get(&printk_fifo, K_FOREVER);` in the infinite loop is a blocking call and that each of the blinking threads suspends itself for the requisite amount of time between toggling its led by the use of `k_msleep(sleep_ms);`.

The messages to be sent are copied, using memcpy, into a dynamically allocated memory block of the correct size, and the pointer to this block of memory is placed in the fifo, as the relevant code snippet shows.

```
char *mem_ptr = k_malloc(size);
        __ASSERT_NO_MSG(mem_ptr != 0);
        memcpy(mem_ptr, &tx_data, size);
        k_fifo_put(&printk_fifo, mem_ptr);
```

Once the message has been sent, the dynamically allocated block of memory is freed by a call to `k_free(rx_data);`.

CHAPTER 4 ZEPHYR RTOS MULTITHREADING

This example can be run on a wide range of boards that are supported by Zephyr. In the case of boards having only one LED, it may be necessary to "wire up" the second LED using a breadboard of some sort. This example can also be run in Renode, using an application targeting a board that is supported by Renode.

An important lesson to be learned from this code walkthrough is that implementing multithreaded applications and studying examples of such applications involve paying careful attention to the various APIs used and their stateful behavior. The comments in the code and descriptions in the Zephyr documentation are brief and do not cover all the details in depth. Understanding and gaining maximum benefit from the various Zephyr examples requires using the example code as a starting point and then thinking about various ways in which it might be extended and modified.

Questions to ponder in connection with this example include things such as the following: What if the priorities of the threads and the UART are all different? What if the flashing rate of one of the LEDs is very fast? Can the code be made more robust by handling `k_malloc()` failures more gracefully?

Synchronizing Threads Using Semaphores and Sleeping

The interleaving of the work done by application threads according to some specified set of requirements is a common need.

For relatively uncomplicated applications, one or more solutions can usually be found without too much effort.

For more complex systems, especially applications involving distributed systems, the challenges are far greater. The pattern/scenario described in this section is one of several potentially useful "building block" patterns.

This scenario demonstrates kernel scheduling, communication, and timing APIs in action.

In this example, two threads (A and B) take turns printing a greeting message to the console. The thread interleaving illustrates the use of sleep requests and binary semaphores to control the order and the rate at which messages are generated.

Figure 4-7 illustrates the strategy used, which involves a thread blocking on a semaphore that is released by the other thread when the other thread has completed its turn.

CHAPTER 4 ZEPHYR RTOS MULTITHREADING

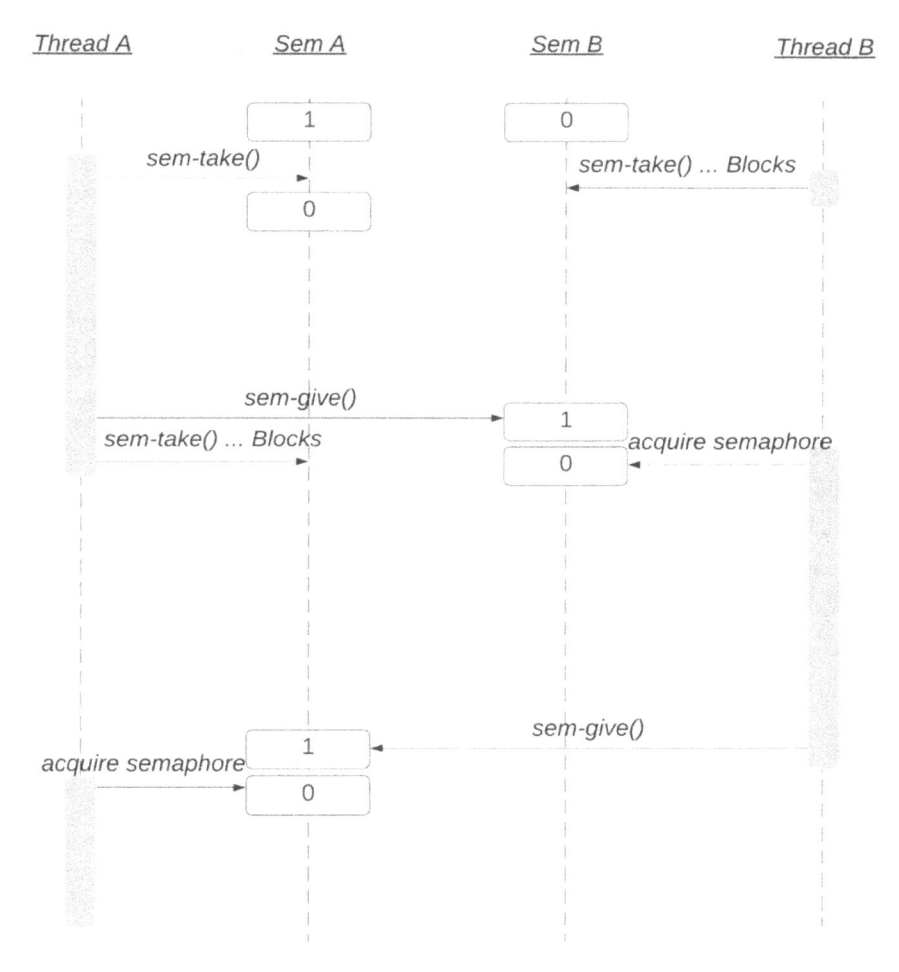

Figure 4-7. Interleaving and synchronizing threads

Although the example described is for an application running on a single core processor, it could be generalized to applications running on multicore processors.

At the heart of the implementation is a `helloLoop()` function that takes three arguments, namely, the string/message to be sent to the console, a semaphore associated with the current thread, and a semaphore

153

CHAPTER 4 ZEPHYR RTOS MULTITHREADING

associated with the other thread. The two threads, each one running the code shown, will bring about the "interleaving" of the threads, via mutually interdependent calls to k_sem_take() and k_sem_give().

```
#include <zephyr.h>
#include <sys/printk.h>/* size of stack area used by each thread */
#define STACKSIZE 1024
#define PRIORITY 7
#define SLEEPTIME 500
void helloLoop (const char *my_name, struct k_sem *my_sem,
                struct k_sem *other_sem) {
    const char *tname;
    uint8_t cpu;
    struct k_thread *current_thread;
    while (true) {
        k_sem_take(my_sem, K_FOREVER);
        current_thread = k_current_get();
        tname = k_thread_name_get(current_thread);
        cpu = 0;
        if (tname == NULL) {
            printk("%s: Hello World from cpu %d
            on %s!\n",
                    my_name, cpu, CONFIG_BOARD);
        } else {
            printk("%s: Hello World from cpu %d
            on %s!\n",
                    tname, cpu, CONFIG_BOARD);
        }
        k_busy_wait(100000);
        k_sem_give(other_sem);
```

k_msleep(SLEEPTIME);
        }
}

Thread A and thread B are instantiated and started in the function main(), and the thread entry point functions, the semaphores, and the thread stacks are defined before main() is defined.

The correct initialization of the initial state of each semaphore is essential if the code is to run as expected.

```
K_SEM_DEFINE(threadA_sem, 1, 1);      /* binary semaphore
                                         starts off "available" */
K_SEM_DEFINE(threadB_sem, 0, 1);      /* binary semaphore
                                         starts off "unavailable" */

void threadB (void *dummy1, void *dummy2, void *dummy3) {
      ARG_UNUSED(dummy1);
      ARG_UNUSED(dummy2);
      ARG_UNUSED(dummy3);
      /* invoke routine to ping-pong hello messages with
      threadA */
      helloLoop(__func__, &threadB_sem, &threadA_sem);
}
K_THREAD_STACK_DEFINE(threadA_stack_area, STACKSIZE);
static struct k_thread threadA_data;

K_THREAD_STACK_DEFINE(threadB_stack_area, STACKSIZE);
static struct k_thread threadB_data;

void threadA(void *dummy1, void *dummy2, void *dummy3) {
      ARG_UNUSED(dummy1);
      ARG_UNUSED(dummy2);
      ARG_UNUSED(dummy3);
```

CHAPTER 4   ZEPHYR RTOS MULTITHREADING

```
        /* invoke routine to ping-pong hello messages with
        threadB */
        helloLoop(__func__, &threadA_sem, &threadB_sem);
}
void main(void) {
        k_thread_create(&threadA_data, threadA_stack_area,
                    K_THREAD_STACK_SIZEOF(threadA_stack_area),
                    threadA, NULL, NULL, NULL,
                    PRIORITY, 0, K_FOREVER);
        k_thread_name_set(&threadA_data, "thread_a");
        k_thread_create(&threadB_data, threadB_stack_area,
                    K_THREAD_STACK_SIZEOF(threadB_stack_area),
                    threadB, NULL, NULL, NULL,
                    PRIORITY, 0, K_FOREVER);
        k_thread_name_set(&threadB_data, "thread_b");
        k_thread_start(&threadA_data);
        k_thread_start(&threadB_data);
}
```

Note ARG_UNUSED is a macro, used to suppress compiler warnings, defined as follows:

`#define ARG_UNUSED(x) (void)(x)`

When the application is built and run on a chosen target board, an nRF52840 DK board, in this case, the output sent to the console will be something like the following:

```
*** Booting Zephyr OS build v2.7.99-ncs1-1  ***
thread_a: Hello World from cpu 0 on nrf52840dk_nrf52840!
thread_b: Hello World from cpu 0 on nrf52840dk_nrf52840!
```

```
thread_a: Hello World from cpu 0 on nrf52840dk_nrf52840!
thread_b: Hello World from cpu 0 on nrf52840dk_nrf52840!
thread_a: Hello World from cpu 0 on nrf52840dk_nrf52840!
thread_b: Hello World from cpu 0 on nrf52840dk_nrf52840!
thread_a: Hello World from cpu 0 on nrf52840dk_nrf52840!
thread_b: Hello World from cpu 0 on nrf52840dk_nrf52840!
thread_a: Hello World from cpu 0 on nrf52840dk_nrf52840!
thread_b: Hello World from cpu 0 on nrf52840dk_nrf52840!
```

Running this sample on some other targets, or as a Renode simulation, or as a QEMU emulation should show similar behavior. Building and running applications on different targets is a good way to get a feel for the "portability" aspects of building Zephyr applications.

Scaling applications to more than two threads can reveal a variety of timing and performance issues. The example shown previously can be generalized to illustrate the use of more than two threads and more complex coordination patterns.

Signalling Using a Condition Variable

The pattern/example implemented in this scenario involves two threads that take turns incrementing a counter and a third thread that watches the count value. The counter incrementing code is enclosed inside a mutex-based critical section so that a thread will not be preempted by another thread in the middle of the counter processing code. Inside the counter incrementing critical section, when the counter value reaches a predefined `COUNT_LIMIT`, a condition variable condition is signalled, which a count watching thread is waiting on. In the example, `k_thread_join()` is used to synchronize the termination of the three threads via a thread join operation.

CHAPTER 4   ZEPHYR RTOS MULTITHREADING

The counter incrementing function is implemented as shown here:

```
void inc_count(void *p1, void *p2, void *p3) {
      int i;
      long my_id = (long) p1;
      for (i = 0; i < TCOUNT; i++) {
            k_mutex_lock(&count_mutex, K_FOREVER);
            count++;
            /* Check the value of count and signal waiting
            thread when condition
             * is reached.  Note that this occurs while mutex
             is locked. */
            if (count == COUNT_LIMIT) {
                  printk("%s: thread %ld, count = %d  Threshold
                  reached.", __func__, my_id, count);
                  k_condvar_signal(&count_threshold_cv);
                  printk("Just sent signal.\n");
            }
            printk("%s: thread %ld, count = %d, unlocking
            mutex\n", __func__, my_id, count);
            k_mutex_unlock(&count_mutex);
            k_sleep(K_MSEC(500)); /* Sleep so    */
         /* threads can alternate on mutex lock */
      }
}
```

The counter watching function is implemented in the following way:

```
void watch_count(void *p1, void *p2, void *p3) {
      long my_id = (long)p1;
      printk("Starting %s: thread %ld\n", __func__, my_id);
      k_mutex_lock(&count_mutex, K_FOREVER);
```

CHAPTER 4 ZEPHYR RTOS MULTITHREADING

```
        while (count < COUNT_LIMIT) {
                printk("%s: thread %ld Count= %d. Going into
                wait...\n", __func__, my_id, count);
                k_condvar_wait(&count_threshold_cv, &count_mutex,
                K_FOREVER);
                printk("%s: thread %ld Condition signal received.
                Count= %d\n", __func__, my_id, count);
        }
        printk("%s: thread %ld Updating the value of
        count...\n", __func__, my_id);
        count += 125;
        printk("%s: thread %ld count now = %d.\n", __func__,
        my_id, count);
        printk("%s: thread %ld Unlocking mutex.\n", __
        func__, my_id);
        k_mutex_unlock(&count_mutex);
}
```

The important thing to be aware of when reading this code is that a thread will block until another thread signals the condition being waited on. However, to make sense of the code, it is important to be aware of the fact that when the thread is blocked, the critical section mutex is released and then re-acquired just before the thread is woken up and the call returns.

Interestingly, the example uses a (global) array of thread structures to manage a collection of threads. The array is set up at the beginning of `main.c` along with macro invocations to create the required mutex and condition variable and to handle the allocation of stack memory.

```
#include <zephyr.h>
#include <arch/cpu.h>
#include <sys/arch_interface.h>
```

159

CHAPTER 4   ZEPHYR RTOS MULTITHREADING

```
#define NUM_THREADS 3
#define TCOUNT 10
#define COUNT_LIMIT 12
static int count;
K_MUTEX_DEFINE(count_mutex);
K_CONDVAR_DEFINE(count_threshold_cv);
#define STACK_SIZE (1024)
K_THREAD_STACK_ARRAY_DEFINE(tstacks, NUM_THREADS, STACK_SIZE);
static struct k_thread t[NUM_THREADS];
```

The threads are created and started in the function main() whose code is given in this code snippet:

```
void main(void) {
      long t1 = 1, t2 = 2, t3 = 3;
      int i;
      count = 0;
      k_thread_create(&t[0], tstacks[0], STACK_SIZE,
      watch_count,
            INT_TO_POINTER(t1), NULL, NULL, K_PRIO_PREEMPT(10),
            0, K_NO_WAIT);
      k_thread_create(&t[1], tstacks[1], STACK_SIZE, inc_count,
            INT_TO_POINTER(t2), NULL, NULL, K_PRIO_PREEMPT(10),
            0, K_NO_WAIT);
      k_thread_create(&t[2], tstacks[2], STACK_SIZE, inc_count,
            INT_TO_POINTER(t3), NULL, NULL, K_PRIO_PREEMPT(10),
            0, K_NO_WAIT);
      /* Wait for all threads to complete */
      for (i = 0; i < NUM_THREADS; i++) {
            k_thread_join(&t[i], K_FOREVER);
      }
```

```
    printk("Main(): Waited and joined with %d threads."
    "Final value of count = %d. Done.\n", NUM_
    THREADS, count);
}
```

When reading the preceding code snippet, note the use of the INT_TO_POINTER (x) macro. It is used to cast x, a signed integer, to a void* pointer.

When built and run, this application will produce output something like the following:

```
*** Booting Zephyr OS build v2.7.0-rc2-7-g0d538447144c   ***
Starting watch_count: thread 1
watch_count: thread 1 Count= 0. Going into wait...
inc_count: thread 2, count = 1, unlocking mutex
inc_count: thread 3, count = 2, unlocking mutex
inc_count: thread 2, count = 3, unlocking mutex
inc_count: thread 3, count = 4, unlocking mutex
inc_count: thread 2, count = 5, unlocking mutex
inc_count: thread 3, count = 6, unlocking mutex
inc_count: thread 2, count = 7, unlocking mutex
inc_count: thread 3, count = 8, unlocking mutex
inc_count: thread 2, count = 9, unlocking mutex
inc_count: thread 3, count = 10, unlocking mutex
inc_count: thread 2, count = 11, unlocking mutex
inc_count: thread 3, count = 12  Threshold reached.Just
sent signal.
inc_count: thread 3, count = 12, unlocking mutex
watch_count: thread 1 Condition signal received. Count= 12
watch_count: thread 1 Updating the value of count...
watch_count: thread 1 count now = 137.
watch_count: thread 1 Unlocking mutex.
```

```
inc_count: thread 2, count = 138, unlocking mutex
inc_count: thread 3, count = 139, unlocking mutex
inc_count: thread 2, count = 140, unlocking mutex
inc_count: thread 3, count = 141, unlocking mutex
inc_count: thread 2, count = 142, unlocking mutex
inc_count: thread 3, count = 143, unlocking mutex
inc_count: thread 2, count = 144, unlocking mutex
inc_count: thread 3, count = 145, unlocking mutex
Main(): Waited and joined with 3 threads. Final value of count
= 145. Done.
```

This program can be run on one or more target boards, on a simulated board using `Renode`, and also as a QEMU emulation.

The Dining Philosophers Problem

This is a classical problem and is included here because of its fame in "computer science circles." It was originally formulated in 1965 by Edsger Dijkstra [7] as a student exam exercise, presented in terms of computers competing for access to tape drive peripherals. Some time later Tony Hoare gave the problem its present formulation.

Here it is (see Figure 4-8):

CHAPTER 4   ZEPHYR RTOS MULTITHREADING

Figure 4-8. Dining philosphers

Five silent philosophers sit at a round table with bowls of spaghetti.
Forks are placed between each pair of adjacent philosophers.
Each philosopher must alternately think and eat.

However, a philosopher can only eat spaghetti when they have both left and right forks.

Each fork can be held by only one philosopher at a time, and so a philosopher can use the fork only if it is not being used by another philosopher.

After an individual philosopher finishes eating, they need to put down both forks so that the forks become available to others.

A philosopher can only take the fork on their right or the one on their left as they become available, and they cannot start eating before getting both forks.

Eating is not limited by the remaining amounts of spaghetti or stomach space; an infinite supply and an infinite demand are assumed.

This problem was designed to illustrate the challenges involved in implementing code that avoids deadlock, a system state in which no progress is possible.

The example solution used in the Zephyr dining philosophers example is based on the use of multiple preemptive and cooperative threads of differing priorities, as well as mutexes and thread sleeping. The solution depends on acquiring resources in a fixed order and then releasing them in a fixed order. In the example code, a philosopher always tries to acquire the lowest fork first, and then, when finished eating, giving back the forks in the reverse order. A philosopher that has two forks is in the EATING state. Otherwise, the philosopher is in the THINKING state. A philosopher alternates between the EATING and the THINKING state in a random manner.

The dining philosophers sample provided in Zephyr is a general-purpose solution that can be built using one of a number of possible synchronization strategies, by defining the synchronization mechanism to use, for example, semaphore, mutex, stack, fifo, or lifo.

The main abstraction used in the sample is the FORK that is #defined in the example `phil_obj_abstract.h` file. For example, the following code snippet shows using mutexes as the underlying synchronization mechanism:

```
#elif FORKS == MUTEXES
    #define fork_t struct k_mutex *
    #if STATIC_OBJS
        K_MUTEX_DEFINE(fork0);
        K_MUTEX_DEFINE(fork1);
```

```
            K_MUTEX_DEFINE(fork2);
            K_MUTEX_DEFINE(fork3);
            K_MUTEX_DEFINE(fork4);
            K_MUTEX_DEFINE(fork5);
    #else
            #define fork_obj_t struct k_mutex
            #define fork_init(x) k_mutex_init(x)
    #endif
    #define take(x) k_mutex_lock(x, K_FOREVER)
    #define drop(x) k_mutex_unlock(x)
    #define fork_type_str "mutexes"
```

The code itself uses the #if 0 ... #endif preprocessor macro construct to (temporarily) remove segments of code.

In certain contexts, this approach is more effective than using the C comment-out notation.

For example, to build the sample using mutexes, main.c might start as follows:

```
#include <zephyr.h>
#if defined(CONFIG_STDOUT_CONSOLE)
#include <stdio.h>
#else
#include <sys/printk.h>
#endif
#include <sys/__assert.h>
#define MUTEXES 2
/* control the behaviour of the demo **/
#ifndef DEBUG_PRINTF
#define DEBUG_PRINTF 0
#endif
#ifndef NUM_PHIL
```

CHAPTER 4   ZEPHYR RTOS MULTITHREADING

```
#define NUM_PHIL 6
#endif
#ifndef STATIC_OBJS
#define STATIC_OBJS 0
#endif
#ifndef FORKS
#define FORKS MUTEXES
#if 0
#define FORKS SEMAPHORES
#define FORKS STACKS
#define FORKS FIFOS
#define FORKS LIFOS
#endif
#endif
#ifndef SAME_PRIO
#define SAME_PRIO 0
#endif
```

The behavior of a philosopher is realized in the philosopher() function, which is the entry point function when a philosopher thread is created.

```
void philosopher(void *id, void *unused1, void *unused2) {
    ARG_UNUSED(unused1);
    ARG_UNUSED(unused2);
    fork_t fork1;
    fork_t fork2;
    int my_id = POINTER_TO_INT(id);
    /* Djkstra's solution: always pick up the lowest numbered
    fork first */
    if (is_last_philosopher(my_id)) {
        fork1 = fork(0);
```

```
            fork2 = fork(my_id);
    } else {
            fork1 = fork(my_id);
            fork2 = fork(my_id + 1);
    }
    while (1) {
            int32_t delay;
            print_phil_state(my_id, " STARVING ", 0);
            take(fork1);
            print_phil_state(my_id, "   HOLDING ONE FORK   ", 0);
            take(fork2);
            delay = get_random_delay(my_id, 25);
            print_phil_state(my_id, "   EATING  [ %s%d ms ] ", delay);
            k_msleep(delay);
            drop(fork2);
            print_phil_state(my_id, "   DROPPED ONE FORK   ", 0);
            drop(fork1);
            delay = get_random_delay(my_id, 25);
            print_phil_state(my_id, " THINKING [ %s%d ms ] ", delay);
            k_msleep(delay);
    }
}
```

The (global) array of forks can be created statically or dynamically. A philosopher is assigned two forks based on the philosopher's id. The fork items are created as follows:

```
static void init_objects(void) {
```

CHAPTER 4　ZEPHYR RTOS MULTITHREADING

```
#if !STATIC_OBJS
    for (int i = 0; i < NUM_PHIL; i++) {
        fork_init(fork(i));
    }
#endif
}
```

Various thread prioritization policies can be experimented with. For example, a configuration having six philosophers with two philosopher threads being cooperative threads (priorities -2/-1) and the other four being preemptive threads (priorities 0-3) can be set up as in the following code snippet:

```
static void start_threads(void) {
    for (int i = 0; i < NUM_PHIL; i++) {
        int prio = new_prio(i);
        k_thread_create(&threads[i], &stacks[i][0], STACK_
        SIZE, philosopher, INT_TO_POINTER(i), NULL, NULL,
        prio, K_USER, K_FOREVER);
#ifdef CONFIG_THREAD_NAME
        char tname[CONFIG_THREAD_MAX_NAME_LEN];
        snprintk(tname, CONFIG_THREAD_MAX_NAME_LEN,
                "Philosopher %d", i);
        k_thread_name_set(&threads[i], tname);
#endif /* CONFIG_THREAD_NAME */
        k_object_access_grant(fork(i), &threads[i]);
        k_object_access_grant(fork((i + 1) % NUM_PHIL),
        &threads[i]);
        k_thread_start(&threads[i]);
    }
}
```

CHAPTER 4 ZEPHYR RTOS MULTITHREADING

The preceding code snippet uses the function k_object_access_grant(). This is necessary because a user thread cannot directly manipulate a kernel object such as a mutex or a semaphore to manipulate a kernel object using system calls. In order to perform a system call on a kernel object, a system call handler function checks that the kernel object address is valid and that the calling thread has the necessary permissions to work with it. More information about system calls and kernel objects can be found in the Zephyr documentation [6].

The code for the main() function is very straightforward:

```
void main(void) {
      display_demo_description();
#if CONFIG_TIMESLICING
      k_sched_time_slice_set(5000, 0);
#endif
      init_objects();
      start_threads();
#ifdef CONFIG_COVERAGE
      /* Wait a few seconds before main() exit, giving the
      sample the opportunity to
         dump some output before coverage data gets emitted */
      k_sleep(K_MSEC(5000));
#endif
}
```

Building and running the application should result in something like the following being displayed in the console window:

```
Demo Description
----------------
An implementation of a solution to the Dining Philosophers
problem (a classic multi-thread synchronization problem).
```

CHAPTER 4 ZEPHYR RTOS MULTITHREADING

This particular implementation demonstrates the usage of multiple
preemptible and cooperative threads of differing priorities, as well as dynamic mutexes and thread sleeping.

```
Philosopher 0 [P: 3]   STARVING
Philosopher 1 [P: 2]   THINKING [  375 ms ]
Philosopher 2 [P: 1]   HOLDING ONE FORK
*** Booting Zephyr OS build v2.7.0-rc2-7-g0d538447144c   ***
Philosopher 4 [C:-1]   THINKING [  650 ms ]
Philosopher 5 [C:-2]   EATING   [  775 ms ] RK
r 0 [P: 3]    EATING   [  750 ms ]
```

The importance of the dining philosophers problem is that it illustrates the power of the imagination and "thought scenarios" in exploring multithreading application development.

As an exercise, try changing the "behavior" of the dining philosophers so that when the code is run, there is a possibility that a deadlock may arise.

Producers and Consumers and Multithreading

Producer-consumer problems crop up frequently in multitasking applications. The first description of the family of producer-consumer problems is due to Edsger Dijkstra, who described some of the initial solutions to these problems. We have already come across Edsger Dijkstra in connection with the dining philosophers problem. Not many people know about him, yet he has been described as "The Man Who Carried Computer Science on His Shoulders" [6].

CHAPTER 4 ZEPHYR RTOS MULTITHREADING

In a producer-consumer scenario, the Producer and Consumer are two separate threads that share a common buffer or queue. The producer produces data of some sort and pushes it onto the buffer, whereas the consumer pulls data from the shared buffer and does something with it (i.e., consumes the data). Producer-consumer implementations have to be aware of and capable of dealing with a variety of problems. The producer and consumer must not try to update the shared queue at the same time as this might result in loss of data, or the data ending up in an inconsistent state. In cases where the rates at which data is being produced and consumed do not match, situations may arise such as where the producer would need to be concerned with the possibility of overflowing a finite sized (bounded) queue, or where the consumer consumes data faster than it is being produced and will have to pause when the queue is empty. It is quite common for real-world scenarios to involve several producers and several consumers using the same shared buffer.

The Zephyr RTOS Producer-Consumer Example

This section will explore the basic Zephyr RTOS consumer-producer example [8]. The example is an "example of many parts" and covers many aspects not covered in simplistic "producer-consumer" examples.

The scenario in this example involves a "sample driver" that receives incoming data from some source and generates an interrupt with a pointer to the received data every time a data item is received.

The data is processed by application code, and then the transformed (processed) data is sent back to the driver. Figure 4-9 illustrates the movement and processing of data from the device, transforming it and then writing the transformed data back to the device.

CHAPTER 4 ZEPHYR RTOS MULTITHREADING

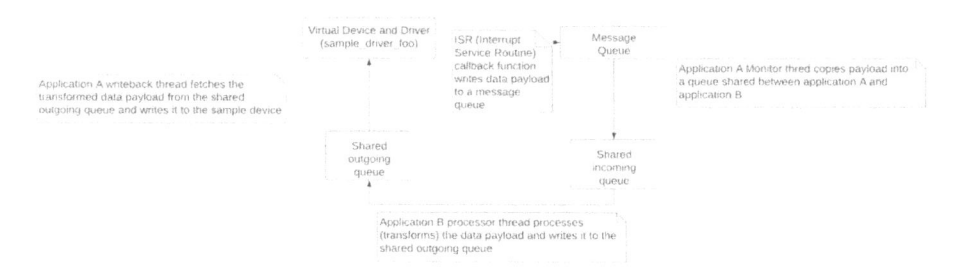

Figure 4-9. Zephyr producer-consumer example message processing flow

Many Zephyr features are used in the sample code. The features used include the use of logical applications with their own memory domains, creating and assigning a kernel system memory heap, a sys_heap, where the heap is assigned to its own memory partition, and also configuring and using a thread resource pool. In the application, a message queue (k_msgq) is used for the transfer of data between the driver and the producer application, and kernel queues (k_queue) are used for exchanging data between application threads.

The prod_consumer example involves two applications: application A and application B.

Application A interfaces with the driver and buffers incoming data, and application B processes the data. The scenario assumes that the data involved is untrusted and possibly malicious and, hence, application B is sandboxed from everything else and has two queues for sending/receiving data items.

A "pseudocode-like" description of the application code describes the essential aspects of the producer-consumer example, to help make better sense of the various code fragments that follow.

Pseudocode for application A

- Define a heap for application A.
- Define a memory partition for application A.

CHAPTER 4 ZEPHYR RTOS MULTITHREADING

- Define a message queue for IPC between the driver callback and the application monitor thread.
- Create a thread entry point function that will take data processed by application B and write it back to the virtual device driver.
- Define an ISR-level callback function (note that this function runs in supervisor mode) that will move data from the device to the user mode worker thread that will do the data processing. A message queue is used in the example because it will perform a data copy automatically when buffering this data.

Shared memory for use by application A and application B is set up by

- Defining an application memory partition
- Defining a memory pool to be placed into this shared memory
- Queues are defined for sharing data between application A and application B

Pseudocode for application B

- Define a heap for application B.
- Define a memory partition for application B.
- Define a processor thread function, which will fetch data from the incoming shared queue, do some processing of that data, and put the processed data into the outgoing shared queue.

173

- Define the application B entry point function, which will reuse the main thread as its processor thread and reuse the default memory domain as its application domain, and add the application B partition and the shared memory partition to this memory domain.

- The entry point function will eventually be the user space monitoring thread. The entry point functions code

  - Assigns a heap resource pool for use by kernel side allocations that will be performed on behalf of application A

  - Adds the necessary partitions to the default memory domain as described previously

  - Grants access to its thread (the thread id of the code it is running) to the shared queue objects

  - Drops the thread privileges to those of a user mode thread running the processor thread code (which is defined in the processor thread function)

Although the exchange of data and the processing of the data in this example are relatively uncomplicated, it is the other details such as thread privileges, assigning permissions for using kernel objects, implementing a driver, and using system calls that are of particular interest here. This is what makes this example interesting; it is an "example of many parts" that demonstrates many of the issues that need to be considered when implementing "fully fledged" real-world applications. The various parts covered will extend your knowledge of interesting features of the feature-rich Zephyr RTOS API.

In the course of exploring this example, the topics covered will include working with Zephyr RTOS system calls, implementing a driver for a virtual interface (which will serve as an introduction to techniques involved in implementing device drivers for real physical devices), the use of memory partitions, working with message queues and queues, heap creation and memory management, and, additionally, making use of supervisor threads.

Another objective of this section is to provide insights into the work involved in developing more complex secure real-world applications. Do not, on a first reading/studying of the code, try to fully understand all the details, but rather try and get a feel for the problems addressed, such as restricting access to kernel resources by user threads, sandboxing of untrusted data processing, and dropping a thread from privileged mode to user mode. You should try to build and run this example on various boards and also in Renode and QEMU.

The example also involves the use of the processor MPU (Memory Protection Unit). In connection with working with a processor MPU, it should be noted that in systems without an embedded OS, the MPU can be programmed to have a static configuration, which can be used to provide functionality such as setting a RAM/SRAM region as read-only so that the data held there is protected from accidental corruption, making a piece of the RAM/SRAM space at the bottom of the stack inaccessible so as to be able to detect stack overflow, and setting a region of RAM/SRAM to be XN (execution no) so as to mitigate code injection attacks.

In systems with an embedded OS, the MPU can be programmed at each context switch, which makes it possible for an application task to have its own task-specific MPU configuration. Using this approach, it is possible to define memory access permissions in such a way that application stack operations in one thread are not able to access the stack of another application in the event of a stack leak, and also to constrain task memory access to only the data and peripherals that the task should be permitted to access.

The producer-consumer example also includes a, fairly trivial, system call example involving a "magic cookie," included in the example, to demonstrate a template to follow for the creation and invocation of system calls.

CHAPTER 4 ZEPHYR RTOS MULTITHREADING

Using Zephyr RTOS System Calls: Essential Concepts and Overview

System calls provide a mechanism that allows a user thread to access resources and perform operations not directly available to it. Access by a user thread to private kernel data is only possible via system call interface functions.

Digging deeper into the "workings" of the Zephyr framework will reveal the presence of various Python scripts that generate code such as linker files and header files. There are also Python scripts for processing devicetree files and Kconfig files and generating code as a result of doing so. This also applies to implementing system calls. A Zephyr system call has a C prototype prefixed with `__syscall` for the API. The prototype is never implemented manually but is created by the `scripts/gen_syscalls.py` script.

Inline functions are used in the implementation of Zephyr system calls. The code for an inline function is actually expanded inline in the code at the point where the function is called. Unlike C macro expansion in which the macro parameters are not checked, the parameters passed to an inline function are checked.

The inline function generated by the `gen_syscalls.py` script either calls the implementation function directly (if called from supervisor mode) or goes through privilege elevation and validation steps if called from user mode. The function that implements the system call can be written on the assumption that all the parameters passed in have been validated if the function was invoked from user mode. The implementation function itself is wrapped by a verification function that performs the validation of all the arguments passed in. The system call code generation process also produces an un-marshalling function, which is an automatically generated handler that must be included by user source code.

CHAPTER 4　ZEPHYR RTOS MULTITHREADING

Architectures that implement Zephyr system calls must implement seven inline functions, _arch_syscall_invoke0() through to _arch_syscall_invoke6(), which marshal arguments into designated CPU registers and perform the necessary privilege elevation and which are a key part of the system call implementation code. The parameters of an API inline function, before being passed as arguments to system call, are cast to a uintptr_t type, which matches the size of a register. However, when passing 64-bit parameters on a 32-bit system, the 64-bit parameter is split into lower and higher parts and passed as two consecutive 32-bit arguments.

The system call execution flow is outlined in the schematic shown in Figure 4-10.

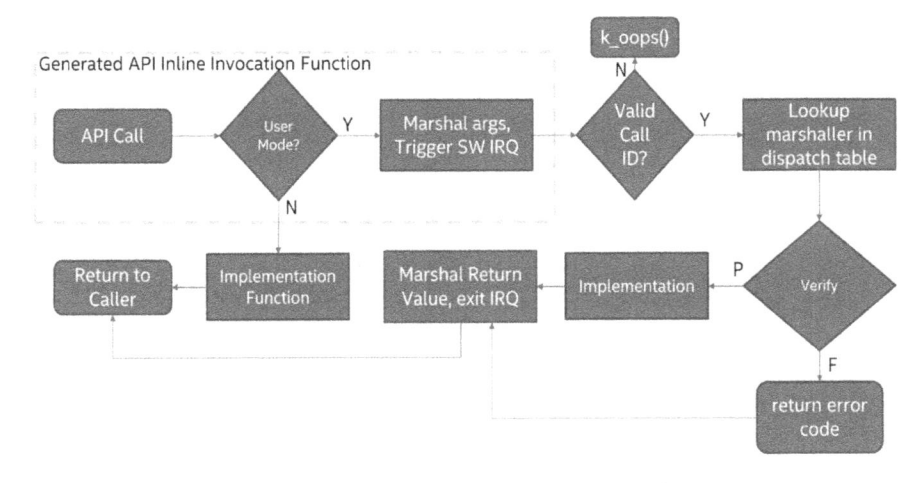

Figure 4-10. Zephyr RTOS system call execution flow

The corresponding example code is in the app_syscall.h and app_syscall.c files.

Code of app_syscall.h:

```
/* app_syscall.h */
#ifndef APP_SYSCALL_H
```

177

CHAPTER 4   ZEPHYR RTOS MULTITHREADING

```
#define APP_SYSCALL_H
__syscall int magic_syscall (unsigned int *cookie);
#include <syscalls/app_syscall.h>
#endif /* MAGIC_SYSCALL_H */
```

Code of app_syscall.c:

```
#include <syscall_handler.h>
#include <logging/log.h>
LOG_MODULE_REGISTER(app_syscall);
/* magic_syscall() is a custom system call , not part of the kernel code
 * It demonstrates  how a  syscall can be defined in application code. */
int z_impl_magic_syscall(unsigned int *cookie) {
      LOG_DBG("magic syscall: got a cookie %u", *cookie);
      if (*cookie > 42) {
            LOG_ERR("bad cookie :(");
            return -EINVAL;
      }
      *cookie = *cookie + 1;
      return 0;
}

static int z_vrfy_magic_syscall (unsigned int *cookie) {
      unsigned int cookie_copy;
      int ret;
      /* Confirm that this user-supplied pointer is valid memory that
       * can be accessed. If it's OK, copy into cookie_copy. */
      if (z_user_from_copy(&cookie_copy, cookie, sizeof(*cookie)) != 0) {
            return -EPERM;
```

        }
     /* Pass *copy* to the implementation the , to
     prevent TOCTOU
     * (time-of-check to time-of-use) attacks */
        ret = z_impl_magic_syscall(&cookie_copy);
     if (ret == 0 && z_user_to_copy(cookie, &cookie_copy,
     sizeof(*cookie)) != 0) {
            return -EPERM;
        }
        return ret;
}
#include <syscalls/magic_syscall_mrsh.c>

Producer-Consumer Example Sample Driver Part

The driver in this sample is a driver for a virtual device. It serves to introduce the topic of implementing device drivers in Zephyr.

The file sample_driver.h defines a number of function pointer types, a driver API structure of function pointer types, a static inline driver API, and driver API-associated functions.

sample_driver.h file:

```
#ifndef ZEPHYR_FAKE_DRIVER_H
#define ZEPHYR_FAKE_DRIVER_H
#include <device.h>
#define SAMPLE_DRIVER_NAME_0       "SAMPLE_DRIVER_0"
#define SAMPLE_DRIVER_MSG_SIZE     128

typedef void (*sample_driver_callback_t)(const struct device *dev, void *context, void *data);
```

```
typedef int (*sample_driver_write_t)(const struct device *dev,
void *buf);
typedef int (*sample_driver_set_callback_t)(const struct
device *dev,
             sample_driver_callback_t cb, void *context);
typedef int (*sample_driver_state_set_t)(const struct device
*dev, bool active);

__subsystem struct sample_driver_api {
      sample_driver_write_t write;
      sample_driver_set_callback_t set_callback;
      sample_driver_state_set_t state_set;
};

/* Write some processed data to the sample driver
 * After processing the data received in the sample driver
callback,
 * write this processed data back to the driver.
 * dev - Sample driver device
 * buf - Processed data, of size SAMPLE_DRIVER_MSG_SIZE
 * return 0 Success, nonzero if an error occurred
 */
__syscall int sample_driver_write(const struct device *dev,
void *buf);

static inline int z_impl_sample_driver_write(const struct
device *dev, void *buf) {
      const struct sample_driver_api *api = dev->api;
      return api->write(dev, buf);
}

__subsystem struct sample_driver_api {
      sample_driver_write_t write;
```

```
        sample_driver_set_callback_t set_callback;
        sample_driver_state_set_t state_set;
};
/* Register a callback function for the sample driver
 * This callback runs in interrupt context.
 * The provided data blob will be of size SAMPLE_DRIVER_
MSG_SIZE.
 * dev - Sample driver device to install callabck
 * cb - Callback function pointer
 * context - Context passed to callback function, or NULL if
not needed
 * return 0 on Success, nonzero if an error occurred
 */
static inline int sample_driver_set_callback(const struct
device *dev, sample_driver_callback_t cb, void *context) {
        const struct sample_driver_api *api = dev->api;
     return api->set_callback(dev, cb, context);
}
#include <syscalls/sample_driver.h>
#endif
```

The fake (virtual) device driver code for the "simple" device type is in the file simple_driver_foo.c, shown here:

```
#include "sample_driver.h"
#include <string.h>
#include <kernel.h>
#include <logging/log.h>

LOG_MODULE_REGISTER(sample_driver);
```

```
/* This fake driver demonstrates how an application can make
system calls to
 *   interact with a device. The driver sets up a timer which is
used to fake interrupts. */
#define DEV_DATA(dev)   ((struct sample_driver_foo_dev_data
*const)(dev)->data)

struct sample_driver_foo_dev_data {
        const struct device *dev;
        sample_driver_callback_t cb;
        void *cb_context;
        struct k_timer timer; /* to fake 'interrupts' */
        uint32_t count;
};

static int sample_driver_foo_write(const struct device *dev,
void *buf) {
        LOG_DBG("%s(%p, %p)", __func__, dev, buf);
        return 0;
}

static int sample_driver_foo_set_callback(const struct
device *dev,
                    sample_driver_callback_t cb, void *context) {
        struct sample_driver_foo_dev_data *data = DEV_DATA(dev);
        int key = irq_lock();
        data->cb_context = context;
        data->cb = cb;
        rq_unlock(key);
        return 0;
}
```

```c
static int sample_driver_foo_state_set(const struct device
*dev, bool active) {
    struct sample_driver_foo_dev_data *data = DEV_DATA(dev);
    LOG_DBG("%s(%p, %d)", __func__, dev, active);
    data->timer.user_data = data;
    if (active) {
        k_timer_start(&data->timer, K_MSEC(100), K_
        MSEC(100));
    } else {
        k_timer_stop(&data->timer);
    }
    return 0;
}

static struct sample_driver_api sample_driver_foo_api = {
    .write = sample_driver_foo_write,
    .set_callback = sample_driver_foo_set_callback,
    .state_set = sample_driver_foo_state_set
};

static void sample_driver_foo_isr(void *param) {
    struct sample_driver_foo_dev_data *data = param;
    char data_payload[SAMPLE_DRIVER_MSG_SIZE];
    LOG_INF("%s: param=%p count=%u", __func__, param,
    data->count);
    /* Just for demonstration purposes; the data payload
        contains arbitrary data*/
    if (data->cb) {
        data->cb(data->dev, data->cb_context, data_
        payload);
    }
    data->count++;
}
```

```
static void sample_driver_timer_cb (struct k_timer *timer) {
    sample_driver_foo_isr (timer->user_data);
}

static int sample_driver_foo_init(const struct device *dev) {
    struct sample_driver_foo_dev_data *data = DEV_DATA(dev);
    k_timer_init(&data->timer, sample_driver_timer_cb, NULL);
    LOG_DBG("initialized foo sample driver %p", dev);
    data->dev = dev;
    return 0;
}

static struct sample_driver_foo_dev_data sample_driver_foo_dev_data_0;

DEVICE_DEFINE( sample_driver_foo_0, SAMPLE_DRIVER_NAME_0,
    &sample_driver_foo_init,
    device_pm_control_nop,
    &sample_driver_foo_dev_data_0, NULL,
    POST_KERNEL, CONFIG_KERNEL_INIT_PRIORITY_DEVICE,
    &sample_driver_foo_api );
```

The file sample_driver_handlers.c contains verification code.

```
#include <zephyr/kernel.h>
#include <zephyr/syscall_handler.h>
#include "sample_driver.h"
int z_vrfy_sample_driver_state_set(const struct device *dev,
bool active)
{
    if (Z_SYSCALL_DRIVER_SAMPLE(dev, state_set)) {
        return -EINVAL;
    }
```

```
        return z_impl_sample_driver_state_set(dev, active);
}
#include <syscalls/sample_driver_state_set_mrsh.c>
int z_vrfy_sample_driver_write(const struct device *dev,
void *buf) {
        if (Z_SYSCALL_DRIVER_SAMPLE(dev, write)) {
              return -EINVAL;
        }
        if (Z_SYSCALL_MEMORY_READ(buf, SAMPLE_DRIVER_MSG_SIZE)) {
              return -EFAULT;
        }
        return z_impl_sample_driver_write(dev, buf);
}
#include <syscalls/sample_driver_write_mrsh.c>
```

The driver example is relatively simple. Writing custom drivers for more complex devices and their associated protocols is a challenging task. The best way of getting started is to study the device driver code that is part of the Zephyr source tree.

Shared Memory Partition, System Heap, Memory Pool, and Kernel Queues Part

The relevant example files are app_share.h and app_share.c.

app_share.h file code:

```
#ifndef PROD_CONSUMER_APP_A_H
#define PROD_CONSUMER_APP_A_H
#include <kernel.h>
#include <app_memory/app_memdomain.h>
void app_a_entry(void *p1, void *p2, void *p3);
```

```
extern struct k_mem_partition app_a_partition;
#define APP_A_DATA      K_APP_DMEM(app_a_partition)
#define APP_A_BSS       K_APP_BMEM(app_a_partition)
#endif /* PROD_CONSUMER_APP_A_H */
```

app_share.c file code:

This file relies on various macros provided by the Zephyr framework to set up the memory region, system heap, and shared memory pool. The details of MPUs (typically optional components when designing ARM Cortex M processors, or RISC-V processors) vary, and one of the goals of Zephyr is to provide a suitable "abstraction" of the underlying functionality.

```
#include "app_shared.h"
/* Define the shared partition, which will contain a memory region that
 * will be accessible by both applications A and B. */
K_APPMEM_PARTITION_DEFINE(shared_partition);

/* Define a memory pool to place in the shared area. */
K_APP_DMEM(shared_partition) struct sys_heap shared_pool;
K_APP_DMEM(shared_partition) uint8_t shared_pool_mem[HEAP_BYTES];
/* queues for exchanging data between App A and App B */
K_QUEUE_DEFINE(shared_queue_incoming);
K_QUEUE_DEFINE(shared_queue_outgoing);
```

Application A Part

app_a.h file code:

```
#ifndef PROD_CONSUMER_APP_A_H
#define PROD_CONSUMER_APP_A_H
```

```
#include <zephyr/kernel.h>
#include <zephyr/app_memory/app_memdomain.h>

void app_a_entry(void *p1, void *p2, void *p3);
extern struct k_mem_partition app_a_partition;
#define APP_A_DATA K_APP_DMEM(app_a_partition)
#define APP_A_BSS  K_APP_BMEM(app_a_partition)
#endif /* PROD_CONSUMER_APP_A_H */
```

app_a.c file code: The comments in the sample code have been edited in order to simplify and clarify what the code is doing. Reading through the commented code should give you an idea of how it works. A deeper understanding will require reading the documentation and "inventing and debugging new examples" to test out your understanding.

```
#include <zephyr/kernel.h>
#include <zephyr/device.h>
#include <zephyr/sys/libc-hooks.h>
#include <zephyr/logging/log.h>
#include "sample_driver.h"
#include "app_shared.h"
#include "app_a.h"
#include "app_syscall.h"

LOG_MODULE_REGISTER(app_a);
#define MAX_MSGS    8
/* The K_HEAP_DEFINE macro defined a resource pool to be used
for allocations made by the kernel on behalf of system calls.
It is needed by k_queue_alloc_append()  */
K_HEAP_DEFINE(app_a_resource_pool, 256 * 5 + 128);
/* The macro K_APPMEM_PARTITION_DEFINE defines app_a_partition,
which is where the globals for this app will be routed to. The
partition starting address and size are populated by build
```

CHAPTER 4 ZEPHYR RTOS MULTITHREADING

```
system and linker magic. */
K_APPMEM_PARTITION_DEFINE(app_a_partition);
/* The memory domain for application A, is set up and installed
in app_a_entry() */
static struct k_mem_domain app_a_domain;
/* The macro K_MSGQ_DEFINE is used to define the message queue
for IPC between the driver callback and the monitor thread.
This message queue is statically initialized, so it is not
necessary call k_msgq_init() on it. */
K_MSGQ_DEFINE(mqueue, SAMPLE_DRIVER_MSG_SIZE, MAX_MSGS, 4);

/* The writeback processing thread takes data that has been
processed by application B and writes it to the sample_
driver */
struct k_thread writeback_thread;
K_THREAD_STACK_DEFINE(writeback_stack, 2048);

/* Global data used by application A. By tagging with APP_A_BSS
or APP_A_DATA,
is linked into the continuous region denoted by app_a_
partition. */
APP_A_BSS const struct device *sample_device;
APP_A_BSS unsigned int pending_count;

/* The ISR-level callback function runs in supervisor mode
and gets the data into the memory that is accessible by the
application. A worker thread running in user mode can then do
further work on this data . */
void sample_callback(const struct device *dev, void *context,
void *data) {
    int ret;
    ARG_UNUSED(context);
    LOG_DBG("sample callback with %p", data);
```

CHAPTER 4   ZEPHYR RTOS MULTITHREADING

```
        /* The callback places the data payload into the
        message queue.
        This will wake up the monitor thread for further
        processing.
        The Zephyr message queue performs a data copy when
        buffering the data. */
        ret = k_msgq_put(&mqueue, data, K_NO_WAIT);
        if (ret) {
              LOG_ERR("k_msgq_put failed with %d", ret);
        }
}

static void monitor_entry(void *p1, void *p2, void *p3)
{
        int ret;
        void *payload;
        unsigned int monitor_count = 0;
        ARG_UNUSED(p1);
        ARG_UNUSED(p2);
        ARG_UNUSED(p3);

        /* The monitor thread runs in user mode and pulls the
        data out of the message
        queue for further writeback.*/
        LOG_DBG("monitor thread entered");
        ret = sample_driver_state_set (sample_device, true);
        if (ret != 0) {
              LOG_ERR("couldn't start driver interrupts");
              k_oops();
        }
```

CHAPTER 4   ZEPHYR RTOS MULTITHREADING

```
while (monitor_count < NUM_LOOPS) {
        payload = sys_heap_alloc(&shared_pool, SAMPLE_
        DRIVER_MSG_SIZE);
        if (payload == NULL) {
                LOG_ERR("couldn't alloc memory from
                shared pool");
                k_oops();
                continue;
        }

        LOG_DBG("monitor thread waiting for data...");
        ret = k_msgq_get(&mqueue, payload, K_FOREVER);
        if (ret != 0) {
                LOG_ERR("k_msgq_get() failed with %d", ret);
                k_oops();
        }
        LOG_INF("monitor thread got data payload #%u",
        monitor_count);
        LOG_DBG("pending payloads: %u", pending_count);
        /* Put the payload in the queue for data to be
        processed by app B. There is no copying of data
        because k_queue is being used from user mode.
        However, the k_queue_alloc_append() variant, is
        used, which needs to allocate some memory on the
        kernel side from the thread resource pool. */
        pending_count++;
        k_queue_alloc_append(&shared_queue_incoming,
        payload);
        monitor_count++;
}
```

```
        /* Shut down after exiting the while loop   */
        ret = sample_driver_state_set(sample_device, false);
        if (ret != 0) {
              LOG_ERR("couldn't disable driver");
              k_oops();
        }
        LOG_DBG("monitor thread exiting");
}
static void writeback_entry(void *p1, void *p2, void *p3)
{
        void *data;
        unsigned int writeback_count = 0;
        int ret;
        ARG_UNUSED(p1);
        ARG_UNUSED(p2);
        ARG_UNUSED(p3);
        LOG_DBG("writeback thread entered");
        while (writeback_count < NUM_LOOPS) {
              /* Retrieve a data payload processed by
              Application B,
              and send it to the driver, and free the buffer. */
              data = k_queue_get(&shared_queue_outgoing, K_
              FOREVER);
              if (data == NULL) {
                    LOG_ERR("no data?");
                    k_oops();
              }
              OG_INF("writing processed data back to the sample
              device");
```

CHAPTER 4   ZEPHYR RTOS MULTITHREADING

```
            sample_driver_write(sample_device, data);
            sys_heap_free(&shared_pool, data);
            pending_count--;
            writeback_count++;
      }

      /* A simplistic example that demonstrates an application-
      defined system
      call being defined and used. */
      ret = magic_syscall(&writeback_count);
      if (ret != 0) {
            LOG_ERR("no more magic!");
            k_oops();
      }
      LOG_DBG("writeback thread exiting");
      LOG_INF("SUCCESS");
}
/* Supervisor mode setup function for application A */
void app_a_entry (void *p1, void *p2, void *p3) {
      int ret;
      struct k_mem_partition *parts[] = {
#if Z_LIBC_PARTITION_EXISTS
            &z_libc_partition,
#endif
            &app_a_partition, &shared_partition
      };
      sample_device = device_get_binding(SAMPLE_DRIVER_NAME_0);
      if (sample_device == NULL) {
            LOG_ERR("bad sample device");
            k_oops();
      }
```

/* Initialize a memory domain with the specified partitions
and add self to this domain. */
ret = k_mem_domain_init(&app_a_domain, ARRAY_SIZE(parts), parts);
__ASSERT(ret == 0, "k_mem_domain_init failed %d", ret);
ARG_UNUSED(ret);
k_mem_domain_add_thread(&app_a_domain, k_current_get());
/* Assign a resource pool to serve for kernel-side allocations on behalf of application A. Needed for k_queue_alloc_append(). */
k_thread_heap_assign(k_current_get(), &app_a_resource_pool);

/* Set the callback function for the sample driver. This has to be done from supervisor mode, as this code will run in supervisor mode in IRQ context. */
sample_driver_set_callback(sample_device, sample_callback, NULL);

/* Set up the writeback thread, which takes processed data from application B and sends it to the sample device. This child thread automatically inherits the memory domain of the thread that created it; it will be a member of app_a_domain. Initialize this thread with K_FOREVER timeout so as to be able to modify its permissions and then start it. */

k_thread_create(&writeback_thread, writeback_stack,
        K_THREAD_STACK_SIZEOF(writeback_stack),
        writeback_entry, NULL, NULL, NULL,
        -1, K_USER, K_FOREVER);

CHAPTER 4   ZEPHYR RTOS MULTITHREADING

```
        k_thread_access_grant(&writeback_thread, &shared_queue_
        outgoing, sample_device);
        k_thread_start(&writeback_thread);

        /* Drop to user mode and become the monitor thread,
        having granted
        ourselves access to the kernel objects required by
        the monitor thread
        Monitor thread needs access to the message queue shared
        with the
        ISR, and the queue to send data to the processing
        thread in
        App B.*/
        k_thread_access_grant(k_current_get(), &mqueue, sample_
        device, &shared_queue_incoming);

        /* One-way transition to user mode, so end up in monitor_
        thread().  */
        k_thread_user_mode_enter(monitor_entry, NULL,
        NULL, NULL);
}
```

APP B Part

app_b.h file code:

```
#ifndef PROD_CONSUMER_APP_B_H
#define PROD_CONSUMER_APP_B_H
#include <zephyr/kernel.h>
#include <zephyr/app_memory/app_memdomain.h>
void app_b_entry(void *p1, void *p2, void *p3);
extern struct k_mem_partition app_b_partition;
```

```c
#define APP_B_DATA      K_APP_DMEM(app_b_partition)
#define APP_B_BSS       K_APP_BMEM(app_b_partition)
#endif /* PROD_CONSUMER_APP_B_H */
```

app_b.c file code (comments edited):

```c
#include <zephyr/kernel.h>
#include <zephyr/device.h>
#include <zephyr/sys/libc-hooks.h>
#include <zephyr/logging/log.h>
#include "app_shared.h"
#include "app_b.h"
LOG_MODULE_REGISTER(app_b);

/* K_HEAP_DEFINE defines the resource pool used for memory
allocations made by the kernel on behalf of system calls, e.g.
for k_queue_alloc_append() */
K_HEAP_DEFINE(app_b_resource_pool, 256 * 4 + 128);
/* K_APPMEM_PARTITION_DEFINE defines app_b_partition, which
is where all the globals for this app will be placed. The
partition starting address and size are populated by the build
system and the linker */
K_APPMEM_PARTITION_DEFINE(app_b_partition);

/* Tagging with APP_B_BSS or APP_B_DATA  will ensure all this
data gets linked into the continuous region denoted by app_b_
partition. An alternative approachwould be for the processor_
thread to put the data on its stack. */
APP_B_BSS unsigned int process_count;

static void processor_thread(void *p1, void *p2, void *p3) {
    void *payload;
    ARG_UNUSED(p1);
    ARG_UNUSED(p2);
```

CHAPTER 4   ZEPHYR RTOS MULTITHREADING

```
        ARG_UNUSED(p3);
        LOG_DBG("processor thread entered");

        /* The sleep call is used, here, to simulate the
        processor_thread taking some initialization time. During
        this time data coming in from the driver will be buffered
        in the incoming queue */
        k_sleep(K_MSEC(400));

        /* This while loop consumes data blobs from shared_
        queue_incoming, does some processing, and then puts the
        processed data into shared_queue_outgoing. */
        while (process_count < NUM_LOOPS) {
                payload = k_queue_get(&shared_queue_incoming,
                K_FOREVER);
                /* the following pretends that some complicated/
                time-consmuming
                data processing is being done on untrusted data
                which is processed in the sandboxed App B */
                LOG_DBG("processing payload #%d", process_count);
                k_busy_wait(100000);
                process_count++;
                LOG_INF("processing payload #%d complete",
                process_count);
                /* The processed data is put into the outgoing queue
                for handling App A's writeback thread.  */
                k_queue_alloc_append(&shared_queue_outgoing,
                payload);
        }
        LOG_DBG("processor thread exiting");
}
```

```c
void app_b_entry(void *p1, void *p2, void *p3) {
    int ret;
    /* Re-use the default memory domain as the domain for
    application B. */
    ret = k_mem_domain_add_partition(&k_mem_domain_default,
                        &app_b_partition);
    if (ret != 0) {
        LOG_ERR("Failed to add app_b_partition to mem domain
        (%d)", ret);
        k_oops();
    }
    ret = k_mem_domain_add_partition(&k_mem_domain_default,
                                            &shared_
                                            partition);
    if (ret != 0) {
        LOG_ERR("Failed to add shared_partition to mem domain
        (%d)", ret);
        k_oops();
    }

    /* Assign a resource pool for kernel-side allocations on
    behalf of application A. Needed for k_queue_alloc_
     append(). */
    k_thread_heap_assign(k_current_get(), &app_b_
    resource_pool);
    /* Drop to user mode and become the monitor thread,
    first granting self access to the kernel objects needed
    by the monitor thread.
    Here, access is required to both the shared queue
    objects. Access to the sample driver is not required as
    it is handled by App A */
```

```
        k_thread_access_grant(k_current_get(), &shared_queue_
        incoming, &shared_queue_outgoing);

        k_thread_user_mode_enter(processor_thread, NULL,
        NULL, NULL);
}
```

The main.c file code:

```
#include <kernel.h>
#include <device.h>
#include <sys/printk.h>
#include <app_memory/app_memdomain.h>
#include <sys/libc-hooks.h>
#include <logging/log.h>
#include "main.h"
#include "sample_driver.h"
#include "app_a.h"
#include "app_b.h"

#define APP_A_STACKSIZE        2048
LOG_MODULE_REGISTER(app_main);
/* Define the shared partition, for a memory region accessible
by both applications A and B.*/
K_APPMEM_PARTITION_DEFINE(shared_partition);
/* Define a memory pool to place in the shared memory area. */
#define BLK_SIZE (SAMPLE_DRIVER_MSG_SIZE + sizeof(void *))
#define HEAP_BYTES (BLK_SIZE * 16)
K_APP_DMEM(shared_partition) struct sys_heap shared_pool;
K_APP_DMEM(shared_partition) uint8_t shared_pool_
mem[HEAP_BYTES];
```

```
/* Define queues for exchanging data between App A and App B */
K_QUEUE_DEFINE(shared_queue_incoming);
K_QUEUE_DEFINE(shared_queue_outgoing);
/* Define a thread for the root of application A.
Application B, will re-use the main thread. */
struct k_thread app_a_thread;
K_THREAD_STACK_DEFINE(app_a_stack, APP_A_STACKSIZE);

void main(void) {
      LOG_INF("APP A partition: %p %zu", (void *)app_a_
      partition.start, (size_t)app_a_partition.size);
      LOG_INF("Shared partition: %p %zu", (void *)shared_
      partition.start, (size_t)shared_partition.size);
#ifdef Z_LIBC_PARTITION_EXISTS
      LOG_INF("libc partition: %p %zu", (void *)z_libc_
      partition.start,
            (size_t)z_libc_partition.size);
#endif
      sys_heap_init(&shared_pool, shared_pool_mem, HEAP_BYTES);
      /* Spawn supervisor entry for application A */
      k_thread_create(&app_a_thread, app_a_stack, APP_A_
      STACKSIZE, app_a_entry, NULL, NULL, NULL, -1,
      K_INHERIT_PERMS, K_NO_WAIT);
      /* Re-use main for app B supervisor mode setup */
      app_b_entry(NULL, NULL, NULL);
}
```

CHAPTER 4　ZEPHYR RTOS MULTITHREADING

Shared Memory, Protected Memory Partitions, and Memory Domains

In Linux, sharing memory between tasks involves using the Linux memory mapping API that uses the Linux kernel virtual memory management framework. Zephyr is designed to run on systems that do not have a memory management unit, but it is designed to make use of a Memory Protection Unit where this is available. The Zephyr Memory Domains framework provides the means by which access to additional blocks of memory can be provided to a user thread. A memory domain is, essentially, just a collection of a specified set of memory partitions. A given MPU has an upper limit on the number of MPU regions that it can support, and this, of course, also places a limit on the number of partitions a memory domain can have in it. In Zephyr, the memory domain APIs can only be used in supervisor mode. From the user mode perspective, a thread's child threads automatically become members of the parent's domain.

In Zephyr, a thread is a member of some memory domain. Zephyr provides a default domain `k_mem_domain_default` that will be assigned to a thread that has not been assigned to some specific domain or inherited a memory domain membership from their parent thread. The main thread starts as a member of the default domain.

Memory Partitions

A memory partition's attributes include a starting memory address, a size, and access attributes. The purpose of memory partitions is to control access to system memory. A partition represents a memory region that can be programmed by the underlying memory management hardware and conforms to the underlying processor implementation design hardware constraints. In the case of an MMU-based system, a partition has to be aligned to a page boundary, and its size is a multiple of the page size. Overlap between partitions in a given memory domain is not permitted. A given partition may be specified in more than one memory domain, for example, in the case of a shared memory area that multiple domains grant access to. For safety and security reasons, user mode access should not be allowed to memory containing private kernel data.

In Zephyr, memory partitions can be defined in one of two ways: manually or automatically.

Defining a memory partition manually, typically, involves declaring a global memory array, declaring a memory partition with appropriate read/write permissions, and then adding the declared array to the specified partition, for example:

```
uint8_t __aligned(32) buf[32];
K_MEM_PARTITION_DEFINE(my_partition, buf, sizeof(buf),
                 K_MEM_PARTITION_P_RW_U_RW);
```

A downside of manually defining memory partitions is that such an approach will not scale well to situations involving assigning multiple objects scattered over multiple C files into a common single partition. In the case of automatic memory partition creation, the globals to be placed inside a partition are tagged with a destination partition. The Zephyr build system will coalesce them into the corresponding single contiguous block of memory, zero any BSS variables at boot time, and define a memory partition of appropriate base address and size, which will contain all of the tagged data.

This is handled by the Zephyr gen_app_partitions.py script, one of a number of Python scripts used in the west-driven application build process (see Figure 4-11).

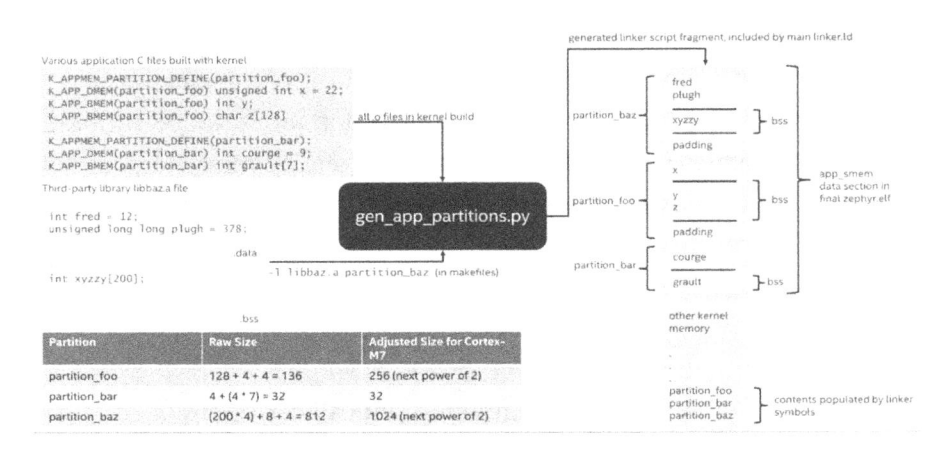

Figure 4-11. Outline of the processing done by gen_app_partitions.py

Automatic memory partitions are only configured as read-write regions and are defined using the macro K_APPMEM_PARTITION_DEFINE(). Global variables are then routed to a given partition by using the macro K_APP_DMEM() for initialized data and K_APP_BMEM() for BSS. The pattern/template to follow is shown in the following code snippet:

```
#include <zephyr/app_memory/app_memdomain.h>

/* Declare a k_mem_partition "my_partition" .
Note that this will be read-write to user mode, and that the
definition does not specify a base address or size. */
K_APPMEM_PARTITION_DEFINE(my_partition);

/* For a global variable var1 to be placed inside the bounds of
my_partition and to be initialized with 37 at boot time   */
K_APP_DMEM(my_partition) int var1 = 37;

/* For a global variable var2 to be placed inside the bounds of
my_partition and to be zeroed at boot time K_APP_BMEM() , which
indicates a BSS variable is used */
K_APP_BMEM(my_partition) int var2;
```

CHAPTER 4   ZEPHYR RTOS MULTITHREADING

The build system ensures that the base address of my_partition will be properly aligned, and the total size of the region will conform to the requirements of the memory management hardware requirements, including adding padding if necessary.

For creating multiple partitions, Zephyr provides a variadic preprocessor macro, the definition of which can be found in app_macro_support.h.

```
FOR_EACH(K_APPMEM_PARTITION_DEFINE, part0, part1, part2);
```

Zephyr RTOS automatically creates partitions for Static Library Globals and provides a number of system predefined partitions such as the z_malloc_partition, which contains the system-wide pool of memory used by libc malloc(), and z_libc_partition for globals required by the C library and runtime.

A memory domain is defined using a variable of type k_mem_domain and must be initialized by calling k_mem_domain_init(), for example:

The following code snippet shows how to define and initialize an empty memory domain:

```
struct k_mem_domain app0_domain;
k_mem_domain_init(&app0_domain, 0, NULL);
```

Memory partitions can be added to a memory domain as part of the memory domain creation process, or they can be added into an initialized memory domain individually.

This, next, code snippet demonstrates adding memory partitions while creating a memory domain:

```
/* the start address of the MPU region needs to align with
its size */
uint8_t __aligned(32) app0_buf[32];
uint8_t __aligned(32) app1_buf[32];
K_MEM_PARTITION_DEFINE(app0_part0, app0_buf, sizeof(app0_buf),
                       K_MEM_PARTITION_P_RW_U_RW);
```

203

```
K_MEM_PARTITION_DEFINE(app0_part1, app1_buf, sizeof(app1_buf),
                       K_MEM_PARTITION_P_RW_U_RO);
struct k_mem_partition *app0_parts[] = {
     app0_part0,
     app0_part1
};
k_mem_domain_init(&app0_domain, ARRAY_SIZE(app0_parts),
app0_parts);
```

The following code snippet, on the other hand, demonstrates how to add memory partitions to an initialized memory domain:

```
/* the start address of the MPU region needs to align with
its size */
uint8_t __aligned(32) app0_buf[32];
uint8_t __aligned(32) app1_buf[32];
K_MEM_PARTITION_DEFINE(app0_part0, app0_buf, sizeof(app0_buf),
                       K_MEM_PARTITION_P_RW_U_RW);
K_MEM_PARTITION_DEFINE(app0_part1, app1_buf, sizeof(app1_buf),
                       K_MEM_PARTITION_P_RW_U_RO);
k_mem_domain_add_partition(&app0_domain, &app0_part0);
k_mem_domain_add_partition(&app0_domain, &app0_part1);
```

Any thread may join a memory domain, and a memory domain can have multiple threads assigned to it. Threads are assigned to memory domains with the API call:

```
k_mem_domain_add_thread(&app0_domain, app_thread_id);
```

Where the thread was already a member of some other domain (including the default domain), it will be removed from that domain in favor of the new one. Also, if a thread is a member of a memory domain and it creates a child thread, that child thread will also belong to that memory domain.

To remove a Memory Partition from a Memory Domain, the `k_mem_domain_remove_partition(&app0_domain, &app0_part1);` API function can be used.

Access control to a memory partition relies on the MPU or MMU present in the processor architecture; hence, the available partition attributes will be architecture dependent, and the relevant data sheets and Zephyr documentation will need to be consulted. Some examples of partition attributes are

```
/* Denote partition is privileged read/write, unprivileged
read/write */
K_MEM_PARTITION_P_RW_U_RW
/* Denote partition is privileged read/write, unprivileged
read-only */
K_MEM_PARTITION_P_RW_U_RO
```

Zephyr Shared Memory Example

Having laid some foundations regarding shared memory and memory partitions, the Zephyr shared memory example is a good starting point for exploring how to make use of shared memory in Zephyr applications.

The Zephyr Shared Memory example involves running multiple threads assigned to unique memory domains with protected partitions. In the example, the threads carry out computations that simulate a simple cryptographic machine. The sample depends on the subsystem `app_memory` and will only run on boards that support the `app_memory` subsystem. When the application is built and run, it will display some starting messages in the console, followed by messages corresponding to the input and output of the enigma-like machine. The second message is the output after processing the first message, and the resulting output is the first message without spaces. In the output, the two messages are marked as 1 and 1', respectively.

Building and running the sample, `zephyr\samples\userspace\shared_mem\src`, should produce output something like the following:

```
*** Booting Zephyr OS build v2.7.0-rc2-7-g0d538447144c ***
ENC Thread Created 0x20020398
Partitions added to enc_domain
enc_domain Created
PT Thread Created 0x20020450
pt_domain Created
CT Thread Created 0x200202e0
ct partitions installed
ENC thread started
PT thread started

PT Sending Message 1
ENC Thread Received Data
ENC PT MSG: PT: message to encrypt

CT Thread Received Message
CT MSG: ofttbhfspgmeqzos

PT Sending Message 1'
ENC Thread Received Data
ENC PT MSG: ofttbhfspgmeqzos
```

The code uses three threads: a PT thread, a CT thread, and an ENC thread.

The PT thread sends a message to be encoded and then, later, an encrypted version of the message for decoding. To send the message, the PT thread checks a flag and, if it is clear, writes the message to a buffer shared with the encrypt thread. After writing the buffer, the flag is set. The encrypt thread copies the memory from the common buffer into the encrypted thread's private memory when the flag is set and then clears the flag. Once the encrypted thread receives the text string, it runs a simulation

CHAPTER 4 ZEPHYR RTOS MULTITHREADING

of the enigma machine to produce cypher text (CT). The CT is copied to a shared memory partition connecting to the third thread. The third thread prints the CT to the console with a banner denoting the content as CYPHER TEXT.

The encryption using an enigma-type engine is used simply to make for an interesting scenario. The aspects to focus on in this example are the setting up and use of memory partitions for sharing data in a controlled manner.

main.c code snippets:

```
#include <zephyr/sys/__assert.h>
#include <zephyr/sys/libc-hooks.h> /* for z_libc_partition */
#include "main.h"
#include "enc.h"
/* the following definition name prefix is to avoid a
conflict */
#define SAMP_BLOCKSIZE 50

/* prepare the memory partition structures   */
FOR_EACH(K_APPMEM_PARTITION_DEFINE, (;), user_part, \
red_part, enc_part, blk_part, ct_part);

/* prepare the memory domain structures   */
struct k_mem_domain pt_domain, enc_domain;

/* Each of the following  variables follows a naming convention
starts with a symbolic name for the corresponding memory
partition - where the names are defined in main.h
#define _app_red_d K_APP_DMEM(red_part)
#define _app_red_b K_APP_BMEM(red_part)

#define _app_blk_d K_APP_DMEM(blk_part)
#define _app_blk_b K_APP_BMEM(blk_part)

#define _app_enc_d K_APP_DMEM(enc_part)
```

207

CHAPTER 4 ZEPHYR RTOS MULTITHREADING

```
#define _app_enc_b K_APP_BMEM(enc_part)
*/
volatile _app_red_b BYTE fBUFIN;
volatile _app_red_b BYTE BUFIN[63];

volatile _app_blk_b BYTE fBUFOUT;
volatile _app_blk_b BYTE BUFOUT[63];

/*  Setting up the threads and associated memory resources
and  asynchronisation semaphore */
K_SEM_DEFINE(allforone, 0, 3);
struct k_thread enc_thread;
K_THREAD_STACK_DEFINE(enc_stack, STACKSIZE);
struct k_thread pt_thread;
K_THREAD_STACK_DEFINE(pt_stack, STACKSIZE);
struct k_thread ct_thread;
K_THREAD_STACK_DEFINE(ct_stack, STACKSIZE);

_app_enc_d char encMSG[] = "ENC!\n";
volatile _app_enc_b char enc_pt[50];   /* Buffer - Copy from
shared pt */
volatile _app_enc_b char enc_ct[50];   /* Buffer - Copy to
shared ct */

_app_user_d char ptMSG[] = "PT: message to encrypt\n";

/* encrypted message when W1 = START_WHEEL */
/* to use add definition ALTMSG   */
#ifdef ALTMSG
_app_user_d char ptMSG2[] = "nfttbhfspfmdqzos\n";
#else
/* encrypted message when W1 = START_WHEEL2 */
_app_user_d char ptMSG2[] = "ofttbhfspgmeqzos\n";
```

```
#endif
_app_ct_d char ctMSG[] = "CT!\n";

void main(void) {
      struct k_mem_partition *enc_parts[] = {
#if Z_LIBC_PARTITION_EXISTS
            &z_libc_partition,
#endif
            &enc_part, &red_part, &blk_part
      };
      struct k_mem_partition *pt_parts[] = {
#if Z_LIBC_PARTITION_EXISTS
            &z_libc_partition,
#endif
            &user_part, &red_part
      };
      k_tid_t tPT, tENC, tCT;
      int ret;
      fBUFIN = 0; /* clear flags */
      fBUFOUT = 0;

/* enigma set up ... */
      calc_rev_wheel((BYTE *) &W1, (BYTE *)&W1R);
      calc_rev_wheel((BYTE *) &W2, (BYTE *)&W2R);
      calc_rev_wheel((BYTE *) &W3, (BYTE *)&W3R);
      IW1 = 0;
      IW2 = 0;
      IW3 = 0;
/* end of enigma setup ... */
      k_thread_access_grant(k_current_get(), &allforone);

      /* create an enc thread, init the memory domain and add
      partitions
```

```
         then add the thread to the domain.    */
tENC = k_thread_create(&enc_thread, enc_stack, STACKSIZE,
            (k_thread_entry_t)enc, NULL, NULL, NULL,
            -1, K_USER,
            K_FOREVER);
k_thread_access_grant(tENC, &allforone);
/* use K_FOREVER followed by k_thread_start*/
printk("ENC Thread Created %p\n", tENC);

ret = k_mem_domain_init(&enc_domain, ARRAY_SIZE
(enc_parts), enc_parts);
__ASSERT(ret == 0, "k_mem_domain_init() on enc_domain
failed %d", ret);
ARG_UNUSED(ret);

printk("Partitions added to enc_domain\n");
k_mem_domain_add_thread(&enc_domain, tENC);
printk("enc_domain Created\n");

tPT = k_thread_create(&pt_thread, pt_stack, STACKSIZE,
            (k_thread_entry_t)pt, NULL, NULL, NULL, -1,
            K_USER,
            K_FOREVER);
k_thread_access_grant(tPT, &allforone);
printk("PT Thread Created %p\n", tPT);

ret = k_mem_domain_init(&pt_domain, ARRAY_SIZE(pt_parts),
pt_parts);
__ASSERT(ret == 0, "k_mem_domain_init() on pt_domain
failed %d", ret);

k_mem_domain_add_thread(&pt_domain, tPT);
printk("pt_domain Created\n");
```

```
tCT = k_thread_create(&ct_thread, ct_stack, STACKSIZE,
        (k_thread_entry_t)ct, NULL, NULL, NULL, -1,
        K_USER,
        K_FOREVER);
k_thread_access_grant(tCT, &allforone);
printk("CT Thread Created %p\n", tCT);

/* Re-using the default memory domain for CT */
ret = k_mem_domain_add_partition(&k_mem_domain_default,
&ct_part);
if (ret != 0) {
    printk("Failed to add ct_part to mem domain
    (%d)\n", ret);
    k_oops();
}
printk("ct partitions installed\n");

ret = k_mem_domain_add_partition(&k_mem_domain_default,
&blk_part);
if (ret != 0) {
    printk("Failed to add blk_part to mem domain
    (%d)\n", ret);
    k_oops();
}
printk("blk partitions installed\n");

k_thread_start(&enc_thread);
/* Start all three threads.  with enc going first to
perform an init step */
printk("ENC thread started\n");
k_thread_start(&pt_thread);
printk("PT thread started\n");
k_thread_start(&ct_thread);
```

CHAPTER 4   ZEPHYR RTOS MULTITHREADING

```
        k_sem_give(&allforone);
        printk("CT thread started\n");
}
/* The enc thread whose work is to copy memory from pt thread
and encrypt to a local buffer, and then then copy to the ct
thread. */
void enc(void) {
        int index, index_out;
        while (1) {
                k_sem_take(&allforone, K_FOREVER);
                if (fBUFIN == 1) { /* 1 is process text */
                        printk("ENC Thread Received Data\n");
                        /* copy message form shared mem and
                        clear flag */
                        memcpy((void *)&enc_pt, (void *)BUFIN, SAMP_
                        BLOCKSIZE);
                        printk("ENC PT MSG: %s\n", (char *)&enc_pt);
                        fBUFIN = 0;

                        /* Encryption work ... */
                        /* reset enigma engine wheel: probably better
                        as a flag option   */
                        IW1 = 7;
                        IW2 = 2;
                        IW3 = 3;
                        /* encode */
                        memset((void *)&enc_ct, 0, SAMP_BLOCKSIZE);
                        for (index = 0, index_out = 0; index < SAMP_
                        BLOCKSIZE; index++) {
                                if (enc_pt[index] == '\0') {
                                        enc_ct[index_out] = '\0';
```

```c
                        break;
                }
                if (enc_pt[index] >= 'a' && enc_
                pt[index] <= 'z') {
                        enc_ct[index_out] =
                                (BYTE) enig_enc((BYTE) enc_
                                pt[index]);
                        index_out++;
                }
            }
            /* test for CT flag */
            while (fBUFOUT != 0) {
                    k_sleep(K_MSEC(1));
            }
            /* ct thread has cleared the buffer */
            memcpy((void *)&BUFOUT, (void *)&enc_ct,
            SAMP_BLOCKSIZE);
            fBUFOUT = 1;
        }
        k_sem_give(&allforone);
    }
}
/* the pt function pushes data to the enc thread. */
void pt(void) {
    k_sleep(K_MSEC(20));
    while (1) {
        k_sem_take(&allforone, K_FOREVER);
        if (fBUFIN == 0) { /* send message to encode */
            printk("\nPT Sending Message 1\n");
            memset((void *)&BUFIN, 0, SAMP_BLOCKSIZE);
```

CHAPTER 4 ZEPHYR RTOS MULTITHREADING

```
                    memcpy((void *)&BUFIN, (void *)&ptMSG,
                    sizeof(ptMSG));
                    fBUFIN = 1;
            }
            k_sem_give(&allforone);
            k_sem_take(&allforone, K_FOREVER);
            if (fBUFIN == 0) { /* send message to decode   */
                    printk("\nPT Sending Message 1'\n");
                    memset((void *)&BUFIN, 0, SAMP_BLOCKSIZE);
                    memcpy((void *)&BUFIN, (void *)&ptMSG2,
                    sizeof(ptMSG2));
                    fBUFIN = 1;
            }
            k_sem_give(&allforone);
            k_sleep(K_MSEC(50));
        }
}

/* ct waits for fBUFOUT = 1 then copies the message, clears the
flag and prints */
void ct(void) {
        char tbuf[60];
        while (1) {
                k_sem_take(&allforone, K_FOREVER);
                if (fBUFOUT == 1) {
                        printk("CT Thread Received Message\n");
                        memset((void *)&tbuf, 0, sizeof(tbuf));
                        memcpy((void *)&tbuf, (void *)BUFOUT, SAMP_
                        BLOCKSIZE);
                        fBUFOUT = 0;
                        printk("CT MSG: %s\n", (char *)&tbuf);
                }
```

```
            k_sem_give(&allforone);
    }
}
```

You should try running this on a number of boards, QEMU and Renode.

References

1. Zephyr RTOS usermode and overview https://docs.zephyrproject.org/latest/kernel/usermode/overview.html)

2. Embedded Software Design: A Practical Approach to Architecture, Processes, and Coding Techniques, Jacob Beningo, publisher Apress, published 2022, ISBN-13: 978-1484282786

3. https://embeddedcomputing.com/application/industrial/industrial-computing/using-a-memory-protection-unit-with-an-rtos

4. https://events19.linuxfoundation.cn/wp-content/uploads/2017/11/Retrofitting-Memory-Protection-in-the-Zephyr-OS_Wayne-Ren-_-Huaqi-Fang.pdf

5. https://docs.zephyrproject.org/latest/kernel/services/scheduling/index.html

6. https://docs.zephyrproject.org/latest/kernel/usermode/kernelobjects.html#kernel-objects

CHAPTER 4　ZEPHYR RTOS MULTITHREADING

7. Edsger Dijkstra. The Man Who Carried Computer Science on His Shoulders https://arxiv.org/abs/2010.00506

8. Zephyr producer consumer example location in the Zephyr source code zephyr\samples\userspace\prod_consumer

CHAPTER 5

Message Queues, Pipes, Mailboxes, and Workqueues

Message queues, mailboxes, and pipes provide both synchronization between a producer and a consumer (sender and receiver) as well as temporary storage of data where necessary. Workqueues represent storage of requests for work to be done.

Underlying these mechanisms are data structures, algorithms, and APIs (Application Programming Interfaces).

In the case of a message queue, the maximum size of a message and the maximum number of messages the circular buffer associated with the message queue can store are fixed when an instance of the message queue is created. A mailbox, on the other hand, allows threads to send and receive messages of any size and makes use of message descriptors, data structures that contain a pointer to the message in question.

Whereas message queues and mailboxes are concerned with whole messages, pipes are used for streaming data. Unlike POSIX pipes, Zephyr pipes are not associated with file descriptors.

Figure 5-1 illustrates a common embedded system application scenario.

CHAPTER 5   MESSAGE QUEUES, PIPES, MAILBOXES, AND WORKQUEUES

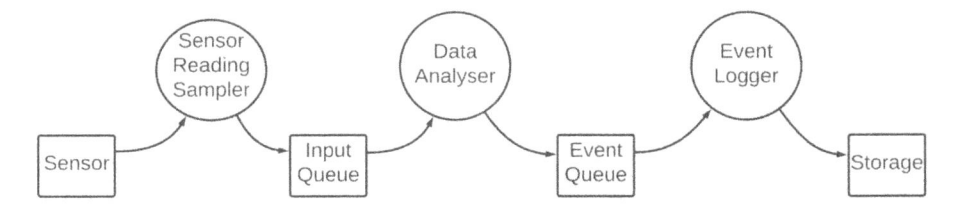

Figure 5-1. Common embedded system application scenario

In this scenario, there are three threads: a thread associated with fetching sensor data and writing it to an input queue, a thread that is responsible for analyzing the input data and identifying application events on the basis of that data, and, finally, a thread that is responsible for retrieving event information from the event queue and writing event details to a log file.

More complex scenarios may involve applications pulling in data from multiple sensors, writing commands to actuators, and receiving instructions and commands over a communications link such as BLE or Ethernet.

Zephyr Message Queue

A Zephyr Message Queue can be thought of as a container that can hold a collection of fixed-size data items. The size of the item and the data it contains is determined by the application being implemented. When a message queue is created, the maximum number of items it can contain is also specified. The Zephyr Message Queue API and implementation provide the logic for adding and removing items from the queue and also provide blocking semantics whereby a thread attempting to retrieve a message from an empty message queue will exhibit configurable blocking behavior (returning immediately (K_NO_WAIT), blocking indefinitely (K_FOREVER), blocking for a specified timeout period). Similarly, attempting to read from an empty queue also exhibits blocking semantics when the message queue is empty.

CHAPTER 5   MESSAGE QUEUES, PIPES, MAILBOXES, AND WORKQUEUES

When working with message queues, it is important to take the possible use case scenarios into account. These will include things such as handling the situation when the message queue is full and a message sender attempts to post a message to the queue, and the situation when the message receiver attempts to receive a message from an empty message queue. When configuring the message queue, it is necessary to decide on the message size to use and the maximum number of messages the queue is to hold.

Message Queue – Technical Details and the Message Queue API

A Zephyr Message Queue is a kernel object that can be used by threads and ISRs (interrupt service routines) to asynchronously send and receive fixed-size data items.

An application can have more than one message queue, and the number of message queues that can be defined is limited by the available RAM. The size of a message queue is fixed and cannot be altered dynamically by a running thread. The main characteristics of a message queue from the application point of view are that it has a ring buffer that contains up to some specified number of data items. The items have a fixed size, measured in bytes, and the number of items that the ring buffer can hold and the size of a data item are defined when a message queue instance is created.

Zephyr requires that the message queue ring buffer is aligned to an N-byte boundary, where N is a power of 2 (i.e., 1, 2, 4, 8, etc.), and the data item size is also a multiple of N bytes. After creation, a message queue must be initialized so that its ring buffer is set to empty (item count of 0).

An ISR or a thread can send a data item to a message queue. When an item is sent, it will be sent to a waiting thread if one is waiting, or otherwise it is copied into the message queue ring buffer. The memory area into which the message is copied must have the same size as that defined for the memory queue data item.

If a thread tries to send a data item when the ring buffer is full, the sending thread may choose to wait for space to become available. Multiple sending threads can wait on a full ring buffer, and when space becomes available, the thread that is unblocked will be the one that has the highest priority, or, in the case of multiple threads with equal priority, the thread that has been waiting the longest.

When data is fetched (received) from a message queue, it is copied into a specified area, whose size equals the size of the data item, provided by the receiving thread.

If a thread tries to fetch a data item from an empty buffer, the attempt can be given a timeout value for which the thread is to wait. Multiple threads can be waiting on an empty mail queue, and, as with sending when data becomes available, the thread that is unblocked will be the one that has the highest priority, or, in the case of multiple threads with equal priority, the thread that has been waiting the longest.

The Zephyr Message Queue API also has a method for peeking at the message at the head of the queue, without removing it from the queue.

An important point to note when working with message queues is the amount of data being transferred via the message queue. Generally a message queue should be used to transfer relatively small amounts of data. This is because the data interrupts are locked when data is being written or read, and hence, the greater the amount of data involved, the greater the latency. Common practice when transferring larger amounts of data is to make use of pointers to the data item in questions as opposed to transferring the data item itself.

CHAPTER 5 MESSAGE QUEUES, PIPES, MAILBOXES, AND WORKQUEUES

Overview of the Message Queue API Functions

The API has functions for creating and initializing a message queue as well as functions for putting a message into and getting a message from a message queue.

They are summarized as follows:

`void k_msgq_init(struct k_msgq *msgq, char *buffer, size_t msg_size, uint32_t max_msgs)` for initializing a message queue after the memory for the message queue structure and the message queue buffer has already been allocated.

`int k_msgq_alloc_init(struct k_msgq *msgq, size_t msg_size, uint32_t max_msgs)`, which initializes a message queue and allocates the memory required from the calling thread's memory resource pool.

`int k_msgq_put(struct k_msgq *msgq, const void *data, k_timeout_t timeout)`, which is used to put (send) messages into the message queue, or into a thread waiting on an empty queue if there is one waiting.

`int k_msgq_get(struct k_msgq *msgq, void *data, k_timeout_t timeout)` for getting a message from the message queue.

There are also methods for peeking at a message item at the head of the queue and for discarding all the unreceived messages in a message queue. In a peek operation, the data item is copied into a specified area large enough to hold the data. One possible use of a peek might be to examine the data for validity and safety, and if the data checks pass, then the data can be retrieved from the message queue for application processing, or retrieved and discarded otherwise.

`int k_msgq_peek(struct k_msgq *msgq, void *data)` performs a read without removing that item from the message queue.

`void k_msgq_purge(struct k_msgq *msgq)` performs a purge on the message queue by discarding all the unreceived messages in the message queue. At the same time any threads that were blocking and waiting to send a message to the message queue are unblocked. The put calls associated with these unblocked threads will return an ENOMSG error code.

Other API methods include the following:

`uint32_t k_msgq_num_free_get(struct k_msgq *msgq)` for inquiring about the available free space in the message queue.

`void k_msgq_get_attrs(struct k_msgq *msgq, struct k_msgq_attrs *attrs)` to inquire about the message queue's attributes.

`uint32_t k_msgq_num_used_get(struct k_msgq *msgq)` to inquire about the number of messages in the message queue, and a method for freeing up the memory associated with the message queue ring buffer.

`int k_msgq_cleanup(struct k_msgq *msgq)`, which releases the allocated buffer for a queue and the memory allocated for the ring buffer.

Message Queue Example

This example involves a scenario where pressing one button triggers the writing of a message to a message queue and pressing a different button triggers the retrieval of a message from that message queue.

The messages contain information used by the recipient of the message.

A message data item contains two fields: one identifying the LED to flash and the other specifying the number of times that LED is to be flashed. The flash period in this example is set to a constant value, 200 msecs in this case. The message items are selected at random from a collection of possible messages that are generated during startup. The thread that retrieves a message item will not only flash the target LED for the specified number of times but will also set a busy flag while it is executing a flashing sequence.

When the busy flag is set, pressing the button that triggers receiving a message will have no effect.

The example demonstrated describes a build for an nRF52840 DK board, but the example can be built for other boards and also run in Renode and QEMU.

The buttons are connected to GPIO pins configured to have edge-triggered interrupts.

Button presses will be acted upon by interrupt handlers detecting edge-triggered interrupts on the target buttons. The interrupts will trigger sending or receiving of data by the use of binary counting semaphores.

In this case, the interrupt handlers will control the behavior of the threads that write and read messages to and from the message queue.

The purpose of this example is to provide some insights into how Zephyr applications can make use of some of the synchronization and message passing mechanisms available in Zephyr, some ways of working with the Zephyr GPIO driver framework, and, additionally, something about how pseudorandom number generation is supported in Zephyr.

Exercise Scenario Description

The gist of this scenario is shown in Figure 5-2.

CHAPTER 5   MESSAGE QUEUES, PIPES, MAILBOXES, AND WORKQUEUES

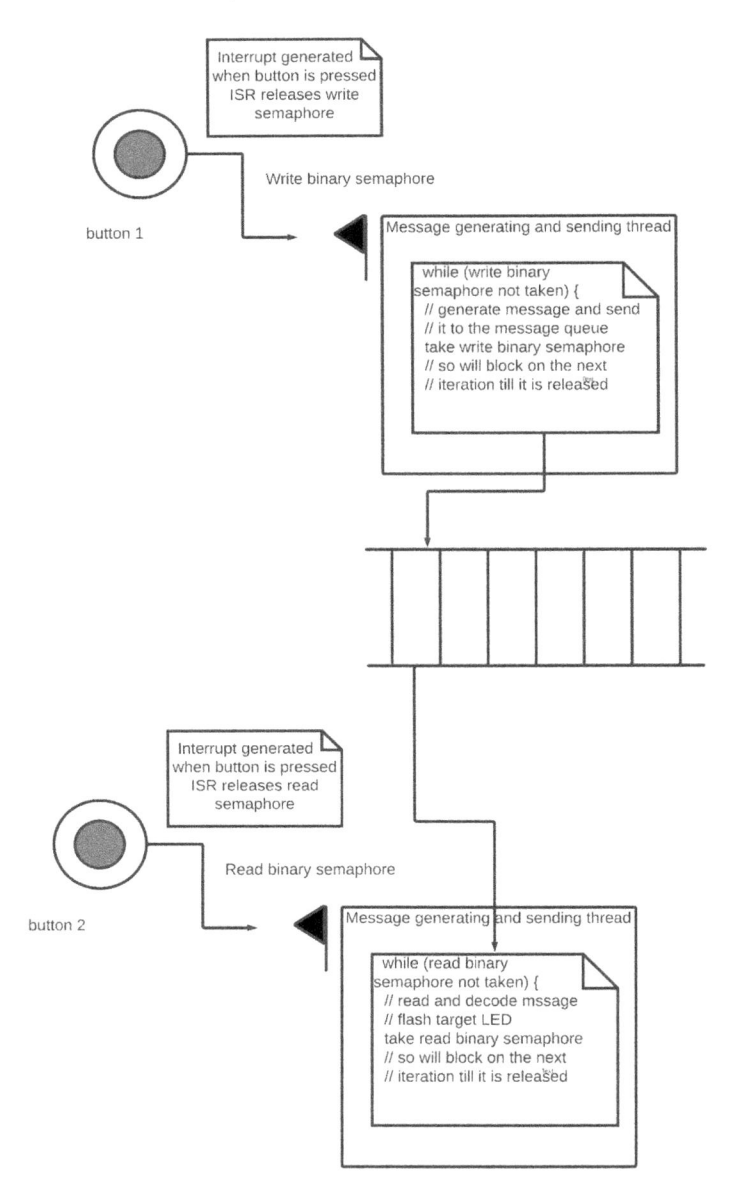

Figure 5-2. Button presses controlling message queue reading and writing

CHAPTER 5   MESSAGE QUEUES, PIPES, MAILBOXES, AND WORKQUEUES

In this scenario, a button 1 press interrupt handler issues a `give` operation to a synchronizing binary semaphore, the sender semaphore, that the message sending thread is blocking on.

The message sending thread, itself, runs in a loop. At the start of the loop, the thread performs a `take` operation on the synchronizing binary semaphore. This means that it will block on the next loop iteration unless a button 1 press has released the synchronizing sender semaphore. Once unblocked, the thread posts a message to the message queue. The message data specifies which led to flash and the number of times to flash it. When the message queue is full, a "mailbox full" message is sent to the console, and the button 1 press will have no other effect.

The button 2 press interrupt handler issues a `give` operation to a synchronizing binary semaphore, the receiving semaphore, that the receiving thread is blocking on. In this case, also, the message receiving thread, itself, runs in a loop. At the start of the loop, the thread performs a `take` operation on the synchronizing binary semaphore. This means that it will block on the next loop iteration unless a button 2 press has released the synchronizing sender semaphore. Once unblocked, the thread will get a message from the message queue. The receiving thread will send details of the received message to the console, and based on the information in the message, it will flash the designated led the specified number of times. While the LED is being flashed, a busy flag is set, and if button 2 is pressed while flashing is in progress, then a "busy" message will be sent to the console, and the button 2 press handler will not retrieve a message from the mail queue. If the message queue is empty, an "empty mailbox" message is sent to the console.

The code snippets for defining the message type to be stored in the message queue and for setting up the circular buffer memory for the message queue is shown as follows:

CHAPTER 5 MESSAGE QUEUES, PIPES, MAILBOXES, AND WORKQUEUES

```
struct k_msgq shd_msgq;
struct data_item_type {
      uint32_t num_flashes;
      uint32_t which_led;
};
char __aligned(4) shd_msgq_buffer[10U * sizeof(struct data_item_type)];

void main(void) {
      ...
      k_msgq_init(
            &shd_msgq, shd_msgq_buffer, sizeof(struct data_item_type), 10U);
      ...
}
```

The array of messages to use in the application is set up and initialized as follows:

```
struct data_item_type {
      uint32_t num_flashes;
      uint32_t which_led;
};

struct data_item_type test_patterns[10];

struct patternsCollection {
      uint32_t size;
      struct data_item_type * patterns;
} patternData;

void init_test_patterns(struct data_item_type* test_patterns_arry, uint32_t arr_size) {
            int i;
```

CHAPTER 5 MESSAGE QUEUES, PIPES, MAILBOXES, AND WORKQUEUES

```
        for (i = 0; i < 10; i++) {
            test_patterns_arry[i].num_flashes =
                        (sys_rand32_get() % 10U) + 1;
            test_patterns_arry[i].which_led =
                        (sys_rand32_get() % 2U) + 1;
        }
}
void main(void) {
    ...
    init_test_patterns(test_patterns,
        sizeof(test_patterns) / sizeof (struct data_
                            item_type));
    patternData.size =
        sizeof(test_patterns) / sizeof (struct data_
                            item_type);
    patternData.patterns = test_patterns;
    ...
}
```

The global variables corresponding to the two buttons and their associated callback structures are defined in the following way:

```
static const struct gpio_dt_spec button1 =
    GPIO_DT_SPEC_GET_OR(SW0_NODE, gpios, {0});
static struct gpio_callback button1_cb_data;
static const struct gpio_dt_spec button2 =
    GPIO_DT_SPEC_GET_OR(SW1_NODE, gpios,{0});
static struct gpio_callback button2_cb_data;
```

The code for the global "working" flag and for the button press interrupt callback functions is defined as shown in the next code snippet:

```
uint32_t working = 0;
```

CHAPTER 5   MESSAGE QUEUES, PIPES, MAILBOXES, AND WORKQUEUES

```c
void button1_pressed(const struct device *dev,
      struct gpio_callback *cb, uint32_t pins)
{
      printk("Button1 pressed at %" PRIu32 "\n", k_cycle_
      get_32());
      /* triggers posting of data to message queue */
      k_sem_give(&b1_sem);
      printk("button1 press sem give \n");
}
void button2_pressed(const struct device *dev,
      struct gpio_callback *cb,uint32_t pins){
      printk("Button2 pressed at %" PRIu32 "\n", k_cycle_
      get_32());
      if (!working){
      /* Triggers retrieval of message from message queue */
            k_sem_give(&b2_sem);}
      else {
            printk("Busy\n");
      }
}
```

The code in main for setting up the button interrupt handlers is shown next:

```c
void main(void) {
      ...
      if (!device_is_ready(button1.port)) {
            printk("Error: button1 device %s is not ready\n",
            button1.port->name);
            return;
      }
      if (!device_is_ready(button2.port)) {
```

CHAPTER 5 MESSAGE QUEUES, PIPES, MAILBOXES, AND WORKQUEUES

```
        printk("Error: button2 device %s is not
        ready\n",  button2.port->name);
        return;
}

ret = gpio_pin_configure_dt(&button1, GPIO_INPUT);
if (ret != 0) {
        printk("Error %d: failed to configure %s pin %d\n",
                ret, button1.port->name, button1.pin);
        return;
}

ret = gpio_pin_configure_dt(&button2, GPIO_INPUT);
if (ret != 0) {
        printk("Error %d: failed to configure %s pin %d\n",
                ret, button1.port->name, button1.pin);
        return;
}

ret = gpio_pin_interrupt_configure_dt(&button1,
                                      GPIO_INT_EDGE_TO_ACTIVE);

if (ret != 0) {
        printk("Error %d: failed to configure interrupt on
        %s pin %d\n",
                ret, button1.port->name, button1.pin);
        return;
}

ret = gpio_pin_interrupt_configure_dt(&button2,
                                      GPIO_INT_EDGE_TO_ACTIVE);

if (ret != 0) {
```

229

```
            printk("Error %d: failed to configure interrupt on
            %s pin %d\n",
                    ret, button2.port->name, button2.pin);
            return;
    }
    gpio_init_callback(&button1_cb_data, button1_pressed,
                                                BIT(button1.pin));
    gpio_add_callback(button1.port, &button1_cb_data);
    printk("Set up button at %s pin %d\n", button1.
    port->name,
                                                        button1.pin);

    gpio_init_callback(&button2_cb_data, button2_pressed,
                                                BIT(button2.pin));
    gpio_add_callback(button2.port, &button2_cb_data);
    printk("Set up button at %s pin %d\n", button2.
    port->name,
                                                        button2.pin);
    ...
}
```

As shown in the diagram illustrating how the code works and a description of how the application works, it can be seen that the application is relatively straightforward. Much of the detailed work lies in understanding Zephyr's GPIO framework and how it is implemented on a particular target processor and target board.

This involves understanding how to use the various convenience macros provided by Zephyr for configuring the GPIO pins as either input pins or output pins. In this example, the output pins of interest are those that drive the leds on the target board. In this example, just two LEDs, led1 and led2, are used. The code snippets for setting these up follow next:

CHAPTER 5   MESSAGE QUEUES, PIPES, MAILBOXES, AND WORKQUEUES

Zephyr convenience macros can be used to define global variables led1 and led2 based on aliases set up in the devicetree configuration file.

```
static struct gpio_dt_spec led1 =
                GPIO_DT_SPEC_GET_OR(DT_ALIAS(led0),
                gpios, {0});
static struct gpio_dt_spec led2 =
                GPIO_DT_SPEC_GET_OR(DT_ALIAS(led1),
                gpios, {0});
```

The leds are configured and set up as shown in the following code:

```
void main (void) {
    ...
    if (led1.port && !device_is_ready(led1.port)) {
        printk("Error %d: LED device %s is not ready;
        ignoring it\n",
              ret, led1.port->name);
        led1.port = NULL;
    }
    if (led1.port) {
        ret = gpio_pin_configure_dt(&led1, GPIO_OUTPUT);
        if (ret != 0) {
            printk("Error %d: failed to configure LED
            device %s pin %d\n",
                   ret, led1.port->name, led1.pin);
            led1.port = NULL;
        } else {
            printk("Set up LED at %s pin %d\n",
                       led1.port->name, led1.pin);
        }
    }
    if (led2.port && !device_is_ready(led2.port)) {
```

231

CHAPTER 5   MESSAGE QUEUES, PIPES, MAILBOXES, AND WORKQUEUES

```
                printk("Error %d: LED device %s is not ready;
                ignoring it\n",
                        ret, led2.port->name);
                led2.port = NULL;
        }
        if (led2.port) {
                ret = gpio_pin_configure_dt(&led2, GPIO_OUTPUT);
                if (ret != 0) {
                        printk("Error %d: failed to configure LED
                        device %s pin %d\n",
                                ret, led2.port->name, led2.pin);
                        led2.port = NULL;
                } else {
                        printk("Set up LED at %s pin %d\n",
                                        led2.port->name, led2.pin);
                }
        }
        ...
}
```

The code for the sending and receiving threads is not particularly complicated.

This is the code for the sending thread function (entry point):

```
void senderTF(struct k_msgq * shd_mqueue, struct k_sem *
postSem, struct
                patternsCollection * patts ) {
        uint32_t which_pattern;
        uint32_t res;

        while(1) {
                k_sem_take(postSem, K_FOREVER);
                which_pattern = (sys_rand32_get() % patts->size);
```

CHAPTER 5 MESSAGE QUEUES, PIPES, MAILBOXES, AND WORKQUEUES

```
                printk("Sending %d %d \n",
                        patts->patterns[which_pattern].which_led,
                        patts->patterns[which_pattern].num_flashes);
                res = k_msgq_put(shd_mqueue,
                        &(patts->patterns[which_pattern]), K_
                        NO_WAIT);
                if (res != 0) {
                        printk("Mailbox full\n");
                }
        }
}
```

And this is the code for the receiving thread function (entry point):

```
void receiverTF(struct k_msgq * shd_mqueue,
                struct k_sem * recvSem, void * param) {
    uint32_t ret;
    struct data_item_type msg;
    struct gpio_dt_spec * ledp = NULL;
    uint32_t num_flashes;
    uint32_t i;
    while(1) {
        k_sem_take(&b2_sem, K_FOREVER);
        ret = k_msgq_get(shd_mqueue, &msg, K_NO_WAIT);
        if(ret != 0) {
            printk("Mailbox empty\n");
        }
        else {
            switch (msg.which_led) {
                case 1:
                    ledp = &led1;
                    break;
```

233

CHAPTER 5   MESSAGE QUEUES, PIPES, MAILBOXES, AND WORKQUEUES

```
                    case 2:
                        ledp = &led2;
                        break;
                    default:
                        printk("Invalid LED\n");
                }
                num_flashes = msg.num_flashes;
                working = 1;
                printk("Led %d, number of flashes %d\n",
                        msg.which_led, msg.num_flashes);
                for (i = 0; i < num_flashes; i++) {
                    ret = gpio_pin_toggle_dt(ledp);
                    if (ret < 0) {
                        return;
                    }
                    k_msleep(SLEEP_TIME_MS);
                    ret = gpio_pin_toggle_dt(ledp);
                    if (ret < 0) {
                        return;
                    }
                    k_msleep(SLEEP_TIME_MS);
                }
                working = 0;
            }
        }
}
```

CHAPTER 5   MESSAGE QUEUES, PIPES, MAILBOXES, AND WORKQUEUES

The receiver and sender threads can be instantiated using Zephyr convenience macros.

K_THREAD_DEFINE(msgq_sender_id, STACKSIZE, senderTF, \
&shd_msgq, &b1_sem, &patternData, PRIORITY, 0, 0);

K_THREAD_DEFINE(msgq_receiver_id, STACKSIZE, receiverTF, &shd_msgq, \ &b2_sem, NULL, PRIORITY, 0, 0);

The prj.conf file is very simple:

CONFIG_GPIO=y
CONFIG_ENTROPY_GENERATOR=y
CONFIG_TEST_RANDOM_GENERATOR=y

Apart from GPIO, the project also makes use of the Zephyr modules needed to generate pseudorandom numbers.

Building the project for the nRF52840 target board and using PuTTY to provide a terminal console produce output such as this:

*** Booting Zephyr OS build v3.1.99-ncs1-1   ***
Set up button at gpio@50000000 pin 11
Set up button at gpio@50000000 pin 12
Set up LED at gpio@50000000 pin 13
Set up LED at gpio@50000000 pin 14
Button1 pressed at 332343
button1 press sem give
Sending 2 5
Button1 pressed at 460261
button1 press sem give
Sending 1 4
Button1 pressed at 658118
button1 press sem give
Sending 1 9
Button2 pressed at 770119

235

```
Led 2, number of flashes 5
Button2 pressed at 862307
Led 1, number of flashes 4
Button2 pressed at 899629
Busy
Button2 pressed at 971006
Led 1, number of flashes 9
Button2 pressed at 1061342
Busy
Button2 pressed at 1102722
Mailbox empty
```

Zephyr Mailbox

A mailbox is a kernel object that extends the capabilities of a message queue object. A mailbox can be used by threads to send and receive messages of any size synchronously or asynchronously, and the number of mailboxes that can be defined is limited only by available RAM. A mailbox instance is referenced by its memory address and has a send queue of messages that have been sent but not yet received and a receive queue of threads that are waiting to receive a message. Before starting to use a mailbox, it must be initialized, setting both of its queues to empty. Because mailboxes are designed for message exchange between threads, ISRs (interrupt service routines) cannot use mailboxes to exchange messages, as an ISR is not associated with any thread.

The use case pattern for mailboxes involves a sending thread sending a message and a receiving thread receiving the message. A message may be received by only one thread because the Zephyr implementation does not support point-to-multipoint (multicast) and broadcast messaging. Furthermore, the messages exchanged using a mailbox are handled non-anonymously. The threads participating in an exchange know the identity of the other thread. In fact, a thread can even specify the identity of the thread whose mail messages it is interested in. This feature can be used, for example, in implementing a managing and monitoring thread that controls several managed threads on the basis of information received from these threads. Where there is a requirement to synchronize multiple tasks, use can be made of Zephyr Events. An event can be used to indicate that some set of conditions has occurred and can notify multiple threads. Where only small amounts of data are involved, an event provides a way of passing small amounts of data to several threads concurrently.

Mailbox Message Format

A mailbox message is associated with a message descriptor, a data structure, which specifies where the starting address of the message data and how the message is to be handled by the mailbox. The mailbox message sending thread and the mailbox message receiving thread need to provide a message descriptor when accessing a mailbox. The message descriptors are required for message exchange between compatible sending and receiving threads to take place. During message exchange, message descriptor fields are modified (updated) by the mailbox so that the sending thread and receiving thread can track the message exchange. The mailbox message itself can contain zero or more bytes of message data. The application defines the size and format of the mail messages that are to be exchanged, and these can vary from message to message. Sending and receiving threads must supply a message buffer memory for holding messages.

A message that has no buffer associated with it and, hence, no bytes of data is an empty message. A message that has a message buffer associated with it and where there is no data in that message buffer is not an empty message in Zephyr mailbox parlance.

CHAPTER 5 MESSAGE QUEUES, PIPES, MAILBOXES, AND WORKQUEUES

Mailbox Message Life Cycle

The mailbox message life cycle is relatively simple. A message is created when and passed to the mailbox by a sending thread. The mailbox has ownership of the message until that message is actually given to the receiving thread. A receiving thread may choose to retrieve the message data when it receives the message from the mailbox, or may carry out the data retrieval in a follow-on mailbox operation. Once data retrieval by the receiving thread has completed, the mailbox message can be deleted by the mailbox.

Mailbox Sending and Receiving Thread Compatibility

In the Zephyr mailbox implementation, a sending thread can specify the address (identity) of the thread or threads to which the message is to be sent, as mentioned earlier. The K_ANY identifier means "sending to any receiving thread." Also, a receiving thread can specify an address of a thread from which it wishes to receive a message. K_ANY can be used to indicate that the thread is willing to receive a message from any sender thread. A message can only be exchanged between compatible threads.

For example, where thread A sends a message to thread B exclusively, then thread B can receive that message if thread B indicates that it is willing to receive messages from thread A or if it is willing to receive any message. The message exchange will not occur if thread B tries to receive a message from thread C. Thread C cannot receive a message sent exclusively to thread B, even where thread C is willing to receive messages from thread A, or to receive messages from any thread.

Mailbox Message Sending – Synchronous and Asynchronous

The sender and receiver of mailbox messages can use either a synchronous approach or an asynchronous approach. Synchronous exchange involves blocking of the sending thread until the message has been fully received by the receiving thread. In asynchronous exchange, the sending thread does not block and can continue running and doing further ongoing work. The sending policy, synchronous or asynchronous, is determined by the sending thread.

Flow control is implicit in synchronous exchange as the sending thread cannot send messages faster than they can be received. Technique provides an implicit form of flow control, preventing a sending thread from generating messages faster than they can be consumed by receiving threads. Flow control can be implemented in asynchronous message exchange by having the sending thread first check whether a previously sent message is still in the mailbox before attempting to send another message.

The Mailbox API – Data Types and Functions

The Zephyr Mailbox API is deceptively simple. Here, the API will be described and explained. The "real fun" begins with implementing real-world applications that make effective use of this API. As always with embedded systems, it is important to take heed of the mantra that "resources are limited and must be used sparingly and effectively." The other important observation is that the Zephyr RTOS API can be used for sending messages having variable sizes (including a size of zero), which can be really useful in applications where the sizes of the data responses from various attached sensors (e.g., different I2C and SPI sensors) may differ.

A Zephyr Mailbox object is created by defining a variable of the correct type and then initializing it. A mailbox variable is of type k_mbox, and the initialization method is k_mbox_init() and the basic code pattern for defining and initializing an empty mailbox is

```
struct k_mbox some_mailbox;
k_mbox_init(&some_mailbox);
```

Zephyr provides the K_MBOX_DEFINE macro for defining and initializing a mailbox at compile time, and the following code snippet will have the same effect as the two-line code in the previous snippet:

```
K_MBOX_DEFINE(some_mailbox);
```

Message Descriptors

Message descriptors are instances of a structure of type k_mbox_msg. This structure contains fields that can be used in applications as well as other fields that are only for internal mailbox use. The fields for application use are info, size, tx_data, tx_target_thread, and rx_source_thread:

- info is an application-defined 32-bit value that can be exchanged between a sender and a receiver. This exchange can occur in both directions. A sender can pass a value to the receiver during message exchange. A receiver can pass a value to the sender in a synchronous message exchange. Recall that in a synchronous exchange, the sending thread blocks until the message has been fully processed by the receiving thread, whereas in an asynchronous exchange, the sending thread does not wait until the message has been received by another thread before continuing.

CHAPTER 5　MESSAGE QUEUES, PIPES, MAILBOXES, AND WORKQUEUES

- `size` is the size of the message data in bytes and can be set to zero when sending an empty message, or when sending a buffer that does not contain any data. When receiving a message, the size specifies the maximum amount of data wanted, or zero if the message data is not wanted. This field is updated by the mailbox to the actual number of data bytes exchanged when the message is received.

- `tx_data` is a pointer to the message buffer used by the sending thread. When sending an empty message, it is set to NULL, and when receiving a message, this field is uninitialized.

- `tx_target_thread` is the address (id) of the thread for which the message is destined. It is set to K_ANY if the intention is to allow any thread to receive the message. This value is not initialized when receiving a message as the mailbox will update this field with the address of the actual receiver that receives the message.

- `rx_source_thread` is the address of the thread from which a message is wanted. It is set to K_ANY in the case where a message sent by any thread is acceptable. This field is not initialized when sending a message as the mailbox will update this field with the address of the actual sender when the message is put into the mailbox.

CHAPTER 5   MESSAGE QUEUES, PIPES, MAILBOXES, AND WORKQUEUES

Sending and Receiving Zephyr Mailbox Messages

The Zephyr Mailbox has many features, and using it to its best advantage will, almost certainly, involve deciding on which features to use and how to use them. An attempt to construct a UML sequence diagram covering all of these features would result in a very large, complicated, and difficult-to-follow diagram, which defeats the whole purpose of working with UML diagrams. A better approach might be to devise various scenarios that illustrate possible use patterns and situations where multiple threads exchange information via the use of a common mailbox, and then, when examining examples, to consider the various patterns that are being followed in practice. It is also worth considering that analyzing such patterns and scenarios can be of considerable help in unit testing of application code.

Here are a couple of example scenarios:

Scenario 1

The mailbox is empty.

A consumer thread is waiting for a message, and it is the only thread in the mailbox receive queue.

The sending thread sends a message that does not target any particular thread id.

The message is sent to the receiving thread directly.

Scenario 2

The mailbox is not empty.

The mailbox receive queue is empty.

The sending thread sends a message that is placed in the mailbox send queue, which sorts messages by priority and time arrival order.

A consumer thread requests a message.

There are variants of these scenarios involving messages targeting particular threads and threads only interested in certain messages.

CHAPTER 5 MESSAGE QUEUES, PIPES, MAILBOXES, AND WORKQUEUES

Sending a Message

The sequence of steps followed when sending a message is perfectly logical. To send a message, the sending thread creates (acquires) the data it wishes to send, if any. It then creates a message descriptor characterizing the message to be sent.

Finally, the sending thread invokes the mailbox send API to start the message exchange. In the case that there already is a waiting compatible thread, the message is passed to that thread straight away; otherwise, the message is added to the send queue of the mailbox.

The mailbox send queue can contain multiple messages, and these are sorted according to the priority of the sending thread. Messages of equal priority are sorted in the order from the oldest to the most recent so that the oldest message can be received first.

In the case of a synchronous send operation, normal completion means that the receiving thread has received the message and has actually retrieved the message data. Where the message is not received before the timeout specified by the sending thread expires, then the message is removed from the send queue of the mailbox, and the send operation is considered to have failed.

When a send operation has completed successfully, the sending thread can find out which thread actually received the message by reading the `rx_source_thread` field of the message descriptor. Similarly, by reading the corresponding fields, it can find out how much data was actually exchanged and also the application-defined info value supplied by the receiving thread.

In synchronous transmission, once a message is received, there is no limit to the time the receiving thread may take to retrieve the message data and unblock the sending thread.

Hence, it is possible that a synchronous send operation may block the sending thread indefinitely, even when the thread specifies a maximum waiting period. This is because the timeout period only limits the amount

243

CHAPTER 5   MESSAGE QUEUES, PIPES, MAILBOXES, AND WORKQUEUES

of time the mailbox will wait for before the message is received by the other thread. The possibility of such a situation needs to be taken into account when implementing and testing an application using a mailbox.

In the case of an asynchronous send operation, the operation completes immediately, and the sending thread can continue doing something else. A sending thread may optionally specify a semaphore that the mailbox gives when the message is deleted by the mailbox, for example, immediately after the message has been received and its data has been retrieved by a receiving thread. The semaphore can be used as part of a flow control mechanism that ensures that the mailbox will, at any given point in time, hold no more than an application-specified number of messages from a sending thread (or a set of sending threads).

It is also worth noting that where a message is sent asynchronously, the sending thread has no way of determining which thread received the message, how much data was exchanged, or the application-defined info value supplied by the receiving thread.

The following code snippet shows the use of a mailbox to synchronously pass 4-byte random values to any consuming thread that needs a random value. In this case, because the message "info" field holds all of the data required, there is no need to make use of the data portion of the message.

```
void producer_thread(void) {
    struct k_mbox_msg send_msg;
    while (1) {
        /* generate random value to send */
        uint32_t some_random_value = sys_rand32_get();

        /* Set up the empty message to be sent*/
        send_msg.info = some_random_value;
        send_msg.size = 0;
        send_msg.tx_data = NULL;
        send_msg.tx_block.data = NULL;
```

CHAPTER 5   MESSAGE QUEUES, PIPES, MAILBOXES, AND WORKQUEUES

```
        send_msg.tx_target_thread = K_ANY;
        /* send message in synchronous mode */
        k_mbox_put(&some_mailbox, &send_msg, K_FOREVER);
    }
}
```

The next code snippet illustrates a coding idiom for synchronously sending data to a mailbox using a message buffer to any consumer thread that wishes to receive that data.

This code uses a mailbox to synchronously pass variable-sized requests from a producing thread to any consuming thread that wants it. Here, the message "info" field is used to exchange information about the maximum size message buffer that each thread can handle.

```
void producer_thread(void){
    char buffer[128];
    int buffer_bytes_used;
    struct k_mbox_msg send_msg;
    while (1) {
        /* generate/acquire the data to send */
        ...
        buffer_bytes_used = ... ;
        memcpy(buffer, data_to_send, buffer_bytes_used);

        /* fill out the k_mbox_msg fields */
        send_msg.info = buffer_bytes_used;
        send_msg.size = buffer_bytes_used;
        send_msg.tx_data = buffer;
        send_msg.tx_block.data = NULL;
        send_msg.tx_target_thread = K_ANY;

        /* send message in synchronous mode */
        k_mbox_put(&some_mailbox, &send_msg, K_FOREVER);
```

245

```
    /* on reaching here the info, size, and tx_
target_thread
        fields will have been updated */

    /* can then check whether the message data was
        fully received */
    if (send_msg.size < buffer_bytes_used) {
        printf("possible loss of data");
        printf("the receiver retrieved %d bytes", send_
        msg.info);
    }
  }
}
```

Receiving a Mailbox Message

The sequence of steps to be taken in order for a thread to receive a mailbox message is straightforward:

- First, the thread creates a message descriptor for the message it wishes to receive.

- It then uses the mailbox receive APIs to retrieve the message.

- The mailbox tries to satisfy the request by searching its send queue, and then in the case where a suitable message is present in the mailbox, it will take the message from the first compatible thread found.

CHAPTER 5   MESSAGE QUEUES, PIPES, MAILBOXES, AND WORKQUEUES

- Where there is no compatible thread, the receiving thread may choose to block for one to arrive, for the time specified in the API call. It is considered a failure if no compatible thread arrives before the expiry time limit is reached.

- Once the receive operation has completed, the receive thread can examine the message details in the message descriptor.

Multiple threads can wait concurrently on the receive queue of the mailbox.

- The threads are sorted in order of priority, and in the case of multiple threads with equal priorities, the thread chosen is the one that has been waiting the longest (i.e., the one that arrived first at the mailbox).

The order in which messages are received will be influenced by the thread compatibility constraints specified in the message descriptors. This may result in threads not necessarily being received in a FIFO order, for example, in a scenario where thread A is waiting to receive a message only from thread X and later on thread B arrives and waits to receive a message from thread Y. In this case, a message from thread Y directed to any thread will be passed to thread B, and thread A will continue waiting.

The receiving thread can control the amount of data it retrieves from the incoming message and where that data will be placed. The thread may, for example, choose to fetch all of the message data, or part of it or none at all.

The possible options for retrieving message data are either to retrieve the data at receive time or to retrieve the data into a designated message buffer at some later point in time.

CHAPTER 5   MESSAGE QUEUES, PIPES, MAILBOXES, AND WORKQUEUES

The following example will outline the idiom for retrieving data from the mailbox at receive time by specifying both the actual location and size of a message buffer when the message is received. In this case, the mailbox will copy the message data to the specified receive buffer as a part of the receive operation. If the size of the message buffer is less than the amount of data sent, then the uncopied data will be lost. Where the amount of data is less than the size of the buffer, then the unused portion of the buffer is left unchanged. The mailbox will update the message descriptor of the receiving thread with the number of bytes (if any) that were copied. The immediate data retrieval technique is well suited for handling small sized messages.

The following code snippet demonstrates a scenario involving using a mailbox to process variable-sized requests from any producing thread, using immediate data retrieval. The message "info" field provides data exchange information about the maximum size message buffer that each thread can handle.

```
void consumer_thread(void) {
    struct k_mbox_msg recv_msg;
    char buffer[128];
    int i;
    int total;
    while (1) {
        /* Set up the receive message fields */
        recv_msg.info = 128;
        recv_msg.size = 128;
        recv_msg.rx_source_thread = K_ANY;

        /* Synchronous retrieval of an arriving message */
        k_mbox_get(&some_mailbox, &recv_msg, buffer,
        K_FOREVER);
```

CHAPTER 5　MESSAGE QUEUES, PIPES, MAILBOXES, AND WORKQUEUES

```
    /* On reaching this section of code the
         info, size, and rx_source_thread fields will
         have been updated */

    /* Check that all the message data was received */
    if (recv_msg.info != recv_msg.size) {
        printf("Some data lost ");
        printf("sender tried to send %d bytes",
        recv_msg.info);
    }

    /* process the received data */
        ...
    }
}
```

The next code snippet illustrates a scenario where the retrieval of the message data takes place at some later point in time.

The receiving thread indicates its intention of retrieving the message data at some later point in time by specifying a message buffer location of NULL and a size indicating the maximum amount of data it is willing to retrieve later.

In this case, the mailbox will not copy any message data sent as part of the receive operation but will update the message descriptor of the receiving thread to indicate how many data bytes are available for retrieval.

The response scenario involving the receiving thread can be one of the following:

- If the message descriptor size is zero, then either the sender's message contained no data or the receiving thread did not want to receive any data. In this case, the receiving thread does not need to take any further action, as the mailbox will have already completed data retrieval and deleted the message.

249

CHAPTER 5   MESSAGE QUEUES, PIPES, MAILBOXES, AND WORKQUEUES

- If the message descriptor size is nonzero and the receiving thread intends to retrieve the data, it will call k_mbox_data_get() and provide a message buffer to hold the data. The mailbox will, then, copy the data into the message buffer and delete the message from the mailbox. If the message descriptor size is nonzero and the receiving thread does not wish to retrieve the data, the thread must call k_mbox_data_get() and specify a message buffer of NULL. In this case, the mailbox will delete the message without copying the data.

The code snippet that follows shows how to use the deferred data retrieval mechanism to fetch the message data from the producing thread if the message meets certain conditions. This mechanism, in effect, filters out unwanted messages. In this example, the message "info" field supplied by the sender acts as a message classifier.

```
void consumer_thread(void) {
    struct k_mbox_msg recv_msg;
    char buffer[10000];
    while (1) {
        /* prepare to receive message */
                recv_msg.size = 10000;
                recv_msg.rx_source_thread = K_ANY;
                /* get the message, but do not retrieve
                its data */
                k_mbox_get(&some_mailbox, &recv_msg, NULL,
                K_FOREVER);
                /* apply a message filter based on the info
                field */
            if (is_message_type_ok(recv_msg.info)) {
                /* retrieve message data and delete message */
                k_mbox_data_get(&recv_msg, buffer);
```

CHAPTER 5   MESSAGE QUEUES, PIPES, MAILBOXES, AND WORKQUEUES

```
        /* process data in "buffer" */
        ...
    } else {
        /* ignore message data and delete message */
        k_mbox_data_get(&recv_msg, NULL);
    }
  }
}
```

Introductory Zephyr Mailbox Example

The scenario in this example involves two threads: a sending thread and a receiving thread. The sending threads post chunks of text from a text file to a shared mailbox, and the receiving thread retrieves these chunks of text and displays them in a console using `printk()`.

In this example, a synchronous mode of transmission is used. Data is fetched by the receiving thread as soon as it arrives at the shared mailbox. In this example, the sending thread sends mail messages to a specific receiving thread, and the receiving thread receives messages from a specific sending thread. Using this example as a starting point, more elaborate Zephyr mailbox scenarios can be explored, as well as different schemes for allocating and managing buffer memory. As with the message queue example, button presses are used to drive the sending and receiving processes.

In the example shown here, the data being sent consists of the title-author and verses of Lewis Carroll's nonsense verse poem "Jabberwocky."

The data to be sent is set up as shown in the following code snippet:

CHAPTER 5   MESSAGE QUEUES, PIPES, MAILBOXES, AND WORKQUEUES

```
const char title[] = "Jabberwocky\nBy Lewis Carroll\n";
const char verse1[] = "\'Twas brillig, and the slithy toves\n\
tDid gyre and gimble in the wabe:\nAll mimsy were the
borogoves,\n\tAnd the mome raths outgrabe.\n";
const char verse2[] = "\"Beware the Jabberwock, my son!\n\tThe
jaws that bite, the claws that catch!\nBeware the Jubjub bird,
and shun\n\tThe frumious Bandersnatch!\"";
const char verse3[] = "He took his vorpal sword in hand;\n\
tLong time the manxome foe he sought—\nSo rested he by the
Tumtum tree\n\tAnd stood awhile in thought.\n";
const char verse4[] = "And, as in uffish thought he stood,\n\
tThe Jabberwock, with eyes of flame,\nCame whiffling through
the tulgey wood,\n\tAnd burbled as it came!\n";
const char verse5[] = "One, two! One, two! And through and
through\n\tThe vorpal blade went snicker-snack!\nHe left it
dead, and with its head\n\tHe went galumphing back.\n";
const char verse6[] = "\"And hast thou slain the Jabberwock?\n\
tCome to my arms, my beamish boy!\nO frabjous day! Callooh!
Callay!\"\n\tHe chortled in his joy.\n";
const char verse7[] = "\'Twas brillig, and the slithy toves\n\
tDid gyre and gimble in the wabe:\nAll mimsy were the
borogoves,\n\tAnd the mome raths outgrabe.";
const char* poem[] = {title, verse1, verse2, verse3, verse4,
verse5, verse6, verse7};
```

Global fixed-sized buffers are used for sending and receiving:

```
char mailbox_send_buffer[256];
char mailbox_receive_buffer[256];
```

and in this example, only one chunk of data is exchanged at a time. A good follow-on exercise would be to devise a scenario involving sending multiple messages to the mailbox and having multiple sender threads and multiple receiver threads.

CHAPTER 5   MESSAGE QUEUES, PIPES, MAILBOXES, AND WORKQUEUES

Convenience macros can be used to define the producer and consumer threads at compile time.

K_THREAD_DEFINE(mbox_sender_tid, STACKSIZE, senderTF, &shd_mbox, &b1_sem, poem, PRIORITY, 0, 0);

K_THREAD_DEFINE(mbox_receiver_tid, STACKSIZE, receiverTF, &shd_mbox, &b2_sem, NULL, PRIORITY, 0, 0);

The code for the sender thread will be something like the following:

```
void senderTF(struct k_mbox * shd_mbox_ptr, struct k_sem * postSem, char ** messages ){
     uint32_t pos = 0;
     uint32_t poem_part_data_len  = 0;
     uint32_t num_parts = sizeof(poem)/sizeof(char*);
     struct k_mbox_msg send_msg;
     int buffer_bytes_used;
     while(1) {
          k_sem_take(postSem, K_FOREVER);
          busy_sending = 1;
          printk("poem part %d\n", pos);
          printk("Sending %s \n", poem[pos]);
          poem_part_data_len =  strlen(poem[pos]) + 1;
          if(poem_part_data_len > 256) {
                    printk("Truncating message\n");
          }
          strncpy(mailbox_send_buffer, poem[pos], 255);
          printk("poem part length %d\n", poem_part_data_len);
          buffer_bytes_used = strlen(mailbox_send_buffer);
          send_msg.info = pos;
          send_msg.size = poem_part_data_len + 1;
                  send_msg.tx_data = mailbox_send_buffer;
```

CHAPTER 5   MESSAGE QUEUES, PIPES, MAILBOXES, AND WORKQUEUES

```
                send_msg.tx_block.data = NULL;
                send_msg.tx_target_thread = mbox_
                receiver_tid;
            k_mbox_put(shd_mbox_ptr, &send_msg, K_FOREVER);
            if (send_msg.size < buffer_bytes_used) {
                printk("possible loss of data");
                    printk("the receiver retrieved %d
                    bytes", send_msg.info);
                }
            pos = (pos + 1)%num_parts;
            busy_sending = 0;
        }
    }
}
```

In this code, the messages are destined for a specific target thread, namely, the receiver thread whose thread id is mbox_receiver_tid, and the data to be sent is copied into a designated buffer, mailbox_send_buffer. The sending is synchronous as the timeout period is K_FOREVER.

The code for the receiver thread will be something like the following:

```
void receiverTF(struct k_mbox * shd_mbox_ptr,
            struct k_sem * recvSem, void * param) {
    struct k_mbox_msg recv_msg;
    while (1) {
    /* Set up the receive message fields */
    recv_msg.size = 256;
    recv_msg.rx_source_thread = mbox_sender_tid;
    /* Synchronous retrieval of a mail message */
    k_mbox_get(shd_mbox_ptr, &recv_msg,
            mailbox_receive_buffer, K_FOREVER);
        busy_reading = 1;
    /* At this point the info, size, and rx_source_thread
```

CHAPTER 5   MESSAGE QUEUES, PIPES, MAILBOXES, AND WORKQUEUES

```
            fields will have been updated */
            printk("Received:\n%s", mailbox_receive_buffer);
            busy_reading = 0;
        }
}
```

Building and running this program produces output like the following:

```
*** Booting Zephyr OS build v3.1.99-ncs1-1  ***
Set up button at gpio@50000000 pin 11
Set up button at gpio@50000000 pin 12
Button1 pressed at 278817
button1 press sem give
poem part 0
Sending Jabberwocky
By Lewis Carroll

poem part length 30
Received:
Jabberwocky
By Lewis Carroll
Button2 pressed at 456169
Button1 pressed at 554245
button1 press sem give
poem part 1
Sending 'Twas brillig, and the slithy toves
       Did gyre and gimble in the wabe:
All mimsy were the borogoves,
       And the mome raths outgrabe.

poem part length 131
Received:
```

255

CHAPTER 5 MESSAGE QUEUES, PIPES, MAILBOXES, AND WORKQUEUES

```
'Twas brillig, and the slithy toves
        Did gyre and gimble in the wabe:
All mimsy were the borogoves,
        And the mome raths outgrabe.
Button1 pressed at 666316
button1 press sem give
poem part 2
Sending "Beware the Jabberwock, my son!
        The jaws that bite, the claws that catch!
Beware the Jubjub bird, and shun
        The frumious Bandersnatch!"
poem part length 137
Received:
"Beware the Jabberwock, my son!
        The jaws that bite, the claws that catch!
Beware the Jubjub bird, and shun
        The frumious Bandersnatch!"
```

Zephyr RTOS Workqueues

A workqueue is, essentially, a thread and a collection of workqueue items. It is a kernel object that uses a dedicated thread to process work items in a first in, first out manner. A work item contains a function pointer to the function that "does the work item work."

Workqueues provide a mechanism by which an ISR or high-priority thread can pass less urgent processing on to a thread of lower priority.

A project can have multiple workqueues, with each workqueue being referenced by its memory address. The priority of the workqueue thread is configurable, which means that it is possible to have either cooperative or preemptive workqueue threads depending on the project requirements. Whatever priority a workqueue thread has, it will yield between each

CHAPTER 5 MESSAGE QUEUES, PIPES, MAILBOXES, AND WORKQUEUES

submitted work item. This prevents a cooperative workqueue thread from starving out other threads.

A workqueue has to be initialized before it can be used. Initialization sets the queue to empty and spawns that workqueue's thread. A workqueue thread runs forever and sleeps when there are no work items in its queue of work items.

The "work" that is submitted to a workqueue is a "work handler" function. No explicit mechanism is provided for passing data to a work handler. One way in which data can be passed to a work handler is to place the work item inside a data structure that contains the data to be used by the work item. The data in the structure can, then, be accessed using the Zephyr CONTAINER_OF() macro, which is defined in include/zephyr/sys/util.h as follows:

```
#define CONTAINER_OF(ptr, type, field) \
      ((type *)(((char *)(ptr)) - offsetof(type, field)))
```

The offsetof() macro is part of the ANSI C library and can be found in stddef.h. It is used to obtain the offset (in bytes) of a given member of a struct or union type. It takes two parameters: first a structure name and secondly the name of a member inside that structure.

A Zephyr application already has a system workqueue, which can be used without having to create an application-specific workqueue. In an application, the system workqueue stack size can be configured by setting the value of CONFIG_SYSTEM_WORKQUEUE_STACK_SIZE to an appropriate value.

The following code snippet demonstrates how to place a work item in the system workqueue in response to a button press.

```
/*Define a button press work handler function */
void button_press_work_handler (struct k_work *work) {
      button_press_response();
}
```

```
/* Register the work handler */
K_WORK_DEFINE(button_press_work, button_press_work_handler);

/* Add a work item to the system workqueue from a button
interrupt handler function */
void button_pressed(const struct device *dev,
            struct gpio_callback *cb, uint32_t pins) {
    k_work_submit(&button_press_work);
}
```

Delayable Work

Zephyr provides a delayable work item that can be added to a workqueue. Such an item can be used by an ISR or a thread to schedule the processing of a work item after a specified time delay. A delayable work item contains a standard work item and a field specifying when and where the item should be submitted. A delayable work item is initialized and scheduled to a workqueue using the API functions and macros for delayable work. When a delayable work item is submitted to workqueue, the kernel starts a timeout mechanism that is triggered after the specified time delay has elapsed. When the timeout has triggered, the kernel submits the work item to workqueue specified. It will, then, be processed as a regular (normal) work item. The work handler used for delayable work receives a pointer to the underlying nondelayable work structure, which is not publicly accessible from k_work_delayable. To access an object that contains the delayable work object, an idiom such as that shown in the following code snippet can be used:

```
static void work_handler(struct k_work *work)
{
        struct k_work_delayable *dwork =
                k_work_delayable_from_work(work);
```

CHAPTER 5 MESSAGE QUEUES, PIPES, MAILBOXES, AND WORKQUEUES

```
    struct work_context *ctx =
            CONTAINER_OF(dwork, struct work_context,
                         timed_work);
    ...
}
```

Simple Workqueue Example 1

This example uses the button press interrupt handler code described earlier. Only a single button is involved.

When the button is pressed, the interrupt handler will add a work item to the system workqueue that will flash an LED associated with that button, led1, five times.

```
#define SW0_NODE DT_ALIAS(sw0)
#if !DT_NODE_HAS_STATUS(SW0_NODE, okay)
#error "Unsupported board: sw0 devicetree alias is not defined"
#endif
#define SLEEP_TIME_MS 200
static const struct gpio_dt_spec button1 = GPIO_DT_SPEC_GET_OR(SW0_NODE, gpios,{0});
static struct gpio_callback button1_cb_data;
extern void led_flash_work_handler(struct k_work *work);
K_WORK_DEFINE(button_press_work, led_flash_work_handler);
static struct gpio_dt_spec led1 = GPIO_DT_SPEC_GET_OR(DT_ALIAS(led0), gpios, {0});
```

The preceding code snippet checks that button 1 (sw0) is supported by the target board and defines the button 1 variable and the button 1 callback data button1_cb_data variable.

CHAPTER 5   MESSAGE QUEUES, PIPES, MAILBOXES, AND WORKQUEUES

The button 1 press event callback handler is defined as in the following code snippet:

```
void button1_pressed(const struct device *dev,
      struct gpio_callback *cb, uint32_t pins){
      printk("Button1 pressed at %" PRIu32 "\n",
      k_cycle_get_32());
      k_work_submit(&button_press_work);
      printk("Work submitted\n");
}
```

The button press work handler function that is in the k_work work item posted to the system workqueue is defined as in this code snippet:

```
void led_flash_work_handler (struct k_work *work) {
      uint32_t num_flashes = 5;
      int ret;
      int i;
      for (i = 0; i < num_flashes; i++) {
            ret = gpio_pin_toggle_dt(&led1);
            if (ret < 0) {return;}
            k_msleep(SLEEP_TIME_MS);
            ret = gpio_pin_toggle_dt(&led1);
            if (ret < 0) {return;}
            k_msleep(SLEEP_TIME_MS);
      }
}
```

The main() function sets up led1 and button 1 and the button press interrupt callback function, using the same approach as shown in an earlier example.

Building and running this code will send output such as the following to the console:

```
*** Booting Zephyr OS build v3.1.99-ncs1-1  ***
Set up button at gpio@50000000 pin 11
Set up LED at gpio@50000000 pin 13
Button1 pressed at 133805
Work submitted
Button1 pressed at 215116
Work submitted
Button1 pressed at 292387
Work submitted
```

and led1 will flash five times when button 1 is pressed.

Simple Workqueue Example 2

This example is similar to the preceding example, except that in this case, a delayed item of work is submitted to the system workqueue. The delay time is set to five seconds. The result is that after button 1 is pressed, there is a delay of five seconds before the led flashing sequence is displayed.

The code for this example is very similar to that for example 1 except that the delayed work submission API is used.

The following code snippet shows the details of setting up the button press interrupt handler to submit a delayed workqueue work item:

```
#define SLEEP_TIME_MS 200
#define DELAY_TIME_MS 5000

static const struct gpio_dt_spec button1 = GPIO_DT_SPEC_GET_OR(SW0_NODE, gpios,{0});
static struct gpio_callback button1_cb_data;
extern void led_flash_work_handler(struct k_work *work);
```

CHAPTER 5   MESSAGE QUEUES, PIPES, MAILBOXES, AND WORKQUEUES

```
K_WORK_DELAYABLE_DEFINE(delayed_button_press_work,
                       led_flash_work_handler);
static struct gpio_dt_spec led1 =
    GPIO_DT_SPEC_GET_OR(DT_ALIAS(led0), gpios,{0});

void button1_pressed(const struct device *dev,
     struct gpio_callback *cb, uint32_t pins){
    printk("Button1 pressed at %" PRIu32 "\n", k_cycle_get_32());
    k_work_schedule(&delayed_button_press_work,
                    K_MSEC(DELAY_TIME_MS));
    printk("Work submitted\n");
}
```

The K_WORK_DELAYABLE_DEFINE macro is used to create a delayable work item that will call the led_flash_work_handler when invoked.

```
K_WORK_DELAYABLE_DEFINE(delayed_button_press_work,
                       led_flash_work_handler);
```

The delayed work is submitted using the API function k_work_schedule and providing a pointer to the work item and the required time delay as arguments.

```
k_work_schedule(&delayed_button_press_work,
                K_MSEC(DELAY_TIME_MS));
```

When the application is built and run, the led flash sequence will start five seconds after the button press. The output sent to the console will be something like the following:

```
*** Booting Zephyr OS build v3.1.99-ncs1-1  ***
Set up button at gpio@50000000 pin 11
Set up LED at gpio@50000000 pin 13
```

```
Button1 pressed at 284551
Work submitted
Button1 pressed at 536600
Work submitted
```

Simple Workqueue Example 3

This example involves buttons 1 and 2. When button 1 is pressed, the interrupt callback submits a work item to the workqueue and passes the led to flash and the number of flashes to the work item function. It does this by using a data structure that contains a data structure that contains a data structure containing the led number and the number of flashes information and a k_work work item and then accessing this information in the work item function using the CONTAINER_OF macro described previously.

The buttons and leds are set up as shown previously. The work items are defined as shown in the next code snippet:

```
extern void led_flash_work_handler(struct k_work *work);
typedef struct work_details {
    uint32_t led_num;
    uint32_t num_flashes;
} work_data;

typedef struct parameterised_work {
    struct k_work work_to_do;
    work_data work_info;
} parameterised_work_instance;

parameterised_work_instance parameterised_work_instance1;
parameterised_work_instance parameterised_work_instance2;

K_WORK_DEFINE(button_press_work1, led_flash_work_handler);
K_WORK_DEFINE(button_press_work2, led_flash_work_handler);
```

CHAPTER 5 MESSAGE QUEUES, PIPES, MAILBOXES, AND WORKQUEUES

The button press interrupt handlers for buttons 1 and 2 are shown next:

```
void button1_pressed(const struct device *dev,
      struct gpio_callback *cb,uint32_t pins){
      printk("Button1 pressed at %" PRIu32 "\n",
      k_cycle_get_32());
      k_work_submit(&parameterised_work_instance1.work_to_do);
      printk("Work submitted\n");
}

void button2_pressed(const struct device *dev,
      struct gpio_callback *cb,uint32_t pins){
      printk("Button2 pressed at %" PRIu32 "\n",
      k_cycle_get_32());
      k_work_submit(&parameterised_work_instance2.work_to_do);
      printk("Work submitted\n");
}
```

Each handler is passed the work item via a pointer to the parameterized work instance structure it is embedded in (i.e., a pointer to a field inside an instance of a data structure, e.g., k_work_submit(&parameterised_work_instance1.work_to_do); for button 1).

Inside the work handler code, the CONTAINER_OF macro is used to get at the parameters that the work handler function is to use. The led number and the number of flashes can then be obtained. The code for the work handler is as follows:

```
void led_flash_work_handler(struct k_work *work_item) {
      uint32_t num_flashes;
      uint32_t led_num;
      int ret;
      int i;
```

CHAPTER 5   MESSAGE QUEUES, PIPES, MAILBOXES, AND WORKQUEUES

```
parameterised_work_instance * pwi_p;
pwi_p = CONTAINER_OF(work_item, struct parameterised_work,\
work_to_do);
num_flashes = (pwi_p->work_info).num_flashes;
led_num = (pwi_p->work_info).led_num;
struct gpio_dt_spec * pled;
switch (led_num) {
      case 1:
            pled = &led1;
            break;
      case 2:
            pled = &led2;
            break;
      default:
            pled = NULL;
            printk("Invalid led\n");
            break;
}

if (pled != NULL) {
      for (i = 0; i < num_flashes; i++) {
            ret = gpio_pin_toggle_dt(pled);
            if (ret < 0) {
                  return;
            }
            k_msleep(SLEEP_TIME_MS);
            ret = gpio_pin_toggle_dt(pled);
            if (ret < 0) {
                  return;
            }
```

CHAPTER 5   MESSAGE QUEUES, PIPES, MAILBOXES, AND WORKQUEUES

```
            k_msleep(SLEEP_TIME_MS);
        }
    }
}
```

parameterised_work_instance1 and parameterised_work_instance2 are initialised in main as shown here:

```
parameterised_work_instance1.work_to_do = button_press_work1;
parameterised_work_instance1.work_info.led_num = 1;
parameterised_work_instance1.work_info.num_flashes = 4;

parameterised_work_instance2.work_to_do = button_press_work2;
parameterised_work_instance2.work_info.led_num = 2;
parameterised_work_instance2.work_info.num_flashes = 7;
```

When the application is built and run, pressing button 1 will result in led1 flashing four times, and pressing button 2 will result in led2 flashing seven times.

The output sent to the console should be something like the following:

```
*** Booting Zephyr OS build v3.1.99-ncs1-1  ***
Set up button at gpio@50000000 pin 11
Set up button at gpio@50000000 pin 12
Set up LED at gpio@50000000 pin 13
Set up LED at gpio@50000000 pin 14
Button1 pressed at 207499
Work submitted
Button2 pressed at 431291
Work submitted
```

Summary

This chapter has introduced key Zephyr RTOS mechanisms (message queues, mailboxes, and pipes) for moving data around in multithreading applications and the synchronization and interprocess communications made possible by using these mechanisms. The various examples explored showed coding idioms and patterns that can be used to provide both synchronization between a producer and a consumer (sender and receiver) as well as temporary storage of data where necessary, and also for the movement of data and information from interrupt handles to threads that consume that data. These idioms and patterns can then be incorporated into more complex real-world applications.

CHAPTER 6

Using Filesystems in Zephyr Applications

Many IoT and IIoT systems and applications running on them fall into the "middle ground" where bare metal multitasking has implications from the point of view of "cross-platform" portability and the use of standardized APIs (Application Programming Interfaces). Applications using systems in this "middle ground" have, sometimes, a requirement to store persistent information in a "structured way" using some kind of file system.

SRAM is a limited resource in the kinds of systems being considered here, and hence, implementing a small file system in RAM may not be an optimal solution.

The file systems discussed in this section, FatFs and LittleFS, are, typically, built on top of QSPI flash memory, or on SD/MMC card-based systems.

This chapter will begin by introducing QSPI flash and SD/MMC and how they are supported in Zephyr RTOS. This will be followed by an introduction and overview of FatFs and LittleFS filesystems and how these are supported in Zephyr RTOS.

This, in turn, will be followed by an introduction and overview of Zephyr RTOS support for a "generic POSIX-like" file system API.

CHAPTER 6 USING FILESYSTEMS IN ZEPHYR APPLICATIONS

Quad-SPI (QSPI)

Quad-SPI [3, 6-9] is, essentially, a serial interface standard, which uses four data lines to read, write, and erase flash memory chips. A QSPI device (peripheral) can be used to interface with flash memory that supports QSPI.

The diagram shown in Figure 6-1 from the ARM mbed-os documentation (4) illustrates a typical configuration.

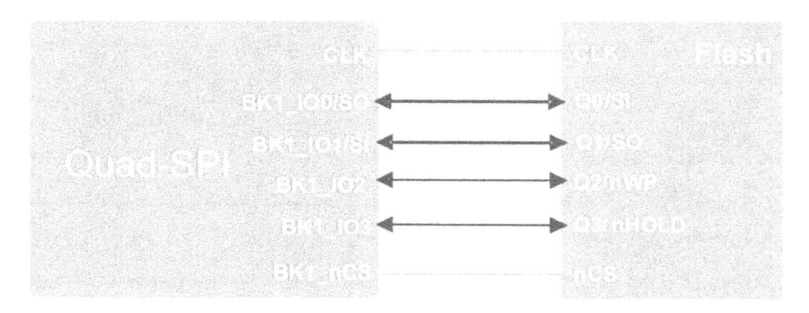

Figure 6-1. Typical Quad-SPI configuration

SPI as Quad-SPI uses four data lines (I0, I1, I2, and I3) as opposed to two data lines (MOSI and MISO) in traditional SPI.

SPI has a data transfer rate of up to 16 Mbps, which is quite sufficient for use cases such as the reading of data from sensors and the sending of data to actuators or output devices.

However, traditional SPI has limitations when it comes to its use as a bus for transferring data to and from flash memory. Although flash memory is cheap and durable (an attractive option when it comes to embedded system applications), it is inherently slow, and flash devices are not capable of sending data at the maximum data rates that SPI is capable of. Prior to the development of QSPI, acceptably high data transfer rates for transferring data from flash memory were based on using parallel memory involving 8, 16, or 32 pins (depending on the address range) to connect external memory devices with the microcontroller. The disadvantages

CHAPTER 6   USING FILESYSTEMS IN ZEPHYR APPLICATIONS

of such an approach were that it resulted in more complicated PCB designs and the need to devote a block of pins exclusively for use with one particular chip to achieve fast performance. But this approach had two major cons.

The QSPI approach was to modify SPI protocols to use two extra and to have all the four data lines bidirectional.

Whereas regular normal SPI uses separate data lines for input and output (MISO and MOSI), the Quad-SPI interface configures the data lines dynamically so that they can best be used as outputs to send data to flash memory, or as inputs to read data from flash memory. The switch from input to output takes two clock cycles, as shown in Figure 6-2.

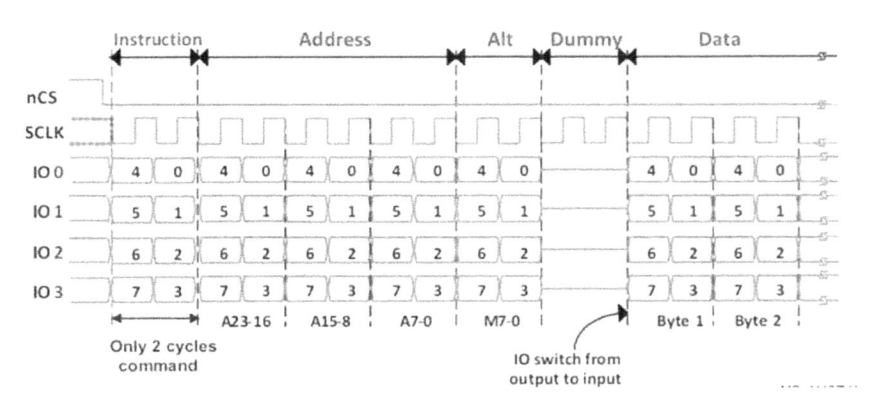

Figure 6-2.   *Quad-SPI clock cycle traces*

Four bits are transferred every clock cycle, and the bit order is that in the first clock cycle, IO0 sends bit0, IO1 sends bit1, and in the second clock cycle, bits 4, 5, 6, and 7 are sent. In effect, a byte can be transmitted in just two clock cycles.

QSPI also defines a double data rate mode, in which the voltage on the data line can change on both the rising edge and the falling edge, the effect of which is to send 2 bits per clock cycle, which doubles the effective transmission rate.

CHAPTER 6   USING FILESYSTEMS IN ZEPHYR APPLICATIONS

This is shown schematically in the diagram in Figure 6-3. In this diagram the top line (trace) is the clock cycle. For dual mode to work, it has to be supported on both the microcontroller and the flash chip.

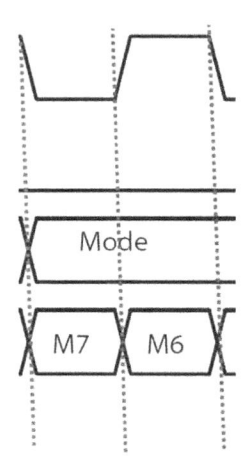

Figure 6-3. QSPI double data rate mode

Modern flash chips are, typically, both SPI and QSPI pin compatible.

The advantages of using Quad-SPI are that it involves a smaller pin count than solutions using a parallel memory bus and that it is possible to link multiple devices to a single QSPI interface, with a chip select pin being used to select a particular device.

The details of QSPI on a particular processor are manufacturer dependent and may include features such as DMA (Direct Memory Access) support. The low-level chip-specific driver code is accessed via suitable HAL (Hardware Abstraction Layer) code provided by the chip vendor.

The next two sections will overview QSPI support in example Nordic Semiconductor and STM32 devices.

The QSPI peripheral in the Nordic nRF52840 processor is a versatile device that supports single/dual/quad SPI input/output, has a clock frequency configurable in the range 2–32 MHz, supports single-word

CHAPTER 6   USING FILESYSTEMS IN ZEPHYR APPLICATIONS

read/write access from/to external flash, and supports DMA (using the Nordic EasyDMA DMA architecture) for block read and write transfers. EasyDMA enables a read rate of up to 16 MB/sec EasyDMA read rate. In addition, the Nordic nRF52840 QSPI peripheral allows for Execute in Place (XIP) execution of program code directly from external flash. A key advantage of XIP is that the code to be executed does not need to be loaded into RAM or processor flash code memory. This is depicted in Figure 6-4.

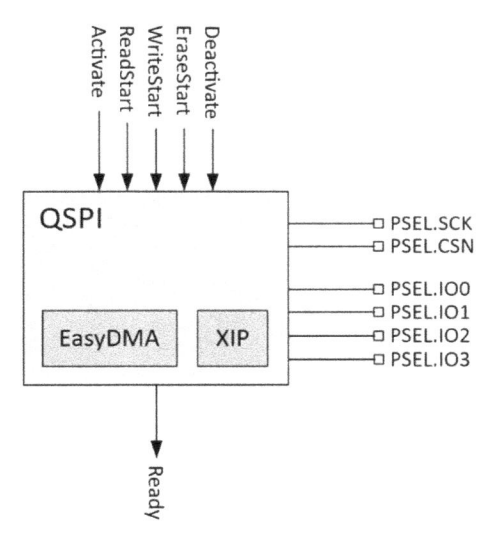

Figure 6-4. *QSPI and Execute in Place (XIP)*

In order to use the QSPI peripheral to execute in place (XIP), the start address of the XIP memory region must be mapped to start at the address XIPOFFSET of external flash (see Figure 6-5).

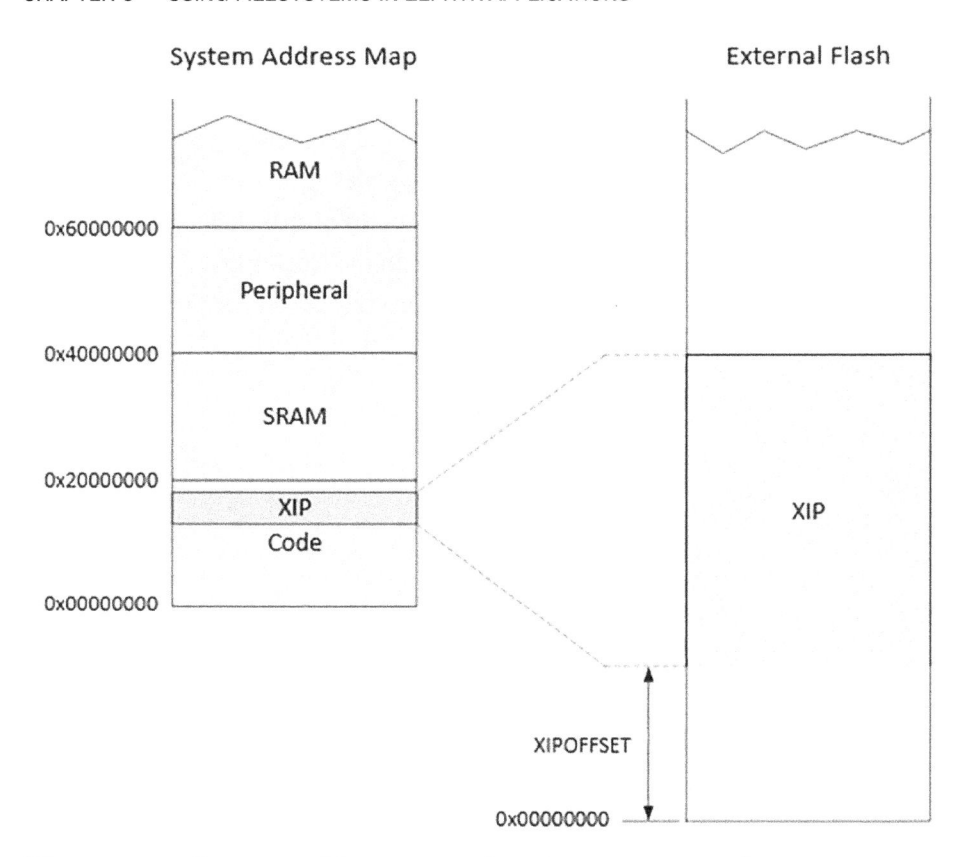

CHAPTER 6   USING FILESYSTEMS IN ZEPHYR APPLICATIONS

Figure 6-5. *System Address Map showing mapping of XIP memory*

Further information on the use of QSPI with Nordic Semiconductor devices can be found in the Nordic Semiconductor documentation [1, 2].

There are variations in how QSPI is implemented in other processor architectures, such as the STM32 family of processors. The details for the QSPI peripheral implementations in various members of the STM32 processor family are given in the ST AN4760 application note, "Quad-SPI interface on STM32 microcontrollers and microprocessors" [3].

The details differ between different processor family members. As an example, the STM32F4 system architecture is built around a 32-bit multilayer AHB bus matrix that interconnects multiple masters to multiple

CHAPTER 6   USING FILESYSTEMS IN ZEPHYR APPLICATIONS

slaves. The external Quad-SPI memory can be accessed by the Cortex-M4 processor through the S-bus. The Quad-SPI peripheral is accessible by all the masters on the AHB bus matrix such as DMA1, DMA2, USB OTG HS, MAC Ethernet, LTDC, and DMA2D. Access to the Quad-SPI can be either a registers-based access or a memory-mapped region access and can use DMA where necessary.

The schematic in Figure 6-6 illustrates how the QSPI device fits into the processor architecture.

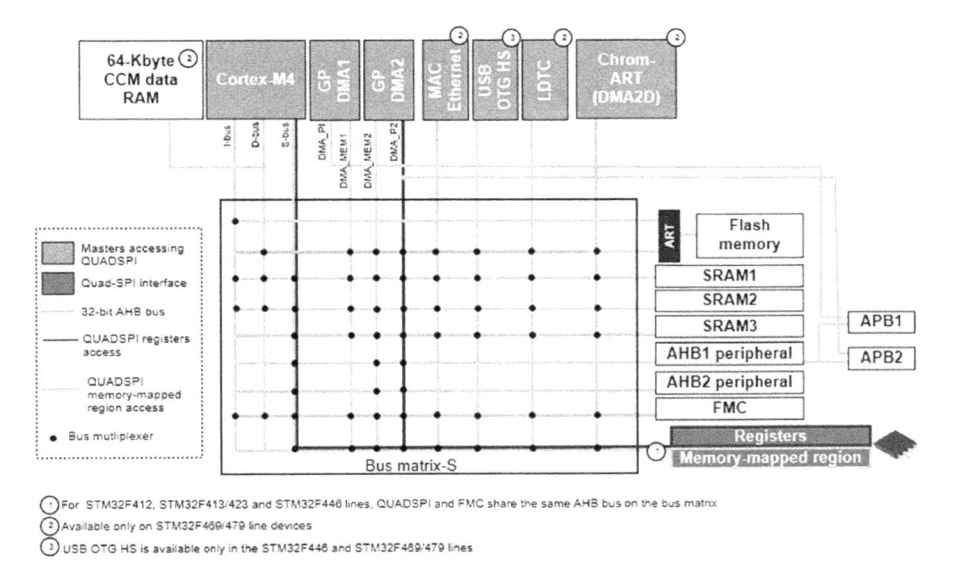

Figure 6-6. QSPI in STM32 processors

The driver code for working with QSPI flash in Nordic devices is in the source code file zephyr/drivers/flash/nrf_qspi_nor.c, and that for working with QSPI flash in STM32 devices is in the source code file zephyr/drivers/flash/flash_stm32_qspi.c.

275

CHAPTER 6   USING FILESYSTEMS IN ZEPHYR APPLICATIONS

SDC and MMC Cards

SDC and MMC cards essentially consist of a flash memory array combined with an on-card (micro)controller inside. The flash memory operations such as reading, writing, erasing, wear levelling, and error handling and reporting take place inside the memory card. The transfer of data between the memory card and the host controller takes place as 512-byte data block transfers. In essence, it is possible, from the perspective of upper-layer software, to think of an SDC or MMC care as a kind of generic hard drive.

The block diagram in Figure 6-7 illustrates, schematically, the architecture of SDC and MMC cards.

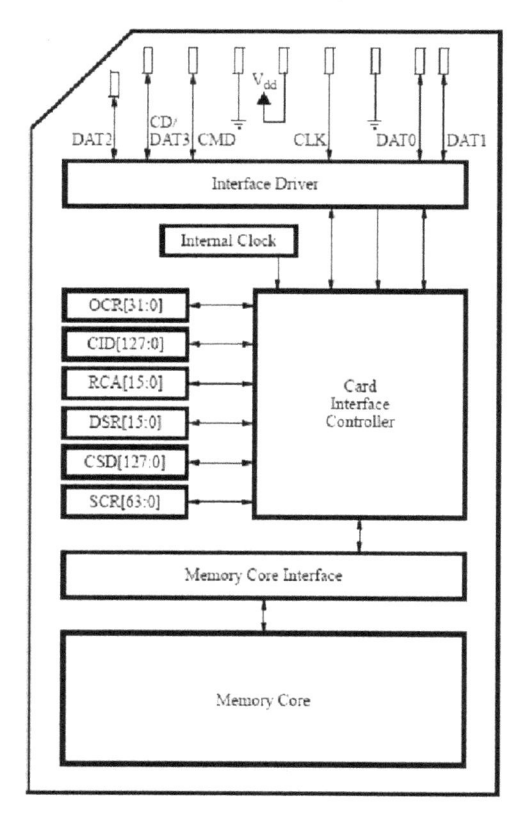

Figure 6-7. Schematic of architecture of SDC and MMC cards

CHAPTER 6   USING FILESYSTEMS IN ZEPHYR APPLICATIONS

Zephyr RTOS supports a number of SD card controllers and also provides support for interfacing SD cards over SPI. The drivers make use of the disk driver interface so that a file system can access the SD cards via the disk access API. Zephyr supports both standard and high-capacity SD cards.

The current Zephyr firmware does not support inserting or removing cards while the system is running, which means that the cards used must be present at boot time and must not be removed while the system is running.

The Zephyr SD Memory Card (SDMMC) subsystem is used transparently by the Zephyr RTOS disk driver API. It can also be used to access data in a memory card directly at the block level. The SDMMC subsystem uses the SD host controller API to communicate with an attached SD card.

SD Card Support via SPI

To build an application that accesses an SD card via SPI, it is necessary to add an appropriate fragment to the devicetree that will add an SD card node to the given processor SPI interface. An introduction to devicetree configuration is given in a following chapter. The devicetree snippet shown shows setting up pin PA27 for chip select and running the SPI bus at 24 MHz once the SD card has been initialized:

```
&spi1 {
        status = "okay";
        cs-gpios = <&porta 27 GPIO_ACTIVE_LOW>;

        sdhc0: sdhc@0 {
                compatible = "zephyr,sdhc-spi-slot";
                reg = <0>;
                status = "okay";
```

```
            label = "SDHC_0";
            mmc {
                compatible = "zephyr,sdmmc-disk";
                status = "okay";
                label = "SDMMC_0";
            };
            spi-max-frequency = <24000000>;
        };
    };
};
```

With a correct devicetree configuration, when the application is built, the SD card will be detected and initialized by the filesystem driver automatically when the board boots.

Zephyr RTOS Disk Access API

The config option is `CONFIG_DISK_ACCESS`.

The API has a function for initialization prior to making any IO calls, `int disk_access_init(const char *pdrv)` where pdrv is the disk name.

There is also a function for retrieving disk status, `int disk_access_status(const char *pdrv)`.

The function that reads data from the disk to a memory buffer is

```
int disk_access_read(const char *pdrv, uint8_t *data_buf,
    uint32_t start_sector, uint32_t num_sector)
```

where `pdrv` is the disk name, `data_buf` is a pointer to the memory buffer into which to put the data that is read, `start_sector` is the starting disk sector to read from, and `num_sector` is the number of disk sectors to be read.

The corresponding write function is

```
int disk_access_write(const char *pdrv, const uint8_t *data_buf,
     uint32_t start_sector, uint32_t num_sector)
```

There is also an `ioctl` function `int disk_access_ioctl(const char *pdrv, uint8_t cmd, void *buff)` that can be used for getting disk parameters and configuring disk parameters.

Zephyr File System API

The Zephyr RTOS file system API is based on the concept of a Virtual Filesystem Switch (VFS), which is used by applications to mount multiple file systems at different mount points such as /fatfs and /lfs. for example.

The mount point is a data structure that contains the information required to instantiate, mount, and operate on a file system. The File System Switch decouples the application from having to directly access the specific API of a given file system. In Zephyr, the file system implementation or library is plugged into or pulled out through a file system registration API. A file system implementation has a globally unique integer identifier. FS_TYPE_EXTERNAL_BASE is used to avoid clashes with in-tree identifiers.

```
int fs_register(int type, const struct fs_file_system_t *fs);
int fs_unregister(int type, const struct fs_file_system_t *fs);
```

The mount point is used as the disk volume name, and it is this which is used by the file system library when formatting or mounting a disk.

A file system is declared as shown in the following code snippet:

```
static struct fs_mount_t mp = {
     .type = FS_FATFS,
```

CHAPTER 6   USING FILESYSTEMS IN ZEPHYR APPLICATIONS

```
        .mnt_point = FATFS_MNTP,
        .fs_data = &fat_fs,
};
```

Here, FS_FATFS is the file system type such as FatFs or LittleFS; for example, FATFS_MNTP is the mount point at which the file system will be mounted, and fat_fs is the file system data that is used by the fs_mount() API.

The Zephyr file system API is very similar to the standard POSIX file system API. The handle to access a given filesystem is a pointer to a data structure of type struct fs_file_t, and it is initialized, prior to first use, with fs_file_t_init().

```
static inline void fs_file_t_init(struct fs_file_t *zfp)
```

For file directories, a struct fs_dir_t type variable is initialized with fs_dir_t_init() prior to calling fs_opendir().

```
static inline void fs_dir_t_init(struct fs_dir_t *zdp)
```

A file is referred to via a struct fs_file_t instance and is opened/created with fs_open() and associated with a data stream.

```
int fs_open(struct fs_file_t *zfp, const char *file_name, fs_mode_t flags)
```

The flags can be 0 or a binary combination of one or more of FS_O_READ open for read, FS_O_WRITE open for write, FS_O_RDWR open for read/write (FS_O_READ | FS_O_WRITE), FS_O_CREATE to create a file if it does not exist, and FS_O_APPEND to move to the end of the file before each write. If flags are set to 0, the function will attempt to open an existing file with no read/write access; this may be used to, for example, check if the file exists.

- `fs_open()` returns 0 on success, -EBUSY if the file is already in use, -EINVAL if the file name is invalid, -EROFS if trying to open a read-only file for write, or attempting to create a file on a system that has been mounted with the FS_MOUNT_FLAG_READ_ONLY flag, -ENOENT if the file path is not possible (because of a bad mount point for example), -ENOTSUP if not implemented by an underlying file system driver. Negative errno codes are dependent on the file system backend being used. A file is closed using `int fs_close(struct fs_file_t *zfp)` and unlinked/deleted using `int fs_unlink(const char *path)`.

Files and directories can be renamed using `int fs_rename(const char *from, const char *to)`.

The source path (`from`) can refer to either a file or a directory. All intermediate directories in the destination path must already exist. If the source path refers to a file, the destination path must contain a full file name path, not just the new parent directory. Where an object already exists at the specified destination path, it will be unlinked prior to the renaming operation taking effect (i.e., the preexisting file at the destination location is deleted). In Zephyr RTOS (currently), files cannot be moved between different mount points.

`fs_read()` is used to read data from a file:

`ssize_t fs_read(struct fs_file_t *zfp, void *ptr, size_t size)`

`fs_read()` reads up to size bytes of data to ptr pointed buffer and returns number of bytes read, and the return value, the number of bytes actually read, may be less than the number of bytes requested if fewer bytes were available at the time of the read request.

CHAPTER 6   USING FILESYSTEMS IN ZEPHYR APPLICATIONS

Data is written to a file with `fs_write()`:

```
ssize_t fs_write(struct fs_file_t *zfp, const void *ptr,
size_t size)
```

The return value is the number of bytes actually written. If a negative value is returned from the function, the file pointer has not been advanced, and if the function returns a non-negative number that is lower than size (the number of bytes to be written), then the global `errno` variable should be checked for an error code, as the device may not have sufficient free space for storing all of the data to be written.

Conceptually, a file can be thought of as a large array of bytes, and when traversing a file, a (conceptual) cursor tracks the current position in the file. The `fs_seek()` function is used to move the cursor to a new file location.

```
int fs_seek(struct fs_file_t *zfp, off_t offset, int whence)
```

The offset is added to file position based on the whence parameter, which can be one of FS_SEEK_SET for the beginning of the file, FS_SEEK_CUR for the current position, and FS_SEEK_END for the end of the file. `fs_tell()` can be used to retrieve the current file position, `off_t fs_tell(struct fs_file_t *zfp)`.

There is also an `fs_truncate()` function that can be used to truncate or extend an open file to some given size.

```
int fs_truncate(struct fs_file_t *zfp, off_t length)
```

The `fs_sync()` function can be used to flush cached write data buffers of an open file.

```
int fs_sync(struct fs_file_t *zfp)
```

A typical use case is to make sure that data gets written to the storage media immediately, for example, to avoid data loss should the power be removed unexpectedly.

CHAPTER 6   USING FILESYSTEMS IN ZEPHYR APPLICATIONS

Working with Directories

A new directory can be created with `fs_mkdir()`:

    int fs_mkdir(const char *path)

where path is the path to the directory to be created, and `fs_readdir()` can be used to read the entries of an open directory.

    int fs_readdir(struct fs_dir_t *zdp, struct fs_dirent *entry)

Directories can be closed using `fs_closedir()`:

    int fs_closedir(struct fs_dir_t *zdp)

The `fs_mount()` command, `int fs_mount(struct fs_mount_t *mp)`, is used for mounting a file system and adding the mount point to the system list of mounted file systems. `fs_unmount()` can be used to unmount a filesystem:

    int fs_unmount(struct fs_mount_t *mp)

The remaining file system API functions are `fs_readmount()`, which iterates through a list of mount points and returns the directory name of the mount point at the given index; `fs_stat()`, which checks the status of a file or directory specified by the path argument; and `fs_statvfs()`, which can be used to obtain the total and available space in the file system volume.

File systems need to be registered with a virtual file system. This is done using

    int fs_register(int type, const struct fs_file_system_t *fs)

The number of allowed file system types to be registered can be controlled with the `CONFIG_FILE_SYSTEM_MAX_TYPES` Kconfig option.

CHAPTER 6   USING FILESYSTEMS IN ZEPHYR APPLICATIONS

File Systems – A High-Level Overview

File systems, essentially, organize storage on disk drives. From the system point of view, the typical file system design is a layered design. The lowest layer is provided by the physical devices on which the file system is installed. Above this layer is an I/O control layer and its associated low-level device drivers. The next layer is the basic file system–level layer that is concerned with retrieving and storing raw blocks of data. Raw blocks or data are read and written without needing to know exactly what is present in each block. The next level up is associated with file organization. A file organization module is aware about files, their logical blocks, and how these map to physical blocks on the disk. Its responsibilities include the translation from logical to physical blocks, maintaining a list of free blocks and allocating free blocks to files as required. The logical file system layer deals with file details (file metadata), which are distinct from the data held in the file itself.

The main advantage of a layered approach to file system realization is that it makes it possible for the same code to be used on various different file systems and only for some file system–specific layers. See Figure 6-8.

CHAPTER 6　USING FILESYSTEMS IN ZEPHYR APPLICATIONS

application programs
⇩
logical file system
⇩
file-organization module
⇩
basic file system
⇩
I/O control
⇩
devices

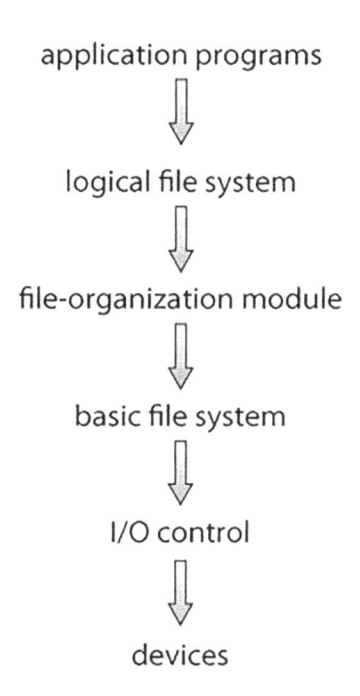

Figure 6-8. *Conceptual diagram showing a layered approach to file systems*

Overview of the FAT File System and FatFs

FAT file system stands for file allocation table (FAT) file system. The original design and implementation was credited to Bill Gates and Marc McDonald. FAT specifies a format and procedures for storing and organizing files on some kind of storage device, which can be, for example, a disk drive or some kind of memory-based storage device. FAT filesystem software provides APIs for accessing files and directories, time stamping file creation or file modification time, and retrieving and storing file attributes such as file size and file read/write attributes, for example, a file may be a read-only file, whether a file should be hidden in the context of displaying the contents of a directory. A fairly detailed history of the origins

CHAPTER 6   USING FILESYSTEMS IN ZEPHYR APPLICATIONS

and evolution of FAT can be found on Wikipedia (https://en.wikipedia.org/wiki/File_Allocation_Table). The technical details of FAT and how its design evolved are described in this Wikipedia article: https://en.wikipedia.org/wiki/Design_of_the_FAT_file_system.

Originally FAT was developed for use with floppy disks, and, later, it was extended to cope with larger hard disk drives. Thus, there are various versions of FAT oriented to file systems of different sizes and include FAT12 (12-bit version – introduced in 1980), FAT16 (16-bit version – introduced in 1984 with DOS 3.0–based PCs), and FAT32 (32-bit version with 28 bits used – introduced in 1996 in Windows 95 OSR2).

Descriptions of file systems include terms such as sector and cluster. A sector is a disk drive unit of storage. It depends on the drive and is typically 256 bytes for a RAM disk and 512 bytes for a hard disk. A cluster is a file system unit of storage and is, typically, an integer multiple of the sector size.

Blocks in a file system can be allocated using a contiguous allocation strategy where all the blocks of a file are contiguous, or a linked allocation strategy where file data blocks are stored as a linked list. FAT uses a linked list approach as shown in the schematic featured in Figure 6-9.

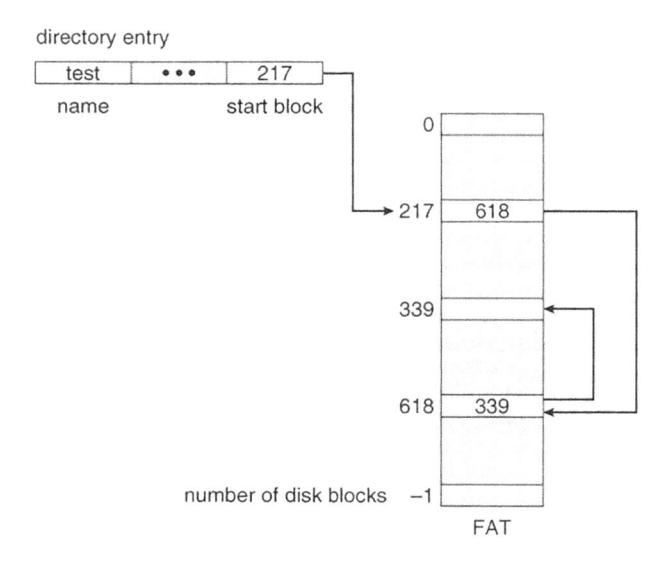

Figure 6-9. *Block allocation in FatFs*

CHAPTER 6   USING FILESYSTEMS IN ZEPHYR APPLICATIONS

The implementation of FAT that is used in many embedded system applications is the one implemented by ChaN, and this is the FAT implementation used in Zephyr RTOS.

FatFs is implemented in ANSI C so as to make it easy to port to a variety of processor architectures. The FatFs code is also designed to be thread safe so as to make it suitable for use in embedded operating systems–based applications. FatFs is not dependent on any particular operating system platform or storage medium and defines a media interface for communication with storage device control modules.

The implementation of the interface for a given device control module is implementation dependent. This approach, in which the user application abstractions and the platform code are separated and where the low-level disk I/O layer (driver) must be implemented separately, means that an application system can have several storage devices, each with their own specific driver. An application needs to ensure that when it is built, the correct libraries and drivers are installed, but from the point of view of the application developer, it is a standard API that is used, and the details of the underlying physical media are hidden.

A minimum driver layer implementation must provide support for the disk_status, disk_initialize, and disk_read interfaces.

disk_status returns the block device status information, disk_initialize initializes the physical device, and disk_read reads blocks of data from the physical device.

A fuller driver layer implementation will also provide support for disk_write(), which writes sector(s) to the disk; disk_ioctl(), which controls device-specified features, and get_fattime(), which returns the current time.

CHAPTER 6   USING FILESYSTEMS IN ZEPHYR APPLICATIONS

Overview of the LittleFS File System

LittleFS is a little fail-safe filesystem for microcontrollers. The original implementation was to experimentally gain knowledge about how to implement a file system that is resilient to power loss and that implements flash wear levelling and, furthermore, one whose implementation uses a limited amount of memory. The typical systems targeted by LittleFS are 32-bit microcontrollers with about 32 KiB of RAM and 512 KiB of ROM and which may, in addition, be paired with SPI NOR flash chips providing about 4 MiB of flash storage.

The key features of LittleFS, namely, power-loss resilience, wear levelling, and small code size, arise because power loss when the embedded system is running may occur at any time, writing to flash memory is destructive, and embedded systems have limited amounts of memory, both RAM and ROM. Corruption of any persistent data structures as a result of power loss may result in an unrecoverable device. Repeatedly writing to the same block of flash memory (i.e., not implementing wear levelling) will cause that block to wear out. Not taking flash memory wear into account when storing frequently updated metadata may result in early failure of a device. Limited device memory means that techniques relying on storing relatively large amounts of temporary filesystem metadata are infeasible.

The design and implementation approaches used in the development of LittleFS are described in detail on the LittleFS GitHub site [4].

Walkthrough of a LittleFS Example Program

This section will explore the LittleFS example provided in the Zephyr source code repository [5]. The example involves creating and mounting a QSPI-based file system on an nRF52840 DK development board, using the SOC (System on Chip) flash memory. The filesystem example involves

CHAPTER 6 USING FILESYSTEMS IN ZEPHYR APPLICATIONS

two files and file that stores a count the number of times the system has been rebooted, and another file that holds a pattern of byte values that are modified systematically on each reboot. The purpose of the demonstration is to show how data can be persisted between reboots and also illustrates how to work with the Zephyr RTOS filesystem API. This application can also be run on a board having an SD/MMC card-based file system by modifying the project configuration files appropriately.

The partition labelled "storage" is used for the file system. If that area does not already have a compatible LittleFS file system, then its contents will be replaced with an empty file system.

Building and running the application and then running it and rebooting several times will produce output something like the following:

```
*** Booting Zephyr OS build v3.3.99-ncs1-1 ***
Sample program to r/w files on littlefs
Area 3 at 0xf8000 on flash-controller@4001e000 for 32768 bytes
I: LittleFS version 2.5, disk version 2.0
I: FS at flash-controller@4001e000:0xf8000 is 8 0x1000-byte blocks with 512 cycle
I: sizes: rd 16 ; pr 16 ; ca 64 ; la 32
E: WEST_TOPDIR/modules/fs/littlefs/lfs.c:1234: Corrupted dir pair at {0x0, 0x1}
W: can't mount (LFS -84); formatting
I: /lfs mounted
/lfs mount: 0
/lfs: bsize = 16 ; frsize = 4096 ; blocks = 8 ; bfree = 6

Listing dir /lfs ...
/lfs/boot_count read count:0 (bytes: 0)
/lfs/boot_count write new boot count 1: [wr:1]
I: Test file: /lfs/pattern.bin not found, create one!
```

CHAPTER 6   USING FILESYSTEMS IN ZEPHYR APPLICATIONS

```
------ FILE: /lfs/pattern.bin ------
01 55 55 55 55 55 55 55 02 55 55 55 55 55 55 55
03 55 55 55 55 55 55 55 04 55 55 55 55 55 55 55
05 55 55 55 55 55 55 55 06 55 55 55 55 55 55 55
07 55 55 55 55 55 55 55 08 55 55 55 55 55 55 55
09 55 55 55 55 55 55 55 0a 55 55 55 55 55 55 55
0b 55 55 55 55 55 55 55 0c 55 55 55 55 55 55 55
0d 55 55 55 55 55 55 55 0e 55 55 55 55 55 55 55
0f 55 55 55 55 55 55 55 10 55 55 55 55 55 55 55
11 55 55 55 55 55 55 55 12 55 55 55 55 55 55 55
13 55 55 55 55 55 55 55 14 55 55 55 55 55 55 55
.... more lines of output
2f 55 55 55 55 55 55 55 30 55 55 55 55 55 55 55
31 55 55 55 55 55 55 55 32 55 55 55 55 55 55 55
33 55 55 55 55 55 55 55 34 55 55 55 55 55 55 55
35 55 55 55 55 55 55 55 36 55 55 55 55 55 55 55
37 55 55 55 55 55 55 55 38 55 55 55 55 55 55 55
39 55 55 55 55 55 55 55 3a 55 55 55 55 55 55 55
3b 55 55 55 55 55 55 55 3c 55 55 55 55 55 55 55
3d 55 55 55 55 55 55 55 3e 55 55 55 55 55 55 55
3f 55 55 55 55 55 55 55 40 55 55 55 55 55 55 55

41 55 55 55 55 55 55 55 42 55 55 55 55 55 55 55
43 55 55 55 55 55 55 55 44 55 55 55 55 55 55 55
45 55 aa
I: /lfs unmounted
/lfs unmount: 0

*** Booting Zephyr OS build v3.3.99-ncs1-1 ***
Sample program to r/w files on littlefs
Area 3 at 0xf8000 on flash-controller@4001e000 for 32768 bytes
I: LittleFS version 2.5, disk version 2.0
```

CHAPTER 6 USING FILESYSTEMS IN ZEPHYR APPLICATIONS

```
I: FS at flash-controller@4001e000:0xf8000 is 8 0x1000-byte
blocks with 512 cycle
I: sizes: rd 16 ; pr 16 ; ca 64 ; la 32
/lfs mount: 0
/lfs: bsize = 16 ; frsize = 4096 ; blocks = 8 ; bfree = 5

Listing dir /lfs ...
[FILE] boot_count (size = 1)
[FILE] pattern.bin (size = 547)
/lfs/boot_count read count:1 (bytes: 1)
/lfs/boot_count write new boot count 2: [wr:1]
------ FILE: /lfs/pattern.bin ------
02 55 55 55 55 55 55 55 03 55 55 55 55 55 55 55
04 55 55 55 55 55 55 55 05 55 55 55 55 55 55 55
06 55 55 55 55 55 55 55 07 55 55 55 55 55 55 55
08 55 55 55 55 55 55 55 09 55 55 55 55 55 55 55
0a 55 55 55 55 55 55 55 0b 55 55 55 55 55 55 55
0c 55 55 55 55 55 55 55 0d 55 55 55 55 55 55 55
0e 55 55 55 55 55 55 55 0f 55 55 55 55 55 55 55
10 55 55 55 55 55 55 55 11 55 55 55 55 55 55 55
12 55 55 55 55 55 55 55 13 55 55 55 55 55 55 55
14 55 55 55 55 55 55 55 15 55 55 55 55 55 55 55
... more lines of output
2c 55 55 55 55 55 55 55 2d 55 55 55 55 55 55 55
2e 55 55 55 55 55 55 55 2f 55 55 55 55 55 55 55
30 55 55 55 55 55 55 55 31 55 55 55 55 55 55 55
32 55 55 55 55 55 55 55 33 55 55 55 55 55 55 55
34 55 55 55 55 55 55 55 35 55 55 55 55 55 55 55
36 55 55 55 55 55 55 55 37 55 55 55 55 55 55 55
38 55 55 55 55 55 55 55 39 55 55 55 55 55 55 55
3a 55 55 55 55 55 55 55 3b 55 55 55 55 55 55 55
3c 55 55 55 55 55 55 55 3d 55 55 55 55 55 55 55
```

CHAPTER 6   USING FILESYSTEMS IN ZEPHYR APPLICATIONS

3e 55 55 55 55 55 55 55 3f 55 55 55 55 55 55 55
40 55 55 55 55 55 55 55 41 55 55 55 55 55 55 55

42 55 55 55 55 55 55 55 43 55 55 55 55 55 55 55
44 55 55 55 55 55 55 55 45 55 55 55 55 55 55 55
46 55 ab
I: /lfs unmounted
/lfs unmount: 0

*** Booting Zephyr OS build v3.3.99-ncs1-1 ***
Sample program to r/w files on littlefs
Area 3 at 0xf8000 on flash-controller@4001e000 for 32768 bytes
I: LittleFS version 2.5, disk version 2.0
I: FS at flash-controller@4001e000:0xf8000 is 8 0x1000-byte blocks with 512 cycle
I: sizes: rd 16 ; pr 16 ; ca 64 ; la 32
/lfs mount: 0
/lfs: bsize = 16 ; frsize = 4096 ; blocks = 8 ; bfree = 5

Listing dir /lfs ...
[FILE] boot_count (size = 1)
[FILE] pattern.bin (size = 547)
/lfs/boot_count read count:2 (bytes: 1)
/lfs/boot_count write new boot count 3: [wr:1]
------ FILE: /lfs/pattern.bin ------
03 aa aa aa aa aa aa aa 04 aa aa aa aa aa aa aa
05 aa aa aa aa aa aa aa 06 aa aa aa aa aa aa aa
07 aa aa aa aa aa aa aa 08 aa aa aa aa aa aa aa
09 aa aa aa aa aa aa aa 0a aa aa aa aa aa aa aa
0b aa aa aa aa aa aa aa 0c aa aa aa aa aa aa aa
0d aa aa aa aa aa aa aa 0e aa aa aa aa aa aa aa
0f aa aa aa aa aa aa aa 10 aa aa aa aa aa aa aa
11 aa aa aa aa aa aa aa 12 aa aa aa aa aa aa aa

```
13 aa aa aa aa aa aa aa 14 aa aa aa aa aa aa aa
15 aa aa aa aa aa aa aa 16 aa aa aa aa aa aa aa
... more lines of output
33 aa aa aa aa aa aa aa 34 aa aa aa aa aa aa aa
35 aa aa aa aa aa aa aa 36 aa aa aa aa aa aa aa
37 aa aa aa aa aa aa aa 38 aa aa aa aa aa aa aa
39 aa aa aa aa aa aa aa 3a aa aa aa aa aa aa aa
3b aa aa aa aa aa aa aa 3c aa aa aa aa aa aa aa
3d aa aa aa aa aa aa aa 3e aa aa aa aa aa aa aa
3f aa aa aa aa aa aa aa 40 aa aa aa aa aa aa aa
41 aa aa aa aa aa aa aa 42 aa aa aa aa aa aa aa

43 aa aa aa aa aa aa aa 44 aa aa aa aa aa aa aa
45 aa aa aa aa aa aa aa 46 aa aa aa aa aa aa aa
47 aa ac
I: /lfs unmounted
/lfs unmount: 0

*** Booting Zephyr OS build v3.3.99-ncs1-1 ***
Sample program to r/w files on littlefs
Area 3 at 0xf8000 on flash-controller@4001e000 for 32768 bytes
I: LittleFS version 2.5, disk version 2.0
I: FS at flash-controller@4001e000:0xf8000 is 8 0x1000-byte
blocks with 512 cycle
I: sizes: rd 16 ; pr 16 ; ca 64 ; la 32
/lfs mount: 0
/lfs: bsize = 16 ; frsize = 4096 ; blocks = 8 ; bfree = 5

Listing dir /lfs ...
[FILE] boot_count (size = 1)
[FILE] pattern.bin (size = 547)
/lfs/boot_count read count:3 (bytes: 1)
/lfs/boot_count write new boot count 4: [wr:1]
```

CHAPTER 6 USING FILESYSTEMS IN ZEPHYR APPLICATIONS

```
------ FILE: /lfs/pattern.bin ------
04 55 55 55 55 55 55 55 05 55 55 55 55 55 55 55
06 55 55 55 55 55 55 55 07 55 55 55 55 55 55 55
08 55 55 55 55 55 55 55 09 55 55 55 55 55 55 55
0a 55 55 55 55 55 55 55 0b 55 55 55 55 55 55 55
0c 55 55 55 55 55 55 55 0d 55 55 55 55 55 55 55
0e 55 55 55 55 55 55 55 0f 55 55 55 55 55 55 55
10 55 55 55 55 55 55 55 11 55 55 55 55 55 55 55
12 55 55 55 55 55 55 55 13 55 55 55 55 55 55 55
14 55 55 55 55 55 55 55 15 55 55 55 55 55 55 55
... more lines of output
2e 55 55 55 55 55 55 55 2f 55 55 55 55 55 55 55
30 55 55 55 55 55 55 55 31 55 55 55 55 55 55 55
32 55 55 55 55 55 55 55 33 55 55 55 55 55 55 55
34 55 55 55 55 55 55 55 35 55 55 55 55 55 55 55
36 55 55 55 55 55 55 55 37 55 55 55 55 55 55 55
38 55 55 55 55 55 55 55 39 55 55 55 55 55 55 55
3a 55 55 55 55 55 55 55 3b 55 55 55 55 55 55 55
3c 55 55 55 55 55 55 55 3d 55 55 55 55 55 55 55
3e 55 55 55 55 55 55 55 3f 55 55 55 55 55 55 55
40 55 55 55 55 55 55 55 41 55 55 55 55 55 55 55
42 55 55 55 55 55 55 55 43 55 55 55 55 55 55 55

44 55 55 55 55 55 55 55 45 55 55 55 55 55 55 55
46 55 55 55 55 55 55 55 47 55 55 55 55 55 55 55
48 55 ad
I: /lfs unmounted
/lfs unmount: 0
```

CHAPTER 6   USING FILESYSTEMS IN ZEPHYR APPLICATIONS

The prj.conf file is fairly straightforward:

```
# Optionally force the file system to be recreated
#CONFIG_APP_WIPE_STORAGE=y
# fs_dirent structures are big.
CONFIG_MAIN_STACK_SIZE=2048
CONFIG_DEBUG=y
CONFIG_LOG=y
CONFIG_LOG_MODE_MINIMAL=y
CONFIG_FLASH=y
CONFIG_FLASH_MAP=y
CONFIG_FLASH_PAGE_LAYOUT=y
CONFIG_FILE_SYSTEM=y
CONFIG_FILE_SYSTEM_LITTLEFS=y
```

The main.c file starts with the required #includes needed for the filesystem, logging and flash_map APIs and their associated data structures, the macro for registering main, some #defines for the maximum length of a path string and the size of the test file used in the example, and a global byte array used to store the test byte pattern.

```
#include <stdio.h>
#include <zephyr/zephyr.h>
#include <zephyr/device.h>
#include <zephyr/fs/fs.h>
#include <zephyr/fs/littlefs.h>
#include <zephyr/logging/log.h>
#include <zephyr/storage/flash_map.h>
LOG_MODULE_REGISTER(main);
/* Matches LFS_NAME_MAX */
#define MAX_PATH_LEN 255
#define TEST_FILE_SIZE 547
static uint8_t file_test_pattern[TEST_FILE_SIZE];
```

The filesystem and mount point are declared with the aid of various helper macros; the corresponding code snippet is the following. If the required partition node does not exist, then it is created.

```
#define PARTITION_NODE DT_NODELABEL(lfs1)
#if DT_NODE_EXISTS(PARTITION_NODE)
FS_FSTAB_DECLARE_ENTRY(PARTITION_NODE);
#else /* PARTITION_NODE */
FS_LITTLEFS_DECLARE_DEFAULT_CONFIG(storage);
static struct fs_mount_t lfs_storage_mnt = {
      .type = FS_LITTLEFS,
      .fs_data = &storage,
      .storage_dev = (void *)FLASH_AREA_ID(storage),
      .mnt_point = "/lfs",
};
#endif /* PARTITION_NODE */
      struct fs_mount_t *mp =
#if DT_NODE_EXISTS(PARTITION_NODE)
            &FS_FSTAB_ENTRY(PARTITION_NODE)
#else
            &lfs_storage_mnt
#endif
            ;
```

The `main()` function starts by calling the function `littlefs_mount(mp)`, which starts by calling `littlefs_flash_erase`, which, in this case, where SOC flash is used (as in the nRF52840 DK board). `littlefs_flash_erase` only erases the flash contents if the application has been configured to do this. Otherwise, it simply tries to open the flash area and print out information about it. An approach such as this where the behavior of a function depends on various #defines being in place can be confusing and would, probably, not be considered best practice. Here is the code for `littlefs_flash_erase`:

CHAPTER 6   USING FILESYSTEMS IN ZEPHYR APPLICATIONS

```
#ifdef CONFIG_APP_LITTLEFS_STORAGE_FLASH
static int littlefs_flash_erase(unsigned int id) {
    const struct flash_area *pfa;
    int rc;
    rc = flash_area_open(id, &pfa);
    if (rc < 0) {
        LOG_ERR("FAIL: unable to find flash area %u: %d\n",
            id, rc);
        return rc;
    }
    LOG_PRINTK("Area %u at 0x%x on %s for %u bytes\n",
            id, (unsigned int)pfa->fa_off, pfa->fa_dev->name,
            (unsigned int)pfa->fa_size);
    /* Optional wipe flash contents */
    if (IS_ENABLED(CONFIG_APP_WIPE_STORAGE)) {
        rc = flash_area_erase(pfa, 0, pfa->fa_size);
        LOG_ERR("Erasing flash area ... %d", rc);
    }
    flash_area_close(pfa);
    return rc;
}
```

littlefs_mount(mp) only mounts the mount point if automount has not been enabled. Its code does show how mount can be carried out explicitly.

```
#ifdef CONFIG_APP_LITTLEFS_STORAGE_FLASH
static int littlefs_mount(struct fs_mount_t *mp) {
    int rc;
    rc = littlefs_flash_erase((uintptr_t)mp->storage_dev);
    if (rc < 0) {
        return rc;
    }
```

CHAPTER 6   USING FILESYSTEMS IN ZEPHYR APPLICATIONS

```
    /* Do not mount if auto-mount has been enabled */
#if !DT_NODE_EXISTS(PARTITION_NODE) ||                \
    !(FSTAB_ENTRY_DT_MOUNT_FLAGS(PARTITION_NODE) &    \
FS_MOUNT_FLAG_AUTOMOUNT)
    rc = fs_mount(mp);

    if (rc < 0) {
        LOG_PRINTK("FAIL: mount id %" PRIuPTR " at %s: %d\n",
                   (uintptr_t)mp->storage_dev, mp->mnt_
                   point, rc);
        return rc;
    }
    LOG_PRINTK("%s mount: %d\n", mp->mnt_point, rc);
#else
    LOG_PRINTK("%s automounted\n", mp->mnt_point);
#endif
    return 0;
}
#endif /* CONFIG_APP_LITTLEFS_STORAGE_FLASH */
```

The work of manipulating the two test files in main involves calling the corresponding functions for manipulating these files as shown in the following code snippet:

```
    rc = littlefs_increase_infile_value(fname1);
    if (rc) {
        goto out;
    }
    rc = littlefs_binary_file_adj(fname2);
    if (rc) {
        goto out;
    }
```

CHAPTER 6   USING FILESYSTEMS IN ZEPHYR APPLICATIONS

These functions are interesting because they provide useful examples of low-level manipulation of file data. `littlefs_increase_infile_value` tracks the number of times the system has been rebooted. Here is the code snippet for that function:

```c
static int littlefs_increase_infile_value(char *fname) {
    uint8_t boot_count = 0;
    struct fs_file_t file;
    int rc, ret;
    fs_file_t_init(&file);
    rc = fs_open(&file, fname, FS_O_CREATE | FS_O_RDWR);
    if (rc < 0) {
        LOG_ERR("FAIL: open %s: %d", fname, rc);
        return rc;
    }

    rc = fs_read(&file, &boot_count, sizeof(boot_count));
    if (rc < 0) {
        LOG_ERR("FAIL: read %s: [rd:%d]", fname, rc);
        goto out;
    }
    LOG_PRINTK("%s read count:%u (bytes: %d)\n", fname, boot_count, rc);
    rc = fs_seek(&file, 0, FS_SEEK_SET);
    if (rc < 0) {
        LOG_ERR("FAIL: seek %s: %d", fname, rc);
        goto out;
    }
    boot_count += 1;
    rc = fs_write(&file, &boot_count, sizeof(boot_count));
    if (rc < 0) {
        LOG_ERR("FAIL: write %s: %d", fname, rc);
```

CHAPTER 6   USING FILESYSTEMS IN ZEPHYR APPLICATIONS

```
        goto out;
    }
    LOG_PRINTK("%s write new boot count %u: [wr:%d]\n", fname,
        boot_count, rc);
    out:
        ret = fs_close(&file);
        if (ret < 0) {
            LOG_ERR("FAIL: close %s: %d", fname, ret);
            return ret;
        }
        return (rc < 0 ? rc : 0);
}
```

The error handling code makes use of a goto to branch to a common function exit point in case of errors.

The edited code snippet with the error handling code left shows how the function works.

```
fs_file_t_init(&file);
rc = fs_open(&file, fname, FS_O_CREATE | FS_O_RDWR);
rc = fs_read(&file, &boot_count, sizeof(boot_count));
LOG_PRINTK("%s read count:%u (bytes: %d)\n", fname, boot_
count, rc);
rc = fs_seek(&file, 0, FS_SEEK_SET);
boot_count += 1;
rc = fs_write(&file, &boot_count, sizeof(boot_count));
LOG_PRINTK("%s write new boot count %u: [wr:%d]\n", fname,
boot_count, rc);
```

It shows a standard file processing pattern, namely:

```
initialise a file handle data structure
open the file for reading and writing
```

300

CHAPTER 6   USING FILESYSTEMS IN ZEPHYR APPLICATIONS

read some data from the file
rewind to the start of the file
overwrite file data with a new value

The `littlefs_binary_file_adj` function makes use of several helper functions that initialize and manipulate test patterns of bytes; they are `incr_pattern`, `init_pattern`, and `print_pattern`. They are relatively simple functions and demonstrate possible ways of creating, modifying, and displaying arrays of bytes that might be useful in an application testing context. The code for `littlefs_binary_file_adj`, with the error handling code edited out, is as follows:

```
static int littlefs_binary_file_adj(char *fname) {
    struct fs_dirent dirent;
    struct fs_file_t file;
    int rc, ret;
    rc = fs_open(&file, fname, FS_O_CREATE | FS_O_RDWR);
    rc = fs_stat(fname, &dirent);
    /* Check if the file exists - if not just write the
    pattern */
    if (rc == 0 && dirent.type == FS_DIR_ENTRY_FILE && dirent.
    size == 0) {
        LOG_INF("Test file: %s not found, create one!", fname);
        init_pattern(file_test_pattern, sizeof(file_test_
        pattern));
    } else {

        rc = fs_read(&file, file_test_pattern, sizeof(file_
        test_pattern));
        incr_pattern(file_test_pattern, sizeof(file_test_
        pattern), 0x1);
    }
    LOG_PRINTK("------ FILE: %s ------\n", fname);
```

301

CHAPTER 6 USING FILESYSTEMS IN ZEPHYR APPLICATIONS

```
    print_pattern(file_test_pattern, sizeof(file_test_
    pattern));
    rc = fs_seek(&file, 0, FS_SEEK_SET);
    rc = fs_write(&file, file_test_pattern, sizeof(file_test_
    pattern));
    ret = fs_close(&file);
    return (rc < 0 ? rc : 0);
}
```

It follows the file data processing pattern described earlier.

Summary

This chapter has overviewed the filesystem APIs that are part of the Zephyr RTOS framework and walked through a sample application showing how these APIs can be used with a particular filesystem littlefs. It has also overviewed the QSPI interface and its uses and the SD/MMC architecture and its possible uses.

References

1. QSPI — Quad serial peripheral interface
   https://infocenter.nordicsemi.com/index.jsp?topic=%2Fps_nrf52840%2Fqspi.html

2. nordic,nrf-qspi
   https://docs.zephyrproject.org/latest/build/dts/api/bindings/flash_controller/nordic,nrf-qspi.html

CHAPTER 6   USING FILESYSTEMS IN ZEPHYR APPLICATIONS

3. Quad-SPI interface on STM32 microcontrollers and microprocessors
   www.st.com/content/ccc/resource/technical/
   document/application_note/group0/
   b0/7e/46/a8/5e/c1/48/01/DM00227538/files/
   DM00227538.pdf/jcr:content/translations/
   en.DM00227538.pdf

4. https://github.com/littlefs-project/
   littlefs/blob/master/DESIGN.md

5. zephyr\samples\subsys\fs\littlefs

6. Quad-SPI, Everything You Need To Know
   https://embeddedinventor.com/quad-spi-
   everything-you-need-to-know/

7. nordic,nrf-qspi
   https://docs.zephyrproject.org/latest/build/
   dts/api/bindings/flash_controller/nordic,nrf-
   qspi.html

8. QuadSPI (QSPI)
   https://os.mbed.com/docs/mbed-os/v6.15/apis/
   spi-apis.html

9. The Quad SPI Protocol
   https://www.jblopen.com/qspi-nor-flash-
   part-3-the-quad-spi-protocol/

10. UM1721 – User manual – Developing applications on STM32Cube™ with FatFs
    www.st.com/content/ccc/resource/technical/
    document/user_manual/61/79/2b/96/
    c8/b4/48/19/DM00105259.pdf/files/
    DM00105259.pdf/jcr:content/translations/
    en.DM00105259.pdf

CHAPTER 7

Developing Zephyr BLE Applications

Zephyr RTOS is becoming increasingly important as an RTOS for developing IoT (Internet of Things) applications, not only smart sensors but also edge computing devices. In the IoT ecosystem, the importance of BLE (Bluetooth Low Energy) is as a short-distance radio communications link for, for example, connecting wearable sensors to mobile devices and for use in wireless connected computer peripherals such as BLE mice and BLE keyboards. BLE support and its APIs are, therefore, a very important part of the Zephyr framework.

This chapter will start by covering BLE (Bluetooth Low Energy) concepts, terminology, and programming and will also overview the differences between BLE 4 and the, newer, BLE 5 standards. The next section will then go on to explore the Nordic Semiconductor BLE-capable SoC (System on Chip) and Nordic's closed source BLE stack and how it is used with Zephyr RTOS, and also introduce Zephyr's open source BLE stack, and explore a number of Zephyr RTOS–based BLE applications.

CHAPTER 7   DEVELOPING ZEPHYR BLE APPLICATIONS

BLE: A Short History

What is now BLE began as a Nokia research project concerned with the development of a wireless technology derived from the Bluetooth standard, which could provide lower power usage while making use of the existing Bluetooth technology standards. Continued development work led to Wibree, which was released in 2006 and was, later, incorporated into evolving Bluetooth standard specification work as a Bluetooth ultra-low-power technology. This was initially called Bluetooth Smart and integrated into version 4.0 of the Core Specification in 2010. The first smartphone to implement the 4.0 specification was the iPhone 4S, released in October 2011.

The latest version of BLE, as part of Bluetooth 5, was announced in 2016 by the Bluetooth SIG. BLE 5 added features such as increasing the range of BLE by using increased the transmit power, use of coded physical layer approaches and increasing the advertising data length of low-energy Bluetooth transmissions as compared to Bluetooth 4.x. In a more recent development, the Bluetooth SIG released a Mesh Profile and Mesh Model specifications in 2017 for use in many-to-many device communications applications such as, for example, home automation and distributed sensor networks.

The range of a BLE transmission depends on the environment of the communicating BLE device and the mode being used, standard mode vs. long-range mode. The typical range is 10–30 meters.

To transfer data from a BLE device to the Internet, another BLE device (BLE Gateway) that has an IP connection is required. Typically this involves connecting a BLE-capable sensor or BLE-capable controller to a BLE Gateway that can connect to the Internet.

CHAPTER 7 DEVELOPING ZEPHYR BLE APPLICATIONS

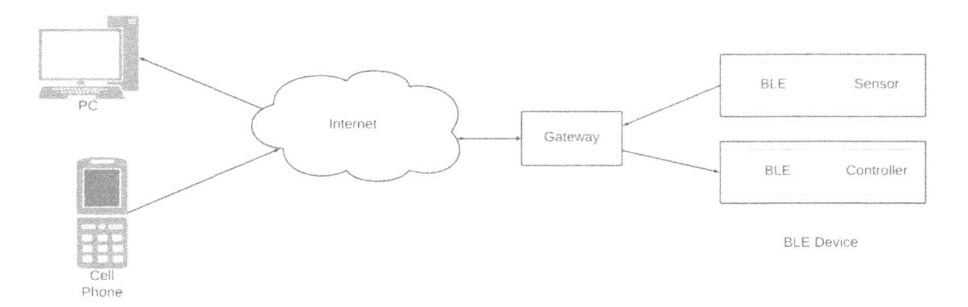

Figure 7-1. *BLE sensor and BLE controller gateway connectivity to computer and mobile devices*

Uses of BLE

BLE can be used for applications such as controlling actuators over a low bandwidth connection, for personal and wearable devices often in combination with a BLE-capable smartphone (cell phone), which can provide a graphical user interface and relay data from a smart BLE sensor to the cloud. Another use is in the deployment of broadcast-only beacon devices, which broadcast data that can be discovered and read by other devices.

BLE Architecture

Like most networking protocols, BLE has a layered architecture. This is illustrated in Figure 7-2, which shows the various layers and sublayers of BLE.

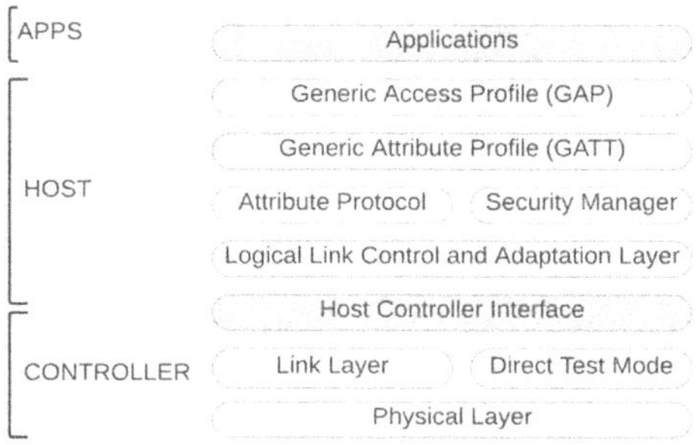

CHAPTER 7   DEVELOPING ZEPHYR BLE APPLICATIONS

Figure 7-2. BLE architecture protocol layers

There are various acronyms associated with BLE. For the host layer, these include Generic Access Profile (GAP), Generic Attribute Profile (GATT), Attribute Protocol (ATT), Security Manager (SM), Logical Link Control and Adaptation Protocol (L2CAP), and the Host Controller Interface (HCI) host side. For the link layer, PHY refers to the physical layer, and HCI refers to the controller side Host Controller Interface.

BLE Physical Layer

The BLE physical layer (PHY) is concerned with the radio hardware used for communication and for modulating/de-modulating the data being transmitted.

BLE operates in the somewhat congested ISM band (2.4 GHz spectrum). In the case of BLE, this is segmented into 40 RF channels, each of which is separated by a 2 MHz (center-to-center) gap. Three of the channels are the Primary Advertising Channels, and the remaining 37 channels are used for Secondary Advertisements and for data transfer during a connection. This is shown schematically in Figure 7-3.

CHAPTER 7 DEVELOPING ZEPHYR BLE APPLICATIONS

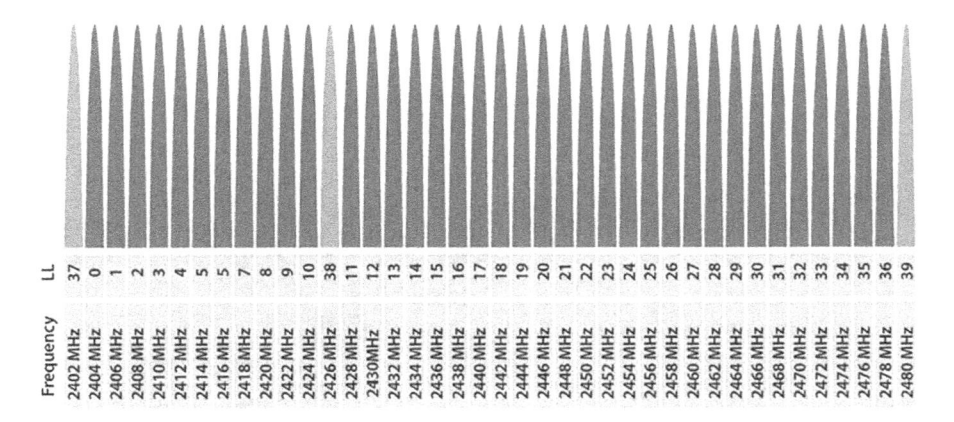

Figure 7-3. BLE RF channels, showing the Primary Advertising Channels (yellow)

Advertising starts with advertisement packets being sent on all or some of the three Primary Advertising Channels. Devices scan for advertisers and read the data being advertised. Some advertisers support scan requests. Here, a scanner can initiate a scan request, and the advertiser can respond and send additional advertisement data to a device requesting this data.

BLE Link Layer

The BLE link layer directly interfaces to the physical layer, and it is this layer that is responsible for advertising, scanning, and creating/maintaining connections. Because driving a transceiver uses significant amounts of energy, transceivers are not turned on continuously. Rather, advertising and scanning activities occur at regular intervals. However, because Advertisers and Scanners are not synchronized, scanning and advertising activities must overlap if discovery is to occur. This involves configuring suitable advertising intervals, for example, 20 ms, and, on the scanner side, configuring scan intervals (e.g., 50 ms) and scan widows, for example, 25 ms, so that discovery can be made in a relatively timely manner, as illustrated in Figure 7-4 [2].

CHAPTER 7 DEVELOPING ZEPHYR BLE APPLICATIONS

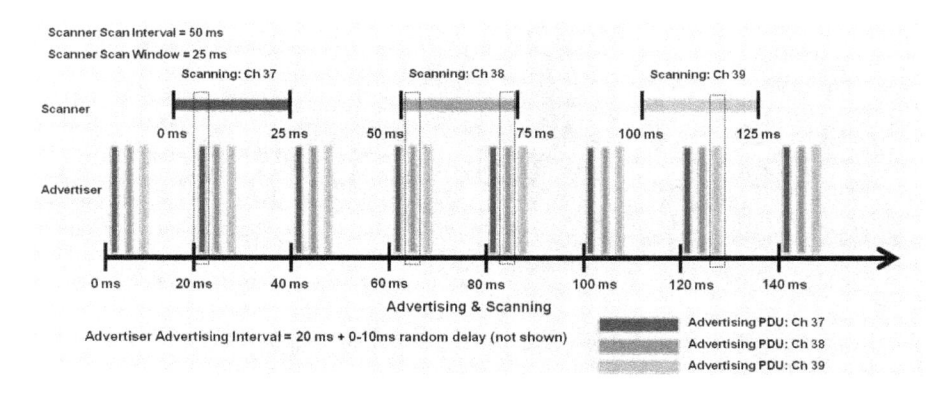

Figure 7-4. BLE link layer advertising and scanning

The three main operational states of a BLE device are the Advertising, Scanning, and Connected states.

In addition to handling timing, the link layer manages hardware-accelerated operations such as CRC checksumming, random number generation, and encryption.

BLE link layer use cases involve role pairs that are played out during the various phases of discovery/connection. These are the Advertiser/Scanner (Initiator), Slave/Master, and Broadcaster/Observer role pairs.

BLE distinguishes between unicast (peer-to-peer) and broadcast connections.

BLE Unicast Connection Scenario

A typical unicast connection scenario involves a sequence of steps that start with a situation in which two BLE hosts, initially in a Standby (unconnected) state, enter a Discovery state in which the device wishing to be discovered becomes the Advertiser and the host wishing to connect becomes a Scanner. The Advertiser sends advertising packets containing basic information about the host it is running on, and all scanners receive these packets. The Scanner (after filtering/analyzing information

CHAPTER 7   DEVELOPING ZEPHYR BLE APPLICATIONS

contained in the advertising packets) may become an Initiator and initiate a connection with a specific advertiser. In the Connecting phase, the Initiator sends a CONNECT_REQ advertising packet to the Advertiser. If the Advertiser accepts the connection request, the connected phase is reached. In this phase, the Advertiser is the Slave, while the Initiator is the Master.

The sequence of exchanges in the unicast scenario looks something like Figure 7-5 [3].

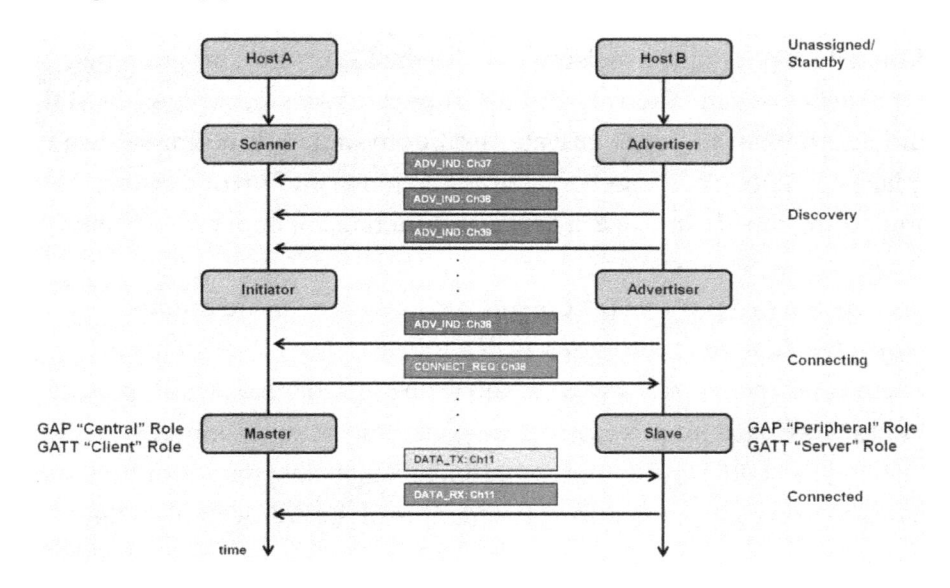

Figure 7-5.   BLE unicast scenario sequence diagram

BLE Broadcast Connect Scenario

In the case of broadcast connections, the link layer roles do not change, and the defined roles are Broadcaster (the host sending the packets) and Observer. The messages are one-way, and the BLE standard defines the allowed types of advertising packets and their structure.

311

CHAPTER 7 DEVELOPING ZEPHYR BLE APPLICATIONS

BLE Link Layer Addressing

A BLE device is identified by a unique 48-bit (6-byte) address. There are two types of device address, public and random, and one or both can be set on a device. A Public Device Address is the standard, IEEE-assigned 48-bit universal LAN MAC address that must be obtained from the IEEE Registration Authority. It is divided into two fields, namely, an IEEE-assigned company ID, held in the 24 most-significant bits, and a Company-assigned device ID, held in the 24 least-significant bits. A Random Device Address does not require registration with the IEEE and is programmed on the device or generated at runtime. There are two kinds (types) of BLE Random Address, static and private. A random static BLE address is used in place of a Public address. It can be generated at bootup or stay the same during the lifetime of the device. If generated at boot time, it cannot change until a power cycle occurs.

There are two private address subtypes: resolvable and nonresolvable. Nonresolvable private addresses, which are not widely used in practice, are temporary addresses with a certain time duration. Resolvable private addresses are used for privacy and are generated using an Identity Resolving Key (IRK) and a random number. Resolvable private addresses change periodically (even during the lifetime of the connection). They are used to avoid being tracked by unknown scanners. However, trusted devices can resolve a resolvable private address using a previously stored IRK.

BLE Packet Types

The (BLE) link layer defines a single packet format that is used for both advertising channel packets and data channel packets. It is structured as illustrated in the schematic featured in Figure 7-6 [4].

CHAPTER 7　DEVELOPING ZEPHYR BLE APPLICATIONS

BLE Packet			
Preamble	Access Address	Protocol Data Unit (PDU)	CRC
1 Byte	4 Bytes	2-257 Bytes	3 Bytes

Advertising Channel PDU

Header	Payload
2 Bytes	0-37 Bytes

Data Channel PDU

Header	Payload	MIC*
2 Bytes	up to 255 Bytes (incl. MIC)	4 Bytes

Ref: BT Specification v4.2, Vol. 6, Part B, Sec. 2.1

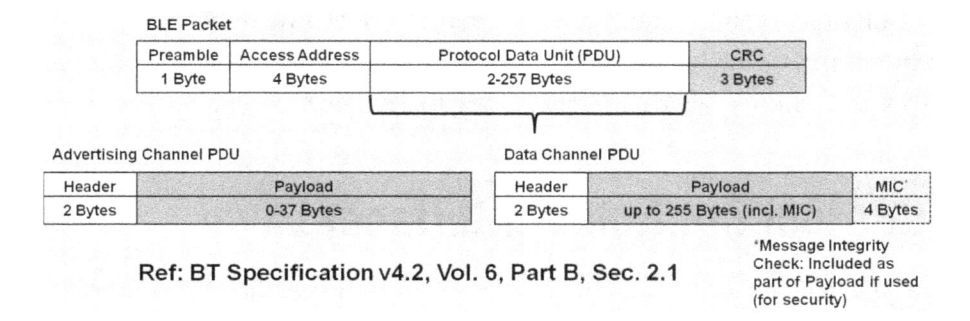

*Message Integrity Check: Included as part of Payload if used (for security)

Figure 7-6. BLE packet types

Their advertising channel PDU (Protocol Data Unit) types are ADV_IND for connected unidirectional advertising, ADV_DIRECT_IND for connectable directed advertising, ADV_NONCONN_IND for nonconnectable undirected advertising, and ADV_SCAN_IND for scannable undirected advertising.

The scanning PDUs are the request and response PDUs SCAN_REQ and SCAN_RSP. The connection initiating PDU CONNECT_REQ defines things such as the frequency hopping interval, the connection interval, and the time between two connection events.

Connections and Connection Events

Connection events are the regular exchanges of data between master and slave. 0-byte data packets are exchanged if there is no data to send. If a packet is not received, the connection event is terminated, and data will have to be resent at the next connection event.

Once a connection has been established, the link layer functions as a reliable data bearer. Received packets are checked against a 24-bit CRC and re-transmissions requested as necessary. The link layer will resend a packet until it is acknowledged.

BLE unicast connections give rise to a piconet (tiny) network architecture in which a master coordinates data transfer with one or more slaves and where a slave can only belong to a single piconet.

HCI (Host Controller Interface) Layer

The HCI layer protocol is defined in the Bluetooth specification, and it defines how the host layer can communicate with the controller layer. The host layer and the controller layer may exist in separate chipsets, or they may exist in the same chipset.

In the case where the host and controller are in separate chipsets, the HCI layer is implemented over a physical communication interface such as UART, USB, or SDIO (Secure Digital Input Output).

In the case where the two layers (host and controller) live on the same chipset, the HCI layer is a logical interface. The task of the HCI layer is to relay commands from the host to the controller and to send events from the controller to the host.

Logical Link Control and Adaptation Protocol (L2CAP) Layer

The Logical Link Control and Adaptation Protocol (L2CAP) layer acts as a protocol multiplexing layer. It takes multiple protocols from the upper layers and places them in standard BLE packets that are passed down to the lower layers. It is responsible for fragmentation and reassembly of larger packets (which exceed the maximum BLE payload size). L2CAP layer handles the BLE Attribute Protocol (ATT) and the BLE Security Manager Protocol (SMP).

BLE Actors – Peripherals, Broadcasters, Centrals, and Observers

From the application development point of view, it is the implementation of the code that realizes the behavior of the BLE actors taking part that is the focus of interest.

BLE Peripheral

A BLE peripheral device announces its presence by sending out advertising packets and can accept a connection from another BLE device (a BLE central), whereas a BLE broadcaster (Beacon) is a device that sends out advertising packets but does not allow a connection from a central device. Beacons are commonly used to provide indoor location services. Broadcasters and peripherals can be distinguished by virtue of the different types of advertising packets they transmit.

BLE Central

A Central is a device that discovers and listens to other BLE devices that are advertising and is capable of establishing a connection to a BLE peripheral. A Central can establish connections with multiple peripherals. An Observer, on the other hand, discovers and listens to other BLE devices but cannot initiate connections with a peripheral device.

The features of the various BLE actors are summarized in the following table:

Broadcaster	Peripheral	Observer	Central
Does not need to have a radio receiver	Must have both a transmitter and a receiver	Does not need to have a radio receiver	Must have both a transmitter and a receiver
There is no bidirectional data transfer	Capable of bidirectional data transfer	There is no bidirectional data transfer	Capable of bidirectional data transfer
Can function with reduced hardware and a reduced BLE software stack	Requires a full BLE software stack	Can function with reduced hardware and a reduced BLE software stack	Requires a full BLE software stack

It is possible to implement a BLE device that can act as both a central and a peripheral.

An example of such a multi-role BLE device is a device that can monitor multiple sensors (peripheral devices) and, concurrently, advertise its presence to a smartphone so as to allow access to sensor data via a mobile app interface.

Important HCI (Host Controller Interface) elements include GAP (Generic Access Profile), GATT (Generic Attribute Profile), and ATT (Attribute Protocol) and are overviewed in the following sections.

HCI – Generic Access Profile (GAP)

The Generic Access Profile (GAP) is mandatory as it defines how BLE devices interact with each other and is what makes it possible for BLE devices to interoperate, communicate, and exchange data with each other. It is concerned with the various modes and roles of BLE devices and includes things such as advertisements (advertising, scanning, advertising parameters, advertising data, scanning parameters), connection establishment (initiating, accepting, connection parameters), and security.

Attribute Protocol (ATT)

An ATT defines how a server exposes data to a client and how that data is structured.

ATT involves two roles: a server role and a client role. The server exposes the data it controls or contains. It may also expose some other aspects of server behavior that other devices may be able to control. The server accepts incoming commands from a peer device and sends responses, notifications, and indications back. For example, a BLE thermometer device will behave as a server when it exposes the temperature of its surrounding environment, as well as other details, which might include details such as the units of measurement, the time intervals at which temperature readings are taken, and, possibly, further information such as, for example, the battery life of the sensor device. Instead of being polled for data by a client, a thermometer device may notify a client when a temperature reading has changed. The client device interfaces with the server in order to read the server's exposed data and/or to control one or more aspects of the server's behavior. The client sends commands and requests and accepts incoming notifications and indications.

Data Attributes

In BLE, the data exposed by a BLE server is structured in the form of attributes. An attribute is a generic term for a type of data exposed by the server and serves to define the structure of that data. An attribute type is a Universally Unique Identifier or UUID. In the case of a Bluetooth SIG-Adopted Attribute, it is a 16-bit number. For a custom attribute type defined by an application developer, it is a 128-bit number. Custom attribute UUIDs are also referred to as vendor-specific UUIDs.

For example, the UUID for a SIG-adopted temperature measurement value is 0x2A1C. SIG-adopted attribute types (UUIDs) share all but 16 bits of a special 128-bit base UUID 0000**0000**-0000-1000-8000-00805F9B34FB.

The published 16-bit UUID value replaces the 2 bytes in bold in the base UUID.

A custom UUID, on the other hand, is a 128-bit number that does not use the SIG-adopted base UUID. A benefit of using a SIG-adopted UUID is that it results in a reduction in packet size as it can be transmitted using a 16-bit representation instead of a full 128-bit UUID value. Data attributes also include an Attribute Handle and Attribute Permissions.

An Attribute Handle is a 16-bit value that the server assigns to its attributes for identification purposes. It is used by the client to reference a given attribute and is guaranteed by the server to uniquely identify that attribute for the duration of the connection between two devices. Handle's values lie in the range 0x0001-0xFFFF, as the value 0x0000 is reserved.

Attribute Permissions determine things such as whether an attribute can be read from or written to, whether that attribute can be notified or indicated, and, also, the security levels required for the attribute operations. Permissions are not defined or discovered via the Attribute Protocol (ATT), but rather defined at a higher layer (GATT layer or Application layer).

The structure of an attribute is shown schematically in Figure 7-7.

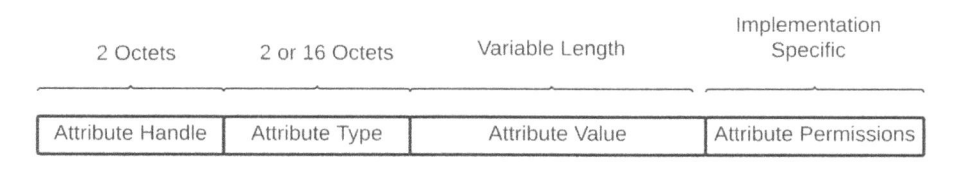

2 Octets	2 or 16 Octets	Variable Length	Implementation Specific
Attribute Handle	Attribute Type	Attribute Value	Attribute Permissions

(An octet is equivalent to a byte)

Figure 7-7. *Structure of an attribute*

GATT Attribute and Data Hierarchy

GATT organizes attributes in a hierarchical way. Attributes are organized as a GATT Server Profile and are grouped into Services, containing Characteristics, containing the Attributes Declaration, Value, and Descriptor. The Descriptor is optional.

A GATT service is made up of one or more include services and one or more characteristics. A characteristic will have a number of properties, a value, and zero or more characteristic descriptors. An include service allows a service to refer to other services for the purpose, for example, of extending the included service.

A Primary Service represents primary functionality of a device, and a Secondary Service provides auxiliary functionality of the device and is referenced (included) by at least one other primary service on the device.

Characteristics

A characteristic is an essential part of a service and represents a piece of information/data that the server wants to provide to a client. For example, the battery level characteristic represents the remaining power level of a battery in a device, and this information can be read by a client. A characteristic is made up of Properties and Descriptors, attributes that are part of the definition of the value held by the characteristic. Properties are represented by bits that define how a characteristic value can be used, for example, read, write, write without response, notify, and indicate. Descriptors contain information related to the characteristic value and include information such as extended properties, a user description, fields used for subscribing to notifications and indications, and also a field defining the presentation of the value such as, for example, the format and the units of the value.

CHAPTER 7   DEVELOPING ZEPHYR BLE APPLICATIONS

Although there are no restrictions or limitations on the characteristics that can be contained within a service, the sensible approach is to group related characteristics together in a way that defines the specific functionality of a device.

Profiles

Profiles have a broader scope than services and are used to define various aspects of the behavior of both the client and server. This covers things such as services, characteristics, connections, and security requirements. This needs to be distinguished from pure server-side definitions, which are concerned only with the implementation of the services and characteristics on the server side.

There are various BLE SIG-adopted profiles for which official specifications have been published. A profile specification will generally contain things such as the definitions of roles and the relationship between the GATT server and client, required services and service requirements, and details of how the required services and characteristics are to be used.

A profile specification also provides details of connection establishment requirements and includes things such as advertising and connection parameters, and security details.

A service can be specified formally as a GATT XML file. The following example shows a specification for a Current Time Service:

```
<server-configuration name="CTS v1.1.0">
    <service uuid="00001805-0000-1000-8000-00805f9b34fb"
    enabled="true">
        <characteristic name="Current Time" uuid="0000
        2A2B-0000-1000-8000-00805f9b34fb" value="00"
        enabled="true">
            <property name="READ" />
            <property name="WRITE" />
```

```xml
            <property name="NOTIFY" />
            <permission name="READ" />
            <permission name="WRITE" />
            <descriptor name="Client Characteristic
            Configuration Descriptor" uuid="00002902-
            0000-1000-8000-00805f9b34fb" value="00"
            enabled="true">
                <permission name="READ" />
                <permission name="WRITE" />
            </descriptor>
        </characteristic>
        <characteristic name="Local Time Information" uuid
        ="00002A0F-0000-1000-8000-00805f9b34fb" value="00"
        enabled="true">
            <property name="READ" />
            <property name="WRITE" />
            <permission name="READ" />
            <permission name="WRITE" />
        </characteristic>
        <characteristic name="Reference Time Information"
        uuid="00002A14-0000-1000-8000-00805f9b34fb"
        value="00" enabled="true">
            <property name="READ" />
            <permission name="READ" />
        </characteristic>
    </service>
</server-configuration>
```

CHAPTER 7   DEVELOPING ZEPHYR BLE APPLICATIONS

Attribute Operations

There are six attribute operations. They are Commands, Requests, Notifications, Responses, Indications, and Confirmations.

- Commands are sent by the client to the server and do not require a response.
- Requests are sent by the client to the server and do require a response.
  - There are two types of request: a Find Information Request and a Read Request.
- Responses are sent by the server in response to a request.
- Notifications that have been enabled for a characteristic of interest by a client are sent by the server to the client to let the client know that the value of a specific characteristic has changed.
  - A notification does not require a response from the client to acknowledge its receipt.
- Indications are sent by the server to the client; they are similar to notifications but require an acknowledgment to be sent back from the client to inform the server that the indication was successfully received.

Notifications and indications are exposed via the Client Characteristic Configuration Descriptor (CCCD) attribute. Writing a "1" to this attribute value enables notifications, writing a "2" enables indications, and writing a "0" disables both notifications and indications.

Confirmation acknowledgment packets are packets sent by the client to the server to inform it that the client successfully received an indication.

Requests – Flow Control, Reading Attributes, and Writing to Attributes

Requests are sequential in the sense that they require a response from the server before a new request can be sent. Indications have a similar requirement; a new indication cannot be sent before a confirmation for the previous indication is received by the server.

Requests and indications, however, are mutually exclusive in terms of the sequence requirement. Thus, an indication can be sent by the server before it responds to a request received earlier.

Commands and notifications do not require any flow control; they can be sent at any time. It is therefore possible that commands and notifications may be missed because of issues such as a buffer and processing limitations. This implies that commands and notifications cannot be considered as reliable. Where reliability is a concern, requests and indications should be used instead of commands and notifications.

Attribute reads are, in effect, requests because they require a response. There are various possible kinds of read. These include a read request that references the attribute to be read by specifying its handle and a read blob request where both a handle and an offset indicating where the read should start are given, and which, therefore, returns only a part of the value of the specified characteristic.

A write to an attribute can be issued either in the form of a write request or in the form of a write command. Write commands do not require a response from the server, whereas write requests do require an acknowledgment from the server that the attribute has been successfully written to.

There are also queued writes that can be used to provide an atomic operation involving several writes. A queued write involves the preparation of the corresponding write requests that will include an offset specifying the position at which the sent value should be written within the attribute value. These sent values are also referred to as prepared values, and they are used whenever a large value needs to be written that will not fit within a single message. The prepared values are stored in a buffer on the server side and not written directly to the attribute. Once all the prepared values have been sent and received, a write request is used to request the server to either execute or cancel the write operation of the prepared values. The server has to respond with a confirmation that the complete attribute value that was sent to the server has been written.

Bluetooth 5

Bluetooth 5 adds a number of extra features to BLE. These include 2M PHY, which specifies how to achieve twice the speed of earlier versions of Bluetooth, and Coded PHY, which makes it possible to extend the range of earlier versions of Bluetooth and make possible BLE communication between devices several hundred meters apart. BLE 5 also supports extended advertisements that make use of secondary advertisement channels to make it possible for a device to advertise more data than allowed on the primary advertisement channels. In the case of extended advertisements, the advertisement packets sent on the primary advertisement channels provide the information necessary to discover the offloaded advertisements that are sent on the secondary advertisement channels. BLE 5 also supports a periodic advertising mode in which two or more devices communicate in a connectionless manner.

In periodic advertising mode, the peripheral device sends out synchronization information and other extended advertisement data that will allow another device to become synchronized with the peripheral and receive the peripheral device's extended advertisements at regular, deterministic intervals.

BLE Security

BLE security is handled by the Security Manager (SM) layer of the architecture.

The Security Manager defines the protocols and algorithms for generating and exchanging keys between two devices and involves mechanisms for pairing, which is the process of creating shared secret keys between two devices; bonding, which is the process of creating and storing shared secret keys on each side (central and peripheral) for use in subsequent connections between the devices; authentication, which is the process of verifying that the two devices share the same secret keys; encryption, which is the process of encrypting the data exchanged between the devices; and, finally, message integrity, which is the process of signing the data sent and verifying the signature at the receiving end.

These steps are illustrated in the sequence diagram shown in Figure 7-8.

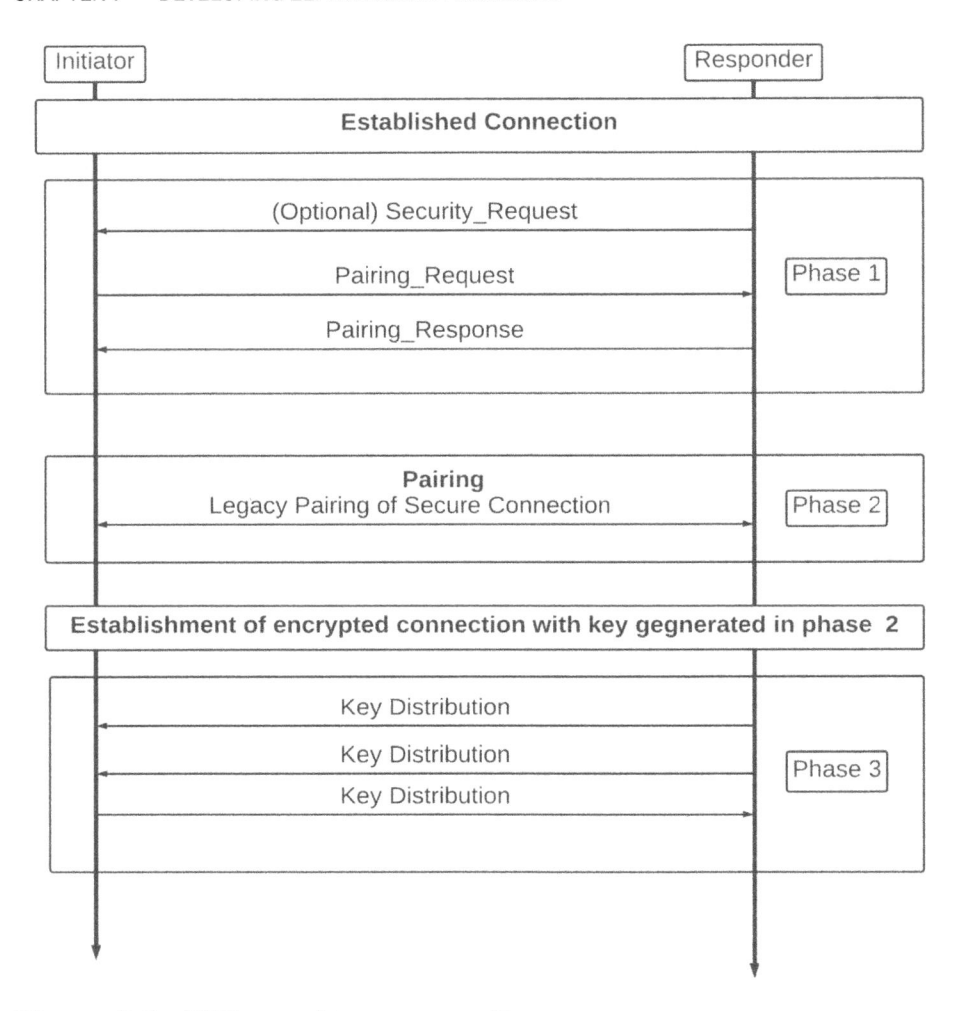

Figure 7-8. *BLE security sequence diagram*

Based on the preceding schematic, pairing is the combination of Phases 1 and 2, and bonding is represented by Phase 3. Pairing is a temporary security measure that does not persist across connections and has to be initiated and completed each time the two devices reconnect and would like to encrypt the connection between them. In order to extend the encryption across subsequent connections, bonding must occur between the two devices.

CHAPTER 7 DEVELOPING ZEPHYR BLE APPLICATIONS

Building and Testing Peripheral and Central BLE Applications

Building and testing BLE applications requires setting up, at a minimum, a small BLE network containing several BLE nodes running, for example, a BLE peripheral application, a BLE central application, and, possibly, a BLE communications scanning and protocol analysis application. The examples covered here involve Nordic Semiconductor nRF devices using a combination of nRF52840 DK, nRF52840 dongle, a mobile phone, and the nRF Connect Bluetooth Low Energy application. An alternative approach is to simulate a BLE network and BLE applications using Renode.

The nRF52840 Dongle and Its Uses

The nRF52840 dongle is a small (compact), low-cost, USB dongle based on the nRF52840 chipset from Nordic Semiconductor that has a few I/O peripherals that include one button, two LEDs (one green, one RGB), and 15 GPIO pins. As a dongle, it can be used to enable nRF Connect PC applications such as the Bluetooth Low Energy application (central and peripheral emulator), the nRF Cloud Gateway application, and the RSSI Viewer application. As a development kit, it can be used to develop custom applications and run sample applications that are provided in the nRF Connect SDK and run BLE example programs. The dongle can also be programmed to work as a BLE sniffer.

CHAPTER 7   DEVELOPING ZEPHYR BLE APPLICATIONS

nRF Connect Bluetooth Low Energy Applications

The nRF Connect application can be thought of as a single hub (access point) for desktop-based nRF applications. As shown in Figure 7-9, the applications include a Bluetooth Low Energy application, a Power Profiler, a Programmer, and an RSSI Viewer.

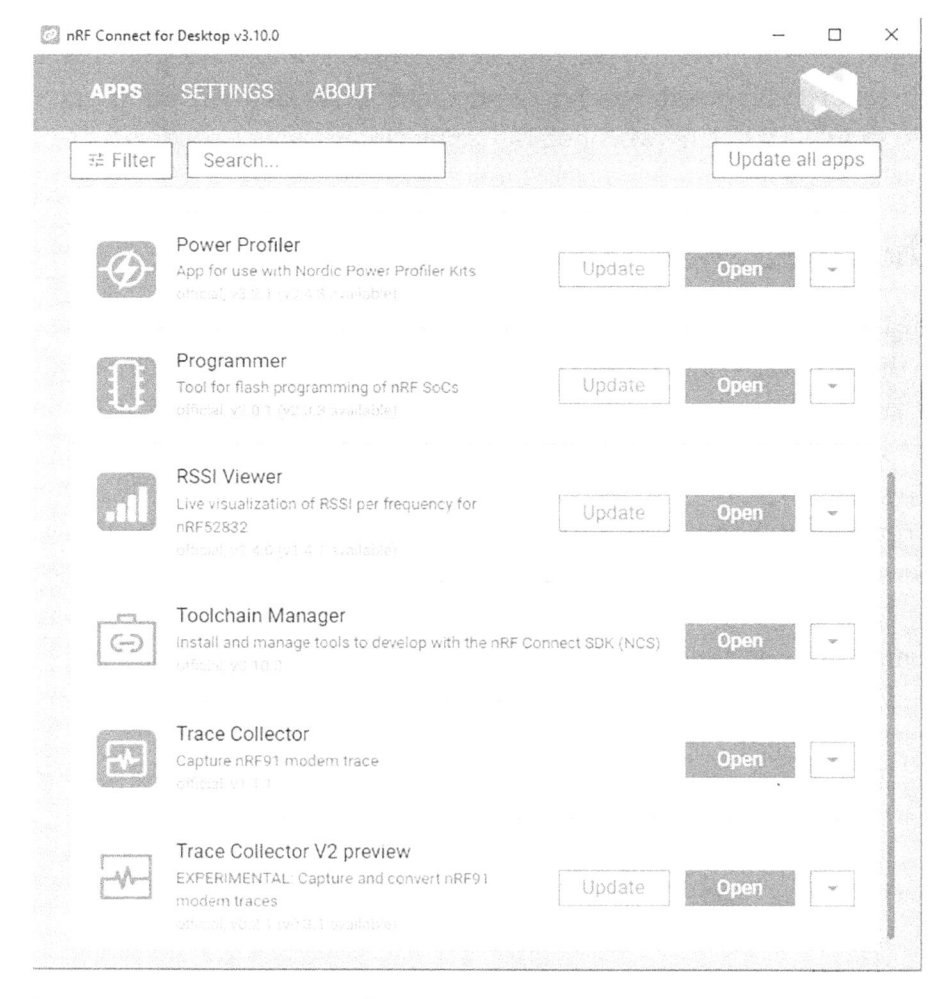

Figure 7-9. nRF Connect for Desktop

CHAPTER 7　DEVELOPING ZEPHYR BLE APPLICATIONS

Note　As the nRF Connect for Desktop moves to newer versions, the screen captures shown here may differ from those actually observed.

A Bluetooth Low Energy application has two modes of operation. It can be run either as a BLE central device that can discover advertising devices (broadcasters and peripherals) or as a BLE peripheral that advertises, allows connections, and exposes a GATT server. The GATT server can be customized with SIG-adopted services and characteristics or, even, with custom services and characteristics.

Setting Up an nRF52840 Dongle for Use with the nRF Connect for Desktop nRF BLE Application

In order to use an nRF52840 dongle with the nRF BLE Application, it needs to be programmed with the appropriate firmware. The steps required are to insert the dongle into a PC USB port, start the nRF Connect for Desktop Bluetooth Low Energy application (see Figure 7-10), and then click on SELECT DEVICE for the discovered device (Figure 7-11) and then go ahead and program it (Figure 7-12).

CHAPTER 7   DEVELOPING ZEPHYR BLE APPLICATIONS

Figure 7-10. Starting the nRF Connect for Desktop Bluetooth Low Energy application

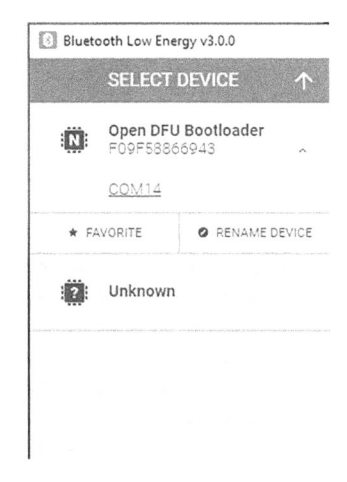

Figure 7-11. Selecting a discovered device

CHAPTER 7　DEVELOPING ZEPHYR BLE APPLICATIONS

Figure 7-12. *Confirming the selection of a discovered device*

After device programming has completed, the device details are displayed as shown in Figure 7-13.

Figure 7-13. *Displaying details of a programmed device*

Once the dongle has been programmed, it can be used as either a BLE central or as a BLE peripheral.

Using the Dongle in BLE Central Mode

In this mode, the application can be used to discover neighboring advertising devices, connect to an advertising device, and interact with the connected peripheral's GATT server via reads and writes, notifications,

CHAPTER 7 DEVELOPING ZEPHYR BLE APPLICATIONS

as well as indications on characteristics. Scanning for BLE peripherals involves scanning for an advertising BLE device by clicking the Start scan button and selecting a device of interest.

The advertising data associated with a device can be displayed by clicking on the Details button. A connection to a peripheral device can, then, be made by clicking the Connect button next to that device in the scan results. Once a connection to a peripheral has been established, it is possible to browse and navigate the different services and characteristics exposed by the GATT server on that device. The nRF Connect Bluetooth Low Energy app allows for concurrent connections to multiple peripherals.

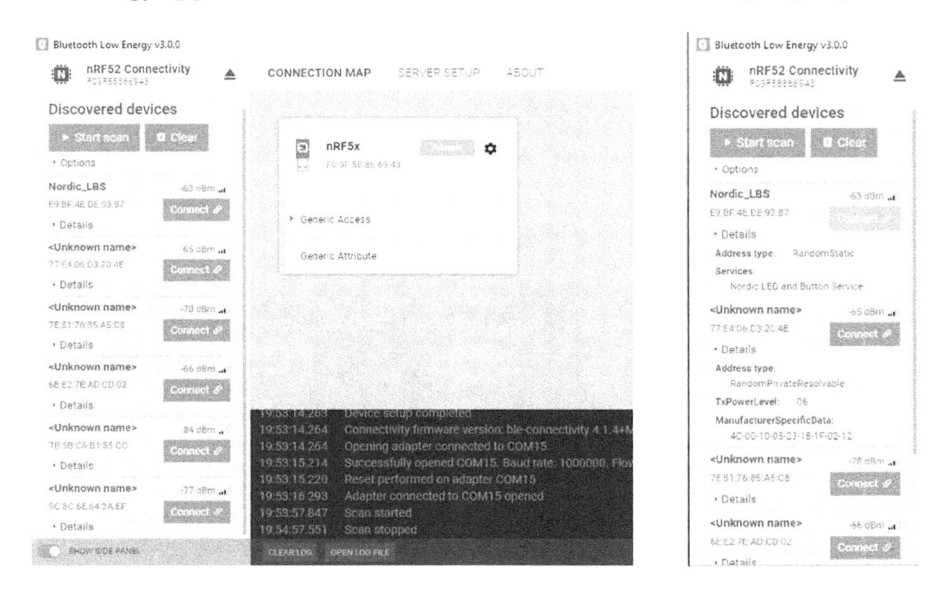

Figure 7-14. Screen captures showing the use of the BLE Dongle in central mode

Clicking on the details option for a device will provide extra information.

CHAPTER 7 DEVELOPING ZEPHYR BLE APPLICATIONS

BLE Network Connection Map

The connection map view in the Bluetooth Low Energy app visualizes the established connections and can be used to inspect and manage connection details, as shown in Figure 7-15.

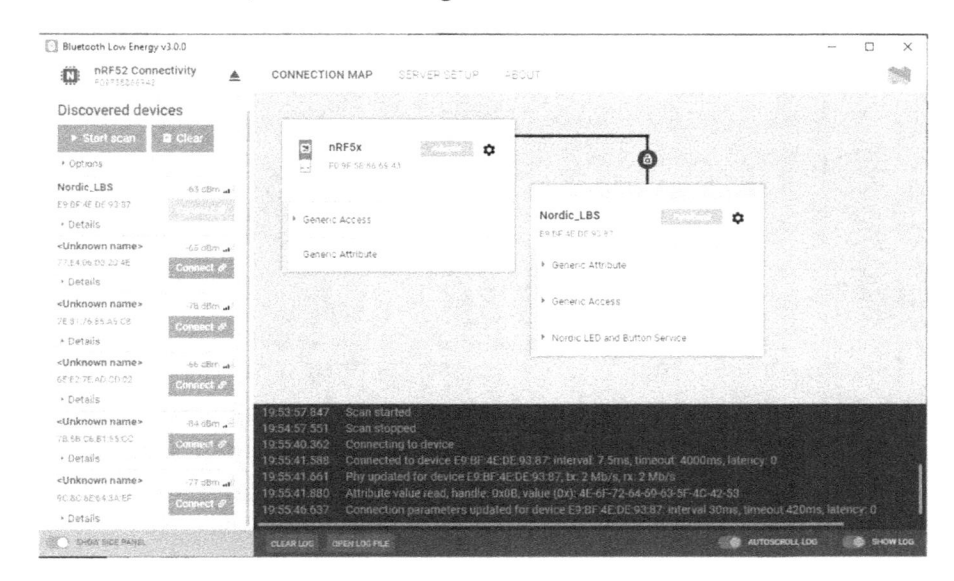

Figure 7-15. BLE network connection map

As an example, a peripheral application that exposes an LED and Button service nrf/samples/bluetooth/peripheral_lbs can be programmed into an nRF52840 DK board, and then the Bluetooth Low Energy app running in central mode can be used to interact with it.

In the Connection Map, hovering over the connection lock icon will display the parameters and properties of the connection such as connection interval, slave latency, supervision timeout, bonding status, and pairing status, as shown in the following screen capture. This feature is demonstrated in Figure 7-16.

CHAPTER 7   DEVELOPING ZEPHYR BLE APPLICATIONS

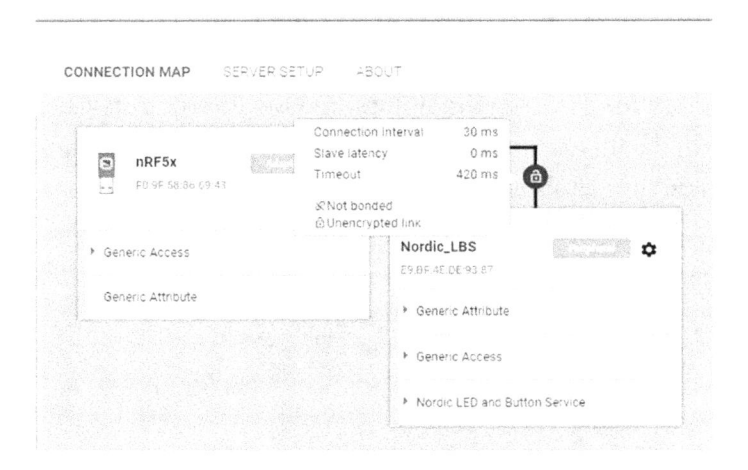

Figure 7-16. Connection details

Clicking on the connection options icon pops up a menu (Figure 7-17), which can be used to change the properties of the connection (since the dongle acts in the central role, and hence it controls the parameters) such as altering the connection parameters, initiating pairing, and disconnecting.

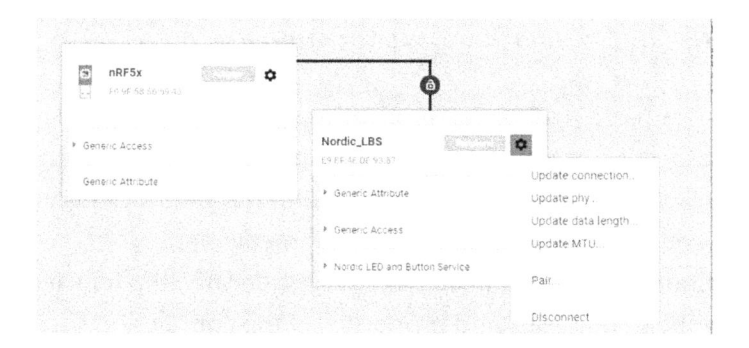

Figure 7-17. Changing the connection properties menu

Clicking on a service associated with a selected link brings up a dialog submenu via which reads and writes, as illustrated in Figures 7-18 and 7-19, to a peripheral can be performed.

CHAPTER 7   DEVELOPING ZEPHYR BLE APPLICATIONS

Figure 7-18. Reading button state

Figure 7-19. Writing button state

335

CHAPTER 7 DEVELOPING ZEPHYR BLE APPLICATIONS

Using the Dongle in BLE Peripheral Mode

When run in peripheral mode, the dongle is set up to act as a peripheral. When running the application in this mode, it is possible to set up and configure the different parameters and services and characteristics exposed by the emulated GATT server. This is done by running the server setup, which can be accessed by navigating to the Server Setup tab, shown in Figure 7-20.

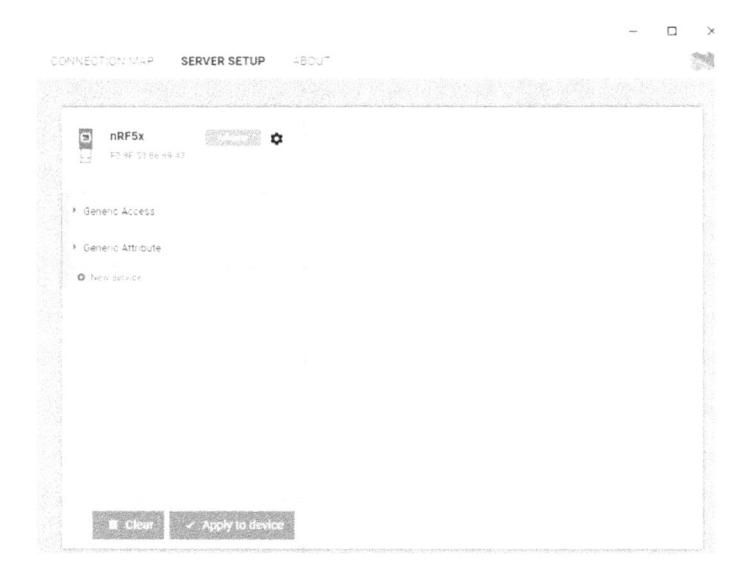

Figure 7-20. Setting up the dongle as a peripheral

The Generic Access service is a mandatory service and is always present. Within the service, the Device Name, Appearance, and Peripheral Preferred Connection Parameters are defined. These characteristics can be modified via the application by clicking on them and then editing the corresponding values and properties. Figure 7-21 illustrates configuring the Device Name.

CHAPTER 7 DEVELOPING ZEPHYR BLE APPLICATIONS

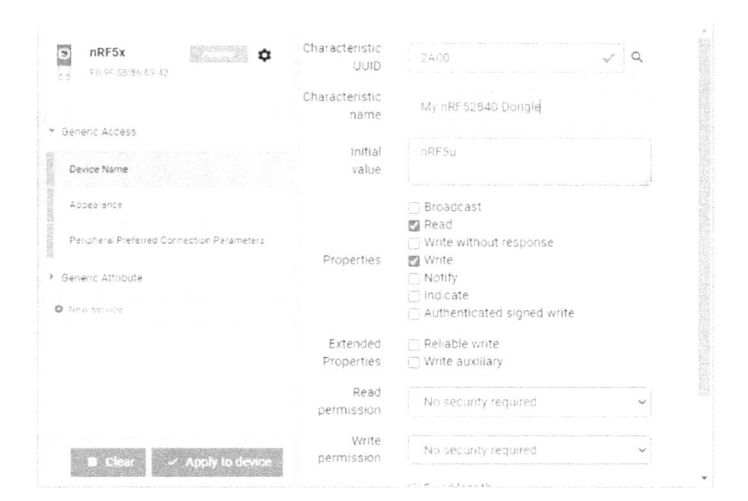

Figure 7-21. *Configuring the Device Name*

Once a service has been configured/customized, it can be applied by clicking on the "Apply to device" button and then, in the Connection Map tab, clicking on the gear button next to the nRF5x dongle listing and then clicking on Start advertising, as shown in Figure 7-22.

CHAPTER 7　DEVELOPING ZEPHYR BLE APPLICATIONS

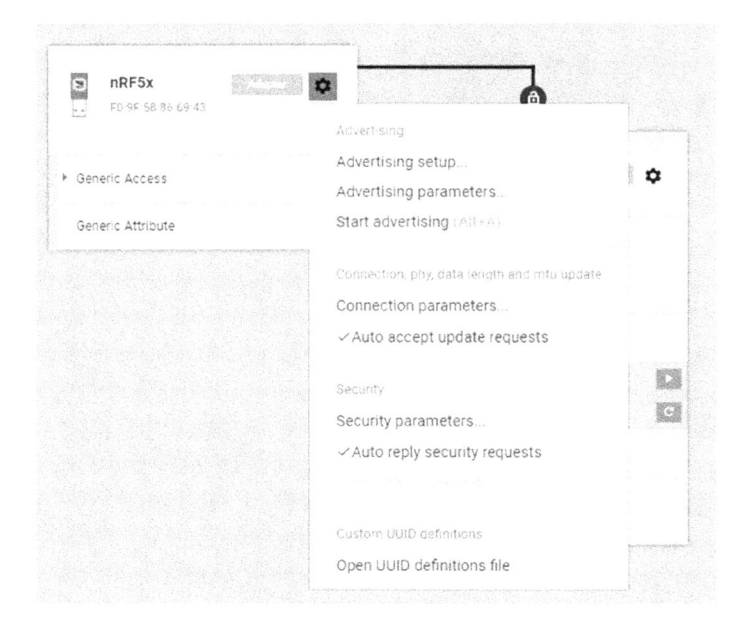

Figure 7-22. Advertising Menu showing Start advertising option

Once the dongle starts advertising, a wireless icon will be displayed (see Figure 7-23). It is then possible to check that the device is advertising and working properly by using a BLE client emulator app such as Nordic nRF Connect or LightBlue Explorer running on a mobile phone.

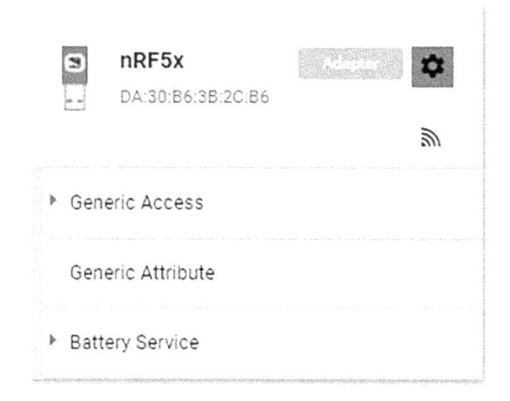

Figure 7-23. Adapter advertising

338

CHAPTER 7　DEVELOPING ZEPHYR BLE APPLICATIONS

Using the Power Mode Emulation to Set Up an Emulated Battery Service

The dongle-based emulation can be set up to act as a peripheral exposing various services and characteristics exposed by the GATT server by navigating to the Server Setup tab and then clicking on the service to be created, having selected it from the list of listed services, for example, the battery service (shown in Figure 7-24).

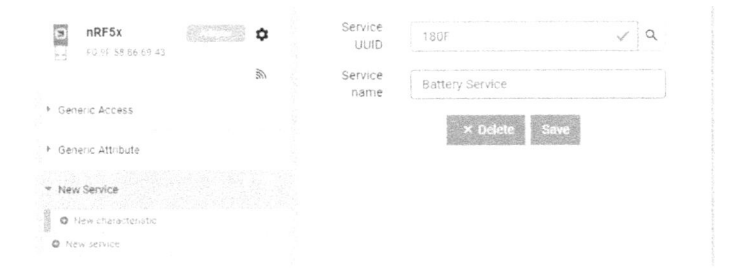

Figure 7-24. Configuring dongle to emulate the battery service

Then, a characteristic can be created by selecting a characteristic from the list of characteristics and clicking on it, for example, the battery level, as in Figure 7-25.

339

CHAPTER 7   DEVELOPING ZEPHYR BLE APPLICATIONS

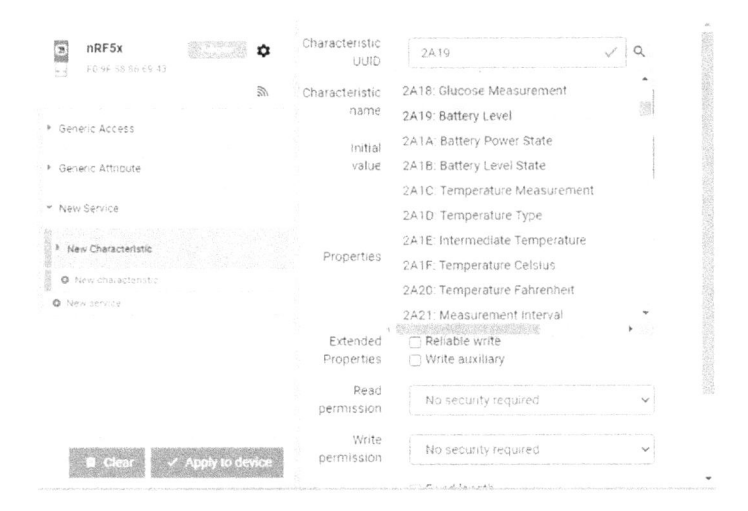

Figure 7-25.   Selecting the Battery Level characteristic

The properties for this characteristic such as its initial value and the read, write, notify, and indicate behaviors can then be set (Figure 7-26).

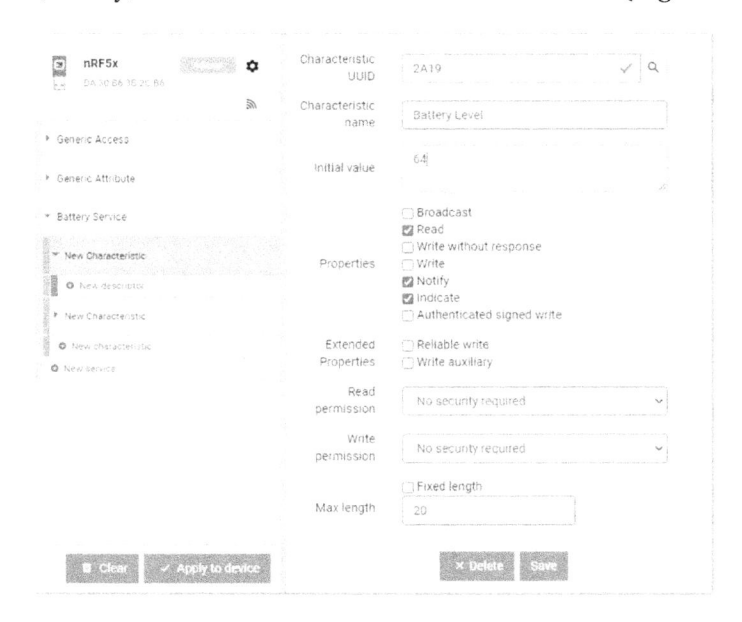

Figure 7-26.   Setting properties for the battery level characteristic

CHAPTER 7 DEVELOPING ZEPHYR BLE APPLICATIONS

If Notify and Indication are set, as in this example, then, it is necessary to create a Client Characteristic Configuration Descriptor for the Battery Level by clicking on New Characteristic, followed by clicking on the newly created characteristic and then selecting the Client Characteristic Configuration Descriptor. This is demonstrated in Figure 7-27.

Figure 7-27. Configuring a Client Characteristic

The configuration can then be applied to the device by clicking on the Apply to device button. If this will involve overwriting an existing configuration, then a dialog asking for confirmation to reset the device will be shown (see Figure 7-28).

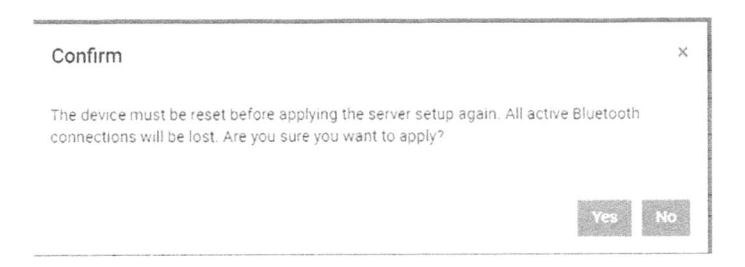

Figure 7-28. Confirming a client characteristic configuration

The last step is to navigate to the Connection Map and click on the gear button next to the nRF5u dongle listing and then click on Start advertising.

341

CHAPTER 7 DEVELOPING ZEPHYR BLE APPLICATIONS

To test out the peripheral, a central is needed. One way is to use a mobile phone, for example, an iPhone application such as LightBlue (see figure 7-29). When this application starts, it will scan for and display a list of nearby peripherals. Selecting the dongle (the nRF5u peripheral) will establish a connection, and the Battery Service can be discovered by interrogating the selected peripheral for the services it provides.

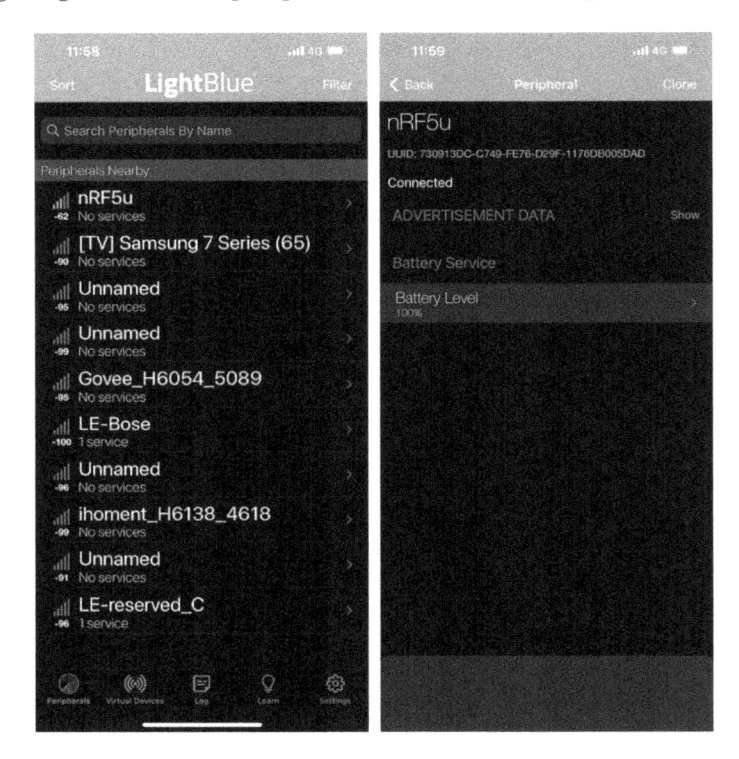

Figure 7-29. LightBlue app selecting a nearby peripheral

Clicking on the Battery Level will show the details and options for interacting with the service over the established connection as shown in the following phone screen image capture.

Clicking on the Battery Service in the Connection Map tab will bring up a dialog for interacting with the Battery Service on the peripheral.

BLE Application Development APIs Provided by Zephyr and the nRF Connect SDK

The Zephyr set of BLE APIs is both large and extensive. Only the most essential APIs needed to get started with BLE application development will be covered here. The core, fundamental, Zephyr BLE APIs are the ATT, GAP, GATT, UUID, SDP (Service Discovery Protocol) API, and Logical Link Control and Adaptation Protocol (L2CAP) APIs.

When developing Zephyr RTOS applications for Nordic nRF devices, it is common practice to use the nRF Connect SDK, which includes standard Zephyr as well as Nordic-specific libraries and source code files. A Bluetooth Low Energy (LE) application must include a Bluetooth LE Controller, which implements the Link Layer, the low-level, real-time protocol that controls Bluetooth LE communications.

The nRF Connect SDK provides two implementations of a Bluetooth LE Controller: the SoftDevice Controller implemented by Nordic Semiconductor and the open source Zephyr Link Layer implementation. Both of these Link Layers integrate with the Zephyr Bluetooth Host firmware, which completes the full Bluetooth LE protocol stack solution in the nRF Connect SDK. In general, either Bluetooth LE Controller can be used for application development.

The SoftDevice Controller was designed for nRF52 and nRF53 Series devices and is provided as a set of precompiled libraries conforming to the Bluetooth 5.2 specification as well as some extensions for high-performance applications such as Low Latency Packet Mode (LLPM) operation.

The Zephyr Bluetooth Low Energy stack includes a Zephyr Bluetooth LE Controller implemented in the form of an upper and a lower implementation suited to supporting multiple hardware platforms. To use Zephyr's Bluetooth LE Controller in an application, it is necessary to include a Controller-only build of the Bluetooth LE stack. Zephyr's Bluetooth LE Controller implementation supports most standard Bluetooth LE features.

Chapter 7 Developing Zephyr BLE Applications

Starting with ATT, the file zephyr\include\zephyr\bluetooth\att.h defines the various error codes for Error response PDUs and for the Common Profile error codes. It also provides an enum for enhanced and unenhanced channels.

```
enum bt_att_chan_opt {
    /** Both Enhanced and Unenhanced channels can be used  */
    BT_ATT_CHAN_OPT_NONE = 0x0,
    /** Only Unenhanced channels will be used  */
    BT_ATT_CHAN_OPT_UNENHANCED_ONLY = BIT(0),
    /** Only Enhanced channels will be used  */
    BT_ATT_CHAN_OPT_ENHANCED_ONLY = BIT(1),
};
```

A good way to learn how to develop Bluetooth Low Energy (BLE) applications with Zephyr RTOS, and the way to follow to go beyond the introductory coverage in this chapter, is to study the basic and the more advanced BLE samples by building them, running them, and then going through the code carefully and looking at the various data structures, macros, and function prototypes in the corresponding header files.

In this section, some basic BLE examples will be explored to serve as a starting point for developing more complex applications and the study of some of the more complex samples given in the nRF Connect SDK and Zephyr sources. Study of these examples will also help in becoming familiar with the way the Zephyr source code tree is structured and becoming proficient in reading and studying the source code.

A key file is `zephyr/subsys/bluetooth/host/att_internal.h,` which is the header file concerned with attribute protocol handling. It defines all the relevant data structures, function pointer types, and the ATT API-associated function prototypes such as those for `bt_att_init, bt_att_create_pdu, bt_att_send,` and `bt_att_req_send.`

CHAPTER 7 DEVELOPING ZEPHYR BLE APPLICATIONS

The code makes extensive use of GNU C extensions to specify details such as the packing and alignment of data structures. For example, the bt_att_signed_write_cmd structure is defined in the following way:

```
/* Signed Write Command */
#define BT_ATT_OP_SIGNED_WRITE_CMD      0xd2
struct bt_att_signed_write_cmd {
    uint16_t handle;
    uint8_t  value[0];
} __packed;
```

Here, although the size of a zero-length array is zero, an array member of this kind may increase the size of the enclosing type as a result of tail padding. The offset of a zero-length array member from the beginning of the enclosing structure is the same as the offset of an array with one or more elements of the same type. The alignment of a zero-length array is the same as the alignment of its elements. The __packed qualifier forces the alignment of all the fields of a structure/union on a single byte boundary (i.e., with no padding). The constraints on using the __packed qualifier are that it cannot be used for structures or unions with floating-point fields. Neither can it be used for structures that were previously declared without __packed, and it applies to all the members of a union or structure when that structure is declared using __packed. In particular, there is no padding between members of the data structure, or at the end of the structure. Also, all the substructures of a packed structure must also have been declared using __packed. This packing and alignment to a byte level is very well suited to transmission of packed byte-oriented data.

The header file dealing with UUIDs is zephyr/includezephyr/bluetooth/uuid.h.

It contains many data structure definitions as well as helper macros and builder macros.

CHAPTER 7   DEVELOPING ZEPHYR BLE APPLICATIONS

```
/** Size in octets of a 128-bit UUID */
#define BT_UUID_SIZE_128            16

struct bt_uuid_128 {
      /** UUID generic type. */
      struct bt_uuid uuid;
      /** UUID value, 128-bit in little-endian format. */
      uint8_t val[BT_UUID_SIZE_128];
};
#define BT_UUID_INIT_128(value...)        \
{                                         \
      .uuid = { BT_UUID_TYPE_128 },       \
      .val = { value },                   \
}
```

For example, #define BT_UUID_INIT_128(value...) is a macro that can be used to initialize a 128-bit UUID where value is a set of 128-bit UUID values in little-endian format. The macro because of the ellipsis (...) is a variadic macro. In C variadic macros, when the macro is invoked, all the tokens in its argument list after the last named argument (this macro has none), including any commas, become the variable arguments.

This, in turn, can be used in a helper macro that declares a 128-bit UUID given a readable form of UUID as shown here:

```
#define BT_UUID_DECLARE_128(value...) \
      ((struct bt_uuid *) ((struct bt_uuid_128[]) \ {BT_UUID_
      INIT_128(value)}))
```

CHAPTER 7 DEVELOPING ZEPHYR BLE APPLICATIONS

The Source BLE Structure in the Zephyr Source Code

The stack source code is organized in the source tree in a reasonably logical manner.

In the Bluetooth subsys directory, the host stack code is in subsys/bluetooth/host. The host code deals with HCI command and event handling, connection tracking, and the implementation of the BLE core protocols including L2CAP, ATT, and SMP.

The controller stack code in subsys/bluetooth/controller implements things such as the controller side of the HCI (Host Controller Interface), the Link Layer, and also the code to access the radio transceiver.

The public API header files, which applications need to include to be able to make use of Bluetooth functionality, are to be found in include/bluetooth/, and the HCI transport drivers are to be found in drivers/bluetooth/.

Building, Programming, and Configuring Host Roles

In Zephyr, corresponding to the GAP roles Peripheral and Central for the connection-oriented roles and broadcaster and observer for the connectionless roles are the corresponding Kconfig build-time configuration options CONFIG_BT_PERIPHERAL, CONFIG_BT_CENTRAL, CONFIG_BT_BROADCASTER, and CONFIG_BT_OBSERVER.

Basic Peripheral Example

The example described here is to be found at zephyr\samples\bluetooth\peripheral_hr and is provided as part of the Zephyr source code tree. The application exposes the HR (Heart Rate) GATT Service, and once a

CHAPTER 7   DEVELOPING ZEPHYR BLE APPLICATIONS

device connects to it, it generates simulated heart rate values. The heart rate profile is documented on the BLE website at www.bluetooth.com/specifications/specs/heart-rate-profile-1-0/.

The command can be built using west; the command to build the application for the nRF52840 DK board is `west build -b nrf52840dk_nrf52840` and then flashed to the target board using the command `west flash`.

Running the application and connecting and disconnecting should produce output something like the following in a terminal console such as PuTTY:

```
*** Booting Zephyr OS build v3.1.99-ncs1-1  ***
[00Bluetooth initialized
Advertising successfully started
:00:00.004,455] <inf> sdc_hci_driver: SoftDevice Controller build revision:
                                    29 5c 92 f1 36 81 92
d1  b7 a9 f0 f1 99 e9 4c 19  |)\..6... ......L.
                                    1f 23 83 4a
|.#.J
[00:00:00.007,354] <inf> bt_hci_core: HW Platform: Nordic Semiconductor (0x0002)
[00:00:00.007,415] <inf> bt_hci_core: HW Variant: nRF52x (0x0002)
[00:00:00.007,415] <inf> bt_hci_core: Firmware: Standard Bluetooth controller (0x00) Version 41.37468 Build 2457941745
[00:00:00.008,575] <inf> bt_hci_core: Identity: E9:BF:4E:DE:93:87 (random)
[00:00:00.008,605] <inf> bt_hci_core: HCI: version 5.3 (0x0c) revision 0x11d8, manufacturer 0x0059
[00:00:00.008,636] <inf> bt_hci_core: LMP: version 5.3 (0x0c) subver 0x11d8
```

CHAPTER 7 DEVELOPING ZEPHYR BLE APPLICATIONS

```
Connected
[00:01:41.754,089] <wrn> bt_l2cap: Ignoring data for unknown
channel ID 0x003a
[00:01:42.384,185] <inf> hrs: HRS notifications enabled
Disconnected (reason 0x13)
[00:02:31.973,510] <inf> hrs: HRS notifications disabled
```

The corresponding iPhone screenshots for the nRF Toolbox app are shown in the following sequence of image captures.

Starting the nRF Toolbox app displays a list of services of possible interest.

Clicking on the heart rate service (HRS) displays a message saying there is no connected device and a Connect button.

Clicking on the Connect button brings up a dialogue showing the result of scanning for services with UUID corresponding to the heart rate service (see Figure 7-30). Clicking on the heart rate service starts the connection process and, once connected, plots the heart rate values as they are sent at regular intervals. The application, as implemented, also supports the battery service, and the battery level is also displayed. The connection can be terminated by clicking on the Disconnect button (Figure 7-31).

CHAPTER 7 DEVELOPING ZEPHYR BLE APPLICATIONS

Figure 7-30. Apple iPhone Connect application scanning for services

CHAPTER 7   DEVELOPING ZEPHYR BLE APPLICATIONS

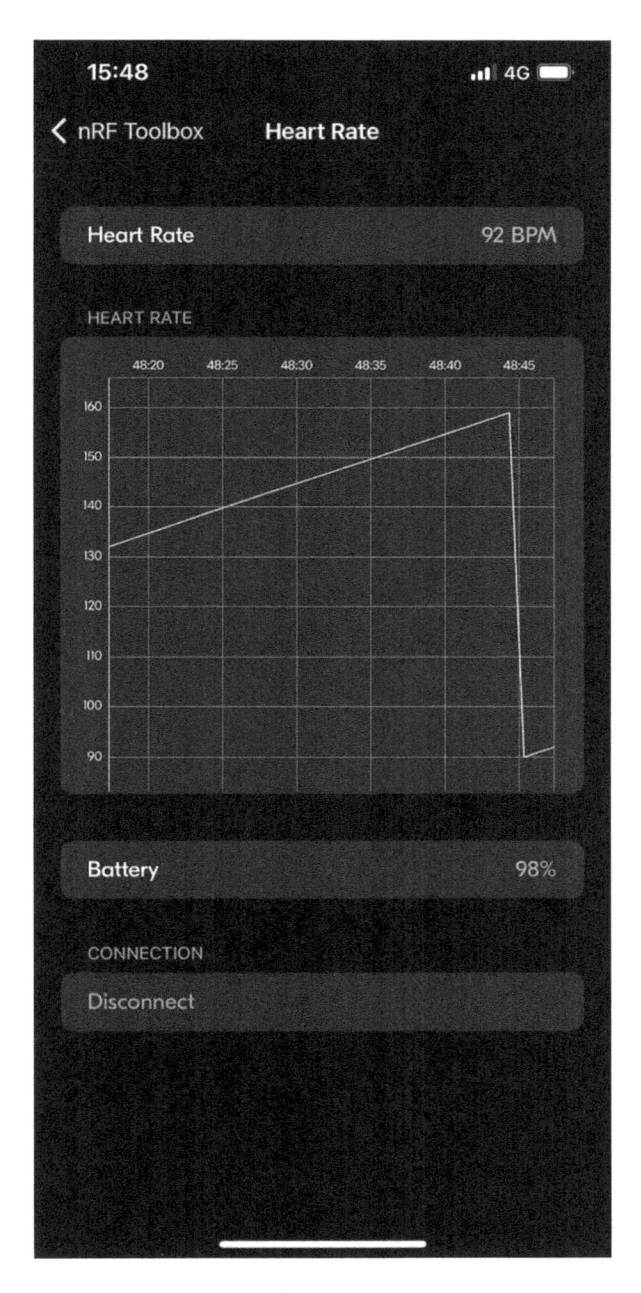

Figure 7-31. Heart Rate Data display

CHAPTER 7 DEVELOPING ZEPHYR BLE APPLICATIONS

The prj.conf file for this project lists the various BLE modules to be included in the application build.

```
CONFIG_BT=y
CONFIG_BT_DEBUG_LOG=y
CONFIG_BT_SMP=y
CONFIG_BT_PERIPHERAL=y
CONFIG_BT_DIS=y
CONFIG_BT_DIS_PNP=n
CONFIG_BT_BAS=y
CONFIG_BT_HRS=y
CONFIG_BT_DEVICE_NAME="Zephyr Heartrate Sensor"
CONFIG_BT_DEVICE_APPEARANCE=833
```

The project consists of a single main.c file.

The include files required by the application are included at the beginning of main.c.

```
#include <zephyr/types.h>
#include <stddef.h>
#include <string.h>
#include <errno.h>
#include <zephyr/sys/printk.h>
#include <zephyr/sys/byteorder.h>
#include <zephyr/zephyr.h>

#include <zephyr/bluetooth/bluetooth.h>
#include <zephyr/bluetooth/hci.h>
#include <zephyr/bluetooth/conn.h>
#include <zephyr/bluetooth/uuid.h>
#include <zephyr/bluetooth/gatt.h>
#include <zephyr/bluetooth/services/bas.h>
#include <zephyr/bluetooth/services/hrs.h>
```

CHAPTER 7   DEVELOPING ZEPHYR BLE APPLICATIONS

The array of services supported by the application is defined as an array of struct bt_data values.

```
static const struct bt_data ad[] = {
    BT_DATA_BYTES(BT_DATA_FLAGS, (BT_LE_AD_GENERAL | BT_LE_
    AD_NO_BREDR)),
    BT_DATA_BYTES(BT_DATA_UUID16_ALL,
              BT_UUID_16_ENCODE(BT_UUID_HRS_VAL),
              BT_UUID_16_ENCODE(BT_UUID_BAS_VAL),
              BT_UUID_16_ENCODE(BT_UUID_DIS_VAL))
};
```

The connection callback functions are defined, and the connection callbacks structure is initialized as shown in the following code snippet:

```
static void connected(struct bt_conn *conn, uint8_t err)
{
    if (err) {
        printk("Connection failed (err 0x%02x)\n", err);
    } else {
        printk("Connected\n");
    }
}
static void disconnected(struct bt_conn *conn, uint8_t reason)
{
    printk("Disconnected (reason 0x%02x)\n", reason);
}

BT_CONN_CB_DEFINE(conn_callbacks) = {
    .connected = connected,
    .disconnected = disconnected,
};
```

353

CHAPTER 7   DEVELOPING ZEPHYR BLE APPLICATIONS

The battery service (BAS) and heart rate service (HRS) notify functions that send simulated values are straightforward, as can be seen from the following code:

```
static void bas_notify(void)
{
      uint8_t battery_level = bt_bas_get_battery_level();
      battery_level--;
      if (!battery_level) {
            battery_level = 100U;
      }
      bt_bas_set_battery_level(battery_level);
}
static void hrs_notify(void)
{
      static uint8_t heartrate = 90U;
      /* Heartrate measurements simulation */
      heartrate++;
      if (heartrate == 160U) {
            heartrate = 90U;
      }
      bt_hrs_notify(heartrate);
}
```

The bt_ready() function in the application code is called after Bluetooth initialization and calls the bt_le_adv_start() function to start advertising, or sends a printk error message if advertising startup fails.

```
static void bt_ready(void)
{
      int err;
      printk("Bluetooth initialized\n");
      err = bt_le_adv_start(BT_LE_ADV_CONN_NAME, ad,
```

CHAPTER 7 DEVELOPING ZEPHYR BLE APPLICATIONS

```
                                    ARRAY_SIZE(ad),
                                    NULL, 0);
    if (err) {
        printk("Advertising failed to start
        (err %d)\n", err);
        return;
    }
    printk("Advertising successfully started\n");
}
```

The callback function auth_cancel reports on pairing cancellation and is used to initialize the authenticated pairing callback structure auth_cb_display as shown in the code that follows:

```
static void auth_cancel(struct bt_conn *conn)
{
    char addr[BT_ADDR_LE_STR_LEN];
    bt_addr_le_to_str(bt_conn_get_dst(conn), addr,
    sizeof(addr));
    printk("Pairing cancelled: %s\n", addr);
}
static struct bt_conn_auth_cb auth_cb_display = {
    .cancel = auth_cancel,
};
```

The application itself, which runs in the thread associated with the main() function, is relatively straightforward to read. The BLE details are taken care of by the BLE libraries provided by Zephyr and Nordic (in the case where the Nordic BLE firmware is used).

```
void main(void)
{
    int err;
```

355

```
        err = bt_enable(NULL);
        if (err) {
                printk("Bluetooth init failed (err %d)\n", err);
                return;
        }
bt_ready();
        bt_conn_auth_cb_register(&auth_cb_display);
        while (1) {
                k_sleep(K_SECONDS(1));
                /* Heartrate measurements simulation */
                hrs_notify();
                /* Battery level simulation */
                bas_notify();
        }
}
```

Here, a mobile phone is acting as a central. The Zephyr source tree contains many examples of implementing centrals on BLE-enabled boards such as the nRF52840 DK. They include a `central_hr` example, which will be reviewed next.

Bluetooth: Central/Heart Rate Monitor

This example, `samples/bluetooth/central_hr`, specifically looks for heart rate monitors and reports the heart rate readings once connected.

The code shows a typical approach to searching for particular peripherals and, then, connecting to a desired peripheral when it is found.

The main() function is very simple:

```
void main(void)
{
        int err;
```

CHAPTER 7   DEVELOPING ZEPHYR BLE APPLICATIONS

```
    err = bt_enable(NULL);
    if (err) {
        printk("Bluetooth init failed (err %d)\n", err);
        return;
    }
    printk("Bluetooth initialized\n");
    start_scan();
}
```

Scanning is initiated by the start_scan() function, which defines and initializes a variable of type struct bt_le_scan_param and then calls the API function bt_le_scan_start() whose first argument is a pointer to struct bt_le_scan_param variable and whose second argument is a function pointer to a callback function that handles the initial processing of device details as devices are found. The details are shown in the following code snippet:

```
static void start_scan(void)
{
    int err;
    /* Use active scanning and disable duplicate filtering to handle any
     * devices that might update their advertising data at runtime. */
    struct bt_le_scan_param scan_param = {
            .type       = BT_LE_SCAN_TYPE_ACTIVE,
            .options    = BT_LE_SCAN_OPT_NONE,
            .interval   = BT_GAP_SCAN_FAST_INTERVAL,
            .window     = BT_GAP_SCAN_FAST_WINDOW,
    };
    err = bt_le_scan_start(&scan_param, device_found);
    if (err) {
```

357

CHAPTER 7 DEVELOPING ZEPHYR BLE APPLICATIONS

```
        printk("Scanning failed to start (err %d)\n", err);
        return;
    }
    printk("Scanning successfully started\n");
}
```

Active scanning (BT_LE_SCAN_TYPE_ACTIVE) involves sending scan requests to all advertisers asking them for their scan response packets in addition to the advertisement packets. In this example, the scan window (how long to scan) and the scan interval (how long to wait between scans) are set to fast so as to provide a faster response.

The callback function type for reporting BLE scan results (bt_le_scan_cb_t) has the following parameters:

- addr – Advertiser LE address and type
- rssi – Strength of advertiser signal
- adv_type – Type of advertising response from the advertiser
- buf – Buffer containing advertiser data, of type struct net_buf_simple

struct net_buf_simple is defined in buf.h and contains three fields:

- uint8_t * data – A pointer to the start of data in the buffer
- uint16_t len – The length of the data pointed to
- uint16_t size – The amount of data that a net_buf_simple::__buf can store

The code for device_found is shown as follows:

```
static void device_found(const bt_addr_le_t *addr, int8_t rssi, uint8_t type,
```

358

CHAPTER 7 DEVELOPING ZEPHYR BLE APPLICATIONS

```
                struct net_buf_simple *ad)
{
    char dev[BT_ADDR_LE_STR_LEN];
    bt_addr_le_to_str(addr, dev, sizeof(dev));
    printk("[DEVICE]: %s, AD evt type %u, AD data len %u,
    RSSI %i\n",
            dev, type, ad->len, rssi);
    if (type == BT_GAP_ADV_TYPE_ADV_IND ||
        type == BT_GAP_ADV_TYPE_ADV_DIRECT_IND) {
           bt_data_parse(ad, eir_found, (void *) addr);
    }
}
```

BT_GAP_ADV_TYPE_ADV_IND - identifies scannable and connectable advertising

BT_GAP_ADV_TYPE_ADV_DIRECT_IND - identifies directed connectable advertising.

The logical expression

```
(type == BT_GAP_ADV_TYPE_ADV_IND ||
type == BT_GAP_ADV_TYPE_ADV_DIRECT_IND)
```

therefore selects connectable advertising events. In the example, the objective is to find a peripheral providing an HR (heart rate) service that can be "connected to."

When such an event is identified, the data associated with it is parsed by calling the API function bt_data_parse(ad, eir_found, (void *) addr). This is a helper function used when parsing basic data types that occur in Extended Inquiry Response (EIR), Advertising Data (AD), and OOB data blocks. Its common use occurs when it is called inside the callback function passed to bt_le_scan_start(). Its function prototype, declared in the header file "bluetooth.h", is

CHAPTER 7   DEVELOPING ZEPHYR BLE APPLICATIONS

```
void bt_data_parse ( struct net_buf_simple * ad,
            bool(*) (struct bt_data *data, void *user_
            data)  func,
            void *  user_data
     )
```

where the parameters are as follows:

- ad - Advertising data as passed to the bt_le_scan_cb_t callback
- func - A callback function that will be called for each element in the advertising data, which returns a boolean, true or false, value, which, if true, causes parsing to continue and, if false, stops parsing
- user_data - A pointer to user data to be passed to the callback function#

void bt_data_parse is destructive, in the sense that it consumes ad when parsing. It is the responsibility of the application to create a copy of the original data if that data is to be used later on.

The code for eir_found is shown in the next code snippet. It looks for an advertisement from a peripheral with the sought for UUID, and if it finds one, it attempts to create a connection to it.

```
static bool eir_found (struct bt_data *data, void *user_data)
{
        bt_addr_le_t *addr = user_data;
        int i;
        printk("[AD]: %u data_len %u\n", data->type,
        data->data_len);
        switch (data->type) {
        case BT_DATA_UUID16_SOME:
        case BT_DATA_UUID16_ALL:
```

CHAPTER 7   DEVELOPING ZEPHYR BLE APPLICATIONS

```
if (data->data_len % sizeof(uint16_t) != 0U) {
    printk("AD malformed\n");
    return true;
}
for (i = 0; i < data->data_len; i +=
sizeof(uint16_t)) {
    struct bt_le_conn_param *param;
    struct bt_uuid *uuid;
    uint16_t u16;
    int err;
    memcpy(&u16, &data->data[i], sizeof(u16));
    uuid = BT_UUID_DECLARE_16(sys_le16_to_
    cpu(u16));
    if (bt_uuid_cmp(uuid, BT_UUID_HRS)) {
        continue;
    }
    err = bt_le_scan_stop();
    if (err) {
        printk("Stop LE scan failed
        (err %d)\n", err);
        continue;
    }
    param = BT_LE_CONN_PARAM_DEFAULT;
    err = bt_conn_le_create(addr, BT_CONN_LE_
    CREATE_CONN, param, &default_conn);
    if (err) {
        printk("Create conn failed
        (err %d)\n", err);
        start_scan();
    }
```

```
            return false;
        }
    }
    return true;
}
```

Recall that advertising data is made up of Advertising Data (AD) elements, where each element has the following structure:

- 1st byte – Length of the element (excluding the length of byte itself)

- 2nd byte – AD type – Specifies the type of data is included in the element

- AD data – The actual data

The possible AD type values are listed on the Bluetooth SIG website [5]. Here, the type values of interest are the following two.

BT_DATA_UUID16_SOME has a #define of 0x02, which implies that the data has 16-bit Service Class UUIDs available, but that this is not a complete list and more are available.

BT_DATA_UUID16_ALL has a #define of 0x03, which implies that the data is a complete list of 16-bit Service Class UUIDs.

data->data_len % sizeof(uint16_t) != 0U checks that the data is well formed, which requires it to be a multiple of 2 bytes.

BT_UUID_DECLARE_16(sys_le16_to_cpu(u16)) returns a pointer to a generic UUID given a 16-bit UUID value in host endian format. sys_le16_to_cpu takes a 16-bit integer in little-endian format and converts it from little-endian to host endianness.

UUIDs are compared with bt_uuid_cmp(), which has the function prototype (defined in the header file uuid.h).

```
int bt_uuid_cmp ( const struct bt_uuid * u1, const struct bt_uuid * u2 )
```

CHAPTER 7   DEVELOPING ZEPHYR BLE APPLICATIONS

It returns a negative value if u1 < u2, 0 if u1 == u2, and a positive value otherwise.

If uuid matches the uuid for the heart rate service, then the value returned is 0. This is interpreted as false, and the next statement executed if there is a match is err = bt_le_scan_stop();. If bt_le_scan_stop() stops scanning without error, then bt_conn_le_create is called.

The bt_conn_le_create function prototype is defined in the header file zephyr/bluetooth/conn.h. bt_conn_le_creat attempts to create an LE connection to a remote device given its address. It uses the BLE General Connection Establishment procedure. It should be noted that an application must disable explicit scanning before attempting to initiate a new BLE connection. The return value is 0 on success or a nonzero error code otherwise. The function prototype and descriptions of the various parameters follow.

```
int bt_conn_le_create ( const bt_addr_le_t *  peer,
            const struct bt_conn_le_create_param
            *   create_param,
            const struct bt_le_conn_param * conn_param,
            struct bt_conn ** conn
    )
```

The parameters are as follows:

- peer – The remote address
- create_param – The connection parameters for the connection to be created
- conn_param – The initial parameters to be used in trying to create the BLE connection
- conn – A pointer to a valid connection object on success

BT_LE_CONN_PARAM_DEFAULT, in zephyr/bluetooth/conn.h, defines the default connection parameters, which are 30–50 ms for the connection interval and 4 s for the timeout value. It is defined as

BT_LE_CONN_PARAM(BT_GAP_INIT_CONN_INT_MIN, \
                                       BT_GAP_INIT_CONN_INT_MAX, \
                                       0, 400)

BT_CONN_LE_CREATE_CONN defines default LE create connection parameters that specify continuous scanning, by setting the scan interval equal to the scan window. It is defined as

BT_CONN_LE_CREATE_PARAM(BT_CONN_LE_OPT_NONE, \
                                       BT_GAP_SCAN_FAST_INTERVAL, \
                                       BT_GAP_SCAN_FAST_INTERVAL)

The connection callbacks for connection events are set up using the macro BT_CONN_CB_DEFINE as follows:

```
BT_CONN_CB_DEFINE(conn_callbacks) = {
     .connected = connected,
     .disconnected = disconnected,
};
```

which invokes other macros to carry out the low-level work involved.

The connected function's main task is to fill out a bt_gatt_discover_params instance, static struct bt_gatt_discover_params discover_params, and then to call bt_gatt_discover. struct bt_gatt_discover_params contains a pointer to the discovery function and is initialized like this discover_params.func = discover_func;. The job of the discovery function is to carry out the discovery process by invoking bt_gatt_discover and then to subscribe to the required service by calling bt_gatt_ subscribe. One of the arguments passed to bt_gatt_discover is a struct bt_gatt_subscribe_params instance subscribe_params, which contains a function pointer to a notify function that will handle notifications.

discover_params and subscribe_params are defined as static global variables.

```
static struct bt_gatt_discover_params discover_params;
static struct bt_gatt_subscribe_params subscribe_params;
```

A static global variable uuid is also defined and initialized to 0.

```
static struct bt_uuid_16 uuid = BT_UUID_INIT_16(0);
```

The whole process of connecting and subscribing is fairly logical, but, as always, the "devil lies in the detail."

Overview of the Connected Function

The code for the connected function is listed in the following code snippet:

```
static void connected(struct bt_conn *conn, uint8_t conn_err)
{
    char addr[BT_ADDR_LE_STR_LEN];
    int err;
    bt_addr_le_to_str(bt_conn_get_dst(conn), addr,
    sizeof(addr));
    if (conn_err) {
        printk("Failed to connect to %s (%u)\n", addr,
        conn_err);
        bt_conn_unref(default_conn);
        default_conn = NULL;
        start_scan();
        return;
```

CHAPTER 7 DEVELOPING ZEPHYR BLE APPLICATIONS

```
      }
      printk("Connected: %s\n", addr);
      if (conn == default_conn) {
            memcpy(&uuid, BT_UUID_HRS, sizeof(uuid));
            discover_params.uuid = &uuid.uuid;
            discover_params.func = discover_func;
            discover_params.start_handle = BT_ATT_FIRST_
            ATTRIBUTE_HANDLE;
            discover_params.end_handle = BT_ATT_LAST_
            ATTRIBUTE_HANDLE;
            discover_params.type = BT_GATT_DISCOVER_PRIMARY;
            err = bt_gatt_discover(default_conn, &discover_
            params);
            if (err) {
                  printk("Discover failed(err %d)\n", err);
                  return;
            }
      }
}
```

On achieving a successful connection (the error code in err is 0), printk prints out a suitable message to this effect. If the connection is the one associated with the application (i.e., conn == default_conn), then the global variable uuid is initialized to hold the information associated with the heart rate service, memcpy(&uuid, BT_UUID_HRS, sizeof(uuid));.

The uuid, func, start_handle, end_handle, and type fields of the discover_params global variable are then initialized before calling bt_gatt_discover. BT_ATT_FIRST_ATTRIBUTE_HANDLE is defined to be 0x0001 as 0x0000 is reserved for future use.

BT_ATT_LAST_ATTRIBUTE_HANDLE is defined to be 0xffff.

BT_GATT_DISCOVER_PRIMARY indicates discovery of primary services.

discover_func function is the discover attribute callback function. If the discovery procedure has completed, the callback function will be called with attr set to NULL. This will not happen if the attribute discovery procedure was stopped by a return value of BT_GATT_ITER_STOP in a prior call to it. The attr argument is a pointer to a struct bt_gatt_att whose definition is

```
struct bt_gatt_attr {
    const struct bt_uuid *uuid;
    bt_gatt_attr_read_func_t read;
    bt_gatt_attr_write_func_t write;
    void *user_data;
    uint16_t handle;
    uint16_t perm;  /* Will be 0 if returned from bt_gatt_
    discover() */
};
```

The following snippet shows its implementation for this application:

```
static uint8_t discover_func(struct bt_conn *conn,
    const struct bt_gatt_attr *attr, struct bt_gatt_discover_
    params *params)
{
    int err;
    if (!attr) {
        printk("Discover complete\n");
        (void) memset (params, 0, sizeof(*params));
        return BT_GATT_ITER_STOP;
    }
    printk("[ATTRIBUTE] handle %u\n", attr->handle);
    if (!bt_uuid_cmp(discover_params.uuid, BT_UUID_HRS)) {
        memcpy(&uuid, BT_UUID_HRS_MEASUREMENT,
        sizeof(uuid));
```

```
                discover_params.uuid = &uuid.uuid;
                discover_params.start_handle = attr->handle + 1;
                discover_params.type = BT_GATT_DISCOVER_
                CHARACTERISTIC;
                err = bt_gatt_discover(conn, &discover_params);
                if (err) {
                        printk("Discover failed (err %d)\n", err);
                }
        } else if (!bt_uuid_cmp(discover_params.uuid,
                        BT_UUID_HRS_MEASUREMENT)) {
                memcpy(&uuid, BT_UUID_GATT_CCC, sizeof(uuid));
                discover_params.uuid = &uuid.uuid;
                discover_params.start_handle = attr->handle + 2;
                discover_params.type = BT_GATT_DISCOVER_DESCRIPTOR;
                subscribe_params.value_handle = bt_gatt_attr_value_
                handle(attr);
                err = bt_gatt_discover(conn, &discover_params);
                if (err) {
                        printk("Discover failed (err %d)\n", err);
                }
        } else {
                subscribe_params.notify = notify_func;
                subscribe_params.value = BT_GATT_CCC_NOTIFY;
                subscribe_params.ccc_handle = attr->handle;
                err = bt_gatt_subscribe(conn, &subscribe_params);
                if (err && err != -EALREADY) {
                        printk("Subscribe failed (err %d)\n", err);
                } else {
                        printk("[SUBSCRIBED]\n");
                }
                return BT_GATT_ITER_STOP;
```

CHAPTER 7   DEVELOPING ZEPHYR BLE APPLICATIONS

```
        }
        return BT_GATT_ITER_STOP;
}
```

If !bt_uuid_cmp(discover_params.uuid, BT_UUID_HRS) is true, the attribute discover_params.uuid matches BT_UUID_HRS. The next step is to modify discover_params, setting the uuid value to BT_UUID_HRS_MEASUREMENT, setting the start_handle to attr->handle + 1 (i.e., adding an offset of 1 to attr->handle), and setting the discover_params.type to BT_GATT_DISCOVER_CHARACTERISTIC to specify discovery of the characteristic value and its properties. The subscribe_params.value_handle is set to bt_gatt_attr_value_handle(attr), and then bt_gatt_discover is called with the newly modified discover_params argument.

The final, else, sets the subscribe_params fields as follows:

```
subscribe_params.notify = notify_func;
subscribe_params.value = BT_GATT_CCC_NOTIFY;
subscribe_params.ccc_handle = attr->handle;
```

and calls bt_gatt_subscribe with these subscribe_params. On success, a printk message indicating successful subscription is sent using printk and the value BT_GATT_ITER_STOP returned.

Having completed a successful subscription, use is then made of the notify callback, notify_func, which prints out data it receives and whose code is shown in the following code snippet:

```
static uint8_t notify_func(struct bt_conn *conn,
      struct bt_gatt_subscribe_params *params,  const void
      *data, uint16_t length)
{
      if (!data) {
            printk("[UNSUBSCRIBED]\n");
            params->value_handle = 0U;
```

369

```
                return BT_GATT_ITER_STOP;
        }
        printk("[NOTIFICATION] data %p length %u\n", data,
        length);
        return BT_GATT_ITER_CONTINUE;
}
```

Building the central_hr example and having a setup where one nRF52840 DK board is running the central_hr code and the other is running the peripheral_hr code will produce printk output something like the following from the board running the central_hr application:

```
*** Booting Zephyr OS build v3.3.99-ncs1-1 ***
[00:00:00.000,366] <inf> bt_sdc_hci_driver: hci_driver_open:
SoftDevice Controller build revision:
                                             e0 7e 2e c1 5e 05
85 23  46 15 dc fa 8e 29 7d 70 |.~..^..# F....)}p
                                             10 93 a5 fc
                              |....
[00:00:00.003,326] <inf> bt_hci_core: hci_vs_init: HW Platform:
Nordic Semiconductor (0x0002)
[00:00:00.003,356] <inf> bt_hci_core: hci_vs_init: HW Variant:
nRF52x (0x0002)
[00:00:00.003,387] <inf> bt_hci_core: hci_vs_init: Firmware:
Standard Bluetooth controller (0x00) Version 224.11902 Build
2231721665
[00:00:00.004,455] <inf> bt_hci_core: bt_dev_show_info:
Identity: E9:BF:4E:DE:93:87 (random)
[00:00:00.004,486] <inf> bt_hci_core: bt_dev_show_info: HCI:
version 5.4 (0x0d) revision 0x1077, manufacturer 0x0059
[00:00:00.004,516] <inf> bt_hci_core: bt_dev_show_info: LMP:
version 5.4 (0x0d) subver 0x1077
```

```
Bluetooth initialized
Scanning successfully started
[DEVICE]: F6:89:DA:3E:20:DE (random), AD evt type 0, AD data
len 11, RSSI -32
[AD]: 1 data_len 1
[AD]: 3 data_len 6
Connected: F6:89:DA:3E:20:DE (random)
[ATTRIBUTE] handle 25
[ATTRIBUTE] handle 26
[ATTRIBUTE] handle 28
[SUBSCRIBED]
[NOTIFICATION] data 0x20007e1b length 2
[NOTIFICATION] data 0x20007e1b length 2
[NOTIFICATION] data 0x20007e1b length 2
[NOTIFICATION] data 0x20007e1b length 2
[NOTIFICATION] data 0x20007e1b length 2
[NOTIFICATION] data 0x20007e1b length 2
[NOTIFICATION] data 0x20007e1b length 2
[NOTIFICATION] data 0x20007e1b length 2
[NOTIFICATION] data 0x20007e1b length 2
[NOTIFICATION] data 0x20007e1b length 2
```

Is It Possible to Run Both a Peripheral and a Central on the Same Board?

The answer is that it is indeed possible to code an application involving both a peripheral and a central running on the same device. The sample \nrf\samples\bluetooth\central_and_peripheral_hr in the nRF Connect SDK shows how to build an application with Central and Peripheral roles running concurrently. As might be expected, this application makes use of multiple threads.

CHAPTER 7   DEVELOPING ZEPHYR BLE APPLICATIONS

What Next?

Between them, the Zephyr framework Bluetooth examples and the nRF Bluetooth examples provided the nRF Connect SDK cover many different scenarios. The nRF Connect SDK documentation [6] provides links to descriptions of the nRF Connect SDK Bluetooth samples, and the Zephyr documentation [7] provides links to descriptions of the Bluetooth samples that have been contributed to the Zephyr framework. Renode can be used for multi-node BLE development and debugging purposes, and the Antmicro blog post [8] describes how to run the central_hr and peripheral_hr applications together in Renode.

Summary

This chapter has covered the basics of the BLE protocol and explained key concepts such as central and peripheral, ATT and GATT, advertising, connecting to a service, and client-server aspects of BLE. It has walked through the Zephyr RTOS examples showing peripheral and central application implementation using an nRF52840 DK and an nRF52840 dongle. Some of the important macros associated with the BLE API have also been overviewed.

References

1. https://docs.nordicsemi.com/bundle/ncs-latest/page/nrf/protocols/bt/index.html

2. https://microchipdeveloper.com/wireless:ble-link-layer-discovery

3. https://microchipdeveloper.com/wireless:ble-link-layer-roles-states

CHAPTER 7 DEVELOPING ZEPHYR BLE APPLICATIONS

4. https://microchipdeveloper.com/wireless:ble-link-layer-packet-types

5. www.bluetooth.com/specifications/assigned-numbers/generic-access-profile

6. https://developer.nordicsemi.com/nRF_Connect_SDK/doc/latest/nrf/samples/bl.html

7. https://docs.zephyrproject.org/latest/samples/bluetooth/bluetooth.html

8. https://antmicro.com/blog/2022/04/developing-and-testing-ble-on-nrf52840-with-renode-and-zephyr/

CHAPTER 8

Zephyr RTOS and Ethernet, Wi-Fi, and TCP/IP

Networking lies at the heart of IoT, and Zephyr provides extensive embedded TCP/IP networking support. This chapter assumes that you have a basic understanding of computer networking and TCP/IP. The focus here will be on developing application using the Zephyr RTOS networking framework.

Zephyr's network stack is a Zephyr OS stack implementation. As with most networking stacks, it has a layered architecture where the interface associated with a given layer provides services to other layers. In Zephyr, the network stack functionality to be incorporated into an application is specified by selecting the required Kconfig options.

Zephyr's network stack has many components, and its architecture is summarized in the diagrams in Figures 8-1 through 8-3, going from application layers and ending up at the physical layer.

CHAPTER 8   ZEPHYR RTOS AND ETHERNET, WI-FI, AND TCP/IP

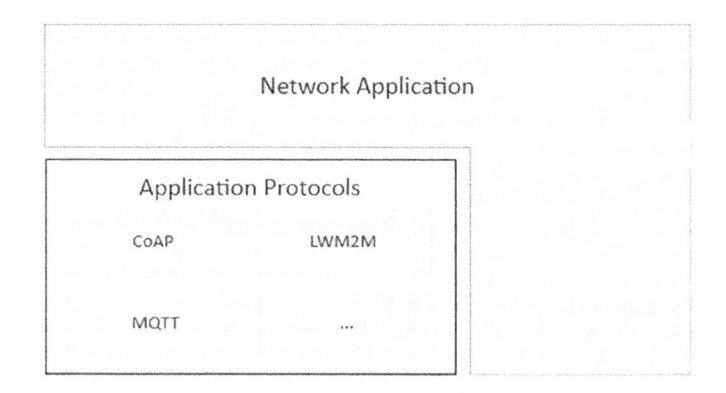

Figure 8-1. Network Application

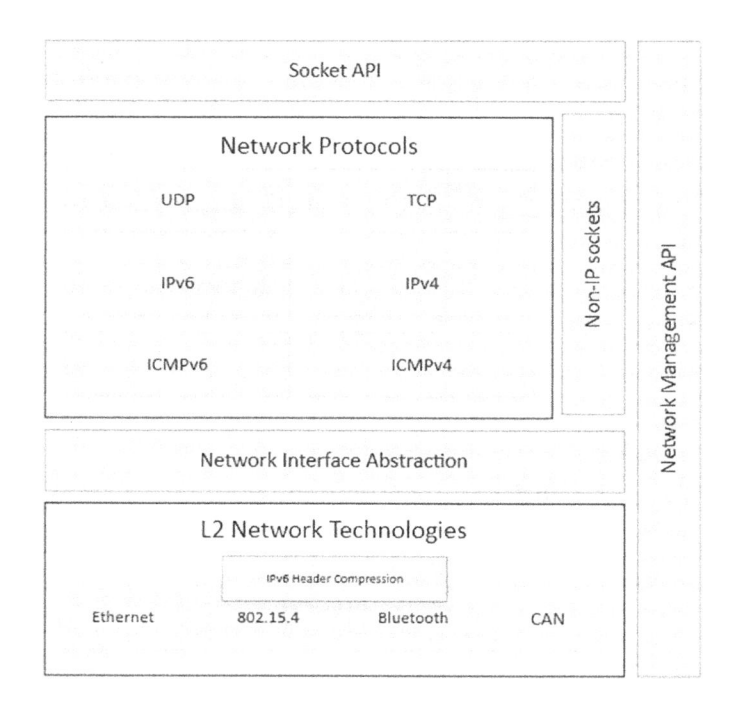

Figure 8-2. Network Protocols

CHAPTER 8   ZEPHYR RTOS AND ETHERNET, WI-FI, AND TCP/IP

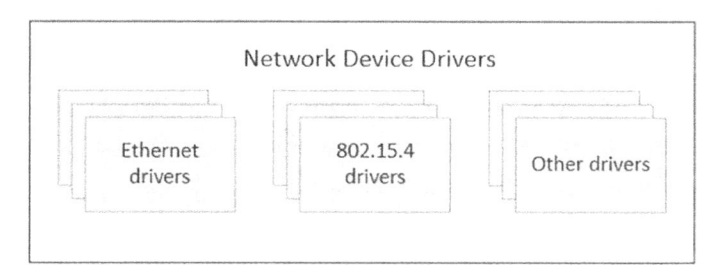

Figure 8-3. Network Device Drivers

A Zephyr network application can use the application-level protocol libraries provided by Zephyr. Alternatively networking applications can be developed that make use of Zephyr's implementation of the BSD Sockets API directly. Zephyr also provides a Network Management API that can be used to configure the network and set networking parameters such as network link options, starting a scan (when applicable), listen for network configuration events, and more. Zephyr's network interface API can be used to perform actions such as assigning an IP address to a network interface, taking a network interface down, and more.

Application layer protocols supported by Zephyr include CoAP, LwM2M, and MQTT.

TCP/IP layer 3 and layer 4 protocols supported by Zephyr include IPv6, IPv4, UDP, TCP, ICMPv4, and ICMPv6, and these protocols are accessed via the BSD Sockets API.

Layer 2 (Link Layer) Network Technologies supported in Zephyr include Ethernet, IEEE 802.15.4, Bluetooth, and CAN bus.

The low-level device drivers are responsible for the physical layer sending and receiving of network packets.

Common practice when implementing Zephyr networking applications is to run the application code in userspace context and the network stack code in kernel context.

CHAPTER 8   ZEPHYR RTOS AND ETHERNET, WI-FI, AND TCP/IP

The Zephyr Network Interface Abstraction layer plays an important role in providing a common API functionality for network interfaces, especially the ability to set network interfaces up or down. Data transfers for sent and received data take place via a network interface. In Zephyr, network interfaces cannot be created at runtime. A special linker section containing information about network interfaces is created as part of the build process and populated with them at linking time. Network interfaces are created by the use of the `NET_DEVICE_INIT()` macro or a more specialized variant. In the case of an Ethernet network, the `ETH_NET_DEVICE_INIT()` macro should be used as it will create VLAN interfaces automatically if `CONFIG_NET_VLAN` is enabled. Network initialization macros are mostly used in network device driver implementation.

A network interface can be turned ON by calling `net_if_up()` and OFF by calling `net_if_down()`. In Zephyr, the default behavior is that when a networking device is powered ON, the network interface is also turned ON. Network interfaces can be referenced via a struct net_if * pointer or via a network interface index. A network interface can be resolved from its index by calling net_if_get_by_index() and from an interface pointer by calling net_if_get_by_iface().

For IP networks, the IP address for a network device must be set correctly. IP addresses can be set automatically via DHCPv4 or manually by using an API function such as `net_if_ipv4_addr_add()`.

The Zephyr networking framework provides a mechanism for prioritizing certain classes of packets. The intention is to enable higher priority packets to be sent or received earlier than lower priority packets. To include support for packet prioritization, Zephyr provides the `CONFIG_NET_TC_TX_COUNT` and `CONFIG_NET_TC_RX_COUNT` options.

`CONFIG_NET_TC_TX_COUNT` is used to define the number of Tx (transmit) traffic classes a network device can have, and `CONFIG_NET_TC_RX_COUNT` is used to define the number of Rx (receive) traffic classes a network device can have.

A network packet priority can then be mapped to the traffic class so that higher prioritized packets can be processed before lower prioritized ones. This involves a queue for each priority with the handling for each queue handled by a separate thread, and a higher traffic class value corresponds to a lower thread priority value. In the case of transmission classes, where the number of classes is 0, transmission network traffic is pushed to the driver directly without any queues. In the case of receive classes, a count value of 0 means that all the network traffic will be pushed from the driver to the application thread without any intermediate RX queue. There is a receive socket queue between the device driver and the application. Disabling the RX thread has the effect that the network device driver, typically running in IRQ context, will handle the packet all the way through to the application. A consequence of this handling is that other incoming packets may be lost if RX processing is time consuming, relative to the packet arrival rate.

Where USERSPACE support is enabled, then in the current implementation, at least 1 TX thread and 1 RX thread need to be enabled.

Zephyr can be used to configure promiscuous mode for network technologies such as Ethernet where this is applicable. If the CONFIG_NET_PROMISCUOUS_MODE is enabled, then all the network packets that the network device driver is able to receive will be accepted. If promiscuous mode is not configured, then only packets destined for the MAC address of the Ethernet device will be accepted. In general, promiscuous mode is used when monitoring all traffic. It is not something that would normally be configured on an embedded system with limited memory and processing resources.

Zephyr and Network Management

The RFC 2863 standard is concerned with that part of the Management Information Base (MIB) concerned with managed objects used for managing network interfaces. It identifies Zephyr's two interface states, namely, the administrative state and the operational state. The administrative state indicates whether an interface is turned ON or OFF. In Zephyr, it is represented by NET_IF_UP flag, which is controlled by the application. Its value can be changed by calling the net_if_up() or net_if_down() function. Just because an interface is up does not mean that it is ready to transmit or receive packets. The operational state represents the internal interface status. It is updated whenever an interface is brought up/down by the application (administrative state changes), or the interface is notified by the driver/L2 that the PHY (layer 1) status has changed, or the interface is notified by the driver/L2 that it joined/left a network.

The PHY status is represented with NET_IF_LOWER_UP flag and can be changed with the functions net_if_carrier_on() and net_if_carrier_off(). By default, this flag is set on for a newly initialized interface. In the case of Ethernet, for example, the carrier state will be changed when an Ethernet cable is connected or disconnected.

The network association status is represented with NET_IF_DORMANT flag and can be changed with net_if_dormant_on() and net_if_dormant_off(). In the case of Wi-Fi, the dormant state is changed when the Wi-Fi driver successfully connects to an access point. The Wi-Fi driver sets the dormant state to ON during initialization, and when it detects that a connection to a Wi-Fi network has been established, the dormant state is set to OFF.

The Zephyr network API provides a number of functions for testing the status of an interface such as `net_if_is_admin_up()`, `net_if_is_carrier_ok()`, and `net_if_is_dormant()`.

Zephyr networking support is quite comprehensive, and the list of available application layer APIs includes many of the protocols that are used in IoT applications, such as

- CoAP
- CoAP client
- HTTP client

- Lightweight M2M (LwM2M)
- MQTT
- MQTT-SN
- SNTP (Simple Network Time Protocol)

Transport and link layer APIs include

- BSD sockets
- APIs for configuring IPv4/IPv6
- API for configuring DNS name resolution
- Various APIs for adding network management and monitoring capabilities to an application

More detailed information can be found in the Zephyr project documentation [1].

When developing a TCP/IP network-based application, it is important to only include and configure only those components that are needed, as the application is the final result of a monolithic build, and including a large number of unnecessary networking features will use up a lot of limited memory resources. This chapter will not aim to provide an encyclopedic coverage of all the networking features that are present in Zephyr. Rather, the aim will be to focus on those components that must be understood and mastered to get started with building useful IoT-oriented applications. As such, the emphasis will be on IPv4. IPv6 is a topic for a more advanced course. The applications explored will use Zephyr's implementation of the BSD Sockets API. The board used will be an STM32 Nucleo board, the Nucleo-F767ZI Board with an ARM Cortex M7 processor with Ethernet built into the SoC (System on Chip).

CHAPTER 8   ZEPHYR RTOS AND ETHERNET, WI-FI, AND TCP/IP

The Nucleo-F767ZI Board

The STM32F767ZI Microcontroller has an ARM Cortex M7 core and has 2 MB Flash and 512 KB SRAM, GPIOs with external interrupt capability, 12-bit ADCs with 24 channels, 12-bit DAC channels, USART and UART Serial peripherals, and I2C and SPI peripherals. The processor also includes General-Purpose Timers, Advanced-Control Timers, Basic Timers, Low-Power Timers, and Watchdog Timers. It also includes CAN 2.0B, SDMMC, USB 2.0 OTG HS/FS, Random Number Generator, and Ethernet peripherals.

The board has three user LEDs, two push buttons (USER and RESET), and an Ethernet RJ45 connector.

The images of the board (Figure 8-4) and its layout (Figure 8-5) are shown.

CHAPTER 8 ZEPHYR RTOS AND ETHERNET, WI-FI, AND TCP/IP

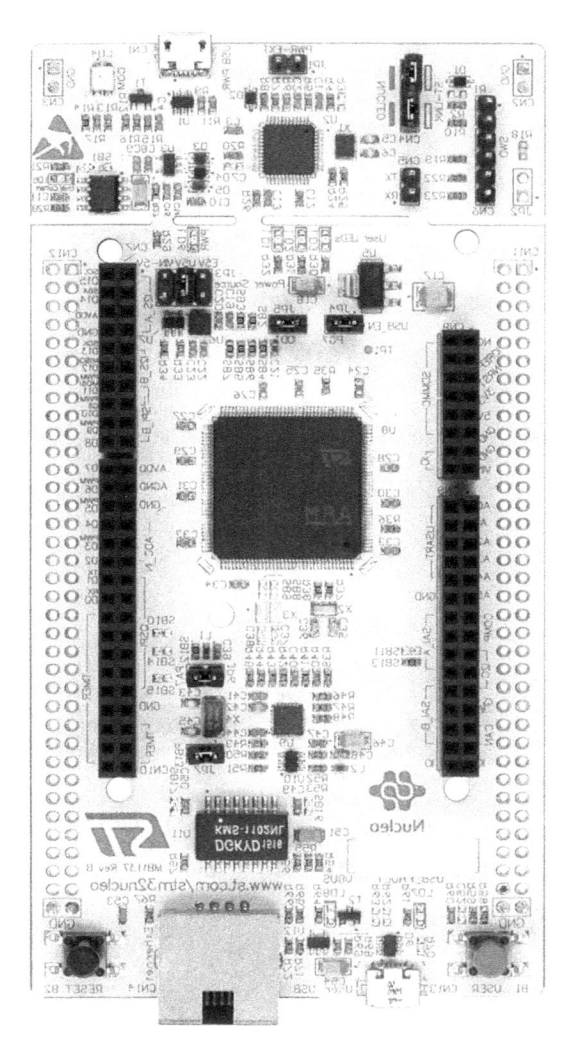

Figure 8-4. Nucleo-F767ZI Board

CHAPTER 8   ZEPHYR RTOS AND ETHERNET, WI-FI, AND TCP/IP

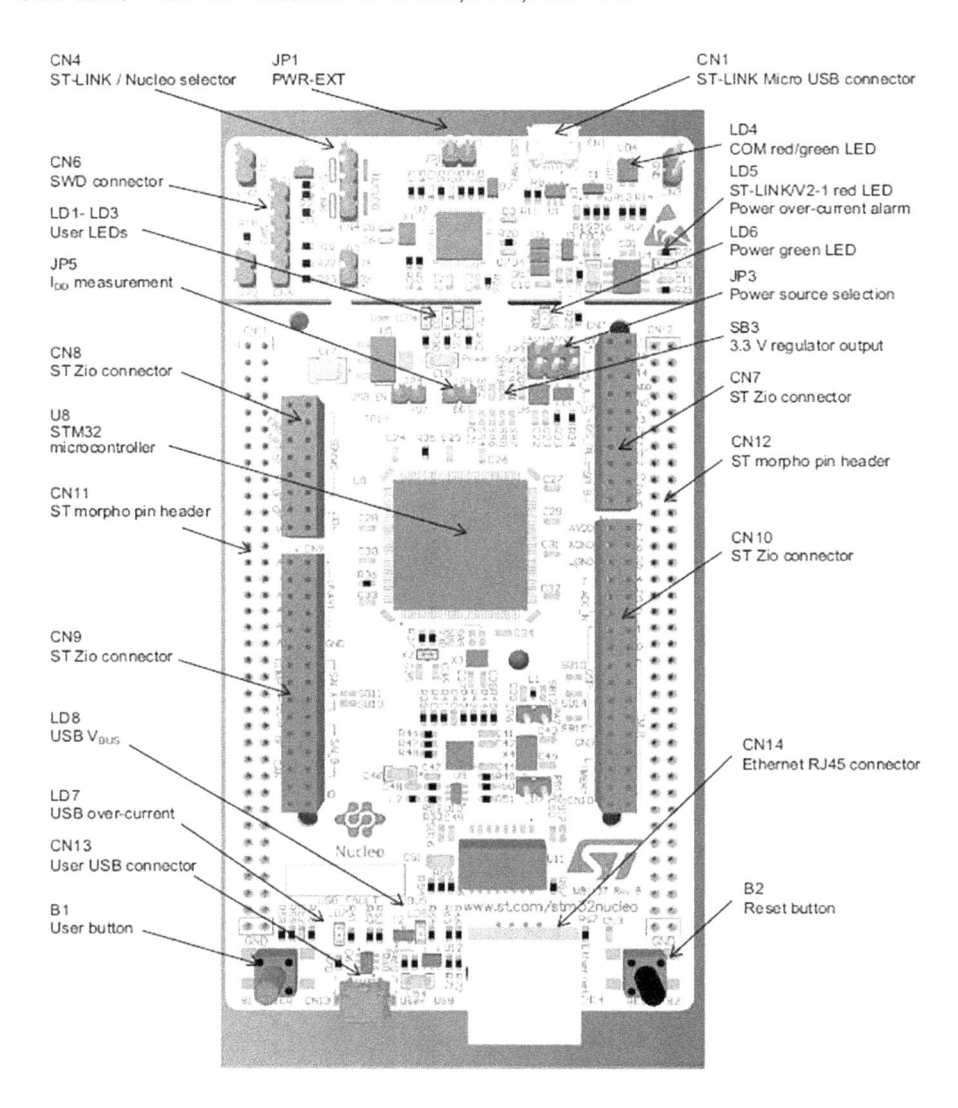

Figure 8-5. *Nucleo-F767ZI Board layout*

CHAPTER 8   ZEPHYR RTOS AND ETHERNET, WI-FI, AND TCP/IP

Building and Troubleshooting the Zephyr Network Programming Examples Using the STM32 Nucleo-F767ZI Board

The Zephyr network programming samples cover many aspects of TCP/IP network programming that include dhcpv4_client, dns_resolve, sockets, ipv4_autoconf, lldp (Link Layer Discovery Protocol, and telnet. There are also IoT-oriented protocol examples that include an lwm2m_client (lightweight M2M client) and an mqtt_publisher example.

When building Zephyr net examples for various boards, problems may arise, because the aim of the Zephyr project is to support a wide range of boards which has the consequence that documentation pertaining to the "quirks and features" of individual boards is sometimes limited. When building and testing network applications, it is often necessary to troubleshoot and carefully check things such as the assignment of IP addresses and subnet masks where IP addresses are being assigned manually, or setting up and configuring DHCP correctly if addresses are being assigned automatically. Running the application in a real network also requires some knowledge of network configuration and troubleshooting. This can include dealing with issues such as configuring firewalls, network routing, and NAT (Network Address Translation) as well as IPv4 and IPv6 configuration details such as the IP address of a default gateway and IP address(es) of DNS resolvers to use.

The Zephyr source code repository has a comprehensive collection of net sockets examples including examples demonstrating a dumb http server, a basic multithreading http server, echo and client servers running over TCP and UDP, an http client, and custom tcp socket client examples. The examples explored in this chapter will be a UDP and TCP echo server example, an asynchronous select example, and a WebSocket client example. These examples correspond, broadly speaking, to the kinds of examples covered when introducing Linux TCP/IP programming. The difference here is that Zephyr applications are monolithic applications and everything that is needed must be built into the application. Historically Zephyr used to incorporate the CivetWeb embedded HTTP server. However, Zephyr's CivetWeb module has been deprecated and removed. The stated cause was complications of maintaining a fork of the, third-party, Civet project in an external module.

The requirements for a Zephyr HTTP server module are that it should interface with existing Zephyr building blocks and support the ZTest Framework, the HTTP, WebSocket, JSON, and mbedTLS libraries and include POSIX API support for socket, threads, and filesystem operations, Kconfig, and Build System to permit tuning of server options. There is also a requirement for Zephyr Iterable Section support, to make possible a more flexible specification of HTTP services and resources.

The BSD Sockets API

The BSD Sockets API (a part of the POSIX standard) was designed at Berkeley in connection with the development of the original version of the TCP/IP protocol.

Zephyr includes an implementation of this protocol, designed to have as minimal an overhead as possible. The Zephyr BSD Sockets API uses a namespacing convention that involves adding a zsock_ prefix to the native BSD Sockets API name, for example, zsock_socket() and zsock_close() for the BSD socket() and close() functions. This is to avoid name conflicts with names such as close(), which may be part of libc or one of the other POSIX compatibility libraries. The Config option CONFIG_NET_SOCKETS_POSIX_NAMES can be enabled to expose native POSIX names. The BSD functions supported are socket(), close(), recv(), recvfrom(), send(), sendto(), connect(), bind(), listen(), accept(), fcntl() (to set nonblocking mode), getsockopt(), setsockopt(), poll(), select(), getaddrinfo(), and getnameinfo().

The implementation of the Zephyr network API makes extensive use of the short-read/short-write property of the POSIX API whenever possible. This is done in order to minimize both overheads and code complexity. This property permits calls such as `recv()` and `send()` on SOCK_STREAM type sockets to actually process (receive or send) less data than was actually requested by the user. For example, a call such as `recv(sock, 1000, 0)` may return 100, meaning that only 100 bytes were read (short read). To retrieve the remaining 900 bytes, the application will need to invoke `call()` repeatedly till all the bytes have been received.

A Zephyr Echo Server Example Overview

The Zephyr echo-server sample application implements a UDP/TCP server that listens for incoming IPv4 (and, if configured to do so, IPv6) packets (sent by an echo client) and simply sends them back. Additionally it is possible to configure the project to include TLS 1.2 support by providing a suitable overlay overlay-tls.conv. The example code can be found in the Zephyr repository [2]. Even though the concept of an echo server is simple, the actual code covers many aspects of implementing TCP and UDP server applications in Zephyr RTOS. In real-world applications, the number of concurrent server applications is likely to be small, because of resource constraints on the kinds of hardware Zephyr RTOS will be running on.

Recent versions of the server example support client connections to the server and the server port number is configured to be 4242. As TCP and UDP port numbers are independent the application will have a TCP port number 4242 and a UDP port number 4242.

The echo server can be tested by setting up a second board running the echo client application, or by implementing a suitable testing program in, for example, C, C++, or Python running on a Windows or Linux PC, for example.

The west command to build the server will be something like the following

```
west build -p -b nucleo_f767zi  <path to echo_server project source code directory>
```

and the code can be flashed to the board using the command west flash --runner jlink.

The board startup messages sent to PuTTY over the USB Serial link are

```
*** Booting Zephyr OS build v2.7.0-rc2-7-g0d538447144c  ***

[00:00:01.560,000] <inf> net_config: Initializing network
[00:00:01.560,000] <inf> net_config: Waiting interface 1 (0x2002260c) to be up...
[00:00:02.051,000] <inf> net_config: Interface 1 (0x2002260c) coming up
```

In fact, the example is an example of many parts, as it also includes the Zephyr OS Services shell command library module, which will be described next.

Zephyr OS Services Module

The Zephyr OS Services module makes it possible to create and deploy an interpreter shell with a user-defined command set. It can be used to provide support for more complex interactions and feedback than possible with simple buttons and LEDs.

The module provides a (simplified) Unix-like shell with many useful features. These include support for multiple instances, cooperation with the logging framework, as well as support for both static (provided at compile time) and dynamic (implemented by the application at runtime) commands.

CHAPTER 8　ZEPHYR RTOS AND ETHERNET, WI-FI, AND TCP/IP

Further useful features include support for dictionary commands, command autocompletion using the Tab key, and a set of useful built-in commands such as clear, shell, colors, echo, history, and resize. Recently executed commands can be viewed by the use of up arrow and down arrow keys or meta keys. Text editing at the command line is available by the use of left arrow and right arrow keys as well as backspace, delete, and home and insert keys. The module additionally supports ANSI escape codes and multiline command editing, a handler for displaying help for commands, support for the use of the wildcard characters * and ?, and support for meta keys. There is also support for getopt and getopt_long. Various Kconfig configuration options associated with this module can be used to only include required features so as to optimize application memory usage.

The shell can be built with support for Zephyr net commands so that Linux command-line networking commands can be run. The available commands are shown in the following screen capture.

The example, zephyr\samples\net\sockets\echo_server, in the Zephyr repository can be used to explore some of the Zephyr shell networking commands. Mode detailed information about incorporating the Zephyr shell into applications can be found in the Zephyr documentation at `https://docs.zephyrproject.org/latest/services/shell/index.html`.

Figure 8-6 shows the networking net subcommands that are available. These subcommands are very useful in network troubleshooting of remote devices.

CHAPTER 8   ZEPHYR RTOS AND ETHERNET, WI-FI, AND TCP/IP

```
uart:~$ net
net - Networking commands
Subcommands:
  allocs     :Print network memory allocations.
  arp        :Print information about IPv4 ARP cache.
  capture    :Configure network packet capture.
  conn       :Print information about network connections.
  dns        :Show how DNS is configured.
  events     :Monitor network management events.
  gptp       :Print information about gPTP support.
  iface      :Print information about network interfaces.
  ipv6       :Print information about IPv6 specific information and
              configuration.
  mem        :Print information about network memory usage.
  nbr        :Print neighbor information.
  ping       :Ping a network host.
  pkt        :net_pkt information.
  ppp        :PPP information.
  resume     :Resume a network interface
  route      :Show network route.
  stacks     :Show network stacks information.
  stats      :Show network statistics.
  suspend    :Suspend a network interface
  tcp        :Connect/send/close TCP connection.
  udp        :Send/recv UDP packet
  virtual    :Show virtual network interfaces.
  vlan       :Show VLAN information.
  websocket  :Print information about WebSocket connections.
uart:~$
uart:~$
```

Figure 8-6. Available net subcommands

The screenshot in Figure 8-7, meanwhile, shows the use of the net iface command to obtain details of a particular network interface.

CHAPTER 8   ZEPHYR RTOS AND ETHERNET, WI-FI, AND TCP/IP

```
uart:~$ net iface

Interface 0x2002260c (Ethernet) [1]
===================================
Link addr : 02:80:E1:8B:6E:B0
MTU       : 1500
Flags     : NO_AUTO_START,IPv4,IPv6
Ethernet capabilities supported:
        10 Mbits
        100 Mbits
IPv6 unicast addresses (max 2):
        fe80::80:e1ff:fe8b:6eb0 autoconf preferred infinite
IPv6 multicast addresses (max 3):
        ff02::1
        ff02::1:ff8b:6eb0
IPv6 prefixes (max 2):
        <none>
IPv6 hop limit           : 64
IPv6 base reachable time : 30000
IPv6 reachable time      : 33529
IPv6 retransmit timer    : 0
IPv4 unicast addresses (max 1):
        192.0.2.1 manual preferred infinite
IPv4 multicast addresses (max 1):
        <none>
IPv4 gateway : 0.0.0.0
IPv4 netmask : 255.255.255.0
uart:~$
```

Figure 8-7. net iface command

Figure 8-8 shows a "ping" in action.

```
uart:~$ net ping 192.0.2.1
PING 192.0.2.1
28 bytes from 192.0.2.1 to 192.0.2.1: icmp_seq=0 ttl=64 time=0 ms
28 bytes from 192.0.2.1 to 192.0.2.1: icmp_seq=1 ttl=64 time=0 ms
28 bytes from 192.0.2.1 to 192.0.2.1: icmp_seq=2 ttl=64 time=0 ms
uart:~$
uart:~$
```

Figure 8-8. net ping command output

The echo_server example [2] also demonstrates how to add a sample command that, in this example, contains a single subcommand quit.

CHAPTER 8 ZEPHYR RTOS AND ETHERNET, WI-FI, AND TCP/IP

Running the sample command in the shell produces the following output:

```
uart:~$ sample - Sample application commands
sample - Sample application commands
Subcommands:
  quit   :Quit the sample application
```

Pinging from the PC to the Nucleo board will produce output such as the following:

```
> ping 192.0.2.1

Pinging 192.0.2.1 with 32 bytes of data:
Reply from 192.0.2.1: bytes=32 time=1ms TTL=64
Reply from 192.0.2.1: bytes=32 time=1ms TTL=64
Reply from 192.0.2.1: bytes=32 time=1ms TTL=64
Reply from 192.0.2.1: bytes=32 time=1ms TTL=64

Ping statistics for 192.0.2.1:
    Packets: Sent = 4, Received = 4, Lost = 0 (0% loss),
Approximate round trip times in milli-seconds:
    Minimum = 1ms, Maximum = 1ms, Average = 1ms
>
```

To Telnet from the PC to the Nucleo board, the command is `telnet 192.0.2.1 4242` brings up a telnet session. Each character sent is echoed back so, for example, typing in abcde will result in aabbccddee being displayed.

Strategies for Studying and Reverse Engineering (Where Necessary) Zephyr Application Code

When reading and trying to understand and analyze a Zephyr application, the key is to try and understand things such as initialization details, interrupt handling details, and the number of threads involved and the interactions between these threads. Also vital is getting to understand how access to resources that are shared between threads is controlled and the various ways blocking and asynchronous calls are used when accessing shared resources.

For complex applications, it can be helpful to split up the application into its components and incorporate combinations of these components into partial applications that are simpler and that can be analyzed in a simpler context.

In the case of the echo_server example, the source code files contain multiple #ifdef ... #endif sections that can be used to control which parts of the code are included in the project build and which are ignored. Here, the focus of interest is on the TCP and UDP echo server services, exploring the shell net subcommands, the use of the basic telnet service capabilities, and the implementation of the shell sample command with a quit menu option. To illustrate the usefulness of Python scripts running on a PC for testing network connectivity with embedded, we will also introduce and explore two Python scripts, a TCP echo client script and a UDP echo client script.

When the basic project (i.e., one not using any of the available, optional, overlays in the project source directory) is built and flashed onto the target board, the output displayed on a terminal (e.g., PuTTY in Windows) console will be something like the following:

CHAPTER 8   ZEPHYR RTOS AND ETHERNET, WI-FI, AND TCP/IP

```
*** Booting Zephyr OS build zephyr-v3.2.0-2577-
gd46b9bd12411 ***
[00:00:03.434,000] <inf> net_config: Initializing network
[00:00:03.434,000] <inf> net_config: Waiting interface 1
(0x20022764) to be up..
[00:00:03.930,000] <inf> net_config: Interface 1 (0x20022764)
coming up
[00:00:03.930,000] <inf> net_config: IPv4 address: 192.0.2.1
[00:00:04.030,000] <inf> net_config: IPv6 address: 2001:db8::1
[00:00:04.030,000] <inf> net_config: IPv6 address: 2001:db8::1
[00:00:04.030,000] <inf> net_echo_server_sample: Run
echo server
[00:00:04.030,000] <inf> net_echo_server_sample: Network
connected
[00:00:04.030,000] <inf> net_echo_server_sample: Starting...
[00:00:04.031,000] <inf> net_echo_server_sample: Waiting for
TCP connection on port 4242 (IPv6)...
[00:00:04.031,000] <inf> net_echo_server_sample: Waiting for
TCP connection on port 4242 (IPv4)...
[00:00:04.031,000] <inf> net_echo_server_sample: Waiting for
UDP packets on port   4242 (IPv6)...
[00:00:04.031,000] <inf> net_echo_server_sample: Waiting for
UDP packets on port   4242 (IPv4)...
uart:~$ sample
```

Compared with some of the projects explored previously, the prj.conf file for this sample project is quite big. Even so, it tries to only include those things that are necessary to demonstrate the various features of interest. For initial learning, the various IPv6 components can be done away with, by, for example, commenting them out from a configuration file that includes all the IPv6 options in the build.

Listing of echo_serverprj.cnf [3]:

```
# Generic networking options
CONFIG_NETWORKING=y
CONFIG_NET_UDP=y
CONFIG_NET_TCP=y
CONFIG_NET_IPV6=y
CONFIG_NET_IPV4=y
CONFIG_NET_SOCKETS=y
CONFIG_NET_SOCKETS_POSIX_NAMES=y
CONFIG_POSIX_MAX_FDS=6
CONFIG_NET_CONNECTION_MANAGER=y

# Kernel options
CONFIG_MAIN_STACK_SIZE=2048
CONFIG_ENTROPY_GENERATOR=y
CONFIG_TEST_RANDOM_GENERATOR=y
CONFIG_INIT_STACKS=y

# Logging
CONFIG_NET_LOG=y
CONFIG_LOG=y
CONFIG_NET_STATISTICS=y
CONFIG_PRINTK=y

# Network buffers
CONFIG_NET_PKT_RX_COUNT=16
CONFIG_NET_PKT_TX_COUNT=16
CONFIG_NET_BUF_RX_COUNT=64
CONFIG_NET_BUF_TX_COUNT=64
CONFIG_NET_CONTEXT_NET_PKT_POOL=y
```

```
# IP address options
CONFIG_NET_IF_UNICAST_IPV6_ADDR_COUNT=3
CONFIG_NET_IF_MCAST_IPV6_ADDR_COUNT=4
CONFIG_NET_MAX_CONTEXTS=10

# Network shell
CONFIG_NET_SHELL=y
CONFIG_SHELL=y

# Network application options and configuration
CONFIG_NET_CONFIG_SETTINGS=y
CONFIG_NET_CONFIG_NEED_IPV6=y
CONFIG_NET_CONFIG_MY_IPV6_ADDR="2001:db8::1"
CONFIG_NET_CONFIG_PEER_IPV6_ADDR="2001:db8::2"
CONFIG_NET_CONFIG_NEED_IPV4=y
CONFIG_NET_CONFIG_MY_IPV4_ADDR="192.0.2.1"
CONFIG_NET_CONFIG_PEER_IPV4_ADDR="192.0.2.2"

# Number of socket descriptors might need adjusting
# if there are more than 1 handlers defined.
CONFIG_POSIX_MAX_FDS=12

# How many client can connect to echo-server simultaneously
CONFIG_NET_SAMPLE_NUM_HANDLERS=1
```

As part of the learning process, changing the resources available to the application such as the number of network transmit and receive buffers and their sizes, the main stack size, and the number of clients the echo server can handle concurrently are parameters that can be experimented with. Experimenting with network setups and configurations is another useful and interesting avenue of research to follow. For instance, it may be necessary when networking with Microsoft Windows to alter some of the restrictive Windows firewall settings if trying to, for example, ping a PC from the embedded target.

Zephyr Network Management API

In order to be robust, an embedded network application needs to be able to respond to network events as well as other events such as sensor interrupt events and user interaction events for example. It may also be necessary to shut down network interfaces or bring up network interfaces under various conditions.

Zephyr provides various Network Management APIs that can be used by network applications as well as network layer code itself, to, for example, call specific network routines at any given network level in the IP stack, or to receive notifications when network events of interest occur. An application should, for example, be able to request notification if a network interface IP address changes. In connection with applications using wireless interfaces, it may be necessary to request that a scan be performed on, for example, a Wi-Fi network interface of a BLE network interface.

In conformity with the Zephyr convention of only including what is necessary in an application, the Network Management API implementation is modular and configurable. As opposed to using statically defined APIs for network management procedures, the Zephyr philosophy is to register defined procedure handlers as required via a `NET_MGMT_REGISTER_REQUEST_HANDLER` macro. The `net_mgmt()` API is used to invoke registered handlers for their corresponding requests.

The Network Management APIs are evolving and should be thought of as "work in progress."

How to Request a Defined Procedure

Network management requests take the form `net_mgmt(mgmt_request, ...)`, where the `mgmt_request` parameter is a bit mask indicating which stack layer is the focus of attention. Where a `net_if` object is involved and a specific management procedure is requested, the procedure request details will depend on what has been implemented in the corresponding network stack. To minimize resource usage, net_mgmt() calls are direct.

Listening for Network Events

Notifications about various network events are handled by registering a callback function and providing a set of events of interest to use to filter incoming events in the context of callback invocation. The net_mgmt_add_event_callback() function is used for registering a callback function, and the net_mgmt_del_event_callback() is used for unregistering a callback. Zephyr also has a net_mgmt_init_event_callback() helper function for initializing the callback structure.

When an event that matches a callback's event set occurs, the associated callback function is called with the actual event code. It is possible for different events to be handled by the same callback function where this makes sense. To deal with false positives, a callback handler function has to check the event code (passed as an argument) against the specific network events it is prepared to handle.

To receive events from multiple layers, multiple listeners need to be registered, one for each layer being listened on. It is possible for a callback handler function to be shared between different layer events.

The following code snippet illustrates, in template style, how to define and register a callback:

```
#define EVENT_IFACE_SET (NET_EVENT_IF_xxx | NET_EVENT_IF_yyy)
#define EVENT_IPV4_SET (NET_EVENT_IPV4_xxx | NET_EVENT_IPV4_yyy)
struct net_mgmt_event_callback iface_callback;
struct net_mgmt_event_callback ipv4_callback;
void callback_handler(struct net_mgmt_event_callback *cb,
      uint32_t mgmt_event, struct net_if *iface)
```

```
{
        if (mgmt_event == NET_EVENT_IF_xxx) {
                /* Handle NET_EVENT_IF_xxx */
        } else if (mgmt_event == NET_EVENT_IF_yyy) {
                /* Handle NET_EVENT_IF_yyy */
        } else if (mgmt_event == NET_EVENT_IPV4_xxx) {
                /* Handle NET_EVENT_IPV4_xxx */
        } else if (mgmt_event == NET_EVENT_IPV4_yyy) {
                /* Handle NET_EVENT_IPV4_yyy */
        } else {
                /* Spurious (false positive) invocation. */
        }
}
void register_cb(void)
{
        net_mgmt_init_event_callback(&iface_callback, callback_handler,
                                        EVENT_IFACE_SET);
        net_mgmt_init_event_callback(&ipv4_callback, callback_handler,
                                        EVENT_IPV4_SET);
        net_mgmt_add_event_callback(&iface_callback);
        net_mgmt_add_event_callback(&ipv4_callback);
}
```

How to Define a Network Management Procedure

Additional management procedures specific to a particular stack implementation can be provided by defining a handler and registering it with an associated `mgmt_request` code.

Management request codes are defined in relevant places depending on the layer being focused on. At layer L2, part of the focus will be on the technology being used. As an example IP layer, management request code will be declared in the include/zephyr/net/net_event.h header, whereas for Ethernet (L2 technology), it will be declared in include/zephyr/net/ethernet.h.

The signature for a handler function will take the form

```
static int some_handler(uint32_t mgmt_event, struct net_if *iface, void *data, size_t len);
```

This handler would be registered with an associated mgmt_request code according to the following pattern:

```
NET_MGMT_REGISTER_REQUEST_HANDLER(<mgmt_request code>, your_handler);
```

and, then, the new management procedure could be called as

```
net_mgmt(<mgmt_request code>, ...);
```

Signalling a Network Event

A specific network event is signalled using the net_mgmt_event_notify() function and providing it with the network event code. Event code can also be found on specific L2 technology mgmt headers, for example, in include/zephyr/net/ieee802154_mgmt.h if listening on events at 802.15.4 L2.

The function pointer net_mgmt_request_handler_t is defined as follows:

```
typedef int (*net_mgmt_request_handler_t)(uint32_t mgmt_request, struct net_if *iface, void *data, size_t len);
```

where `mgmt_request` is the request value the handler is being called, `iface` is a pointer to a struct net_if if the request is meant to be bound to a network interface (NULL otherwise), `data` is a valid pointer to the data to be used by the handler (NULL otherwise), and len is the length in bytes of the memory pointed to by data.

The user's callback handler function signature is defined as follows:

```
typedef void (*net_mgmt_event_handler_t)(struct net_mgmt_event_
callback *cb, uint32_t mgmt_event, struct net_if *iface);
```

where `cb` is the struct net_mgmt_event_callback owning this handler, `mgmt_event` is the network event being notified, and `iface` is a pointer to a `struct net_if` to which the event belongs to, if that event is an iface event (NULL otherwise).

Network Management Interface Functions

Zephyr's Network Management API functions include event callback initialization functions, functions to add and delete callback events, an event notification function, functions for waiting synchronously or asynchronously on an event mask, and a function used by the core of the network stack to initialize network event processing.

```
static inline void net_mgmt_init_event_callback(
    struct net_mgmt_event_callback *cb,
    net_mgmt_event_handler_t handler,
    uint32_t mgmt_event_mask)
```

is a helper function to initialize a `struct net_mgmt_event_callback`. The parameters it takes are `cb`, a valid application callback structure pointer; handler, a valid handler function pointer; and `mgmt_event_mask`, a mask of relevant events for the handler.

void net_mgmt_add_event_callback(struct net_mgmt_event_callback *cb) is the function to add a user callback, and void net_mgmt_del_event_callback(struct net_mgmt_event_callback *cb) is the function to delete a user callback.

Events are notified using the function

```
void net_mgmt_event_notify_with_info(uint32_t mgmt_event,
    struct net_if *iface,
    const void *info,
    size_t length)
```

In connection with the notify function, info and length are disabled if CONFIG_NET_MGMT_EVENT_INFO is not defined.

The function for waiting synchronously on an event is

```
int net_mgmt_event_wait(uint32_t mgmt_event_mask, uint32_t *raised_event, struct net_if **iface, const void **info, size_t *info_length, k_timeout_t timeout)
```

where mgmt_event_mask is a mask of events to wait on, raised_event is a pointer on a uint32_t, which is where the raised event is stored (it can be NULL if that information is not of interest), iface is a pointer to a placeholder for the interface from which the event originated, info is a valid pointer in the use case where the user wishes to get the information associated with the event (NULL otherwise), info_length is the size of the info memory area (only valid if the info is not NULL), and timeout is a timeout delay (a timeout of K_FOREVER means waiting indefinitely). The return values are 0 on success, a negative error code otherwise. -ETIMEDOUT is returned if a timeout occurred.

```
int net_mgmt_event_wait_on_iface(struct net_if *iface,
    uint32_t mgmt_event_mask, uint32_t *raised_event,
    const void **info,  size_t *info_length, k_timeout_t
    timeout)
```

is used to wait synchronously on an event mask for a specific interface. The parameters have the same meaning as explained previously.

Finally, void net_mgmt_event_init(void) is used by the core of the network stack to initialize the network event processing.

The struct net_mgmt_event_callback structure is defined in net/net_mgmt.h as follows:

```
struct net_mgmt_event_callback {
      sys_snode_t node;
      union {
            /* Actual callback function being used to notify
            the owner */
            net_mgmt_event_handler_t handler;
            /* Semaphore meant to be used internally for the
            synchronous * net_mgmt_event_wait() function. */
            struct k_sem *sync_call;
      };
#ifdef CONFIG_NET_MGMT_EVENT_INFO
      const void *info;
      size_t info_length;
#endif
      union {
            uint32_t event_mask;
            uint32_t raised_event;
      };
};
```

It is used in conjunction with registering a callback into the network management event part, in order to allow the owner of this struct to obtain network event notification based on a given event mask. Its members are a sys_snode_t node; which is used internally, to insert the callback into a list, a union made up of a net_mgmt_event_handler_t handler,

CHAPTER 8 ZEPHYR RTOS AND ETHERNET, WI-FI, AND TCP/IP

the actual callback function used to notify the owner, and a `struct k_sem *sync_call,` a semaphore used internally for the synchronous `net_mgmt_event_wait()` function; and a union made up of a `uint32_t event_mask,` a mask of network events on which the handler should be called when those events occur, and `uint32_t raised_event,` an internal place holder for when a synchronous event wait is successfully unlocked on an event.

`union net_mgmt_event_callback.[anonymous] [anonymous]` is a mask of network events on which the handler should be called when those events occur. This kind of mask can be modified as necessary to control whether a handler will be called or not.

A shell module instance can be connected to various transports for command input and output. Supported transport layers include Segger RTT, SMP, Telnet, UART, and USB.

Zephyr Shell Module

As previously discussed, the shell module is a Unix-like shell that can be extended by adding user-defined command sets.

Shell Commands

Shell commands are organized as a tree structure and are grouped into several categories. Root commands (level 0 commands) are collected together and organized in an alphabetically sorted manner in a dedicated memory section. Static subcommands (level > 0) are commands whose number and syntax are known at compile time and are created in software. Dynamic subcommands (level > 0) are created dynamically in software, and their number and syntax do not have to be known at compile time.

Command Creation Macros

Zephyr provides an extensive set of macros for adding shell commands that are listed here together with brief descriptions. Root commands must have distinct names and can be created using the SHELL_CMD_REGISTER macro. For root commands that are created conditionally, if a compile time flag is set, there is the SHELL_COND_CMD_REGISTER macro.

It is possible to create a root command that takes arguments, and in this case, the SHELL_CMD_ARG_REGISTER macro should be used. The variant that creates commands that take arguments conditionally on a compile time flag being set is SHELL_COND_CMD_ARG_REGISTER. Further macros include SHELL_CMD for initializing a command and its conditional variant SHELL_COND_CMD. Other macros include the SHELL_EXPR_CMD for initializing a command if a given compile time expression is nonzero and SHELL_CMD_ARG for initializing a command with arguments. Additionally there are the macros SHELL_COND_CMD_ARG for initializing a command with arguments if a compile time flag is set, and SHELL_EXPR_CMD_ARG for initializing a command with arguments if a compile time expression is non-zero. For creating arrays of static subcommands, the SHELL_STATIC_SUBCMD_SET_CREATE macro is provided, and for creating a dictionary subcommands array, the corresponding macro is SHELL_SUBCMD_DICT_SET_CREATE.

Finally, a dynamic subcommands array can be created using the SHELL_DYNAMIC_CMD_CREATE macro.

Commands can be created in any file in the system that includes include/zephyr/shell/shell.h, and these created commands are available for all shell instances.

Creating Static Commands

The following code snippet, based on the Zephyr documentation [4], illustrates the process of creating a root command and a set of associated subcommands.

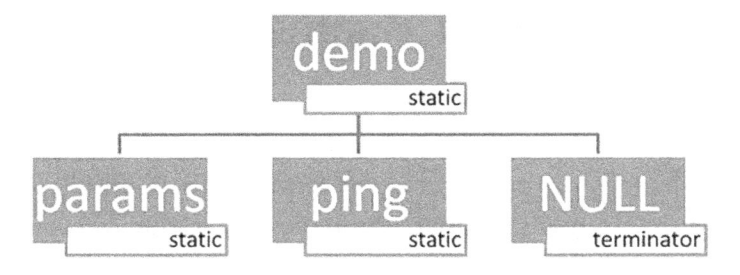

Figure 8-9. Schematic of root command and subcommands [4]

```
/* Creating subcommands (level 1 command) array for command
"demo". */
SHELL_STATIC_SUBCMD_SET_CREATE(sub_demo,
       SHELL_CMD(params, NULL, "Print params command.",
                                             cmd_demo_
                                             params),
       SHELL_CMD(ping,   NULL, "Ping command.",
       cmd_demo_ping),
       SHELL_SUBCMD_SET_END
);
/* Creating root (level 0) command "demo" */
SHELL_CMD_REGISTER(demo, &sub_demo, "Demo commands", NULL);
```

Dictionary Commands

These are static commands where the command handler processes a key-value pair that consists of a string (the key) and data corresponding to that key (the value). The string is typically a description of the given data. The underlying concept is to use the string as a command prompt syntax and to have the corresponding data used in the command processing.

CHAPTER 8   ZEPHYR RTOS AND ETHERNET, WI-FI, AND TCP/IP

An illustrative example is the following, which is concerned with the implementation of a command to set the gain on an amplifier associated with an ADC converter. Here, the string would indicate the gain value, and the value would be the corresponding integer value, which would be used in the ADC driver API. The command handler code for this scenario might be implemented along the lines shown in the following code snippet:

```
static int gain_cmd_handler(const struct shell *shell,
            size_t argc, char **argv, void *data)
{
        int gain;
        /* data value corresponds to called command syntax */
        gain = (int)data;
        adc_set_gain(gain);
        shell_print(shell, "ADC gain set to: %s\n"
                            "Value send to ADC driver: %d",
                            argv[0],
                            gain);
        return 0;
}
SHELL_SUBCMD_DICT_SET_CREATE(sub_gain, gain_cmd_handler,
        (gain1, 1), (gain2, 2), (gain3, 3), (gain4, 4)
);
SHELL_CMD_REGISTER(gain, &sub_gain, "Set ADC gain", NULL);
```

The Zephyr shell also supports the dynamic addition of subcommands. Adding subcommands dynamically in a real-world project needs to be considered carefully at the application design stage. The security aspects of adding subcommands dynamically must be taken into account, and this will involve careful testing and analysis.

CHAPTER 8 ZEPHYR RTOS AND ETHERNET, WI-FI, AND TCP/IP

The Shell and the Echo Server Example

The configuration for this project is shown as follows:

```
# Network shell
CONFIG_NET_SHELL=y
CONFIG_SHELL=y
# Generic networking options
CONFIG_NETWORKING=y
CONFIG_NET_UDP=y
CONFIG_NET_TCP=y
CONFIG_NET_IPV6=y
CONFIG_NET_IPV4=y
CONFIG_NET_SOCKETS=y
CONFIG_NET_SOCKETS_POSIX_NAMES=y
CONFIG_POSIX_MAX_FDS=6
CONFIG_NET_CONNECTION_MANAGER=y
```

`CONFIG_SHELL=y`

means that the echo server application will include the shell and the shell net commands.

The prj.conf statement

`CONFIG_NET_CONNECTION_MANAGER=y`

means that the application is built with support for IPv4, Ipv6, UDP, and TCP.

Echo server application initialization is handled by the function `init_app()`.

If the application is built with TLS support configured in (not the case here), then code for initializing TLS will be conditionally included. In the `init_app()` snippets explored here, the TLS-related code will not be covered.

init_app() edited code snippet :
```
static void init_app(void) {
#if defined(CONFIG_USERSPACE)
        struct k_mem_partition *parts[] = {
#if Z_LIBC_PARTITION_EXISTS
              &z_libc_partition,
#endif
              &app_partition
        };
        int ret = k_mem_domain_init(&app_domain, ARRAY_
        SIZE(parts), parts);
        __ASSERT(ret == 0, "k_mem_domain_init() failed %d", ret);
        ARG_UNUSED(ret);
#endif
        k_sem_init(&quit_lock, 0, K_SEM_MAX_LIMIT);
        LOG_INF(APP_BANNER);
        if (IS_ENABLED(CONFIG_NET_CONNECTION_MANAGER)) {
              net_mgmt_init_event_callback(&mgmt_cb, event_
              handler, EVENT_MASK);
              net_mgmt_add_event_callback(&mgmt_cb);
              net_conn_mgr_resend_status();
        }
        init_vlan();
        init_tunnel();
        init_usb();
}
```

The following statement in this code is significant:

`k_sem_init(&quit_lock, 0, K_SEM_MAX_LIMIT);`

It initializes the application's `quit_lock` semaphore. The effect is that any thread attempting to acquire this semaphore will block.

In the application, the semaphore is released when the user runs the sample quit command in the shell. The last few lines of the function main() show how this affects the application thread associated with main():

```
    k_sem_take(&quit_lock, K_FOREVER);
    if (connected) {
        stop_udp_and_tcp();
    }
}
```

After the call to k_sem_take, the thread will block till the semaphore is released. Once unblocked, it will (gracefully) stop the UDP and TCP services.

In main(), after the call to init_app(), the lines of code that follow are responsible for starting TCP and UDP and the echo server services:

```
    if (!IS_ENABLED(CONFIG_NET_CONNECTION_MANAGER)) {
        /* If the config library has not been configured to
         * start the app only after we have a connection,
         * then we can start it right away.
         */
        k_sem_give(&run_app);
    }
    /* Wait for the connection. */
    k_sem_take(&run_app, K_FOREVER);
    start_udp_and_tcp();
```

The code for starting and stopping TCP and UDP is straightforward.

```
static void start_udp_and_tcp(void){
    LOG_INF("Starting...");
    if (IS_ENABLED(CONFIG_NET_TCP)) {
        start_tcp();
    }
```

CHAPTER 8   ZEPHYR RTOS AND ETHERNET, WI-FI, AND TCP/IP

```
        if (IS_ENABLED(CONFIG_NET_UDP)) {
                start_udp();
        }
}
static void stop_udp_and_tcp(void) {
        LOG_INF("Stopping...");
        if (IS_ENABLED(CONFIG_NET_UDP)) {
                stop_udp();
        }
        if (IS_ENABLED(CONFIG_NET_TCP)) {
                stop_tcp();
        }
}
```

The real work is done by the functions start_udp(), start_tcp(), stop_udp(), and stop_tcp().

The echo server code makes use of the following TCP and UDP configuration and processing related data structures, struct data and struct configs, whose details are shown in the following code snippet.

```
struct data {
        const char *proto;
        struct {
                int sock;
                char recv_buffer[RECV_BUFFER_SIZE];
                uint32_t counter;
                atomic_t bytes_received;
                struct k_work_delayable stats_print;
        } udp;
        struct {
                int sock;
                atomic_t bytes_received;
```

411

CHAPTER 8 ZEPHYR RTOS AND ETHERNET, WI-FI, AND TCP/IP

```
            struct k_work_delayable stats_print;
            struct {
                    int sock;
                    char recv_buffer[RECV_BUFFER_SIZE];
                    uint32_t counter;
            } accepted[CONFIG_NET_SAMPLE_NUM_HANDLERS];
      } tcp;
};

struct configs {
      struct data ipv4;
      struct data ipv6;
};

extern struct configs conf;
```

`struct configs conf` is defined and initialized in echo_server.c as follows:

```
APP_DMEM struct configs conf = {
      .ipv4 = {
             .proto = "IPv4",
      },
      .ipv6 = {
             .proto = "IPv6",
      },
};
```

Getting to the bottom of what APP_DMEM does requires some "detective work."

It turns out that APP_DMEM is #defined in the file common.h as follows:

```
#if defined(CONFIG_USERSPACE)
#include <zephyr/app_memory/app_memdomain.h>
extern struct k_mem_partition app_partition;
```

412

CHAPTER 8   ZEPHYR RTOS AND ETHERNET, WI-FI, AND TCP/IP

```
extern struct k_mem_domain app_domain;
#define APP_BMEM K_APP_BMEM(app_partition)
#define APP_DMEM K_APP_DMEM(app_partition)
#else
#define APP_BMEM
#define APP_DMEM
#endif
```

If CONFIG_USERSPACE is defined, then in the application, the user threads run at a different privilege level to kernel threads then. Many of the processors on which Zephyr RTOS applications are implemented have an MPU (Memory Protection Unit), and Zephyr provides various mechanisms for creating and managing memory partitions.

The echo server application defines an app_partition and a struct k_mem_domain variable app_domain in the file echo-server.c.

```
#if defined(CONFIG_USERSPACE)
K_APPMEM_PARTITION_DEFINE(app_partition);
struct k_mem_domain app_domain;
#endif
```

Automatic memory partitions such as app_partition are configured as read-write regions and are defined with K_APPMEM_PARTITION_DEFINE(). Global variables are then routed to this partition using K_APP_DMEM() for initialized data and K_APP_BMEM() for BSS.

The way APP_BMEM and APP_DMEM are defined in common.h (in the snippet shown previously) means that if CONFIG_USERSPACE is not defined, they expand to nothing, but if it is defined, they expand to K_APP_BMEM and K_APP_DMEM, respectively.

The code snippet for start_udp() is

```
void start_udp(void){
      if (IS_ENABLED(CONFIG_NET_IPV6)) {
#if defined(CONFIG_USERSPACE)
            k_mem_domain_add_thread(&app_domain,
            udp6_thread_id);
#endif
            k_work_init_delayable(&conf.ipv6.udp.stats_print,
            print_stats);
            k_thread_name_set(udp6_thread_id, "udp6");
            k_thread_start(udp6_thread_id);
      }

      if (IS_ENABLED(CONFIG_NET_IPV4)) {
#if defined(CONFIG_USERSPACE)
            k_mem_domain_add_thread(&app_domain,
            udp4_thread_id);
#endif
            k_work_init_delayable(&conf.ipv4.udp.stats_print,
                                                  print_stats);
            k_thread_name_set(udp4_thread_id, "udp4");
            k_thread_start(udp4_thread_id);
      }
}
```

In start_udp(), the threads udp4_thread_id and udp6_thread_id (if the application is configured to support IPv6) are added to the app_domain memory domain by calls to k_mem_domain_add. The print_stats handler is associated with the delayable workqueue items conf.ipv4.udp.stats_print and conf.ipv6.udp.stats_print (if application is configured for IPv6) for carrying out the printing of statistics; the thread names are assigned, and the udp4 and udp6 threads are started.

CHAPTER 8 ZEPHYR RTOS AND ETHERNET, WI-FI, AND TCP/IP

The start_tcp() code follows the same pattern.

```
void start_tcp(void) {
      int i;
      for (i = 0; i < CONFIG_NET_SAMPLE_NUM_HANDLERS; i++) {
            conf.ipv6.tcp.accepted[i].sock = -1;
            conf.ipv4.tcp.accepted[i].sock = -1;
#if defined(CONFIG_NET_IPV4)
            tcp4_handler_in_use[i] = false;
#endif
#if defined(CONFIG_NET_IPV6)
            tcp6_handler_in_use[i] = false;
#endif
      }
#if defined(CONFIG_NET_IPV6)
#if defined(CONFIG_USERSPACE)
      k_mem_domain_add_thread(&app_domain, tcp6_thread_id);
      for (i = 0; i < CONFIG_NET_SAMPLE_NUM_HANDLERS; i++) {
            k_mem_domain_add_thread(&app_domain,
                                    &tcp6_handler_thread[i]);
            k_thread_access_grant(tcp6_thread_id,
                                    &tcp6_handler_thread[i]);
            k_thread_access_grant(tcp6_thread_id,
                                    &tcp6_handler_stack[i]);
      }
#endif
      k_work_init_delayable(&conf.ipv6.tcp.stats_print,
      print_stats);
      k_thread_start(tcp6_thread_id);
#endif
#if defined(CONFIG_NET_IPV4)
#if defined(CONFIG_USERSPACE)
```

415

CHAPTER 8   ZEPHYR RTOS AND ETHERNET, WI-FI, AND TCP/IP

```
        k_mem_domain_add_thread(&app_domain, tcp4_thread_id);
        for (i = 0; i < CONFIG_NET_SAMPLE_NUM_HANDLERS; i++) {
            k_mem_domain_add_thread(&app_domain,
                                            &tcp4_handler_
                                            thread[i]);
            k_thread_access_grant(tcp4_thread_id,
                                            &tcp4_handler_
                                            thread[i]);
            k_thread_access_grant(tcp4_thread_id,
                                            &tcp4_handler_
                                            stack[i]);
        }
#endif
        k_work_init_delayable(&conf.ipv4.tcp.stats_print,
        print_stats);
        k_thread_start(tcp4_thread_id);
#endif
}
```

The difference in the case of TCP is that because TCP is connection oriented, an application may have to support a number of connections concurrently, and this is why there are multiple handlers, each with an associated thread. The number of handlers is configurable and depends on both the processing resources available and the number of concurrent TCP connections that a particular implementation should support.

The threads for processing udp4 and udp6 are defined in the file udp.c using `K_THREAD_DEFINE` and in the file `tcp.c using K_THREAD_DEFINE`.

```
K_THREAD_DEFINE(udp4_thread_id, STACK_SIZE,
            process_udp4, NULL, NULL, NULL,
            THREAD_PRIORITY,
```

CHAPTER 8   ZEPHYR RTOS AND ETHERNET, WI-FI, AND TCP/IP

```
            IS_ENABLED(CONFIG_USERSPACE) ? K_USER : 0, -1);

K_THREAD_DEFINE(udp6_thread_id, STACK_SIZE,
            process_udp6, NULL, NULL, NULL,
            THREAD_PRIORITY,
            IS_ENABLED(CONFIG_USERSPACE) ? K_USER : 0, -1);
```

and the threads for processing tcp4 and tcp6 are defined similarly in `tcp.c`.

```
K_THREAD_DEFINE(tcp4_thread_id, STACK_SIZE,
            process_tcp4, NULL, NULL, NULL,
            THREAD_PRIORITY,
            IS_ENABLED(CONFIG_USERSPACE) ? K_USER : 0, -1);

K_THREAD_DEFINE(tcp6_thread_id, STACK_SIZE,
            process_tcp6, NULL, NULL, NULL,
            THREAD_PRIORITY,
            IS_ENABLED(CONFIG_USERSPACE) ? K_USER : 0, -1);
```

The functions `process_udp4()` and `process_udp6()` are very similar, differing in the socket creation details. The following code snippet shows how `process_udp4()` is implemented:

```
static void process_udp4(void) {
    int ret;
    struct sockaddr_in addr4;
    (void)memset(&addr4, 0, sizeof(addr4));
    addr4.sin_family = AF_INET;
    addr4.sin_port = htons(MY_PORT);
    ret = start_udp_proto(&conf.ipv4, (struct sockaddr *)
    &addr4, sizeof(addr4));
    if (ret < 0) {
        quit();
```

CHAPTER 8 ZEPHYR RTOS AND ETHERNET, WI-FI, AND TCP/IP

```
        return;
    }
    k_work_reschedule(&conf.ipv4.udp.stats_print,
                                        K_SECONDS(STATS_
                                        TIMER));
    while (ret == 0) {
        ret = process_udp(&conf.ipv4);
        if (ret < 0) {
            quit();
        }
    }
}
```

The preceding function initializes a sockaddr_in structure by specifying the protocol member, sin_family, as AF_INET (which means IPv4). In process_udp6(), the protocol is AF_INET6 (which means IPv6). The sin_port member is initialized to the server port number (#defined as MY_PORT), with the function htons() being used to ensure that the byte ordering for sending data over IP, the network-byte-order, is correct (i.e., big-endian). The next step in udp processing is carried out by the function start_udp_proto(). The following code snippet shows the details of socket binding carried out in this function:

```
static int start_udp_proto(struct data *data,
       struct sockaddr *bind_addr,socklen_t bind_addrlen) {
    int ret;
    data->udp.sock = socket(bind_addr->sa_family,
                            SOCK_DGRAM, IPPROTO_UDP);
    if (data->udp.sock < 0) {
        NET_ERR("Failed to create UDP socket (%s):
        %d",  data->proto, errno);
        return -errno;
    }
```

```
        ret = bind(data->udp.sock, bind_addr, bind_addrlen);
        if (ret < 0) {
                NET_ERR("Failed to bind UDP socket (%s):
                %d", data->proto, errno);
                ret = -errno;
        }
        return ret;
}
```

Back in process_udp4, if start_udp_proto returns success, then k_work_reschedule() is called to update work for the network statistics printing workqueue, and, then, process_udp() is called to process the udp data received. Because udp is the same whether running over IPv4 or IPv6, process_udp() is also used to handle udp data sent over IPv6.

process_udp() uses recvfrom() to handle UDP datagrams as they arrive and sendto() to send response datagrams. The process_udp() function implements the UDP echo server behavior. In essence, this function copies the received datagram into a receive buffer and then sends it back out to the originating client, as can be seen in the following code snippet showing the process_udp() code:

```
static int process_udp(struct data *data) {
        int ret = 0;
        int received;
        struct sockaddr client_addr;
        socklen_t client_addr_len;
        NET_INFO("Waiting for UDP packets on port %d
        (%s)...", MY_PORT, data->proto);
        do {
                client_addr_len = sizeof(client_addr);
                received = recvfrom(data->udp.sock,
```

```
                        data->udp.recv_buffer,
                        sizeof(data->udp.recv_
                        buffer), 0,
                        &client_addr, &client_
                        addr_len);
    if (received < 0) {
        /* Socket error */
        NET_ERR("UDP (%s): Connection error %d",
        data->proto, errno);
        ret = -errno;
        break;
    } else if (received) {
        atomic_add(&data->udp.bytes_received,
        received);
    }
    ret = sendto(data->udp.sock, data->udp.recv_buffer,
        received, 0, &client_addr, client_addr_len);
    if (ret < 0) {
        NET_ERR("UDP (%s): Failed to send %d",
                    data->proto, errno);
        ret = -errno;
        break;
    }
    if (++data->udp.counter % 1000 == 0U) {
        NET_INFO("%s UDP: Sent %u packets",
        data->proto,
            data->udp.counter);
    }
    NET_DBG("UDP (%s): Received and replied with %d
    bytes",
        data->proto, received);
```

```
    } while (true);
    return ret;
}
```

The UDP echo server service can be tested out by running a simple Python script such as the following on a PC:

```
import socket
testMessageStart      = "Test message number"
serverAddressAndPort  = ("192.0.2.1", 4242)
bufferSize            = 1024
# Create a client side UDP socket
with socket.socket(family=socket.AF_INET, type=socket.SOCK_DGRAM)\
as UDPClientSocket:
    # Send a few test messages to the Echo Server
    for num in ("1","2","3","4","5","6","7","8","9") :
        message = testMessageStart + " " + num
        messageSize = str.encode(message)
        UDPClientSocket.sendto(messageSize,
        serverAddressAndPort)
        serverResponse = UDPClientSocket.recvfrom(bufferSize)
        response = "Echo from UDP Server{}" \
.format(serverResponse[0].decode("utf-8"))
        print(response)
```

In the TCP echo server code, in the file `tcp.c`, the functions `process_tcp4()` and `process_tcp6()` follow the same pattern as `process_udp4()` and `process_udp6()` and ultimately end up calling the tcp processing function `process_tcp()`. Because TCP is a connection-oriented streaming protocol, reading and writing of data over TCP are analogous to reading and writing to a file. The code for `process_tcp()` is different to the code for `process_udp()`.

CHAPTER 8   ZEPHYR RTOS AND ETHERNET, WI-FI, AND TCP/IP

The following code snippet shows the code within `process_tcp()` for handling IPv4-based TCP requests and responses. The code for handling IPv4-based TCP requests and responses is similar, and the original source code can be consulted to see the details.

```
static int process_tcp(struct data *data) {
    int client;
    int slot;
    struct sockaddr_in client_addr;
    socklen_t client_addr_len = sizeof(client_addr);
    LOG_INF("Waiting for TCP connection on port %d (%s)...",
        MY_PORT, data->proto);
    client = accept(data->tcp.sock,
                (struct sockaddr *)&client_addr, &client_
                addr_len);
    if (client < 0) {
        LOG_ERR("%s accept error (%d)", data->proto,
        -errno);
        return 0;
    }
    slot = get_free_slot(data);
    if (slot < 0) {
        LOG_ERR("Cannot accept more connections");
        close(client);
        return 0;
    }
    data->tcp.accepted[slot].sock = client;
    LOG_INF("TCP (%s): Accepted connection", data->proto);
#define MAX_NAME_LEN sizeof("tcp4[0]")
    if (client_addr.sin_family == AF_INET) {
        tcp4_handler_in_use[slot] = true;
        k_thread_create(
```

```
                &tcp4_handler_thread[slot],
                tcp4_handler_stack[slot],
                K_THREAD_STACK_SIZEOF(tcp4_handler_
                stack[slot]),
                (k_thread_entry_t)handle_data,
                INT_TO_POINTER(slot), data,
                &tcp4_handler_in_use[slot],
                THREAD_PRIORITY,
                IS_ENABLED(CONFIG_USERSPACE) ? K_USER |
                                        K_INHERIT_PERMS : 0,
                K_NO_WAIT);
        if (IS_ENABLED(CONFIG_THREAD_NAME)) {
                char name[MAX_NAME_LEN];
                snprintk(name, sizeof(name),
                "tcp4[%d]", slot);
                k_thread_name_set(&tcp4_handler_
                thread[slot], name);
        }
    }
    return 0;
}
```

Because TCP is connection oriented, it is necessary to track the activity associated with an active connection. The maximum number of TCP connections associated with a server socket is configurable. There are several possible approaches to tracking connections. One is a single threaded approach where a single thread tracks all the connections, and another is to dedicate a separate processing thread to each connection. The sample echo server implementation allocates a separate thread to each connection, and the code involved is explored next.

Configuring a TCP Server Application to Use a Separate Thread for Each Connection

The first thing is to get a working understanding of the various data structures and API functions involved in setting up TCP/IP connections, both on the server side and on the client side.

Data Structures Associated with TCP/IP Server-Side Connections

The conf global variable conf.ipv4.tcp element is of type

```
struct {
        int sock;
        atomic_t bytes_received;
        struct k_work_delayable stats_print;
        struct {
            int sock;
            char recv_buffer[RECV_BUFFER_SIZE];
            uint32_t counter;
        } accepted[CONFIG_NET_SAMPLE_NUM_HANDLERS];
    }
```

The element conf.ipv4.tcp.accepted is an array of elements of type

```
struct {
    int sock;
    char recv_buffer[RECV_BUFFER_SIZE];
    uint32_t counter;
}
```

The `accepted` array can be thought of as an array of slots, where a slot may be allocated to a given connection handling thread, or may be unallocated. The function `get_free_slot()` iterates through the accepted array looking for a free slot, one for which the sock value is less than zero, and returns the first "free" slot it finds.

```
static int get_free_slot(struct data *data)
{
    int i;
    for (i = 0; i < CONFIG_NET_SAMPLE_NUM_HANDLERS; i++) {
        if (data->tcp.accepted[i].sock < 0) {
            return i;
        }
    }
    return -1;
}
```

The `accepted` array is initialized in the function `start_tcp()` using this piece of code:

```
    for (i = 0; i < CONFIG_NET_SAMPLE_NUM_HANDLERS; i++) {
        conf.ipv6.tcp.accepted[i].sock = -1;
        conf.ipv4.tcp.accepted[i].sock = -1;
#if defined(CONFIG_NET_IPV4)
        tcp4_handler_in_use[i] = false;
#endif
        ...
    }
```

Thread Structures Pool for Handling Threads Involved in TCP/IP Server Connections

The pool of thread structures for the connection handling threads is defined in tcp.h as a global variable array of struct k_thread type elements; here is the definition:

```
static struct k_thread
    tcp4_handler_thread[CONFIG_NET_SAMPLE_NUM_HANDLERS];
static APP_BMEM bool
    tcp4_handler_in_use[CONFIG_NET_SAMPLE_NUM_HANDLERS];
```

and the elements in this array are initialized so that for all valid index values

```
tcp4_handler_in_use[i] = false;
```

The code in start_tcp that deals with access permissions when CONFIG_USERSPACE is enabled has the following lines:

```
#if defined(CONFIG_NET_IPV4)
#if defined(CONFIG_USERSPACE)
    k_mem_domain_add_thread(&app_domain, tcp4_thread_id);
    for (i = 0; i < CONFIG_NET_SAMPLE_NUM_HANDLERS; i++) {
        k_mem_domain_add_thread(&app_domain,
                    &tcp4_handler_thread[i]);
        k_thread_access_grant(tcp4_thread_id,
                    &tcp4_handler_thread[i]);
        k_thread_access_grant(tcp4_thread_id,
                    &tcp4_handler_stack[i]);
    }
#endif
```

CHAPTER 8   ZEPHYR RTOS AND ETHERNET, WI-FI, AND TCP/IP

Having located a "free slot," the next step is to actually use it for handling the data associated with that TCP connection. Here is the relevant piece of code, inside the function process_tcp() for carrying out the handling for an IPv4 connection.

```
slot = get_free_slot(data);
    if (slot < 0) {
        LOG_ERR("Cannot accept more connections");
        close(client);
        return 0;
    }
    data->tcp.accepted[slot].sock = client;
    LOG_INF("TCP (%s): Accepted connection", data->proto);
#if defined(CONFIG_NET_IPV4)
    if (client_addr.sin_family == AF_INET) {
        tcp4_handler_in_use[slot] = true;

        k_thread_create(
            &tcp4_handler_thread[slot],
            tcp4_handler_stack[slot],
            K_THREAD_STACK_SIZEOF(tcp4_handler_
            stack[slot]),
            (k_thread_entry_t)handle_data,
            INT_TO_POINTER(slot), data,
                    &tcp4_handler_in_use[slot],
            THREAD_PRIORITY,
            IS_ENABLED(CONFIG_USERSPACE) ? K_USER |
                    K_INHERIT_PERMS : 0,
                K_NO_WAIT);
        if (IS_ENABLED(CONFIG_THREAD_NAME)) {
            char name[MAX_NAME_LEN];
            snprintk(name, sizeof(name),
            "tcp4[%d]", slot);
```

427

CHAPTER 8   ZEPHYR RTOS AND ETHERNET, WI-FI, AND TCP/IP

```
                k_thread_name_set(&tcp4_handler_
                thread[slot], name);
        }
    }
#endif
```

The important thing to note is the dynamic creation of a thread to handle the data. The thread will terminate once the handle_data function returns.

Here is the static (hence private to tcp.h) handle_data function code. The TLS code has been omitted as it is not used in this example.

```
static void handle_data(void *ptr1, void *ptr2, void *ptr3) {
    int slot = POINTER_TO_INT(ptr1);
    struct data *data = ptr2;
    bool *in_use = ptr3;
    int offset = 0;
    int received;
    int client;
    int ret;
    client = data->tcp.accepted[slot].sock;
    do {
        received = recv(client,
            data->tcp.accepted[slot].recv_buffer
            + offset,
            sizeof(
                data->tcp.accepted[slot].recv_
                buffer) - offset,
            0);
        if (received == 0) {
            /* Connection closed */
            LOG_INF("TCP (%s): Connection closed",
            data->proto);
```

428

```
            break;
    } else if (received < 0) {
        /* Socket error */
        LOG_ERR("TCP (%s): Connection error %d",
                data->proto, errno);
        break;
    } else {
        atomic_add(&data->tcp.bytes_received,
           received);
    }
    offset += received;
    /* To prevent fragmentation of the response,
    reply only
     * if buffer is full or there is no more
     data to read
     */
    if (offset ==
            sizeof(data->tcp.accepted[slot].recv_
            buffer) ||
        (recv(client,
            data->tcp.accepted[slot].recv_buffer
            + offset,
            sizeof(
                data->tcp.accepted[slot].recv_
                buffer)-offset,
            MSG_PEEK | MSG_DONTWAIT) < 0 &&
           (errno == EAGAIN || errno ==
           EWOULDBLOCK))) {
        ret = sendall(client,
                    data->tcp.accepted[slot].
                    recv_buffer,
```

```
                                    offset);
                        if (ret < 0) {
                                LOG_ERR("TCP (%s): Failed to send, "
                                        "closing socket", data->proto);
                                break;
                        }
                        LOG_DBG("TCP (%s): \
Received and replied with %d bytes",
                                data->proto, offset);
                        if (++data->tcp.accepted[slot].counter %
                        1000 == 0U
                        {
                                LOG_INF("%s TCP: Sent %u packets",
                                data->proto,
                                        data->tcp.accepted[slot].
                                        counter);
                        }
                        offset = 0;
                }
        } while (true);
        *in_use = false;
        (void)close(client);
        data->tcp.accepted[slot].sock = -1;
}
```

The TCP server-side code may look complicated, but it is quite logical and can be considered as providing an idiom for how a TCP server might be implemented.

CHAPTER 8   ZEPHYR RTOS AND ETHERNET, WI-FI, AND TCP/IP

Echo Server on the STM32 Nucleo-F767ZI Board

Different target boards will present their own "quirks and idiosyncrasies" depending, for example, on whether vendor-implemented code has been fully incorporated into the Zephyr code tree or only partially incorporated. Flashing code to the board can also be an issue. For instance, STM32 Nucleo boards, typically, have ST-LINK firmware loaded into them. In order to use Segger JLink, this firmware needs to be replaced with Segger JLink firmware. With Segger JLink firmware, there may, occasionally, be licensing problems, even when attempting to work with the "free" noncommercial use licensing provided by Segger for use on, for example, STM32 Nucleo boards. This means that, sometimes, if running into difficulties when running a command such as west flash --runner jlink, it might be necessary to flash the code using some other Segger tool, such as, for example, the Segger Ozone debug tool, which, by the way, is a really good integrated debugging tool.

Running the Python echo server udp and tcp clients will produce the following output (in the Idle IDE):

```
Python 3.10.6 (tags/v3.10.6:9c7b4bd, Aug  1 2022, 21:53:49) [MSC v.1932 64 bit (AMD64)] on win32
Type "help", "copyright", "credits" or "license()" for more information.

= RESTART: C:\zsdk_Dec_2022\zephyrproject\f767zi_net_prj1-python-clients\udp_client.py
Echo from UDP Server Test message number 1
Echo from UDP Server Test message number 2
Echo from UDP Server Test message number 3
Echo from UDP Server Test message number 4
Echo from UDP Server Test message number 5
```

CHAPTER 8   ZEPHYR RTOS AND ETHERNET, WI-FI, AND TCP/IP

```
Echo from UDP Server Test message number 6
Echo from UDP Server Test message number 7
Echo from UDP Server Test message number 8
Echo from UDP Server Test message number 9

= RESTART: C:/zsdk_Dec_2022/zephyrproject/f767zi_net_prj1-python-clients/tcp_client.py
Echo from TCP Server Test message number 1
Echo from TCP Server Test message number 2
Echo from TCP Server Test message number 3
Echo from TCP Server Test message number 4
Echo from TCP Server Test message number 5
Echo from TCP Server Test message number 6
Echo from TCP Server Test message number 7
Echo from TCP Server Test message number 8
Echo from TCP Server Test message number 9
```

The corresponding output in a PuTTY console will be something like the following:

```
*** Booting Zephyr OS build zephyr-v3.2.0-2577-gd46b9bd12411 ***
[00:00:01.614,000] <inf> net_config: Initializing network
[00:00:01.614,000] <inf> net_config: Waiting interface 1 (0x20022764) to be up...
[00:00:02.110,000] <inf> net_config: Interface 1 (0x20022764) coming up
[00:00:02.110,000] <inf> net_config: IPv4 address: 192.0.2.1
[00:00:02.211,000] <inf> net_config: IPv6 address: 2001:db8::1
[00:00:02.212,000] <inf> net_echo_server_sample: Run echo server
[00:00:02.212,000] <inf> net_echo_server_sample: Network connected
```

CHAPTER 8 ZEPHYR RTOS AND ETHERNET, WI-FI, AND TCP/IP

[00:00:02.212,000] <inf> net_echo_server_sample: Starting...
[00:00:02.212,000] <inf> net_echo_server_sample: Waiting for TCP connection on port 4242 (IPv6)...
[00:00:02.212,000] <inf> net_echo_server_sample: Waiting for TCP connection on port 4242 (IPv4)...
[00:00:02.213,000] <inf> net_echo_server_sample: Waiting for UDP packets on port 4242 (IPv6)...
[00:00:02.213,000] <inf> net_echo_server_sample: Waiting for UDP packets on port 4242 (IPv4)...
[00:00:29.570,000] <dbg> net_echo_server_sample: process_udp: (udp4): UDP (IPv4): Received and replied with 21 bytes
[00:00:29.582,000] <dbg> net_echo_server_sample: process_udp: (udp4): UDP (IPv4): Received and replied with 21 bytes
[00:00:29.588,000] <dbg> net_echo_server_sample: process_udp: (udp4): UDP (IPv4): Received and replied with 21 bytes
[00:00:29.593,000] <dbg> net_echo_server_sample: process_udp: (udp4): UDP (IPv4): Received and replied with 21 bytes
[00:00:29.597,000] <dbg> net_echo_server_sample: process_udp: (udp4): UDP (IPv4): Received and replied with 21 bytes
[00:00:29.602,000] <dbg> net_echo_server_sample: process_udp: (udp4): UDP (IPv4): Received and replied with 21 bytes
[00:00:29.608,000] <dbg> net_echo_server_sample: process_udp: (udp4): UDP (IPv4): Received and replied with 21 bytes
[00:00:29.613,000] <dbg> net_echo_server_sample: process_udp: (udp4): UDP (IPv4): Received and replied with 21 bytes
[00:00:29.619,000] <dbg> net_echo_server_sample: process_udp: (udp4): UDP (IPv4): Received and replied with 21 bytes
[00:01:02.213,000] <inf> net_echo_server_sample: IPv4 UDP: Received 3 B/sec
[00:01:19.815,000] <inf> net_echo_server_sample: TCP (IPv4): Accepted connection

```
[00:01:19.815,000] <inf> net_echo_server_sample: Waiting for
TCP connection on port 4242 (IPv4)...
[00:01:19.816,000] <dbg> net_echo_server_sample: handle_data:
TCP (IPv4): Received and replied with 21 bytes
[00:01:19.833,000] <dbg> net_echo_server_sample: handle_data:
TCP (IPv4): Received and replied with 21 bytes
[00:01:19.841,000] <dbg> net_echo_server_sample: handle_data:
TCP (IPv4): Received and replied with 21 bytes
[00:01:19.848,000] <dbg> net_echo_server_sample: handle_data:
TCP (IPv4): Received and replied with 21 bytes
[00:01:19.853,000] <dbg> net_echo_server_sample: handle_data:
TCP (IPv4): Received and replied with 21 bytes
[00:01:19.858,000] <dbg> net_echo_server_sample: handle_data:
TCP (IPv4): Received and replied with 21 bytes
[00:01:19.864,000] <dbg> net_echo_server_sample: handle_data:
TCP (IPv4): Received and replied with 21 bytes
[00:01:19.869,000] <dbg> net_echo_server_sample: handle_data:
TCP (IPv4): Received and replied with 21 bytes
[00:01:19.874,000] <dbg> net_echo_server_sample: handle_data:
TCP (IPv4): Received and replied with 21 bytes
[00:01:19.884,000] <inf> net_echo_server_sample: TCP (IPv4):
Connection closed
uart:~$
```

Summary

In this chapter, the data structures and APIs for implementing and configuring basic TCP/IP applications, both UDP and TCP, were overviewed. The example of how to implement a multithreaded TCP server application was walked through carefully. Additionally the basic command-line interface provided by Zephyr was introduced.

References

1. https://docs.zephyrproject.org/latest/connectivity/networking/api/index.html

2. zephyr/samples/net/sockets/echo_server/src

3. zephyr/samples/net/sockets/echo_serverprj.cnf

4. https://docs.zephyrproject.org/latest/services/shell/index.html

CHAPTER 9

Understanding and Working with the Devicetree in General and SPI and I2C in Particular

When developing applications involving a custom board, or adding peripherals such as I2C or SPI peripherals to an existing board, an understanding of the Zephyr devicetree and how it is used in application development is required.

The devicetree concept as used in Zephyr has its origins in Linux, where the main purpose of the devicetree was to provide a means of describing nondiscoverable hardware, namely, hardware that is connected via nondiscoverable protocols such as I2C, SPI, UART, and GPIO. The kernel, which controls the hardware, needs to know what the connected devices are and how it is to communicate with these attached devices.

Prior to the introduction of the devicetree approach, information about such devices had to be hard-coded in the source code. The devicetree

CHAPTER 9   UNDERSTANDING AND WORKING WITH THE DEVICETREE IN GENERAL AND SPI AND I2C IN PARTICULAR

approach itself had its origins in the Sun Microsystems OpenBoot framework, which was, later, incorporated into the IEEE Open Firmware standard. In the context of the Zephyr application development, the devicetree framework provides a way to describe hardware in a format that can be made use of by the Zephyr Device Driver model.

Working with devicetrees makes use of the devicetree syntax as well as a devicetree schema syntax, which can be used for describing the structural and syntactic details of different types of device. There are also tools for parsing and processing devicetree information and tools for checking a particular devicetree section against a corresponding schema definition. In Zephyr, the devicetree associated with a project is built up by including various devicetree components, which are then processed to produce header files that are, in turn, used in the creation of the device driver instances used in the application itself.

Firmware Development Aspects of Application Development

Developing applications running on specialized and resource-constrained embedded systems requires, typically, a much deeper understanding of the underlying hardware than developing Windows, Linux, and Mac OS X applications running on PC or server machines.

Firmware design issues that need to be considered include, for example, things such as deciding on the hardware that should be used to control a particular device, details of working with device drivers for the hardware devices involved, the implementation of the code required to support the hardware involved, and understanding how the hardware interacts with the application code.

CHAPTER 9 UNDERSTANDING AND WORKING WITH THE DEVICETREE IN GENERAL AND SPI AND I2C IN PARTICULAR

The Zephyr approach to implementing device drivers involves classifying drivers in various types of driver. A given type of driver has a generic API (Application Programming Interface) associated with it. Zephyr defines a device model and the mechanisms for configuring the drivers used in an application.

The Zephyr device model provides a consistent device model for configuring the drivers that are part of a system. The device model is responsible for initializing all the drivers configured into the system. The API can be thought of as a collection of interface functions for the corresponding device type, and an instance of a given type of device is defined by a variable of type `struct device`, which has the following structure:

```
struct device {
      const char *name;
      const void *config;
      const void *api;
      void * const data;
};
```

In this structure, the `config` member points to an area of memory that holds read-only device configuration data that is set at build time. The configuration data includes things such as the base memory-mapped IO addresses of the device and the IRQ line numbers associated with the device. The `data` element points to an area of memory that is used by the driver at runtime and may contain objects such as reference counts, semaphores, and scratch buffers required by the driver. The `api` element points to a collection of function pointers that define the actual behavior of the driver. Typically this element is read-only and is populated with pointers to the actual API methods at build time.

The different firmware components in a given device can be thought of as a collection of subsystems. In general, the drivers used in an application will implement (use) a device-independent subsystem-specific API for

CHAPTER 9   UNDERSTANDING AND WORKING WITH THE DEVICETREE IN GENERAL AND SPI AND I2C IN PARTICULAR

that type of device. This has the consequence that when an application uses a device instance, it does not need to know the details of the internal implementations of the various API functions involved. An approach like this goes a long way toward simplifying the task of porting applications from one architecture to another.

The following code snippets illustrate this approach:

```
typedef int (*subsys_api_func1)(const struct device *dev,
int param1, int param2);
typedef void (*subsys_api_func2)(const struct device *dev, void
*pparam);
struct subsystem_api {
      subsys_api_func1 do_it;
      subsys_api_func2 do_other;
};

static inline int subsys_do_this(const struct device *dev, int param1, int param2)
{
      struct subsystem_api *api;
      api = (struct subsystem_api *)dev->api;
      return api->do_it(dev, param1, param2);
}

static inline void subsys_do_other(const struct device *dev, void *pparam)
{
      struct subsystem_api *api;
      api = (struct subsystem_api *)dev->api;
      api->do_other(dev, pparam);
}
```

CHAPTER 9   UNDERSTANDING AND WORKING WITH THE DEVICETREE IN GENERAL AND SPI AND I2C IN PARTICULAR

The real API for a particular subsystem will be realized by code that implements the actual API functions. The corresponding function pointer values will be used in the initialization of the collection of function pointers data structure for the API. In the case of the code snippet shown previously, suppose that the actual driver functions were defined as follows:

```
static int real_driver_do_it(const struct device *dev, int param1, int param2)
{
      ...
}
static void real_driver_do_other(const struct device *dev, void *pparam)
{
      ...
}
```

Then the collection of function pointers of the API could be initialized as follows:

```
static struct subsystem_api real_driver_api_funcs = {
      .do_it = real_driver_do_this,
      .do_other = real_driver_do_other,
};
```

Implementing device drivers is something that must be learned by experience and studying actual device driver implementations. A more advanced aspect of device driver implementation in Zephyr includes implementing device-specific extensions, for example, where a particular driver can be cast to an instance of a driver subsystem such as a GPIO subsystem, but provides added functionality that cannot be exposed through the standard API. Another advanced topic is where there are multiple instances of a device subsystem where the instances differ in their

CHAPTER 9   UNDERSTANDING AND WORKING WITH THE DEVICETREE IN GENERAL AND
            SPI AND I2C IN PARTICULAR

`config` and `data` elements. Yet other complex topics involve scenarios where drivers may depend on other drivers being initialized first, or where a driver requires the use of kernel services, or where a driver involves multiple MMIO (Memory-Mapped Input/Output) regions. Scenarios such as these are advanced topics that are not covered in this book.

Overview of SPI and I2C

The examples studied in this chapter will involve I2C and SPI sensors and peripherals. The number of available I2C and SPI devices is large and includes devices such as accelerometer sensors, gas sensors, SPI EEPROM, SPI flash, SPI Ethernet controllers, and SPO CAN bus controllers.

I2C is a serial bus that consumes only a small number of the pins of a microcontroller and to which multiple devices can be attached. SPI consumes a relatively small number of pins when only a few SPI devices are attached. However, because each SPI device requires a chip select line, then the more devices that are attached to an SPI, the greater the number of pins that will be required. For instance, five SPI devices would require five chip selects and together with the three pins for the bus itself, eight pins will be required in total.

The basic, general, plan of action when deciding to use SPI or I2C devices in a project, typically, involves coming up with answers to questions such as which pins are available for I2C or SPI use and whether these pins are fixed or configurable. Then there is the issue of whether the use of an I2C or SPI peripheral is appropriate and, for a given functionality, whether an I2C or SPI device variant should be used. Where power consumption is important, then the power consumption characteristics of the various possible devices that are being considered also need to be taken into account.

CHAPTER 9   UNDERSTANDING AND WORKING WITH THE DEVICETREE IN GENERAL AND SPI AND
            I2C IN PARTICULAR

Although serial protocols such as SPI, I2C, and UART are significantly slower than higher-speed serial protocols such as USB, Ethernet, Bluetooth, and Wi-Fi, they have the advantage of being much simpler and more economical in the use of code and hardware. They are well suited for scenarios involving communications between microcontrollers or between microcontrollers and sensors where the amount of data to be transferred is relatively small and where high data transmission rates are not needed.

In serial protocols, the actual data bits are sent through a single wire, and there are two main strategies for sending the serial data, namely, asynchronous vs. synchronous. In a synchronous protocol as well as sending the data bits along one wire, a clocking signal is sent along another wire. The clocking signal tells the receiver when to read the signal level on the data wire. In an asynchronous protocol, only the data bits are sent, and the sender and receiver need to have agreed on a common data rate. Additionally, in asynchronous protocols, it is necessary to also send start bits and stop bits to "frame" the data bits.

SPI Explained

The Serial Peripheral Interface (SPI) is widely used in embedded system applications. It is used, for example, in SD memory card modules, RFID card reader modules, and also in 2.4 GHz wireless transmitter/receivers in order to communicate with a microcontroller. SPI is a synchronous protocol. This means that a clock signal is sent on one wire and a data signal on another wire. This makes it possible to send data bits as a continuous stream rather than as individual framed data packets. The SPI protocol has been around for quite some time, being developed, originally, by Motorola in the mid-1980s.

Chapter 9 Understanding and Working with the Devicetree in General and SPI and I2C in Particular

Multiple SPI devices can be attached to an SPI bus; however, at any point in time, only two devices can be involved in the movement of data. In the case of SPI, one device is the master, and it controls the clock signal. The other device is a slave, and it can only send data when permitted to do so by the master. In order to select from one of several attached slave devices, each device has a "slave select" (SS) pin, and a "slave select" line goes from a pin on the master device to the "select" pin on the slave device. Hence, a master can control multiple slaves. However, the addition of an extra slave consumes an extra pin on the microcontroller.

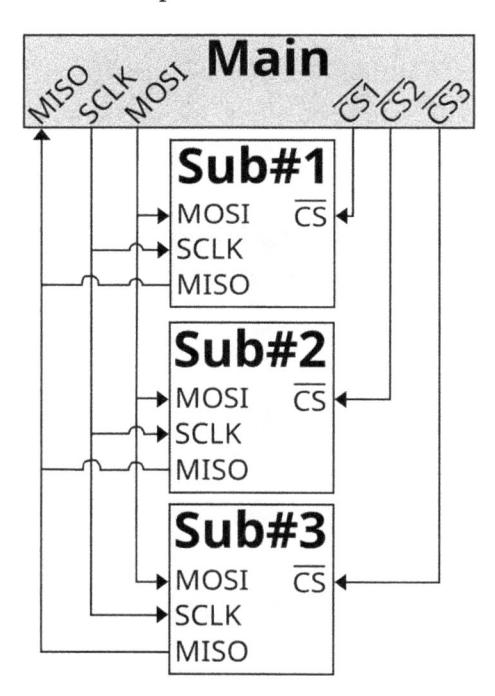

Figure 9-1. Simple SPI network schematic

CHAPTER 9   UNDERSTANDING AND WORKING WITH THE DEVICETREE IN GENERAL AND SPI AND I2C IN PARTICULAR

The setup for a simple SPI network involving a master and three slaves in a multidrop bus configuration is shown in Figure 9-1 [1].

- MOSI (Master Output/Slave Input) – The line used by the master to send data to the slave
- MISO (Master Input/Slave Output) – The line used by the slave to send data to the master
- SCLK (Clock) – The line for the clock signal
- SS/CS (Slave Select/Chip Select) – The line used by the master to select the slave device it will be sending data to

SPI is a "full duplex" protocol because data can be sent from master to slave and slave to master concurrently. The data is sent on two separate lines, namely, the MOSI and MISO lines.

The maximum speed for SPI is 10 Mbps; however, in practice, lower speeds are used. The maximum number of slaves is theoretically unlimited; however, in practice, only a few SPI slaves are attached to a microcontroller at a time in real-world applications.

Data transmission requires that the bus master configures the SPI clock to a frequency that the slave device supports, typically up to several MHz. Transmission itself involves the master selecting a slave device by asserting a logic level of 0 on the chosen select line. After a suitable delay, if required, for example, where the device needs time to complete an analog-to-digital conversion, the master starts the transmission by beginning to issue clock cycles. On each SPI clock cycle, a full duplex data transmission takes place. The master sends a bit on the MOSI line and the slave reads it, and concurrently, the slave sends a bit on the MISO line, which the master reads. This sequence is used even when only one-directional data transfer is being performed.

Advantages and Disadvantages of SPI

Advantages

- As there are no start and stop bits, data can be streamed continuously without interruption.
- Because slaves are selected explicitly, there is no addressing system in I2C, which would add extra complexity to the application.
- SPI is capable of faster data transfer rates than I2C.
- The presence of separate MISO and MOSI lines means that data can be sent and received at the same time.

Disadvantages

- SPI uses up more I/O pins as compared to I2C (SPI involves four wires, whereas I2C involves two wires).
- In SPI, unlike I2C, there is no automatic acknowledgment that the data has been successfully received.
- SPI provides no form of error checking.
- An SPI network can only have a single master.

I2C Explained

I2C was developed by Philips in the early 1980s as a simple serial protocol that supported a two-wire interface that could be used to connect relatively low-speed devices such as microcontrollers, EEPROMs, A/D and D/A converters, I/O interfaces, and various other peripheral chips in embedded systems. Because multiple I2C devices could be attached to the

CHAPTER 9   UNDERSTANDING AND WORKING WITH THE DEVICETREE IN GENERAL AND SPI AND
             I2C IN PARTICULAR

same bus, and there were no select pins, each attached device had to have a unique address. The original version of I2C could only run at speeds up to 100 kHz, and addresses were 7 bits wide. Later, in 1992, in the first public specification, the specification included a 400 kHz fast-mode and an enhanced 10-bit-wide address space. Further additions to the specification included three extra modes: a fast mode, at 1 MHz; a high-speed mode, at 3.4 MHz; and an ultra-fast mode, at 5 MHz, although, such speeds are not commonly found in standard microcontrollers.

There is also an I2C variant of I2C that was developed by Intel called SMBus (System Management Bus), which was, originally, designed to provide more predictable communications between ICs deployed on PC motherboards. SMBus is relatively low speed with speeds from 10 kHz to 100 kHz. In addition to "vanilla" I2C, Intel introduced a variant in 1995 called "System Management Bus" (SMBus). SMBus also has a clock timeout mode designed to make very low-speed operations illegal.

The I2C bus uses two lines: SDA (data line) and SCL (clock line). Data transmission between master and slave is half-duplex, either from master to slave or from slave to master. Data transfer between slave and master is always initiated by the master. The master initiates the data transfer and generates all the synchronization signals. A slave will only start sending data when requested to do so by the master. In addition to multiple slaves, it is also possible to have more than one master on a bus. However, only one master can be active at any one time.

I2C devices are connected to the bus via an open collector or open drain. This means that a device may output either a logic zero or nothing at all (the output is in the high impedance state). If the outputs of all the connected devices are in the high-impedance state, two external pull-up resistors, Rp, which must be present, will hold the lines at a high voltage level (logic 1 state). The resistors have values, typically, in the range from 1K to 10K. The schematic in Figure 9-2 shows a typical setup [2].

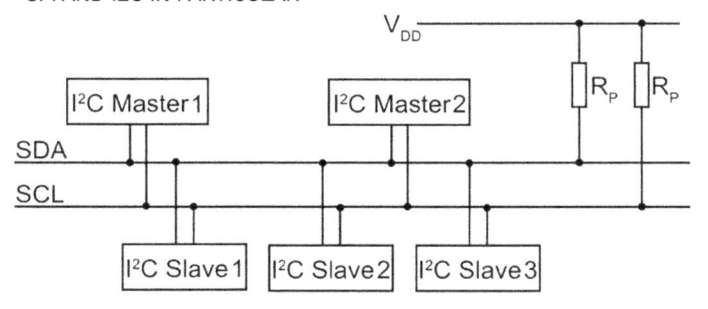

CHAPTER 9 UNDERSTANDING AND WORKING WITH THE DEVICETREE IN GENERAL AND SPI AND I2C IN PARTICULAR

Figure 9-2. Simple I2C network schematic

Devicetree Configuration

The aforementioned introduction to I2C and SPI devices should provide a sufficient background to be able to follow the I2C and SPI devicetree configuration and programming examples that will be introduced later in this chapter. First, however, it is necessary to acquire some familiarity with the devicetree syntax and how devicetrees are processed during a Zephyr application build.

The whole point of devicetrees is to minimize the number of separate application code projects involving devices and boards in applications that are broadly similar but which differ in the details of the devices being used. A devicetree is, essentially, a hierarchical data structure that describes hardware.

The devicetree specification defines both source and binary representations. In Zephyr projects, devicetrees are used to describe the hardware available on supported Boards, as well as the initial configuration of that hardware. Two types of devicetree input files are involved, namely, the devicetree sources, which contain the devicetree itself, and the devicetree bindings, which describe its contents, including data types.

CHAPTER 9   UNDERSTANDING AND WORKING WITH THE DEVICETREE IN GENERAL AND SPI AND
            I2C IN PARTICULAR

The Zephyr build system uses devicetree sources and bindings to produce a "generated" C header. The contents of this generated header are abstracted by the devicetree.h API, which contains a collection of macros that can be used to extract device-related information from the project's devicetree. This usage pattern is outlined in the schematic in Figure 9-3.

Figure 9-3.   Generating devicetree.h

Zephyr and application source code files can include and use `devicetree.h`. In Zephyr projects, the devicetree is used in conjunction with Kconfig. With Kconfig, overrides of default values taken from devicetree are possible, and furthermore, devicetree information can be referenced from Kconfig by the use of Kconfig functions.

Device Tree Source (DTS) Representation of Devicetrees

The following several sections are a "distillation" of the Zephyr devicetree documentation and various Zephyr examples put together to provide a basic understanding of devicetree syntax and how devicetree files are processed when building Zephyr applications.

Device Tree Source code provides a human-readable representation of a devicetree. The complete syntax is to be found in the devicetree specification [3]

A devicetree has its origin in a starting root node, below which is a collection of nodes that, in turn, have subnodes (child nodes) and so on. A node has named properties and property values. These are denoted as name-value pairs.

CHAPTER 9 UNDERSTANDING AND WORKING WITH THE DEVICETREE IN GENERAL AND SPI AND I2C IN PARTICULAR

The example in Figure 9-4 shows a very simple devicetree [4].

```
/dts-v1/;
/ {
    a-node {
        subnode_label: a-sub-node {
            foo = <3>;
        };
    };
};
```

Figure 9-4. *Simple devicetree example*

The `/dts-v1/;` statement in the first line states that the file's contents conform to version 1 of the DTS syntax.

The tree has three nodes:

- A root node: /
- A node labeled (named) a-node, which is a child of the root node
- A node labeled (named) a-sub-node, which is a child of a-node

A node label can be used as a unique shorthand for the node that can be used to refer to that node from some other place in the devicetree. A devicetree node can, in fact, have zero or more node labels. The location of a node in a devicetree is given by the path from the root to that node. A devicetree path is made up of strings separated by slashes (/).

The path of the root node is a single slash: /. For a non-root node, the devicetree path to that node is formed by concatenating the node's ancestors' names with the name of the node itself. In the case of the example devicetree given, the full path to a-sub-node is

/a-node/a-sub-node

CHAPTER 9 UNDERSTANDING AND WORKING WITH THE DEVICETREE IN GENERAL AND SPI AND I2C IN PARTICULAR

The properties of a devicetree node are name/value pairs. A property value is a sequence of bytes, and a value can be an array of cells, where a cell is simply a 32-bit unsigned integer. In the preceding devicetree snippet, the node a-sub-node has a property named foo, and the value of foo is a cell with a value of 3. The size and type of the value associated with foo are implied by the enclosing angle brackets (< and >) in the DTS.

Normally, in a devicetree, devicetree nodes correspond to hardware components, and the node hierarchy is related to the physical organization of the hardware.

For example, in the case of a board with three I2C peripherals connected to an I2C bus controller built into an SoC, this could be represented in the devicetree fragment shown in the next figure.

The I2C peripheral nodes would be children of the bus controller node, and the corresponding DTS describing this setup would look something like that shown in Figure 9-5 [4].

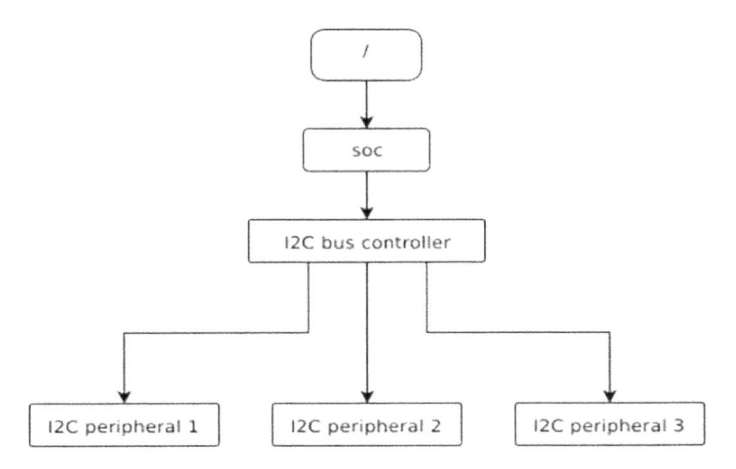

Figure 9-5. *A devicetree fragment describing an on-chip I2C bus controller with three attached I2C peripherals*

CHAPTER 9   UNDERSTANDING AND WORKING WITH THE DEVICETREE IN GENERAL AND SPI AND I2C IN PARTICULAR

```
/dts-v1/;
/ {
    soc {
        i2c-bus-controller {
            i2c-peripheral-1 {
            };
            i2c-peripheral-2 {
            };
            i2c-peripheral-3 {
            };
        };
    };
};
```

The nodes would have properties, and a more realistic devicetree fragment might look something like that in Figure 9-6 [4].

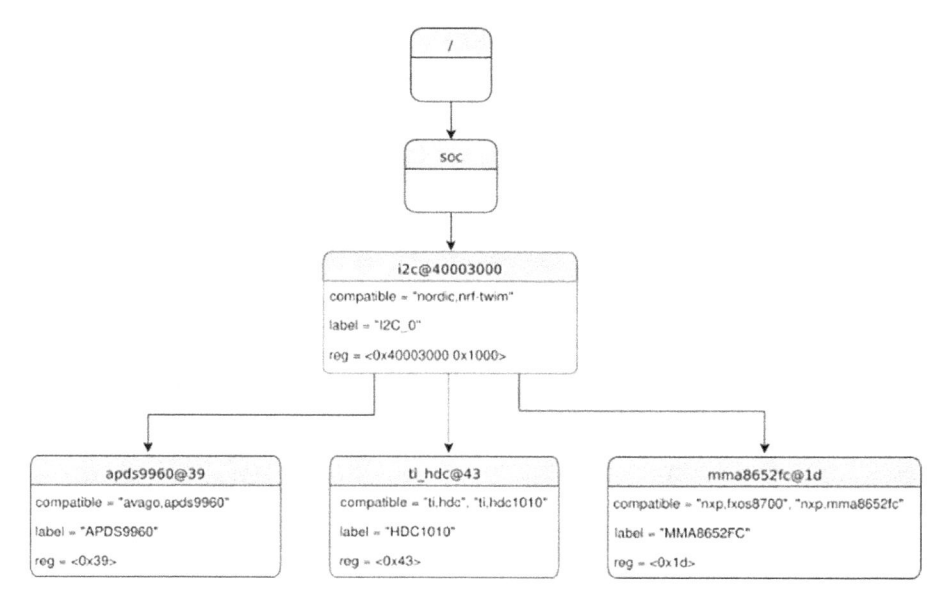

```
/
│
▼
soc
│
▼
i2c@40003000
compatible = "nordic,nrf-twim"
label = "I2C_0"
reg = <0x40003000 0x1000>
```

```
apds9960@39                    ti_hdc@43                      mma8652fc@1d
compatible = "avago,apds9960"  compatible = "ti,hdc", "ti,hdc1010"  compatible = "nxp,fxos8700", "nxp,mma8652fc"
label = "APDS9960"             label = "HDC1010"              label = "MMA8652FC"
reg = <0x39>                   reg = <0x43>                   reg = <0x1d>
```

Figure 9-6. More realistic devicetree fragment

CHAPTER 9   UNDERSTANDING AND WORKING WITH THE DEVICETREE IN GENERAL AND SPI AND
            I2C IN PARTICULAR

Unit Addresses and the Devicetree

Understanding and working with unit addresses is the key to the successful use of devicetrees. Unit addresses are those parts of node names after an "at" sign (@), such as 40003000 in i2c@40003000, or 39 in apds9960@39.

Unit addresses are optional; for example, in the soc node in the devicetree example shown previously, there is no unit address associated with the SoC node. Technically, in a devicetree, the unit address is the address of a node in the address space of the parent node of that node. A unit address must be appropriate for the hardware type of the component that is associated with that node.

In the case of a memory-mapped peripheral, the unit address is the register map base address of the peripheral. For example, in the case of a node named i2c@40003000, the name represents an I2C controller whose register map base address is 0x40003000. In the case of an I2C peripheral, the address is the address of the peripheral on the I2C bus.

Thus, for a child node apds9960@39 of the I2C controller, the address being referred to is an I2C bus address. For an SPI peripheral, the address would be an index representing the chip select line number for that particular peripheral. (If there is no chip select line, 0 is used.) When referring to memory, the address is the start address of a physical block of memory. For example, in the case of a node named memory@2000000, the address represents RAM starting at the physical address 0x2000000.

Memory, such as flash memory, for example, can be partitioned. The devicetree snippet shown in Figure 9-7 demonstrates how partitions are handled in a devicetree [4].

453

CHAPTER 9 UNDERSTANDING AND WORKING WITH THE DEVICETREE IN GENERAL AND SPI AND I2C IN PARTICULAR

```
Example of flash device and its partitions:
    flash@8000000 {
        /* ... */
        partitions {
            partition@0 { /* ... */ };
            partition@20000 { /* ... */ };
            /* ... */
        };
    };
```

Figure 9-7. Devicetree fragment describing flash partitions

Physical flash memory has a starting address. Thus, a node named flash@8000000 represents a flash device whose physical start address is 0x8000000. The partition components for fixed flash memory partitions are identified by providing the offset from the start address. In the preceding example, the node named partition@0 is a partition with offset 0 from the start of its flash device. The base address of this partition is therefore 0x8000000. Similarly, the base address of a node named partition@20000 is 0x8020000.

The `compatible` property can be used to represent the name of the hardware device represented by a given node. A standard format for the compatible string property value consists of a starting vendor name followed by a comma, followed by the name of the device part (`"vendor,device"`), for example, `"avago,apds9960"`, or a sequence of such strings, for example, `"ti,hdc"` and `"ti,hdc1010"`. The vendor part is, usually, an abbreviated name of the vendor. In the Zephyr distribution, the file `dts/bindings/vendor-prefixes.txt` contains a list of generally accepted vendor names. The device part is the one used in the data sheet for that device. In the case of generic hardware values such as `"gpio-keys"`, `"mmio-sram"` or `"fixed-clock"` can be used.

The importance of the compatible property is that it can be used to find the correct bindings for a particular node. Device drivers use `devicetree.h` to find nodes with relevant compatibles, to determine the actual hardware to manage. The compatible property can have multiple values. Additional values are useful in situations where the device is a specific instance of a more general family. The use of additional values makes it possible, during the build process, to match from the most- to the least-specific device drivers. Formally speaking, according to Zephyr's bindings syntax, the `compatible` property has type string-array.

The `label` property is the name of a device according to Zephyr's Device Driver Model. Its value can be passed to the function `device_get_binding()` to retrieve the corresponding driver-level `struct device*` pointer. This pointer can then be passed to the correct driver API in the application code used when interacting with the device. For example, calling `device_get_binding("I2C_0")` should return a pointer to a device structure, which can be passed to I2C API functions such as `i2c_transfer()`. The generated C header will contain a macro that expands to this string.

The `reg` devicetree node property holds the information used to address the device. The value is specific to the device (it depends on the `compatible` property). The `reg` property itself is a sequence of (address, length) pairs. Each pair is called a "register block." In the case of devices accessed via memory-mapped I/O registers such as i2c@40003000, for example, the address is normally the base address of the I/O register space for that device, and the length is the number of bytes occupied by the registers.

In the case of I2C devices, such as apds9960@39 and its siblings, the address is a slave address on the I2C bus. In the case of SPI devices, the address is a chip select line number, and in this case, there is no length value.

The devicetree `status` property is a string that describes whether the node is enabled or not. The permitted values for this property, according to the devicetree specifications, are `"okay"`, `"disabled"`, `"reserved"`, `"fail"`, and `"fail-sss"`. In the case of Zephyr, only the values `"okay"` and `"disabled"` are used. In Zephyr, a node is considered enabled if its status property is either `"okay"` or it is not defined (i.e., it does not exist in the

CHAPTER 9   UNDERSTANDING AND WORKING WITH THE DEVICETREE IN GENERAL AND
            SPI AND I2C IN PARTICULAR

devicetree source). Nodes with status `"disabled"` are explicitly disabled. Devicetree nodes that correspond to physical devices must be enabled for the corresponding `struct device` in the Zephyr driver model to be allocated and initialized.

The `interrupts` property has information about interrupts generated by the device, encoded as an array of one or more interrupt specifiers. Each interrupt specifier has a number of cells, and each cell in an interrupt specifier can be given a name.

The following table provides a summary of property value types and how they are represented in the devicetree source.

Property type	How to write	Example
string	Double quoted	a-string = "hello, world!";
int	between angle brackets (< and >)	an-int = <1>;
boolean	for true, with no value (for false, use /delete-property/)	my-true-boolean;
array	between angle brackets (< and >), separated by spaces	foo = <0xdeadbeef 1234 0>;
uint8-array	in hexadecimal *without* leading 0x, between square brackets ([and]).	a-byte-array = [00 01 ab];
string-array	separated by commas	a-string-array = "string one", "string two", "string three";
phandle	between angle brackets (< and >)	a-phandle = <&mynode>;
phandles	between angle brackets (< and >), separated by spaces	some-phandles = <&mynode0 &mynode1 &mynode2>;
phandle-array	between angle brackets (< and >), separated by spaces	a-phandle-array = <&mynode0 1 2>, <&mynode1 3 4>;

CHAPTER 9 UNDERSTANDING AND WORKING WITH THE DEVICETREE IN GENERAL AND SPI AND I2C IN PARTICULAR

In a Zephyr devicetree, a node can also be specified without having to use its entire path by the use of aliases or chosen nodes. The /aliases and /chosen nodes do not refer to an actual hardware device – they are used to specify some other node in the devicetree.

The /chosen node's properties can be used to configure system- or subsystem-wide values. This is illustrated in the following example code snippet in which my-uart is an alias for the node with path /soc/serial@12340000.

Using its node label uart0, that node can be set as the value of the chosen zephyr,console node, as shown in the devicetree snippet in Figure 9-8.

```
/dts-v1/;
/ {
    chosen {
        zephyr,console = &uart0;
    };
    aliases {
        my-uart = &uart0;
    };
    soc {
        uart0: serial@12340000 {
            ...
        };
    };
};
```

Figure 9-8. Devicetree fragment illustrating the use of chosen and aliases

Devicetree Processing

Devicetree processing is fairly complicated, and only an outline will be given here. It, typically, involves multiple input files and generates multiple output files.

There are four types of devicetree input files, namely, sources (.dts file extension), includes (.dtsi file extension), overlays (.overlay file extension), and bindings (.yaml file extension). In the Zephyr repository

CHAPTER 9   UNDERSTANDING AND WORKING WITH THE DEVICETREE IN GENERAL AND
            SPI AND I2C IN PARTICULAR

board, specific devicetree files are to be found in directories described by the patterns `boards/<ARCH>/<BOARD>/<BOARD>.dts`, `dts/common/skeleton.dtsi`, `dts/<ARCH>/.../<SOC>.dtsi`, and `dts/bindings/.../binding.yaml`.

Typically, a supported board has a `BOARD.dts` file describing its hardware, which includes one or more `.dtsi` files such as `.dtsi` files describing the CPU or System on Chip that Zephyr runs on, and these, in turn, may include other `.dtsi` files. A `BOARD.dts` file also describes the board's specific hardware.

Devicetree processing is outlined in the schematic in Figure 9-9 provided in the Zephyr documentation [4].

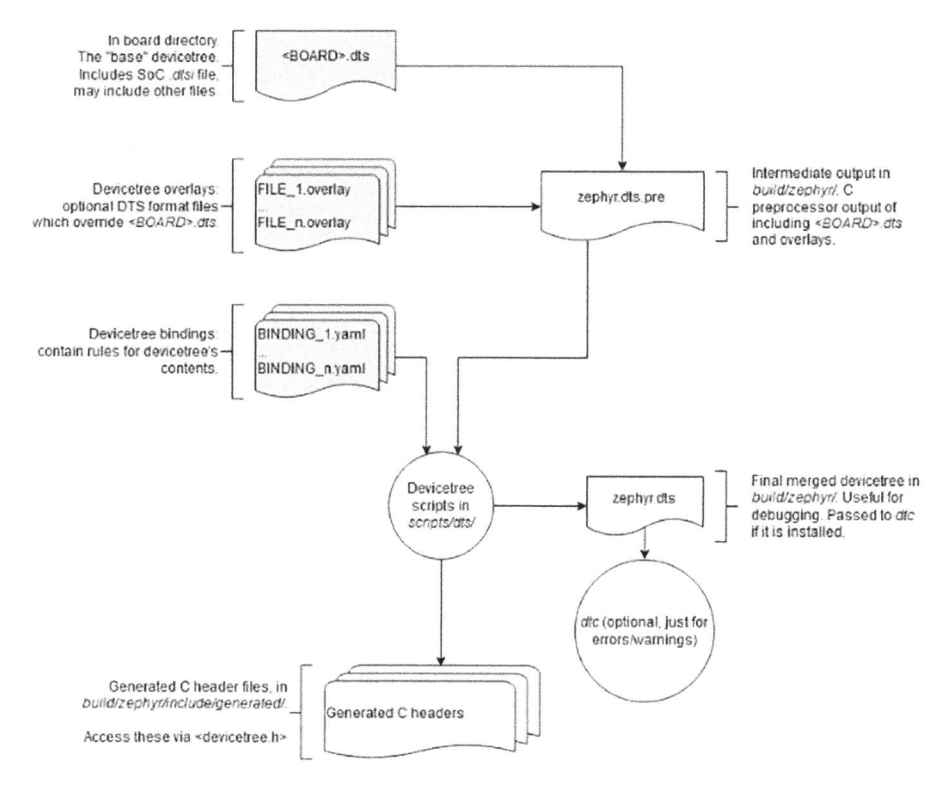

Figure 9-9. *Schematic outline of the devicetree processing procedures*

CHAPTER 9　UNDERSTANDING AND WORKING WITH THE DEVICETREE IN GENERAL AND SPI AND I2C IN PARTICULAR

At the heart of devicetree processing lies the dts/common directory that contains skeleton.dtsi, a minimal include file for defining a complete devicetree. Architecture-specific subdirectories (dts/<ARCH>) contain .dtsi files for CPUs or SoCs that extend skeleton.dtsi. The C preprocessor is run on all devicetree files to expand macro references. Includes are typically via #include <filename> directives. DTS also supports a /include/ "<filename>" syntax. A BOARD.dts file can be extended or modified using overlays. An overlay is also a DTS file, and it is used to adapt the base devicetree for specific target purposes.

Zephyr applications can use overlays for various purposes such as enabling a peripheral that is disabled by default or for selecting a sensor on a target board for some application-specific purpose. By using the devicetree together with Kconfig, it is possible to reconfigure the kernel and the device drivers without needing to modify the application source code. Overlays can also be used for setting up shields attached to development boards or kits.

The Zephyr build system automatically picks up overlay files stored from certain defined locations. A list of overlays to include can also be specified explicitly via the DTC_OVERLAY_FILE CMake variable. The build system combines BOARD.dts and .overlay files by concatenating them. The overlays are added in last. This process makes use of the DTS syntax, which permits merging overlapping definitions of nodes in the devicetree.

Devicetree bindings are YAML files. Their purpose is to describe the contents of devicetree sources, includes, and overlays that can be considered valid. Devicetree bindings are used by the build system to generate C macros that can then be used in device driver and application code.

Much of the work of processing devicetree and devicetree-related files is performed by Python scripts. The scripts/dts/ directory and the scripts/dts/python-devicetree directories contain the libraries and scripts used to create output files from input files in the course of

CHAPTER 9 UNDERSTANDING AND WORKING WITH THE DEVICETREE IN GENERAL AND
            SPI AND I2C IN PARTICULAR

devicetree processing. They include `dtlib.py,` a low-level DTS parsing library; `edtlib.py,` a library layered on top of `dtlib` that uses bindings to interpret properties and provide a higher-level view of the devicetree; and `gen_defines.py,` which uses `edtlib` to generate C preprocessor macros from the devicetree and bindings. The standard `dtc` (devicetree compiler) tool, if installed, can be run on the final devicetree to catch errors or warnings.

The output files generated from devicetree processing during a Zephyr application build are created in the application's build directory. These include header files that are not intended to be used directly but, rather, to be accessed from C/C++ code. The header files in question are `devicetree_unfixed.h` and `device_fixups.h,` which are included via `#include` statements at the start of `devicetree.h. devicetree.h` is part of the Zephyr distribution source code and can be found at `zephyr/include/zephyr/devicetree.h`.

From the previous overview, it can be seen that devicetree construction and building as part of the Zephyr application build process is quite complex and involves the use of some "powerful and nontrivial" Python scripts. In the "great scheme of things," the advantages of this approach are that it makes for flexibility, API consistency, code reuse, and portability.

Devicetree Bindings

Devicetree bindings provide more detailed hardware descriptions by declaring requirements that the contents of a node must satisfy and also semantic information about the contents of a node. During the configuration phase of the build process, the build system attempts to match each node in the devicetree to a binding file. The information in the binding file is used both to validate the contents of a node and also in the process of generating macros for working with that node in an application.

CHAPTER 9 UNDERSTANDING AND WORKING WITH THE DEVICETREE IN GENERAL AND SPI AND
          I2C IN PARTICULAR

The following basic example, based on the Zephyr documentation, illustrates various aspects of the binding process. It concerns a hypothetical DTS node bar-device and a matching YAML binding.

Suppose the node entry in a DTS file for bar-device is

```
bar-device {
      compatible = "foo-company,bar-device";
      num-foos = <3>;
};
```

and the matching YAML binding is

```
compatible: "foo-company,bar-device"
Properties:
      Num-foos:
      type: int
      required: true
```

The build system will match the bar-device node to its YAML binding because the node's `compatible` property matches the binding's `compatible:` line. When converting the devicetree's contents into a generated `devicetree_unfixed.h` header file, the build system will use the given binding to check that the required num-foos property is present in the bar-device node and that its value, <3>, has the correct type. The build system will then generate a macro for the bar-device node's `num-foos` property, which will expand to the integer literal 3. This macro can be used to get the value of that property in the C/C++ application program code.

Where a node has more than one string in its compatible property, the build system looks for compatible bindings in the listed order and uses the first match it finds. In the case of a node that does not have compatible properties, matching will be attempted on bindings associated with the parent node. In the case where a node describes hardware on a bus, such as an I2C or SPI bus, then the bus type is also taken into account when matching the node to its binding.

461

CHAPTER 9   UNDERSTANDING AND WORKING WITH THE DEVICETREE IN GENERAL AND SPI AND I2C IN PARTICULAR

The build system looks for bindings in dts/bindings subdirectories in the Zephyr repository, the application source directory, the board directory of the application as well as directories specified in the DTS_ROOT CMake variable, and also in any module that defines a dts_root in its Build settings. When matching nodes to bindings, the build system will consider any YAML file in any of these locations, including their subdirectories.

The Syntax of Binding Files

The aim of this section is to provide a practical introduction to the syntax of binding files that will be sufficient to make sense of binding files that you will come across in Zephyr example projects and in actual Zephyr applications encountered in development work. The top-level value in a binding file is a YAML mapping, which is a collection of key:value pairs. The contents of such a file can be illustrated by a didactic example file like the one shown here, which consists of comments and associated key:value combinations.

```
# A high level description of the device the binding applies to:
description: |
      This is the Vendomatic company's foo-device.

      Descriptions which span multiple lines
      (like this) are OK,
      and are encouraged for complex bindings.
See https://yaml-multiline.info/ for formatting help.
# You can include definitions from other bindings using this syntax:
include: other.yaml
```

CHAPTER 9 UNDERSTANDING AND WORKING WITH THE DEVICETREE IN GENERAL AND SPI AND
            I2C IN PARTICULAR

```
# Used to match nodes to this binding as discussed above:
compatible: "manufacturer,foo-device"
Properties:
      # Requirements for and descriptions of the properties
      that this
      # binding's nodes need to satisfy go here.
Child-binding:
      # You can constrain the children of the nodes
      matching this
      # binding using this key.
# If the node describes bus hardware, like an SPI bus
controller
# on an SoC, use 'bus:' to say which one, like this:
bus: spi
# If the node instead appears as a device on a bus, like an
external
# SPI memory chip, use 'on-bus:' to say what type of bus,
like this.
# Like 'compatible', this key also influences the way
nodes match
# bindings.
on-bus: spi

Foo-cells:
      # "Specifier" cell names for the 'foo' domain go here;
      # example 'foo' values are 'gpio', 'pwm', and 'dma'.
      # See below for more information.
```

The Properties key describes the properties that nodes which match the binding can contain. The following example illustrates what the binding for a UART peripheral might look like:

```
compatible: "manufacturer,serial"
```

CHAPTER 9 UNDERSTANDING AND WORKING WITH THE DEVICETREE IN GENERAL AND
          SPI AND I2C IN PARTICULAR

```
Properties:
    Reg:
        type: array
        description: UART peripheral MMIO register space
        required: true
    Current-speed:
        type: int
        description: current baud rate
        required: true
    Label:
        type: string
        description: human-readable name
        required: false
```

A devicetree node such as the one shown in the following example snippet will be validated by the binding shown previously.

```
my-serial@abcdcdef {
    compatible = "manufacturer,serial";
    reg = <0x abcdcdef 0x1000>;
    current-speed = <115200>;
    label = "UART_0";
};
```

Except for special properties, such as reg, whose meanings are defined by the devicetree specification itself, only properties listed in the properties: key will have generated macros associated with them.

Each property entry in a binding must obey the following syntax:

```
<property name>:
    required: <true | false>
    type: <string | int | boolean | array | uint8-array |
    string-array | phandle | phandles | phandle-array
```

CHAPTER 9 UNDERSTANDING AND WORKING WITH THE DEVICETREE IN GENERAL AND SPI AND I2C IN PARTICULAR

```
 | path |
compound>
deprecated: <true | false>
default: <default>
description: <description of the property>
Enum:
      - <item1>
      - <item2>
      ...
      - <itemN>
const: <string | int>
```

The following snippets illustrate how this syntax might be used in practice:

```
Properties:
     # Describes a property, 'current-speed = <115200>;'
     which is
     # obligatory for this example node, so, set
     'required: true'.
     Current-speed:
          type: int
          required: true
          description: Initial baud rate for bar-device
     # 'keys = "foo", "bar";' describes an optional property
     Keys:
          type: string-array
          required: false
          description: Keys for bar-device
     # 'maximum-speed = "full-speed";' is an optional string
     property, and,
     # the enum specifies known values that the string
     property may take
     Maximum-speed:
```

```
            type: string
            required: false
            description: Configures USB controllers to work up
            to a specific speed.
            enum:
                  - "low-speed"
                  - "full-speed"
                  - "high-speed"
                  - "super-speed"
      # The next entry describes an optional property, here,
      'resolution = <16>;'
      # the enum specifies known values that the int property
      may take
      resolution:
            type: int
            required: false
            enum:
                  - 8
                  - 16
                  - 24
                  - 32
      Array-with-default:
            type: array
            required: false
            default: [1, 2, 3] # Same as 'array-with-default =
                              <1 2 3>'

      String-with-default:
            type: string
            required: false
            default: "foo"

      String-array-with-default:
```

```
          type: string-array
          required: false
          default: ["foo", "bar"] # Same as
          # 'string-array-with-default = "foo", "bar"'
      uint8-array-with-default:
          type: uint8-array
          required: false
          default: [0x12, 0x34] # Same as 'uint8-array-with-
          default = [12 34]'
```

In the case of default values for properties, YAML data types are used for the default value, and it only makes sense to combine `default:` with `required: false`. Combining `default` with `required: true` will raise an error. A possible risk in using default is that the value in the binding may be incorrect for some particular board or hardware configuration. In such cases, a better approach might be to make the property `required: true`, which will require the devicetree maintainer to provide the required value explicitly.

Where a node has children that share the same properties, a `child-binding` can be used. In this case, each child will be assigned the contents of the child-binding as its binding. However, an explicit `compatible = ...` on the child node will take precedence, if a binding for it can be found. The following example shows a binding for a PWM LED node where the child nodes are required to have a `pwms` property:

```
pwmleds {
     compatible = "pwm-leds";
     red_pwm_led {
          pwms = <&pwm3 4 15625000>;
     };
     green_pwm_led {
          pwms = <&pwm3 0 15625000>;
     };
```

Chapter 9 Understanding and Working with the Devicetree in General and
           SPI and I2C in Particular

```
        /* ... */
};
```

A corresponding binding would, then, be something like the following:

```
compatible: "pwm-leds"
child-binding:
      description: LED that uses PWM
      properties:
            pwms:
                  type: phandle-array
                  required: true
```

Child-binding also works recursively, and, for example, the following binding

```
compatible: foo
child-binding:
      child-binding:
            Properties:
                  My-property:
                  type: int
                  required: true
```

will apply to the grandchild node in the code snippet shown here:

```
parent {
      compatible = "foo";
      child {
            grandchild {
            my-property = <123>;
            };
      };
};
```

468

CHAPTER 9 UNDERSTANDING AND WORKING WITH THE DEVICETREE IN GENERAL AND SPI AND I2C IN PARTICULAR

Binding and Bus Controller Nodes

Where a node is a bus controller, `bus:` is used in the binding to specify the type of the bus. For example, a binding for an SPI peripheral on an SoC would be written as

```
compatible: "manufacturer,spi-peripheral"
bus: spi
```

The presence of the `bus` key in the binding tells the build system that the children of any node matching this binding correspond to devices appearing on this type of bus. This influences the way `on-bus:` is used to match bindings for the child nodes. Where a node appears as a device on a bus, the `on-bus:` key is used in the binding of that node to specify the type of bus involved, for example, `on-bus: spi` in the case of an external SPI, or `on-bus: i2c` in the case of an I2C-based temperature sensor. When searching for a binding for a node attached to a bus, the build system checks to see if the binding for the parent node contains `bus: <bus type>`. If it does, then only bindings with a matching `on-bus: <bus type>` and bindings without an explicit `on-bus` key will be considered.

Bindings with an explicit `on-bus: <bus type>` are searched for before bindings without an explicit on-bus. Hence, it is possible for the same device to have different bindings depending on what bus it appears on; for example, a sensor device with a compatible `manufacturer,sensor` value could be used via either I2C or SPI. This is illustrated in the next devicetree fragment code snippet:

```
spi-bus@0 {
    /* ... some compatible with 'bus: spi', etc. ... */
    sensor@0 {
        compatible = "manufacturer,sensor";
        reg = <0>;
        /* ... */
```

CHAPTER 9   UNDERSTANDING AND WORKING WITH THE DEVICETREE IN GENERAL AND SPI AND I2C IN PARTICULAR

```
        };
    };
    i2c-bus@0 {
        /* ... some compatible with 'bus: i2c', etc. ... */
        sensor@79 {
            compatible = "manufacturer,sensor";
            reg = <79>;
            /* ... */
        };
    };
```

In a scenario such as this, it is possible for there to be two separate binding files that match these individual sensor nodes, even though they have the same compatible, for example:

```
# manufacturer,sensor-spi.yaml,
# which matches sensor@0 on the SPI bus:
compatible: "manufacturer,sensor"
on-bus: spi
# manufacturer,sensor-i2c.yaml,
# which matches sensor@79 on the I2C bus:
compatible: "manufacturer,sensor"
properties:
    uses-clock-stretching:
        type: boolean
        required: false
on-bus: i2c
```

Only `sensor@79` can have a `use-clock-stretching` property.

The bus-sensitive logic ignores the file `manufacturer,sensor-i2c.yaml` when searching for a binding for `sensor@0`.

CHAPTER 9 UNDERSTANDING AND WORKING WITH THE DEVICETREE IN GENERAL AND SPI AND I2C IN PARTICULAR

Phandles, Phandle-Array Type Properties, and Specifier Cell Names

In devicetree terminology, a phandle value provides a means to reference another node in the devicetree. Any node that can be referenced defines a phandle property with a unique <u32> value, and that number is used for the value of properties with a phandle value type. A phandle-array is a list of comma-separated p-values. For example a phandle-array describing pulse width modulation values for a device might be written as follows:

```
my-device {
        pwms = <&pwm0 1 2>, <&pwm3 4>;
};
```

When an entry such as this is being processed, the tooling strips away the final s from the property name of this property, resulting in pwm. Then the value of the #pwm-cells property is looked up in each of the PWM controller nodes pwm0 and pwm3, as shown here:

```
pwm0: pwm@0 {
        compatible = "foo,pwm";
        #pwm-cells = <2>;
};
pwm3: pwm@3 {
        compatible = "bar,pwm";
        #pwm-cells = <1>;
};
```

The &pwm0 1 2 part of the property value has two cells, 1 and 2, which matches #pwm-cells = <2>;, so these cells are considered as the specifier associated with pwm0 in the phandle array. Similarly, cell 4 is the specifier associated with pwm3.

CHAPTER 9   UNDERSTANDING AND WORKING WITH THE DEVICETREE IN GENERAL AND
            SPI AND I2C IN PARTICULAR

The number of PWM cells in the specifiers in pwms must match the corresponding #pwm-cells values, as is the case in the preceding example. An error will be raised if there is a mismatch. A node such as the following, for example, will result in an error:

```
my-bad-device {
        /* wrong: 2 cells given in the specifier,
        but #pwm-cells is 1 in pwm3. */
        pwms = <&pwm3 5 6>;
};
```

The binding for each PWM controller must also have a *-cells key, where * in an actual file will be replaced with some particular string. In the pwm example given, it will be pwm-cells. It is this which provides names to the cells in each specifier.

The following .yaml file snippets show the kinds of bindings that can be written:

```
# foo,pwm.yaml
compatible: "foo,pwm"
...
pwm-cells:
        - channel
        - period
# bar,pwm.yaml
compatible: "bar,pwm"
...
pwm-cells:
        - period
```

A *-names (e.g., pwm-names) property can appear on a node as well, thus providing a name to each entry. This makes it possible for the cells in the specifiers to be accessed by name, by using APIs such as DT_PWMS_

CHANNEL_BY_NAME, for example. Because other property names are derived from the name of the property by removing the final s, the property name must end in s, and an error will be raised if it does not. A special case to be aware of concerns *-gpios properties. Here, something like foo-gpios will resolve to gpio-cells rather than foo-gpio-cells.

In the case of phandle-array type properties, these support mapping through

*-map properties, e.g. gpio-map .

Including .yaml Binding Files

Commonly needed property definitions bindings can be shared by including other files by using the include: key whose value is either a string or a list. For example, include: foo.yaml will result in any file named foo.yaml that is found being included into the binding. Included files are merged into a binding file by means of a recursive dictionary merge. The build system will check that the resulting merged binding is well formed. With one exception, it is an error if a key appears with a different value in a binding and in a file that that binding includes. That exception is where a binding has a required: true for a property definition and the included file has a required: false. In this particular case, the required: true will take precedence. This illustrates how a binding can strengthen requirements from included files. A pattern based on strengthening is where a file base.yaml, for example, contains definitions for many common properties and a strengthening merge is used to make a property defined in base.yaml obligatory.

The converse, the weakening of requirements, is a pattern where the binding has required: false and where the included file has required: true. This is not allowed and will result in an error.

CHAPTER 9 UNDERSTANDING AND WORKING WITH THE DEVICETREE IN GENERAL AND SPI AND I2C IN PARTICULAR

Multiple files can be included by specifying a list of files using either the syntax

```
Include:
    - foo.yaml
    - bar.yaml
```

or the syntax [`foo.yaml, bar.yaml`] to include, for example, the files `foo.yaml` and `bar.yaml`.

When including multiple files, any overlapping required keys on properties in the included files are ORed together to ensure that a `required: true` will always be respected.

In a map element, it is possible to have either a `property-allowlist` or a key but not both. A map element with neither `property-allowlist` nor `property-blocklist` is valid and means that no additional filtering will be done.

It is also possible to intermix strings and mappings in a single `include:` list, as illustrated in the next code snippet:

```
Include:
    - foo.yaml
    - name: bar.yaml
      Property-blocklist:
            - do-not-include-this-one
            - or-this-one
```

It is also possible to filter from a child-binding as this next code snippet demonstrates:

```
include:
- name: bar.yaml
      Child-binding:
            Property-allowlist:
                - child-prop-to-allow
```

CHAPTER 9   UNDERSTANDING AND WORKING WITH THE DEVICETREE IN GENERAL AND SPI AND I2C IN PARTICULAR

Accessing the Devicetree in C and C++ Application Code

The Zephyr devicetree build process generates a C header in which all the required devicetree data is abstracted behind a macro API framework. Information about a particular devicetree node is obtained by using a corresponding C macro, which is referred to as a node identifier for that device. The devicetree build process that goes from a devicetree to `struct device` definitions is sometimes referred to as the "Cheshire Cat model of setting up devices" [5]. This is a metaphor based on Lewis Carroll's *Alice in Wonderland* in which a character, the Cheshire Cat, fades away and all that remains is its smile. Loosely speaking, the Zephyr approach to setting up devices involves "messing around with the devicetree," then "fighting with the build system" so that when the build system is run, the devicetree "disappears" and all that is left are the "devices."

A Zephyr application uses APIs to ask drivers to do real work on real hardware. The APIs are to be found in C headers, and the drivers are to be found in C files. This is shown schematically in Figure 9-10.

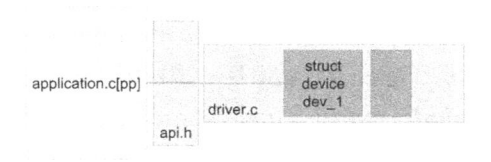

Figure 9-10.   APIs found in C headers and drivers found in .c files

The key device driver abstraction in Zephyr is that, from the device perspective, everything is a `struct device`, and particular kinds of `struct device` correspond to particular kinds of driver.

An application will have a `.conf` Kconfig file specifying which drivers are needed. For a supported board, there will be a base devicetree in the Zephyr source code. This base devicetree can be modified for application-specific purposes by providing a devicetree overlay file. The final devicetree is consumed by the device driver source code files, which will use it to allocate the corresponding struct device structures. Access to the devices in the application code will be via pointers to actual device structure instances.

Working with Devices in Applications

To work with a device in an application, it is necessary to "get hold of" a node identifier from the application devicetree. There are various ways in which this can be done, which involve the use of devicetree (DT) macros. If the full path to the node in the devicetree is known, then the macro DT_PATH() can be used by supplying the full path to the node in the devicetree. The macro DT_NODELABEL() can be used to get a node identifier from a node label. Node labels are often provided by the SoC .dtsi, which gives node names that match the SoC data sheet, such as i2c1, spi2, and so on.

The DT_ALIAS() macro can be used to get a node identifier for a property of the special /aliases node. The DT_INST() macro can be used when an instance number is available. Still other approaches include using the macro DT_CHOSEN() to get a node identifier for /chosen node properties, or using DT_PARENT() and DT_CHILD() to get a node identifier for a parent or child node, starting from some given node identifier.

From the coding perspective, two node identifiers that refer to the same node are identical and can be used interchangeably. This rich "ecosystem" of macros is an example of TIMTOWODI (There Is More Than One Way Of Doing It), pronounced as "tim tau dee," in action.

The use of the macros is not nearly as daunting as it might first appear to be. Hopefully the next few examples will show that the use of the various DT_ macros is reasonably straightforward.

The examples explored in this section are based on those in the Zephyr documentation.

CHAPTER 9　UNDERSTANDING AND WORKING WITH THE DEVICETREE IN GENERAL AND SPI AND I2C IN PARTICULAR

They will be based on the following dts example code snippet:

```
/dts-v1/;
/ {
    aliases {
        sensor-controller = &i2c1;
    };
    soc {
        i2c1: i2c@40002000 {
            compatible = "vnd,soc-i2c";
            label = "I2C_1";
            reg = <0x40002000 0x1000>;
            status = "okay";
            clock-frequency = < 100000 >;
        };
    };
};
```

Possible ways for getting node identifiers for the i2c@40002000 node are

```
DT_PATH(soc, i2c_40002000)
DT_NODELABEL(i2c1)
DT_ALIAS(sensor_controller)
DT_INST(x, vnd_soc_i2c) for some unknown number x.
```

When working with the DT_ macros, non-alphanumeric characters such as dash (-) and the at sign (@) in devicetree names are converted to underscores (_), and the names in a DTS are converted to lowercase.

To avoid errors, it is important to remember that node identifiers are not values and a node identifier cannot be stored in a variable.

477

CHAPTER 9   UNDERSTANDING AND WORKING WITH THE DEVICETREE IN GENERAL AND
            SPI AND I2C IN PARTICULAR

Statements such as the following will result in compiler errors:

```
void *i2c_0 = DT_INST(0, vnd_soc_i2c);
unsigned int i2c_1 = DT_INST(1, vnd_soc_i2c);
long my_i2c = DT_NODELABEL(i2c1);
```

Given the variables

```
void *i2c_0;
unsigned int i2c_1;
long my_i2;
```

the Zephyr way to initialize these variables is to use C macros, for example:

```
#define MY_I2C DT_NODELABEL(i2c1)
#define INST(i) DT_INST(i, vnd_soc_i2c)
#define I2C_0 INST(0)
#define I2C_1 INST(1)
```

The DT_NODE_HAS_PROP() macro can be used to check whether a node has a particular property or not. For example, in the case of the example devicetree shown earlier:

```
DT_NODE_HAS_PROP(DT_NODELABEL(i2c1), clock_frequency)
/*expands to 1 */
DT_NODE_HAS_PROP(DT_NODELABEL(i2c1), not_a_property) /*
expands to 0 */
```

The DT_PROP(node_id, property) macro can be used to read basic integer, boolean, string, numeric array, and string array properties. For example, the clock-frequency property value in the preceding example can be read in several different ways:

```
DT_PROP(DT_PATH(soc, i2c_40002000), clock_frequency)
DT_PROP(DT_NODELABEL(i2c1), clock_frequency)
DT_PROP(DT_ALIAS(sensor_controller), clock_frequency)
```

CHAPTER 9 UNDERSTANDING AND WORKING WITH THE DEVICETREE IN GENERAL AND SPI AND I2C IN PARTICULAR

Recall that the DTS property clock-frequency is spelled clock_frequency in C, because of the rule that replaces special characters with underscores and converts names to all lowercase.

The DT_PROP() macro expands to a string literal in the case of strings and the number 0 or 1 in the case of booleans, for example:

```
#define I2C1 DT_NODELABEL(i2c1)
DT_PROP(I2C1, status) /* expands to the string literal "okay" */
```

In the case of properties with type array, uint8-array, and string-array, DT_PROP() expands to an array initializer.

In the case of the following example devicetree fragment:

```
foo: foo@1234 {
        a = <1000 2000 3000>; /* array */
        b = [aa bb cc dd]; /* uint8-array */
        c = "bar", "baz"; /* string-array */
};
```

its properties can be accessed as shown here:

```
#define FOO DT_NODELABEL(foo)
int a[] = DT_PROP(FOO, a); /* {1000, 2000, 3000} */
unsigned char b[] = DT_PROP(FOO, b);/* {0xaa, 0xbb, 0xcc, 0xdd} */
char* c[] = DT_PROP(FOO, c); /*{"foo", "bar"} */
```

Zephyr provides the DT_PROP_LEN() macro to obtain logical array lengths, for example:

```
size_t a_len = DT_PROP_LEN(FOO, a); /* 3 */
size_t b_len = DT_PROP_LEN(FOO, b); /* 4 */
size_t c_len = DT_PROP_LEN(FOO, c); /* 2 */
```

DT_PROP_LEN() cannot, however, be used with the special reg or interrupts properties.

CHAPTER 9   UNDERSTANDING AND WORKING WITH THE DEVICETREE IN GENERAL AND SPI AND I2C IN PARTICULAR

Working with reg and interrupts Properties

There are special (specific) macros for working with reg and interrupts properties.

For a node that only has one register block, DT_REG_ADDR(node_id) can be used to obtain the register block address for that node, and DT_REG_SIZE(node_id) can be used to obtain its size.

Where a node has multiple register blocks, the macro DT_REG_ADDR_BY_IDX(node_id, idx) or DT_REG_SIZE_BY_IDX(node_id, idx) should be used instead. DT_REG_ADDR_BY_IDX(node_id, idx) gives the address of register block at index idx, and DT_REG_SIZE_BY_IDX(node_id, idx) gives the size of the block at index idx. The idx argument must be an integer literal or a macro that expands to an integer literal without requiring any arithmetic. In particular, idx cannot be a variable. The following code snippet will result in a compiler error:

```
for (size_t i = 0; i < DT_NUM_REGS(node_id); i++) {
    size_t addr = DT_REG_ADDR_BY_IDX(node_id, i);
}
```

There are also macros for working with interrupts properties.

Given a node identifier node_id, DT_NUM_IRQS(node_id) can be used to get the total number of interrupt specifiers in the interrupts property for that node. Interrupt specifiers can be accessed with the macro DT_IRQ_BY_IDX(node_id, idx, val) where idx is the logical index into the interrupts array and the val argument is the name of a cell within the interrupt specifier.

The DT_PHANDLE(), DT_PHANDLE_BY_IDX(), and DT_PHANDLE_BY_NAME() macros provide a means for converting a phandle to a node identifier.

CHAPTER 9 UNDERSTANDING AND WORKING WITH THE DEVICETREE IN GENERAL AND SPI AND I2C IN PARTICULAR

Working with Devices

The skills to master include knowing how to allocate and configure a device and how to create a device instance and use it in an application. For illustrative purposes, a scenario involving a Bosch BME280 environmental sensor and a nRF52840-based board will be considered. The BME280 is quite a versatile sensor and is a popular component in "weather station" projects. It is a humidity sensor that not only measures relative humidity but also barometric pressure and ambient temperature. It was developed for use in mobile applications and wearables where size and low power consumption are key design parameters. The humidity sensor has a low power consumption and has a high accuracy over a fairly wide temperature range.

An overlay file for working with the BME sensor could be written along the following lines:

```
&spi3 {
    compatible = "nordic,nrf-spim";
    status = "okay";
    cs-gpios = <&gpio1 12 GPIO_ACTIVE_LOW>;
    mysensor: bme280@0 {
        compatible = "bosch, bme280";
        label = "BME280";
        reg = <0>;
        spi-max-frequency = <1000000>;
    };
};
```

Nodes in the devicetree are segmented by the kinds of hardware they describe. In this example, the spi3 node describes nordic, nrf-spim hardware. Nodes for different hardware elements will have different compatible properties. For example, in the case of `mysensor: bme280`, it is necessary to describe how the sensor device attached to the SPI bus is configured.

CHAPTER 9   UNDERSTANDING AND WORKING WITH THE DEVICETREE IN GENERAL AND SPI AND I2C IN PARTICULAR

The Zephyr documentation provides information about bindings. The top-level web page for API documentation can be found at https://docs.zephyrproject.org/latest/develop/api/overview.html. It has a table that lists the various Zephyr APIs and has links to information about them. The I2C link takes you to the I2C documentation API, which contains details of the Zephyr I2C API.

Information about bindings can be found in the devicetree bindings web page at https://docs.zephyrproject.org/latest/build/dts/api/bindings.html. This page has a section that contains an index of hardware vendors. Clicking on a vendor's name will bring up a list of bindings for that vendor. Clicking on the Bosch Sensortec GmbH (bosch) goes to the subsection with links to various bosch sensors, including bosch,bme280 (on SPI bus) and bosch,bme280 (on I2C bus). Clicking on a link leads to a page containing a table of base properties and a table of properties that are not inherited from the base binding file.

For the bosch,bme280 on an SPI bus, the base properties table is as follows:

Name	Type	Details
status	string	Indicates the operational status of a device Legal values: 'ok', 'okay', 'disabled', 'reserved', 'fail', 'fail-sss'
compatible	string-array	Compatible strings This property is required.
reg	array	Register space This property is required.
reg-names	string-array	Name of each register space
interrupts	array	Interrupts for device
interrupts-extended	compound	extended interrupt specifier for device

(continued)

CHAPTER 9   UNDERSTANDING AND WORKING WITH THE DEVICETREE IN GENERAL AND SPI AND I2C IN PARTICULAR

Name	Type	Details
interrupt-names	string-array	Name of each interrupt
interrupt-parent	phandle	Phandle to interrupt controller node
label	string	Human-readable string describing the device (used as device_get_binding() argument) This property is deprecated.
clock-names	string-array	Name of each clock
#address-cells	int	Number of size cells in reg property
#size-cells	int	Number of size cells in reg property
dmas	phandle-array	DMA channel specifiers
dma-names	string-array	Provided names of DMA channel specifiers
io-channels	phandle-array	IO channels specifiers
io-channel-names	string-array	Mailbox/IPM channels specifiers
mboxes	phandle-array	Mailbox/IPM channels specifiers
mbox-names	string-array	Provided names of mailbox/IPM channel specifiers

(*continued*)

483

CHAPTER 9   UNDERSTANDING AND WORKING WITH THE DEVICETREE IN GENERAL AND SPI AND I2C IN PARTICULAR

Name	Type	Details
wakeup-source	boolean	Property to identify that a device can be used as wakeup source. When this property is provided, a specific flag is set into the device that tells the system that the device is capable of waking up the system. Wakeup capable devices are disabled (interrupts will not wake up the system) by default, but they can be enabled at runtime if necessary.
power-domain	phandle	Power domain the device belongs to. The device will be notified when the power domain it belongs to is either suspended or resumed.

and for the bosch bme280 on an SPI bus, the node-specific properties table is as follows:

Name	Type	Details
friendly-name	string	Human-readable string describing the sensor. It can be used to distinguish multiple instances of the same model (e.g., lid accelerometer vs. base accelerometer in a laptop) to a host operating system.
spi-max-frequency	int	Maximum clock frequency of a device's SPI interface in Hz This property is required.
duplex	int	Duplex mode, full or half. By default, it's always full duplex, thus 0, as this is, by far, the most common mode. Use the macros, not the actual enum value; here is the concordance list (see dt-bindings/spi/spi.h): 0 SPI_FULL_DUPLEX 2048 SPI_HALF_DUPLEX Legal values: 0, 2048

(*continued*)

CHAPTER 9　UNDERSTANDING AND WORKING WITH THE DEVICETREE IN GENERAL AND SPI AND I2C IN PARTICULAR

Name	Type	Details
frame-format	int	Motorola or TI frame format. By default, it's always Motorola's, thus 0, as this is, by far, the most common format. Use the macros, not the actual enum value; here is the concordance list (see dt-bindings/spi/spi.h): 0　SPI_FRAME_FORMAT_MOTOROLA 32768　SPI_FRAME_FORMAT_TI Legal values: 0, 32768
supply-gpios	phandle-array	GPIO specifier that controls power to the device. This property should be provided when the device has a dedicated switch that controls power to the device. The supply state is entirely the responsibility of the device driver. Contrast with vin-supply.
vin-supply	phandle	Reference to the regulator that controls power to the device. The referenced devicetree node must have a regulator compatible. This property should be provided when device power is supplied by a shared regulator. The supply state is dependent on the request status of all devices fed by the regulator. Contrast with supply-gpios. If both properties are provided, then the regulator must be requested before the supply GPIOS is set to an active state, and the supply GPIOS must be set to an inactive state before releasing the regulator.

485

CHAPTER 9   UNDERSTANDING AND WORKING WITH THE DEVICETREE IN GENERAL AND SPI AND I2C IN PARTICULAR

Nordic nRF processors support a Nordic-specific form of DMA (Direct Memory Access) called EasyDMA. An SPI master with EasyDMA is a `nordic,nrf-spim` device. This device is an SPI bus node. The base properties in the previous table are those of base for SPI devices. The table that follows summarizes the node-specific properties for Nordic nRF family SPIM (SPI master with EasyDMA) nodes.

Name	Type	Details
miso-pull-up	boolean	Enable pull-up on MISO line
miso-pull-down	boolean	Enable pull-down on MISO line
anomaly-58-workaround	boolean	Enables the workaround for the nRF52832 SoC SPIM PAN 58 anomaly. Must be used in conjunction with CONFIG_SOC_NRF52832_ALLOW_SPIM_DESPITE_PAN_58=y
rx-delay-supported	boolean	Indicates if the SPIM instance has the capability of delaying MISO sampling. This property needs to be defined at SoC level DTS files.
rx-delay	int	Number of 64 MHz clock cycles (15.625 ns) delay from the sampling edge of SCK (leading or trailing, depending on the CPHA setting used) until the input serial data on MISO is actually sampled. This property does not have any effect if the rx-delay-supported property is not set. Legal values: 0, 1, 2, 3, 4, 5, 6, 7
max-frequency	int	Maximum data rate the SPI peripheral can be driven at, in Hz. This property must be set at SoC level DTS files. This property is required.

(*continued*)

CHAPTER 9   UNDERSTANDING AND WORKING WITH THE DEVICETREE IN GENERAL AND SPI AND I2C IN PARTICULAR

Name	Type	Details
overrun-character	int	The overrun character (ORC) is used when all bytes from the TX buffer are sent, but the transfer continues due to RX. Defaults to 0xff (line high), the most common value used in SPI transfers. Default value: 255
clock-frequency	int	Clock frequency the SPI peripheral is being driven at, in Hz.

CHAPTER 9   UNDERSTANDING AND WORKING WITH THE DEVICETREE IN GENERAL AND SPI AND I2C IN PARTICULAR

Name	Type	Details
cs-gpios	phandle-array	An array of chip select GPIOs to use. Each element in the array specifies a GPIO. The index in the array corresponds to the child node that the CS gpio controls. Example: ```\nspi@... {\n cs-gpios = <&gpio0 23 GPIO_ACTIVE_LOW>,\n <&gpio1 10 GPIO_ACTIVE_LOW>,\n ...;\n spi-device@0 {\n reg = <0>;\n ...\n };\n spi-device@1 {\n reg = <1>;\n ...\n };\n ...\n};\n``` The child node "spi-device@0" specifies an SPI device with chip select controller gpio0, pin 23, and devicetree GPIO flags GPIO_ACTIVE_LOW. Similarly, "spi-device@1" has CS GPIO controller gpio1, pin 10, and flags GPIO_ACTIVE_LOW. Additional devices can be configured in the same way. If unsure about the flags cell, GPIO_ACTIVE_LOW is generally a safe choice for a typical "CSn" pin. GPIO_ACTIVE_HIGH may be used if intervening hardware inverts the signal to the peripheral device or the line itself is active high. If this property is not defined, no chip select GPIOs are set. SPI controllers with dedicated CS pins do not need to define the cs-gpios property.

(*continued*)

488

CHAPTER 9 UNDERSTANDING AND WORKING WITH THE DEVICETREE IN GENERAL AND SPI AND I2C IN PARTICULAR

Name	Type	Details
pinctrl-0	phandles	Pin configuration/s for the first state. Content is specific to the selected pin controller driver implementation.
pinctrl-1	phandles	Pin configuration/s for the second state. Content is specific to the selected pin controller driver implementation.
pinctrl-2	phandles	Pin configuration/s for the third state. Content is specific to the selected pin controller driver implementation.
pinctrl-3	phandles	Pin configuration/s for the fourth state. Content is specific to the selected pin controller driver implementation.
pinctrl-4	phandles	Pin configuration/s for the fifth state. Content is specific to the selected pin controller driver implementation.
pinctrl-names	string-array	Names for the provided states. The number of names needs to match the number of states.
memory-regions	phandle-array	List of memory region phandles
memory-region-names	string-array	A list of names, one for each corresponding phandle in memory-region

For the cs-gpios property, the GPIO port and pin number and flags for the chip select must be given, for example, in the following code snippet:

```
&spi3 {
     compatible = "nordic,nrf-spim";
     status = "okay";
     cs-gpios = <&gpio1 12 GPIO_ACTIVE_LOW>;
     mysensor: bme280@0 {
          compatible = "bosch,bme280";
          label = "BME280";
          reg = <0>;
```

CHAPTER 9   UNDERSTANDING AND WORKING WITH THE DEVICETREE IN GENERAL AND SPI AND I2C IN PARTICULAR

```
            spi-max-frequency = <1000000>;
    };
};
```

In the line `cs-gpios = <&gpio1 12 GPIO_ACTIVE_LOW>;`:

- `&gpio1` refers to the GPIO port
- 12 is the pin number
- `GPIO_ACTIVE_LOW` is a flag

From the preceding snippet, it can be deduced that active low drives the chip select. Zephyr has a driver compatible for bme280 sensor, but the sensor is not built into the board. The node is a child of the bus controller. With an SPI device, it is necessary to specify the chip select for the particular sensor, and this is taken care of by the `reg` property. Here, `reg = <0>` means use index 0 of the cs-gpios property.

`mysensor` (on line 5) is a node label … and is not to be confused with the label property (line 6). Either of these can be used to get the device pointer when implementing application code.

The following code snippet shows how to write the code to get a pointer to the device structure and then make use of the device. It shows the use of the macro `DEVICE_DT_GET` and of the `DT_NODELABEL` macro.

```
const struct device *dev = DEVICE_DT_GET(DT_NODELABEL(mysensor));
if (!device_is_ready(dev)) { return; }
struct sensor_value temp;
sensor_sample_fetch(dev);
sensor_channel_get (dev, SENSOR_CHAN_AMBIENT_TEMP, &temp);
printk("temperature in degrees C: %d.%06d\n", temp.val1, temp.val2);
```

CHAPTER 9   UNDERSTANDING AND WORKING WITH THE DEVICETREE IN GENERAL AND SPI AND
           I2C IN PARTICULAR

If using the I2C interface on an nRF5 device and using EasyDMA, the node will be an "i2c" bus node of the Nordic nRF family TWIM (TWI master with EasyDMA), namely, nordic,nrf-twim. The node specific properties for this type of node can be found in Zephyr documentation [8] and the nRF Connect SDK documentation [9].

The overlay for the BME280 sensor attached to an I2C bus controller is shown as follows:

```
&i2c0 {
     compatible = "nordic, nrf-twim";
     status = "okay";
     sda_pin = <26>;
     scl-pin = <27>;
     mysensor: bme280@77 {
          compatible = "bosch, bme280";
          reg = <0x77>;
          label = "BME280";
     };
};
```

When setting up the sensor device attached to the I2C bus, the sensor is a child of the I2C bus controller – where the bus node is i2c0. The BME280 node has the same compatible as for the SPI example covered previously, but because of the bus tree hierarchy, the driver will know that the communication is for I2C and that I2C should be used. Here, reg = <0x77>, which is the address to be used by the i2c0 bus master to communicate with the sensor.

Using the preceding overlay, the code for using the I2C sensor that corresponds to that shown previously for the SPI sensor will be the same:

```
const struct device *dev = DEVICE_DT_GET(DT_
NODELABEL(mysensor));
if (!device_is_ready(dev)) { return; }
```

```
struct sensor_value temp;
sensor_sample_fetch(dev);
sensor_channel_get (dev, SENSOR_CHAN_AMBIENT_TEMP, &temp);
printk("temperature in degrees C: %d.%06d\n", temp.val1,
temp.val2);
```

Overview of How the DEVICE_DT_GET Macro Works

The expansion of the invocation of the DEVICE_DT_GET macro is shown as follows:

```
const struct device *dev = DEVICE_DT_GET(DT_NODELABEL(mysensor));
```

expands to

```
const struct device *dev = (&__device_dt_ord_63);
```

To understand this expansion, it is necessary to understand the concept of instance numbers as they relate to the compatible.

In the file zephyr/drivers/sensor/bme280/bme280.h, the following macro is defined:

```
#define DT_DRV_COMPAT bosch_bme280
```

The value is a token as opposed to a string. The underlying idea is that for every driver, there will be a corresponding compatible.

CHAPTER 9 UNDERSTANDING AND WORKING WITH THE DEVICETREE IN GENERAL AND SPI AND
            I2C IN PARTICULAR

In the file zephyr/drivers/sensor/bme280/bme280.c, the following snippet can be found:

```
#define BME280_DEFINE(inst)                                         \
    static struct bme280_data bme280_data_##inst;                   \
    static const struct bme280_config bme280_config_##inst =        \
        COND_CODE_1(DT_INST_ON_BUS(inst, spi),                      \
            (BME280_CONFIG_SPI(inst)),                              \
            (BME280_CONFIG_I2C(inst)));                             \
                                                                    \
    PM_DEVICE_DT_INST_DEFINE(inst, bme280_pm_action);               \
                                                                    \
    DEVICE_DT_INST_DEFINE(inst,                                     \
            bme280_chip_init,                                       \
            PM_DEVICE_DT_INST_REF(inst),                            \
            &bme280_data_##inst,                                    \
            &bme280_config_##inst,                                  \
            POST_KERNEL,                                            \
            CONFIG_SENSOR_INIT_PRIORITY,                            \
            &bme280_api_funcs);

/* Create the struct device for every status "okay" node in the devicetree. */
DT_INST_FOREACH_STATUS_OKAY(BME280_DEFINE)
```

In the preceding snippet from the bme280.c driver, BME280_DEFINE(inst) takes an instance number. The BME280_DEFINE macro is passed into the macro DT_INST_FOREACH_STATUS_OKAY(BME280_DEFINE), and this macro is expanded. Then the macros inside it are further expanded. The effect of running this macro is to allocate a device for every BME280 node in the devicetree, which is enabled with status okay set.

493

CHAPTER 9   UNDERSTANDING AND WORKING WITH THE DEVICETREE IN GENERAL AND
           SPI AND I2C IN PARTICULAR

Expanding the macro

```
DEVICE_DT_INST_DEFINE(inst,                         \
                bme280_chip_init,                   \
                PM_DEVICE_DT_INST_REF(inst),        \
                &bme280_data_##inst,                \
                &bme280_config_##inst,              \
                POST_KERNEL,                        \
                CONFIG_SENSOR_INIT_PRIORITY,        \
                &bme280_api_funcs);
```

involves the use of the ## concatenation operator, whose purpose, here, is to generate global variables with unique names, where the uniqueness comes, in effect, from information in the devicetree.

In the driver, macro expansion results in something like the following:

```
const struct device __device_dts_ord_63 = {
    ...
}
```

in the driver, so that the global variable token contains the ordinal number 63.

The ordinal number is the result of enumerating the nodes in the devicetree. Each node will have a distinct ordinal number associated with it, and this ensures that devices will be associated with uniquely named global variables.

In the case of a multi-instance driver application, there will be multiple different struct devices from different devicetree nodes, all with the same compatible. This is illustrated in the following example involving two compatibles, one for a device attached to an I2C bus and the other for a device attached to an SPI bus.

CHAPTER 9 UNDERSTANDING AND WORKING WITH THE DEVICETREE IN GENERAL AND SPI AND I2C IN PARTICULAR

```
&spi3 {
       /* ... */
       onspi: bme280@0 {
             compatible = = "bosch,bme280";
             label = "BME280";
             reg = <0>;
             spi-max-frequency = <1000000>
       };
};
```

Driver macro expansion will result in device global variables with unique names being created in the C file that is to be compiled, as shown in the following:

```
const struct device __device_dts_ord_65 = {
       ...
}
const struct device __device_dts_ord_70 = {
       ...
}
```

It should be noted that instance numbers are not the same thing as ordinal numbers. In this, next, example, the instance numbers are 0 and 1. In the application, there will be two devices produced as a result of macro expansion. The macro expansion of

```
const struct device
       *spidev = DEVICE_DT_GET(DT_NODELABEL(onspi)),
       *i2cdev = DEVICE_DT_GET(DT_NODELABEL(oni2c));
```

results in the following:

```
const struct device
       *spidev = (&__device_dts_ord_70),
       *i2cdev = (&__device_dts_ord_65);
```

CHAPTER 9   UNDERSTANDING AND WORKING WITH THE DEVICETREE IN GENERAL AND SPI AND I2C IN PARTICULAR

The devicetree processing generates a header file that pre-declares all the potential devices in that header file so that they do not have to be declared by the application developer before taking their addresses.

Codewise the results will have the same footprint as one involving an access to a global data structure. However, the macro-based approach combines a hierarchical configuration language without incurring the footprint and performance penalty of having to explicitly carry out tree-walking.

In summary, the devicetree-based design achieves the following outcome:

- The devicetree captures dependencies, and this dependency information is available at build time.

- The ordinals capture the dependency structure of the devicetree, and this dependency information is available at preprocessor time.

- There are also devicetree APIs for querying the forward and reverse dependencies of a node, and having dependency information available in device structures makes it possible to control the sequence of the device initialization steps at link time so that when the application is run, the devices are initialized in the correct order.

- Knowing device dependencies is also important in connection with device power management as it helps ensure that things are shut down in the correct order, for example, when entering sleep mode.

CHAPTER 9　UNDERSTANDING AND WORKING WITH THE DEVICETREE IN GENERAL AND SPI AND I2C IN PARTICULAR

I2C Case Study Example

This example is based on the X-NUCLEO-IKS01A2 board, which is a motion MEMS and environmental sensor expansion board for the STM32 Nucleo with an Arduino UNO R3 connector layout. It contains a selection of sensors, namely, an LSM6DSL 3D accelerometer and 3D gyroscope, an LSM303AGR 3D accelerometer and 3D magnetometer, an HTS221 humidity and temperature sensor, and an LPS22HB pressure sensor. The X-NUCLEO-IKS01A2 interfaces with the STM32 microcontroller via I^{2}C.

An image of this board is shown in Figure 9-11.

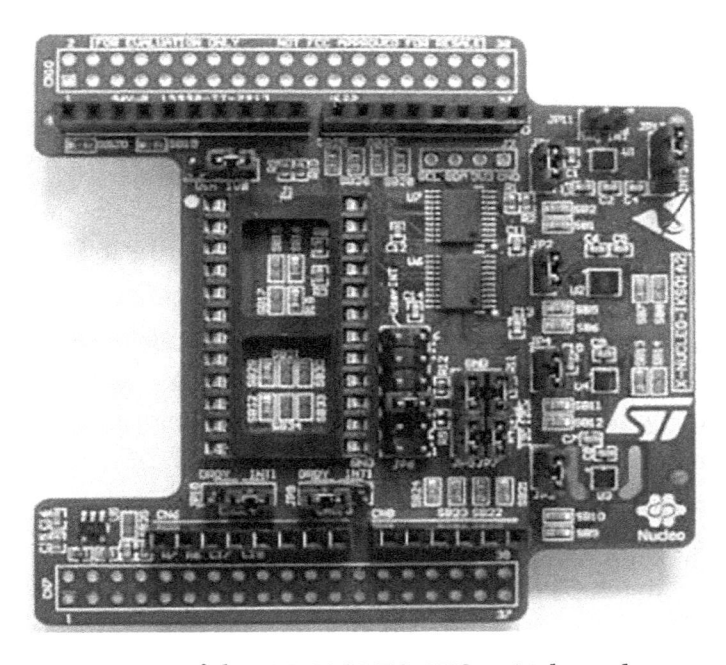

Figure 9-11. Image of the X-NUCLEO-IKS01A2 board

The LSM6DSL has an I^{2}C sensor hub through which it can be an I^{2}C master of other devices (slaves) connected to an I^{2}Caux bus. The Zephyr example for this shield requires the board be configured for Mode 2 (Sensor hub I2C mode). In sensor hub I^{2}C mode, the LSM6DSL is connected to an external main board by an I²C bus; all other devices are slaves connected to LSM6DSL via I²Caux. This requires configuring the board by setting some jumpers on it as in Figure 9-12, JP7: 2-3 (I²C1 = I²Cx) and JP8: 2-3 (I²C1 = I²Cx).

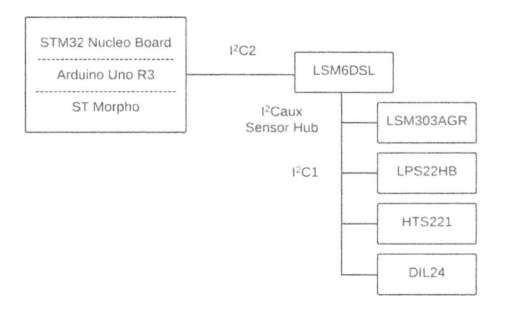

Figure 9-12. Schematic showing the I2C connections of the LSM6DSL device

The schematic in Figure 9-12 illustrates the logical configuration used in this scenario. The example that will be explored here is to be found in the Zephyr sources [6].

This sample enables LSM6DSL sensors, and since all the other on shield devices are connected to LSM6DSL, the LSM6DSL driver is configured in sensorhub mode (`CONFIG_LSM6DSL_SENSORHUB=y`) with a selection of one slave only from `LPS22HB` and `LSM303AGR` (default is `LSM303AGR`). The application code displays the following sensor data periodically: LSM6DSL 6-Axis acceleration and angular velocity and LSM6DSL 3-Axis magnetic field intensity (from the LSM303AGR's magnetometer) as the primary option. There is secondary option that displays LSM6DSL ambient temperature and atmospheric pressure (from LPS22HB).

The example can be built and flashed by running the following commands:

```
west build -p -b nucleo_f767zi \
./zephyr/samples/shields/x_nucleo_iks01a2/sensorhub/

west flash --runner jlink
```

CHAPTER 9 UNDERSTANDING AND WORKING WITH THE DEVICETREE IN GENERAL AND SPI AND I2C IN PARTICULAR

The output sent by the application over the serial link will look something like the following:

```
X-NUCLEO-IKS01A2 sensor dashboard

LSM6DSL: Accel (m.s-2): x: 0.0, y: -0.5, z: 9.9
LSM6DSL: Gyro (dps): x: -0.014, y: -0.029, z: -0.516
LSM6DSL: Magn (gauss): x: 0.093, y: 0.059, z: -0.386
38:: lsm6dsl acc trig 7633
```

The prj.conf file contains the following configuration settings:

```
CONFIG_LOG=y
CONFIG_STDOUT_CONSOLE=y
CONFIG_I2C=y
CONFIG_SENSOR=y
CONFIG_SENSOR_LOG_LEVEL_DBG=y
CONFIG_LSM6DSL=y
CONFIG_LSM6DSL_TRIGGER_OWN_THREAD=y
# The LSM6DSL shub driver only permits one sensor
# connected at a time
CONFIG_LSM6DSL_SENSORHUB=y
CONFIG_LSM6DSL_EXT0_LPS22HB=n
CONFIG_LSM6DSL_EXT0_LIS2MDL=y
CONFIG_CBPRINTF_FP_SUPPORT=y
```

The CMakeLists.txt file script used for this project is shown next:

```
cmake_minimum_required(VERSION 3.20.0)

# This sample is specific to x_nucleo_iks01a2 shield. Enforce -DSHIELD option
set(SHIELD x_nucleo_iks01a2_shub)
find_package(Zephyr REQUIRED HINTS $ENV{ZEPHYR_BASE})
```

CHAPTER 9   UNDERSTANDING AND WORKING WITH THE DEVICETREE IN GENERAL AND SPI AND I2C IN PARTICULAR

```
project(x_nucleo_iks01a2_sensorhub)
FILE(GLOB app_sources src/*.c)
target_sources(app PRIVATE ${app_sources})
```

and the overlay file for the project, which is to be found at zephyr\boards\shields\x_nucleo_iks01a2\x_nucleo_iks01a2.overlay its contents are shown as follows:

```
&arduino_i2c {
    hts221@5f {
        compatible = "st,hts221";
        reg = <0x5f>;
        label = "HTS221";
    };
    lps22hb-press@5d {
        compatible = "st,lps22hb-press";
        reg = <0x5d>;
        label = "LPS22HB";
    };
    lsm6dsl@6b {
        compatible = "st,lsm6dsl";
        reg = <0x6b>;
        label = "LSM6DSL";
        irq-gpios = <&arduino_header 10 GPIO_ACTIVE_
        HIGH>; /*D4*/
    };
    lsm303agr-magn@1e {
        compatible = "st,lis2mdl","st,lsm303agr-magn";
        reg = <0x1e>;
        label = "LSM303AGR-MAGN";
        irq-gpios = <&arduino_header 3 GPIO_ACTIVE_
        HIGH>;         /*A3*/
    };
```

CHAPTER 9   UNDERSTANDING AND WORKING WITH THE DEVICETREE IN GENERAL AND SPI AND I2C IN PARTICULAR

```
        lsm303agr-accel@19 {
            compatible = "st,lis2dh", "st,lsm303agr-accel";
            reg = <0x19>;
            label = "LSM303AGR-ACCEL";
            irq-gpios = <&arduino_header 3 GPIO_ACTIVE_
            HIGH>;         /*A3*/
        };
    };
};
```

The zephyr\drivers\sensor\lsm6dsl directory contains the driver code for the lsm6dsl. It contains .h files and .c files for sensor functionality, SPI functionality, I2C functionality, and I2C hub functionality. Studying this code is best done with the corresponding data sheet (which weighs in at 114 pages of technical detail) to hand [7] and is not covered here. The application code file main.c is shown in the following. It follows the classical embedded system application programming pattern of first initializing the system and then entering an infinite data acquisition and display loop.

```
#include <zephyr.h>
#include <device.h>
#include <drivers/sensor.h>
#include <stdio.h>
#include <sys/util.h>
#ifdef CONFIG_LSM6DSL_TRIGGER
static int lsm6dsl_trig_cnt;
static void lsm6dsl_trigger_handler(const struct device *dev,
struct sensor_trigger *trig) {
    sensor_sample_fetch_chan(dev, SENSOR_CHAN_ALL);
    lsm6dsl_trig_cnt++;
}
#endif
```

```c
#define LSM6DSL_DEVNAME      DT_LABEL(DT_INST(0, st_lsm6dsl))
void main(void) {
#ifdef CONFIG_LSM6DSL_TRIGGER
    int cnt = 1;
#endif
#ifdef CONFIG_LSM6DSL_EXT0_LPS22HB
    struct sensor_value temp, press;
#endif
#ifdef CONFIG_LSM6DSL_EXT0_LIS2MDL
    struct sensor_value magn[3];
#endif
    struct sensor_value accel[3];
    struct sensor_value gyro[3];
    const struct device *lsm6dsl =
                device_get_binding(LSM6DSL_DEVNAME);
    if (lsm6dsl == NULL) {
        printf("Could not get LSM6DSL device\n");
        return;
    }
    /* set LSM6DSL accel/gyro sampling frequency to 104 Hz */
    struct sensor_value odr_attr;
    odr_attr.val1 = 104;
    odr_attr.val2 = 0;
    if (sensor_attr_set(lsm6dsl, SENSOR_CHAN_ACCEL_XYZ,
     SENSOR_ATTR_SAMPLING_FREQUENCY, &odr_attr) < 0) {
     printk("Cannot set sampling frequency for
     accelerometer\n");
     return;
    }
    if (sensor_attr_set(lsm6dsl, SENSOR_CHAN_GYRO_XYZ,
                SENSOR_ATTR_SAMPLING_FREQUENCY, &odr_
                attr) < 0) {
```

```
            printk("Cannot set sampling frequency for gyro.\n");
            return;
        }
#ifdef CONFIG_LSM6DSL_TRIGGER
        struct sensor_trigger trig;
        trig.type = SENSOR_TRIG_DATA_READY;
        trig.chan = SENSOR_CHAN_ACCEL_XYZ;
        sensor_trigger_set(lsm6dsl, &trig, lsm6dsl_trigger_handler);
#endif
        while (1) { /* Get sensor samples */
#ifndef CONFIG_LSM6DSL_TRIGGER
            if (sensor_sample_fetch(lsm6dsl) < 0) {
                printf("LSM6DSL Sensor sample update error\n");
                return;
            }
#endif
            /* Get sensor data */
            sensor_channel_get(lsm6dsl,
                SENSOR_CHAN_ACCEL_XYZ, accel);
            sensor_channel_get(lsm6dsl, SENSOR_CHAN_GYRO_
            XYZ, gyro);
#ifdef CONFIG_LSM6DSL_EXT0_LPS22HB
            sensor_channel_get(lsm6dsl,
                SENSOR_CHAN_AMBIENT_TEMP, &temp);
            sensor_channel_get(lsm6dsl, SENSOR_CHAN_PRESS,
            &press);
#endif
#ifdef CONFIG_LSM6DSL_EXT0_LIS2MDL
            sensor_channel_get(lsm6dsl, SENSOR_CHAN_MAGN_
            XYZ, magn);
```

CHAPTER 9   UNDERSTANDING AND WORKING WITH THE DEVICETREE IN GENERAL AND SPI AND I2C IN PARTICULAR

```
#endif
            /* Display sensor data and erase previous data */
            printf("\0033\014");
            printf("X-NUCLEO-IKS01A2 sensor dashboard\n\n");
            /* lsm6dsl accel */
            printf("LSM6DSL: Accel (m.s-2):"
                " x: %.1f, y: %.1f, z: %.1f\n",
             sensor_value_to_double(&accel[0]),
                        sensor_value_to_
                        double(&accel[1]),
                    sensor_value_to_double(&accel[2]));
            /* lsm6dsl gyro */
            printf("LSM6DSL: Gyro (dps):"
            " x: %.3f, y: %.3f, z: %.3f\n",
             sensor_value_to_double(&gyro[0]),
             sensor_value_to_double(&gyro[1]),
                  sensor_value_to_double(&gyro[2]));
#ifdef CONFIG_LSM6DSL_EXT0_LPS22HB
            printf("LSM6DSL: Temperature: %.1f C\n",
             sensor_value_to_double(&temp));
            printf("LSM6DSL: Pressure:%.3f kpa\n",
             sensor_value_to_double(&press));
#endif
#ifdef CONFIG_LSM6DSL_EXT0_LIS2MDL
            printf("LSM6DSL: Magn (gauss):"
            " x: %.3f, y: %.3f, z: %.3f\n",
                 sensor_value_to_double(&magn[0]),
                 sensor_value_to_double(&magn[1]),
                 sensor_value_to_double(&magn[2]));
```

CHAPTER 9 UNDERSTANDING AND WORKING WITH THE DEVICETREE IN GENERAL AND SPI AND
            I2C IN PARTICULAR

```
#endif
#ifdef CONFIG_LSM6DSL_TRIGGER
            printk("%d:: lsm6dsl acc trig %d\n",
                            cnt++, lsm6dsl_trig_cnt);
#endif
            k_sleep(K_MSEC(2000));
    }
}
```

Summary

This chapter introduced the Zephyr RTOS device driver model and the key role played in it by devicetrees. The devicetree syntax was reviewed and also the use of binding files (which are written in YAML syntax) to describe the rules to be obeyed by the devicetree contents, including data types. The process of generating the devicetree-based device header files and how these are used in actual applications was reviewed. The basics of the I2C and SPI protocols were reviewed, and, finally, an example involving an application using an actual I2C sensor device was explored.

References

1. By Em3rgent0rdr – Own work, CC0 https://commons.wikimedia.org/w/index.php?curid=134759387
2. www.electronicshub.org/how-to-use-i2c-in-stm32f103c8t6/
3. https://github.com/devicetree-org/devicetree-specification/releases/download/v0.4-rc1/devicetree-specification-v0.4-rc1.pdf

4. Zephyr project devicetree documentation https://docs.zephyrproject.org/2.7.5/guides/dts/intro.html

5. Zephyr Developer Summit (2021) presentation. "A deep dive into the Zephyr 2.5 (and 2.6) device model www.youtube.com/watch?v=sWaxQyIgEBY

6. Zephyr\samples\shields\x_nucleo_iks01a2\sensorhub\

7. www.st.com/resource/en/datasheet/lsm6dsl.pdf

8. https://docs.zephyrproject.org/latest/build/dts/api/bindings/i2c/nordic,nrf-twim.html

9. https://developer.nordicsemi.com/nRF_Connect_SDK/doc/latest/nrfx/drivers/twim/index.html

CHAPTER 10

Building Zephyr RTOS Applications Using Renode

When developing relatively complex embedded systems applications, it can be useful to start developing firmware and application software before actual hardware is available. Development kits based on the selected target processor are useful but are limited because they may not support all the peripherals that will be used in the actual application. Many development kits support the addition (plugging in) of peripherals either because they provide Arduino connectors to which shields containing the needed peripherals can be used or because they provide connectors such as PMod [1] connectors or Mikroe [2] connectors for attaching various sensors and peripherals. An alternative approach is to use an emulator such as Renode to emulate the target system and develop and test application code on.

The use of Zephyr RTOS in the development of IoT embedded applications, in other words, applications that involve multiple devices that are part of a network which can involve both wired and wireless communications links, is growing rapidly, driven by the adoption of Zephyr RTOS by companies such as Nordic, STM, Microchip, and Silabs.

CHAPTER 10 BUILDING ZEPHYR RTOS APPLICATIONS USING RENODE

More and more complex applications are being developed to tighter and tighter development deadlines. Some of the applications have safety-critical and security applications in addition to having to satisfy real-time requirements. There is therefore a need to develop and test application code and associated firmware in parallel with the development of the hardware.

Modern continuous integration and continuous delivery approaches depend on being able to automate testing, version control, and delivery. Testing and test automation can benefit from the availability of a powerful and extensible emulator such as Renode.

In addition to being used for developing and testing networked multi-node applications, Renode can be used for the development of single node applications, especially where actual target boards are not yet available.

An emulator is not the same thing as a simulator. A good way of distinguishing between the two is to imagine a car simulator or flight simulator. If the car or flight simulator could actually carry the user from place to place, it would be an emulator.

Complex application development may involve part simulation and part emulation, for instance, emulating a microcontroller core, but simulating peripherals and sensors or communications links.

To place Renode in context, it is important to distinguish between simulators and emulators and to consider the advantages and disadvantages of using emulators and simulators in the development of embedded systems applications.

	Emulator	**Simulator**
Purpose	Substitutes an actual device	Reveals application behavior
Coding	Both assembler and compiled high level language code	High-level language using the simulator API
Environment being imitated	Both software and hardware aspects	End behavior of the software (what the user will experience)

(*continued*)

CHAPTER 10　BUILDING ZEPHYR RTOS APPLICATIONS USING RENODE

	Emulator	**Simulator**
Performance	Can be slow	Typically, runs compiled code, hence faster
Use cases	Testing at the level of detailed internal behavior	Testing the external (visible/experienced) behavior

Simulator Use Cases

- Developing software when the target devices have not been decided on or are not available, or are expensive
- When evaluating how an application interacts with users or some external environment
- Checking effects of using different kinds of peripheral, for example:
  - Using UI (User Interface) devices with different screen sizes and different screen resolutions

Emulator Use Cases

- Checking how application software interacts with the hardware or a combination of the hardware and an OS (Operating System)
  - Note: It may not be possible to emulate all hardware units.

509

CHAPTER 10   BUILDING ZEPHYR RTOS APPLICATIONS USING RENODE

- In continuous integration testing approaches, for example, when using an Agile development methodology where there is a requirement to carry out testing during the early stages of the project life cycle
- Emulator-based automation testing makes it possible to test in parallel with the development process life cycle
- More powerful/insightful debugging involving measuring things such as
  - CPU load
  - Memory consumption
  - Network loads

Advantages of Simulators and Emulators

- Saving money when testing network application performance as it is not necessary to actually build and administer a physical network
- Ability to use scalability and pay-as-you-go benefits of cloud computing to scale up as needed
  - As well as relative ease of cloud deployment
- The convenience of using virtual emulator and simulator devices for test automation purposes

Disadvantages of Simulators and Emulators

- Because simulators and emulators are virtual copies and not the actual devices, the test results may not be completely accurate. It will be necessary to be aware of the possibility of false-positive and false-negative results.
- Not all features can be tested with emulators and simulators, for example:
  - Battery performance
  - CPU performance
  - Memory consumption
  - Video and audio quality
  - Connectivity issues involving, for example, Wi-Fi and BLE networks
  - Color display details
- Staying up to date with the underlying physical devices and their peripherals and drivers.

Renode

- Renode [3] is designed to be a "whole-system emulator" that can be used in continuous integration and continuous development (CI/CD) scenarios on multiple devices.
- It is capable of simulating systems with multiple cores and multiple heterogenous CPUs.

- It supports a variety of network protocols.
- It has built-in emulation for commonly used processor architectures such as ARM, RISC-V, PowerPC, and x86.
- It is a good environment for exploring Zephyr RTOS programming in a hardware-agnostic environment.
- Renode can use the same firmware as that used in production and run it against emulated cores, peripherals, and even sensors and actuators.
- Because of its extensive networking support and multisystem emulation capabilities, it is well suited for testing systems made up of multiple communicating devices.
- It makes it possible to start development before the hardware is ready, to test the firmware on multiple target architectures.
- Makes for faster iteration cycles because it avoids the flash loading delays inherent when loading compiled code to actual targets.
- Because Renode is built using the Mono/C# framework, it can run on multiple workstation operating systems without modification.
- It is focused on embedded devices, unlike QEMU, which is more focused on emulating systems designed for use with higher-level OSes (e.g., Linux computers).
    - However, Zephyr applications can be run on systems emulated using QEMU.

CHAPTER 10   BUILDING ZEPHYR RTOS APPLICATIONS USING RENODE

Renode Installation

Renode is implemented in C# and requires a recent version of .Net to run on Windows.

.Net is normally already installed in Windows 10.

On Linux systems and macOS, a recent version of Mono (> 5.2) is required.

The simplest way to install Renode on Windows is to download a `.msi` installer from the Renode GitHub site. When the Microsoft installation is started by clicking on the .msi file in File Explorer, a warning is displayed. Installation in Program Files requires administrator privileges – activated by allowing installation in the modal dialog box that appears.

Figure 10-1. Renode setup and installation

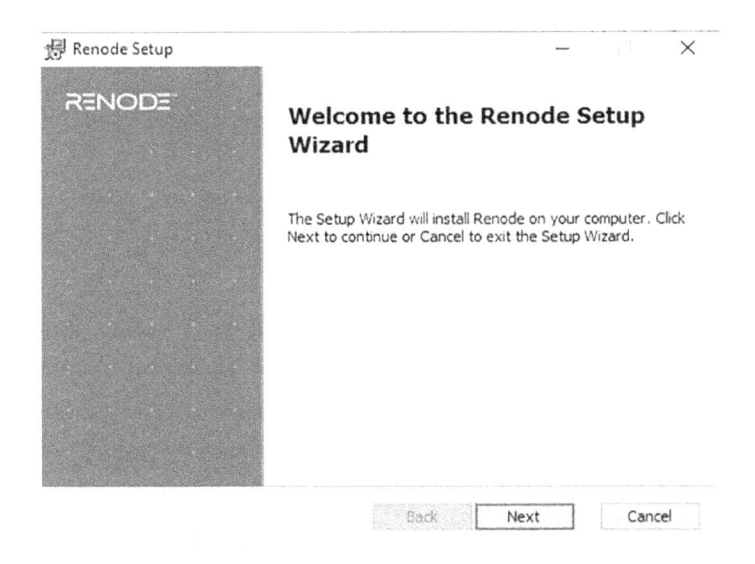

CHAPTER 10   BUILDING ZEPHYR RTOS APPLICATIONS USING RENODE

Figure 10-2. Renode setup and installation ctd

Clicking the Run anyway button brings up a welcome from the installation wizard, and clicking the Next button brings up a dialog in which to specify an installation directory, and then clicking the Next button brings up an Install options dialog box.

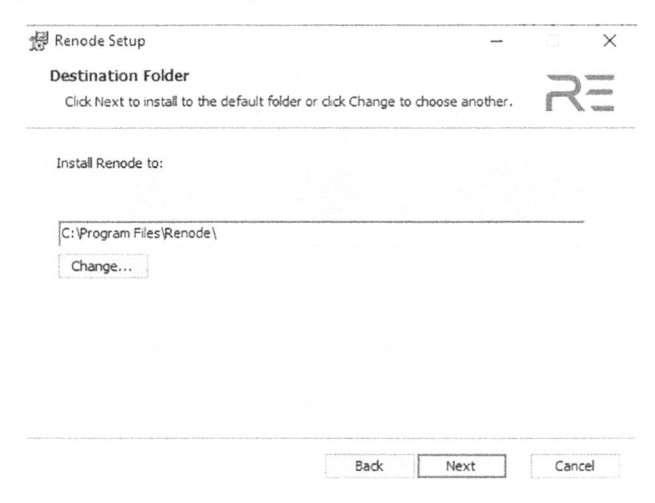

Figure 10-3. Renode setup and installation ctd

CHAPTER 10   BUILDING ZEPHYR RTOS APPLICATIONS USING RENODE

Clicking the Next button again brings up the dialog to start installation. Clicking the Install button starts the installation process during which a dialog with a progress bar is displayed. Finally, a dialog confirming successful installation is displayed, and clicking the `Finish` button completes the installation process.

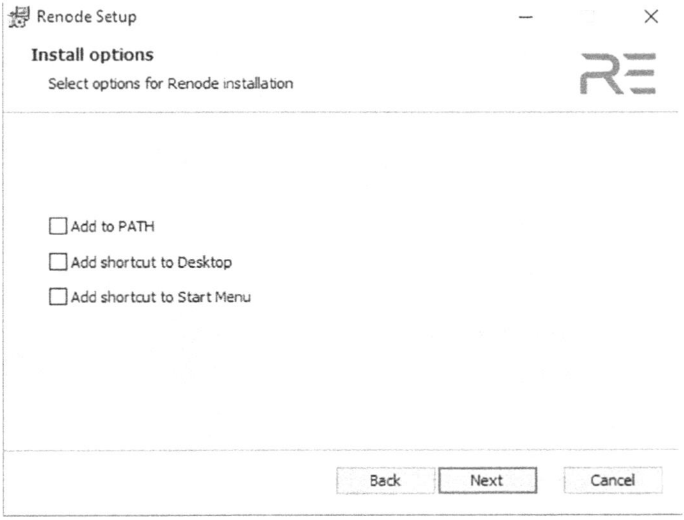

Figure 10-4. Renode setup and installation ctd

515

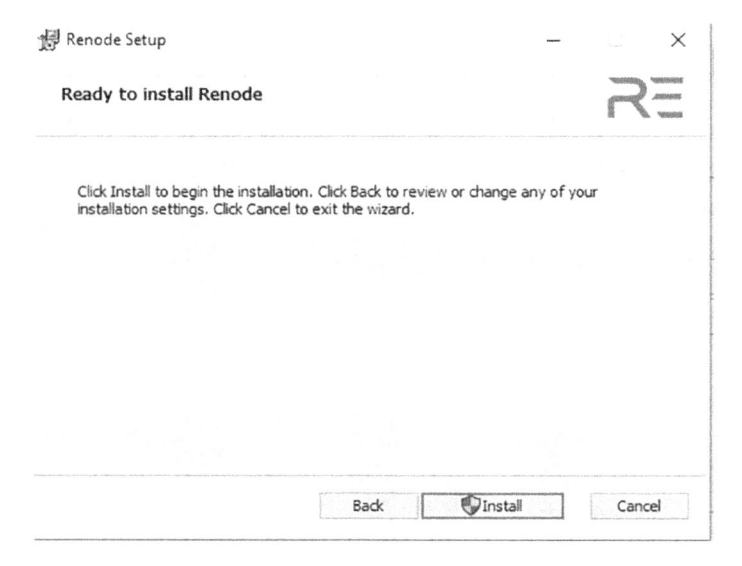

CHAPTER 10   BUILDING ZEPHYR RTOS APPLICATIONS USING RENODE

Figure 10-5. Renode setup and installation ctd

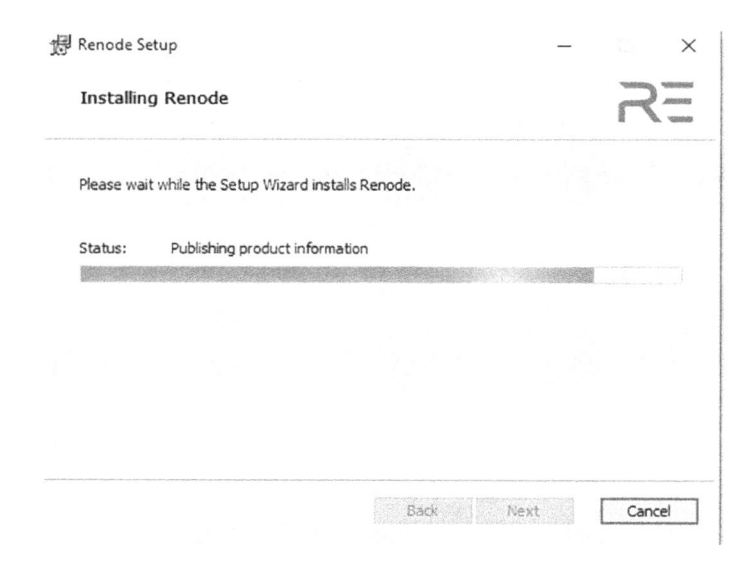

Figure 10-6. Renode setup and installation ctd

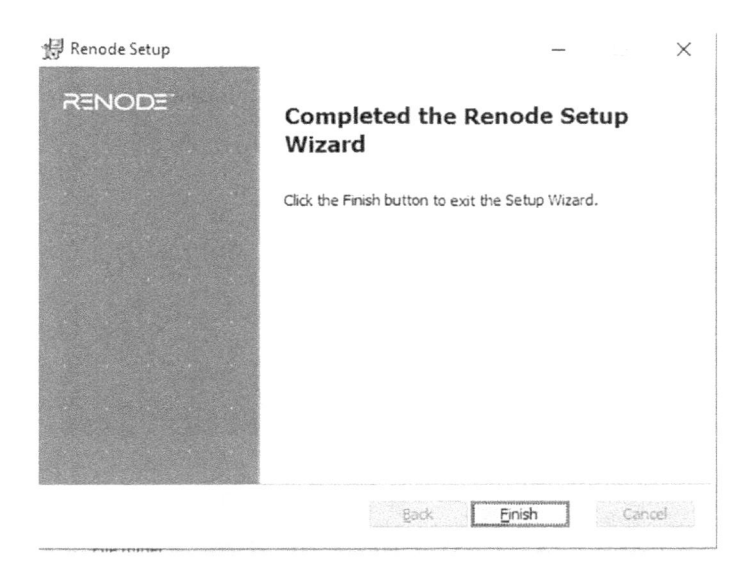

CHAPTER 10   BUILDING ZEPHYR RTOS APPLICATIONS USING RENODE

Figure 10-7.   Renode setup and installation ctd

Renode can be started by entering the renode command in a terminal shell window.

The current terminal will now act as the Renode log window, and a new window will pop up for "the Monitor" – the CLI (command-line interface) for Renode.

```
PS C:\> renode
15:01:46.3231 [INFO] Loaded monitor commands from: C:\Program Files\Renode\scripts/monitor.py
```

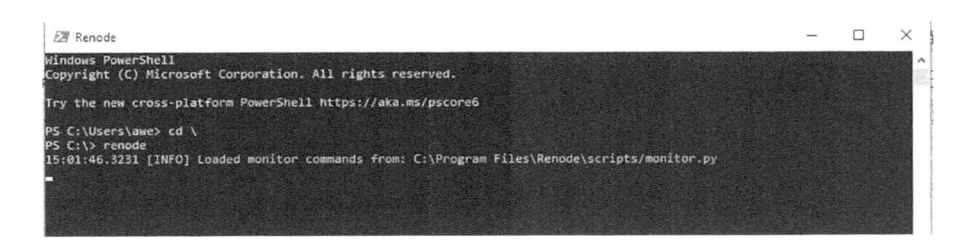

Figure 10-8.   Starting Renode with the renode command

517

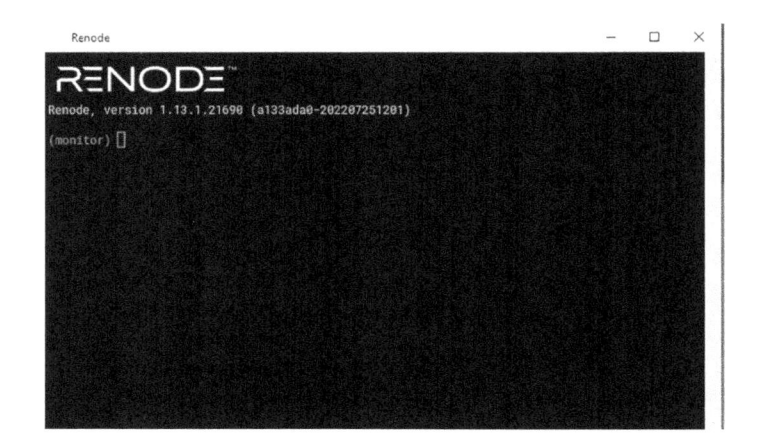

CHAPTER 10   BUILDING ZEPHYR RTOS APPLICATIONS USING RENODE

Figure 10-9. Renode monitor window

Typing help at the monitor prompt will list the available commands.

Typing in help <some command> will provide some help information about that command, for example:

start [s]
starts the emulation.
Usage:
start - starts the whole emulation
start @path - executes the script and starts the emulation

The Renode CLI shell has features such as

- Printing a help string for a command when incorrect or incomplete arguments are used.
- Basic autocompletion
  - Pressing the Tab key once completes the current command.
  - Pressing the Tab key will show all available suggestions.
- When providing file arguments, the @ sign represents a path to a file, for example, @/path/to/script.resc.

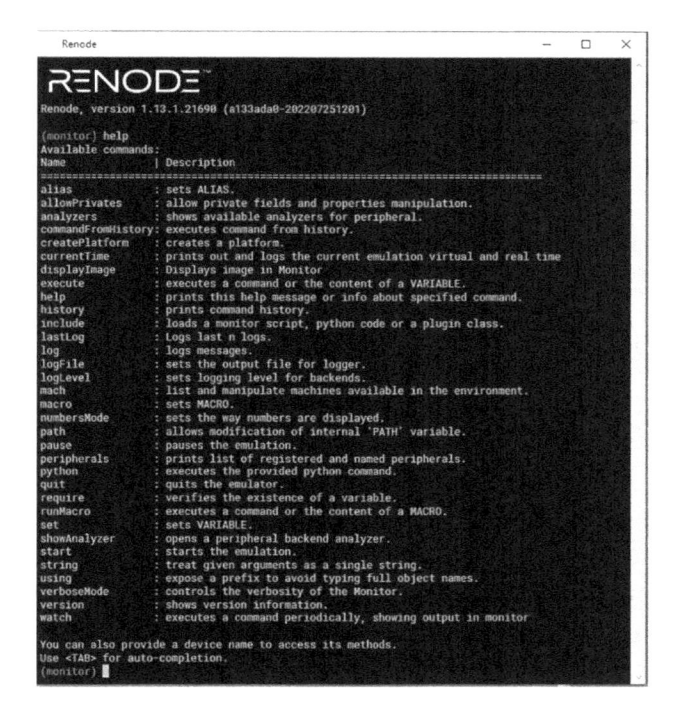

CHAPTER 10   BUILDING ZEPHYR RTOS APPLICATIONS USING RENODE

Figure 10-10. Renode commands

Commonly used renode commands have one-letter abbreviations, for example:

start - s
quit - q

Similarly to Bash, in Renode:

- The monitor CLI has a command history (arrow up/down) with interactive search (Control-r), which speeds up the task of re-executing previous commands.

- Pasting with Control-Shift-v, as well as via the context menu on right click, is also available.

- Control-c erases the current command and returns to a clean prompt.

519

CHAPTER 10   BUILDING ZEPHYR RTOS APPLICATIONS USING RENODE

Renode Scripts

Renode is a scripting language.

- The simplest scripts are one-line Renode commands.
- Scripts can be constructed by combining commands.
- Scripts, in turn, can include both commands and other scripts.

Renode scripts are concerned with creating and running emulations of a single emulated (guest) platform or a networked collection of platforms.

Renode commands can be used to interact with the external interfaces (peripherals) of the emulated machines such as UARTs or Ethernet controllers.

When running Renode interactively, the user would normally start with creating the emulation through a sequence of commands building up, configuring, and connecting the relevant emulated (guest) platform or platforms (called "machines").

This is normally done using nested `.resc` scripts, which help encapsulate some of the repeatable elements in this activity (normally, the user will want to create the same platform over and over again in between runs, or even script the execution entirely).

When the emulation is created and all the necessary elements (including, e.g., binaries to be executed) are loaded, the emulation itself can be started – to do this, the `start` command is entered in the Monitor.

At this point, it is possible to see a lot of information about the operation of the emulated environment in the log window, extract additional information, and manipulate the running emulation using the Monitor (or plug-ins such as Wireshark) – as well as interact with the external interfaces of the emulated machines like UARTs or Ethernet controllers.

Renode scripts can be saved in files, which, typically, have a `.resc` extension.

CHAPTER 10 BUILDING ZEPHYR RTOS APPLICATIONS USING RENODE

A script can be loaded with the `include` command, for example:

`include @/path/to/script.resc`

- The Renode framework can be used to set up and configure various embedded systems to be emulated.
- Renode has a steep learning curve, and here only a few scripts corresponding to sample embedded systems target platforms will be used.
- The Zephyr applications running in Renode built as if they were being targeted for a real embedded system board, however
  - The compiled code is being run on an emulated device, and the output logs can be used to study the application in action.
  - This makes it possible to focus on Zephyr RTOS programming without having to worry about flashing compiled code to a target device and running it on that device.

What Is Needed to Emulate a Zephyr Application Using Renode?

- An emulator for the processor core
- Some kind of emulation for various devices and peripherals
  - Emitting some kind of text message (e.g., a logging message) when the state of a peripheral changes

521

CHAPTER 10 BUILDING ZEPHYR RTOS APPLICATIONS USING RENODE

- Using some kind of graphical "animation"/"visualization" to illustrate peripherals such as, for example, an LED or the value of an input pin or the position of a servo
  - However, the code to do this would need to be implemented explicitly, typically in C#, as Renode, itself, is a C# application.
- Implementation of actual device drivers for devices for which there is no Zephyr device driver implementation

Boards and Processors Supported by Zephyr That Are Also Supported by Renode

The Renode website has a dashboard that is generated by a CI (continuous integration) run, which builds all boards supported in Zephyr RTOS and tries to run them in Renode.

Figure 10-11 shows the dashboard web page (https://zephyr-dashboard.renode.io/).

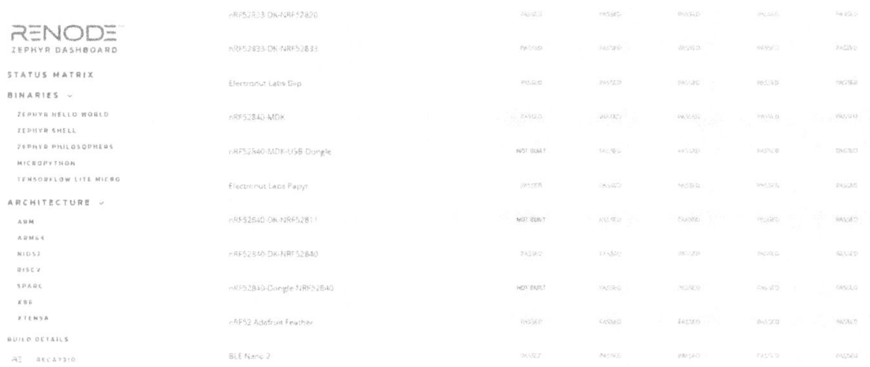

Figure 10-11. Renode dashboard

CHAPTER 10   BUILDING ZEPHYR RTOS APPLICATIONS USING RENODE

The focus will be on applications built for the nRF52840 DK developer kit board. The Renode dashboard information for the nRF52840 DK board is shown in Figure 10-12.

Figure 10-12.   Renode dashboard – information for the nRF52840 DK board

The uart output produced by running a sample application can be displayed in the UART output window on the dashboard processor web page.

523

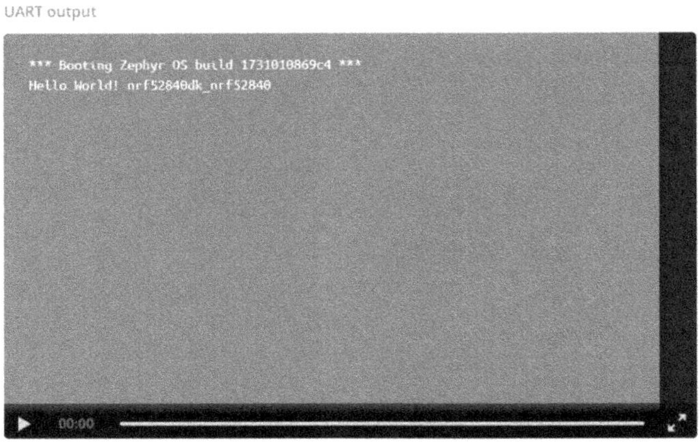

CHAPTER 10   BUILDING ZEPHYR RTOS APPLICATIONS USING RENODE

Figure 10-13. Renode Hello World for the nRF52840 DK board

Clicking the Peripherals tab provides information about the various device peripherals that are supported in the Renode emulation.

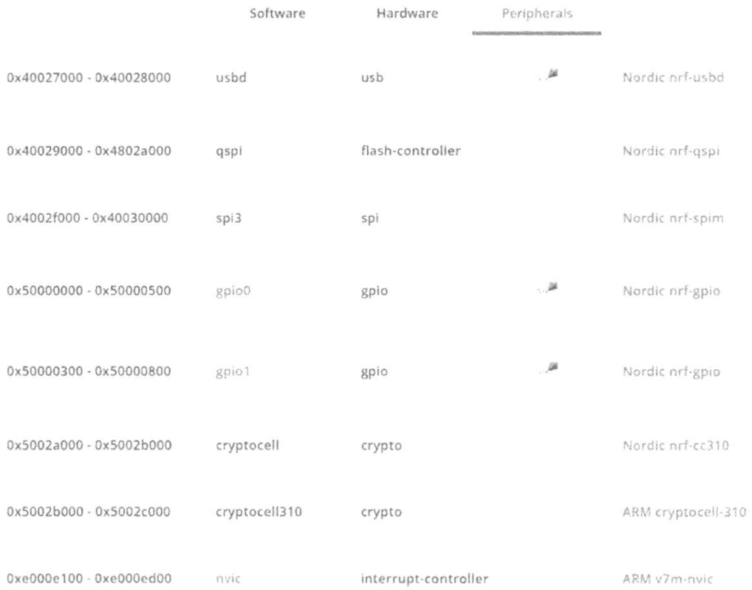

Address range	Software	Hardware	Peripherals
0x40027000 - 0x40028000	usbd	usb	Nordic nrf-usbd
0x40029000 - 0x4802a000	qspi	flash-controller	Nordic nrf-qspi
0x4002f000 - 0x40030000	spi3	spi	Nordic nrf-spim
0x50000000 - 0x50000500	gpio0	gpio	Nordic nrf-gpio
0x50000300 - 0x50000800	gpio1	gpio	Nordic nrf-gpio
0x5002a000 - 0x5002b000	cryptocell	crypto	Nordic nrf-cc310
0x5002b000 - 0x5002c000	cryptocell310	crypto	ARM cryptocell-310
0xe000e100 - 0xe000ed00	nvic	interrupt-controller	ARM v7m-nvic

Figure 10-14. Renode – supported emulated peripherals available in simulation

CHAPTER 10   BUILDING ZEPHYR RTOS APPLICATIONS USING RENODE

Clicking on the zephyr (blue kite) icon brings up the Zephyr device driver source code.

Clicking on a link in the second column of the table in the Peripherals tab (where one exists) will bring up the emulator code in C#, for example, for uart0.

Figure 10-15. Renode – C# source code for UART driver emulation

Studying the device driver source code and the emulator source code is a good way to learn about how to write driver code for new devices and also how to write emulator code for these devices.

525

CHAPTER 10 BUILDING ZEPHYR RTOS APPLICATIONS USING RENODE

Building an nRF52840 DK Application and Running It in Renode

The "dining philosophers" example is a widely used scenario to demonstrate multithreading and the "possibility of deadlock" occurring.

It is one of the examples used in testing target boards and their Renode emulations. When the example is run in Renode, the results are displayed in the Renode boards dashboard.

The dining philosophers example can be run in Renode by entering the appropriate monitor command manually. Later these commands can be collected together as a Renode script.

The first step is to build the dining philosophers demo for a particular target board using the Zephyr west tool, for example:

```
west build -b nrf52840dk_nrf52840 -p=auto --force -d \ dining_philosophers_demo ./zephyr/samples/philosophers
```

The west tool creates a build directory in which the project is built.

If all goes well, it will contain a zephyr subdirectory in which the compiled application, called `zephyr.elf`, will be located.

To run the application code in Renode, it is necessary to start renode and then, in the monitor window, enter individual commands, or, alternatively, invoke a renode script file that contains multiple commands.

In the directory containing renode, run the `renode` command, which brings up the renode monitor window.

As commands are entered into the monitor window, output is written to the PowerShell window from which renode was started.

CHAPTER 10   BUILDING ZEPHYR RTOS APPLICATIONS USING RENODE

The basic pattern for running an emulation in renode is as follows:

1. Create a machine (if you do not provide an explicit name, then one, e.g., `machine-0`, will be generated automatically) `mach create`.

2. Load a renode platform description for the target device `machine, LoadPlatformDescription @platforms/cpus/nrf52840.repl`.

3. Load the binary to run in the renode emulator `sysbus LoadELF @C:\ncs\dining_philosophers_demo\zephyr\zephyr.elf`.

4. Display the uart console in which uart messages will be displayed:

    - `showAnalyzer sysbus.uart0`

5. Start the emulation with the `start` command.

6. Note: An emulation can be paused with the pause command.

The following screen capture images demonstrate running the emulation.

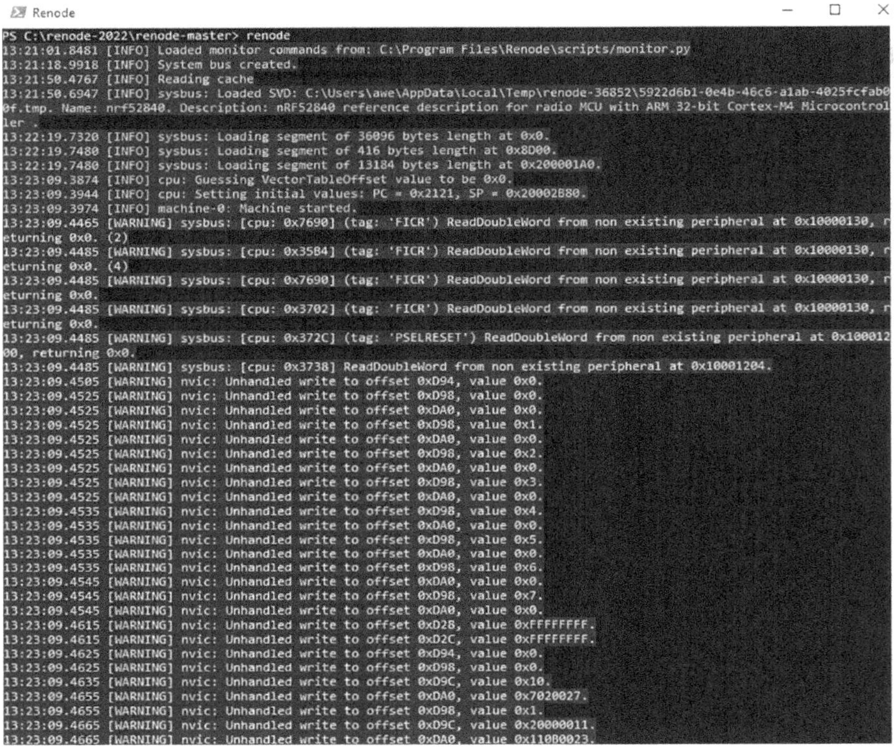

CHAPTER 10   BUILDING ZEPHYR RTOS APPLICATIONS USING RENODE

Figure 10-16. PowerShell Console output when running application

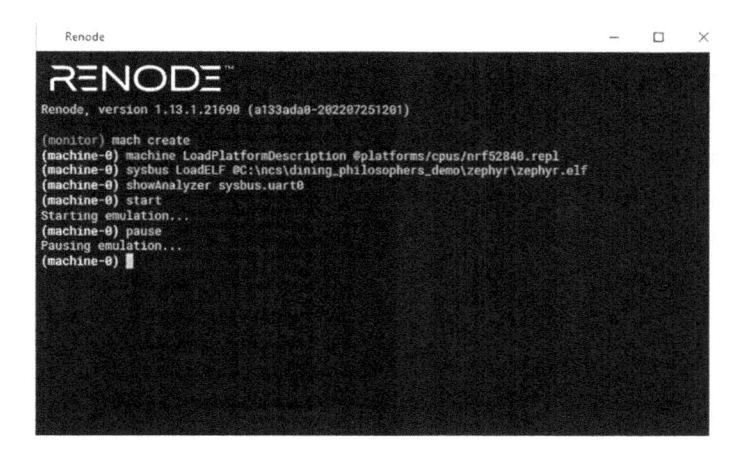

CHAPTER 10   BUILDING ZEPHYR RTOS APPLICATIONS USING RENODE

Figure 10-17. Renode Monitor Console output when running application

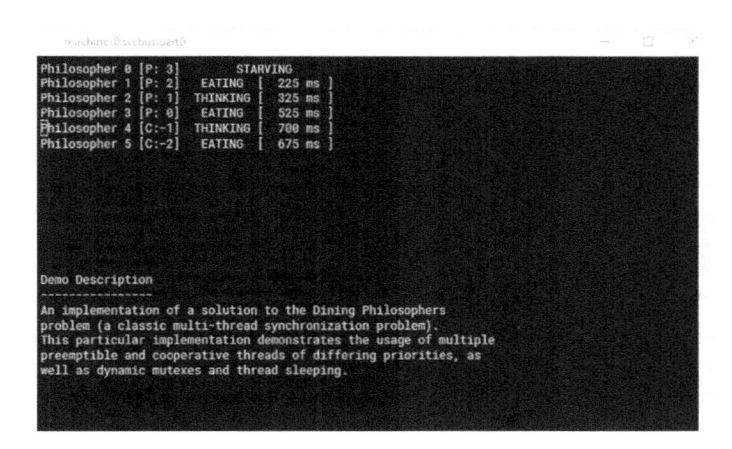

Figure 10-18. Renode UART Terminal Window output when running application

529

Summary and Where Next?

This chapter has provided an overview of Renode and its usefulness in developing and testing Zephyr applications. Renode is a large and complex tool and has a steep learning curve. Areas to explore include the use of C# to create emulations of devices and peripherals [4] and developing automated testing procedures making use of the Robot framework testing suite with which Renode is integrated [5]. Renode provides various Python hooks [6]. Python can be used to emulate simple devices, and Python scripts can be invoked from the Renode command-line monitor.

References

1. https://en.wikipedia.org/wiki/Pmod_Interface
2. www.mikroe.com/click-boards
3. https://renode.io/
4. https://renode.readthedocs.io/en/latest/advanced/writing-peripherals.html
5. https://renode.readthedocs.io/en/latest/introduction/testing.html
6. https://renode.readthedocs.io/en/latest/basic/using-python.html

CHAPTER 11

Understanding and Using the Zephyr ZBus in Application Development

Zephyr ZBus

ZBus has many concepts in common with DBus, which is used in Linux-based systems. Whereas DBus is concerned with communication between processes running in separate virtual memory spaces, ZBus is concerned with communication between Zephyr RTOS threads.

The pattern underlying ZBus is an observer pattern in which a thread can broadcast messages to all observers interested in receiving such messages. ZBus can be used for many-to-many communication purpose as well. The communication patterns supported by ZBus are publish/subscribe and message passing. ZBus-based communication makes use of shared memory and can be either synchronous or asynchronous in nature.

CHAPTER 11 UNDERSTANDING AND USING THE ZEPHYR ZBUS IN APPLICATION DEVELOPMENT

The essential ZBus abstraction is the channel. Zephyr threads publish messages to and read messages from channels. Threads can also observe channels and receive notifications from the bus when the channels are modified.

The ZBus architecture is illustrated conceptually in Figure 11-1.

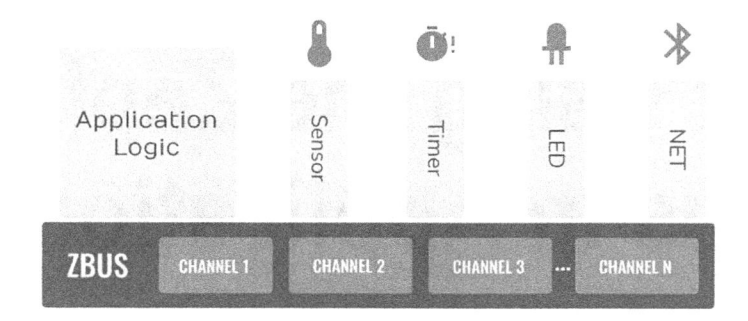

Figure 11-1. Conceptual overview of the ZBus architecture

The application logic that uses ZBus is hardware independent. An application thread communicates with other threads over this bus. Threads communicating with one another over the ZBus do not need to know each other's details. In this sense, the threads are decoupled from one another.

ZBus Architecture

The architecture of the ZBus, as outlined in the following schematic, consists of

- A set of channels with each channel having a unique identifier and control metadata information
- A virtual distributed event dispatcher (VDED), which provides the bus logic for sending notifications to the observers

CHAPTER 11   UNDERSTANDING AND USING THE ZEPHYR ZBUS IN APPLICATION DEVELOPMENT

- Threads (subscriber threads) and callbacks (listener threads), which do the publishing, reading, and receiving of notifications from the bus

This is outlined in Figure 11-2.

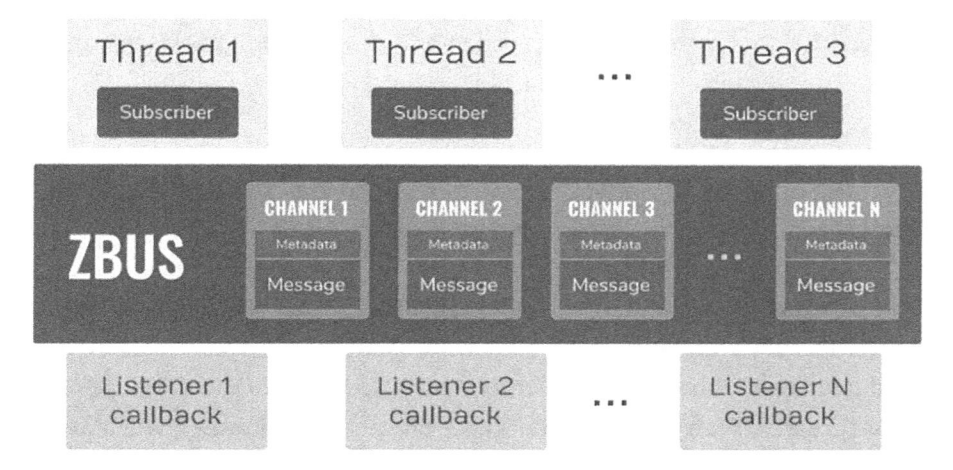

Figure 11-2. *Schematic overview of the ZBus architecture*

The ZBus actions that can be performed over a channel are publish, read, and subscribe.

Publishing and reading cannot be used in an ISR (interrupt service routine) context because the underlying operations may block. This is because publishing and copying involve a mutex locking step followed by a memory copy to or from a shared memory region.

The registration of a ZBus observer can be either static or dynamic. A static observer registration is defined at compile time and cannot be removed. It can, however, be suppressed via a call to the zbus_obs_set_enable() method. Dynamic observer registrations can be added and removed at runtime as required.

The Zephyr documentation provides an example of a fairly typical possible use of the ZBus in a sensor-based application. The scenario underlying this example is illustrated in Figure 11-3.

533

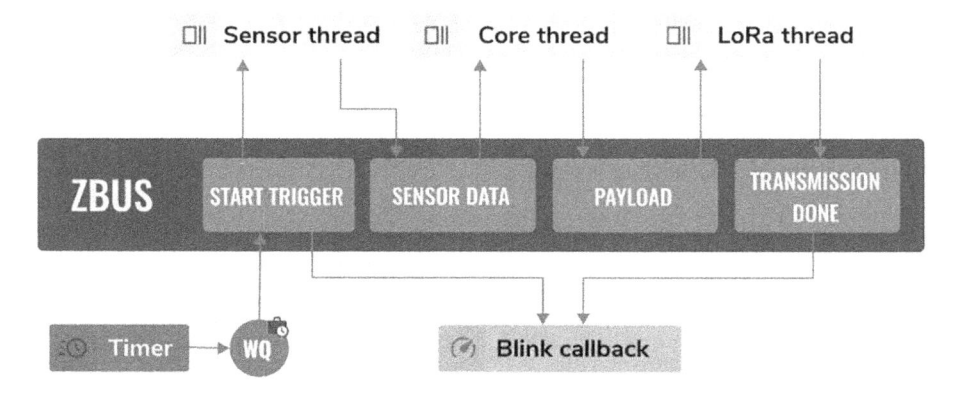

CHAPTER 11   UNDERSTANDING AND USING THE ZEPHYR ZBUS IN APPLICATION DEVELOPMENT

Figure 11-3. Example ZBus usage scenario

In this scenario, when the timer is triggered, it pushes an action to a workqueue that publishes to the Start trigger channel. This is the standard way of getting an interrupt handler to send something to the ZBus. The sensor thread, which is subscribed to the Start trigger channel, will start retrieving the sensor data when notified. The event dispatcher will execute the blink callback because it listens to the Start trigger channel. Once the sensor data is ready, the sensor thread publishes it to the Sensor data channel.

The core thread, which is a Sensor data channel subscriber, retrieves and processes the sensor data that was sent over the ZBus and stores it in its internal sample buffer. This process is repeated till the sample buffer becomes full. At this point, the core thread aggregates the stored sample information, packages it up, and publishes it to the Payload channel. The LoRa thread, as a subscriber to the Payload channel, receives this message and transmits it. Once it has finished transmitting, the LoRa thread publishes a suitable event as this callback is a listener on the Transmission done channel.

The power of the ZBus comes from the flexible way in which it can be used. For example, instead of using a timer interrupt to trigger the sequence of events described, the code could be modified to use a button press interrupt. Changing the transmission medium from LoRa to Bluetooth Low Energy (BLE) would only require replacing the LoRa thread with an analogous BLE thread.

The ZBus and Code Reusability

Suppose a given module has a set of well-defined behaviors and only uses ZBus channels as opposed to hardware channels. Such a module can readily be reused in other applications. If the new application implements the interfaces (set of channels) that the module needs to work with, then this new application can be made to work together with that module.

Limitations of the ZBus

The ZBus is better suited to some problems than to others, and it is important to be aware of the limitations of the ZBus. For example, ZBus benchmarking will reveal that the ZBus is not well suited for sending a high-speed stream (megabits per second or higher) of bytes from one thread to another. That particular requirement might be better met by using a Pipe kernel object. Limitations to take into account include those concerning message delivery guarantees and those concerning message delivery sequence guarantees.

ZBus Message Delivery Guarantees and Message Delivery Rates

Although Zbus will always deliver messages to listeners, this will not necessarily be the case for subscribers. This is because a subscriber will be sent a notification, and the reading of the message will depend on the way the subscriber has been implemented.

Heuristics to use to increase the delivery rate include the following:

- Making the listeners fast and, where necessary, offloading more time-consuming processing by submitting that work to a workqueue
- Assigning producer threads a high priority to avoid losses
- Ensuring there are sufficient CPU resources available for observers to consume the data produced in a timely manner
- Considering the use of message queues or pipes for fast transfer of streams of bytes

ZBus Message Delivery Sequence Guarantees

Listeners, being synchronous observers, will follow the channel definition sequence as their notification and message consumption sequence. Subscribers, on the other hand, which behave asynchronously, although they will receive notifications in the channel definition sequence, will consume the data when they run next. As a result, the priority assigned to the subscribers will serve to define the reaction sequence.

In ZBus applications, all listeners (whether static or dynamic) will receive a given message before any of the subscribers receive the notification for that message. The rule for the sequence of delivery is that the order, from first to last, will be (SRLSRS)

- Static listeners, then
- Runtime listeners, then
- Static subscribers, and finally
- Runtime subscribers

CHAPTER 11   UNDERSTANDING AND USING THE ZEPHYR ZBUS IN APPLICATION DEVELOPMENT

ZBus Programming in Practice

This involves defining ZBus channels, ZBus messages, necessary callback functions, subscribers, and listeners. As with most "things Zephyr," the practical details involve getting to grips with the various ZBus Framework macros, data structures, and the ZBus API. These are overviewed in this section.

The message is defined by some application-dependent data structure.

For example, a data structure for accelerometer sensor reading might be something like the following:

```
struct acc_msg {
        int x;
        int y;
        int z;
};
```

The ZBus framework makes extensive use of macros, which help to hide many lower-level code details. The `ZBUS_CHAN_DEFINE` macro is used to define a channel.

```
ZBUS_CHAN_DEFINE(_name, _type, _validator, _user_data, _observers, _init_val)
```

The parameters have the following meanings:

- _name – The channel's name.
- _type – The Message type. It must be a struct or union.
- _validator – The validator function.
- _user_data – A pointer to the user data.
- _observers – The observers list. The sequence indicates the priority of the observer. The first, the highest priority.
- _init_val – The message initialization.

537

CHAPTER 11 UNDERSTANDING AND USING THE ZEPHYR ZBUS IN APPLICATION DEVELOPMENT

and the following code snippet illustrates how to use it:

```
ZBUS_CHAN_DEFINE(acc_chan,                          /* Name */
        struct acc_msg,                             /* Message type */
        NULL,                                       /* Validator */
        NULL,                                       /* User Data */
        ZBUS_OBSERVERS(my_listener, my_subscriber), /* observers */
        ZBUS_MSG_INIT(.x = 0, .y = 0, .z = 0)       /* Initial
                                                    value {0} */
);
```

In fact, every ZBus channel has a `zbus_channel` structure associated with it, which contains the information required to control the channel access and usage.

```
struct zbus_channel {
    const char *const name;
    void *const message;
    const size_t message_size;
    void *const user_data;
    bool (*const validator)(const void *msg, size_t msg_size);
    struct zbus_channel_data *const data;
};
```

- name – The Channel name
- message_size – The size of the channel's message
- user_data – Data that can be used to extend the ZBus features, however, the channel must first be claimed before using this field
- message – A reference to the message that points to the actual shared memory region where the message is

CHAPTER 11   UNDERSTANDING AND USING THE ZEPHYR ZBUS IN APPLICATION DEVELOPMENT

- `validator` – A function pointer to the message validator function that will carry out validation before actually publishing the message

  - An invalid message will not be published.

  - If this field is empty, then every message will be considered valid.

- `mutex` – A pointer to the access control mutex, which is used to avoid race conditions when accessing the channel

- `observers` – The channel observer list, which can be empty or contain listeners and subscribers mixed in any sequence

The following code snippet shows how a callback can be implemented:

```
void listener_callback_example (const struct zbus_
channel *chan)
{
        const struct acc_msg *acc;
        if (&acc_chan == chan) {
                acc = zbus_chan_const_msg(chan);
                LOG_DBG("From listener -> Acc x=%d, y=%d,
                z=%d", acc->x, acc->y, acc->z);
        }
}
```

After `acc = zbus_chan_const_msg(chan);`, `acc` points directly to the message.

In the preceding example, the fields in the message data structure are accessed, here, `acc->x, acc->y, acc->z`, and then used as arguments to `LOG_DBG`.

539

CHAPTER 11   UNDERSTANDING AND USING THE ZEPHYR ZBUS IN APPLICATION DEVELOPMENT

Zephyr provides the following utility macros for defining listeners and subscribers.

ZBUS_LISTENER_DEFINE for defining listeners and ZBUS_SUBSCRIBER_DEFINE for defining subscribers.

ZBUS_SUBSCRIBER_DEFINE(_name, _queue_size) defines and initializes a subscriber.

It defines a subscriber type of observer and the message queue where the subscriber will asynchronously receive the notification, by initializing the struct zbus_observer instance that defines the subscriber.

_name is the subscriber name.

_queue_size is the size of the notification queue.

ZBUS_LISTENER_DEFINE(_name, _cb) defines and initializes a listener, providing the callback function to use when the listener is notified, by initializing the struct zbus_observer instance that defines the observer.

_name is the listener's name.

_cb is the callback function.

The struct zbus_observer structure source code is full of Doxygen documentation, which can be conditionally included by defining DOXYGEN. This documentation code, associated with conditional includes #if defined(__DOXYGEN__), is edited out in most of the code snippets that follow.

```
struct zbus_observer {
#if defined(CONFIG_ZBUS_OBSERVER_NAME)
    const char *const name;
#endif
    enum zbus_observer_type type;
    bool enabled;
    union {
        struct k_msgq *const queue;
        void (*const callback)(const struct zbus_
        channel *chan);
```

CHAPTER 11   UNDERSTANDING AND USING THE ZEPHYR ZBUS IN APPLICATION DEVELOPMENT

```
#if defined(CONFIG_ZBUS_MSG_SUBSCRIBER)
            struct k_fifo *const message_fifo;
#endif /* CONFIG_ZBUS_MSG_SUBSCRIBER */
      };
};
```

In this structure:

- name is the observer name.
- enabled is the enabled flag that indicates whether the observer is receiving notifications or not.
- queue is the observer message queue, which, in effect, turns the observer into a subscriber.
- callback is the function pointer to the observer callback function.
- message_fifo is the fifo for a message subscriber.

The actual details of the structure are dependent on the outcome of the preprocessing stage and will depend on whether CONFIG_ZBUS_OBSERVER_NAME and CONFIG_ZBUS_MSG_SUBSCRIBER have been #defined.

The following code snippets from the Zephyr documentation show how these helper macros can be used:

```
ZBUS_LISTENER_DEFINE(my_listener, listener_callback_example);
ZBUS_SUBSCRIBER_DEFINE(my_subscriber, 4);

void subscriber_task (void) {
    const struct zbus_channel *chan;
    while (!zbus_sub_wait(&my_subscriber, &chan, K_FOREVER)) {
        struct acc_msg acc = {0};
        if (&acc_chan == chan) {
            // Indirect message access
            zbus_chan_read(&acc_chan, &acc, K_NO_WAIT);
```

CHAPTER 11   UNDERSTANDING AND USING THE ZEPHYR ZBUS IN APPLICATION DEVELOPMENT

```
            LOG_DBG("From subscriber -> Acc x=%d, y=%d, z=%d",
            acc.x, acc.y, acc.z);
        }
    }
}
```

The subscriber task is associated with a thread that must be defined appropriately, for example:

```
K_THREAD_DEFINE(subscriber_task_id, 512, subscriber_task, \
NULL, NULL, NULL, 3, 0, 0);
```

The subscriber task uses the ZBus API function

```
int zbus_sub_wait(const struct zbus_observer *sub,
     const struct zbus_channel **chan, k_timeout_t timeout)
```

to wait for a channel notification. The arguments are the subscriber reference (sub), the channel notification reference (chan), and a timeout, which can be either K_NO_WAIT or K_FOREVER or an explicit timeout value.

The possible return values are as follows:

- 0 – Notification received.
- -ENOMSG – Returned without waiting.
- -EAGAIN – Waiting period timed out.
- -EINVAL – The observer is not a subscriber.
- -EFAULT – A parameter is incorrect, or the function context is invalid (e.g., inside an ISR). The function only returns this value when CONFIG_ZBUS_ASSERT_MOCK is enabled.

Hard Channels and Message Validation

A hard channel is a channel that only allows valid messages to be published. This requirement is enforced by providing a Validator function. The following code snippet in the Zephyr documentation demonstrates the implementation of a channel that will only publish move messages whose values are equal to 0.

The following code defines and initializes a hard channel and its dependencies. Only valid messages can be published to a hard channel. This is possible because a Validator function is passed to the channel's definition. In this example, only messages with move equal to 0, 1, or -1 are valid.

```
struct control_msg {
        int move;
};
bool control_validator(const void* msg, size_t msg_size) {
        const struct control_msg* cm = msg;
        bool is_valid = (cm->move == -1) || (cm->move == 0) || (cm->move == 1);
        return is_valid;
}
static int message_count = 0;
ZBUS_CHAN_DEFINE(control_chan,      /* Name */
        struct control_msg,         /* Message type */
        control_validator,          /* Validator */
        &message_count,             /* User data */
        ZBUS_OBSERVERS_EMPTY,       /* observers */
        ZBUS_MSG_INIT(.move = 0)    /* Initial value {.move=0} */
);
```

CHAPTER 11   UNDERSTANDING AND USING THE ZEPHYR ZBUS IN APPLICATION DEVELOPMENT

Overview of ZBus Features and Their Uses

The key ZBus API functions (operations) include functions for

- Publishing to a channel
- Reading from a channel
- Forcing channel notification
- Declaring channels and observers
- Iterating over channels and observers
- Claiming and finishing a channel
- Runtime observer registration

Publishing and Reading to and from a Channel

Publishing to a channel uses the function zbus_chan_pub:

int zbus_chan_pub (const struct zbus_channel *chan, const void *msg, k_timeout_t timeout)

and reading from a channel uses the function zbus_chan_read:

int zbus_chan_read (const struct zbus_channel *chan, void *msg, k_timeout_t timeout)

For both functions, chan is the channel reference, and timeout is a timeout that can be either K_NO_WAIT or K_FOREVER or an explicit timeout value.

The possible return values are 0 on success or an error value, which can be one of the following:

- `-ENOMSG` – Returned without waiting.
- `-EAGAIN` – Waiting period timed out.
- `-EINVAL` – The observer is not a subscriber.
- `-EFAULT` – A parameter is incorrect, or the function context is invalid (e.g., inside an ISR). The function only returns this value when `CONFIG_ZBUS_ASSERT_MOCK` is enabled.

In the case of `zbus_chan_pub,` the parameter `msg` is a reference to where the publish function copies the channel's message data from, whereas in the case of `zbus_chan_read,` the parameter `msg` is a reference to where the message read is copied to.

Claiming and Finishing a Channel

The `user_data` pointer in the zbus_channel structure can be used to associate metadata (extra information) with a ZBus channel. Working with this metadata in a multithreading context requires the ability to access this data safely. To this end, the API functions `zbus_chan_claim()` and `zbus_chan_finish()` have been provided. Once a channel has been claimed, the actions associated with that channel will not be available. For the actions to become available again, the finish operation needs to be performed on that channel.

The Zephyr document provides an example snippet showing how channel claiming and finishing might be used in a scenario involving counting how many times the channels exchange messages. In this scenario, the user_data is a 32-bit integer. A code snippet such as the following would, typically, be part of the listener code:

```
if (!zbus_chan_claim(&acc_chan, K_MSEC(200))) {
        int *message_counting = (int *) zbus_chan_user_
        data(acc_chan);
        *message_counting += 1;
        zbus_chan_finish(&acc_chan);
}
```

Because claiming and finishing are operations that can block, they should not be used in ISRs.

Ensuring a Message Will Not Be Changed During a Notification

Listeners can access the receiving channel message directly as they have a mutex lock for it. To access the message without changing it, the zbus_chan_const_msg function should be used instead of zbus_chan_read. The reason for doing so is that the channel passed as an argument to the listener function is a constant pointer to the channel, the intention being that the message itself will be kept unchanged during the notification process.

The following code snippet shows this:

```
void listener_callback_example(const struct zbus_channel *chan) {
        const struct acc_msg *acc;
        if (&acc_chan == chan) {
                acc = zbus_chan_const_msg(chan); // Use this
                LOG_DBG("From listener -> Acc x=%d, y=%d,
                z=%d", acc->x, acc->y, acc->z);
        }
}
```

Iterating over Channels and Observers

Because the use of the ZBus envisages multiple channels and multiple observers, the need for a convenient mechanism to iterate over such collections of channels and of observers is obvious. Zephyr's solution to this is Iterable Sections and its associated API.

An iterable area is a block of memory containing a number of equally sized data structures that can be iterated over using the `STRUCT_SECTION_FOREACH` macro.

When setting an iterable section, background linker processing is necessary. As part of the compilation process, the linker has to be instructed to place the iterable structure in a contiguous memory segment using one of the linker macros such as `ITERABLE_SECTION_RAM` or `ITERABLE_SECTION_ROM`. Custom linker snippets can be declared using one of the `zephyr_linker_sources()` CMake functions, providing the appropriate section identifier, namely, `DATA_SECTIONS` for RAM structures and `SECTIONS` for ROM-based structures.

The ZBus subsystem provides an implementation of Iterable Sections for channels and observers and supporting API functions such as `zbus_iterate_over_channels()`, `zbus_iterate_over_channels_with_user_data()`, `zbus_iterate_over_observers()`, and `zbus_iterate_over_observers_with_user_data()`. This makes it possible to call a procedure over all the declared channels, with a procedure parameter of type pointer to a zbus_channel. The execution sequence proceeds in the alphabetical name order of the channels.

ZBus implements a similar feature for zbus_observer.

The following code snippet shows a typical implementation pattern for iterating over channels and observers. It involves implementing suitable "iterator" functions that can be used to collect and extract information during the iteration process and then applying these functions.

```
static bool print_channel_data_iterator(const struct zbus_
channel *chan, void *user_data) {
      int *count = user_data;
      LOG_INF("%d - Channel %s:", *count, zbus_chan_
      name(chan));
      LOG_INF("      Message size: %d", zbus_chan_msg_
      size(chan));
      LOG_INF("      Observers:");
      ++(*count);
      struct zbus_channel_observation *observation;

      for (int16_t i = *chan->observers_start_idx, limit =
      *chan->observers_end_idx;
                        i < limit; ++i) {
          STRUCT_SECTION_GET(zbus_channel_observation, i,
          &observation);
          LOG_INF("      - %s", observation->obs->name);
      }

      struct zbus_observer_node *obs_nd, *tmp;

      SYS_SLIST_FOR_EACH_CONTAINER_SAFE(chan->observers,
      obs_nd, tmp, node) {
          LOG_INF("      - %s", obs_nd->obs->name);
      }
      return true;
}
static bool print_observer_data_iterator(const struct zbus_
observer *obs, void *user_data) {
      int *count = user_data;
      LOG_INF("%d - %s %s", *count, obs->queue ? "Subscriber" :
      "Listener", \ zbus_obs_name(obs));
```

CHAPTER 11   UNDERSTANDING AND USING THE ZEPHYR ZBUS IN APPLICATION DEVELOPMENT

```
      ++(*count);
      return true;
}
int main(void) {
      int count = 0;
      LOG_INF("Channel list:");
      zbus_iterate_over_channels_with_user_data(print_channel_
      data_iterator, &count);
      count = 0;
      LOG_INF("Observers list:");
      zbus_iterate_over_observers_with_user_data(print_
      observer_data_iterator, &count);
      return 0;
}
```

Running the preceding code will produce output such as the following:

```
D: Channel list:
D: 0 - Channel acc_chan:
D:        Message size: 12
D:        Observers:
D:         - my_listener
D:         - my_subscriber
D: 1 - Channel version_chan:
D:        Message size: 4
D:        Observers:
D: Observers list:
D: 0 - Listener my_listener
D: 1 - Subscriber my_subscriber
```

549

CHAPTER 11   UNDERSTANDING AND USING THE ZEPHYR ZBUS IN APPLICATION DEVELOPMENT

Overview of the Virtual Distributed Event Dispatcher (VDED)

The virtual distributed event dispatcher (VDED) implements the bus logic responsible for sending notifications/messages to the observers. The VDED logic runs inside the publishing action in the same thread context as the publishing action. Because it might block, a VDED cannot run inside an interrupt service routine (ISR), and consequently, ISRs should only access channels indirectly, using some kind of deferred processing mechanism such as a workqueue.

The sequence of VDED steps involved in dispatching an event conforms to the following pattern:

- Acquire the channel mutex.

- Receive the new message to be dispatched into the channel via a direct raw memcpy().

- Execute the listener callback methods.

- Send a copy of the message to each of the message subscribers, and push the channel's reference to the notification message queue of each subscriber in the same sequence they appear on the channel observers' list.

- The listeners can perform a non-copy quick access to the constant message reference directly, using the zbus_chan_const_msg() function, as the channel is still locked.

- Finally, the publishing function unlocks the channel.

Walkthrough of a VDED Execution Scenario

The following example, from the Zephyr documentation, illustrates a basic VDED execution scenario. Implementing all the low-level code for even such a relatively simple scenario would involve a considerable amount of effort and code testing. It is worth noting that the Zephyr RTOS code undergoes quite rigorous testing before being published.

Consider a scenario consisting of four threads in ascending priority, S1, MS2, MS1, and T1 (the highest priority); two listeners, L1 and L2; and a single channel, A. In this scenario, L1, L2, MS1, MS2, and S1 observe channel A. The priority ordering is T1 > MS1 > MS2 > S1, with T1 having the highest priority.

Figure 11-4 shows the aforementioned state of affairs.

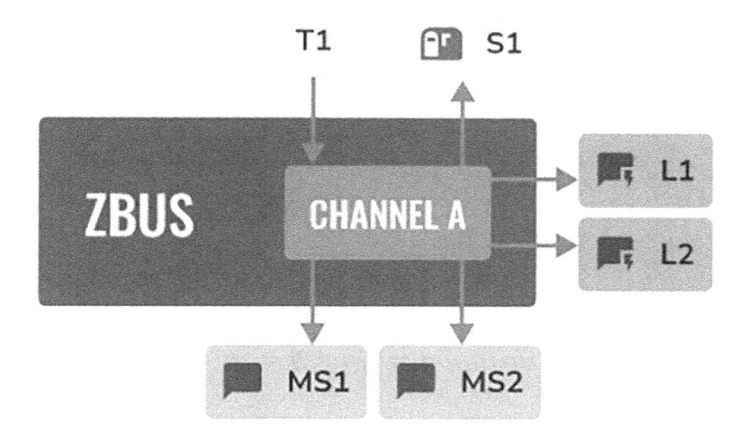

Figure 11-4. Example virtual distributed event dispatcher (VDED) scenario

CHAPTER 11   UNDERSTANDING AND USING THE ZEPHYR ZBUS IN APPLICATION DEVELOPMENT

Suppose that channel A is defined (for illustrative purposes) as follows:

```
ZBUS_CHAN_DEFINE(a_chan,                    /* Name */
    struct a_msg,                           /* Message type */
    NULL,                                   /* Validator */
    NULL,                                   /* User Data */
    ZBUS_OBSERVERS(L1, L2, MS1, MS2, S1),   /* observers */
    ZBUS_MSG_INIT(0)                        /* Initial value {0} */
);
```

Figure 11-5 illustrates VDED execution for this particular scenario.

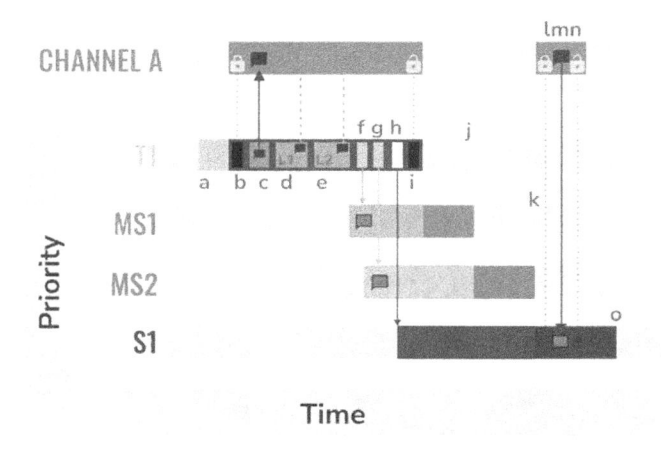

Figure 11-5. Example virtual distributed event dispatcher (VDED) scenario timing

The steps (actions) involved are as follows:

- a – T1 starts and, at some point, publishes to channel A.
- b – The publishing (VDED) process starts.
  - The VDED locks channel A's mutex.

552

- c – The VDED copies the T1 message to the channel A message.
- d, e – The VDED executes L1 and L2 in sequence.
  - Inside the listeners, there is, typically, a call to the `zbus_chan_const_msg()` function, which accesses channel A's message directly without the need to copy it.
- f, g – The VDED copies the message and sends it to MS1 and MS2 sequentially.
  - These threads become ready to execute immediately after receiving the notification.
  - However, they enter a pending state because they have a lower priority than T1.
- h – The VDED pushes the notification message to the queue of S1.
  - The thread becomes ready to execute immediately after receiving the notification.
  - However, it enters a pending state as it cannot access the channel, which, at this stage, is still locked.
- i – The VDED finishes the publishing operation by unlocking channel A.
  - MS1 leaves the pending state and starts executing.
- j – MS1 finishes execution.
  - MS2 leaves the pending state and starts executing.
- k – MS2 finishes execution.
  - S1 leaves the pending state and starts executing.

CHAPTER 11   UNDERSTANDING AND USING THE ZEPHYR ZBUS IN APPLICATION DEVELOPMENT

- l, m, n – S1 leaves the pending state since channel A is no longer locked.
  - S1 starts executing.
  - Because S1 received a notification from channel A, it performs a channel read (using a lock, memory copy, unlock sequence) and then continues execution.
- o – S1 completes its workload.

In the following VDED execution scenario, the priority ordering is, now, T1 < MS1 < MS2 < S1.

Figure 11-6 illustrates this scenario, and the sequence of steps involved is given after that.

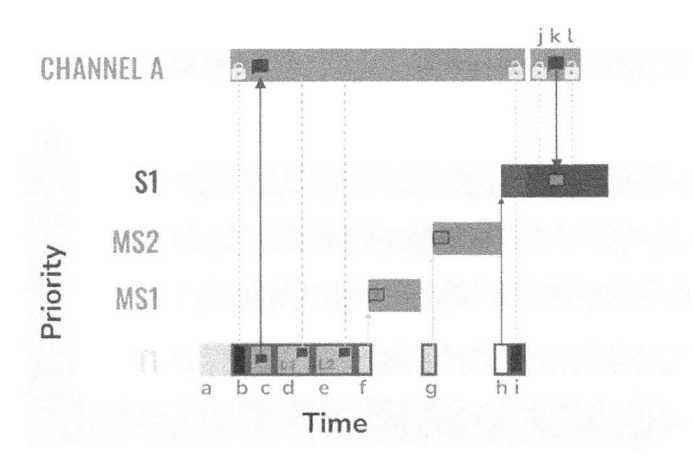

Figure 11-6. *Example virtual distributed event dispatcher (VDED) scenario timing after priorities have been altered*

554

CHAPTER 11   UNDERSTANDING AND USING THE ZEPHYR ZBUS IN APPLICATION DEVELOPMENT

- a – T1 starts and, at some point, publishes to channel A.
- b – The publishing (VDED) process starts, and VDED locks channel A's mutex.
- c – The VDED copies the T1 message to the channel A message element.
- d, e – The VDED executes the listeners L1 and L2 in that order.
  - Typically, listeners call zbus_chan_const_msg() to access the message directly without having to copy it.
- f – The VDED copies the message and sends that to MS1.
  - MS1 preempts T1 and starts working.
  - When MS1 has completed, T1 can continue executing.
- g – The VDED copies the message and sends it to MS2.
  - MS2 preempts T1 and starts working.
  - After T1 can execute.
- h – The VDED pushes the notification message to the queue of S1.
  - That thread becomes ready to execute on receiving the notification but enters the pending state because the channel, at this stage, is till locked.
  - At this point, the priority of the T1 thread is elevated (priority inheritance mechanism of the mutex) to the highest pending thread (the one blocked by the unavailability of channel A). In this case, it is the priority of S1.

555

- This should make it possible that T1 will finish the VDED execution in a timely manner without preemption from threads with priorities below those of the engaged threads.
- i – The VDED finishes the publishing by unlocking channel A.
- j, k, l – The S1 leaves the pending state since channel A is not locked.
- S1 can now run and start executing.
  - Because it received a notification from channel A, it will perform a channel read (using a lock, memory copy, unlock sequence) and continue execution to complete the work at hand.

Walking Through Some Selected Zephyr ZBus Examples

The Zephyr repository contains several examples demonstrating various ways of using the ZBus in Zephyr RTOS applications. In the documentation, the description of these examples involves running the code in the QEMU emulator. They can also be run using Renode and on various target boards.

In this section, the Zephyr repository ZBus examples explored were run on the nRF52840 DK board.

The final section explores a prototype controller application involving a sensor, an actuator, and a Wi-Fi network controller. It uses the nRF70002 DK and shows how some of the examples in the Zephyr Wi-Fi chapter might be extended or refactored to make use of the ZBus framework.

CHAPTER 11   UNDERSTANDING AND USING THE ZEPHYR ZBUS IN APPLICATION DEVELOPMENT

Zephyr ZBus Hello World

This example can be found at samples/subsys/zbus/hello_world.

It involves setting up several threads and setting up communications between them by means of ZBus channels. The importance of this example is that it covers most of the ZBus API functionality and can be readily adapted and modified for real-world applications.

The prj.conf file shows the configuration required for a typical ZBus application. These are

```
CONFIG_LOG=y
CONFIG_LOG_MODE_MINIMAL=y
CONFIG_BOOT_BANNER=n
CONFIG_MAIN_THREAD_PRIORITY=5
CONFIG_ZBUS=y
CONFIG_ZBUS_LOG_LEVEL_INF=y
CONFIG_ZBUS_CHANNEL_NAME=y
CONFIG_ZBUS_OBSERVER_NAME=y
CONFIG_ZBUS_RUNTIME_OBSERVERS=y
```

The CMakeLists.txt file is fairly simple:

```
# SPDX-License-Identifier: Apache-2.0
cmake_minimum_required(VERSION 3.20.0)
find_package(Zephyr REQUIRED HINTS $ENV{ZEPHYR_BASE})
project(hello_world)
FILE(GLOB app_sources src/*.c)
target_sources(app PRIVATE ${app_sources})
```

The application involves two kinds of messages whose structures are shown in the following code snippet, which also shows the header files that need to be included and the declaration of the logging module.

CHAPTER 11   UNDERSTANDING AND USING THE ZEPHYR ZBUS IN APPLICATION DEVELOPMENT

```
#include <stdint.h>
#include <zephyr/kernel.h>
#include <zephyr/logging/log.h>
#include <zephyr/zbus/zbus.h>
LOG_MODULE_DECLARE(zbus, CONFIG_ZBUS_LOG_LEVEL);
struct version_msg {
      uint8_t major;
      uint8_t minor;
      uint16_t build;
};
struct acc_msg {
      int x;
      int y;
      int z;
};
```

One of the message types provides version and build information; the other message provides accelerometer sensor reading information.

The three channels involved in this example are `version_chan` for use with version information, `acc_data_chan` for use with accelerometer sensor reading information, and `simple_chan`, which is a hard channel because it has a validator. The data type for `simple_chan` is int.

These are defined as shown in the next code snippet:

```
ZBUS_CHAN_DEFINE(version_chan,         /* Name */
         struct version_msg, /* Message type */
         NULL,                           /* Validator */
         NULL,                           /* User data */
         ZBUS_OBSERVERS_EMPTY, /* observers */
         ZBUS_MSG_INIT(.major = 0, .minor = 1,
                     .build = 2) /* Initial value major 0,
                                 minor 1, build 2 */
);
```

CHAPTER 11   UNDERSTANDING AND USING THE ZEPHYR ZBUS IN APPLICATION DEVELOPMENT

```
ZBUS_CHAN_DEFINE(acc_data_chan,  /* Name */
         struct acc_msg, /* Message type */
         NULL,              /* Validator */
         NULL,              /* User data */
         ZBUS_OBSERVERS(foo_lis, bar_sub),    /* observers */
         ZBUS_MSG_INIT(.x = 0, .y = 0, .z = 0) /* Initial
                                                  value */
);
ZBUS_CHAN_DEFINE(simple_chan, /* Name */
         int,        /* Message type */
         simple_chan_validator, /* Validator */
         NULL,       /* User data */
         ZBUS_OBSERVERS_EMPTY,  /* observers */
         0           /* Initial value is 0 */
);
```

In this example, version_chan and simple_chan have no observers, and acc_data_chan has two observers named foo_lis, a listener, and bar_sub, a subscriber.

The validator for simple_chan is very simple as its purpose is to demonstrate how to set up and use a validator. Here is the code for it:

```
static bool simple_chan_validator(const void *msg, size_t msg_size) {
    ARG_UNUSED (msg_size);
    const int *simple = msg;
    if ((*simple >= 0) && (*simple < 10)) {
          return true;
    }
    return false;
}
```

Note the presence of the ARG_UNUSED macro to suppress compiler warnings.

The listener callback function simply extracts some message data and logs it, as the next code snippet shows:

```
static void listener_callback_example(const struct zbus_channel *chan) {
      const struct acc_msg *acc = zbus_chan_const_msg(chan);
      LOG_INF("From listener -> Acc x=%d, y=%d, z=%d", acc->x, acc->y, acc->z);
}
```

foo_lis and bar_sub are defined as shown here:

```
ZBUS_LISTENER_DEFINE (foo_lis, listener_callback_example);
ZBUS_SUBSCRIBER_DEFINE (bar_sub, 4);
```

A subscriber task and a thread running this task can be set up as shown in this example code snippet:

```
static void subscriber_task(void) {
    const struct zbus_channel *chan;
    while (!zbus_sub_wait(&bar_sub, &chan, K_FOREVER)) {
        struct acc_msg acc;
        if (&acc_data_chan == chan) {
            zbus_chan_read(&acc_data_chan, &acc, K_MSEC(500));
            LOG_INF("From subscriber -> Acc x=%d, y=%d, z=%d",
            acc.x, acc.y, acc.z);
        }
    }
}

K_THREAD_DEFINE (subscriber_task_id, CONFIG_MAIN_STACK_SIZE,
\         subscriber_task, NULL, NULL, NULL, 3, 0, 0);
```

CHAPTER 11   UNDERSTANDING AND USING THE ZEPHYR ZBUS IN APPLICATION DEVELOPMENT

The subscriber runs an infinite loop involving making a blocking zbus_sub_wait call on each iteration of the loop and only exiting the loop when zbus_sub_wait returns with an error code. In the body of the loop, the message data is retrieved by calling zbus_chan_read to obtain the data and then processing the data and acting on it as required by the application. In this example, the extracted data is simply output to a logger.

The thread itself is defined using the K_THREAD_DEFINE macro.

The example includes a couple of iterator functions: a channel iterator and a data iterator.

This is the code for the print_channel_data_iterator() function:

```
static bool print_channel_data_iterator(const struct zbus_
channel *chan, void *user_data) {
    int *count = user_data;
    LOG_INF("%d - Channel %s:", *count, zbus_chan_name(chan));
    LOG_INF("      Message size: %d", zbus_chan_msg_
                size(chan));
    LOG_INF("      Observers:");
    ++(*count);
    struct zbus_channel_observation *observation;
    for (int16_t i = chan->data->observers_start_idx,
         limit = chan->data->observers_end_idx;
         i < limit; ++i) {
            STRUCT_SECTION_GET (zbus_channel_observation, i,
            &observation);
            __ASSERT(observation != NULL, "observation must be
            not NULL");
            LOG_INF("      - %s", observation->obs->name);
    }
    struct zbus_observer_node *obs_nd, *tmp;
    SYS_SLIST_FOR_EACH_CONTAINER_SAFE (&chan->data-
    >observers, \
```

```
        obs_nd,tmp, node) {
            LOG_INF("        - %s", obs_nd->obs->name);
        }
        return true;
}
```

This function prints out information about a channel starting with its name and the message size, by the string "Observers:", followed by the count value, which is post incremented, and then the observers observing on that channel. The for loop performs an array traversal. The SYS_SLIST_FOR_EACH_CONTAINER_SAFE is used for ZBus observers.

The observer data iterator function is shown next:

```
static bool print_observer_data_iterator(const struct zbus_
observer *obs, void *user_data) {
    int *count = user_data;
    LOG_INF("%d - %s %s", *count,
        obs->type == ZBUS_OBSERVER_LISTENER_TYPE ? "Listener" :
        "Subscriber",
        zbus_obs_name(obs));
    ++(*count);
    return true;
}
```

This counts the number of observers and also prints out information about the type of observer (listener or subscriber) and the observer name.

The application's main() function code is as follows:

```
int main(void) {
    int err, value;
    struct acc_msg acc1 = {.x = 1, .y = 1, .z = 1};
    const struct version_msg *v = zbus_chan_const_msg
    (&version_chan);
```

CHAPTER 11   UNDERSTANDING AND USING THE ZEPHYR ZBUS IN APPLICATION DEVELOPMENT

```c
    LOG_INF("Sensor sample started raw reading, version %u.%u-%u!", v->major, v->minor, v->build);

    int count = 0;
    LOG_INF("Channel list:");
    zbus_iterate_over_channels_with_user_data (print_channel_data_iterator, &count);

    count = 0;
    LOG_INF("Observers list:");
    zbus_iterate_over_observers_with_user_data(print_observer_data_iterator, &count);
    zbus_chan_pub(&acc_data_chan, &acc1, K_SECONDS(1));
    k_msleep(1000);
    acc1.x = 2;
    acc1.y = 2;
    acc1.z = 2;
    zbus_chan_pub(&acc_data_chan, &(acc1), K_SECONDS(1));
    value = 5;
    err = zbus_chan_pub(&simple_chan, &value, K_MSEC(200));
    if (err == 0) {
        LOG_INF("Pub a valid value to a channel with validator successfully.");
    }
    value = 15;
    err = zbus_chan_pub(&simple_chan, &value, K_MSEC(200));
    if (err == -ENOMSG) {
        LOG_INF("Pub an invalid value to a channel validator successfully.");
    }
    return 0;
}
```

CHAPTER 11   UNDERSTANDING AND USING THE ZEPHYR ZBUS IN APPLICATION DEVELOPMENT

The application initializes a struct acc_msg variable acc1.

It also initializes a constant pointer to the version information in the version channel:

```
const struct version_msg *v = zbus_chan_const_msg
(&version_chan);
```

and writes the details out to the logger:

```
LOG_INF("Sensor sample started raw reading, version %u.%u-%u!",
        v->major, v->minor, v->build);
```

Information about the channels and observers is provided by using the corresponding iterators print_channel_data_iterator and print_observer_data_iterator, respectively.

Two sets of (dummy) accelerometer readings are then published to the accelerometer channel acc_data_chan.

The correctness of the validator method on the simple_chan channel is then checked by attempting to publish a valid integer value and then an invalid integer value.

The output sent using LOG_INF to a serial terminal is as follows:

I: SI: Sensor sample started raw reading, version 0.1-2!

```
I: Channel list:
I: 0 - Channel acc_data_chan:
I:         Message size: 12
I:         Observers:
I:         - foo_lis
I:         - bar_sub
I: 1 - Channel simple_chan:
I:         Message size: 4
I:         Observers:
I: 2 - Channel version_chan:
I:         Message size: 4
```

```
I:         Observers:
I: Observers list:
I: 0 - Subscriber bar_sub
I: 1 - Listener foo_lis
I: From listener -> Acc x=1, y=1, z=1
I: From subscriber -> Acc x=1, y=1, z=1
I: From listener -> Acc x=2, y=2, z=2
I: From subscriber -> Acc x=2, y=2, z=2
I: Pub a valid value to a channel with validator successfully.
I: Pub an invalid value to a channel with validator successfully.
```

Zephyr Bus Workqueue Example

Since ZBus operations cannot be used directly in an interrupt service routine (ISR), an ISR must use some second-stage deferred processing to publish information over the ZBus. One way of doing this effectively is to delegate this work to a workqueue, and the workqueue sample demonstrates the way to do this.

The example can be found in the Zephyr or Nordic repositories at zephyr/samples/subsys/zbus/work_queue.

In addition to showing scheduling ZBus work by pushing it to the system workqueue, this sample also demonstrates using a listener callback for reacting rapidly to ZBus events and the use of a subscriber thread for retrieving messages posted on the ZBus.

The message structures in this example (defined in message.h) are shown here:

```
struct version_msg {
    uint8_t major;
    uint8_t minor;
    uint16_t build;
};
```

CHAPTER 11   UNDERSTANDING AND USING THE ZEPHYR ZBUS IN APPLICATION DEVELOPMENT

```
struct sensor_msg {
      uint32_t temp;
      uint32_t press;
      uint32_t humidity;
};
```

One structure is for publishing version information messages, and the other is for publishing sensor reading messages.

Sensor readings are simulated in a peripheral thread, the thread function code for which is given in sensors.c and is created at compile time using K_THREAD_DEFINE.

```
// sensors.c
#include <zephyr/logging/log.h>
#include <zephyr/zbus/zbus.h>
LOG_MODULE_DECLARE(zbus, CONFIG_ZBUS_LOG_LEVEL);
ZBUS_CHAN_DECLARE(sensor_data_chan);
void peripheral_thread (void) {
      struct sensor_msg sm = {0};
      while (1) {
            LOG_DBG("Sending sensor data...");
            sm.press += 1;
            sm.temp += 10;
            sm.humidity += 100;
            zbus_chan_pub(&sensor_data_chan, &sm, K_MSEC(250));
            k_msleep(500);
      }
}
K_THREAD_DEFINE (peripheral_thread_id, 1024, peripheral_thread,
NULL, NULL, NULL, 5, 0, 0);
```

In this example, the simulated pressure, temperature, and humidity sensor readings are published every 500 msecs.

CHAPTER 11   UNDERSTANDING AND USING THE ZEPHYR ZBUS IN APPLICATION DEVELOPMENT

The example uses two ZBus channels: version_chan and sensor_data_chan, defined as shown in the next code snippet:

```
#include <stdint.h>
#include <zephyr/kernel.h>
#include <zephyr/logging/log.h>
#include <zephyr/sys/util_macro.h>
#include <zephyr/zbus/zbus.h>
LOG_MODULE_DECLARE(zbus, CONFIG_ZBUS_LOG_LEVEL);

ZBUS_CHAN_DEFINE (version_chan,         /* Name */
    struct version_msg, /* Message type */
    NULL,               /* Validator */
    NULL,               /* User data */
    ZBUS_OBSERVERS_EMPTY, /* observers */
     ZBUS_MSG_INIT(.major = 0, .minor = 1,
                    .build = 1023) /* Initial value major 0,
                    minor 1, build 1023 */
);

ZBUS_CHAN_DEFINE(sensor_data_chan,   /* Name */
    struct sensor_msg, /* Message type */
    NULL, /* Validator */
    NULL, /* User data */
    ZBUS_OBSERVERS(fast_handler1_lis, fast_handler2_lis, fast_
    handler3_lis,
                delay_handler1_lis, delay_handler2_lis, delay_
                handler3_lis,
                thread_handler1_sub, thread_handler2_sub,
                thread_handler3_sub), /* observers */
    ZBUS_MSG_INIT(0)            /* Initial value {0} */
);
```

567

CHAPTER 11   UNDERSTANDING AND USING THE ZEPHYR ZBUS IN APPLICATION DEVELOPMENT

The version data channel has no observers, and the sensor data channel has a variety of observers, both listeners and subscribers. The listener callbacks demonstrate various ways of handling messages, and the various subscribers show various ways of implementing subscriber behavior.

The callback code for the three fast handlers is essentially the same; all three print out logging information using LOG_INF.

The following code snippet is that for the fast_handler1_lis listener and also shows how that listener is defined:

```
static void fh1_cb(const struct zbus_channel *chan) {
    const struct sensor_msg *msg = zbus_chan_const_msg(chan);
    LOG_INF("Sensor msg processed by CALLBACK fh1: temp = %u,
    press = %u, humidity = %u", msg->temp, msg->press,
    msg->humidity);
}
ZBUS_LISTENER_DEFINE (fast_handler1_lis, fh1_cb) ;
```

The three "delay" handlers submit work to the system workqueue, and all run esentially the same code.

The following code snippet is that for the delay_handler1_lis listener and also shows how that listener is defined and how the workqueue and channel callbacks are set up:

```
struct sensor_wq_info {
    struct k_work work;
    const struct zbus_channel *chan;
    uint8_t handle;
};
static struct sensor_wq_info wq_handler1 = {.handle = 1};

static void wq_dh_cb(struct k_work *item) {
    struct sensor_msg msg;
```

568

```
    struct sensor_wq_info *sens = CONTAINER_OF (item, struct
    sensor_wq_info, work);
    zbus_chan_read(sens->chan, &msg, K_MSEC(200));
    LOG_INF("Sensor msg processed by WORK QUEUE handler dh%u:
    temp = %u,
        press = %u, humidity = %u",
        sens->handle, msg.temp, msg.press, msg.humidity);
}
static void dh1_cb (const struct zbus_channel *chan) {
    wq_handler1.chan = chan;
    k_work_submit(&wq_handler1.work);
}
ZBUS_LISTENER_DEFINE(delay_handler1_lis, dh1_cb);
```

The three subscriber observers and their associated threads are also essentially the same, and the following code snippet shows how one of these subscribers is set up:

```
ZBUS_SUBSCRIBER_DEFINE (thread_handler1_sub, 4);

static void thread_handler1_task(void) {
    const struct zbus_channel *chan;
    while (!zbus_sub_wait(&thread_handler1_sub, &chan,
    K_FOREVER)) {
        struct sensor_msg msg;
        zbus_chan_read(chan, &msg, K_MSEC(200));
        LOG_INF("Sensor msg processed by THREAD handler 1:
        temp = %u, "
            "press = %u, humidity = %u",
            msg.temp, msg.press, msg.humidity);
    }
}
```

CHAPTER 11   UNDERSTANDING AND USING THE ZEPHYR ZBUS IN APPLICATION DEVELOPMENT

```
K_THREAD_DEFINE (thread_handler1_id, 1024, thread_handler1_
task, NULL, NULL, NULL, 3, 0, 0);
```

The threads for each subscriber task are created at compile time using K_THREAD_DEFINE.

The code for main(), shown here, is fairly simple:

```
int main(void) {
    k_work_init(&wq_handler1.work, wq_dh_cb);
    k_work_init(&wq_handler2.work, wq_dh_cb);
    k_work_init(&wq_handler3.work, wq_dh_cb);
    struct version_msg *v = zbus_chan_msg(&version_chan);
    LOG_DBG("Sensor sample started, version %u.%u-%u!",
        v->major, v->minor, v->build);
    return 0;
}
```

It simply sets up the workqueue and then retrieves version information from the version channel and prints it out using LOG_DBG.

When this application is run, the output sent to the connected serial terminal will be something like the following:

```
*** Booting Zephyr OS build v3.3.99-ncs1-1 ***
I: Sensor msg processed by CALLBACK fh1: temp = 10, press = 1, humidity = 100
I: Sensor msg processed by CALLBACK fh2: temp = 10, press = 1, humidity = 100
I: Sensor msg processed by CALLBACK fh3: temp = 10, press = 1, humidity = 100
I: Sensor msg processed by WORK QUEUE handler dh1: temp = 10, press = 1, humidity = 100
I: Sensor msg processed by WORK QUEUE handler dh2: temp = 10, press = 1, humidity = 100
```

```
I: Sensor msg processed by WORK QUEUE handler dh3:
temp = 10, press = 1, humidity = 100
I: Sensor msg processed by THREAD handler 1: temp = 10,
press = 1, humidity = 100
I: Sensor msg processed by THREAD handler 2: temp = 10,
press = 1, humidity = 100
I: Sensor msg processed by THREAD handler 3: temp = 10,
press = 1, humidity = 100
I: Sensor msg processed by CALLBACK fh1: temp = 20, press = 2,
humidity = 200
I: Sensor msg processed by CALLBACK fh2: temp = 20, press = 2,
humidity = 200
I: Sensor msg processed by CALLBACK fh3: temp = 20, press = 2,
humidity = 200
I: Sensor msg processed by WORK QUEUE handler dh1: temp = 20,
press = 2, humidity = 200
I: Sensor msg processed by WORK QUEUE handler dh2: temp = 20,
press = 2, humidity = 200
I: Sensor msg processed by WORK QUEUE handler dh3: temp = 20,
press = 2, humidity = 200
I: Sensor msg processed by THREAD handler 1: temp = 20,
press = 2, humidity = 200
I: Sensor msg processed by THREAD handler 2: temp = 20,
press = 2, humidity = 200
I: Sensor msg processed by THREAD handler 3: temp = 20,
press = 2, humidity = 200
I: Sensor msg processed by CALLBACK fh1: temp = 30, press = 3,
humidity = 300
I: Sensor msg processed by CALLBACK fh2: temp = 30, press = 3,
humidity = 300
I: Sensor msg processed by CALLBACK fh3: temp = 30, press = 3,
humidity = 300
```

```
I: Sensor msg processed by WORK QUEUE handler dh1: temp = 30,
press = 3, humidity = 300
I: Sensor msg processed by WORK QUEUE handler dh2: temp = 30,
press = 3, humidity = 300
I: Sensor msg processed by WORK QUEUE handler dh3: temp = 30,
press = 3, humidity = 300
I: Sensor msg processed by THREAD handler 1: temp = 30,
press = 3, humidity = 300
I: Sensor msg processed by THREAD handler 2: temp = 30,
press = 3, humidity = 300
I: Sensor msg processed by THREAD handler 3: temp = 30,
press = 3, humidity = 300
I: Sensor msg processed by CALLBACK fh1: temp = 40, press = 4,
humidity = 400
I: Sensor msg processed by CALLBACK fh2: temp = 40, press = 4,
humidity = 400
I: Sensor msg processed by CALLBACK fh3: temp = 40, press = 4,
humidity = 400
I: Sensor msg processed by WORK QUEUE handler dh1: temp = 40,
press = 4, humidity = 400
I: Sensor msg processed by WORK QUEUE handler dh2: temp = 40,
press = 4, humidity = 400
I: Sensor msg processed by WORK QUEUE handler dh3: temp = 40,
press = 4, humidity = 400
```

CHAPTER 12

Zephyr RTOS Wi-Fi Applications

Wi-Fi is the brand name for a wireless networking technology that can be used by devices such as computers (laptops and desktops), mobile devices (smartphones and wearables), and other equipment such as printers, video cameras, and Wi-Fi-enabled sensors to interface with the Internet and exchange information with one another.

The standards underlying Wi-Fi belong to the IEEE 802.11 family of standards. The device that provides wireless connectivity to the Internet is commonly referred to as an access point. A Wi-Fi router is an access point that is also a router.

Wireless LAN protocols work at the physical and link layers of the ISO-OSI 7 layer model.

The 802.11 data link layer is made up of two sublayers: a Logical Link Control (LLC) layer and a Media Access Control (MAC) layer. 802.11 uses the same 802.2 LLC and 48-bit addressing as other 802 LANs. The MAC protocol details of a wireless LAN are not the same as those for a wired LAN. For 802.3 Ethernet LANs, the Carrier Sense Multiple Access with Collision Detection (CSMA/CD) protocol controls how Ethernet stations establish access to the wire and how they detect and handle collisions that occur when two or more devices try to simultaneously communicate over the LAN.

The problems (scenarios) that result in the Wi-Fi MAC protocol being the way it is include the following [1]:

- The "near/far" problem
    - For a station (network interface) to detect a collision, it has to be able to transmit and listen at the same time. However, in an 802.11 WLAN, transmission will drown out the ability of the station to detect a collision.
- The "hidden node" issue
    - This arises where two stations on opposite sides of an access point may both hear activity from that access point, but not from each other. This may be due to distance effects, or the presence of some obstruction.
- The need for power efficiency that arises when using Wi-Fi in battery-powered devices, in which battery life considerations are important

Approaches to Tackling the Various Wi-Fi MAC Problems

The 802.11 CSMA/CA (Carrier Sense Multiple Access with Collision Avoidance) protocol, or the Distributed Coordination Function (DCF), was designed to handle the "near/far" problem. In this protocol, a station wishing to transmit listens for wireless transmission activity; if no activity is detected, it waits for an additional, randomly selected period of time and then transmits if the medium is still free. This strategy will tend to reduce the probability that two or more stations will begin transmitting at the same time and will tend to ensure a degree of fairness.

Because CSMA/CA cannot guarantee that a collision will not occur, 802.11 uses an explicit acknowledgment (ACK) scheme, which involves the receiving station sending an ACK packet to confirm that the data packet arrived intact. If the sending station does not detect an ACK frame, it assumes that the packet was not received and retransmits it after waiting for a random period of time. This acknowledgment mechanism imposes an overhead, which means that an 802.11 LAN will have a lower performance than an equivalent Ethernet LAN.

The 802.11 RTS/CTS protocol represents an attempt to address the "hidden node" issue. When RTS/CTS is being used, a sending station transmits an RTS and waits for the access point to reply with a CTS. As all stations in the network can hear the access point, the CTS will cause them to delay any intended transmissions, thus giving the sending station the opportunity to transmit and receive a packet acknowledgment without a collision occurring. Because RTS/CTS adds a further processing overhead to the network by temporarily reserving the medium, it is typically only used when sending large packets, the retransmission of which would be costly.

Security Issues

IEEE 802.11 involves authentication and encryption. Authentication proves that a particular station is the one it claims to be and, therefore, is authorized to communicate with a second station in a given coverage area. In the infrastructure mode, authentication is established between an AP (access point) and each station.

802.11 specifies two methods of authentication: open system or shared key.

An open system allows any client to authenticate as long as it conforms to any MAC address filter policies that may have been set. All authentication packets are transmitted without encryption.

Various shared key authentication schemes have been developed as the Wi-Fi standards have evolved. The sequence of authentication schemes from least secure to most secure is WEP, WPA, WPA2, and then WPA3 [2].

The newer protocols were developed as weaknesses were discovered in the earlier protocols. Wired Equivalent Privacy (WEP) was shown to have many flaws and should no longer be used. There are readily available tools that can be used to break WEP encryption. For this reason, the Wi-Fi Alliance officially retired the WEP Wi-Fi encryption standard in 2004.

WPA launched in 2003 served as a stepping stone to WPA2, which was launched in 2004.

WPA3, developed in light of vulnerabilities discovered in WPA2, was released in 2018.

The features added in WPA3 include

- Brute-force protection by protecting from brute-force dictionary attacks
- Public network privacy
- Security support for the Internet of Things (IoT)
- Stronger encryption by supporting 192-bit encryption

Modern WPA3 routers support WPA2/WPA3 Transitional mode because not all devices connecting to the access point will support WPA2, a special mixed mode that uses WPA3-Personal (more on this in the following) and WPA2-Personal, allowing older devices without WPA3 support to connect to the router.

WPA2 is vulnerable to the Key Reinstallation Attack (KRACK), which can be used by a hacker to intercept and manipulate the creation of new encryption keys within the secure connection process. However, it is a relatively sophisticated attack, and so WPA2 can provide a useful level of security where WPA3 is not possible.

WPA3 requires all connections to use Protected Management Frames (PMF), which provide additional security. WPA3 can use 128-bit AES, but for WPA3-Enterprise connections, 192-bit AES is required.

There are three versions of WPA3:

- WPA3-Personal
- WPA3-Enterprise
- Wi-Fi Enhanced Open

Wi-Fi Enhanced Open was designed to provide Wi-Fi encryption to users on "open" networks. A wireless router encrypts network traffic using a key. In the case of WPA-Personal, this key is calculated from the Wi-Fi passphrase set up on the router. For security reasons, it is important to use strong passphrases that are difficult to guess.

WPA3 SAE Key Exchange Protocol

SAE (Simultaneous Authentication of Equals) is a key exchange protocol that eliminates the reuse of encryption keys and also provides "forward secrecy." Forward secrecy prevents an attacker from decrypting a previously recorded Internet connection, even if they know the WPA3 password. SAE also uses peer-to-peer connection to establish the exchange, which can protect against man-in-the-middle key interception attacks.

How Wi-Fi Uses the Radio Spectrum Allocated to It

Wi-Fi can use the 2.4 GHz ISM (Industrial Scientific Medical) band and the 5 GHz band. The 2.4 GHz band is very congested because it is relatively narrow and is also used by other protocols such as BLE and Zigbee. By contrast, the 5 GHz band is far less congested. Although in theory Wi-Fi should move over entirely to using the 5 GHz spectrum, in practice, this is unlikely to happen any time soon because there are so many Wi-Fi devices out there that work at 2.4 GHz.

Wi-Fi has been evolving continually in a never ceasing effort to provide faster data rates, better security, and lower power consumption. The standards have both IEEE names and Wi-Fi Alliance names. For example, 802.11ac is also referred to as Wi-Fi 5.

The evolution of Wi-Fi is summarized in the next several bullet points [3]:

- IEEE 802.11 is the original 2.4 GHz Wi-Fi standard, introduced in 1997, which kicked off the development of Wi-Fi, one of the most widely used wireless computer networking protocols.

- IEEE 802.11b, or Wi-Fi 1, was introduced in 1999 and used a direct-sequence spread spectrum/ complementary code keying (DSSS/CCK) so as to cope with interference from other devices such as microwave ovens, cordless phones, and baby monitors, for example. It had an indoor range of around ~38 m and an outdoor range of ~140 m.

- IEEE 802.11a, or Wi-Fi 2, was introduced in 1999 as the successor to IEEE 802.11b. It used OFDM (Orthogonal Frequency Division Multiplexing) modulation to provide higher data rates and also supported 5 GHz operation.

- IEEE 802.11g, or Wi-Fi 3, was introduced in 2003 and provided faster data rates of up to 54 Mbit/s in the same 2.4 GHz frequency band as IEEE 802.11b, using various enhancements of OFDM. It was popular in the mass market for such devices because 2.4 GHz devices were less expensive than 5 GHz devices.

- IEEE 802.11n, or Wi-Fi 4, was introduced in 2009 as a standard that supported both the 2.4 GHz and 5 GHz frequency bands, with data rates up to 600 Mbit/s. IEEE 802.11n data throughputs led to the development and deployment of WLAN networks in place of wired networks.

- IEEE 802.11ac, or Wi-Fi 5, was introduced in 2013 to support data rates of up to 3.5 Gbit/s, providing greater bandwidth, additional channels, and improved modulation. It was the first Wi-Fi standard to enable the use of multiple input/multiple output (MIMO) technology.

- IEEE 802.11ax, or Wi-Fi 6, was published in 2021. It supports a theoretical data rate of up to 9.6 Gbit/s; however, the underlying design was to address the fact that the very pervasive use of Wi-Fi usage may cause performance degradation in areas of dense Wi-Fi traffic, such as sports stadiums, concert halls, and public transportation hubs, and in office and home environments where routers have to communicate simultaneously with a large number of digital gadgets.

Wi-Fi Frames and the 802.11 Packet Structure – An Overview

Wi-Fi frames are of three main types:
- Management frames
- Control frames
- Data frames

Management frames packets are used to discover APs (access points) and to join a BSS (Basic Service Set). They include frames such as Beacon, Probe Request and Response, Authentication and Deauthentication, Association, and Disassociation frames.

Control frame packets are used to acknowledge successful transmission and reserve the wireless medium. Control frame packets are used for the delivery of management and data information. Common control frame subtypes are ACK, request-to-send, and clear-to-send.

Data frame packets contain actual data and are the only packets that will be forwarded from the wireless network to the wired network. Data frame types include Data and null function packets.

The Wi-Fi layer header is more complex than the corresponding wired Ethernet layer header. It provides information such as channel, data rate, and signal strength.

- Channel (frequency) is necessary because a wireless LAN may support anywhere from 3 to 25 different channels.

- Data rate information about the data rates that are being used.

- Signal strength – Indicates the power level in dBm. It is a measure of the expected quality of the signal.

Access Points

An access point can be thought of as a bridge that bridges traffic between a client (mobile station) and other devices on an accessible network. Before a mobile station can send traffic through an AP, it must set up an association that puts it into an appropriate connection state [4].

Discovering an Access Point

Scanning for nearby access points can use either a passive or an active approach.

In an active approach, the seeking device tunes its radio to each supported channel in turn, transmits a Probe Request frame, and waits for about 20–40 ms to collect Probe Response frames from APs on that channel and then moves on to the next channel.

In a passive scan, the seeking device tunes to each channel in turn and waits for the duration of a typical Beacon Interval (about 100 ms) to collect Beacons. Passive scanning is slower than active scanning.

Authentication and Association

The three 802.11 connection states are as follows:

- Not authenticated or associated
- Authenticated but not yet associated
- Authenticated and associated

For bridging to take place, a mobile station must be in an authenticated and associated state. Authentication involves the mobile station and the AP exchanging a series of 802.11 management frames.

The sequence of exchanges is shown in the following schematic:

CHAPTER 12 ZEPHYR RTOS WI-FI APPLICATIONS

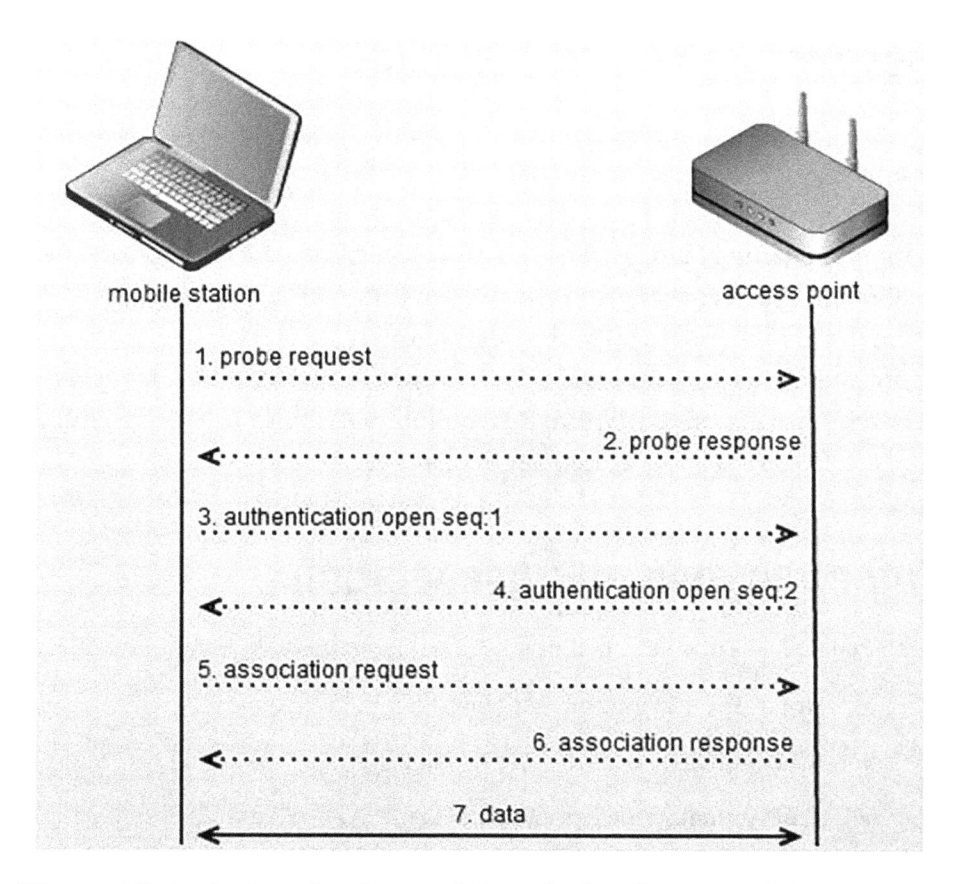

Figure 12-1. Authentication and Association Sequence Diagram

1. A mobile station sends probe requests to discover 802.11 networks within its vicinity. Probe requests advertise the mobile station's supported data rates and 802.11 capabilities such as 802.11ac. Because the probe request is sent from the mobile station to the destination layer 2 address with a BSSID (48-bit MAC address of an access point's radio card) of ff:ff:ff:ff:ff:ff, all APs that receive it will respond.

582

CHAPTER 12 ZEPHYR RTOS WI-FI APPLICATIONS

2. APs receiving the probe request check to see if the mobile station has at least one common supported data rate. If this is found to be the case, a probe response is sent advertising the SSID (wireless network name), supported data rates, encryption types if required, and also other 802.11 capabilities of the AP.

   A mobile station chooses compatible networks from the probe responses it receives. Compatibility may take encryption type into account. When a compatible to connect to has been discovered, the mobile station will attempt low-level 802.11 authentication with the compatible AP. Initial 802.11 authentication uses authentication frames that are open and should, almost, always succeed.

3. The mobile station sends a low-level 802.11 authentication frame to an AP, setting the authentication to open and the sequence to 0x0001.

4. The AP receives the authentication frame and responds to the mobile station with an authentication frame set to open indicating a sequence of 0x0002.

   If an AP receives any frame other than an authentication or probe request from a mobile station that is not authenticated, it will respond with a deauthentication frame placing the mobile into an unauthenticated and unassociated state. The station will have to begin the association process from the low-level authentication step again. At this point, the mobile station is authenticated but not yet associated.

583

Some 802.11 capabilities allow a mobile station to low-level authenticate to multiple APs, which can speed up the association process when moving between APs. Although a mobile station may be 802.11 authenticated to multiple APs, it can only be actively associated and transferring data through a single AP at a time.

5. Once a mobile station determines which AP it would like to associate to, it will send an association request to that AP. The association request contains chosen encryption types if required and other compatible 802.11 capabilities.

   Once an AP receives a frame from a mobile station that is authenticated but not yet associated, it responds with a disassociation frame placing the mobile into an authenticated but unassociated state.

6. If the elements in the association request match the capabilities of the AP, the AP will create an Association ID for the mobile station and respond with an association response success message granting network access to the mobile station.

7. Now the mobile station is successfully associated to the AP, and data transfer can begin.

Where WPA/WPA2/WPA3 or 802.1X authentication is required on the wireless network, the mobile station will not be able to send data until dynamic keying and authentication have taken place after the 802.11 Association is complete.

CHAPTER 12   ZEPHYR RTOS WI-FI APPLICATIONS

Zephyr RTOS and Wi-Fi Application Development

The Zephyr RTOS framework includes support for Wi-Fi, typically by supporting various shields and boards. Examples of Arduino-compatible shields include the Inventek es-WIFI Shield, the Adafruit WINC1500 WiFi Shield, and the MikroElektronika WIFI and BLE Shield, which is based on an ESP32 processor. Zephyr also supports various ESP32 boards having an ESP32 processor on-chip Wi-Fi, such as the Olimex ESP32 EVB.

As this book has used Nordic Semiconductor nRF boards extensively, the main board used in this chapter will be the nRF7002 DK, which incorporates Nordic's nRF7002 as a Wi-Fi 6 companion IC [8, 9]. The nRF7002 DK uses an nRF5340 multiprotocol System-on-Chip (SoC) as the host processor for the nRF7002. The nRF7002 Wi-Fi Companion IC is designed to be power efficient and supports 2.4 GHz and 5 GHz dual-band Wi-Fi, Wi-Fi 6 Station (STA), compliance with 802.11a/b/g/n/ac/ax as well as OFDMA (Orthogonal Frequency Division Multiple Access), both Downlink and Uplink, Wi-Fi BLE co-existence interfaces, Beamforming, and Target Wake Time. It also supports WPA3.

CHAPTER 12 ZEPHYR RTOS WI-FI APPLICATIONS

nRF7002 DK Board – An Overview

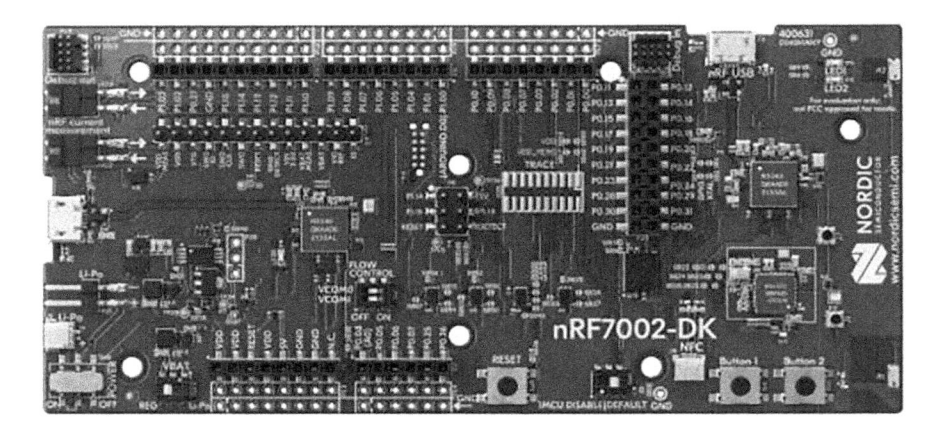

Figure 12-2. Top view of the nRF7002 DK board

Because the DK combines the Wi-Fi 6 capabilities of the nRF7002 companion Integrated Circuit (IC) with the nRF5340 System on Chip (SoC), it can also be used to build BLE as well as Wi-Fi applications.

The nRF7002 Wi-Fi companion IC provides the following:

- Dual-band 2.4 GHz and 5 GHz Wi-Fi 6

- Compatible with IEEE 802.11ax (known as Wi-Fi 6) and earlier standards IEEE 802.11a/b/g/n/ac.

- 20 MHz wide channels, 1x1 (SISO) operation, and up to 86 MHz 802.11 PHY rate

- Open source Wi-Fi driver – L2 Network Technologies layer compatible

- SPI or QSPI host interface, 3-wire or 4-wire coexistence interface

- Secure, 64-word One Time Programmable (OTP) memory with logical and voltage-level-based protection mechanisms

CHAPTER 12 ZEPHYR RTOS WI-FI APPLICATIONS

The capabilities provided by the nRF5340 SoC include the following:

- Bluetooth Low Energy
- Near Field Communication (NFC)
- Other wireless protocols
- Onboard 2.4 GHz and 2.4/5 GHz antennas
- NFC antenna
- 2 user-programmable LEDs and 2 buttons
- Segger J-link on-board programmer/debugger
- UART interface through a virtual serial port
- Pins for measuring power consumption
- 1.8 V power supply from Universal Serial Bus (USB) or external lithium-polymer (Li-Poly) battery
- 3.6 V power supply from USB or external Li-Poly battery to the VBAT of the nRF7002 companion IC

The nRF5340 SoC is a dual core ARM Cortex M33 processor and has support for ARM TrustZone security.

Wi-Fi Scanning Example Walkthrough Using the nRF7002 DK

This example is to be found in the nRF Connect SDK repository at nrf\samples\wifi\scan. It is an example application that shows how to implement an application that shows that the nRF7002 DK board can discover local Wi-Fi access points.

The sample code shows how to run Wi-Fi scan operations in the 2.4 GHz and 5 GHz bands. Scans can be performed on the basis of various profiles, namely:

CHAPTER 12 ZEPHYR RTOS WI-FI APPLICATIONS

- Default scan
- Active scan
- Passive scan
- 2.4 GHz Active scan
- 2.4 GHz Passive scan
- 5 GHz Active scan
- 5 GHz Passive scan
- Scan only non-overlapping channels in the 2.4 GHz band
- Scan only non-DFS (Dynamic Frequency Selection) channels in the 5 GHz band
- Scan only non-overlapping channels in the 2.4 GHz and non-DFS channels in the 5 GHz band

Understanding the code in this example requires a basic understanding of the Zephyr Network Management APIs, how to invoke them, and how to register application-specific callback functions.

Zephyr Network Management – An Overview

The purpose of the Zephyr Network Management APIs [5] is to make it possible for applications and network layer code to call specific defined routines as well as to receive notifications of network events of interest at any level in the network protocol stack. These APIs can, for example, be used to invoke scans on a Wi-Fi- or Bluetooth-based network interface, or to request notification if the IP address of a network interface changes.

Because Zephyr applications are monolithic and include the operating system itself, only those routines that are required are compiled into the application, and application-specific network management code is provided by defining and registering handlers using a NET_MGMT_REGISTER_REQUEST_HANDLER macro. Procedure requests are then invoked with a single net_mgmt() API that invokes the handler that has been registered for the corresponding request. Function prototypes and macros for collecting information concerning receive and transmit packets are defined in the net_private.h header file located in the zephyr/subsys/net/ip folder.

Requesting a Defined Network Management Procedure

A network management request takes the form net_mgmt(mgmt_request, ...).

The mgmt_request parameter is a bit mask that indicates the stack layer being targeted, if a net_if object is implied and a specific management procedure is being requested. The procedure requests that are available depend on the way the stack has been implemented.

Listening to Network Events

The procedure to follow to receive notifications on network events is to register a callback function and to specify a filter to select the events of interest for which the callback will be invoked.

CHAPTER 12 ZEPHYR RTOS WI-FI APPLICATIONS

A callback can be registered with a call to the `net_mgmt_add_event_callback()` function and unregistered with a call to the `net_mgmt_del_event_callback()` function. The net_mgmt_init_event_callback() function can be used to initialize the corresponding `struct net_mgmt_event_callback` data structure correctly.

When an event occurs that matches one in the event set associated with the callback, the callback function will be invoked with the actual event code. Because set filtering may pass through false positive events to the callback function, it is the responsibility of the callback function to check that the event code (passed as an argument) does correspond to one of the specific network events it will handle.

In order to receive events from multiple layers, multiple listeners need to be registered, one for each layer being listened on. With this proviso, a callback handler function can be shared between different layer events.

Defining Network Management Procedures

Management procedures specific to a custom stack implementation can be provided by defining a handler and registering it with an associated `mgmt_request` code.

Management request codes are defined in relevant places depending on the targeted layer or eventually, if L2 is the layer, on the technology also. For example, IP layer management request code is to be found in the `include/zephyr/net/net_event.h` header file. In the case of the L2 technology Ethernet, for example, these codes will be found in `include/zephyr/net/ethernet.h`.

Signalling Network Events

The occurrence of particular network events can be signalled by calling the `net_mgmt_event_notify()` function and providing the corresponding network event code as an argument.

Building the Wi-Fi Scan Example from the nRF Connect SDK Repository

The build target for the nRF7002 DK passed to West is the "nrf7002dk_nrf5340_cpuapp" build target. Various command-line options can be used to specify the type of scan application to be built.

- Build to fetch only Device scan results
  - west build -b nrf7002dk_nrf5340_cpuapp
- Build to fetch only Raw scan results
  - `west build -b nrf7002dk_nrf5340_cpuapp -- -DCONFIG_WIFI_MGMT_RAW_SCAN_RESULTS=y -DCONFIG_WIFI_MGMT_RAW_SCAN_RESULTS_ONLY=y`
- Build to fetch both Raw and Device scan results
  - `west build -b nrf7002dk_nrf5340_cpuapp -- -DCONFIG_WIFI_MGMT_RAW_SCAN_RESULTS=y`

CHAPTER 12 ZEPHYR RTOS WI-FI APPLICATIONS

Structured Overview of the Code of the Scan Example from the nRF Connect SDK Repository

The various aspects of the Wi-Fi protocol standards and how active and passive Wi-Fi scanning work and also the Zephyr Network Management APIs can be explored by studying the code for the scan application in the single function main.c.

As one would expect, there are various #includes and #defines at the start of this file and an invocation of LOG_MODULE_REGISTER so that the results of scanning can be output. Quite a few of the included header files are from the zephyr/net folder as one would expect. There is also a condition include for specifying WIFI_SHELL_MGMT_EVENTS based on the various defines passed into the build process.

```
#include <zephyr/logging/log.h>
LOG_MODULE_REGISTER(scan, CONFIG_LOG_DEFAULT_LEVEL);
#include <zephyr/kernel.h>
#if defined(CLOCK_FEATURE_HFCLK_DIVIDE_PRESENT) || NRF_CLOCK_HAS_HFCLK192M
#include <nrfx_clock.h>
#endif
#include <stdio.h>
#include <stdlib.h>
#include <zephyr/shell/shell.h>
#include <zephyr/sys/printk.h>
#include <zephyr/init.h>
#include <zephyr/net/net_if.h>
#include <zephyr/net/wifi_mgmt.h>
#include <zephyr/net/wifi_utils.h>
#include <zephyr/net/net_event.h>
#include <zephyr/net/ethernet.h>
```

```
#include <zephyr/net/ethernet_mgmt.h>
#include "net_private.h"
#define WIFI_SHELL_MODULE "wifi"
#ifdef CONFIG_WIFI_MGMT_RAW_SCAN_RESULTS_ONLY
#define WIFI_SHELL_MGMT_EVENTS (NET_EVENT_WIFI_RAW_SCAN_RESULT |    \
                    NET_EVENT_WIFI_SCAN_DONE)
#else
#define WIFI_SHELL_MGMT_EVENTS (NET_EVENT_WIFI_SCAN_RESULT |        \
                    NET_EVENT_WIFI_SCAN_DONE |         \
                    NET_EVENT_WIFI_RAW_SCAN_RESULT)
#endif
#define SCAN_TIMEOUT_MS 10000
```

The global variable test is an array of elements of type `const struct wifi_scan_params,` which is initialized appropriately based on the type of scan requested, as shown in the following code snippet:

```
const struct wifi_scan_params tests[] = {
#ifdef CONFIG_WIFI_SCAN_PROFILE_DEFAULT
    {
    },
#endif
#ifdef CONFIG_WIFI_SCAN_PROFILE_ACTIVE
    {
    .scan_type = WIFI_SCAN_TYPE_ACTIVE,
    .dwell_time_active = CONFIG_WIFI_MGMT_SCAN_DWELL_
    TIME_ACTIVE
    },
#endif
```

CHAPTER 12　ZEPHYR RTOS WI-FI APPLICATIONS

The callback structure details are held in the global variable wifi_shell_mgmt_cb defined as shown here:

```
static struct net_mgmt_event_callback wifi_shell_mgmt_cb;
```

This structure is defined in zephyr/include/zephyr/net/net_mgmt.h and is used internally by the network management code. Its components, some of which are unions, are as follows:

```
struct net_mgmt_event_callback {
    sys_snode_t node;
    union {
        net_mgmt_event_handler_t handler;
        struct k_sem *sync_call;
    };
#ifdef CONFIG_NET_MGMT_EVENT_INFO
    const void *info;
    size_t info_length;
#endif
    union {
        uint32_t event_mask;
        uint32_t raised_event;
    };
};
```

The purpose of sys_snode_t node is to allow the callback to be inserted into a list.

- net_mgmt_event_handler_t handler is the actual callback function being used to notify the owner.
- struct k_sem * sync_call is a semaphore used internally for the synchronous net_mgmt_event_wait() function.

CHAPTER 12   ZEPHYR RTOS WI-FI APPLICATIONS

- uint32_t event_mask is a mask of network events on which the aforementioned handler should be called in case those events arise.

- uint32_t raised_event is an internal place holder used when a synchronous event wait is successfully unlocked on an event.

A scan result is processed by the application-specific function handle_wifi_scan_result, which processes and formats the scan data for output. The code for this function shows the kinds of techniques used to process scan result data.

```
static void handle_wifi_scan_result(struct net_mgmt_event_callback *cb)
{
    const struct wifi_scan_result *entry =
        (const struct wifi_scan_result *) cb->info;
    uint8_t mac_string_buf[sizeof("xx:xx:xx:xx:xx:xx")];
    scan_result++;
    if (scan_result == 1U) {
        printk("%-4s | %-32s %-5s | %-4s | %-4s | %-5s | %s\n",
                "Num", "SSID", "(len)", "Chan", "RSSI",
                "Security", "BSSID");
    }
    printk("%-4d | %-32s %-5u | %-4u | %-4d | %-5s | %s\n",
            scan_result, entry->ssid, entry->ssid_length,
            entry->channel, entry->rssi,
            (entry->security == WIFI_SECURITY_TYPE_PSK ?
                "WPA/WPA2" : "Open    "),
            ((entry->mac_length) ?
```

595

CHAPTER 12 ZEPHYR RTOS WI-FI APPLICATIONS

```
            net_sprint_ll_addr_buf(entry->mac, WIFI_MAC_
            ADDR_LEN,
                 mac_string_buf, sizeof(mac_string_
                 buf)) : ""));
}
```

The application code includes several helper utility functions for processing raw scan results, such as handling frequency information, for example, wifi_freq_to_channel, wifi_frequency_to_band, and handle_raw_scan_result shown here to demonstrate the techniques used.

```
static int wifi_freq_to_channel(int frequency) {
    int channel = 0;
    if (frequency == 2484) { /* channel 14 */
        channel = 14;
    } else if ((frequency <= 2472) && (frequency >= 2412)) {
        channel = ((frequency - 2412) / 5) + 1;
    } else if ((frequency <= 5895) && (frequency >= 5180)) {
        channel = ((frequency - 5000) / 5);
    } else {
        channel = frequency;
    }
    return channel;
}

static enum wifi_frequency_bands wifi_frequency_to_band(int
frequency) {
    enum wifi_frequency_bands band = WIFI_FREQ_BAND_2_4_GHZ;
    if ((frequency >= 2401) && (frequency <= 2495)) {
        band = WIFI_FREQ_BAND_2_4_GHZ;
    } else if ((frequency >= 5170) && (frequency <= 5895)) {
        band = WIFI_FREQ_BAND_5_GHZ;
    }
```

Chapter 12   Zephyr RTOS Wi-Fi Applications

```c
        return band;
}
static void handle_raw_scan_result(struct net_mgmt_event_
callback *cb) {
        struct wifi_raw_scan_result *raw = (struct wifi_raw_scan_
        result *)cb->info;
        int channel;
        int band;
        int rssi;
        int i = 0;
        int raw_scan_size = raw->frame_length;
        uint8_t mac_string_buf[sizeof("xx:xx:xx:xx:xx:xx")];
        scan_result++;
        if (scan_result == 1U) {
                printk("%-4s | %-13s | %-4s |   %-15s | %-15s | 
                %-32s\n", "Num", "Channel (Band)", "RSSI", "BSSID",
                        "Frame length", "Frame Body");
        }
        rssi = raw->rssi;
        channel = wifi_freq_to_channel(raw->frequency);
        band = wifi_frequency_to_band(raw->frequency);

        printk("%-4d | %-4u (%-6s) | %-4d | %s |       %-4d          ",
                scan_result, channel,
                wifi_band_txt(band),
                rssi,
                net_sprint_ll_addr_buf(raw->data + 10, WIFI_MAC_
                ADDR_LEN,
                mac_string_buf,  sizeof(mac_string_buf)), raw_
                scan_size);
```

```
        if (raw->frame_length >
                CONFIG_WIFI_MGMT_RAW_SCAN_RESULT_LENGTH) {
            raw_scan_size =
                    CONFIG_WIFI_MGMT_RAW_SCAN_RESULT_LENGTH;
        }
        if (raw_scan_size) {
            for (i = 0; i < 32; i++) {
                printk("%02X ", *(raw->data + i));
            }
        }
        printk("\n");
}
```

The utility function handle_wifi_scan_done prints out scan completion information and also releases the semaphore associated with the scanning action.

```
static void handle_wifi_scan_done(struct net_mgmt_event_callback *cb) {
    const struct wifi_status *status =
            (const struct wifi_status *)cb->info;
    if (status->status) {
        LOG_ERR("Scan request failed (%d)", status->status);
    } else {
        printk("Scan request done\n");
    }
    scan_result = 0U;
    k_sem_give(&scan_sem);
}
```

CHAPTER 12   ZEPHYR RTOS WI-FI APPLICATIONS

The Wi-Fi management event handler is responsible for invoking the appropriate result handler based on the management event involved. It uses a simple switch statement as shown here:

```
static void wifi_mgmt_event_handler(struct net_mgmt_event_
callback *cb, uint32_t mgmt_event, struct net_if *iface) {
      switch (mgmt_event) {
      case NET_EVENT_WIFI_SCAN_RESULT:
            handle_wifi_scan_result(cb);
            break;
#ifdef CONFIG_WIFI_MGMT_RAW_SCAN_RESULTS
      case NET_EVENT_WIFI_RAW_SCAN_RESULT:
            handle_raw_scan_result(cb);
            break;
#endif
      case NET_EVENT_WIFI_SCAN_DONE:
            handle_wifi_scan_done(cb);
            break;
      default:
            break;
      }
}
```

The function wifi_scan drives the actual scanning and runs in an infinite loop in the thread associated with the main() function.

```
static int wifi_scan(void) {
      struct net_if *iface = net_if_get_default();
      int band_str_len;
      struct wifi_scan_params params = tests[0];
      band_str_len = sizeof(CONFIG_WIFI_SCAN_BANDS_LIST);
```

599

```
if (band_str_len - 1) {
    char *buf = malloc(band_str_len);
    if (!buf) {
        LOG_ERR("Malloc Failed");
        return -EINVAL;
    }
    strcpy(buf, CONFIG_WIFI_SCAN_BANDS_LIST);
    if (wifi_utils_parse_scan_bands(buf, &params.
    bands)) {
        LOG_ERR("Incorrect value(s) in
                CONFIG_WIFI_SCAN_BANDS_LIST: %s",
                CONFIG_WIFI_SCAN_BANDS_LIST);
        free(buf);
        return -ENOEXEC;
    }
    free(buf);
}
if (sizeof(CONFIG_WIFI_SCAN_CHAN_LIST) - 1) {
    if (wifi_utils_parse_scan_chan(CONFIG_WIFI_SCAN_
    CHAN_LIST,
                    params.chan)) {
        LOG_ERR("Incorrect value(s) in
                CONFIG_WIFI_SCAN_CHAN_LIST: %s",
                CONFIG_WIFI_SCAN_CHAN_LIST);
        return -ENOEXEC;
    }
}
if (net_mgmt(NET_REQUEST_WIFI_SCAN, iface, &params,
        sizeof(struct wifi_scan_params))) {
    LOG_ERR("Scan request failed");
    return -ENOEXEC;
}
```

```
    printk("Scan requested\n");
    k_sem_take(&scan_sem, K_MSEC(SCAN_TIMEOUT_MS));
    return 0;
}
```

As the preceding code shows, it does a lot of initializing and setting up before, finally, calling

```
net_mgmt(NET_REQUEST_WIFI_SCAN, iface, &params,
            sizeof(struct wifi_scan_params))
```

Another useful helper application tests to see if the Wi-Fi interface MAC address is set, and if not, it assigns a default MAC address.

```
static bool is_mac_addr_set(struct net_if *iface) {
    struct net_linkaddr *linkaddr = net_if_get_link_addr(iface);
    struct net_eth_addr wifi_addr;
    if (!linkaddr || linkaddr->len != WIFI_MAC_ADDR_LEN) {
        return false;
    }
    memcpy(wifi_addr.addr, linkaddr->addr, WIFI_MAC_ADDR_LEN);
    return net_eth_is_addr_valid(&wifi_addr);
}
```

The main function is a typical embedded application function that performs a whole lot of initialization and then enters an infinite loop, in this case a loop that performs scanning.

```
int main(void) {
    scan_result = 0U;
    net_mgmt_init_event_callback(&wifi_shell_mgmt_cb,
            wifi_mgmt_event_handler, WIFI_SHELL_MGMT_EVENTS);
    net_mgmt_add_event_callback(&wifi_shell_mgmt_cb);
```

```
#if defined(CLOCK_FEATURE_HFCLK_DIVIDE_PRESENT) || NRF_CLOCK_
HAS_HFCLK192M
    nrfx_clock_divider_set(NRF_CLOCK_DOMAIN_HFCLK,
                    NRF_CLOCK_HFCLK_DIV_1);
#endif
    k_sleep(K_SECONDS(1));
    printk("Starting %s with CPU frequency: %d MHz\n",
        CONFIG_BOARD, SystemCoreClock / MHZ(1));
    if (!is_mac_addr_set(net_if_get_default())) {
        struct net_if *iface = net_if_get_default();
        int ret;
        struct ethernet_req_params params;
        /* Set a local MAC address with a Nordic OUI */
        if (net_if_is_up(iface)) {
            ret = net_if_down(iface);
            if (ret) {
                LOG_ERR("Cannot bring down iface
                    (%d)", ret);
                return ret;
            }
        }
        ret = net_bytes_from_str(params.mac_address.addr,
            sizeof(CONFIG_WIFI_MAC_ADDRESS),
            CONFIG_WIFI_MAC_ADDRESS);
        if (ret) {
            LOG_ERR("Failed to parse MAC address:
            %s (%d)", CONFIG_WIFI_MAC_ADDRESS, ret);
            return ret;
        }
```

CHAPTER 12 ZEPHYR RTOS WI-FI APPLICATIONS

```
            net_mgmt(NET_REQUEST_ETHERNET_SET_MAC_
            ADDRESS, iface,
                    &params, sizeof(params));
            ret = net_if_up(iface);
            if (ret) {
                    LOG_ERR("Cannot bring up iface (%d)", ret);
                    return ret;
            }
            LOG_INF("OTP not programmed, proceeding with local
            MAC: %s",
                    net_sprint_ll_addr(
                            net_if_get_link_addr(iface)->addr,
                            net_if_get_link_addr(iface)->len));
        }
        while (1) {
                wifi_scan();
                k_sleep(K_SECONDS(CONFIG_WIFI_SCAN_INTERVAL_S));
        }
        return 0;
}
```

The output when the basic scanning options are chosen should be something like the following:

```
*** Booting Zephyr OS build v3.3.99-ncs1-1 ***
[00:00:00.403,625] <inf> wifi_nrf: Firmware (v1.2.8.1) booted
successfully
```

603

CHAPTER 12   ZEPHYR RTOS WI-FI APPLICATIONS

```
Starting nrf7002dk_nrf5340_cpuapp with CPU frequency: 128 MHz
Scan requested
Num   | SSID                          (len) | Chan | RSSI |
Security | BSSID
1     | BTWi-fi                       7     | 6    | -64  |
Open     | EA:AD:A                                  6:E0:83:23
2     | BTBHub6-35MR                  12    | 6    | -66  |
WPA/WPA2 | E8:AD:A                                  6:E0:81:22
3     | BTWifi-X                      8     | 36   | -67  |
Open     | EA:AD:A                                  6:E0:82:21
4     | SKYJ6AQ5                      8     | 11   | -72  |
WPA/WPA2 | 9C:31:C                                  3:7E:A0:1A
5     | HPE710n.83B7E9                14    | 6    | -72  |
Open     | 02:27:5                                  7:0F:E3:0D
6     | CommunityFibre10Gb_4B8AD      24    | 6    | -73  |
WPA/WPA2 | E8:9F:8                                  0:94:B8:AE
7     | DIRECT-95-HP ENVY 7640 series 29    | 6    | -73  |
WPA/WPA2 | D0:BF:9                                  C:69:AC:96
8     |                               0     | 6    | -74  |
WPA/WPA2 | EE:9F:8                                  0:94:B8:AE
9     | SKYPVCF8                      8     | 11   | -75  |
WPA/WPA2 | 50:70:4                                  3:D0:96:AA
10    | VM2185960                     9     | 1    | -77  |
WPA/WPA2 | 94:98:8                                  F:F0:33:4D
11    | Granie's house                16    | 9    | -80  |
Open     | 10:27:F5:                                25:96:66
12    | TP-Link_Guest_5DC0            18    | 2    | -81  |
Open     | BA:AF:9                                  7:88:5D:B2
13    | FFFFFF                        6     | 11   | -82  |
WPA/WPA2 | 90:70:6                                  5:0E:8C:19
```

```
14    | CommunityFibre10Gb_73C2E      24    | 120   | -83   |
WPA/WPA2 | 80:69:1                                  A:77:3C:31
15    |                                0    | 6     | -84   |
WPA/WPA2 | 86:69:1                                  A:77:3C:2F
16    | VM3343038                      9    | 1     | -85   |
WPA/WPA2 | AC:F8:C                                  C:50:07:6E
17    | Virgin Media                   12   | 1     | -85   |
Open     | BE:F8:C                                  C:50:07:6E
Scan request done
```

The prj.conf file shows the configuration details to use for this kind of application.

```
CONFIG_WIFI=y
CONFIG_WIFI_NRF700X=y
CONFIG_NET_L2_WIFI_MGMT=y
CONFIG_HEAP_MEM_POOL_SIZE=25000
# System settings
CONFIG_NEWLIB_LIBC=y

# Networking
CONFIG_NETWORKING=y
CONFIG_NET_L2_ETHERNET=y
CONFIG_NET_NATIVE=n
CONFIG_NET_OFFLOAD=y
CONFIG_INIT_STACKS=y

# Memories
CONFIG_MAIN_STACK_SIZE=4096

# Debugging
CONFIG_STACK_SENTINEL=y
CONFIG_DEBUG_COREDUMP=y
CONFIG_DEBUG_COREDUMP_BACKEND_LOGGING=y
CONFIG_DEBUG_COREDUMP_MEMORY_DUMP_MIN=y
```

CHAPTER 12 ZEPHYR RTOS WI-FI APPLICATIONS

```
# Logging
CONFIG_LOG=y
CONFIG_PRINTK=y
# If below config is enabled, printk logs are
# buffered. For unbuffered messages, disable this.
CONFIG_LOG_PRINTK=n

# A higher timeout should be used for a crowded environment.
CONFIG_NET_MGMT_EVENT_QUEUE_TIMEOUT=5000

# Raw scan Options
CONFIG_WIFI_MGMT_RAW_SCAN_RESULTS=n
CONFIG_WIFI_MGMT_RAW_SCAN_RESULTS_ONLY=n

CONFIG_WIFI_MGMT_SCAN_DWELL_TIME_ACTIVE=50
CONFIG_WIFI_MGMT_SCAN_DWELL_TIME_PASSIVE=130
```

The CMakeLists.txt file is quite straightforward:

```
cmake_minimum_required(VERSION 3.20.0)
find_package(Zephyr REQUIRED HINTS $ENV{ZEPHYR_BASE})
project(nrf_wifi_scan)
target_include_directories(app PUBLIC ${ZEPHYR_BASE}/
subsys/net/ip)
target_sources(app PRIVATE
     src/main.c
)
```

It provides the path to the include file "net_private.h" discussed in the aforementioned walkthrough.

CHAPTER 12   ZEPHYR RTOS WI-FI APPLICATIONS

Exploring the nRF Connect SDK Wi-Fi Shell Example

This example implements a UART CLI shell that has Wi-Fi commands that can be used to test out the nRF7002 chip. It provides not only basic TCP/IP commands but also Wi-Fi subcommands such as scan, connect, disconnect, status, and statistics, and subcommands for configuring power saving modes and options and an add subcommand for adding a network to the credential storage with <SSID>, <Passphrase>, and other parameters. The example documentation at nrf/samples/wifi/shell/README.rst should be consulted for the full details.

Once the application has been built and a connection with a terminal such as, for example, PuTTY on Windows or minterm on Linux has been established, various shell commands can be run to, for example, connect to an access point router, check the DHCP IP address and DNS configuration of the nRF7002 DK Wi-Fi interface by the access point router, and then test connectivity by, for example, pinging another device on the local network and pinging a DNS server.

```
uart:~$
[00:00:00.357,086] <inf> wifi_nrf: Firmware (v1.2.8.1) booted successfully

[00:00:00.516,204] <inf> fs_nvs: 6 Sectors of 4096 bytes
[00:00:00.516,235] <inf> fs_nvs: alloc wra: 0, fe8
[00:00:00.516,235] <inf> fs_nvs: data wra: 0, 0
*** Booting Zephyr OS build v3.3.99-ncs1-1 ***
Starting nrf7002dk_nrf7001_nrf5340_cpuapp with CPU frequency: 128 MHz
[00:00:00.516,662] <inf> wpa_supp: Successfully initialized wpa_supplicant
uart:~$
```

CHAPTER 12   ZEPHYR RTOS WI-FI APPLICATIONS

uart:~$ wifi connect BTBHub6-35MR *passphrase*
Connection requested
[00:05:39.711,303] <inf> wpa_supp: wlan0: CTRL-EVENT-DSCP-POLICY clear_all
[00:05:41.388,397] <inf> wpa_supp: wlan0: SME: Trying to authenticate with e8:ad:a6:e0:81:22 (SSID='BTBHub6-35MR' freq=2462 MHz)
[00:05:41.391,326] <inf> wifi_nrf: wifi_nrf_wpa_supp_authenticate:Authentication request sent successfully

[00:05:41.652,191] <inf> wpa_supp: wlan0: Trying to associate with e8:ad:a6:e0:81:22 (SSID='BTBHub6-35MR' freq=2462 MHz)
[00:05:41.657,806] <inf> wifi_nrf: wifi_nrf_wpa_supp_associate: Association request sent successfully

[00:05:41.673,492] <inf> wpa_supp: wlan0: Associated with e8:ad:a6:e0:81:22
[00:05:41.673,553] <inf> wpa_supp: wlan0: CTRL-EVENT-SUBNET-STATUS-UPDATE status=0
Connected
[00:05:42.694,183] <inf> wpa_supp: wlan0: WPA: Key negotiation completed with e8:ad:a6:e0:81:22 [PTK=CCMP GTK=CCMP]
[00:05:42.694,305] <inf> wpa_supp: wlan0: CTRL-EVENT-CONNECTED - Connection to e8:ad:a6:e0:81:22 completed [id=0 id_str=]
[00:05:49.830,993] <inf> net_dhcpv4: Received: 192.168.1.87
uart:~$ wifi status
Status: successful
==================
State: COMPLETED
Interface Mode: STATION
Link Mode: WIFI 4 (802.11n/HT)
SSID: BTBHub6-35MR

```
BSSID: E8:AD:A6:E0:81:22
Band: 2.4GHz
Channel: 11
Security: WPA2-PSK
MFP: Optional
RSSI: -73
Beacon Interval: 100
DTIM: 3
TWT: Not supported
uart:~$ net ipv4
IPv4 support                            : enabled
IPv4 fragmentation support              : disabled
Max number of IPv4 network interfaces in the
system          : 1
Max number of unicast IPv4 addresses per network
interface    : 1
Max number of multicast IPv4 addresses per network
interface : 1

IPv4 addresses for interface 1 (0x200016a8) (Ethernet)
======================================================
Type            State              Lifetime (sec)   Address
DHCP      preferred          192.168.1.87/255.255.255.0
uart:~$

uart:~$ net dns google.com
Query for 'google.com' sent.
dns: 142.250.187.238
dns: All results received
uart:~$ net ping 142.250.187.238
PING 142.250.187.238
28 bytes from 142.250.187.238 to 192.168.1.87: icmp_seq=1
ttl=117 time=24 ms
```

CHAPTER 12 ZEPHYR RTOS WI-FI APPLICATIONS

```
28 bytes from 142.250.187.238 to 192.168.1.87: icmp_seq=2
ttl=117 time=16 ms
28 bytes from 142.250.187.238 to 192.168.1.87: icmp_seq=3
ttl=117 time=20 ms
uart:~$
```

To ping a PC on a Wi-Fi network, turn the private firewall off (for testing purposes) and then try to ping:

```
uart:~$ net ping 192.168.1.86
PING 192.168.1.86
28 bytes from 192.168.1.86 to 192.168.1.87: icmp_seq=1 ttl=128 time=14 ms
28 bytes from 192.168.1.86 to 192.168.1.87: icmp_seq=2 ttl=128 time=13 ms
28 bytes from 192.168.1.86 to 192.168.1.87: icmp_seq=3 ttl=128 time=14 ms
uart:~$
```

If the private firewall is on the ping will fail.

```
uart:~$ net ping 192.168.1.86
PING 192.168.1.86
Ping timeout
uart:~$
```

The code in main relevant to the nRF7002 DK board is quite simple.

```
#ifdef CONFIG_NET_CONFIG_SETTINGS
    /* With the code as written here
            DHCPv4 always starts on the Wi-Fi interface
        independent of the ordering.
    */
    const struct device *dev = device_get_binding("wlan0");
```

```
        struct net_if *wifi_iface = net_if_lookup_by_dev(dev);
        /* As both are Ethernet, need to set a specific
        interface*/
        net_if_set_default(wifi_iface);
        net_config_init_app(dev, "Initializing network");
#endif
```

The prj.conf file contains a great deal of network configuration, memory, protocol stack, and shell configuration entries and is shown here:

```
CONFIG_WIFI=y
CONFIG_WIFI_NRF700X=y

# WPA supplicant
CONFIG_WPA_SUPP=y
CONFIG_NET_L2_WIFI_SHELL=y

# System settings
CONFIG_NEWLIB_LIBC=y
CONFIG_NEWLIB_LIBC_NANO=n

# Networking
CONFIG_NETWORKING=y
CONFIG_NET_SOCKETS=y
CONFIG_NET_LOG=y
CONFIG_NET_IPV6=y
CONFIG_NET_IPV4=y
CONFIG_NET_UDP=y
CONFIG_NET_TCP=y
CONFIG_NET_DHCPV4=y
CONFIG_DNS_RESOLVER=y

CONFIG_NET_STATISTICS=y
CONFIG_NET_STATISTICS_WIFI=y
CONFIG_NET_STATISTICS_USER_API=y
```

CHAPTER 12   ZEPHYR RTOS WI-FI APPLICATIONS

```
CONFIG_NET_PKT_RX_COUNT=8
CONFIG_NET_PKT_TX_COUNT=8

# Below section is the primary contributor to SRAM and is currently
# tuned for performance, but this will be revisited in the future.
CONFIG_NET_BUF_RX_COUNT=16
CONFIG_NET_BUF_TX_COUNT=16
CONFIG_NET_BUF_DATA_SIZE=128
CONFIG_NRF700X_RX_NUM_BUFS=16
CONFIG_NRF700X_MAX_TX_AGGREGATION=4
# nRF700x is main consumer: (16 + 8) * 1600 = ~40KB + ~40KB control path (experimental)
CONFIG_HEAP_MEM_POOL_SIZE=80000
CONFIG_NET_TC_TX_COUNT=1

CONFIG_NET_IF_UNICAST_IPV6_ADDR_COUNT=4
CONFIG_NET_IF_MCAST_IPV6_ADDR_COUNT=5
CONFIG_NET_MAX_CONTEXTS=5
CONFIG_NET_CONTEXT_SYNC_RECV=y

CONFIG_INIT_STACKS=y

CONFIG_NET_L2_ETHERNET=y
CONFIG_NET_SHELL=y

# Memories
CONFIG_MAIN_STACK_SIZE=4096
CONFIG_SHELL_STACK_SIZE=4096
CONFIG_SYSTEM_WORKQUEUE_STACK_SIZE=2048
CONFIG_NET_TX_STACK_SIZE=4096
CONFIG_NET_RX_STACK_SIZE=4096
```

```
# Debugging
CONFIG_STACK_SENTINEL=y
CONFIG_DEBUG_COREDUMP=y
CONFIG_DEBUG_COREDUMP_BACKEND_LOGGING=y
CONFIG_DEBUG_COREDUMP_MEMORY_DUMP_MIN=y
CONFIG_SHELL_CMDS_RESIZE=n
#CONFIG_DEBUG=y
CONFIG_WPA_SUPP_LOG_LEVEL_INF=y

# Kernel options
CONFIG_ENTROPY_GENERATOR=y

# Logging
CONFIG_LOG=y
CONFIG_PRINTK=y
CONFIG_SHELL=y
CONFIG_SHELL_GETOPT=y
CONFIG_DEVICE_SHELL=y
CONFIG_POSIX_CLOCK=y
CONFIG_DATE_SHELL=y
CONFIG_NET_CONFIG_AUTO_INIT=n

CONFIG_WIFI_MGMT_EXT=y
CONFIG_WIFI_CREDENTIALS=y
CONFIG_WIFI_CREDENTIALS_BACKEND_SETTINGS=y
CONFIG_FLASH=y
CONFIG_FLASH_PAGE_LAYOUT=y
CONFIG_FLASH_MAP=y
CONFIG_NVS=y
CONFIG_SETTINGS=y
CONFIG_SETTINGS_NVS=y
```

CHAPTER 12 ZEPHYR RTOS WI-FI APPLICATIONS

```
# printing of scan results puts pressure on queues in
new locking
# design in net_mgmt. So, use a higher timeout for a crowded
# environment.
CONFIG_NET_MGMT_EVENT_QUEUE_TIMEOUT=5000
```

The complexity of all the configurations is that the application being built is a monolithic application, in contrast to a similar Linux application where much of the functionality is built into the kernel and is accessible via suitable utilities and system calls.

Basic TCP/IP Application Programming Using the nRF7002 DK

A Wi-Fi access point has hub-like behavior as well as bridge-like behavior. Only one frame can be successfully transmitted at a time, and collisions do occur, as is the case for a hub. An access point must receive an entire frame before forwarding it, and the frame is forwarded or filtered based on the destination MAC address, which is bridge-like behavior. The wireless clients associated with an access point (AP) constitute a Local Area Network (LAN), and it is possible to configure these clients with static (manually configured) IP addresses. An alternative is to configure the client IP addresses dynamically using the DHCP protocol. One way to do this would be to set up a DHCP server on the local Wi-Fi LAN. Alternatively, if the access point is combined with a router (i.e., is part of a Wi-Fi router) it is possible to makeuse of the DHCP server on the router itself. More complex Wi-Fi setups can be created using APs that can act as mesh repeaters [6], for example, by using Cisco Meraki MR access points. Because such repeaters also support wired clients plugged into their wired interfaces, they can also be used to bridge remote LAN segments to the main network. Using this approach, a large Wi-Fi sensor network can be deployed, for example, in an office or warehouse building.

Once an nRF7002-based device has been assigned an IP address, it is possible to build regular TCP/IP applications and both client and server applications and run them on that device. In the following section, applications implementing some relatively simple TCP and UDP clients and servers will be explored. The examples are based on the nRF Connect SDK sta (station) example and the BSD sockets programming case study from "abluethinginthecloud" (`https://github.com/abluethinginthecloud/nrf7002-bsd-sockets-example`).

Structured Exploration of the nRF Connect SDK Wi-Fi sta Example

The Station example is located at v2.5.0/nrf/samples/wifi/sta in the nRF Connect SDK repository. It shows how to implement application code to connect the Wi-Fi station on the nRF7002 DK board to a specified access point using the Dynamic Host Configuration Protocol (DHCP) to configure IP addressing and TCP/IP.

The example implements LED support to indicate connection and disconnection events.

LED 1:

- Starts blinking when the sample is connected to the access point
- Stops blinking when the sample is disconnected from the access point

The Wi-Fi credentials for a given AP must be provided in the "prj.conf" file, namely:

- Network name (SSID)
- Key management protocol to use
- Password

In the example, Zephyr's power management policy is enabled by default, which sets the nRF5340 processor into low-power mode whenever it is idle.

The example uses DHCP to obtain an IP address for the Wi-Fi interface. However, a static IP address can be configured to handle networks without DHCP servers, or to deal with the case where the DHCP server is not available. A successful DHCP handshake overrides the default static IP address configuration.

The default static IP address configuration is provided in the prj.conf file, for example:

```
CONFIG_NET_CONFIG_MY_IPV4_ADDR="192.168.1.98"
CONFIG_NET_CONFIG_MY_IPV4_NETMASK="255.255.255.0"
CONFIG_NET_CONFIG_MY_IPV4_GW="192.168.1.1"
```

The build target for the application is "nrf7002dk_nrf5340_cpuapp".

The prj.conf file is quite large, and it is important, for the application to work, to ensure that the configuration settings are correct for the type of AP being used. The configuration settings are listed as follows:

```
CONFIG_WIFI=y
CONFIG_WIFI_NRF700X=y
# WPA supplicant
CONFIG_WPA_SUPP=y
# Choose the setting that matches the security capabilities
of the AP
```

```
# CONFIG_STA_KEY_MGMT_NONE=y
# CONFIG_STA_KEY_MGMT_WPA2=y
# CONFIG_STA_KEY_MGMT_WPA2_256=y
# CONFIG_STA_KEY_MGMT_WPA3=y
CONFIG_STA_SAMPLE_SSID="Myssid"
CONFIG_STA_SAMPLE_PASSWORD="Mypassword"
# System settings
CONFIG_NEWLIB_LIBC=y
CONFIG_NEWLIB_LIBC_NANO=n
# Networking
CONFIG_NETWORKING=y
CONFIG_NET_SOCKETS=y
CONFIG_NET_LOG=y
CONFIG_NET_IPV4=y
CONFIG_NET_UDP=y
CONFIG_NET_TCP=y
CONFIG_NET_DHCPV4=y
CONFIG_NET_PKT_RX_COUNT=8
CONFIG_NET_PKT_TX_COUNT=8
# These configurations influence SRAM usage for Wi-Fi
# and can be tuned as necessary based on performance
requirements
CONFIG_NET_BUF_RX_COUNT=16
CONFIG_NET_BUF_TX_COUNT=16
CONFIG_NET_BUF_DATA_SIZE=128
CONFIG_HEAP_MEM_POOL_SIZE=153600
CONFIG_NET_TC_TX_COUNT=1
CONFIG_NET_IF_UNICAST_IPV4_ADDR_COUNT=1
CONFIG_NET_MAX_CONTEXTS=5
CONFIG_NET_CONTEXT_SYNC_RECV=y
CONFIG_INIT_STACKS=y
```

```
CONFIG_NET_L2_ETHERNET=y
CONFIG_NET_CONFIG_SETTINGS=y
CONFIG_NET_CONFIG_INIT_TIMEOUT=0
CONFIG_NET_SOCKETS_POLL_MAX=6
# Memories
CONFIG_MAIN_STACK_SIZE=4096
CONFIG_SYSTEM_WORKQUEUE_STACK_SIZE=2048
CONFIG_NET_TX_STACK_SIZE=4096
CONFIG_NET_RX_STACK_SIZE=4096
# Debugging
CONFIG_STACK_SENTINEL=y
CONFIG_DEBUG_COREDUMP=y
CONFIG_DEBUG_COREDUMP_BACKEND_LOGGING=y
CONFIG_DEBUG_COREDUMP_MEMORY_DUMP_MIN=y
CONFIG_SHELL_CMDS_RESIZE=n
# Kernel options
CONFIG_ENTROPY_GENERATOR=y
# Logging
CONFIG_LOG=y
CONFIG_LOG_BUFFER_SIZE=2048
CONFIG_POSIX_CLOCK=y
CONFIG_NET_CONFIG_MY_IPV4_ADDR="192.168.1.99"
CONFIG_NET_CONFIG_MY_IPV4_NETMASK="255.255.255.0"
CONFIG_NET_CONFIG_MY_IPV4_GW="192.168.1.1"
# printing of scan results puts pressure on queues in new locking
# design in net_mgmt. So, use a higher timeout for a crowded environment.
CONFIG_NET_MGMT_EVENT_QUEUE_TIMEOUT=5000
```

The nRF Connect SDK documentation should be consulted for information about these parameters.

CHAPTER 12 ZEPHYR RTOS WI-FI APPLICATIONS

The project build requires the IP networking code, and the location needs to be given in the CMakeLists.txt file:

```
cmake_minimum_required(VERSION 3.20.0)
find_package(Zephyr REQUIRED HINTS $ENV{ZEPHYR_BASE})
project(nrf_wifi_sta)
target_include_directories(app PUBLIC ${ZEPHYR_BASE}/subsys/net/ip)
target_sources(app PRIVATE
     src/main.c
)
```

The Station code is made up of one file `main.c`, which will be explored next.

It begins with logging module registration followed by a whole lot of #defines:

```
#include <zephyr/logging/log.h>
LOG_MODULE_REGISTER(sta, CONFIG_LOG_DEFAULT_LEVEL);
#include <nrfx_clock.h>
#include <zephyr/kernel.h>
#include <stdio.h>
#include <stdlib.h>
#include <zephyr/shell/shell.h>
#include <zephyr/sys/printk.h>
#include <zephyr/init.h>
#include <zephyr/net/net_if.h>
#include <zephyr/net/wifi_mgmt.h>
#include <zephyr/net/net_event.h>
#include <zephyr/drivers/gpio.h>
#include <qspi_if.h>
#include "net_private.h"
```

619

CHAPTER 12   ZEPHYR RTOS WI-FI APPLICATIONS

There then follow some definitions for symbolic constants.

```
#define WIFI_SHELL_MODULE "wifi"
#define WIFI_SHELL_MGMT_EVENTS \
            (NET_EVENT_WIFI_CONNECT_RESULT |                  \
            NET_EVENT_WIFI_DISCONNECT_RESULT)
#define MAX_SSID_LEN        32
#define STATUS_POLLING_MS   300
/* 1000 msec = 1 sec */
#define LED_SLEEP_TIME_MS   100
/* The devicetree node identifier for the "led0" alias. */
#define LED0_NODE DT_ALIAS(led0)
```

Next are some global variables for things such as context, event callbacks, and devicetree spec.

```
static const struct gpio_dt_spec led = GPIO_DT_SPEC_GET(LED0_NODE, gpios);
static struct net_mgmt_event_callback wifi_shell_mgmt_cb;
static struct net_mgmt_event_callback net_shell_mgmt_cb;

static struct {
    const struct shell *sh;
    union {
        struct {
            uint8_t connected              : 1;
            uint8_t connect_result         : 1;
            uint8_t disconnect_requested   : 1;
            uint8_t _unused                : 5;
        };
        uint8_t all;
    };
} context;
```

620

CHAPTER 12 ZEPHYR RTOS WI-FI APPLICATIONS

Next the toggle led task and its associated thread are defined. The thread infinite polling loop checks the value of the context variable periodically and switches to led toggling or led off mode as appropriate.

```
void toggle_led(void) {
    int ret;
    if (!device_is_ready(led.port)) {
        LOG_ERR("LED device is not ready");
        return;
    }
    ret = gpio_pin_configure_dt(&led, GPIO_OUTPUT_ACTIVE);
    if (ret < 0) {
        LOG_ERR("Error %d: failed to configure LED
        pin", ret);
        return;
    }
    while (1) {
        if (context.connected) {
            gpio_pin_toggle_dt(&led);
            k_msleep(LED_SLEEP_TIME_MS);
        } else {
            gpio_pin_set_dt(&led, 0);
            k_msleep(LED_SLEEP_TIME_MS);
        }
    }
}
K_THREAD_DEFINE(led_thread_id, 1024, toggle_led, NULL, NULL,
NULL, 7, 0, 0);
```

621

CHAPTER 12   ZEPHYR RTOS WI-FI APPLICATIONS

The command for reporting Wi-Fi status is fairly straightforward and depends on knowing the various WI-FI API methods to use and how to generate suitably formatted text strings to use with LOG_INF.

```
static int cmd_wifi_status(void)
{
    struct net_if *iface = net_if_get_default();
    struct wifi_iface_status status = { 0 };
    if (net_mgmt(NET_REQUEST_WIFI_IFACE_STATUS, iface,
    &status, sizeof(struct wifi_iface_status))) {
        LOG_INF("Status request failed");
        return -ENOEXEC;
    }
    LOG_INF("==================");
    LOG_INF("State: %s", wifi_state_txt(status.state));
    if (status.state >= WIFI_STATE_ASSOCIATED) {
        uint8_t mac_string_buf[sizeof("xx:xx:xx:xx:xx:xx")];
        LOG_INF("Interface Mode: %s",
            wifi_mode_txt(status.iface_mode));
        LOG_INF("Link Mode: %s",
            wifi_link_mode_txt(status.link_mode));
        LOG_INF("SSID: %-32s", status.ssid);
        LOG_INF("BSSID: %s",
            net_sprint_ll_addr_buf(
                status.bssid, WIFI_MAC_ADDR_LEN,
                mac_string_buf, sizeof(mac_
                string_buf)));
        LOG_INF("Band: %s", wifi_band_txt(status.band));
        LOG_INF("Channel: %d", status.channel);
        LOG_INF("Security: %s", wifi_security_txt(status.
        security));
```

```
            LOG_INF("MFP: %s", wifi_mfp_txt(status.mfp));
            LOG_INF("RSSI: %d", status.rssi);
    }
    return 0;
}
```

Next come the various event handling setup functions, which illustrate a fairly standard pattern for doing such things and which assume knowledge of the Wi-Fi protocols as described earlier in this chapter and the Wi-Fi API functions and macros.

```
static void handle_wifi_connect_result(struct net_mgmt_event_
callback *cb) {
        const struct wifi_status *status = (const struct wifi_
        status *) cb->info;
        if (context.connected) {
            return;
        }
        if (status->status) {
            LOG_ERR("Connection failed (%d)", status->status);
        } else {
            LOG_INF("Connected");
            context.connected = true;
        }
        context.connect_result = true;
}

static void handle_wifi_disconnect_result(struct net_mgmt_
event_callback *cb) {
        const struct wifi_status *status = (const struct wifi_
        status *) cb->info;
```

```
        if (!context.connected) {
            return;
        }
        if (context.disconnect_requested) {
            LOG_INF("Disconnection request %s (%d)",
                    status->status ? "failed" : "done",
                        status->status);
            context.disconnect_requested = false;
        } else {
            LOG_INF("Received Disconnected");
            context.connected = false;
        }
        cmd_wifi_status();
}

static void wifi_mgmt_event_handler(struct net_mgmt_event_callback *cb, uint32_t mgmt_event, struct net_if *iface) {
    switch (mgmt_event) {
    case NET_EVENT_WIFI_CONNECT_RESULT:
        handle_wifi_connect_result(cb);
        break;
    case NET_EVENT_WIFI_DISCONNECT_RESULT:
        handle_wifi_disconnect_result(cb);
        break;
    default:
        break;
    }
}
```

CHAPTER 12   ZEPHYR RTOS WI-FI APPLICATIONS

```
static void print_dhcp_ip(struct net_mgmt_event_callback *cb)
{
      /* Get DHCP info from struct net_if_dhcpv4 and print */
      const struct net_if_dhcpv4 *dhcpv4 = cb->info;
      const struct in_addr *addr = &dhcpv4->requested_ip;
      char dhcp_info[128];
      net_addr_ntop(AF_INET, addr, dhcp_info,
      sizeof(dhcp_info));
      LOG_INF("DHCP IP address: %s", dhcp_info);
}

static void net_mgmt_event_handler(struct net_mgmt_event_
callback *cb, uint32_t mgmt_event, struct net_if *iface) {
      switch (mgmt_event) {
      case NET_EVENT_IPV4_DHCP_BOUND:
            print_dhcp_ip(cb);
            break;
      default:
            break;
      }
}
```

The preceding code is, pretty much, boilerplate code. It provides a template for use in typical Wi-Fi applications. The print_dhcp_ip() function shows how to implement a function that will extract an IPv4 address and then to convert it into string form using the net_addr_ntop() utility function.

The __wifi_args_to_params() function shows how to initialize the Wi-Fi connection request parameters data structure.

```
static int __wifi_args_to_params(struct wifi_connect_req_params
*params) {
        params->timeout = CONFIG_STA_CONN_TIMEOUT_SEC * MSEC_
        PER_SEC;
```

625

CHAPTER 12 ZEPHYR RTOS WI-FI APPLICATIONS

```
        if (params->timeout == 0) {
                params->timeout = SYS_FOREVER_MS;
        }

        /* SSID */
        params->ssid = CONFIG_STA_SAMPLE_SSID;
        params->ssid_length = strlen(params->ssid);
#if defined(CONFIG_STA_KEY_MGMT_WPA2)
        params->security = 1;
#elif defined(CONFIG_STA_KEY_MGMT_WPA2_256)
        params->security = 2;
#elif defined(CONFIG_STA_KEY_MGMT_WPA3)
        params->security = 3;
#else
        params->security = 0;
#endif
#if !defined(CONFIG_STA_KEY_MGMT_NONE)
        params->psk = CONFIG_STA_SAMPLE_PASSWORD;
        params->psk_length = strlen(params->psk);
#endif
        params->channel = WIFI_CHANNEL_ANY;
        /* MFP (optional) */
        params->mfp = WIFI_MFP_OPTIONAL;
        return 0;
}
```

The MFP protocol alluded to in params->mfp = WIFI_MFP_OPTIONAL; is a protocol for providing Wi-Fi Management Frame Protection. The Cisco Meraki documentation provides a useful introduction [7].

For the application to work, it is important that the level of security required can be provided by the access point being used.

CHAPTER 12   ZEPHYR RTOS WI-FI APPLICATIONS

The function `wifi_connect()` attempts to set up a Wi-Fi connection. Conceptually it is a straightforward function that initializes a `struct wifi_connect_req_params` connection parameters structure, and the context structure that controls LED0 behavior, and then calls the Wi-Fi API `net_mgmt()` function with the arguments needed to request a Wi-Fi connection.

```
static int wifi_connect(void) {
    struct net_if *iface = net_if_get_default();
    static struct wifi_connect_req_params cnx_params;
    context.connected = false;
    context.connect_result = false;
    __wifi_args_to_params(&cnx_params);

    if (net_mgmt(NET_REQUEST_WIFI_CONNECT, iface,
            &cnx_params, sizeof(struct wifi_connect_req_
            params))) {
        LOG_ERR("Connection request failed");
        return -ENOEXEC;
    }
    LOG_INF("Connection requested");
    return 0;
}
```

It is possible to configure the example so that it encrypts data being sent over the QSPI bus. The example code also contains a utility function `bytes_from_str()` for converting a string into a sequence of bytes in connection with decryption of the QSPI encryption key if programmed into the device. The Nordic Semiconductor documentation should be consulted for the necessary details, and in the demonstration program tested, it was not used as it is an optional feature.

The application `main()` function sets up the various callbacks, enables QSPI configuration if the board has been configured to use it, and then enters an infinite loop in which it calls `wifi_connect()` until a WI-FI connection is established.

```
int main(void)
{
    memset(&context, 0, sizeof(context));
    net_mgmt_init_event_callback(&wifi_shell_mgmt_cb,
                    wifi_mgmt_event_handler,
                    WIFI_SHELL_MGMT_EVENTS);
    net_mgmt_add_event_callback(&wifi_shell_mgmt_cb);
    net_mgmt_init_event_callback(&net_shell_mgmt_cb,
            net_mgmt_event_handler, NET_EVENT_IPV4_
            DHCP_BOUND);
    net_mgmt_add_event_callback(&net_shell_mgmt_cb);
    LOG_INF("Starting %s with CPU frequency: %d MHz",
        CONFIG_BOARD, SystemCoreClock/MHZ(1));
    k_sleep(K_SECONDS(1));
#if defined(CONFIG_BOARD_NRF7002DK_NRF7001_NRF5340_CPUAPP) || \
    defined(CONFIG_BOARD_NRF7002DK_NRF5340_CPUAPP)
    if (strlen(CONFIG_NRF700X_QSPI_ENCRYPTION_KEY)) {
        char key[QSPI_KEY_LEN_BYTES];
        int ret;
        ret = bytes_from_str(CONFIG_NRF700X_QSPI_
        ENCRYPTION_KEY, key, sizeof(key));
        if (ret) {
            LOG_ERR("Failed to parse encryption key:
            %d\n", ret);
            return 0;
        }
```

```
            LOG_DBG("QSPI Encryption key: ");
            for (int i = 0; i < QSPI_KEY_LEN_BYTES; i++) {
                    LOG_DBG("%02x", key[i]);
            }
            LOG_DBG("\n");
            ret = qspi_enable_encryption(key);
            if (ret) {
                    LOG_ERR("Failed to enable encryption:
                    %d\n", ret);
                    return 0;
            }
            LOG_INF("QSPI Encryption enabled");
      } else {
            LOG_INF("QSPI Encryption disabled");
      }
#endif /* CONFIG_BOARD_NRF700XDK_NRF5340 */
      LOG_INF("Static IP address (overridable): %s/%s -> %s",
            CONFIG_NET_CONFIG_MY_IPV4_ADDR,
            CONFIG_NET_CONFIG_MY_IPV4_NETMASK,
            CONFIG_NET_CONFIG_MY_IPV4_GW);
      while (1) {
            wifi_connect();
            while (!context.connect_result) {
                    cmd_wifi_status();
                    k_sleep (K_MSEC(STATUS_POLLING_MS));
            }
            if (context.connected) {
                    k_sleep(K_FOREVER);
            }
      }
      return 0;
}
```

The default clock frequency is 64 MHz, but it can be set to 128 MHz, if necessary, by calling the function

nrfx_clock_divider_set(NRF_CLOCK_DOMAIN_HFCLK,
                       NRF_CLOCK_HFCLK_DIV_1);

as is done in the "shell" example program.

The output when this application is run will be something like the following:

```
OK
*** BooOK
...
OK
OK
ting nRF Connect SDK v2.5.0 ***
[00:00:00.446,105] <OK
inf> net_config: Initializing network
[00:00:00.446,105] <inf> net_config: Waiting interface 1 (0x20001478) to be up...
[00:00:00.446,228] <inf> net_config: IPv4 address: 192.168.1.99
[00:00:00.446,289] <inf> net_config: Running dhcpv4 client...
[00:00:00.446,563] <inf> sta: Starting nrf7002dk_nrf5340_cpuapp with CPU frequency: 128 MHz
[00:00:01.446,594] <inf> sta: QSPI Encryption disabled
[00:00:01.446,624] <inf> sta: Static IP address (overridable): 192.168.1.99/255.255.255.0 -> 192.168.1.1
[00:00:02.230,560] <inf> sta: Connection requested
[00:00:02.230,590] <inf> sta: ===================
[00:00:02.230,590] <inf> sta: State: SCANNING
[00:00:02.530,700] <inf> sta: ===================
....
```

```
[00:00:05.531,768] <inf> sta: State: SCANNING
[00:00:05.831,848] <inf> sta: ==================
[00:00:05.831,848] <inf> sta: State: SCANNING
[00:00:06.131,927] <inf> sta: ==================
[00:00:06.131,958] <inf> sta: State: AUTHENTICATING
[00:00:06.409,027] <inf> sta: Connected
[00:00:06.483,825] <inf> net_config: IPv6 address: fe80::f6ce:36ff:fe00:270a
[00:00:08.495,269] <inf> net_config: IPv6 address: fdaa:bbcc:dd ee:0:f6ce:36ff:fe00:270a
[00:00:10.445,343] <inf> net_dhcpv4: Received: 192.168.1.87
[00:00:10.445,404] <inf> net_config: IPv4 address: 192.168.1.87
[00:00:10.445,434] <inf> net_config: Lease time: 86400 seconds
[00:00:10.445,434] <inf> net_config: Subnet: 255.255.255.0
[00:00:10.445,465] <inf> net_config: Router: 192.168.1.254
[00:00:10.445,495] <inf> sta: DHCP IP address: 192.168.1.87
```

Wi-Fi BSD Sockets Programming

Once a Wi-Fi interface has been successfully configured, it is possible to start experimenting with implementing simple BSD sockets client and server applications using the Zephyr RTOS BSD sockets programming API. The following example, based on abluethinginthecloud nrf7002-bsd-sockets-example, shows how this can be done and serves as a starting point for more ambitious projects.

nRF7002 DK – Basic TCP and UDP Example

This example involves implementing basic echo server code, both client and server variants: one using UDP and the other using TCP that will run as separate threads on the nRF7002 DK board. Complementing these

CHAPTER 12   ZEPHYR RTOS WI-FI APPLICATIONS

components will be Python echo client and echo server applications, both UDP and TCP variants running on a PC and using a Wi-Fi interface that uses the same access point as used by the nRF7002 DK board.

The importance of this exercise is to show the basic techniques involved in implementing TCP and UDP applications running over a Wi-Fi interface and how to test them out using Python script-based applications running on a PC. Instead of using a PC, an embedded Linux system such as a Raspberry Pi can also be used.

The main() function of the application simply creates and starts a number of threads that do all the work, as shown in the following code snippet:

```
#include <zephyr/logging/log.h>
LOG_MODULE_REGISTER(sta, CONFIG_LOG_DEFAULT_LEVEL);
#include <zephyr/kernel.h>
#include "Task/Wifi_Setup.h"
#include "Task/Led.h"
#include "Task/TCP_Server.h"
#include "Task/TCP_Client.h"
#include "Task/UDP_Server.h"
#include "Task/UDP_Client.h"
#include "Task/deviceInformation.h"
// added
#include <nrfx_clock.h>
#include <zephyr/device.h>
#include <zephyr/net/net_config.h>
void main( void ) {
    nrfx_clock_divider_set(NRF_CLOCK_DOMAIN_HFCLK,
                    NRF_CLOCK_HFCLK_DIV_1);
    printk("Starting %s with CPU frequency: %d MHz\n",
    CONFIG_BOARD, SystemCoreClock/MHZ(1));
```

```
    printk("Starting with CPU frequency: %d MHz\n",
    SystemCoreClock/MHZ(1));
       Task_Wifi_Setup_Init();
    Task_Toggle_Led_Init();
    Task_TCP_Client_Init();
    Task_TCP_Server_Init();
    Task_UDP_Client_Init();
    Task_UDP_Server_Init();
    k_sleep( K_FOREVER );
}
```

Project source code directory structure

In multithreaded applications, one way of structuring the code is to have the application main.c file in the project src directory and to put the various tasks and task-related .c and .h files in a task-related subdirectory called, for example, Task. Then, in CMakeLists.txt, there will be an entry such as

```
target_sources(app PRIVATE
      src/main.c
      src/Task/Led.c
      src/Task/TCP_Client.c
      src/Task/TCP_Server.c
      src/Task/UDP_Client.c
      src/Task/UDP_Server.c
      src/Task/Wifi_Setup.c
)
```

Device-related configuration details can be placed in an appropriate header file called, for example, "deviceinformation.h" containing actual and default parameter values as #defines and a Wi-Fi connection context information data structure along the lines of the following struct:

CHAPTER 12 ZEPHYR RTOS WI-FI APPLICATIONS

```
typedef struct sContext{
    const struct shell *pShell;
    union {
        struct {
            uint8_t connected       ;
            uint8_t connect_result ;
            uint8_t disconnect_requested;
            uint8_t _unused ;
        };
        uint8_t all;
    };
} tContext;
```

Whether to place the code for setting up a Wi-Fi connection into the application's main() function or whether to run it as a separate thread is a design decision. In this example, the work is delegated to a separate thread, and the thread-related code is in the file Wifi_Setup.c. Wifi_Setup.c has the code for Wi-Fi event handling, utilities for printing out logging and error information, as well as the details of DHCP interface configuration.

The initialization and creation of the thread that sets up and manages the Wi-Fi connection are carried out by the function ask_Wifi_Setup_Init(), the code for which is shown in the following code snippet:

```
void Task_Wifi_Setup_Init( void ){
    k_thread_create      (                                        \
                         &wifiThread,                             \
                         WIFI_STACK,                              \
                         WIFI_STACK_SIZE,                         \
                         (k_thread_entry_t) Wifi_Setup,           \
                         NULL,                                    \
                         NULL,                                    \
                         NULL,                                    \
```

CHAPTER 12 ZEPHYR RTOS WI-FI APPLICATIONS

```
                        WIFI_PRIORITY,                          \
                        0,                                      \
                        K_NO_WAIT);
    k_thread_name_set(&wifiThread, "wifiSetup");
    k_thread_start(&wifiThread);
}
```

The Wifi_Setup() function takes care of the details of setting up a connection with a Wi-Fi access point, setting up the various event handlers, and carrying out reporting and logging. In general, the details are application dependent. The implementation for this example is shown here:

```
void Wifi_Setup( void ) {
    int i;
    memset( &context, 0, sizeof( context ));
    net_mgmt_init_event_callback (                              \
                        &wifiEventsCallback,                    \
                        Handle_Wifi_Events,                     \
                        SHELL_EVENTS_FLAG );
    net_mgmt_add_event_callback( &wifiEventsCallback );
    net_mgmt_init_event_callback(                               \
                        &netEventsCallback,                     \
                          Handle_Net_Events,                    \
                            NET_EVENT_IPV4_DHCP_BOUND );
    net_mgmt_add_event_callback( &netEventsCallback );
    // to set the clock speed to 128 MHz
    nrfx_clock_divider_set(NRF_CLOCK_DOMAIN_HFCLK,
                    NRF_CLOCK_HFCLK_DIV_1);
    LOG_INF( "Starting %s with CPU frequency: %d MHz",          \
                CONFIG_BOARD, SystemCoreClock/MHZ( 1 ));
    k_sleep( K_SECONDS( 10 ));
    LOG_INF( "Static IP address (overridable): %s/%s -> %s",    \
```

```
        CONFIG_NET_CONFIG_MY_IPV4_ADDR,                    \
        CONFIG_NET_CONFIG_MY_IPV4_NETMASK,                 \
        CONFIG_NET_CONFIG_MY_IPV4_GW );
    while ( 1 ) {
        Wifi_Connect();
        for ( i = 0; i < TIMEOUT_MS; i++ ) {
            k_sleep( K_MSEC( STATUS_POLLING_MS ));
            Cmd_Wifi_Status();
            if ( context.connect_result ) {
                break;
            }
        }
        if ( context.connected ) {
            LOG_INF( "============" );
            k_sleep( K_FOREVER );
        }
        else if ( !context.connect_result ) {
            LOG_ERR( "Connection Timed Out" );
        }
    }
}
```

The Led Toggling Task

The code for the thread work and for initializing and starting the thread is to be found in the file Led.c.

The function `Task_Toggle_Led_Init( void )` creates and starts the thread.

The thread function `Toggle_Led()` blinks the LED when the board is ready to receive TCP or UDP connections. The code is shown in the following code snippet:

```
void Toggle_Led( void ) {
    int returnCode;
    if( !device_is_ready ( led.port ) ) {
        LOG_ERR( "LED device is not ready" );
        return;
    }

    returnCode = gpio_pin_configure_dt( &led, GPIO_OUTPUT_
    ACTIVE );

    if( returnCode < 0 ) {
        LOG_ERR( "Error %d: failed to configure LED pin",
        returnCode );
        return;
    }

    while( 1 ) {
        if( context.connected ) {
            gpio_pin_toggle_dt( &led );
            k_msleep ( LED_SLEEP_TIME_MS );
        } else {
            gpio_pin_set_dt( &led, 0 );
            k_msleep( LED_SLEEP_TIME_MS );
        }
    }
}
```

UDP Server Task on Target Board

The UDP_Server.c file contains two functions: Task_UDP_Server_Init(), which creates and starts the UDP server thread, and UDP_Server(void), which contains the UDP server code. This server is a simple echo server

CHAPTER 12 ZEPHYR RTOS WI-FI APPLICATIONS

that simply echoes back any messages it receives to the client that sent the message. The code shown in the following is a standard implementation using the BSD Sockets API as supported by Zephyr RTOS. Essentially it creates and initializes a socket, binds the socket, and waits for connections.

For each connection, it extracts the sent data and sends it back to the client. The following code shows the implementation used in the example, here. At the start of the function, the code polls (waits) till a connection is established with the access point and DHCP assigns an IP address to the board.

```
void UDP_Server(void) {
      int udpServerSocket;
      struct sockaddr_in bindingAddress;
      int bindingResult;
      struct sockaddr clientAddress;
      socklen_t clientAddressLength;
      int receivedBytes;
      int sentBytes = 0;
      uint8_t *pTransmitterBuffer;
         // Poll intermittently till a DHCP IP address is
         assigned to the board
      while( !context.connected ) {
            k_msleep( UDP_SERVER_SLEEP_TIME_MS );
      }

      // Create the server side socket
      ( void ) memset( &bindingAddress, 0, sizeof
      ( bindingAddress ));
      bindingAddress.sin_family = AF_INET;
      //bindingAddress.sin_port = htons( UDP_SERVER_PORT );
      bindingAddress.sin_port = htons( 31337 );
```

CHAPTER 12 ZEPHYR RTOS WI-FI APPLICATIONS

```
udpServerSocket = socket(                              \
                    bindingAddress.sin_family,         \
                    SOCK_DGRAM,                        \
                    IPPROTO_UDP);
    if ( udpServerSocket < 0 ) {
      LOG_ERR( "UDP Server error: socket: %d\n", errno );
      k_sleep( K_FOREVER );
}

// Bind the socket
bindingResult = bind(                                  \
    udpServerSocket,                                   \
    ( struct sockaddr * )&bindingAddress,              \
    sizeof( bindingAddress ));
if ( bindingResult < 0 ) {
    LOG_ERR( "UDP Server error: bind: %d\n", errno );
    k_sleep( K_FOREVER );
}

// Server Sending/receiving loop
while ( 1 ) {
    LOG_INF( "UDP Server waiting for UDP packets on
    port %d...",          \
        UDP_SERVER_PORT );
    do {
        // Receive
        clientAddressLength = sizeof( clientAddress );
        receivedBytes = recvfrom(                      \
            udpServerSocket,                           \
            receiverBuffer,                            \
            sizeof( receiverBuffer ),                  \
            0,                                         \
```

639

CHAPTER 12   ZEPHYR RTOS WI-FI APPLICATIONS

```
                    &clientAddress,                      \
                    &clientAddressLength );              \
            if ( receivedBytes <= 0 ) {
                if( receivedBytes < 0 ) {
                    LOG_ERR( "UDP Server: Connection
                    error %d",
                                                      errno );
                    sentBytes = -errno;
                }
                        break;
            }
        // Send the echo
            pTransmitterBuffer = receiverBuffer;
                sentBytes = sendto (                     \
            udpServerSocket,                             \
                            receiverBuffer,              \
                            receivedBytes,               \
                            0,                           \
                            &clientAddress,              \
                        clientAddressLength );           \
            if ( sentBytes < 0 ) {
                LOG_ERR( "UDP Server: Failed to send
                %d", errno );
                sentBytes = -errno;
                break;

            } else {
                pTransmitterBuffer += sentBytes;
                receivedBytes -= sentBytes;
            }
            LOG_INF( "UDP Server mode: Received and
            replied with %d "    \
```

```
                                "bytes", sentBytes );
        } while ( true );
        if ( sentBytes < 0 ) {
            k_sleep( K_FOREVER );
        }
    }
}
```

Python UDP Client to Test Out UDP Server on Target Board

For testing purposes, a simple Python script such as the following can be used:

```
import socket
import sys
# Create a UDP socket
sock = socket.socket(socket.AF_INET, socket.SOCK_DGRAM)
server_address = ('192.168.1.87', 31337)
message = b'This is the message.  It will be repeated.'
try:
    # Send data
    print ('sending "%s"' % message)
    sent = sock.sendto(message, server_address)
    # Receive response
    print ('waiting to receive')
    data, server = sock.recvfrom(4096)
    print ('received "%s"' % data)
finally:
    print('closing socket')
    sock.close()
```

The IP address and the port number could either be hardwired into the code, as shown here, or could be passed in via command-line arguments by modifying the script accordingly.

TCP Server Task on Target Board

The TCP_Server.c file contains a function Task_TCP_Server_Init() for creating and starting the TCP server thread and the function TCP_Server(), which initializes and starts the TCP Server itself. The Task_TCP_Server_Init () function follows the same pattern as for the UDP server. The following code snippet shows the implementation of the TCP_Server() function:

```
void TCP_Server( void ){
      int tcpServerSocket;
      int tcpClientSocket;
      struct sockaddr_in bindAddress;
      int connectionsNumber = 0;
      int bindingResult;
      struct sockaddr_in clientAddress;
      socklen_t clientAddressLength = sizeof( clientAddress );
      uint8_t addressString[32];
      int receivedBytes;
      uint8_t *pTransmitterBuffer;
      int sentBytes;
      // Keep checking periodically until a DHCP IP is assigned to
      the board
      while ( !context.connected ) {
            k_msleep( TCP_SERVER_SLEEP_TIME_MS );
      }
      // Create a server socket instance
      tcpServerSocket = socket( AF_INET, SOCK_STREAM, IPPROTO_TCP );
```

CHAPTER 12   ZEPHYR RTOS WI-FI APPLICATIONS

```
if ( tcpServerSocket < 0 )     {
    LOG_ERR( "TCP Server error: socket: %d\n", errno );
    k_sleep( K_FOREVER );
}
// Bind the socket
bindAddress.sin_family = AF_INET;
bindAddress.sin_addr.s_addr = htonl(INADDR_ANY);
//bindAddress.sin_port = htons(TCP_SERVER_PORT);
bindAddress.sin_port = htons(31337);

bindingResult = bind(                                        \
                    tcpServerSocket,                         \
                    ( struct sockaddr * )&bindAddress,       \
                    sizeof( bindAddress ));
if ( bindingResult < 0 )     {
    LOG_ERR( "TCP Server error: bind: %d\n", errno );
    k_sleep( K_FOREVER );
}

/* Listen for connection requests*/
if ( listen ( tcpServerSocket, 5 ) < 0 )     {
    LOG_ERR( "TCP Server error: listen: %d\n", errno );
    k_sleep( K_FOREVER );
}
LOG_INF( "TCP server waits for a connection on port %d...",  \
                                    TCP_SERVER_PORT );
while ( 1 ) {
    // Accept connection
    tcpClientSocket = accept( tcpServerSocket,
    ( struct sockaddr * )&clientAddress,
        &clientAddressLength );
    if ( tcpClientSocket < 0 ) {
        LOG_ERR( "TCP Server error: accept: %d\n", errno );
        continue;
    }
```

643

CHAPTER 12 ZEPHYR RTOS WI-FI APPLICATIONS

```
        // Convert the network address from internal to numeric
        ASCII form
        inet_ntop( clientAddress.sin_family,
                   &clientAddress.sin_addr, addressString,
                   sizeof( addressString ));
        LOG_INF( "TCP Server: Connection #%d from %s",    \
                 connectionsNumber++, addressString );

        // Receiving data loop
        while ( 1 ) {
            // Receive
            receivedBytes = recv( tcpClientSocket,
            ( char *) receiverBuffer,
                            sizeof( receiverBuffer ), 0 ) ;
            if ( receivedBytes <= 0 ) {
                if ( receivedBytes < 0 ) {
                    LOG_ERR( "TCP Server error: recv:
                    %d\n", errno );
                }
                break;
            }

            // Send
            pTransmitterBuffer = receiverBuffer;
            do {
                // Echoing back the received message bytes
                sentBytes = send ( tcpClientSocket,
                                   pTransmitterBuffer,
                                   receivedBytes, 0 ) ;
                if ( sentBytes < 0 ) {
                    LOG_ERR( "TCP Server error: send: %d\n",
                    errno );
                    close( tcpClientSocket );
                    LOG_ERR( "TCP server: Connection from %s
                    closed\n", addressString );
```

```
                }
                pTransmitterBuffer += sentBytes;
                receivedBytes -= sentBytes;
                    LOG_INF( "TCP Server mode. "
                        "Received and replied with %d bytes",
                        sentBytes );
            } while ( receivedBytes );
        }
    }
}
```

In this implementation, the data receiving process is handled in an infinite while(1) loop, which contains, inside it, a do ... while() loop for echoing back the received bytes. For a small embedded application where the amount of data being received or transmitted is relatively small and where multiple concurrent client requests are unlikely, the approach shown previously is probably adequate. For more demanding applications, a more rigorous design, testing, and tuning approach will be required. Some of this will probably also require careful network design by including, for example, security appliances, firewalls, and proxy servers.

The Python client code, running on a PC, that can be used to test out the aforementioned TCP server is relatively straightforward, and an example implementation is shown in the following code snippet:

```
import socket
HOST = "192.168.1.87"   # The server's hostname or IP address
PORT = 31337   # The port used by the server
with socket.socket(socket.AF_INET, socket.SOCK_STREAM) as s:
    s.connect((HOST, PORT))
    print("Sending data ",b"Hello, world - test message")
    s.sendall(b"Hello, world - test message")
    data = s.recv(1024)
print(f"Received {data!r}")
```

CHAPTER 12   ZEPHYR RTOS WI-FI APPLICATIONS

UDP Echo Client Task on Target Board

The client task thread is created in the same way as the other application work threads. The thread function that executes the client code is shown as follows:

```
void UDP_Client() {
      struct sockaddr_in serverAddress;
      int connectionResult;
      int sentBytes = 0;
      int errorCode = 0;
      // Starve the thread until a DHCP IP is assigned to
      the board
      while( !context.connected ) {
            k_msleep( UDP_CLIENT_SLEEP_TIME_MS );
      }
      // Server IPV4 address configuration
      serverAddress.sin_family = AF_INET;
      //serverAddress.sin_port = htons( UDP_CLIENT_PORT );
      // port number and ip address should be altered as
      necessary
      serverAddress.sin_port = htons( 31337 );
      errorCode = inet_pton( AF_INET,  "192.168.1.86",          \
                  &serverAddress.sin_addr );
      // Create client socket
      udpClientSocket = socket( serverAddress.sin_family,
      SOCK_DGRAM,
       IPPROTO_UDP );
      if ( udpClientSocket < 0 ) {
            LOG_ERR( "UDP Client error: socket: %d\n", errno );
            k_sleep( K_FOREVER );
      }
```

CHAPTER 12   ZEPHYR RTOS WI-FI APPLICATIONS

```
    // Attempt to connect with the server.
    connectionResult = connect( udpClientSocket,
                        ( struct sockaddr * )&serverAddress, \
                        sizeof( serverAddress ));
    if ( connectionResult < 0 ) {
          LOG_ERR( "UDP Client error: connect: %d\n",
        errno );
          k_sleep( K_FOREVER );
    }
    LOG_INF( "UDP Client connected correctly" );
    // Send the a udp message
    k_msleep( UDP_CLIENT_WAIT_TO_SEND_MS );
    sentBytes = send(    udpClientSocket, udpClientMessage,
    sizeof( udpClientMessage ), 0 );
    LOG_INF( "UDP Client mode. Sent: %d", sentBytes );

    if ( sentBytes < 0 ) {
          LOG_ERR( "UDP Client error: send: %d\n", errno );
          close( udpClientSocket );
          LOG_ERR( "UDP Client error Connection from
          closed\n" );
    }
}
```

An example Python script implementing a simple echo reply UDP server running on a PC is shown in the following code snippet:

```
import socket
sock = socket.socket(socket.AF_INET, socket.SOCK_DGRAM)
server_address = '192.168.1.86'
server_port = 31337
server = (server_address, server_port)
sock.bind(server)
```

CHAPTER 12　ZEPHYR RTOS WI-FI APPLICATIONS

```
print("Listening on " + server_address + ":" +
str(server_port))
while True:
      payload, client_address = sock.recvfrom(1000)
      print("data received: ", payload)
      print("Echoing data back to " + str(client_address))
      sent = sock.sendto(payload, client_address)
```

TCP Echo Client Task on Target Board

The implementation strategy for this task is similar to that used for the other tasks. The details of the TCP_Client() function are shown as follows:

```
void TCP_Client( void ) {
      int tcpClientSocket;
      struct sockaddr_in serverAddress;
      int connectionResult;
      uint8_t *pTransmitterBuffer;
      int sentBytes;
      int missingBytesToSend = sizeof( TCPClientMessage );
      // Keep checking until a DHCP IP is assigned to the board
      while( !context.connected ){
            k_msleep( TCP_CLIENT_SLEEP_TIME_MS );
      }
      // Server IPV4 address configuration
      serverAddress.sin_family = AF_INET;
      //serverAddress.sin_port = htons( TCP_CLIENT_PORT );
      serverAddress.sin_port = htons( 31337 );
/*    inet_pton( AF_INET, CONFIG_NET_CONFIG_PEER_IPV4_ADDR,
                  &serverAddress.sin_addr ); */
      INET, "192.168.1.86", &serverAddress.sin_addr );
```

CHAPTER 12   ZEPHYR RTOS WI-FI APPLICATIONS

```
// Client socket creation
tcpClientSocket = socket( serverAddress.sin_family,
SOCK_STREAM, IPPROTO_TCP );
if ( tcpClientSocket < 0 )     {
    LOG_ERR( "TCP Client error: socket: %d\n", errno );
    k_sleep( K_FOREVER );
}
// Connect to TCP echo server
k_msleep( TCP_CLIENT_WAIT_TO_SEND_MS );
connectionResult = connect ( tcpClientSocket,
    ( struct sockaddr * )&serverAddress,
    sizeof( serverAddress ));
if ( connectionResult < 0 )     {
    LOG_ERR( "TCP Client error: connect: %d\n",
    errno );
    k_sleep( K_FOREVER );
}
LOG_INF( "TCP Client connected correctly" );
pTransmitterBuffer = TCPClientMessage;
do {
    sentBytes = send(       tcpClientSocket,
    TCPClientMessage,
        sizeof( TCPClientMessage ), 0 );
    if ( sentBytes < 0 ) {
        LOG_ERR( "TCP Client error: send: %d\n",
        errno );
        close( tcpClientSocket );
        LOG_ERR( "TCP Client error Connection
        closed\n" );
    }
    LOG_INF( "TCP Client mode. Sent: %d", sentBytes);
    pTransmitterBuffer += sentBytes;
```

CHAPTER 12   ZEPHYR RTOS WI-FI APPLICATIONS

```
            missingBytesToSend -= sentBytes;
    } while ( missingBytesToSend );
}
```

An example of a PC side TCP echo server written in Python is given in this, next, code snippet:

```python
import socket
import sys
import string
import random
server_ip_address = '192.168.1.86'
size = 1024
server_port = 31337
sock = socket.socket(socket.AF_INET, socket.SOCK_STREAM)
server_address = (server_ip_address, server_port)
sock.bind(server_address)
# Listen for incoming connections
sock.listen(1)
while True:
    print('waiting for a connection')
    connection, client_address = sock.accept()
    try:
        print('connection from', client_address)
        # Receive the data pieces and retransmit them as
        they arrive
        while True:
            data = connection.recv(size)
            if data:
                print("data received: ", data)
                connection.send(data)
    finally:
        connection.close()
```

Testing Out the BSD Sockets Example

The "big bang" approach is to start the PC side UDP and TCP servers running, flash the application to the target board, and then run the PC side UDP and TCP clients and collect the log messages sent from the target board to the PC terminal emulator and to note the output messages from the PC side Python servers and clients.

Alternatively by only starting up some of the threads in the target board application (by modifying the main() function), the individual components can be tested one at a time.

References

1. https://www3.nd.edu/~mhaenggi/NET/wireless/802.11b/Data%20Link%20Layer.htm
2. www.makeuseof.com/tag/wep-wpa-wpa2-wpa3-explained/
3. https://standards.ieee.org/beyond-standards/the-evolution-of-wi-fi-technology-and-standards/
4. https://documentation.meraki.com/General_Administration/Tools_and_Troubleshooting/Analyzing_Wireless_Packet_Captures
5. https://developer.nordicsemi.com/nRF_Connect_SDK/doc/latest/zephyr/connectivity/networking/api/net_mgmt.html
6. https://documentation.meraki.com/MR/Wi-Fi_Basics_and_Best_Practices/Extending_the_LAN_with_a_Wireless_Mesh_Link

CHAPTER 12　ZEPHYR RTOS WI-FI APPLICATIONS

7. https://documentation.meraki.com/MR/
Wi-Fi_Basics_and_Best_Practices/802.11w_
Management_Frame_Protection_MFP

8. www.nordicsemi.com/-/media/Software-and-
other-downloads/Product-Briefs/nRF7002-DK_
Product-Brief-v1.0.pdf

9. https://docs.nordicsemi.com/bundle/ncs-
latest/page/nrf/gsg_guides/nrf7002_gs.html

Index

A

Access point, 580
　　mobile station, 580
Acknowledgment (ACK)
　　scheme, 575
Actions View, 95, 97
Active scanning, 358
Activity synchronization, 56, 59, 60
Actual driver functions, 105, 441
ADC (Analog to Digital)
　　conversion, 3, 20, 445
Advertising Data (AD), 359, 362
An entry, 56, 128, 471
APP_BMEM and APP_DMEM, 413
APP_DMEM, 412
Application Programming
　　Interfaces (APIs), 217,
　　439, 441
Applications View, 91
app_memory subsystem, 205
_arch_syscall_invoke0(), 177
_arch_syscall_invoke6(), 177
Architecture-specific
　　subdirectories
　　(dts/<ARCH>), 459
Arduino connectors, 507
ARG_UNUSED, 156, 560

ARM Cortex M7 processor, 381, 382
ARM Cortex M devices, 26
ARM Cortex M microcontroller, 51
ARM processor–based boards, 126
ARM TrustZone security, 587
__ASSERT() macro, 146
Asynchronous exceptions, 50
Asynchronous protocol, 443
Attribute protocol (ATT), 308, 314,
　　317, 318, 343, 344, 347, 372
Automatic memory partitions,
　　202, 413
AVR, 19
AWS FreeRTOS, 25, 26
Azure RTOS ThreadX, 25, 26

B

Bar-device, 461
Barrier synchronization, 56, 57
Battery service (BAS)
　　characteristics, 339, 340
　　Client Characteristic
　　　　Configuration
　　　　Descriptor, 341
　　configuring dongle to
　　　　emulate, 339

INDEX

Battery service (BAS) (cont.)
   in Connection Map, 342
   and HRS, 354
   LightBlue app, 342
   properties, 340
BBC Microbit v2, 75
Big bang approach, 651
Binary semaphore, 34, 35, 38, 40, 41, 43
Binding and bus controller nodes, 469–470
BLE actors
   central, 315, 316
   peripheral, 315
BLE APIs
   nRF Connect SDK, 343–346
   Zephyr, 343–346
BLE peripheral
   application, 327, 333
   array of services, 353
   Battery Service, 342
   BLE broadcaster, 315
   BLE central, 315
   bt_ready() function, 354
   and central, 316, 325
   and central running, 371
   connection callback functions, 353
   dongle, 336–338
   GAP roles, 347
   GATT server, 331
   heart rate service (HRS), 349–351

HR (Heart Rate) GATT Service, 347
I/O, 327
LightBlue app, 342
nRF5u, 342
nRF52840 DK, 356
nRF53840 DK, 348
nRF Toolbox app, 349
prj.conf file, 352
PuTTY, 348
Zephyr source code tree, 347
BLE security, 325–326
BLE thermometer, 317
blink() helper function, 149
Blinky application, 105
Bluetooth, 356–365
Bluetooth 5, 324
Bluetooth Low Energy (BLE), 26, 74, 535
   actors, 315, 316
   APIs, 343–346
   architecture, 307, 308
   ATT, 317, 318, 343, 344, 347, 372
   attribute operations, 322
   Bluetooth 5, 324
   broadcast connections, 311
   building and testing applications, 327
   building, programming, and configuring host roles, 347
   callback function, 358
   characteristics, 319, 320
   client emulator app, 338

INDEX

connected function, 365–371
connection map, 333–335
connections and connection events, 313, 314
controller gateway connectivity, 307
data attributes, 317, 318
data hierarchy, 319
dongle
    in central mode, 331, 332
    in peripheral mode, 336–338
GATT attribute, 319
HCI, 314, 316
keyboards, 305
link layer, 309, 310
link layer addressing, 312
logical link control and adaptation protocol (L2CAP) layer, 314
mice, 305
nRF52840 dongle, 327, 329–331
nRF Connect, 328, 329
packet types, 312, 313
peripheral (*see* BLE peripheral)
physical layer (PHY), 308, 309
power mode emulation, 339–342
profiles, 320
requests, 323, 324
sensor, 307
standards, 306
structure in Zephyr source code, 347
transfer data, 306
transmission range, 306
unicast connections, 310, 311, 314
uses, 307
version, 306
Bluetooth SIG, 306
Bluetooth Smart, 306
BME280_DEFINE macro, 493
BME280 sensor, 481, 491
BOARD.dts file, 458, 459
Bosch BME280 environmental sensor, 481
BSD functions, 386
BSD Sockets API, 377, 386, 387
Build-specific actions, 92
bytes_from_str(), 627

C

Callback handler function, 398
Callbacks, 533
callback structure, 594
Central/heart rate monitor, 356–365
Cheshire Cat model, 475
Child-binding, 467, 468, 474
Chip flash memory, 20
CivetWeb embedded HTTP server, 386
CivetWeb module, 386
Client Characteristic Configuration Descriptor (CCCD), 322
CMake, 28
CMakeLists.txt file, 146, 606

655

INDEX

CMSIS v2 APIs, 28
Code reusability, 24
Command Creation Macros, 405
Command-line interface (CLI), 28, 517
Common embedded system application scenario, 217, 218
Communication patterns, 58, 59
Communications serial link, 19
Compatible property, 454, 461
Complex application development, 508
concatenation operator, 494
Concurrency, 29
Condition variables, 48
CONFIG_DISK_ACCESS, 278
CONFIG_NET_PROMISCUOUS_MODE, 379
CONFIG_NET_TC_RX_COUNT, 378
CONFIG_NET_TC_TX_COUNT, 378
CONFIG_NET_VLAN, 378
CONFIG_THREAD_CUSTOM_DATA, 141
CONFIG_USERSPACE, 133, 141, 142, 413, 426
connected function, 365–371
CONTAINER_OF macro, 263, 264
Continuous integration and continuous development (CI/CD), 508, 511
Cooperative threads, 139

Copy Build Command, 93
Cortex-M23 and Cortex-M33, 135
Counter watching function, 158
Counting semaphore, 35, 36, 38
COUNT_LIMIT, 157
C preprocessor, 459
Credit tracking synchronization, 39
Critical section, 59
Custom linker snippets, 547
Cypher text (CT) thread, 207

D

Data attributes, 317, 318
Data-centric communication, 58
Data transfer, 62
Data transmission, 445
DBus, 531
#defines, 146, 295, 619
Delayable work, 258–259
Details View, 93
Development kits, 507
Device driver model, 97, 98, 103, 455
Device drivers, 66, 67
Device driver types, 103
DEVICE_DT_GET macro, 492–496
device_get_binding(), 455
Device-related configuration, 633
Devicetree
    binding and bus controller nodes, 469–470
    binding files syntax, 462–468
    bindings, 459–462

INDEX

BME280, 481
bosch,bme280, SPI bus
　base properties table, 482
　node-specific properties table, 484
C and C++ application code, 475–476
configuration, 126, 448–449
cs-gpios property, 489
DEVICE_DT_GET macro, 492–496
devicetree fragment, 452
device tree schema syntax, 438
devicetree syntax, 438
DTS, 449–452
firmware development aspects, application development, 438–442
humidity sensor, 481
I2C interface, nRF5 device, 491
I2C peripherals, 451
I2C sensor, 491
input files types, 457
Kconfig files, 127
kernel, 437
mysensor, 490
nodes, 481
nondiscoverable hardware, 437
Nordic nRF processors, node-specific properties, 486
overlay, BME280 sensor, 491
phandle-array type properties, 471–473
phandles, 471–473
processing, 457–460
reg and interrupts properties, 480
source and binary representations, 448
sources and bindings, 449
specifier cell names, 471–473
spi3 node, 481
Sun Microsystems OpenBoot framework, 438
unit addresses, 453–457
work with device, application, 476–480
.yaml binding files, 473–474
Zephyr, 437
Devicetree-based design, 496
Devicetree compiler (dtc), 460
devicetree.h, 460
devicetree.h API, 126, 449
Devicetree node, 99–101, 450
　hardware components, 451
　physical devices, 456
　properties, 451
Device Tree Source (DTS), 449–452
Devicetree View, 94
DHCP protocol, 614
Dictionary commands, 406, 407
Digital sensors, 19
Digital-to-analog converters, 19
Dining philosophers problem, 162–170, 526
Direct Memory Access (DMA), 486
Directories, 283
disk_write(), 287

657

INDEX

Distributed Coordination Function (DCF), 574
DNS server, 607
Dongle
    BAS, 339
    in central mode, 331, 332
    nRF5u, 341
    nRF42840, 327
    nRF52840, 327, 329
    in peripheral mode, 336–338
Doxygen documentation, 540
DT_ALIAS() macro, 476
DT_CHILD(), 476
DT_CHOSEN(), 476
DT_INST() macro, 476
DT_INST_FOREACH_STATUS_OKAY(BME280_DEFINE), 493
DT_macros, 477
DT_NODE_HAS_PROP() macro, 478
DT_PARENT(), 476
DT_PROP() macro, 100, 479
DT_PROP_LEN() macro, 479
DT_PWMS_CHANNEL_BY_NAME, 472
DT_REG_ADDR(node_id), 480
DT_REG_SIZE(node_id), 480
dts/bindings subdirectories, 462
DTS_ROOT CMake variable, 462
Dynamic Host Configuration Protocol (DHCP), 615
Dynamic observer registrations, 533
Dynamic subcommands, 404

E

EasyDMA, 486
Echo server
    application, 413
    code, 411
    example, 393, 408–423
    STM32 Nucleo-F767ZI Board, 431, 432
echo_serverprj.cnf, 395
Echo-server sample application, 387, 388
Embedded systems, 21
    big loop design, 21–23
    real-time requirements, 21
    software development strategies/options
        automotive system, 25
        characteristics, 24, 25
        level of complexity, 25
        operating systems, 25
        Zephyr RTOS, 26–28
Emulated machines, 520
Emulator-based automation testing, 119, 510
Emulators, 117, 508
Emulator use cases, 509, 510
Encryption, 207
ENC thread, 206

INDEX

Enigma-type engine, 207
Entry point function, 128
Espressif ESP32 processors, 79
Ethernet, 379
ETH_NET_DEVICE_INIT()
    macro, 378
Event objects (event registers), 47
Exceptions, 49–52
Execute in Place (XIP), 273
Extended Inquiry Response
    (EIR), 359

F

FatFs, 269, 280, 285–287
File allocation table (FAT) file
    system, 285–287
File organization module, 284
File systems, 279
    advantage, layered
        approach, 284
    basic file system-level layer, 284
    directories, 283
    FAT and FatFs, 285–287
    file organization module, 284
    I/O control layer, 284
    layered approach, 285
    LittleFS, 288–302
    logical file system layer, 284
    lowest layer, 284
    organize storage, disk
        drives, 284
    partition labelled storage is, 289

Finite State Machine (FSM) model,
    31, 35, 37, 42
First in, first out (FIFO), 147–151
Flash memory, 270
Flash memory operations, 276
foo.yaml, 473
FreeRTOS, 5, 6, 128, 142
FS_FATFS, 280
fs_mount() command, 283
fs_read(), 281
fs_readmount(), 283
fs_sync() function, 282
fs_truncate() function, 282

G

GATT server, 331, 332, 336
GATT service, 319
GDB debugger, 116
Generated C header, 449, 455
Generic Access Profile (GAP), 316
Generic Access service, 336
Generic API approach, 103, 439
gen_syscalls.py script, 176
get_free_slot(), 425
Global Actions
    application-specific icons, 92
    View Actions, 91
Global variables, 227
Global variable test, 593
GNU cross compiler, 27
GNU debugger, 27
gpio peripherals, 146

659

INDEX

GPIO Inputs
    configuration flags, 107
    CPU, 107
GPIO subsystem, 441

H

handle_data function, 428
Hard channel, 543
Hard real-time system, 3, 5
HART, 19
HCI
    GAP, 316
The heap, 53
Heart rate service (HRS), 349–351, 354
helloLoop() function, 153
Humidity sensor, 481

I, J

I2C
    case study example, 497–501
    data transmission, master vs. slave, 447
    LSM6DSL device, 498
    open collector/open drain, 447
    pins, 442
    power consumption, 442
    SCL (clock line), 447
    SDA (data line), 447
    simple I2C network schematic, 448
    SMBus, 447
    two-wire interface, 446
I2C-based temperature sensor, 469
I2C peripheral nodes, 451
I2C peripherals, 451
i2c_transfer(), 455
IDE, 2, 27, 28
Idle thread, 143
IEC 61508, 9
#includes, 146
Inline functions, 176
Interleaving and synchronizing threads, 153
Internet of Things/Industrial Internet of Things (IoT/IIoT), 1
Interrupt handler, 50, 225
Interrupts, 49–52
Interrupt service routines (ISRs), 38, 39, 41, 43, 219, 533, 565
Interrupt specifiers, 480
INT_TO_POINTER (x) macro, 161
IoT embedded applications, 507
IP networking code, 619
IPv6, 377, 381, 394, 418
Iterator functions, 547, 561, 562

K

K_APP_BMEM(), 202
K_APP_DMEM(), 202
K_APPMEM_PARTITION_DEFINE(), 202
Kconfig, 449, 459

INDEX

autoconf.h, 126
configuration options, 125
configuration Zephyr kernel and subsystems, 125
devicetree files, 127
executable, 125
initial configuration, application, 126
Linux build framework, 124
Kernel mode, 134
_KERNEL_STACK_SIZEOF, 131
Kernel thread, 136
k_fifo_get(), 147, 150
k_free(rx_data), 150
K_KERNEL_STACK, 131
K_MBOX_DEFINE macro, 240
k_mem_domain_default, 200
Message queue (k_msgq), 172
K_NO_WAIT, 131
k_object_access_grant() function, 169
kernel queues (k_queue), 172
k_thread, 128
k_thread_create(), 131
k_thread_custom_data_get() function, 141
k_thread_custom_data_set() function, 141
K_THREAD_DEFINE, 416, 561
k_thread_join(), 157
K_THREAD_STACK, 131
K_THREAD_STACK _SIZEOF(), 131

k_thread_user_mode_enter() API function, 141
K_WORK_DELAYABLE_DEFINE macro, 262
k_work_reschedule(), 419
k_work_schedule function, 262

L

Label property, 455
Led blinking helper function blink(), 148
LED support, 615
LightBlue Explorer, 338
Linker macros, 547
Linux application, 614
Linux Foundation, 79
littlefs_binary_file_adj function, 301
LittleFS file system
    example, 288–302
    features, 288
    limited device memory, 288
    microcontrollers, 288
littlefs_flash_erase, 296
littlefs_mount(mp), 297
Local Area Network (LAN), 614
Logger module
    API, 111
    architecture design, 113
    features, 111
    fine control, 113
    libraries, 112
    LOG_HEXDUMP_X macro, 112

INDEX

Logging, 114
Long-Term Evolution (LTE), 26
LoRa thread, 534
Low-cost ARM Cortex M processor, 75
Low Latency Packet Mode (LLPM) operation, 343
Low-level device drivers, 377
LSM6DSL sensors, 497, 498
LTE Link Monitor app, 82

M

MAC address, 601, 614
Macro-based approach, 496
Mailbox, 60, 217
    API, data types and functions, 239, 240
    definition, 236
    life cycle, 238
    message descriptors, 240–241
    message exchange, 236
    message format, 237
    message sending, 243–250
    scenarios, 242
    sending and receiving thread compatibility, 238
    synchronous and asynchronous approach, 239
    threads, 236
    use case pattern, 236
Mailbox instance, 236
main() function, 142, 143, 155, 169, 260, 296, 599, 632, 634

Management Information Base (MIB), 379
Management procedures, 590
Manually defining memory partitions, 201
Master Input/Slave Output (MISO), 445
Master Output/Slave Input (MOSI), 445
memcpy, 150
Memory, 453
Memory domain, 200, 201, 203, 204
Memory domain API, 137
Memory management, 53–56
Memory Management Unit (MMU), 137
Memory-Mapped Input/Output (MMIO), 442
Memory-mapped peripheral, 453
Memory partition, 205
    access control, 205
    attributes, 200
    automatic, 202
    automatic memory partition creation, 201
    definition, 201
    gen_app_partitions.py script, 201, 202
    manually defining memory partitions, 201
    memory domain, 203, 204
    memory region, 200
    MMU-based system, 201
    Static Library Globals, 203

INDEX

Memory protection, 135
Memory Protection Unit (MPU), 127, 134, 137, 138, 175, 200
Message descriptors
    definition, 240
    info, 240
    rx_source_thread, 241
    size, 241
    tx_data, 241
    tx_target_thread, 241
Message queue, 41–43, 217
    API functions, 221, 222
    characteristics, 219
    data fetching, 220
    definition, 219
    ISRs/thread, 220
    items, 218
    multiple threads, 220
    ring buffer, 219
    scenario, 222–236
    use case scenarios, 219
Message queueing, 41–43
Message sending thread, 225
mgmt_event, 401
mgmt_event_mask, 402
mgmt_request parameter, 397, 401, 589
Microcontrollers, 19
Mikroe, 78
MISRA, 9
Mobile station, 582–584
Modular RTOS, 11
Motor controller, 2
Mount point, 279

Multi-instance driver application, 494
Multiple MMIO regions, 442
Multiple SPI devices, 444
Multithreaded applications, 633
Multithreading
    app_a.h file code, 186, 187
    app_b.h file code, 194
    example, 145, 146
    kernel queues part, 185, 186
    memory domain, 200
    memory pool, 185, 186
    producer-consumer example, 171–175
    producer-consumer example sample driver part, 179–185
    producer-consumer problems, 170–175
    protected memory partitions, 200
    scenarios, 144–145
    shared memory, 200
    shared memory partition, 185, 186
    signal, condition variable, 157–162
    system heap, 185, 186
    Zephyr FIFO, 147–151
    Zephyr shared memory example, 205–215
Multithreading in Zephyr
    entry point function, 128
    execution mode, 129

INDEX

Multithreading in Zephyr
    FreeRTOS, 128
    guard-based stack overflow detection, 131
    K_FOREVER, 131
    K_KERNEL_STACK macros, 132
    K_KERNEL_STACK_DEFINE, 131
    K_NO_WAIT, 131
    k_thread_create(), 131
    K_THREAD_DEFINE macro, 132
    K_THREAD_STACK_DEFINE, 131
    life cycle, 131
    Microsoft Windows, 128
    MPU, 127
    operating system, 127
    properties, 128
    small 32-bit SoC devices, 127
    stack area, 128
    stack buffer, 131
    thread control block, 128
    thread options, 129
    _THREAD_STACK macros, 132
    thread states, 130
    user mode threads, 129
    Zephyr framework, 130
mutex/semaphore, 169
Mutual exclusions semaphore (Mutex), 36–38

N

NET_DEVICE_INIT() macro, 378
net_if object, 397
net_if_ipv4_addr_add(), 378
NET_IF_UP flag, 380
net_mgmt(), 398
net_mgmt() API, 397
net_mgmt_add_event_callback() function, 398
net_mgmt_del_event_callback() function, 398
net_mgmt_event_callback() function, 401, 404
net_mgmt_event_callback structure, 403
net_mgmt_event_callback() function, 401
net_mgmt_event_handler_t handler, 403
net_mgmt_event_init(void), 403
net_mgmt_event_notify() function, 400
net_mgmt_event_wait() function, 404
net_mgmt_init_event_callback() helper function, 398
net_mgmt_request_handler_t, 400
Network Address Translation (NAT), 385
Network connection map, BLE feature, 333, 334

INDEX

inspect and manage, 333
parameters and properties, 333
properties, 334
reading button state, 335
writing button state, 335
Network events, 398, 400, 401, 589, 591
Network initialization macros, 378
Network interfaces, 378
Network Management API functions, 377, 397, 401–404
Network management procedure, 399, 400
Network packet priority, 379
Node label, 450
Non-alphanumeric characters, 477
Nonresolvable private addresses, 312
Nordic development kit boards, 96
Nordic nRF Connect, 338
Nordic nRF devices, 343
Nordic recommendation, 83
Nordic Semiconductor, 27
Nordic Semiconductor devices, 274
Nordic Semiconductor nRF devices, 327
Nordic Semiconductor processors, 26, 81
nRF5340 SoC, 587
nRF7002-based device h, 615
nRF7002 DK board, 586
nRF52840 DK board, 95, 223, 356
nRF52840 dongle, 327, 329–331
nRF Connect, 81, 82, 328, 329

Desktop nRF BLE application, 329, 330
nRF Connect for Desktop, 27
nRF Connect SDK, 27, 83, 84, 343–346, 372
nRF Connect Sidebar Views, 88
Nucleo boards, 75
Nucleo-F401RE, 76
Nucleo-F767ZI Board, 381, 383, 384
Bar-device node's num-foos property, 461

O

One-way data communication, 43, 44
Open source GitHub repository, 15
Open source RTOS
   in functional safety applications, 5
   certification authorities, 8
   characteristics, 7
   developing and testing, 7
   features, 7
   FreeRTOS, 5, 6
   IEC 61508, 9
   MISRA guidelines, 9
   SAFERTOS, 6
   standards, 6
   use of code, 5
   V-Model, 8
   reconciling certification, 10
OS abstraction layers (OSALs), 28

INDEX

OS Services module
  echo_server example, 391
  net iface command, 391
  net ping command output, 391
  net subcommands, 390
  Tab key, 389
  Unix-like shell, 388
  zephyr\samples\net\sockets\
    echo_server, 389
Overlays, 459

P

Packet-oriented communications protocols, 4
Passive scanning, 581
Phandle-array, 471
phil_obj_abstract.h file, 164
philosopher() function, 166
Physical flash memory, 454
Pipes, 45–47
Port expanders, 19
POSIX file system API, 280
Powershell Console output, 528
Preemptible thread, 139
printk(), 145, 146
Priority inheritance mechanism, 555
Priority inversion avoidance, 37
Privileged thread, 133
Privilege mode, 134
prj.conf file, 611, 616
Probe Request frame, 581

process_tcp() function, 421, 422, 427
process_udp() function, 419
process_udp4() function, 417, 419
process_udp6() function, 418
Producer-consumer problems, 170–175
Property value, 451
Prototyping technology, 78
Pseudocode, 32, 33
PT thread, 206
Public Device Address, 312
Pulse-width modulation (PWM), 20
PuTTY, 348
PWM cells, 472
PWM controller nodes, 471
pwms property, 467
Python, 115, 632, 650, 651
Python client code, 645
Python environment, 73
Python packages, 72
Python programming, 75
Python script, 641, 647
Python virtual environment, 72

Q

QSPI-based file system, 288
Quad-SPI (QSPI)
  advantages, 272
  clock cycle traces, 271
  definition, 271

INDEX

details, particular processor, 272
disadvantages, 270
double data rate mode, 272
EasyDMA, 273
external Quad-SPI memory, 275
flash memory, 270
four data lines, 270
interface with flash memory, 270
modern flash chips, 272
Nordic devices, 275
Nordic nRF52840 processor, 272
Nordic nRF52840 QSPI
    peripheral, 273
Nordic Semiconductor
    devices, 274
STM32F4 system
    architecture, 274
STM32 processors, 275
typical configuration, 270
XIP, 273
Queue Control Block (QCB), 41

R

RAM/SRAM region, 175
Random Device Address, 312
Real Time, 3
Receiving mailbox message
    data control, 247
    data retrieval mechanism, 250
    message buffer, 248, 249
    message descriptor, 248
    multiple threads, 247
    response scenario, 249
    thread, 246
    thread compatibility
        constraints, 247
    variable-sized requests, 248
Receiving thread, 251
Reconciling certification
    open source, 10
Recursive mutex, 37
reg and interrupts properties, 480
reg devicetree node property, 455
Rendezvous
    synchronization, 56, 57
Renode, 121, 122, 162
    basic pattern, emulation, 527
    built-in emulation, 512
    capabilities, 511
    dashboard, 522, 523
    definition, 511
    embedded devices, 512
    emulator, 507
    extensive networking
        support, 512
    firmware, 512
    Mono/C# framework, 512
    scripting language, 520
    single node applications, 508
    supported emulated
        peripherals, 524
    UART driver emulation, 525
    Zephyr application emulator,
        521, 522
Renode installation
    CLI, 517, 518
    commands, 519

INDEX

Renode installation (*cont.*)
    confirmation dialog, 515
    directory, 514
    monitor prompt, 518
    .msi installer, 513
    setup, 513-517
    terminal shell window, 517
Renode Monitor Console
    output, 529
Renode scripts, 520
Renode simulator/emulator, 115
Renode UART Terminal Window
    output, 529
Resolvable private addresses, 312
Resource synchronization, 56, 61, 62
RFC 2863 standard, 379
RISC-V machine, 117
Robot framework, 116
Robot framework testing suite, 530
Root commands, 405, 406
Root node, 450
RS232, 19
RTOS
    APIs, 32
    buttons, 21
    commercial, 23
    communication patterns, 58, 59
    condition variables, 48
    consumer devices, 20
    critical section, 59
    design and implementation, 4
    device drivers, 66, 67
    embedded systems (*see* Embedded systems)
    event objects (event registers), 47
    handling multiple data items and multiple inputs, 65, 66
    home-brewed, 23
    IDE, 2
    infinite loop tasks, 32
    interlocked
        one-way data communication, 43, 44
        two-way data communication, 44, 45
    interrupts and exceptions, 49-52
    intertask communication, 33
    kernels, 32
    LEDs, 21
    memory management, 53-56
    message queue, 41-43
    message queueing, 41-43
    microcontrollers, 19
    multitasking, 3
    networked devices, 3
    open source software (*see* Open source RTOS)
    operating system, 3, 4
    packet-oriented communications protocols, 4
    pipes, 45-47

predictable and reproducible behavior, 5
priority inversion, 37
run-to-completion task, 32
semaphore (*see* Semaphore)
sending urgent/high priority data between tasks, 66
Silabs 8051, 19
smart devices, 20
software libraries, 25
synchronization (*see* Synchronization)
task (thread), 29–33
thread interaction patterns, 62–64
RTOS programming, 75
RTOS Wi-Fi Applications
authentication schemes, 576
CSMA/CA, 575
CTS, 575
802.11 data link layer, 573
evolution, 578
2.4 GHz ISM, 577
IEEE 802.11, 575
IEEE 802.11 family, 573
RTS/CTS protocol, 575
WPA, 576
WPA2, 576
WPA3, 576

S

SAFERTOS, 5, 6
Safety model and threats
assumptions, 135
kernel object, 136
kernel resources/kernel objects, 136
kernel thread, 136
memory domain API, 137
Python scripts, 137
user mode perspective, 136
user threads, 136
sample_driver.h file, 179
Scan application, 591
Scanning options, 603
Scan result, 595
Scheduling algorithm, 29
Scheduling mechanism, 22
Scheduling strategies, 29
scripts/dts/ directory, 459
scripts/dts/python-devicetree directories, 459
SDC and MMC cards, 276–277
SD card support via SPI, 277, 278
SD Memory Card (SDMMC) subsystem, 277
Security Manager (SM) layer, 325
Segger JLink firmware, 431
Segger Ozone debug tool, 431
Semaphore, 244, 410
binary, 34, 35
counting, 35, 36
Mutex, 36–38
SCB, 34
synchronization or mutual exclusion, 34
usage patterns, 38

INDEX

Semaphore control block (SCB), 34
Sending mailbox message
    application-defined info value, 244
    asynchronous send operation, 244
    4-byte random values, 244
    message buffer, 245
    send queue, 243
    synchronous send operation, 243
    synchronous transmission, 243
    thread, 243
    variable-sized requests, 245
Sending thread, 251
Sensor data channel subscriber, 534
Sensor thread, 534
Serial Peripheral Interface (SPI)
    advantages, 446
    chip select line, 442
    data transfer rate, 270
    data transmission, 445
    disadvantages, 446
    embedded system applications, 443
    "full duplex" protocol, 445
    Lpins, 442
    master, 444
    10 Mbps speed, 445
    MISO, 445
    MOSI, 445
    multiple SPI devices, 444
    power consumption, 442
    as Quad-SPI, four data lines, 270
    SCLK (Clock), 445
    simple SPI network schematic, 444
    slave, 444
    SS/CS, 445
    synchronous protocol, 443
    traditional SPI, limitations, 270
Serial protocols, 443
Shared memory, 200, 205–215
Shell commands, 404, 408–423
SHELL_COND_CMD_ARG_REGISTER, 405
SHELL_DYNAMIC_CMD_CREATE macro, 405
Shell module, 404
SHELL_STATIC_SUBCMD_SET_CREATE macro, 405
Signal-centric communication, 58
Simulation/emulation frameworks, 114
Simulators and emulators, 119, 120
    advantages, 510
    disadvantages, 511
Simulators *vs.* emulators, 508
Simulator use cases, 118, 509
Simultaneous Authentication of Equals (SAE), 577
sin_port member, 418
Skip timers, 22
Slave Select/Chip Select (SS/CS), 445
Slave select (SS) pin, 444
SoC devices, 19

INDEX

SoC processor architectures, 2
SoftDevice Controller, 343
Soft real time applications, 5
Soft real-time system, 3
Software Development Kit
    (SDK), 27, 73
SRAM, 269
SRLSRS, 536
Stack overflow protection, 134
Stack protection, 134
start_scan() function, 357
start_tcp() function, 415, 425
start_udp() function, 414
start_udp_proto() function, 418
Static commands, 405, 406
Static observer registration, 533
Static subcommands, 404
Station code, 619
STM32F405 board, 77
STM32F405 Express board, 78
STM32F767ZI Microcontroller, 382
STM32 Nucleo boards, 431
STM32 Nucleo-F767ZI Board
    Echo Server, 431–434
    network programming
        examples
            build and troubleshooting,
                385, 386
STM32 processors, 275
struct k_thread, 426
STRUCT_SECTION_FOREACH
    macro, 547
Sun Microsystems OpenBoot
    framework, 438

Swedish-Polish research
    company, 115
Synchronization
    access to shared
        resource, 40, 41
    activity, 56, 59, 60
    barrier, 56, 57
    credit tracking, 39
    patterns and strategies, 56–58
    rendezvous, 56, 57
    resource, 61, 62
    wait and signal, 38, 39
Synchronizing threads
    semaphores, 151–157
    sleeping, 151–157
Synchronous exceptions, 49, 50
Synchronous protocol, 443
sys_heap, 172
sys_snode_t node, 403, 594
System calls, 174
    access by user thread to private
        kernel data, 176
    app_syscall.h and app_syscall.c
        files, 177
    architectures, 177
    execution flow, 177
    implementation function, 176
    inline functions, 176
    Python scripts, 176
System Management Bus
    (SMBus), 447
System on a Module (SoM), 2
System on Chip (SoC), 109
System threads, 142, 143

INDEX

T

Task flexibility, 24
Task (thread), 29–33
TCP, 423
TCP_Client() function, 648
TCP echo server, 385, 421, 650
TCP/IP network-based
 application, 381
TCP/IP server-side connections
 data structures, 424, 425
 thread structures pool, 426–430
TCP_Server.c file, 642
Thread, 62–64, 218, 533
Thread custom data, 141
Thread priorities
 cooperative thread, 139
 integer value, 139
 K_ESSENTIAL option, 140
 K_FP_REGS option, 140
 K_INHERIT_PERMS option, 141
 K_USER option, 141
 limits, 139
 preemptible thread, 139
 preemptive multitasking
  operating systems, 139
 priority ranges
  cooperative thread, 140
  preemptive thread, 140
 Zephyr documentation,
  cooperative threads, 139
 Zephyr kernel, 139
Thread prioritization policies, 168
Thread termination, 142

ThreadX, 25
Time-critical event handling, 21
Timers, 52, 53
Time-sensitive activities, 52
Timing, 52, 53
Toggle_Led(), 636
Toolchain Manager, 82, 83
Two-way data
 communication, 44, 45

U

UART Communications
 MCU, 108
 nRF52840 DK board, 109
 TXD line, 110
 USB connection, 110
uart_out thread blocks, 150
UART peripheral, 463
UART thread entry function, 150
UDP_Client(), 646
UDP echo server service, 421
UDP_Server.c file, 637
UML sequence diagram, 242
Unit addresses, device trees
 /aliases and /chosen nodes, 457
 /chosen node's properties, 457
 Compatible property, 454
 interrupts property, 456
 label property, 455
 reg devicetree node
  property, 455
Unit addresses, device trees
 additional values, 454

INDEX

flash memory, 453
flash partitions, 454
I2C controller, 453
I2C devices, 455
memory-mapped
    peripheral, 453
node named
    memory@2000000, 453
node names, 453
physical flash memory, 454
property value types, 456
soc node, 453
SPI peripheral, 453
devicetree status property, 455
Unprivileged level status
    thread, 133
Unprivileged user threads, 134
User mode threads, 129, 133
User's callback handler function
    signature, 401
USERSPACE, 379
User syscalls, 138
User threads, 136
UUIDs, 317, 345, 346, 362, 363

V

VDED execution scenario
    low-level code, 551
    priority ordering, 554–556
    scenario timing, 552, 553
    threads, 551
View Toolbar, 91
Virtual distributed event dispatcher
    (VDED), 532

bus logic, 550
event dispatching steps, 550
execution scenario (see VDED
    execution scenario)
ISR, 550
Virtual Filesystem Switch
    (VFS), 279
V-Model, 7
VS Code
    nRF Connect, 85, 96
    nRF Connect SD Extension, 86
    nRF Connect SDK project, 85
    terminal window, 97
    welcome page, 90
VS Code IDE, 85
vTaskStartScheduler()
    function, 142

W

Wait and signal
    synchronization, 38, 39
Welcome View, 90
west init command, 124
west tool
    command, 124
    multiple repositories
        management, 123
    Python 3, 124
    third-party projects, 124
    workspace, 123, 124
    YAML file, 124
while() loop, 645
Wi-Fi, 380

673

INDEX

Wi-Fi access point, 614
__wifi_args_to_params() function, 625
wifi_connect(), 627, 628
Wi-Fi connection, 634
Wi-Fi frames, 579
    control frames packets, 580
    null function packets, 580
Wi_Fi interface, 631
Wi-Fi management, 599
Wi-Fi protocols, 623
Wi-Fi protocol standards, 592
Wi-Fi scan operations, 587
Wifi_Setup() function, 635
Wi-Fi subcommands, 607
Wired Equivalent Privacy (WEP), 576
Wireless interfaces, 397
Wireless technologies, 26
Workqueues
    application-specific, 257
    definition, 256
    initialization, 257
    mechanism, 256
    offsetof() macro, 257
    project, 256
    response, 257
    scenario 1, 259–261
    scenario 2, 261, 262
    scenario 3, 263, 264, 266
    "work handler" function, 257

X

X-NUCLEO-IKS01A2 board, 497

Y

YAML data types, 467

Z

ZBus
    abstraction, 532
    API functions, 544
    application logic, 532
    architecture, 532, 533
    claiming and finishing channel, 545
    code reusability, 535
    iterating over channels, 547, 549
    limitations, 535
    Linux-based systems, 531
    many-to-many communication, 531
    message delivery rates and guarantees, 535, 536
    message delivery sequence guarantees, 536
    observer pattern, 531
    publishing and reading channel, 544, 545
ZBus benchmarking, 535
zbus_chan_const_msg function, 546

INDEX

ZBus observer registration, 533
zbus_obs_set_enable()
    method, 533
ZBus programming
    application-dependent data structure, 537
    callback implementation, 539
    channel notification, 542
    data structure, 539
    helper macros, 541
    macros, 537
    parameters, 537
    return values, 542
    struct zbus_observer instance, 540, 541
    subscriber task, 542
    utility macros, 540
    zbus_channel structure, 538
ZBus usage scenario, 533, 534
Zephyr and network management
    administrative state, 380
    application layer APIs, 380
    BSD Sockets API, 381
    functions, testing status, 380
    IoT-oriented applications, 381
    network association status, 380
    operational state, 380
    PHY status, 380
    RFC 2863 standard, 379
    TCP/IP network-based application, 381
    transport and link layer APIs, 381
Zephyr application code, 393–396

Zephyr applications, 69, 71, 73, 74, 97, 101
    C and C++ compilers, 70
    CMake files, 71
    Microsoft VS Code, 69
    QEMU and Renode, 70
    Renode and QEMU, 69
    RTOS application, 70
Zephyr Bluetooth LE Controller, 343
Zephyr Bus Workqueue
    callback code, 568
    "delay" handlers, 568
    fast_handler1_lis listener, 568
    ISR, 565
    listeners and subscribers, 568
    LOG_DBG, 570
    message structures, 565
    scheduling, 565
    sensor readings, 566
    subscriber observers, 569
    ZBus channels, 567
Zephyr convenience macros, 231, 235
Zephyr device model, 439
Zephyr documentation, 533
Zephyr file system API
    FATFS_MNTP, 280
    fs_read(), 281
    fs_sync() function, 282
    fs_truncate() function, 282
    FS_TYPE_EXTERNAL_BASE, 279
    struct fs_file_t instance, 280

675

INDEX

Zephyr file system API
   bytes, 282
   file directories, 280
   flags, 280
   FS_FATFS, 280
   mount point, 279
   offset, 282
   return value, 282
   source path, 281
Zephyr framework, 102
Zephyr HTTP server module, requirements, 386
Zephyr kernel mode thread, 133
Zephyr Mailbox object, 240
Zephyr mailbox scenarios, 251–256
Zephyr Message Queue API, 218, 220
Zephyr network application, 377
Zephyr networking framework, 378
Zephyr Network Interface Abstraction layer, 378
Zephyr Network Management, 588
   API, 589
Zephyr/Nordic repositories, 565
Zephyr OS, 11
   framework, 27
Zephyr repository, 556
Zephyr repository ZBus, 556
Zephyr RTOS, 25, 77
   advantages, 1
   APIs, 28
   arguments, 14, 15
   ARM Cortex M devices, 26
   BLE (see Bluetooth Low Energy (BLE))
   by Linux Foundation, 15
   CLI tools, 28
   CMake, 28
   components, 51
   features, 12–14
   framework, 26
   framework components, 13, 14
   functional safety, 8
   IDE, 28
   Kconfig and devicetree, 2
   message queue implementation, 42
   modular, 11
   multitasking (multithreading), 26
   Nordic Semiconductor processors, 26, 27
   OSALs, 28
   pre-certified version, 5
   real-world real-time RTOS-based project, 1
   and security, 15–16
   setup and installation, 27
   source code tree, 347
   statement, 7
   timers, 52, 53
   timing, 52, 53
   wireless technologies, 26
Zephyr RTOS applications, 81, 82, 97
   device tree syntax, 98

INDEX

Zephyr RTOS disk access API, 278, 279
Zephyr RTOS framework, 585
Zephyr RTOS mechanisms, 267
Zephyr RTOS
    programming, 98, 521
Zephyr SDK, 79
Zephyr SDK CLI
    Chocolatey website, 72
    CMake, 71, 73
    tools, 72
    virtual environment, 73
Zephyr SDK samples, 90
Zephyr's GPIO framework, 230
Zephyr's network stack
    network application, 376
    network device drivers, 377
    network protocols, 376
    Zephyr OS stack implementation, 375
Zephyr's power management policy, 616
Zephyr ZBus Hello World
    accelerometer readings, 564
    ARG_UNUSED macro, 560
    channels, 558

channels and observers information, 564
CMakeLists.txt file, 557
header files, 557
infinite loop, 561
iterator functions, 561
listener callback function, 560
LOG_INF, 564
main() function, 562
observer data iterator function, 562
observers, 559
string "Observers:", 562
print_channel_data_iterator() function, 561
prj.conf file, 557
struct acc_msg variable acc1, 564
subscriber task, 560
threads and communications setting up, 557
validator, 559
validator method, 564
version and build information, 558

677